D1563832

The Hebrew Folktale

ELI YASSIF

The Hebrew Folktale: History, Genre, Meaning

TRANSLATED FROM HEBREW BY
Jacqueline S. Teitelbaum

INDIANA UNIVERSITY PRESS

Bloomington and Indianapolis

This book is a publication of

Indiana University Press
601 North Morton Street
Bloomington, Indiana 47404-3797 USA

www.indiana.edu/~iupress

Telephone orders   800-842-6796
Fax orders   812-855-7931
Orders by email   iuporder@indiana.edu

© 1999 by Eli Yassif

The paper used in this publication meets the minimum
requirements of American National Standard for Information
Sciences—Permanence of Paper for Printed Library
Materials, ANSI Z39.48-1984.

Manufactured in the United States of America

Library of Congress Cataloging-in-Publication Data

Yassif, Eli, date
     [Sipur ha-' am ha-' Ivri.   English]
     The Hebrew folktale : history, genre, meaning / Eli Yassif ;
translated from Hebrew by Jacqueline S. Teitelbaum.
          p.   cm. — (Folklore studies in translation)
     Includes bibliographical references and index.
     ISBN 0-253-33583-3 (cl : alk. paper)
     1. Folk literature, Hebrew—History and criticism.   2. Jewish folk
literature—History and criticism.   3. Tales—History and criticism.
4. Jews—Folklore.   I. Title.   II. Series.
GR98.Y3713   1999
398.2'089'924—dc21   98-11004

1   2   3   4   5   04   03   02   01   00   99

Contents

Foreword   *Dan Ben-Amos* vii
Acknowledgments xix

1. INTRODUCTION: JEWISH CULTURE AND THE HEBREW FOLKTALE 1

2. THE BIBLICAL PERIOD: THE FOLKTALE AS SACRED HISTORY 8
    A. The Myth 10
    B. The Legend 15
    C. The Fable 23
    D. The Novella 27
    E. The Story Cycle 30
    F. Developments and Transitions 33

3. THE SECOND TEMPLE PERIOD: THE CASTING OF NARRATIVE PATTERNS 38
    A. Narrative in the Apocrypha and Pseudepigrapha:
       Continuation and Renewal 38
    B. The Historical Legend 40
    C. The Expanded Biblical Tale 46
    D. The Martyrological Narrative as Folktale 52
    E. The Hagiographical Cycle 57
    F. The Novella and Wisdom Tale 61
    G. The Fairytale 64
    H. The Contribution to the History of Hebrew Narrative 67

4. THE FOLKTALE IN THE RABBINIC PERIOD: BETWEEN FOLK CULTURE AND
   RABBINIC LITERATURE 70
    A. Introduction 70
    B. Performance Events 72
    C. The Expanded Biblical Story 79
    D. Narrative Traditions from the Second Temple Period 89
    E. The Biographical Legend 106
    F. The Exemplum 120
    G. The Historical Legend 132
    H. Tales of Magic and Demonology 144
    I. The Comic Tale 166
    J. Parables and Fables 191
    K. The Story Cycle 209

5. THE MIDDLE AGES: EXTERNAL PERILS AND INTERNAL TENSIONS 245
    A. Introduction 245
    B. Rabbinic Aggadah as Folk Narrative 250
    C. Tales from International Folklore 265
    D. The Exemplum 283
    E. The Historical Legend 297
    F. The Saint's Legend 321
    G. The Novella and Gender Stories 343
    H. Tales of Magic and Demonology 351

6. THE LATER GENERATIONS: THE FOLKTALE IN CONFRONTATION WITH
A CHANGING WORLD 371
    A. The Hasidic Story as Folk Literature 371
        1. Performance Events 374
        2. Oral and Written 376
        3. Traditional Narrative Patterns 380
        4. The Absorption of Medieval Narrative Traditions 385
        5. The Hidden Zaddik and Social Conflict 393
        6. The Child Taken Captive to the New World 397
        7. Theme, Character, Space 402
        8. "We Saw with Our Own Eyes, in Our Own Generation" 406
    B. Legends of the Saints and Israeli Society 407
        1. Saints' Legends and Contemporary Folk Literature 407
        2. The Reappearance of the Saints 408
        3. Local Saints, Local Reality 411
        4. Saints as War Heroes 415
        5. Saints and Medicine 418
        6. The Struggle over Life and Death: Tradition vs. Modernity 423
        7. Life as Miracle: The Religious Meaning of Society 426
    C. "Return to the Faith" Stories: Religious Rhetoric in a
        Secular World 429
        1. Medium and Ideology 429
        2. The Text 433
        3. Interpretation 436
        4. "Return to the Faith" Narratives and Ancient Jewish Traditions 455
        5. The Meaning and Function in Israeli Culture 459

Notes 461
Abbreviations Used in the Notes 543
Index 549

Foreword
Dan Ben-Amos

From the ancient Israelites to modern Israel, the history of the Hebrew folktale spans a period of three millennia. Rooted in oral tradition, and documented first on parchment, the transmission of Hebrew folktales continued into the medieval, Renaissance, and modern periods, leaving its traces in manuscripts and print, and now resonating in the cassette culture of contemporary mass media.

There are older folktale traditions,[1] but none is more resilient. None of the others sustained the collapse of empires, the death of languages, and the dispersion of its speakers, yet persevered and revived. The tales of Mesopotamia were written on clay only to be covered by dust, and the stories of ancient Egypt remained on papyrus in a language without speakers. But throughout the turbulent history of the Jews, their Hebrew folktales maintained a dual course of orality and literacy, in mutual support. As alternating links in a transmission chain, the oral tales of one generation entered literary canon of the next generation, and in turn became the staging ground for new oral performances. These drew upon as yet uncanonized oral tradition, verbal play, and newly created narratives that imagine the past.

The transition from orality to literacy is a selective and purposeful process controlled by scribes and their religious or political patrons, who tend to be self-serving or, at best, to adhere to normative cultural values. Consequently, the literary guardians of tradition may manage for a while to keep out objectionable oral themes. In succeeding generations, however, when the gatekeepers of literacy change, their control loosens, or social values shift, the suppressed subjects emerge or are imagined anew. What are, for example, the riddles that the Queen of Sheba posed to King Solomon? As Yassif points out, in later Jewish, Islamic, Christian, and Ethiopian traditions, their relationship evolved into a romantic sensual story, but the writers of I Kings 10:2–3 and 2 Chronicles 9:1–2 kept that aspect of the tale toned down and did not spell out the riddles or any other lascivious details. Their texts simply state that *she asked him all that she had in mind. Solomon had answers for all her questions; there was nothing that the king did not know, [nothing] to which he could not give her an answer.* The actual riddles and anything else "she had in mind" are left out of the written records of this momentous event. A perceptive reader might find in the biblical text only a hint of sexuality in the repeated use of the verb "to come" (*va-tavo*) to describe the Queen of Sheba's visit (I Kings 10:1–2; 2 Chronicles 9:1).[2] The Talmudic sages shied away from her feminine image altogether and barely mention her by name, imposing a blackout on her relationship with the builder of the holy Temple. Yet, other texts clearly evidence her presence as a heroine in a tradition about a biblical political-demonic romance. The first-century Josephus Flavius retells the story of the Queen of Sheba, referring to her as "the Queen of Egypt and Ethiopia";[3] she was similarly known in Matthew (12:42), Luke (11:31), and Acts (8:27).[4] In The Testament of Solomon, which "reflects first-century Judaism in Palestine,"[5] she is "Sheeba, Queen of the South, who was a witch" (19:3). This demonic character also resonates in the Aramaic translation of Job that renders the verse *and the Sabeans made a raid* (1:15) as "and suddenly Lilith, the Queen of Samargad, fell upon them."

Throughout the first millennium, the affair between King Solomon and the Queen of Sheba simmered in the oral traditions of the region, but only in the eighth to tenth centuries did the sexual liaison between them, her demonic nature, and the riddles she asked appear in literature. In Jewish sources, only in the *Targum Sheni* to the Book of Esther and *Midrash Mishlei*, both texts likely from the eighth or ninth centuries from Palestine, do riddles actually appear. The tenth-century *Sefer Ben-Sira* states explicitly her demonic character, represented by her hairy legs. Theoretically, the details in the late traditions could have been the product of latent or belated imagination as much as oral transmission. But since the biblical text and the first-century sources foretell elements that later narratives articulate, it is likely that early generations already knew orally what later generations consented to write down.

The arrival of script did not stop the oral circulation and expansion of narrative. The number of riddles multiplied from three and four in the respective eighth- or ninth-century sources to nineteen in a fifteenth-century *Midrash Ha-Hefez* in which, according to Jacob Lassner, there is "a residue of a Yemenite oral tradition."[6] An early-eighteenth-century Yemenite manuscript further expands the basic themes of this ancient oral romance, which by that time had been documented in different versions in Islamic and Ethiopic traditions. Yet Yehuda Avida, who published it, comments: "Our narrator lived in the Hebrew-Moslem world, but it is unlikely that he borrowed the relevant parts of his story directly from the Koran or Thousand and One Nights and the other Arabic sources where they are found. Rather, he took his tales from other narrators and not books—from the oral tradition that circulated in the Hebrew-Arabic world."[7]

In his search for such oral traditions, Yassif scans Hebrew literature from ancient to modern times with a folkloristic sonar, looking for the pulsing discourse of folktales. He listens to the voice of Jewish oral narrators that speaks from beneath the surface of literacy. His diagnostic and analytical tools are formulaic language, oral genres, thematic and typological comparisons, and literary descriptions of oral performances—all concepts and methods of modern folklore.

There are several comprehensive histories of Jewish literature in Hebrew and Yiddish.[8] They acknowledge the debt of writers and poets to Jewish myths, legends, and folktales, but so far none has attempted to chart the historical course of the Hebrew folktales themselves. Nineteenth-century scholars such as Leopold Zunz (1794–1886) and Moritz Steinschneider (1816–1907) laid the foundation and prepared the bibliographical tools for such a literary history. Subsequent research continued to explore the respective periods of Jewish folk literature. Twentieth-century researchers expanded its scope and added to it the Hasidic tales and the narratives of Jewish communities in the Mediterranean and Asian countries. The nineteenth-century scholars of the "Science of Judaism" could consider neither chronologically nor conceptually oral tradition as living literature in Jewish societies. At the same time that they formulated the scientific principles for the study of Jewish history, cultures, and literatures, the Hasidim bubbled with new oral narratives, to which Jewish intellectuals could begin to respond only at the wane of the nineteenth and the beginning of the twentieth centuries as neo-romanticism swept their ranks. They began attending to the traditions of Jews who lived in Islamic countries only in modern times, when travel and migration brought them in contact with one another.

The only previous major study of Jewish folktales, available exclusively in Hebrew, builds upon a major folktale anthology that Micha Joseph Bin Gorion (Berdyczewski) (1865–1921) prepared under the influence of this neo-romantic movement. It appeared first in German as *Der Born Judas: Legenden, Märchen und Erzählungen* (1916–1923), and then in Hebrew as *Mimekor Yisrael* (1939–1945; 1952[2]; 1966[3]), and in English as *Mimekor Yisrael: Classical Jewish Folktales* (1976; 1990[2]). On the basis of this anthology, Emanuel Bin Gorion, Micha Joseph's son, wrote a study of folktales in Hebrew, *Shevilei Aggadah* ["The Paths of Aggadah"] (1955; 1974[2]), which, like his father's anthology, focuses primarily on medieval sources. Yassif delves into this rich scholarship, makes his own insightful contributions to it, and in a graceful summative analysis offers for the first time a panoramic view of the Hebrew folktale that extends from the biblical period to the present.

In writing a history of the Hebrew folktale, Yassif faces an almost impossible, inherently paradoxical task. Oral narration is ephemeral, but historical analysis requires positive tangible evidence. He overcomes this dilemma by breaking down the dichotomy between orality and literacy. For the past thirty years, the interface between the written and the oral, to use the apt title of Jack Goody's book, has been the subject of intensive anthropological, psychological, and literary studies. Orality and literacy have been construed as two opposite modes of thought that generate mutually exclusive verbal representations: analogical vs. logical, poetic vs. scientific, magical vs. philosophical. Literacy produced an environment that excluded orality and its consequences.[9] Departing from this approach, Yassif proposes a historical method for the study of the oral within the written, as it is appropriate for Hebrew literature. In biblical Israelite society, and later even more so in Jewish societies, literacy and orality were not incompatible but reciprocal paradigms. The extent of literacy may have varied with respect to period, country, gender, and class.[10] But these differences opened the way for an examination of orality and literacy not as two abstract categories but as dynamic social forces in society, for which the conflicts between them have significant consequences.

The Hebrew Bible is at the center of Jewish national, cultural, and religious identity. It is the basis upon which all subsequent traditions developed. In narrative patterns, biographical models, and the literary representation of ethical values, the Hebrew Bible has become the basic reference for subsequent tales. It interprets and mediates Jewish historical experiences as an ideal, a model, a prophecy, and a charter. By the time of its assembly into a literary canon in the post-exilic period,[11] the Hebrew Bible itself cast in mythic terms the history about which it tells. Literacy in that case sanctioned traditional narratives as holy and true. Having been in their formative stage in pre-exilic times, some of these narrative texts represent in style, vocabulary, theme, and structure a primary transitional phase from orality to literacy. As Yassif points out, as much as the David and Goliath story (1 Samuel 17) is ingrained in Jewish consciousness as a basic historical metaphor, it is but a fictional tale that follows the fairytale pattern of a youngest son, David, who kills the monster, Goliath, and is rewarded with marriage to the king's beautiful daughter, Michal (1 Samuel 17–18). In structure and content it bears extraordinary similarity to Tale Type 300 "The Dragon-Slayer."[12] Later in the post-exilic period, when the Hebrew Bible achieved the status of a central culturally scripted text, ritualistically read, interpreted, and translated in public, it enabled the articulation of older noncanonic oral traditions and the literary creation of new tales on biblical themes.

As a canon, biblical literacy solidified religious beliefs and did not tolerate competing attitudes. Hence a rabbinical authority of the second century such as Rabbi Akiba is alleged to have condemned the Apocrypha and Pseudepigrapha in the strongest possible terms (Jerusalem Talmud *Sanhedrin* 10:1). As books these texts were more of a threat to the canon than the rejected theme that remained in oral tradition. They owed their origin to the literary mode, and as written text par excellence, their anonymous individual (and often sectarian) authors attributed them falsely to biblical figures in order to sanction them religiously and socially. Though they are replete with references to their literate rather than oral character (see 2 Enoch J, 33:8–9; see also 48:7; The Fourth Book of Ezra 14:45–48), as Yassif demonstrates in chapter 2, the presence of oral traditions is evident in these books as well. The cosmological views, the visions of heaven and the apocalyptic descriptions in Enoch, Baruch, and the Apocalypses of Abraham, Adam, Daniel, Elijah, Sedrach, and Zephania bear the stamp of cultural or sectarian ideas with a broad social basis rather than the imagination of a single author. Several of their stories draw upon oral traditions and recur independently in later rabbinical literature. They expand the biblical narrative, recording some folk legends, even fictive folk tales, of the Second Temple period.

While in the biblical period literacy was restricted in Israelite society, in the post-biblical period it gained ground and attained ritualistic status. Reading Scripture aloud in public became an integral part of religious worship. In order to reach its audience, however, the written fixed text required the mediation of oral tradition, or interpretation through free verbal, sometimes playful, association generated by the speech act of performance. The midrash, the oral literature that was text-bound and accompanied Bible reading in the synagogues, skirted the boundaries between literacy and orality and mediated between restricted and elaborated tradition.[13] In the performance process, the line of demarcation between orality and literacy blurred. The strong rabbinical edict "You shall not deliver/transmit sayings (transmitted) in writing orally; you shall not deliver/transmit sayings (transmitted) orally in writing" (Babylonian Talmud, *Gittin* 60b; *Temurah* 14b) evidences the transgression and its culturally disruptive consequences.

Under the pressure of critical historical circumstances, with the dwindling of the Jewish population in ancient Palestine and decline of support for public reading and oral interpretation of the Scripture, the very literature that oral performances generated, and the tradition that orally circulated, succumbed to the cultural urge of preservation that literacy affords. From the fourth century onward, editors and writers compiled midrashic books that transformed oral deliveries of sermons and narratives into cohesive works. Similarly, the edited Talmuds converted oral learned deliberations into literate arguments, nevertheless maintaining features and genres of orality. Yassif sifts through the rubble that the editors made of the speaking voice and recovers folktales in Hebrew and Aramaic that occur in several preserves of this vast literature. In the history of the Hebrew folktale that Yassif narrates, orality and literacy are contested dichotomies with fragile boundaries, switching their positions as transmission links in changing times and cultural authorities.

In the Middle Ages, the edited and scripted oral tradition of the talmudic-midrashic periods achieved the status of a cultural canon in Jewish societies. The narrative part of these books became a subject of oral and literary retelling and further editing into narrative anthologies, which included later medieval oral stories. The further dispersion of the Jews enabled individuals to escape the tight rabbinical control over literacy. These medieval writers and editors were learned people, but unlike the sages of previous generations, they did not have to submit to any moral or religious communal authority. Consequently, their books and manuscripts include immoral, even vulgar, traditions that no previous editor could have included, even if they were known orally. Such are some of the stories in the *Midrash on the Ten Commandments* (*Midrash 'aseret ha-dibrot*) and the *Alphabet of Ben-Sira*, two major tale collections that most likely originated in Iraq, the first dated from not earlier than the seventh and not later than the eleventh centuries, and the second from the tenth century. A later book from central Europe, *Book of the Pietists* (*Sefer Hasidim*), had a sectarian origin, yet it drew heavily upon the medieval German folk belief system. Its stories about demons, witches, and werewolves are steeped in European folk traditions and are not found in talmudic-midrashic sources.[14]

Individual professional scribes made records of Jewish folk literature in the Middle Ages, creating with their labor milestones that indicated the spread of tales through either oral or manuscript cultures. Probably the most prominent among these is Ms. no. 135 in the Oriental collection of the Bodleian Library at Oxford, which contains several medieval narrative and fable collections, such as *Alephbet of Ben-Sira, The Mishle Shu'alim (Fox Fables) of Rabbi Berechiah ha-Nakdan, Tales of Sendebar, A Chronicle of Moses, Midrash of the Ten Commandments, and Midrash va-Yosha,* and also includes a collection of sixty-one tales, twenty-four of which draw upon the talmudic-midrashic literature, nineteen of which have parallels in other Jewish medieval collections, and eighteen of which are newly recorded. The scribe wrote the manuscript in the northern Champagne region of France during the second quarter of the thirteenth century, not later than 1250.[15] Yassif considers this manuscript a milestone in the history of the Hebrew folktale and has edited a large part of it critically.[16]

By the Middle Ages, Jews in Asia and Europe spoke and wrote, using the Hebrew alphabet, in new Jewish languages such as Judeo-Arabic, Judeo-Berber, Judeo-Greek, Judeo-Italian, Judeo-Persian, Judeo-Spanish, and Yiddish. The diglossia in Jewish societies had two contrasting literary consequences, vernacularization and linguistic elevation. On the one hand writers and poets rendered biblical themes in vernacular languages, and on the other hand they wrote down spoken narratives in a literary medieval Hebrew. For example Rabbi Nissim ben Jacob ibn Shahin of Kairouan, Tunis (c. 990–1062), wrote one of the earliest medieval collection of talmudic-midrashic tales in Judeo-Arabic, *An Elegant Composition Concerning Relief after Adversity* (*Hibbur Yafe me-ha-Yeshu'ah*).[17] In Iran, Mawlana Shahin of Shiraz, the leading Judeo-Persian poet, wrote epic poems such as *Musa-Nameh* (c. 1327), an account of the biblical narrative of Moses; the *Ardashir-Nameh,* which retells the stories of the Book of Esther (c. 1332); and a poetic rendition of the book of Genesis (c. 1358) that includes some classical tales of Jewish biblical and oral tradition.[18] Literary compositions on traditional themes in Yiddish also date back to the fourteenth century. The earliest among them, known as "The Cambridge

Codex," was discovered in a cache of manuscripts (*genizah*) in Cairo. It dates from 1382 and includes poetic renditions of biblical themes which incorporate some of their oral literary elaboration.[19]

Aware of this process, Yassif focuses on the opposite trend, the elevation of spoken narratives into medieval literary Hebrew. He traces oral narratives in themes, traditional biographical patterns of cultural heroes, and historical and legendary accounts in medieval and later Hasidic Hebrew texts. During and after the Middle Ages, Jewish writers had available to them both possibilities, writing their texts in Hebrew or writing them in another, vernacular, Jewish language. Their choice of Hebrew for rendering oral and popular tales signified a clear authorial or scribal intention. They wished to ascribe to popular tales a cultural and ethical function similar to that of the traditional canonic tales. Regardless of their generic category, be it legend, fable, or fictive magical story, the entertaining narratives acquired a moral religious dimension that other texts in the same language had. In focusing on tales available only in Hebrew, Yassif excludes a rich tradition of oral tales, but at the same time he is able to highlight the thematic continuity and intertextuality of the Hebrew folktale tradition. Together with literacy, language itself provides a framework for cultural literary creativity. By their use of Hebrew, a language that had a restricted use in their society, the writers and scribes of folktales attributed to the oral texts they heard qualities similar to those they perceived in texts they read. Latin enjoyed a status among the European vernacular languages similar to that of Hebrew among other Jewish languages.

Such relations between language and religion continued in Jewish traditional societies beyond the chronological medieval period, well into the eighteenth and nineteenth centuries, and up to the threshold of modern times. During these centuries in Hasidic circles, Yiddish was the language of oral narration, and Hebrew was the language of books, including folk books. Around the turn of the twentieth century, Hebrew experienced a dramatic recovery and once again became a spoken language in the Jewish settlements in what was then Palestine.[20] For a while, as the Hebrew author Yosef Hayyim Brenner (1881–1921) laments,[21] there was no folklore in Hebrew, only in other Jewish languages, but now there is. As in previous historical periods, the literary evidence, and even the mass-media recordings, trail behind the speaking voices of the people. However, language offers Yassif a thread of continuity, which he follows up to present-day Israel. In all historical periods he captures the Hebrew folktale in the critical moment of transformation from orality to literacy, offering in the process a glimpse of folktales in other Jewish languages.

The continuity that language and literacy offer to the Hebrew oral tale unfolds a narrative tradition that comparative scholarship has considered only in terms of its mediating function. As Stith Thompson wrote in mid-century in his classic study of *The Folktale*,

There still exist in various parts of Asia Minor and Syria Jewish traditions which come down in many instances from antiquity. These Jewish peoples played an important part in the transmission of tales between Europe and Asia. Many of their stories certainly became known to Jewish communities scattered throughout Europe, but accurate understanding of their role in the dissemination of folktales has never been reached.[22]

For Thompson, these communities, at the gateway between Asia and Europe, were bridges on the silk road of oral narrative diffusion, in much the same way that medieval translators were the mediating agents between Eastern and Western literate traditions. Much has changed since Thompson made his observation. The communities he describes are no longer there. Indeed, these and many other Jewish communities in the Islamic and Mediterranean countries had a rich narrative tradition that infused narratives from East and West. After the establishment of Israel in 1948, they migrated to the new state and other parts of the world. The specific Syrian Jews that Thompson mentions are members of a global community today.[23] In Israel, many of their tales, and those of other Jewish communities from around the world, have been recorded and are on deposit at the Israel Folktale Archives (IFA). But for Thompson then, and for many folklorists in Europe and America yet, the mediating function made the Hebrew folktale important.

Yassif offers a new perspective—the Hebrew folktale as no longer just a bridge, a diffusing agent, or a link, but an oral literary tradition that has its own set of narrative figures, roles, themes, and patterns. It has a unique history that is bound up with the historical experience of the Jewish people and with the particular modes of communication that are distinctive to the Jewish culture. As with all narrative traditions in any other language, there are universal themes, ideas, and plots in the Hebrew folktale. Some are borrowed from other traditions; some evolved independently among the Jews. Influenced by and influencing other traditions, the Hebrew folktale also served as a transmission channel in the global routes of folktale dispersion. But this role in the international diffusion of folktales was incidental to its function in its own Jewish culture. Negotiating their performances between orality and literacy, Jewish narrators told their stories within a vibrant tradition that was alive in diverse ethnic communities in the past and continues to resonate today.

Notes

1. Heda Jason and A. Kempinski, "How Old Are Folktales?" *Fabula* 22 (1981):1–27.
2. When employed sexually in the Hebrew Bible, the verb "to come" refers to the male act; see Genesis 16:14; Genesis 29:30; 30:4; 2 Samuel 16:22; Ezekiel 23:33. When this verb is employed sexually in reference to a female, the formulaic use is "she came [went] and lay"

(*va-tavo—va-tishkav*); see Genesis 19:33; Ruth 3:7. This formula does not occur in the biblical rendition of the Queen of Sheba story.

3. *Jewish Antiquities* 8.6.5–6.

4. See E. Ullendorff, "Candace (Acts VIII.27) and the Queen of Sheba," *New Testament Studies* 2, no. 1 (1955): 53–56.

5. D.C. Duling, "Testament of Solomon (First to Third Century A.D.)," in James H. Charlesworth, ed., *The Old Testament Pseudepigrapha: Apocalyptic Literature and Testaments* (Garden City: Doubleday, 1983), I: 942.

6. Jacob Lassner, *Demonizing the Queen of Sheba: Boundaries of Gender and Culture in Postbiblical Judaism and Medieval Islam* (Chicago: University of Chicago Press, 1993), p. 14. Solomon Schechter identifies the manuscript compiler as Yachya Ben Sulieman, who wrote it as late as 1430. The riddles themselves have parallels in earlier Jewish sources, as well as in the traditions of other peoples. See his article "The Riddle of Solomon in Rabbinic Literature," *Folk-Lore* 1 (1890): 349–58.

7. Y. Avida, "The Queen of Sheba Story," pp. 1–17 in *Sefer Assaf: A Collection of Essays in Honor of Simha Assaf,* ed. M. D. Cassuto, J. Klausner, and J. Guttman (Jerusalem: Mossad Harav Kook, 1953). For further bibliographical references to the relevant sources and literature about the tale of King Solomon and the Queen of Sheba, see M. J. Bin Gorion, *Mimekor Yisrael: Classical Jewish Folktales—Abridged and Annotated Edition* (Bloomington: Indiana University Press, 1990), no. 25, pp. 39–43, as well Lassner, *Demonizing the Queen of Sheba;* Dina Stein, "The Queen of Sheba vs. Solomon: Riddles and Interpretation in Midrash Mishlei A," *Jerusalem Studies in Jewish Folklore* 15 (1993): 7–36 (Hebrew); Burton L. Visotzky, *The Midrash on Proverbs* (New Haven: Yale University Press, 1992), pp. 18–19.

8. For example, Meyer Waxman, *A History of Jewish Literature,* 5 vols. (New York: T. Yoseloff, 1960); Israel Zinberg, *A History of Jewish Literature,* trans. and ed. Bernard Martin, 12 vols. (Cleveland: Press of Case Western Reserve University, 1972–78). The literatures in other Jewish languages have been studied, but their comprehensive histories are yet to be written.

9. Orality and its transition to literacy have received serious scholarly attention in recent years. Selected studies of these processes are M. T. Clanchy, *From Memory to Written Record: England 1066–1307* (Cambridge, Mass.: Harvard University Press, 1979); James Collins, "Litereacy and Literacies," *Annual Review of Anthropology* 24 (1995):7 5–93; A. N. Doane and Carol Braun Pasternack, eds., *Vox Intexta: Orality and Textuality in the Middle Ages* (Madison: University of Wisconsin Press, 1991); Bruno Gentili and G. Paioni, eds., *Oralità: Cultura, Letteratura, Discorso: atti del convegno internazionale (Urbino 21–25 luglio 1980)* (Rome: Edizioni dell' Ateneo, 1985); Ruth Finnegan, *Literacy and Orality* (Oxford: Blackwell, 1988); J. Goody, *Literacy in Traditional Societies* (Cambridge: Cambridge University Press, 1968); idem, *The Domistication of the Savage Mind* (Cambridge: Cambridge University Press, 1977); idem, *The Logic of Writing and the Organization of Society* (Cambridge: Cambridge University Press, 1986); idem, *The Interface between the Written and the Oral* (Cambridge: Cambridge University Press, 1987); W. V. Harris, *Ancient Literacy* (Cambridge, Mass.: Harvard University Press, 1989); Marcel Jousse, *Le parlant, la parole et le souffle* (Paris: Gallimard, 1978); idem, *The Oral Style,* trans. Edgard Sienaert and Richard Whitaker, The Albert Bates Lord Studies in Oral Tradition 6 (New York: Garland, 1990); Werner H. Kelber, *The Oral and the Written Gospel: The Hermeneutics of Speaking and Writing in the Synoptic Tradition, Mark, Paul, and Q* (Bloomington: Indiana University Press, 1997); K. O. O'Keefe, *Visible Song: Transitional Literacy in Old English Verse* (Cambridge: Cambridge University Press, 1990); Walter J. Ong, *Interfaces of the Word: Studies in the Evolution of Consciousness and Culture* (Ithaca: Cornell University Press, 1971); idem, *Rhetoric, Romance, and Technology:*

Studies in the Interaction of Expression and Culture (Ithaca: Cornell University Press, 1971); idem, *Orality and Literacy: The Technologizing of the Word* (New York: Methuen, 1982); K. Schousboe and M. T. Larsen, eds., *Literacy and Society* (Copenhagen: Akademisk Forlag, 1989); Brian V. Street, *Literacy in Theory and Practice* (Cambridge: Cambridge University Press, 1985; Deborah Tannen, ed., *Spoken and Written Language: Exploring Orality and Literacy*, Advances in Discourse Processes 9 (Norwood, N.J.: Ablex, 1982); Rosalind Thomas, *Literacy and Orality in Ancient Greece* (Cambridge: Cambridge University Press, 1992); Y. Zakovitch, "From Oral to Written Tale in the Bible," *Jerusalem Studies in Jewish Folklore* 1 (1981): 9–43 (Hebrew).

10. See, for example, M. Haran, "On the Diffusion of Literacy and Schools in Ancient Israel," in *Congress Volume: Jerusalem 1986*, ed. J. A. Emerton, Vetus Testamentum Supplement 40 (Leiden: Brill, 1988), 81–95.

11. Menahem Haran, *The Biblical Collection: Its Consolidation to the End of the Second Temple Times and Changes of Form to the End of the Middle Ages* (Jerusalem: The Bialik Institute, 1996) (Hebrew).

12. Heda Jason, "The Story of David and Goliath: A Folk Epic?" *Biblica* 60 (1979): 23–41; and see Pamela J. Milne, *Vladimir Propp and the Study of Structure in Hebrew Biblical Narrative*, Bible and Literature Series (Sheffield: Almond Press, 1988).

13. There is a voluminous scholarship about the midrash. For a recent summary see Dan Ben-Amos, "Midrasch," *Enzyklopädie des Märchens* 9: 641–52. The contrasting pair of restricted and elaborated tradition is borrowed here from Basil Bernstein, *Class, Codes and Control*, vol. 1: *Theoretical Studies towards a Sociology of Language* (London: Routledge and Kegan Paul, 1971), 76–94. In Bernstein's use the terms have different methodological applications, although he considers "ritualistic modes of communication" to be a pure form of a restricted code (p. 77).

14. See Tamar Alexander-Frizer, *The Pious-Sinner: Ethics and Aesthetics in the Medieval Hasidic Narrative*, Text and Studies in Medieval and Early Modern Judaism 5 (Tübingen: J. C. B. Mohr [Paul Siebeck], 1991); Micha Joseph bin Gorion, *Mimekor Yisrael: Classical Jewish Folktales, Abridged and Annotated Edition*, ed. Emanuel bin Gorion, trans. I. M. Lask, annotated by Dan Ben-Amos (Bloomington: Indiana University Press, 1990): 441–47 [nos. 227–34]; Joseph Dan, *The Esoteric Theology of the Ashkenazi Hasidim* (Jerusalem: The Bialik Institute, 1968) [Hebrew]; I. G. Marcus, *Piety and Society: The Jewish Pietists of Medieval Germany* (Leiden: E. J. Brill, 1981); Eli Yassif. "Entre culture populaire et culture savante: les exempla dans le *Sefer Hasidim*," *Annales: Histoires, Sciences Sociales* 5 (1994): 1197–1222.

15. See Eli Yassif, "Sepher ha-Ma'asim," *Tarbiz* 53 (1984): 409–29 (Hebrew); Malachi Beit-Arié, "Ms. Oxford, Bodleian Library, Bodl. Or. 135," *Tarbiz* 54 (1985): 631–634 (Hebrew).

16. Forthcoming by the Bialik Institute.

17. See Shraga Abramson, *Nissim Gaon: Libelli Quinque* (Jerusalem: Mekizei Nirdamim, 1965) [Hebrew and Arabic in Hebrew letters]; Nissim ben-Jacob ibn Shahin, *An Elegant Composition Concerning Relief after Adversity* trans. William M. Brinner, Yale Judaica Series vol. 20 (New Haven: Yale University Press, 1977); Julian Oberman, ed., *The Arabic Original of Ibn Shâhîn's Book of Comfort Known. Hibbûr Yaphê of R. Nissîm b. Ya'aqobh*, Yale Oriental Series, Researches vol. 17 (New Haven: Yale University Press, 1933).

18. See Ulrich Marzolph, "Judeo-Persian Narratives," *Jewish Folklore and Ethnology Review* 14, nos. 1–2 (1992): 14; Vera B. Moreen, "The Legend of Adam in the Judeo-Persian Epic *Bereshit* [*Namah*] (14th Century)," *Proceedings of the American Academy for Jewish Research* 57 (1991): 156–78; idem, "Moses, God's Shepherd: An Episode from a Judeo-Persian Epic," *Prooftexts* 11 (1991): 107–30; idem, "Dialogue between God and Satan in Shahin's *Bereshit Nama*," in *Irano-Judaica III*, ed. Shaul Shaked and Amnon Netzer (Jerusalem: Ben-Zvi Insistute, 1994): 127–41.

19. See Jean Baumgarten, *Introduction á la littérature yiddish ancienne* (Paris: CERF, 1993), 163–200; L. Fuks, *The Oldest Known Literary Documents of Yiddish Literature (c. 1382)*, 2 vols. (Leiden: E. J. Brill, 1957); H. J. Hakkarainen, *Studien zum Cambridge Codex T-S. 10. K. 22* (Turku: Turun Yliopisto, 1967–73); Khone Shmeruk, *Yiddish Literature: Aspects of Its History*, Literature, Meaning, Culture vol. 4 (Tel Aviv: The Porter Institute for Poetics and Semiotics, Tel Aviv University, 1978), 117–36; Chava Turniansky, "Two Old-Yiddish Biblical Epics on the Book of Joshua," *Tarbiz* 51 (1982): 589–632; Israel Zinberg, *A History of Jewish Literature*, trans. and ed. Bernard Martin, 12 vols. (Cincinnati: Hebrew Union College Press; New York: Ktav, 1975), 7, 49–118.

20. See Benjamin Harshav, *Language in Time of Revolution* (Berkeley: University of California Press, 1993).

21. See Dan Ben-Amos, "Nationalism and Nihilism: The Attitudes of Two Hebrew Authors toward Folklore," *International Folklore Review* 1 (1981): 10–12.

22. S. Thompson, *The Folktale* (New York: Holt, Rinehart and Winston, 1946), 17.

23. See Joseph A. D. Sutton, *Magic Carpet: Aleppo-in-Flatbush—The Story of a Unique Ethnic Jewish Community* (New York: Thayer-Jacoby, 1986); Walter Zenner, *Aram Soba: The Story of a Global Jewish Community*, forthcoming in the Raphael Patai Series for Jewish Folklore and Anthropology (Detroit: Wayne State University Press).

Acknowledgments

This book is a monograph dedicated to a special branch of Jewish culture—the folktale (or folk narrative). It chronologically describes the main periods of folk creativity from the Hebrew Bible to our own time. However, its orientation is by no means historical, but generic. By using generic distinctions, it describes the major characteristics of the Hebrew folktale in each of the main periods of the history of Jewish culture. The generic distinctions in the following study are not an end, but rather the means through which the main goal of this book will be achieved: exploring and understanding the social function and cultural meaning of the Hebrew folktale.

Although this book is dedicated to one branch of Jewish literature, its goal is much wider: it strives to define and emphasize the place of folk creativity in Jewish culture. The folkloric elements act in complex relationships of contest and adaptation with the elite, institutional Jewish culture. The history of Jewish culture is, essentially, the history of this struggle. This book was not written only for the scholar and expert. Its purpose is to open for everyone who is interested in Jewish culture a rich, variegated, and important domain only recently recognized as a legitimate part of Jewish culture.

This goal is the reason for the book's division into two main parts: the text and the notes. In the text I tried to avoid esoteric terms and concepts and scholarly controversies on methodology and interpretation of texts. The main emphasis of the book's first part is the texts themselves: I attempt to present in full or paraphrase the main and representative texts of each major period, genre, and theme of Hebrew folk literature. My purpose is to present to readers, especially those for whom the Hebrew sources are not available, each one of the major periods through its own authentic, folkloric sources.

The second part of this book consists of the notes. This part is dedicated mainly to the scholar and student. Here I describe in detail the sources of the texts and their variants, the relevant scholarly works regarding each theme and text discussed in the book, and scholarly controversies of definition, interpretation, and methodology. These notes are written in the form of condensed monographs and not simply of bibliographic citations. The two parts of the book are intended for different readers: the reader of general, intellectual interest may read only the text and the student might use the notes independently, as a bibliographical summary and methodological discussion.

The original Hebrew edition of this book was published in 1994. The English translation is essentially the same, excepting some omissions in the last chapter

("The Later Generation"), which I consider of interest only to Israeli readers of Hebrew—in order to rewrite these sections for the English reader would mean to write another book. In addition, I revised the bibliographical notes to include publications up to the beginning of 1998, and so update the status of research in the field.

This book was formulated during the years I taught the introductory course of Jewish folklore at Ben-Gurion and Tel Aviv Universities in Israel, at London University, and the University of California–Berkeley. I am thankful and proud to acknowledge the contribution of my students to the dialogue which led to the writing of this book.

The long process of translating and updating this work could not have been achieved without the help of two institutions: the President, Rector, and Dean of Humanities of Tel Aviv University contributed generously to this project, and the Memorial Foundation for Jewish Culture, which admirably contributes to Jewish studies all over the world, helped me achieve this end as well.

The translation of this book was started right after its publication in Hebrew by Nathan Reisner, who translated the first two chapters. The translation of the book as a whole has been done by Jacqueline Teitelbaum, whose diligence, precision, and good understanding carried the project to its completion. The translation of a book which extensively uses texts written in Biblical Hebrew, Rabbinical style, Medieval Hebrew vernacular, and Hasidic jargon is almost an impossible achievement, and it was done here with courage and precision.

My friend and senior colleague Dan Ben-Amos is the single person without whose advice, debate, and encouragement this book could never appear in English. His deep understanding of the folklore phenomenon, mastery of folkloric research, and wide knowledge of Jewish folklore were sources of support, positive criticism, and encouragement.

I dedicate this book to my children Na'ama, Efrat, and Yinon, and to my wife, Shoshi, who walked with me the long and difficult road of writing and translating this work.

Tel Aviv University
September, 1998

The Hebrew Folktale

1   Introduction

Jewish Culture and the Hebrew Folktale

Varied and complex motives underlie the need for a comprehensive history of the Hebrew folktale. The foremost of these motives is the predisposition of each generation to reexamine its cultural heritage. The openness of recent cultural studies to areas of creativity largely ignored in the past, along with the notion that all branches of life and creativity are dynamically intertwined, has brought the scholarly study of folk culture out of the academic wilderness. This examination of the folk foundation of Hebrew storytelling throughout the history of Jewish culture is anchored in that notion. To be sure, attempts to understand the folk component of many works, and of more general folk phenomena, as well, have been made in the discipline known as "Jewish studies." However, an inclusive study with regard for the uniqueness and development of Hebrew storytelling is important and productive in its own right. The first comprehensive work in this field, Emanuel bin-Gorion's *Shevilei ha-Aggadah* (*Pathways of the Aggadah*, Jerusalem: The Bialik Institute, 1950) was published half a century ago. Despite its initial importance as a pioneering work, it was too eclectic—comprising a popular survey of international folk literature, some comments on folkloristics and its development through the 1940s, and a review of the main periods of Jewish folk literature—along with a healthy dollop of the author's personal musings derived from nineteenth-century German Romanticism as well as the individualistic outlook of his father, the great Hebrew writer and thinker, Micha Josef Berdyczewski. Bin-Gorion's volume served as the Hebrew primer on the subject for some forty years. Since its appearance, drastic changes have taken place in folklore research in general, in the study of Jewish folk literature, and in the academic status of folkloristics within the field of Jewish Studies. Thus, it is no longer possible to regard bin-Gorion's work as a reflection of the status of the discipline in the latter part of the twentieth century.

The study of Jewish folk literature has taken great strides forward in recent decades. The intensive activity of Dov Noy and his students continued the trail blazed by S. D. Goitein, E. Brauer, R. Patai, D. Sadan, and Y. T. Lewinski before the institutional establishment of the field as an academic discipline in Israel. The flourishing of the discipline is evident now in the publication of academic periodicals and doctoral dissertations on Hebrew folk literature and in the founding of large folk literature departments in Israeli universities. Perhaps the pinnacle of Hebrew folktale research in this generation is The Israel Folktale Archives (IFA), which has attracted and inspired hundreds of professional scholars, amateur folklorists, storytellers, authors, and students.

Another outstanding development in Jewish folkloristics of the past generation is a new openness to international folklore research. In generations past, unlike today, awareness and use of the general research literature were most rare. The international literature constitutes a basis for new approaches to the Hebrew folktale. The beginning student, as well as the scholar, requires an in-depth recognition of these developments in general theory. Researchers of the Jewish folktale now participate regularly in international forums and conventions for the study of international folk literature. Thus Jewish folk literature and its study have joined the list of research topics considered by the international community. This openness to general and theoretical research is of great importance in determining the image of the field in the academic world and in society at large.[1]

The escape of Jewish folkloristics from marginality in Jewish studies, similar to that of the study of folklore in the humanities and social sciences, spares us the need to apologize. No longer need we seek justification for dealing with folk literature in the various purposes to which this author or that philosopher applied folktales. We cannot hope to fully comprehend a culture if we focus only on its elite. Parallel to the displays of individualistic, original, and innovative creativity, there exists the culture of the society in its broadest sense, whose creations are traditional and archetypical. The true expression of a society's being, from its intelligentsia through its most marginal cultural sub-strata, are those "traditional" creations that were produced by generations of anonymous artists and transmitted onward as part of the society's spiritual heritage. Any attempt to understand the culture of the past, and certainly that of the present, while ignoring its most candid and unbiased expressions of creativity, can no longer be considered valid. Study of the folktale has a value and importance of its own, both as an investigation of a literary phenomenon whose existence is as old as Jewish culture, and as a medium that faithfully reflects Jewish society through the ages, with all its tensions and hidden aspirations, illuminating its view of itself and of the world around it.[2]

These are the premises that underlie this examination of the history of the Hebrew folktale. This book's chief purpose is to present as complete and nuanced a picture of folk narrative as possible. The premises, definitions, distinctions, and conclusions presented below are based on research conducted in recent generations into Jewish and general folk literature. They should not be taken solely as the author's individual approach, but as the result of the past two hundred years of folk literature research. This said, it must also be stated that the responsibility for applying this wealth of research to the description of the history of the Hebrew folktale, in general outlines as in details, falls entirely upon the author.

Any study of the folktale of the periods that preceded the modern age must contend with an intrinsic problem: the tale is documented in literary, religious, historical, and contemplative sources and serves in them as a vehicle for the purposes of the host text. The folktales have thus undergone radical changes to suit these functions and goals. While their very commission to writing in literary contexts did, in a sense, uproot them from the natural contexts of their creation and dissemination, it also made possible their preservation for later generations. The attitude of the contextual school to these literary context-bound texts is skeptical because they were wrenched from the soil of their societal growth, underwent changes, and were preserved in a way that erased the traces of their place and function in "real life." I view the literary context as no less a place for the growth and legitimate development of the folktale than any other social context. While it is no longer possible to reconstruct in any valid fashion the social context in which the folktale of the past was created or used, we may well ask what function a folktale serves in the literary context in which it is found, what changes it underwent in order to fulfill this function, and how a given literary formulation influenced later development of the folktale. Authors and poets, thinkers and moralists, travelers and historians have always made intensive use of folktales. The versions which they created or borrowed constitute objects of investigation as legitimate as any version recorded in fieldwork. To be sure, scholarship must be alert to the differences between versions recorded orally and those found in literary sources, but, in principle, the latter should not be ranked as inferior. After all, writers, historians, and philosophers also have a right to be part of "the folk."

The folktale was preserved as part of a sacred and normative cultural canon in two main periods in the history of Jewish literature: the biblical and the rabbinic periods. This hinders any description of the folktale in these periods, for neither the Bible, the Talmud, nor the Midrash are folk literature. They do not meet its basic conditions, and the circumstances of their emergence are so complex that it is impossible to identify in these works, even dimly, the motives of their compilers and authors. By contrast, it is possible to retrieve, or discern, the impulses that drove the editors and authors of folk books dating from later periods. Adding to the difficulties of forming a general picture are the numerous contexts that frame the folktale. The historical, theological, halachic, and homiletic contexts place the folktales at the very center of debates about the meaning of the texts, which has always made it difficult to read them as ordinary folktales (e.g., the biblical tale of the parting of the Red Sea, which is incorporated in the section on the Exodus from Egypt and the consolidation of the nation, or the talmudic fable of the fox and the fish, which is at the heart of the story about the martyr's death of Rabbi Akiva).

The current study had first to determine the principles that would govern the location and classification of folktales from the distant past. This was no simple task, for we do not know whether any distinction even existed between folk literature and learned literature during the biblical, Second Temple, and rabbinical periods. Nor can we know for certain if the denizens of these bygone ages distinguished between the various genres of the folktale, or if they even recognized these genres. In sifting through the vast narrative material of the Bible or rabbinic literature for evidence of the existence of folktales, we must rely on those principles learned from the narrative traditions of our time. With these tools, we can attempt to describe the tales of the past. The basic assumption of this method is that the character of folk narrative—and how it is told— has not changed fundamentally in spite of the thousands of years that have elapsed between then and now. Indeed, studies of the folk traditions of ancient Middle Eastern cultures—Egypt, Sumer, Babylonia, and Israel—show that, apart from known changes stemming from social and cultural context, they were told in the same form as are folktales today. The subjects of the tales, the genres to which they can be ascribed, their literary construction, and even their context (in those cases where it has survived) are similar to those of contemporary folk literature. Hence, the means most suited for defining the folktales in the historical sources are those that were developed in the study of contemporary narrative traditions. The genres of the folktales, their cultural contexts, literary structure, and social functions are the basic principles according to which we examine contemporary folktales, and are the tools we must employ in our study of the folk narrative of the past.[3]

Another basic difficulty is that the Bible, the Talmud, and the Midrash are almost the sole extant sources regarding the Jewish culture of their times, and they contain the only evidence of the folk literature of the period. Every description of a Hebrew folktale in the biblical or rabbinic period has only this source—these books—for the culture of these periods. It bears reemphasis that the Bible, the Talmud, and the Midrash are not folk-books. Hence, not all the stories they contain are folktales. Much, if not most, of the vast narrative material they comprise was produced in the literary circles or academies of the rabbinic period and is, in every sense, scholarly material. Still, these works provide unique and significant testimony to the richness of Hebrew folk literature in the two central periods of Jewish culture. Hebrew literature from the Middle Ages and thereafter is less problematic because of the separation of the disciplines: that is, the creation of special compositions for various fields (commentaries, Halacha, linguistics, history, liturgy, etc.) also led to the creation of special works for narrative. In these compositions, the folk component is dominant, facilitating the location of folktales.

Another difficulty intrinsic to the present investigation is posed by the concept of a "Hebrew folktale" as distinct from a "Jewish folktale." Linguistic criteria determine the former, while the latter has a national characteristic. The folktale told and written in Hebrew was always linked to folktales told by Jews in other languages, primarily those termed "Jewish languages." Too narrow a focus on Hebrew folktales, as separate from those told in languages such as Yiddish, Judeo-Arabic, and Judeo-Spanish, dangerously limits the phenomenon that we seek to treat here. It is, furthermore, clear to every student of Jewish culture that, for long periods of time, Hebrew was an unspoken language, and that Jewish life was conducted in languages borrowed from the cultures among which Jews resided, languages which they adapted to their needs. Hence a large number of the folktales in Jewish society were not told in Hebrew at all.

These and similar limitations and reservations, it seems to me, cannot negate the relevance and importance of the notion of the "Hebrew folktale." There is no denying that the vicissitudes of Jewish history have been matched by those of the folktale that accompanied it. Yet the Jewish culture forged in Hebrew had clear characteristics that distinguished it from those created in other languages. This culture, though neither more Jewish nor less, is different. The great bilingual authors, such as Maimonides, knew precisely which of their works should be written in Hebrew and which would best serve in other Jewish languages. In other words, even though all phenomena in Jewish culture are intertwined, we may not skirt the attempt to understand them as individual entities. The Hebrew folktale influenced and was itself influenced by works in other Jewish languages, and it was translated and adapted from such works, just as it underwent these same processes in relation to the international folktale. While these links are discussed in the following study, the basic premise of the work is that the history of the Hebrew folktale is unique and has clearly identifiable markers.

This work must also contend with the claim that Hebrew was not the living, spoken language of Jewish society and therefore not the language of its folk literature. As Latin was the written language for the European peoples during the Middle Ages, so Hebrew was, for the Jews, the language of communication, unfettered by barriers of time and geography. Even if the folktales were told in Aramaic, Judeo-Arabic, or Yiddish, two crucial points must be understood: first, most Jewish folktales have reached us in Hebrew, not in the other languages. Attempts to reconstruct their original tongue are limited to the realm of conjecture. Research can relate only to the folktales as they exist in Hebrew, for only thus have they survived the ravages of time. Second, Hebrew was the only language of communication common to all communities of the Jewish people across the lands of its dispersion. Jewish emissaries that roamed Europe, gathering contributions for their academies, spoke with their co-religionists there in Hebrew. Jewish travelers from Europe who went to tour the wonders of the Holy Land, or visited the Jewish communities in Yemen, heard the stories of their brethren there only in Hebrew. It is known and acknowledged that at no stage of Jewish history was the Hebrew language truly "dead." Even though it did not serve as a living, day-to-day language, but as the language of cultural activity, its place was ever central. The folktale, as one means of forging cultural communication and the place of the tale that survived in Hebrew, orally and in writing, requires our attention.[4]

The variety of narratives contained in the literary sources, the particular problems of each period, and the involvement of the folktale in the most important components of Jewish culture in each period, would seem to justify the writing of separate books on the folktales of each period. Indeed, at least as concerns the folk literature of the Bible (here and throughout this work, the term "Bible" refers solely to the Hebrew Bible), a number of monographs have already been written. In this study, I do not concentrate on questions of the history of the folktale within a specific period, the extensive scholarly literature, or the various ramifications for the culture of each given period. Important as such subjects are, they are liable to divert discussion from its primary objective: to describe and define, by means of essential evidence, the place of the folktale in the history of Jewish culture, with an encompassing view of the tale against the background of its time and locale, and with special emphasis on the changing character of the tales in transition between the periods. The intention is to see the folktale in the history of Hebrew literature as a continuous factor developing synchronously with Jewish culture and history through the generations, influenced by the trends characteristic of each period.

The nature of the folktale caused it to reflect, and react to, the dominant events of Jewish history. Consequently, it cannot be separated from historical events, cultural developments, or the main currents of thought to wind their way through the long years of Jewish history. The tracing of a single cultural phenomenon, as variegated as it may be, cannot, and is not intended to, be all-encompassing. Still, the examples from each period selected for analysis, and the narrative genres discussed, are the most salient and representative of their respective cultural periods. They were chosen because of their high level of representation in the evidence from that period. In this regard, the following chapters also describe the history of the Hebrew folktale, although they cannot cite or discuss every folktale ever recounted in Hebrew.

Among the most interesting and difficult questions pertaining to the description of the Hebrew folktale, two in particular require attention: Is it possible to indicate a continuum in its history? Are there specific qualities that set it apart from the folk narrative of other cultures? The answers to these important questions must follow, rather than precede, historical description. Still, a recurring phenomenon in the structure of this book is noteworthy at this juncture: each chapter (except for that treating the biblical period, of course) opens with a description of the tales of that period whose origin lies in the previous cultural period. The chapter on the folktales of the Second Temple period opens with the place of biblical tales at that time, and the chapter on the tale in the rabbinic period opens likewise, with the transition of the Second Temple period traditions to the folk literature of the rabbinic period. It bears emphasis that this structure was not a result of a predetermined historiographical orientation, but flowed from the factual evidence of the period itself. In other words, the most prominent and certain characteristic of Hebrew folk narrative is its self-perception as an ongoing cultural continuum.

With reverential awe, I embark on this long, difficult, and fascinating journey, on the trail of one of the most dynamic phenomena in the history of Jewish culture.

2   The Biblical Period

The Folktale as Sacred History

Every critical reader of the books of the Hebrew Bible accepts the premise that these literary creations were penned by numerous authors, in various places, over a period of a great many years. The vast similarity between the literature of the Bible and the sacred literatures created in other cultures has, moreover, raised the possibility that the current versions of the biblical books underwent extensive development in the course of which their content, form, and character changed beyond recognition. Accepted, too, is the supposition that, during at least part of the period in which the biblical books evolved, they were created and transmitted orally among many ancient peoples, particularly in the cultures of nomadic tribes—which designation of course includes the ancient Hebrew tribes. This bespeaks an obvious connection between folkloric creativity and various parts of the Bible. Indeed, since the work of Hermann Gunkel in the late nineteenth and early twentieth centuries, scholarship applying folkloristic research methods to biblical literature has gained tremendous momentum. Works of biblical folkloristics are today so numerous and variegated that they cover a large proportion of biblical narrative, poetry, historical chapters, and the Wisdom books. The primary (and often sole) aim of these studies is biblical inquiry: analysis of the sources and development of the biblical texts; comparison of different versions of tales to facilitate the understanding and interpretation of biblical topics; analysis of the pattern and style of various biblical texts; understanding the social background from which the biblical literature grew; bringing historical criticism to bear on the truth of the events recounted, employing, *inter alia*, archaeological finds.[1]

Biblical scholars saw the folktale as a point of departure from which to investigate the biblical text. Not so this discussion; herein the Bible is taken as a source for the description and comprehension of the Hebrew folktale in the biblical period. The Bible stands nearly alone in testimony to the Hebrew culture of this period. The tales and the evidence of the folk culture of the ancient Middle East that survived in Sumer, Babylonia, Phoenicia, Canaan, and Egypt can serve as parallels and can be used to fill in the historical details, but in and of themselves are not considered part of the study of the Hebrew folktale of the period. It bears reemphasis that the Hebrew Bible is not ethnographic-folk material. It contains the only extant evidence from the biblical period of the rich and multifaceted folk culture that was set down in writing out of religious, historical, national, and artistic motives. The reconstruction of the image of Hebrew folk narrative of the biblical period relies solely upon that complex and multifaceted written literature.

The initial difficulty in examining the biblical folk narrative is the (usually impossible) task of separating it from its biblical context. This context, the concern of biblical scholars, very much hampers a description of the Hebrew folktale based on biblical material. This is perhaps also the reason for the occasionally contradictory interpretations of biblical tales—the meaning of the biblical text itself was inadequately severed from that of the folktale that was its foundation, as we shall see further on. The meaning of the ancient folktale was sometimes attributed to the literary text in the Bible, and sometimes the reverse was true. Biblical research in the last generation has improved its methods in striving to reach a basic distinction between the folktale and its literary formulation in Scripture. Such a distinction is most important for describing the character of the folktale in the biblical period, and I intend to deal below only with those tales that can with (relative) certainty be considered folktales. This identification is based on folkloristic definition of a folktale: it must have a multiple existence (i.e., different versions of a tale in the Bible itself, in literary remnants of the ancient Near East, or in international folk narrative); a literary structure that fulfills the basic conditions of folk literature; the main narrative motifs of which it is constructed must belong to the defined constellation of international folk motification, and its intended function in the narrating society.[2]

An examination of the biblical folktale repertoire must consider its variety and complexity. This is hardly surprising, as biblical literary creation spans a period of over a thousand years of culture. It follows that the folk literature created during this time frame will also be complex and multifaceted. This complexity manifests itself on several levels. These are the narrative genres, the narrative types and their structure, the subjects and motifs therein, the overall contexts of the tales, and their social functions.

All the books of the Bible contain folktales and elements of folk literature, and the scope of germane material in this regard is vast. This is not meant to be an exhaustive compendium of the noteworthy folkloric aspects of biblical folk literature. I have chosen to present examples characteristic of the folktale in the biblical period according to the generic division that has become standard in the study of folk literature. This is because the generic model is not bound by the contextual or chronological chains that bind the biblical folkloric materials. Division by genre enables the highlighting of these materials against the background of international folklore, with emphasis on their pattern, typical themes, and social function. In biblical research, there is much discussion of generic classification but, with few exceptions, this research does not employ precisely the generic terminology accepted in the study of folk literature. The description below will be based completely on the generic distinctions developed in folk-literature research from its beginnings in the work of Jakob and Wilhelm Grimm.[3]

The abundant and intensive scholarship of the Bible as folklore is due to the general and comprehensive interest in Scripture itself. As a result, investigation of the folk literature of the biblical period is more developed than that of all other periods of Jewish culture. I felt it unnecessary to deal with all the folk motifs or tales in the Bible. I treat the predominant ones and refer the reader to studies dealing in greater detail with texts not discussed here.

[A] The Myth

The seminal folk genre, and perhaps the oldest, is the myth. It is found in the Bible in its two common, classical, forms: a narrative of the world of the gods, detailing their struggles with other primal forces and their relationships with the human world; and the myth as an account of the origin of things and the various phenomena of our world (the "etiological myth"). Such are, for example, the tales of God's struggles with monsters (Rahab, Tannin, Leviathan, Serpent, Yamm), which have not survived in full and are scattered as secondary motifs in various places in the Bible (Isa. 27:1 and 51:9; Pss. 74:13-14; Job 7:12, 9:13, 26:12-13, 38:10). Various attempts have been made to reconstruct such tales by drawing parallels with the mythology of the ancient Near East and post-biblical Jewish sources, such as the various Midrash. Other typical myths that belong to this category are the Garden of Eden story (Gen. 2:4-3:24) and the tale of the sons of God(s) and the daughters of men (Gen. 6:1-4). The former should be seen as a myth describing the confrontation between the father of the gods and his creatures against the background of their struggle for world dominion. Death and expulsion are the standard mythological punishment for rebellion against the gods. The tale of the Tower of Babel is also couched in characteristic mythological terms:

> The Lord came down to see the city and the tower, which the children of men were building. And the Lord said, Behold, the people is one, and they have all one language; and this they begin to do: and now nothing will be withheld from them, which they have schemed to do. Come, let us go down, and there confound their language, that they may not understand one another's speech. (Gen. 11:5-7)

God descends to visit, as it were, and to ascertain whether man's deeds might pose a threat to his dominion. When, indeed, the rebellious character of the builders of the city and the tower becomes evident, the third person singular voice changes to the first person plural, and a number of gods descend from the heavens for a struggle with the recalcitrant children of men. There is something in this of a general "declaration of war" against mortals who would pursue the course of rebellion.

Of singular mythic force is the tale of carnal relations between the sons of God and the daughters of men. The tale is very widespread in world mythology: it details the process whereby the demigods or mythological giants were created:

> And it came to pass, when men began to multiply on the face of the earth, and daughters were born to them, the sons of God saw that the daughters of men were fair; and they took them wives of all whom they chose. And the Lord said, My spirit shall not always strive on account of man, for that he also is flesh: and his days shall be a hundred and twenty years. There were Nefilim in the earth in those days; and also after that, when the sons of God came in to the daughters of men, and they bore children to them; the same were mighty men of old, men of renown. (Gen. 6:1–4)

The birth of such giants is a challenge against divinely-ordained mortality, for the "hybrid" offspring of god and man would be immortal. These beings are the "Nefilim," i.e., the giants or champions of the culture of the ancient mythologies. This version of the myth, as it appears in the Bible, had already undergone a process of demythologization. It emphasizes that "My spirit shall not always strive on account of man, for that he also is flesh: and his days shall be a hundred and twenty years" (verse 3). In other words, the denial of the existence of demigods as these, who, according to common mythological beliefs, are immortal. This text preserves some of the most compelling evidence of Scripture's struggle against myth, a struggle that retained the original mythological story in conjunction with the monotheistic perception. This particular development is beyond the purview of this book and therefore will not be dealt with further. As a stage in Hebrew folk culture, the story proves that myths about sexual relations between gods and men, about the existence of demigods on earth, and the divine origin of giants and cultural heroes, were part of the repertoire of traditions prevalent among the folk. In this sense, there is no difference between the contents and mythological forms that circulated widely among the Hebrews of the biblical period, and those of the other peoples of the region. The demythologization reflected in the biblical versions of the myths is theological and certainly not to be construed as part of the mythological stories in their folk origin.[4]

The various versions of the Creation stories and the various motifs in the tales of the Garden of Eden and the Flood (such as the origin of death and of agriculture, the pain of childbirth, the serpent's crawling on its belly, divinely controlled rain, the origin of the rainbow, etc.) belong to the second mythic type mentioned above, namely, the etiological myth. Typical examples of this category are the two versions of the myth about the creation of woman in

Genesis 1:27–31 and 2:18–24. According to the first version, the creation of woman is part of the general Creation process; God brings her into being at the same time as Adam: "So God created Mankind in his own image, in the image of God he created him; male and female he created them." According to the second version, woman was a singular creation; she was not created *ex nihilo* (or from the earth) like the other creatures, but from Adam's rib, i.e., from one of the new beings. This relationship of dependency engenders the explicit etiological explanations in the story, "That is why a man leaves his father and his mother, and cleaves to the wife: and they become one flesh" (verse 24), and the designation given to the female: "she shall be called Woman, because she was taken out of Man" (verse 23), as well as that which is not explicitly stated but clearly implied—that man is the superior of the two beings, as he was created first and provided the raw material from which woman was created.

The Bible offers two versions of the creation of woman. The tale bears comparison with others on the same topic in international folklore, and it can stand alone, independent of the biblical context in which it is currently set. As for the original form of this mythic story, and whether or not it was told apart from its present context in the framework of the creation stories, one can only speculate. Nor are these the only textual problems posed by the story. A straightforward reading of verse 23 ("And the man said, *This is now* bone of my bones, and flesh of my flesh: she shall be called Woman, because she was taken out of Man") indicates the existence of an earlier, unsatisfactory mate (including the animals mentioned just earlier in verse 19). In this context, the sages (*Gen. Rabbah* 17:7; 22:7) spoke of "the first Eve" returning to the dust from which she was formed. This presupposes the existence of an ancient myth on the creation of a woman, before Eve, who left Adam, that was the basis of both biblical accounts. Only remnants of such a story remain in the Bible's two versions of woman's creation.

Another tale with an interesting blend of both the mythic forms mentioned thus far—a confrontation between gods and men, and the etiological myth— appears in the account of Jacob's struggle with the angel (Gen. 32:22–32). The story opens with Jacob's journey from Laban's home in Haran to his father's in Canaan, and with the fording of the Jabbok. After sending his family and possessions across, Jacob remains alone on the riverbank, "and there wrestled a man with him until the breaking of the day." When that "man" saw that Jacob was stronger than he, "he touched the hollow of his thigh; and the hollow of [Jacob's] thigh was put out of joint." With the break of dawn, his opponent asks Jacob to free him, but Jacob refuses until the "man" blesses him. The man declares that Jacob shall from then onward be called by the name of Israel, "for thou hast contended with God and with men, and hast prevailed." Jacob names the place "So it is: for I have seen God face to face, and my life is preserved." The tale ends with a typical etiological pronouncement: "Therefore the children of Israel eat not of the sinew of the vein, which is upon the hollow of the thigh, to this day: because he touched the hollow of [Jacob's] thigh in the sinew of the vein" (verse 33).

The story describes a patently mythical-demonical framework in which the hero wishes to make some sort of use of a water source (a spring or river), but the demon, angel, or local god appointed to guard that place (the guardian angel) tries to harm him. The proof of such an interpretation is that the "man" who wrestles Jacob must leave at dawn, like all demonic beings who must flee daylight. Even the plot line (the morphology) of the story bears a surprising resemblance to that of other mythological tales. The structure of mythological plots (the magical fairytale included) is composed of a fixed sequence of narrative stages: according to one of the main approaches in the structural study of folk narrative, the plot is divided into a series of thirty-one such stages. Since the story of Jacob and the angel is not a myth that survived in its entirety but is only an episode or "remnant" of a mythological tale, it exhibits only five of these (located in the middle of the morphological pattern of full-fledged myths):

(A) the hero moves from one location to another (Jacob's journey from Canaan to Haran).
(B) the hero and the antagonist engage in physical combat (verses 24–27).
(C) the hero is "marked"—the princess or other hero "marks" him with an identifying sign, or gives him a ring to facilitate his identification later on (verses 25–32, the injury to Jacob's thigh).
(D) the hero bests his rival (verse 26).
(E) the hero successfully achieves his goal (Jacob crosses the river).

Analyzing and defining the structure of the tale of Jacob and the angel in this way elucidates the fact that it belongs to the mythological sphere.

Another interesting observation in this regard: the figure of Jacob is not known for his physical prowess or heroism in battle. On the contrary, the Bible sees him as antithetical to the violent Esau, hunter and man of arms. This tale of Jacob wrestling physically, like other mythological heroes, with a supernatural being seems unsuited to the protagonist's image as it is drawn in his story cycle. It follows that the original hero of the story, before his incorporation into the literature of the Bible, was not Jacob at all, but some mythological hero along the lines of the Greek Hercules or the biblical Samson.

The etiological aspect also has great significance in the tale, which offers two important etymologies: one geographical (the derivation of the name, "Penuel"), and the other, national (the derivation of the name, "Israel"), as well as the mythical explanation of the origin of an ancient food taboo—the prohibition against eating the sinew of the femoral vein—which links the mythological tale to religious dietary practice.

Not all of these etiological motifs belong to the same level of mythopoetic creation. One can assume that the etymology of the name "Israel" is late. It is perhaps the chief reason that this myth is told about Jacob, of all figures, since it was customary to call him by the name of "Israel." This would explain why so blatantly demonological a tale was admitted to the Bible at all. The obvious etiological nature of the story points to a myth of great social significance in the cultural region wherein it circulated, even without any connection to the sacred history in the Bible. Even if the source of the myth is not Israelite, as has often been suggested, the tale of Jacob and the angel was absorbed into the Israelite culture of the period, and must therefore be seen as a remnant of an ancient mythological tale which was part of the Hebrew folktale repertoire of the biblical period.[5]

The myth was a widespread genre in the folk narrative of the biblical period. It existed in different versions, of which only a handful of fragments survived in the Bible, and it subdivided into the acknowledged categories of myth as a description of the world of the gods and myth as an account of the origins of things. The primary concern of the Hebrew myth of the biblical period is to describe the shaping and origin of the basic life-forms and of the world surrounding them: the myths of God's war with the monster, the creation of the world, the Garden of Eden, the tower of Babel, and the Flood. The sons of the gods and the daughters of men deal with the emergence of the first life-forms as a result, at least in part, of God's struggle with other primal forces. The etiological character of the Hebrew myth is expressed in subjects such as the border between land and sea (God and the sea monster), human mortality, the travail of childbirth and of working the soil, the spread of mankind over the face of the earth and the variety of his languages, woman's dependence upon man, and the like. These are the principal themes of the Hebrew myth whose traces have survived in the Bible.

No complete and comprehensive mythological story as found in the cultures of other peoples has been located in the Bible. This apparently stems from the "monotheistic censorship" that the Scribes imposed on the Holy Scriptures. The fragmentation characteristic of Hebrew myths as conveyed in the Bible is inadequate to prove the character of the Hebrew myths that were transmitted orally, myths undoubtedly more complete and encompassing. These mythological segments, or motifs, scattered throughout biblical literature indicate the genre's dissemination in the Hebrew culture of the biblical period, along with its chief subjects and its affinity to the mythological subjects of other cultures. Biblical literature alludes to these myths and cites them fragmentarily, almost paradoxically indicating that they were widespread and well-known in the region, for the authors who formulated these texts expected their readers and listeners to recognize the allusions from familiar tales.

The real mythical hero in the Bible is always the One God. In contrast to other mythologies that contain tales of many gods, the biblical myth recounts the deeds of the One. To be sure, the remnants of the myths that survived in the Bible allude to the existence of tales of other gods, but it is not surprising that they did not find their full expression there. Even in this regard, the Bible does not completely reflect the repertoire of mythological tales that undoubtedly existed among the ancient Hebrews. The myths underwent basic revision and transformation upon entering biblical literature. The resulting changes, the tales' new significance in the context of the biblical narrative, and their relation to the Israelite *weltanschauung* and theology are the concern of biblical research and have been extensively treated there.

[B] The Legend

The Bible's dominant category in terms of distribution and importance is the legend. This genre is perceived here, as in the genre theory of folk literature, as a folktale anchored in a known historical time and defined geographical location, regarded by its listeners or readers as something that actually happened. Since the Bible describes a continuum of events presented as the history of the Hebrew people, it is no wonder that most of the folktales included therein belong to the category of legend, whose basic characteristic is the claim of authenticity. Here too, the genre's representation in biblical literature does not necessarily reflect its actual distribution in the biblical period. It may be that the authors of the biblical books included only those tales of a legendary nature and ignored the others. Another possibility is that the legends found in the Bible originally belonged to other categories and underwent generic changes in the course of incorporation into biblical literature. This would have had the intended effect of making them more credible—in other words, shaping them into the sacred history of the Hebrews as perceived by the biblical authors, and not necessarily by the people at large.[6]

Legends figure in the historical and wisdom books of the Bible, as well as in biblical poetry, as motifs that recall familiar legends. Yet although legends are found throughout the Hebrew Bible, discussion should center on the two great narrative cycles: those of the Patriarchs in Genesis and that of the Prophets in the Book of Kings. Discussion of these complex story cycles may begin either from the isolated tale or from the encompassing cycle of stories, depending upon the reader's point of view. Those who see the biblical story as the end of the creative process and of oral transmission will certainly prefer the first course; scholars who regard the biblical tale as a written, literary-historical creation will prefer to proceed from the complete text to an examination of the isolated tales which comprise it. Both methods are acceptable as long as the basic premise is clear: the extant literary text is based in various ways upon folk traditions that were transmitted over hundreds of years orally and in writing, and that the laws of folk literature affected their creation just as they did that of every other folk tradition.

One outstanding characteristic of these story cycles is the relative ease with which their basic units can be discerned. Most of the tales they comprise are constructed as completely independent units, their plots and the consecutive stages of development, climax, and resolution all of independent design. These tales hardly require the context of the Abraham or Jacob story cycles, or the general context of the tales of the Patriarchs, in order to sustain narrative tension and artistic unity. Examples of such legends are the stories of Abram and Sarai in Egypt (Gen. 12:10–20), Abraham and Sarah in Gerar (Gen. 20:1–18), and Isaac and Rebecca in Gerar (Gen. 26:1–16). Despite indications that the two later versions (in the biblical chronology) "knew" the first—and one can theorize that these indications were the work of the editor of the Book of Genesis—from a folkloristic point of view, these are three versions of a single tale type. Each was told by a different storyteller in the course of a new and independent creative process and for different ends. They originated as stories that, even if copied from one another or influenced by a single literary source, were told at different performance events, as in every folk tradition, and thus were transmitted to the biblical text.[7]

The three versions of this story are legends by definition. They are set in a distinct time and place, and the Bible strives to strengthen and emphasize these elements of the text and to link them with historic and geographic facts already familiar to its listeners. The three versions are designed according to literary conventions characteristic of the legend genre: the perfectly realistic development of the plot until the denouement or narrative climax in a supernatural event, almost always the direct intervention of a divine force that acts decisively in favor of the story's hero. The sparing and precise use of supernatural motifs in the legend—as opposed to the concentration of supernatural motifs that arouse disbelief, characteristic of the fairytale—and the employment of the force sacred to the society precisely at the decisive point in the plot, are the main characteristics of this genre. Such a careful use of supernatural motifs and their integration into a plot which is mostly realistic endows even the supernatural aspect with a dimension of authenticity from which stems the credibility basic to legend. This is the reason for the intensive use of the supernatural in religious literature.

The supernatural motif differs between the three versions of the story: in the first, God smites Pharaoh with severe afflictions because he approached Sarai, a married woman. In the second version, Avimelekh takes Sarah for himself, but before he can approach her, God appears in a dream to warn him that she is married. In the third version, Avimelekh, king of the Philistines, "looked out at a window, and saw, and behold, [Isaac] was sporting with [Rebecca] his wife" (ibid., 26:8). Moderation of the power of the supernatural motif is clearly discernable: In the first version, the injury caused by the supernatural force is direct and real. In the second version, the revelation of the supernatural force in a dream is a motif bordering on reality, for it is less impressive and more plausible than a manifestation before wakeful eyes. The third version offers no revelation of any supernatural force at all, unless divine intervention is perceived as having caused Avimelekh to look out the window at the precise moment that Isaac "sported with" Rebecca (and it is entirely feasible that most people who heard the tale in this period did indeed understand it that way). The moderation of the supernatural motif may indicate phases in the story's evolution from "supernatural" to more realistic versions. The question of the literary contexts, i.e., the location of the story's versions in the Book of Genesis, is treated at length in biblical research and is not germane to this discussion. It is, however, relevant that these three legends, or three different versions of a single story, each express the folk legend recounted at various performance events as an answer to social, religious, or political circumstances which cannot be reconstructed today.

The category called "legend" is not homogenous. Its primary subdivisions are the biographical (or historical) legend and the local legend. The distinction between them is somewhat ambiguous, since every historical or biographical legend has a geographical basis and every local legend is closely tied with an historical event or acknowledged hero. In most instances, it is possible to determine whether the tale focuses on a historical figure or seeks to explain the origin of a prominent geographical phenomenon, such as an ancient tree or an unusual well or spring. Examples of this sort of integration of historical and local legends include the legends of Hagar and the Lahai-Ro'i well (Gen. 16:13), the story of Lot's wife (Gen. 19:26), Jacob's struggle with the angel (Gen. 32:22–32), and "En-haqqorre, which is in Lehi" in the story of Samson (Judg. 15:11–19).

Most biblical legends belong to the subgenre of biographical legend (or in the terminology that acquired currency in later Jewish culture, the "praise," that is, hagiography). That is the primary raw material of which the tales of the Patriarchs in Genesis, and those of the Prophets in the Books of Kings, are composed. These are treated below, in the section on story cycles in the Bible. Relevant here is the main difference between the types of biographical legends in the two cycles. Elijah and Elisha in the tales of the Books of Kings (1 Kings 16:29–19:18; 1 Kings, 19:19–2 Kings 13:21) are typical wonder-workers. They miraculously provide food for the hungry, cure the ill and the barren, revive the dead, and punish with death those who infringe upon their honor. The image of these legendary heroes as wonder-workers, and the character of their deeds, render these tales sacred in their own right. In these sacred legends, the protagonists, through the magic powers they possess, act to save the communities they represent, to strike the enemies of the narrating society, to rescue individuals, and provide solutions to crises that erupt within that society. The sacred legends have various functions: to strengthen the faith of the community in the power of its leadership, or to reduce the individual and communal tensions of daily life. The sacred legend serves also to deepen the identity of individuals within the community and to preserve and strengthen social equilibrium.

All this is easily discernible in the tales of Elijah and Elisha. To the generic distinctions should also be added the many parallels between the Elijah and Elisha stories and the literature of the ancient Near East, especially the Canaanite and the Ugaritic. Motifs such as the Man of God, rain-making, providing oil and wheat, granting (or resurrecting) a child, or ascending to heaven are also found in ancient Near Eastern literature. These variants are not to be seen as proof of direct borrowing from non-Jewish sources. These motifs belong to the stock of widespread and available folk traditions of the Fertile Crescent in the biblical period that almost assuredly lent their form to the legends of Elijah and Elisha.

These motifs served in the ancient Near East as the raw material of ancient myths, whereas in the stories of Elijah and Elisha they form sacred legends. This is a phenomenon typical of demythologization, already mentioned above, which occurred as part of the internal development of the folk traditions, not particularly as a result of monotheistic censorship. That is to say, these sacred legends apparently reached the biblical authors already crystallized as legends rather than myths; the process occurred gradually as a social development and was not necessarily driven by theological considerations. Such processes are familiar from the development of folk traditions in other cultures. To these developments and purposes of folk legends in general there should be added the special significance that the Elijah and Elisha tales gained in the biblical context, in the struggle against idolatry, and in shaping the structure of prophet–king relationships.[8]

The legends in the cycle of Patriarchal tales belong to another type. Abraham, Isaac, and Jacob are not performers of folk miracles and wield no magical powers—the folk do not turn to them with requests to solve personal difficulties. The Patriarchal tales are true biographical legends, since they deal with events in the heroes' lives. The stories do not describe unusual deeds of the Patriarchs, who wander, develop a complex web of relationships with the inhabitants of Canaan and the neighboring lands, take wives, father children, and leave legacies. The importance of these tales is primarily historical—a story of the first steps of the Jewish people. The legend filled the role of the written sacred history transmitted by the priests and the various guardians of their traditions. The tales of the Patriarchs differ in purpose and literary character, but it seems they can all be seen as belonging to the genre of the historical legend. In contrast to the Elijah and Elisha tales, all the Patriarchal stories have implications for the future of the Jewish people, the nature of its relationships with surrounding peoples, the composition of the nation itself (for example, the tribes), the history of the worship of God and the holy places, and so on. From this perspective, it is possible to see the Patriarchal stories as typical "legendary history," a comprehensive historical narrative made up of legends.

The important conclusion to be drawn from this is that the historical legend was a central component of the folk narrative repertoire of the biblical period. It was the semi-official history of the Hebrew tribes, like the historical legends of other nations. It consisted of traditions whose raw materials were the individual legends. These traditions crystallized over hundreds of years, during which time they were transmitted orally and, when they reached their final form, were passed on both orally and in writing, in a more or less fixed form, until their incorporation into the biblical text. There is no reason to assume that the historical traditions of the Hebrew tribes in the biblical period were crystallized and transmitted in a form different from that known to us from the study of other cultures. The alteration of the biographical-historical legend in the process of its integration into biblical literature is a topic better suited to biblical research.[9]

The biblical legend also appears outside the framework of the large story cycles, as an independent literary unit. An example of this is the Book of Jonah, whose length and complexity do not allow it to be taken in its present form as a folktale. Yet, in different parts of the book, there are clearly recognizable signs of the legend genre: typical motifs such as the wondrous storm at sea and its miraculous stilling; the swallowing of the protagonist and his rescue from the innards of the fish; and the task assigned the hero by a supreme power. Even the book's general construction around sin and its wages befits the pattern of the religious legend, which is essentially a tale of reward and punishment. These narrative motifs or episodes can be seen as independent legends combined to create a literary composition with religious and moral aims that differ from those of its constituent legends.

Another example, similar in this respect to the Book of Jonah, is the story of Job. Biblical research has discerned the major differences in style, theme, literary structure, and worldview between the framework tale of the Book of Job and the philosophical set of monologues upon which most of the book is built. The narrative framework (Job 1; 2:1–10; 42:10–17) most clearly and convincingly maintains the structure of the folk legend. Stylistically, the story employs techniques characteristic of the folktale in general: opening phrases such as "There was a man in the land of Uz . . . " and "Again there was a day when the sons of God came to present themselves before the Lord"; the intensive use of repetitive linguistic phrasings: "While he was yet speaking, there came also another" (three times) and "Now there was a day when the sons of God came to present themselves before the Lord" (twice); and the dialogue between God and the Adversary (i.e., Satan) which recurs twice in the same stylistic pattern. Furthermore, there is the constant use of proverbs as the essence of folk wisdom: "Naked I came out of my mother's womb, and naked I shall return there," "the Lord gave, and the Lord has taken away," "for all that a man has he will give for his life," "What? shall we receive good at the hand of God, and shall we not receive evil?" The literary structure that characterizes the religious folk legend is the double, balanced pattern: sin and its punishment; fulfilling a precept or withstanding a trial, and its reward. Thus are the stories of Elijah the Prophet in Jewish folk legends, the numerous legends about the Thirty-Six Hidden Saints and the theodicy legends abundant in the religious folklore of many cultures. Such a pattern is clearly discernible in this tale: Job withstands the trial and accordingly receives his due, his wife and friends who fail are punished, and their shame made public.

The framework tale of the Book of Job fulfills the basic conditions of folk narrative. The epic law of the opening and ending stipulates that a folktale begin with an episode of tranquility and balance between the opposing forces at work in the story. Confrontation then develops between the active forces or characters, while the story line strives toward resolution in favor of the protagonist and a restoration of the situation to its initial equilibrium. This epic law is fully upheld in the story of Job. So, too, are the epic laws of the three and repetition, manifested in the stylistic structure of the recurring episodes of God's meeting with the Adversary, in the frequent tragedies befalling Job, in the nature of the descriptions such as "and that man was perfect and upright, and one who feared God, and turned away from evil," and the extreme and superlative style ("so that this man was the greatest of all the men of the east," "And in all the land were no women found so fair as the daughters of [Job]"). Upheld, too, are the epic law of formulaic numbers, which in Job are always three and seven, and the model of "two to the scene," which limits to two the *dramatis personae* in the forefront of the action. In Job these are God and the Adversary, Job and his wife, Job and his friends (who function as a single narrative entity), and Job and each of the messengers who come in turn to inform him of the catastrophes that have befallen him.

The most central epic law is the "law of contrast" (or the binary opposition, to use another term). This law is based equally on the folktale's narrative structure and its basic worldview. The polarization between the forces at work in the story appears in the very first episode and shapes the continuation of the plot and its narrative development. From a thematic perspective, the belief structure of the folktale is characterized by absolute concepts of good and evil, rich and poor, old and young, man and woman, Jew and Gentile. These diametrically opposed categories determine the tale's meaning, thus the tale cannot be understood without identifying the contrast in question.

The law of contrast appears in the Book of Job in three main forms: the contrast between God and the Adversary, between Job and the Adversary, and between Job and his wife and friends. If we seek to interpret the story in terms of the first model, we must define the story of Job as a *myth*. According to this application of the law of contrast, Job, the righteous one in the story, is not its main protagonist, but a plaything in the hands of mightier supreme forces (God and the Adversary). Job, his happiness, and his fate are merely pawns in their struggle. Stories with this basic pattern are familiar from international folk literature, especially from Greek mythology. It is important to emphasize at this juncture that such tales were also part of the Hebrew narrative repertoire of the biblical period. The second model of polarity, between the Adversary and Job, presents a typical *sacred legend* situation since the confrontation here is between the representative of the narrating society (the saint, Job) and the primary instigator (Satan), with the very powerful presence of God in the background. The protagonist's ability to withstand the temptations of demonic forces is among the chief characteristics of the sacred legend. The third model—Job against his friends and his wife—removes the supernatural forces from the main confrontation and sets at its center the set of human relationships. Here the legend is neither theological nor mythological, but *social*—it displays man's ability to act according to his personal conviction, and the path which he has chosen to follow, despite the pressure of social forces.

In interpreting this version of the story, all three approaches must be considered simultaneously. They all figure in some way and at various levels of importance and power during the story. These levels of importance, and the significance of the Job story as it appears in the Bible, are not our concern, since it was not preserved as a folktale in its final form. Analysis of the story with the tools developed for the study of folk narrative has facilitated our understanding of the folktale of the period. The analysis hints at the possibility that a number of versions of this story existed: a mythical version or group of versions that focused primarily on the confrontation between supernatural forces; another group of versions which told the story of a righteous man standing against the forces of darkness seeking to deflect him from his path, and who bests them by dint of his ethical perfection; and another cluster of variants which pit the hero against the forces at work in his society. Why this particular legend was taken to serve as the setting for the dramatic-contemplative Book of Job, and what its function is in the overall framework of the Book of Job, are questions already addressed by many Bible scholars.

External proof that Job was the hero of legends of the ancient Near East exists in the Book of Ezekiel (14:14) which attests that "though these three men,

Noah, Dani'el, and Job, were in it, they should only save their own lives by their righteousness, says the Lord God." Legends have been found in the ancient Ugaritic literature about the righteous Dani'el (as distinct from Daniel), and such tales about the righteousness of Job undoubtedly existed also. Taken together, this evidence shows that the main condition required for a story to be defined as a folktale exists here—i.e., the existence of additional versions.[10]

An exception among the biblical legends is the story of the battle of David and Goliath (1 Sam. 17). At its center is the narrative pattern of the folk hero's rise from anonymity to greatness, but the means differs from the norm of Hebrew folk narrative. This is a tale of heroic courage, not of spiritual greatness, withstanding trial, or the performance of wondrous deeds, as in the other biblical legends discussed. Yet, an analysis of the tale's morphology reveals the basic characteristics of the folk epic: the youngest son, venturing forth to rescue his brothers, struggles with a monster, wins the hand of the princess, and encounters and ultimately overcomes additional obstacles to the throne. As in the legend of Job, there is further proof of the story's folkloric origin: the existence of additional versions. In the Bible itself, another version of the story of the slaying of the Philistine giant has survived, whose protagonist is Elhanan, son of Yaare-oregim the Bethlehemite (2 Sam. 21:19; 1 Chron. 20:5): "And there was again a battle in Gov with the Pelishtim, where Elhanan the son of Yaare-oregim, the [Bethlehemite] slew [Goliath] the Gittite, the staff of whose spear was like a weaver's beam." The prevailing assumption in folkloristics, that tales of lesser-known heroes were transferred by the storytellers to famous figures, raises the possibility that it was originally told as the victory of a local hero over the Philistine giant, and later transferred to the cycle of David stories. Here, then, the tale describes an early stage leading to the establishment of the Davidic dynasty.[11]

Folk legend is the literary category closest to historical narrative. It demands that its hearers believe what is being told and seeks to strengthen society's faith in the events related. The status of the legend as historical or pseudo-historical narrative, along with the fact that it often constitutes sole testimony to the events related therein, places it midway between history and fiction. The well-known debate in biblical research on the "historicity" of the Patriarchal tales in the Book of Genesis stems from the question of whether legend is closer to history or fiction. Folkloristics has long deliberated the authenticity of folk legend. It has developed a complex theory to describe the emergence of legend from an actual event (customarily called "the historical kernel") via the accounts of eyewitnesses relating what they saw in the first person (*memorate*). This story passes into third person speech with those who hear it from their predecessors, a literary form already close to the chronicle (*chronikate*). From here, the oral and written story proliferates, with endless additions of folkloric motifs and traditional narrative forms, until the final stage—the ultimate crystallization of the legend. This process, known as "the crystallization [or folklorization] of the folk legend" could explain the transformations in Hebrew folk traditions over the hundreds of years that passed until they were committed to writing in the Bible. Questions regarding the historical authenticity of the Patriarchal stories, for example, and the possibility of reconstructing the historical "kernels" around which legends grew to their final narrative form, are not a concern of folklore research. It is sufficient to say that these legends, in their present form, exhibit clearly discernible features of folk traditions that circulated in different versions over the course of hundreds of years among the Hebrew tribes of the biblical period. Folktale study recognizes this process of crystallization from the development of folk literatures throughout all cultural expanses, and has proven that the dubious authenticity of the final literary text as an historical document stems from the basic characteristics of the folk legend.[12]

[C] The Fable

The fable in folk literature is a story that takes place in the world of animals, plants, or inanimate objects, told in the past tense but applied to the present by virtue of the epimythium. The source of ancient Near Eastern fables lies apparently in mythological animal tales, of which only remnants have survived. These stories are testimony to the animistic phase of various peoples, including the developed cultures of the ancient Near East. Only much later was the moral application added to the animal tale, turning it into a fable. Evidence of such a development consists of the relatively few fables, as compared with the abundance of animal tales, that remained in the literature of the ancient Near East. This indicates the antiquity and spread of the animal tale genre. Further proof lies in the same ancient stories about animals that are found in later sources as fables in every respect. One known example of this process is the story of Etana, concerning the rivalry of the eagle and the serpent, which survived in different versions in ancient Near Eastern literature, and later appeared as a fable in Aesop and in other versions. A literary-cultural process turned the mythological animal tale of Etana into a wisdom fable.

The Bible does not abound with narrative fables such as these. To be sure, the concept of "mashal" in the Bible has various meanings, such as oration, proverb, metaphor, and poetical rhetoric (such as the Book of Proverbs, which is a collection of proverbs and statements of wisdom and morality). This study, however, approaches the fable according to its definition as a folktale and not as a rhetorical device. Such are Jotham's fable (Judg. 9:6–20); the fable of the poor man's ewe lamb (2 Sam. 12:1–4); Jeho'ash's fable about the thistle and the cedar in Lebanon (2 Kings 14:8–11; 2 Chron. 25:17–19), and the fable of the vineyard (Isa. 5:1–7).[13]

Biblical fables do not fit neatly into the aforementioned definition of the fable as a folktale. The only two fables that are set outside the human realm are not animal but plant fables. All the rest take place in the world of men, though animals figure in some. One example is that of Balaam's ass (Num. 22:21–34); there is no justification for seeing it as an animal tale; the events themselves take place entirely in the human world, and the motif of the ass that speaks is taken in the story as a miracle and in no way resembles the natural speech of animals in fable. Even though the fable of the poor man's ewe lamb has the characteristic pattern of a narrative unit and its epimythium, animals are not the active figures in the story, and it takes place within the confines of the human dimension. Unlike those in ancient Near Eastern literature, fables in the Bible are not based on animal tales.

The fable of Jotham is the best-known in biblical literature. Some consider it one of the most ancient to have survived in world literature. Many have dealt with various aspects of its literary and historical contexts, its significance, and its variants. These are important questions in biblical research, but the aim here is to discover how Jotham's fable reflects the themes and the literary structure of the Hebrew fable in the biblical period. Some have already pointed out the lack of correspondence between the plant tale and the historical context into which it is incorporated—i.e., the story of Avimelekh and the citizens of Shekhem. The trees in the tale approach the olive, the fig, and the vine, but in the historical context, the men of Shekhem made no such appeal to the sons of Gideon; three trees appear in the story, in the context, seventy sons of Gideon (one might have expected some sort of numeric correlation, such as seven trees); in the tale, the bramble must be persuaded to rule over the trees, and consents only after they accept its harsh conditions. In the historical context, Avimelekh subjugates the people of Shekhem. The most convincing explanation of these inconsistencies holds that the fable and the historical account of the events were not created together. Instead, there existed an independent plant tale that was incorporated in the story of the descendants of Gideon at a later stage (perhaps in one of the stages of the creation of the oral or written Book of Judges). The style and construction of the plant tale conform completely to the characteristics of folk literature.

The style of the fable is direct and informative; each syntactical unit is weighed and measured, balancing the others. The technique of fixed stylized pattern is so precise that each utterance recurs three times, with only the addressee differing ("and they said to the olive tree, Reign over us. But the olive tree said to them, Should I [forsake] . . . and go to hold sway over the trees? And the trees said to the fig tree, Come thou, and reign over us. But the fig tree said to them, Should I forsake . . . and go to hold sway over the trees? Then said the trees to the vine, Come thou, and reign over us. And the vine said to them,

Should I [forsake] . . . and go to hold sway over the trees?") Students of the fable have emphasized the stylized, compressed, and succinct nature of the folk fable. It is this characteristic that is primarily responsible for the fable's forceful impact upon its hearers (and readers). This stylistic feature is realized fully in the Jotham fable. The other epic laws of folk narrative, such as the plot's progression from an initial, balanced situation, through the presentation of the conflict, on to the resolution, and ultimately to a restoration of the opening balance (the opening and the closing); the law of the three, the two to the stage (the trees and the vine, the trees and the fig tree, etc.); and the repetitions, are clearly upheld in this case, and prove it to be a consummate folk fable. Variants of this plant fable have been found in Akkadian and Egyptian literature (more on this below), attesting to the dissemination and "multiple" existence of the story—basic conditions for its definition as folk narrative.

The meaning of the biblical Jotham fable stems from its immediate context, the epimythium, given it by Jotham, and from the overall meaning of the Book of Judges ("the broad context"). According to these, the "good" trees are the sons of Gideon, the forest trees are the citizens of Shekhem, the power-hungry bramble is Avimelekh, who forcibly seized control of the city. Now that the Jotham fable is proven to be a folktale, we must consider the meaning of the original plant tale—that which does not depend on the context of the Book of Judges. Here, too, the epic law of contrast can facilitate an understanding of the story's original meaning. The polarity in the story is not, as it is customary to think after reading the fable, between those trees who declined the crown (the fig, the olive, and the vine) and the bramble (the "good" vs. the "bad"). Seeing things this way stems from the implication of the epimythium to the plant tale: in the historical context the conflict is between the sons of Gideon, the good (the trees) and Avimelekh, the bad (the bramble). The binary opposition between the positive and negative poles is resolved after the neutral pole (God, king, wise judge, and the like) joins with the positive pole and decides the plot in favor of the values accepted by the narrating society. If, following the usual interpretation of the fable, the fruit trees are set at the positive pole of the story, the bramble at the negative, the neutral force would consequently, of all things, tip the scale in favor of the bramble, i.e., the negative pole, a movement which completely distorts the conceptual structure of the fable as a folktale.

This may indeed have been the precise intention of the storyteller (or creator of the fable): perhaps he sought to show the complete absurdity of selecting Avimelekh over Jotham's "good" brothers, by turning the basic structure of the folk fable upside down. But it seems that in such an instance one would have expected a greater compatibility between the fable and its epimythium— the history of Gideon's sons. If the storyteller intended to break the original pattern of the folk fable here, why then did he not also change some of the details to better fit the historical context?

A more plausible explanation is that the fable, in its independent form, presented a different set of values. The fruit trees stood at the negative pole of the story, the bramble at the positive. Here the neutral pole (i.e., the trees of the forest, representing society) aligns with the bramble and resolves the plot in favor of the positive pole, in keeping with the accepted structure of the folk narrative. What, then, is the meaning of the fable in its folk origin?

In the plant story divested of its Book of Judges' context, there is no justification to designate the bramble as the negative pole. It is not a party to the discussion and does not initiate action. Rather, it responds to the appeal of the trees of the forest. Those who reject their appeal are the three "good" trees, convinced that their own welfare takes priority over that of the forest in which they exist. Support for this interpretation of the fable can be seen in its ancient Near Eastern variants. According to these, the debate between the tamarisk and the palm tree is over which is superior. The bramble (or some other thorny bush), trying to intervene and make peace between them, is immediately scorned as inferior compared to their exalted status. This is further proof that the bramble is the positive protagonist in the plant stories of this kind, and that the narrating society identified actually with the lowly and useless one for whom the general welfare took precedence over his own.[14]

This study of the Jotham fable illustrates that folkloristic research methods further our understanding of the biblical story beyond the background of its contexts and functions within the biblical text. The description of its characteristics as a folktale and a more precise definition of its "core meaning"—the meaning it held when still an independent story—make it possible to grasp the full significance of the changes it underwent in its transition to biblical literature. Unfortunately, examples of the Hebrew folk fable are too few to enable a description of its character and development with any degree of certitude. Two other fables, that of the thistle and the cedar (2 Kings 14:9; 2 Chron. 25:18), and that of the vineyard (Isa. 5:1–6), are literary fables, and serve mainly as rhetorical devices; the first, as a proud boast before the battle of Jeho'ash, King of Israel; the second, as a prophetic vision of the punishment awaiting Israel. In both, use is made of the plant kingdom, but not in the manner in which it appears in folk fable literature. This also curtails our ability to draw general observations about the folk fable in the biblical period. Still, it does seem possible to posit the following: (a) the Hebrew fable preferred the plant story type to the animal tale; (b) it is primarily a prose fable (we have no real examples of a poetic fable); (c) its themes, from the few examples that survive in the Bible, are in the realm of the set of relationships between the ruler and his subjects and the folk views of society's injustice.

[D] The Novella

The Joseph story in Genesis has always piqued the interest of Bible scholars who examined its unique literary qualities in great detail. Compared to the short, concise Patriarch stories, the Joseph story is exceptional in its impressive literary design, its narrative unity, the shaping of the *dramatis personae*, and the narrative development of its smallest details. These literary characteristics delineate the biblical Joseph story as the exemplary novella. The novella is a realistic story whose time and place are determined. Its protagonists are mainly ordinary people, as opposed to heroes and kings. These people seek their fortune in the realm of human, realistic existence, but their appetite for adventure, or their luck, cause them to venture far from home and endure difficult trials. The novella emphasizes such human traits as cleverness, eroticism, loyalty, and wiliness, that drive the plot forward more than any other element. A further distinction germane to the present discussion is that the sources of the novella are literary.[15]

The biblical story of Joseph perfectly fits this definition. It resembles legend in that it is anchored in a definite time and place, almost completely devoid of supernatural motifs, in that the narrative emerges from the hero's character traits, and the story's style and complexity indicate a literary source. The Joseph story is set between two defined boundaries: his vision of his future greatness at the beginning of the story, and its complete realization at the story's end. From start to finish and in all its many twists, the plot advances steadily toward the fulfillment of the vision revealed to the protagonist at its outset. The capricious ways by which the words of that vision are fulfilled, become here, as in many other novellae, the essence of the narrative tension preserved throughout and a primary means of unifying the plot.

Sudden reversals of fortune are a basic feature of the novella. In the Joseph story, this set of turning points (*wendepunkt*) steers the plot: Joseph dreams of the sheaves in the field and of the lights in the sky, an incident which downgrades him from the pampered favorite of Jacob's sons to a slave sold to the Ishmaelites. His success in the house of Potiphar boosts him back to glory, but the lust of his master's wife reduces him once again to the lowliest of states. The dreams of Pharaoh's eunuchs, and of Pharaoh himself, propel Joseph back to the height of society. The hunger in the land of Canaan raises him to true greatness in the eyes of the biblical author—senior status as head of Jacob's family. These reversals of fortune lead gradually to the fulfillment of the vision at beginning of the story.

Different versions of the Joseph story presumably spread as folktales in a less perfected form than that which we now have. It is customary to indicate the entertaining quality of the novella, in that it lacks the compelling authority of the legend, for example. But a folktale cannot exist solely for purposes of pleasure and amusement. The design of the Joseph story, employing the model of a vision and its realization and detailing the ups and downs of the protagonist's fate, apparently seeks to confirm the presence of a hand guiding that fate and determining events in the hero's life from start to finish.

We know of one ancient variant to the Joseph story: the Egyptian tale of Two Brothers. This story, from about the thirteenth century B.C.E., describes the attempts of the elder brother's wife to seduce the younger one, who flees. The woman tells her husband that his brother tried to rape her. The husband pursues his brother and the latter, endeavoring to prove his innocence, castrates himself. The Two Brothers story is an encompassing novella whose second part is actually a mystical treatise that has nothing in common with the biblical Joseph narrative. The two stories are not parallel in all respects, only in the one narrative episode about a woman who seeks to seduce a young member of her household and, later on, denounces him to the master of the house. From the folk literature point of view, it is irrelevant whether or not the Joseph story borrowed from that of the Two Brothers. The existence of such a variant to the Joseph story (alongside additional folk motifs such as the rise to greatness of the youngest of the sons, the vision of future greatness, solution of riddles as proof of wisdom and the rise to greatness, and the catastrophe of famine and the salvation therefrom as a result of the wondrous knowledge of a magician or a saint) proves that different fundamentals of the novella were widespread in the folk traditions of the biblical period in both Egypt and Canaan. The opinion of novella scholars that the source of folk novellae lies in literary works does not rule out a wide circulation of different, less developed versions of the Joseph tale (and other similar novellae) in the folk traditions of the period.[16]

Another biblical narrative that should be seen as a novella is the Scroll of Esther. It also takes place in the realm of human and historical events, the fate of the protagonists hinges on their characters, and its pattern is established by a decree which appears at the start of the story—such that the entire plot is a drive to undo its consequences. The set of tensions built into the story is incorporated on two main planes: the personal—the fate of the active characters—and the national—the fate of the Jewish community. The complexity of the Esther story, the painstaking design of the plot's details, the construction of the images, and the stylized richness of the realia, are indicative of a literary source. And again, folktales about Mordecai and Esther, the two heroes that saved their people, were presumably widespread prior to the time the novella was set down in writing. An analysis of the set of meanings inherent in the story can contribute to the identification of other versions of the Mordecai and Esther story that preceded the literary version in Scripture.[17]

The same law of contrast that was applied to other folktales of the biblical period reveals an interesting phenomenon in this case. In the story of Esther, there are two sets of binary oppositions: The first model sets the two courtiers, Mordecai and Haman, in the two poles, their rivalry and enmity as the driving force behind the narrative plot. This presents the story as the first diaspora tale in Hebrew literature. A Jewish courtier struggles with a Gentile minister to save the community from impending disaster. This narrative model became one of the most common in the Jewish folk narratives of the coming generations. According to such an interpretation, the story should be defined not as a novella, but as a folk legend, like the tales about Maimonides in the court of the Gentile ruler and many other tales of this type.

The second model of binary opposition presents the Scroll as a tale on the theme of the "romantic triangle," wherein Haman, trying to seduce one of the king's wives, is discovered and punished. According to this model, the story is indeed a novella, one of whose most prevalent themes is the lovers' triangle, complete with romantic and erotic motifs. Theoretically, at least, there is the possibility of another model, in which God, rather than the Gentile ruler, who is but a tool in the hands of the God of Israel, is the force resolving the conflict between Mordecai and Haman. Although God is never mentioned in the Scroll of Esther, one may surmise that those who read or heard the story understood God to be the true motive force behind the fateful events. According to this opposition, the story of the Scroll can be defined as a sacred legend in which the official religious force resolves the plot in favor of the narrating community.

The outcome of this analysis is that when the miracle of Purim was recounted in the Jewish community of Persia and other places, it appeared in a variety of narrative forms: a legend about a wise Jewish courtier, who bests his hateful foe, the Gentile minister, and thus brings about the salvation of the Jewish community; a novella about the king's beautiful, wily concubine (or wife) who succeeds in bringing down an evil minister by a ruse of an unquestionably erotic character; a sacred legend in which the hand of God, the sacred force of the narrating society, brought about the miracle. The author of the Scroll of Esther made use of all three folk traditions. How they coalesced to form the final literary creation is not our concern here. The chief significance of this text is the opportunity it affords to ascertain the various ways in which a single theme—the miracle of Purim—was expressed in the Jewish folk narrative of the biblical period.

A third example of the novella genre in the Bible is the tale of Solomon's Judgment (1 Kings 3:15–27). From many perspectives, this story is closer to the folk novella than are the stories of Joseph and the Scroll of Esther. While the versions of these stories reached us as encompassing and complex literary compositions which could not exist as folk literature in this form, the tale of Solomon's judgment of the Prostitutes is concentrated, its plot is unidirectional, and the number of its protagonists is limited—indeed it fulfills all conditions of folk narrative. Certain proof of this is that it belongs to an internationally known tale type (AT 926) for which close variants were found in both the ancient Near East (Babylonia and Sumeria) and in international folk literature (India, primarily).

From the thematic perspective, the story of Solomon and the Prostitutes belongs to the wisdom novellae: in the course of the story, the wise judge faces a problem which legal reasoning alone cannot solve. As in other wisdom novellae, the judge becomes the main hero of the story, since his reputation and credibility are on the line. Such is the case here, in the context in which it is integrated in the Book of Kings—the wisdom with which God graced Solomon is on public trial for the first time. We cannot now know what the nature of the tale was when it was told in real life before being committed to writing. Still, one can surmise that, in at least some of its versions, Solomon—the wise king—already was the story's protagonist, and the editor of the Book of Kings did not take a tale about another hero and replace him with Solomon. It is hard to imagine that the author of the Book of Kings, who certainly saw himself as a reliable recorder of events, would "invent" such a tradition had it not come to him already attributed to the figure of Solomon. In any case, this is a typical folk novella which attests to the existence of folk judgment and wisdom tales that were as widespread in Israel during the biblical period as they were within other cultures. Another important conclusion drawn from this example is that the figure of King Solomon as folk hero existed already in biblical times, which certainly was one of the reasons for him to become the second most important hero of Jewish folklore (after Elijah the Prophet).[18]

[E] The Story Cycle

The most common literary context of the biblical folktale is the grouping (or cycle) of tales. The story cycle generally constitutes evidence of an abundance of stories available to the storyteller or editor and author of written material. It is an accepted assumption that the folktale is not usually told as a solitary tale. At various storytelling events revolving around a narrative theme, be it an historical event or sacred hero, numerous tales are told about the subject with alternating storytellers. The story cycle was not created only at the stage at which it was set down in writing. In many instances, collections of stories were crystallized and recounted orally long before reaching that stage.[19]

Most biblical narratives can indeed be seen as if arranged in story cycles. The narrative of Moses, the Exodus, and the journey through the wilderness is a report of a connected sequence of events, each of which can be seen as a tale in its own right. Here, the story cycle is arranged in a pattern similar to travel books, in which events that happened to the traveler are reported in an order corresponding with an itinerary. Samson's biography in the Book of

Judges should be viewed similarly. It is a collection of tales that separately recount some story or event involving the hero. These tales—his heroic struggles against enemies that seek to do him harm, against the forces of nature (the lion), against internal enemies from within his own tribe, his loves, and his folk wisdom (the contest of riddles)—are so arranged to encompass his entire life, from birth to death. Here the story cycle is built upon the biographical model, just as other famous story cycles are arranged around culture heroes. The two important story cycles about Elijah and Elisha, with which we dealt above, reflect a similar literary pattern. In these, the editorial hand is not so apparent: the individual tales are presented side by side, without being bound by any principle of cause-and-effect. The tales are set, to be sure, over the period of the Prophet's activity, but it is clear from reading the story cycles that no particular story need necessarily appear after or before another. In this sense, the two story cycles of Elijah and Elisha, in spite of the editing done by the biblical author, resemble folktale cycles as told at actual storytelling events.

One of the most encompassing and complex story cycles in the Bible is that of the Patriarchs in the Book of Genesis. Assembled here are dozens of tales detailing the life stories of the fathers of the nation, their travels in Canaan and neighboring lands, the complex array of their relationships with the inhabitants of those lands, the history of their relationships within the extended family itself, and the development of the dynasty from Abraham to Joseph. A group of stories whose main interest is a description of a central family, while concentrating on the family patriarchs and emphasizing their special connections to a geographic expanse to underscore their right thereto, is defined in the study of literature as a 'saga.' The term, like other generic terms, grew out of a cultural, historical, and geographical realm apart from that of the Bible. Sagas evolved in lands of the far North, mainly Iceland and Norway, between the eleventh and thirteenth centuries C.E., and were set down in writing after a lengthy period of creation and oral transmission. They are made up primarily of stories describing the history of the patriarchs of the founding families and move chronologically from generation to generation. Their chief purpose is to strengthen the status of these dynasties within society and their right to the land in their possession.[20]

In spite of the obvious differences of culture and period, the tales of the Patriarchs seem to have the basic indicators of the saga genre. This similarity can also explain much of their character and function. Many questions that arose in biblical research connected with the Patriarchal tales also arose independently in study of the saga, but the relative historical proximity of the period of the sagas, the greater documentation of the events related in them, and the ways they emerged (such as the names and histories of their authors), made for much more confident answers to these questions. The final literary form of the saga is similar to that of the cycle of the Patriarchal tales: it is composed of various narrative categories—legend, fable, folk chronicle, myth, etiological narrative, paeans of praise, and travel tales. The forms of the tales are different and diverse: there are short, truncated stories that indicate story versions in the making, alongside long, complex novelistic tales, like the biblical Joseph story. This variety and complexity are explained in the study of the sagas by the use an author-editor made of diverse sources—historical documentation, story cycles already consolidated by oral tradition, independent tales that originally were not related to the subject but that the author-editor saw fit to incorporate. The composition of material available to the author or authors of the cycle of the Patriarchal tales was such or similar. This assumption enables a reconciliation of the disparate levels of the material's literary development, the existence of similar tales about various personalities, and the sometimes curious placement of stories that do not "fit" their context.

Another question of interest to many scholars is the degree to which sagas reflect historical truth. Sagas are a complex blend of fiction and historical reality; their primary source of raw material is legend (as explained above), whose nature engenders this blending as well as the claim of authenticity. Furthermore, the perception of history in the ancient world and in the Middle Ages was a mixture of "poetry and history." Likewise for the question of the historical accuracy of the Patriarch stories in the Book of Genesis: historical and archaeological studies have proven factual more than a few details recounted therein, but it is clear that each such "fact" is only one piece of a complex mosaic of artistic fiction, folkloric imagination, various political and national aims, heartfelt desires, and deep religious faith. Like the sagas, the cycle of Patriarchal tales is neither truth nor fiction, a collection of legends nor history, but both at the same time, and much more.[21]

The function of the saga in society illuminates the role played by the cycle of Patriarchal tales in the Book of Genesis. The sagas tell of the first families who settled in particular regions of the land, those who became royalty or large feudal dynasties. The creators of the sagas were court scribes or poets who worked for the rulers. Their political and social purpose was to establish and fortify the status of the ruling family and its right to the land it held or to which it claimed ownership. Such a functional view of the Patriarchal tales might clarify the motives for their creation, the purpose for the collection and classification of the ancient traditions by the Hebrew court scribes, and explain the strong emphasis on the geographical aspect of these tales. As was mentioned earlier, legendary-historic traditions about the fathers of the nation were widespread in their basic form as folktales among the Hebrew tribes. At this stage of their existence as folk traditions, they served as the people's oral history, and fulfilled additional functions as the basis of the connection with geographic locations of national or ritual importance, as an explanation of core religious principles, and the like. Only at a relatively later stage, after they had been collected and molded into encompassing story cycles, did they assume their familiar form, the saga. This literary phase was driven by motives that, in essence, were no different from those that underlay the creation and transmission of the individual tales. At the same time, these motives undoubtedly were the product of a broader political and nationalist outlook that sought to weave the disparate traditions into a tapestry that would emphasize the unity of the people and its title to the land.

[F] Developments and Transitions

Are the traits shared by Hebrew folktales of the biblical period discernible? There is no simple answer to the question. If examination is limited to their literary form as reflected in the Hebrew Bible, the answer is yes. Here they reflect the national, religious, and ethical perception of the world of the biblical authors and they evince uniform identifying traits. It is not, however, quite so simple when the frame of reference is expanded to include the folk traditions of the biblical period (and not just the biblical books). The resemblance to the folktale repertoire of other ancient Middle Eastern cultures is apparent, although there is a clear difference in the proportions between the genres. Tales of the deeds of the gods dealing with the origin of the universe; the exploits and wanderings of the fathers of the nation as the foundation for gathering together its various components and legitimizing its ownership of the land; tales of folk saints that deal with the daily life of ordinary people and their influence on historical events; tales about folk heroes who defeat giants or entire armies; stories of sin and punishment, religious precept and its reward; stories of fateful reversals and the rise of the youngest son to greatness; the origins of the nation's greatest leaders (the Scroll of Ruth), or of various geographic and social phenomena; and stories of the wondrous rescue of an endangered community—these themes or "folk ideas" were not the province solely of biblical folk narrative. They grew out of the very life of the people, were influenced by the traditions of other peoples, drawn from the artistic and religious literature of the period, and told in different versions, like folk literature everywhere. The principal difference between the folk literature of the biblical period and that of other peoples and periods is that it became one of the most sublime creations ever produced by humanity.

There is nothing to suggest that the folktales of the Bible exhaust the repertoire of folktales that were prevalent in the Israelite traditions of the period. Biblical authors, like any author, historian, or story cycle editor, only drew on what they could use to further their own purposes. Hence the Bible offers no intentionally humorous anecdotes, magic fairytales, erotic stories, or animal fables—at least some of which undoubtedly circulated in the Hebrew folk traditions of the period.

The generic discussion above also has clear thematic aspects. The myth and legends of the saints, the saga, the novella, and the fable, are narrative genres whose definition is based not only on their basic pattern, but also on their particular contents and social function. The typical theme of the creation myth is cosmogonic description. Other characteristic themes of Hebrew myth are God's struggle with other entities, including God's own creation, humankind, competing for mastery of the world. This is how the story of the Garden of Eden and the origin of death are to be understood, and thus, as well, the tale of the Tower of Babel and the punishment of those who dared strive to reach the abode of the Almighty. Fables revolve primarily around a set of relationships within ancient Israelite society, between the king and his subjects and between different classes; their universe of images is drawn mostly from the plant world, as opposed to the animal kingdom, as in the fables of other nations.

Yet, it seems that the most prevalent theme of the Hebrew folktale in the biblical period is the hero and the surrounding world. The cycles of the Patriarchal tales, of Elijah and Elisha, of Joseph, Samson, and David, and even the tales that encompass entire biblical books, such as Jonah, Job, Ruth, and Esther, focus on the diverse manifestations of the folk hero. These folk heroes belong to various types: the image of the founder of the tribe, unique in faith, devotion, and deeds that are so significant to the future of the nation (the Patriarchs); the image of the folk wonder-worker, who heals the sick, provides food for the faithful, punishes detractors, and is from time to time involved in state and international events (Elijah and Elisha). Another type is the heroic protagonist. Two in particular, Samson and David, stand out. To these should be added the stories of David's warriors, such as the sons of Zeruya, Benayahu, son of Yehoyada, and others, that without doubt were plentiful in the folk traditions but lost some of their impact when written down alongside the David stories. The tales of Gideon and Deborah and the other Judges are typical stories of heroism, disseminated in song and prose, that described the physical prowess of famed heroes. A folk hero of a new type hitherto unknown in the Bible is Mordecai. He is designed in the image of the Jewish courtier involved in the intrigues at the Gentile ruler's court, and whose alertness, multifaceted abilities, and proximity to the ruler protect an entire Jewish community. This image, a biblical novelty, became, in medieval Jewish folk narrative and thereafter, the model of the Jewish hero. The figure of Mordecai unveils a new and major subject in Jewish folk narrative—the role of the minister or courtier in the survival of the Jewish community under Diaspora conditions.[22]

Is it possible to discern developmental lines in the biblical folktale? I shall attempt to separate this question into two aspects: the development of the biblical tale from variants known from the tales of the other Middle Eastern cultures in the biblical period, and the development of the stories in their assorted versions in the Bible itself. Both parts of the question have complex aspects which cannot possibly be dealt with in the present framework; the characteristic trends will suffice here.

A comparison of the mythological tales and prevalent folk motifs of the ancient Near East with those of the Bible, has shown enough similarity to suggest common sources. At the same time, enough differences exist to suggest thorough revision and substitution. The general purpose has been defined as demythologization. The Creation stories, the flood, Samson, and God's war with the sea monster evidently underwent a process to dull their mythic power, minimize expressions substantiating the pagan myths, and remove allusions to the existence of other gods and their relationships with mortals. The demythologization process presumably did not commence when the stories were committed to writing and inserted into the books of the Bible. It is more likely that the eclipse of their mythic power began during their diffusion as oral folk traditions.

One example of this process is the story of the Binding of Isaac. According to the biblical tale, Abraham is tested, with no explanation or reason, and Isaac is never actually sacrificed. In all the mythological stories about offering up the firstborn son or heir to the throne as a sacrifice to the gods, a period of severe plague, an enemy attack (as in the case of the King of Moab), or a life-threatening danger to the king precedes the action. Offering up the firstborn as a sacrifice is a conventional method of appeasing a vengeful god. The absence of so fundamental a motif in the story of Isaac's binding, along with its surprise ending—the substitution of an animal sacrifice for a human one—clearly indicate the process of moderating the demonic and mythological foundations of folktales that were widespread in the cultural milieu of the Bible.

The story of the infant Moses sailing down the river in his basket also has a famous variant in the literature of the Middle East—the monologue of Sargon, King of Agade. He tells of being born to the High Priestess by an unknown sire (an obvious allusion to divine parentage). She bore him in secret, prepared for him a wicker basket covered with pitch, and sent him forth upon the river. He was retrieved by Akki, a drawer of water, who raised him as his son, until the goddess Ishtar (Astrate) adopted him and prepared him for the kingship. The similarity between this story and that of Moses is self-evident, but important here are the modifications in the process of transition to the Bible. All traces of divine parentage are erased completely; Moses is the son of a mortal Israelite male. He was set afloat not because his mother sought to hide her deeds but to save him from the decree issued against all Israelite male children. And, finally, he was raised and trained not by a goddess but by the daughter of Pharaoh. In its biblical version, the story is incorporated in the history of the Israelites in Egypt and the forces acting in it are fully flesh and blood.

Another, similar example of a typical demythologization process is the story of Samson. Only a faint hint of supernatural parentage remains in the biblical tale of Samson's birth ("And the angel of the Lord appeared to the woman . . . Then the woman came and told her husband, saying, A man of God came to me, and his appearance was like the appearance of an angel of God, very terrible . . . but he said to me, Behold, thou shalt conceive, and bear a son . . . " [Judg. 13:3–7]). In the folk mythologies, however, divine descent is characteristic of the birth of the culture hero. Also, the hero's hair as fortress of his strength is explained in the biblical tale as a phenomenon of religious asceticism, but with the mythological cultural heroes and demigods, this is a thoroughly magical phenomenon.[23]

Manifest developments of the form and contents of the folktale are also discernible in the Bible itself. One example, discussed above, involved three versions of the story of Abraham and Sarah, the wife-sister. There is an unmistakable transition from a folktale with sharp, coarse lines—the hero brazenly lying, using his wife as he would a concubine to achieve security and wealth for himself, followed by the immediate supernatural intervention of the Supreme Power. The other versions progressively moderate the crude, demonic atmosphere of the tale; the protagonist's behavior is less churlish, and the intervention of the supernatural force is only suggested, or eliminated entirely. Even the transition from the heroic tale of Elhanan defeating the Philistine giant to the story of David and Goliath, is a clear progression from the short, concentrated heroic story which, at least in the sole surviving version, has no political purposes, to the David story, loaded with historical, religious, and national significance. In the stories of Elijah and Elisha, there is a salient evolution from folk traditions that offer "unbiased evidence" to the biblical tale heavy with significance. The comparison between the parallel stories in the narrative cycles about Elijah and Elisha, such as those about the revival of the son of the woman in whose house the prophet was staying, the provision of food for the widow and her children, and the punishment of those who demean the honor of the Prophet, indicate evident levels of evolution. All the developed stories, such as Elijah and the prophets of the Ba'al, Elisha and Na'aman, captain of the host, and Elijah's ascension to heaven, indicate a tendency to incorporation in the historic edifice of the period, an aspiration to influence the great state events and the cultural struggle against idolatry. The short, compressed folktales whose concern is limited to a local event, with the one-time performance of a miracle for his faithful or in the immediate vicinity of the prophet, are folk legends closest to those told in the oral traditions of the period.

The development of Hebrew folktales in the biblical period tends to demythologization, didacticism, and the adaptation of independent tales to the great cycles in which they fulfill a historic and religious-ethical mission. Scholars of Jewish folk narrative have long understood that an outstanding characteristic of the Jewish folktale is its explicit didacticism. Even though the repertoire of

Jewish folktales includes magical, erotic, and humorous stories, the quantitative proportion between them and those with a didactic orientation is different from that of the story repertoires of other peoples.

In my opinion, this phenomenon can be traced to the development of the Hebrew tale in the biblical period. The Bible is a purposeful religious, ethical, and national work. The incorporation of folk traditions into the literature of the Bible could not but make fundamental changes in their pattern, their atmosphere, and their purpose. Thus the early Hebrew folktales evolved from their mythological and magical origins toward didactic literary forms with ethical and national goals. The biblical narrative, in its sanctified written form, was the basis for the literary traditions of the periods that followed. It seems evident that this aspect of the biblical story was a primary cause of the didactic orientation of the majority of Hebrew folktales in the following generations. The transition stage of the folk traditions into the Bible can be discerned in the consolidation of this approach that determined their character for the generations to come.[24]

3 The Second Temple Period
The Casting of Narrative Patterns

[A] Narrative in the Apocrypha and Pseudepigrapha: Continuation and Renewal

The literary material upon which we base a description of the post-biblical Jewish folktale is fragmentary and scattered, and mostly second- or third-hand. Spanning an estimated five hundred years of Jewish history, the age commonly termed "The Second Temple period" or "The Second Commonwealth" witnessed such decisive historical events as the Return to Zion, the Hasmonean Revolt, Hellenistic inroads into Palestine, the rise of Christianity, and the establishment of the two primary Jewish centers in Babylonia and Egypt. The apocryphal and pseudepigraphal literature reflects key historical events. In Hebrew, literary creation of the period is termed, relative to Scripture, "the hidden" and "external" books. That is, as these works were not included in the biblical literature, they were "hidden," or else they were fraudulently attributed to Scripture and thus considered non-canonical. In any case, the literature of the Second Temple period tends to view itself as a continuation and broadening of the scriptural literature in its themes, forms, and world-view.[1]

The Bible reached us as a complete book in its original language and form. It is very close to the version in which it was set in writing in its own time, as the profound reverence accorded it as a sacred book kept it relatively free of modification in the course of its transmission. The non-canonical books, by contrast, were scattered and fragmented over time. Not even one survived intact in the original Hebrew. We find these books in Greek translation as part of the Septuagint; in Latin as part of the Vulgate; in Armenian and Aramaic manuscripts; and in Slavic, Ethiopian, and Arabic translations. From the first stage of their adaptation and translation, and throughout the centuries that followed, the Apocrypha and Pseudepigrapha underwent extensive modifications in the spirit of Christianity. This process obscured their initial Jewish character, leading to incessant controversies over their purpose and origin and considerably hampering the scholarly treatment of this complex literature, such that a description of the Hebrew folktale of the period is fraught with difficulty.

In the time of the Second Temple, as in the preceding biblical period, profound changes marked the passage of the tales from independent folk versions to the written medium. In Scripture, however, the initial literary distillation of the tales is preserved and sometimes, as we have shown in the preceding chapter, in a version that is close to the tales' original folk form. Conversely, tales of the Second Temple, as they survived in translated and adapted versions, are a vast departure from their independent appearance as folktales. In other words, a description of the Hebrew folktale in the Second Temple period, perhaps more than in any other period, to some extent borders on assumption and conjecture, as reliable evidence is not always available.

It bears mention in this context that medieval Hebrew literature preserved versions of some apocryphal and pseudepigraphal books. These versions have no relevance to the Second Temple. They are translations and free adaptations by medieval Jews from the Latin versions of the Apocrypha or from versions that they heard orally. Medieval Jews apparently identified them as Jewish tales, and sought to "restore" them to Jewish culture, which were viewed as their legitimate place.[2]

Two items warrant further emphasis: the first is the determination of the boundaries of the period under discussion. Some of the apocryphal books we will treat below were written at the end of the biblical period, and some after rabbinic literature began to crystallize. *The Book of Ahikar*, for example, was written around the seventh century B.C.E., whereas the pseudepigraphal *Book of Joseph and Asenath* was, apparently, originally penned by a Jewish author in Greek, and the extant versions exhibit a prominent Christian influence. At the same time, it seems there is no justification for exclusion of these two borderline examples from the description of the Hebrew folktale of the period. *The Book of Ahikar* had vast influence on the folk narrative of the Second Temple. It is extant in a number of languages (Greek, Armenian, Arabic, and in a more ancient Aramaic version from the fifth century B.C.E., copied on papyrus from the Jewish colony at Elephantine, in Egypt). There is no extent Hebrew version, yet the existence of one may be presumed, and the *Book of Ahikar*, in spite of its non-Hebrew origin, belonged in the Second Temple period to Jewish folk literature. Likewise for *Joseph and Asenath*, even though it is not a Hebrew book, as has already been proven beyond a doubt. Its author made intensive use of Jewish folk literature of the period, and the work in turn exerted a considerable influence on Jewish folk literature after its publication.[3]

These difficulties need not hinder efforts to treat the folktale of the Second Temple period. Not merely an interval between two great eras of Jewish history—the biblical and the rabbinic—this period was a time of intensive cultural activity and decisive historical events that influenced the character of the Jewish people down through the ages. Likewise for the importance of the folktale of the period; it picked up where the folktale of the biblical period left off, perpetuating its themes, forms, principal narrative motifs, and association with the narrating society and historical events.

Many of these books deemed "external" by the Talmud are pseudepigraphal in nature, that is, they profess biblical authorship. The tales of the various "Testaments" (*Testaments of the Twelve Patriarchs, The Testament of Job*), and the various additions to biblical stories (to the Scroll of Esther, to the Book of Daniel) that were written, as it were, by the heroes of the Bible, or by the authors of their books, are unequivocal proof of the continuous nature of the tale in the Second Temple period. This continuity is not manifested solely in themes and content. The folktale of the period employs the same narrative genres and forms as its antecedent: the historical legend and the sacred legend, the etiological tale, the mythical motifs, and cycle of hagiographical tales.

Still, the folktale of apocryphal literature displays narrative qualities and purposes not found earlier in the biblical narrative. These contributed decisively to the development of the folk literature of the following generations. The folktale of the Second Temple period developed in new directions; a central theme of Jewish folk narrative—survival in conditions of exile—made its vivid debut here, and the primary subjects of this theme evolved accordingly— tales of the rescue of an imperiled community, and the supernatural punishment of the one who harms the Jewish people. These subjects became the foundation of Jewish folk literature of later periods. Furthermore, important narrative forms developed into full and independent narrative genres only in this period. Alongside the expanded (or rewritten) biblical tale (which had in fact acquired some currency as early as the biblical period), the martyrological tale, an utterly new phenomenon in Jewish narrative (and perhaps in world literature as well), and the magic fairy tale, whose absence from the biblical tale stood out in the previous chapter, took an estimable place in this literature.

[B] The Historical Legend

As in the Hebrew Bible, folktales appear in the apocryphal literature primarily in historical contexts. For our purposes, it is irrelevant if this context is factual or fictive, for denizens of the period were inclined to see the tales as part of history's march and to make them the vehicle for memories of the past. This inclination is reflected in the works themselves. It indicates the tales' cultural status and explains their predisposition to inspire faith and convey a sense of authenticity. Those tales that are given a historical context, that depict the biblical period, as it were, belong unquestionably to fictional convention, and therefore should be seen as expanded biblical tales (more on this below) rather than as historical legends. Other books, such as Maccabees, Judith, Tobit,

Susannah, the *Letter of Aristeas*, and Apocryphal Esdras, take place against the historical backdrop of the Second Temple itself.[4]

Maccabees II preserved the tale of Heliodorus and the Temple treasures: Seleucus, ruler of Asia, sends his viceroy, Heliodorus, to plunder them after a Jew denounces his countrymen. The priests and Jerusalemites try to prevent this by means of fasting, prayer, processions, and supplications. Upon entering the Temple, Heliodorus sees a menacing horseman. The horse rears up and strikes him with his hooves, and two youths standing at his sides rain heavy blows upon him. By the time Heliodorus's bodyguards pull him out, he is half-dead. Only the High Priest's prayer revives him, whereupon he returns to his king, full of praise for the Temple and the God of Israel. Maccabees III preserves a similar tale, concerning Ptolemy Philopator who, after his great victory near Rafa, paid courtesy calls to local temples, among them the Holy of Holies. Here too we have the same picture of priests falling prostrate, pleading with him not to enter; Ptolemy insists, and after the High Priest's prayer the king is stricken by a mysterious power. He lies unconscious on the floor of the Temple, where his guards find him almost lifeless.

The two tales belong to the same tale type—"defiler of the sacred is punished." A foreign potentate or overlord seeks to harm a place, sacred object, or holy figure of the narrating society, and is punished in a supernatural manner by the holy power with whom the place or object is associated. Such a tale type (that can appear also as a narrative motif) is indeed found as early as the Bible, in tales featuring contact with the Ark of the Covenant or entry into the Holy of Holies, but only now, in the apocryphal literature, do these motifs become full narratives. The difference goes beyond the tale's form and scope to affect its meaning as well. In the Bible, the tales are connected principally by the centrality of the Temple in Jerusalem as opposed to other centers of ritual, and by the acknowledged folk awe of sanctified entities and spaces; in the historical legend of the Second Temple period, the national significance becomes paramount.

More than a place of ritual, the Temple is a symbol of the Jewish people, such that brutal trespass of its inner sanctum expresses their sense of physical weakness and vulnerability in the face of the foreign ruler. Here Jewish folk literature makes manifest for the first time the theme of confrontation between the Jewish people and the other nations. In the generations to come, this theme evolves into the central theme of Jewish folk narrative. The story of Titus, who entered the Holy of Holies in rabbinic aggadah, tales of the willful destruction of synagogues and sacred books, and of injury to holy rabbis in medieval folk narrative, as well as tales told among ethnic communities in Israel in recent generations, all descend from the themes of the literature of the Second Temple.[5]

The conclusion of the tale in Maccabees II is also typical of tales wherein the "defiler of the sacred is punished." Heliodorus returns home full of praises for the God of Israel and Jerusalem, an ardent admirer of the Jewish people. Hence the tale is constructed according to the well-known structure of folk narrative: it opens with a description of a situation in balance; the Jewish community and the foreign sovereign live side-by-side. The desire to cause injury to something held holy by the narrating society, whether out of avarice (Maccabees II) or pride (Maccabees III), leads to the ensuing imbalance and conflict. The development of the narrative plot reflects the drive for a restoration of balance. Also characteristic of the construction of historical legend is the insertion of a supernatural motif in the plot: the tale takes place almost entirely in the historical, realistic mode—anchored in a known point in time and a defined geographical location. All these augment the atmosphere of authenticity—as is usually the manner of historical legend. Consequently, the "eruption" of supernatural into the tale, at a particular moment and in concentrated form (the event in the Temple), is all the more powerful and awe-inspiring. The awe stems from the surprise and dread that accompany a supernatural occurrence in the midst of such familiar and realistic surroundings. This also contributes to the acceptance of the supernatural in these tales by the listeners or readers as part of the realistic-historical plot. This combination of a credible historical background with a flash of the supernatural is one of the legend's artistic and psychological foundations, and is clearly manifested in the tales of *The Books of the Maccabees.*

The conclusion of the tale in the version from Maccabees III differs a great deal from that in Maccabees II. Not only is Ptolemy Philopator unimpressed by the greatness of the God of Israel and the Temple, the incident stokes his fury to the point of violence. Upon his return to Egypt, he writes a vicious indictment against the Jews and unleashes a tremendous wave of hatred toward them. He rounds up all of Alexandrian Jewry, and sends them to the municipal hippodrome, where five hundred intoxicated elephants are to be loosed upon them.

This tale, like most of the other narratives of Second Temple literature, includes lengthy speeches and prayers of Greeks and Jews, and long and winding versions of letters and various royal orders, all in the spirit of the Hellenistic rhetoric of the day. This self-glorification of rhetoric is undoubtedly the work of the writers who penned the tales and gave them their final form, and perhaps also the added touch of those who translated them into Greek. In any case, they clearly have nothing to do with the art of folk narrative of the period, of which none of its original, oral style survived as evidence.

After the Greeks' speeches and Jews' prayers, God sends two angels down from heaven to frighten the elephants, who ignore the Jews huddled in their corner in favor of the soldiers and spectators. The beasts' rampage effectively squelches the crowd's eager anticipation of carnage, as they themselves become the quarry, and many are killed. Only now does the king change his mind and become a Judeophile. The community inaugurates a great festival to commemorate the rescue, and even creates a special dance to be performed each year on that date. Another version of the same tale is found in Josephus Flavius's *Against Apion*.[6]

One of the most famous tales of Second Temple literature, the *Book of Judith*, also belongs to this narrative theme. Holofernes, commander in chief of Nebuchadnezzar, has laid seige to the town of Bethulia. With no aid in sight from Jerusalem, its residents are on the verge of surrender. The beautiful widow, Judith, accompanied by her maidservant, goes to Holofernes. She encourages him, assures him he will indeed conquer Bethulia, and even consents to give herself over to him. Having won his trust, she promptly decapitates him, and brings his head home for all to see. The Bethulians attack the enemy officers who, deprived of their leader, flee for their lives. Their pursuers overtake them and Holofernes's advisor, Achior, converts to Judaism upon witnessing the power of the God of Israel.

The tale of Judith, and that of Ptolemy Philopator in Maccabees III, are prototypes of another Jewish oicotype, "rescue of the Jewish community from calamity." Prototypes in the plural because each of these two tales has a different orientation. The tale of Judith is realistic, and in it the representative of the community takes her life in her hands and, with a mixture of courage and wiliness, brings about the salvation of the community in a realistic manner. Such a line of development appears still earlier in the biblical *Scroll of Esther*. In both tales (and some add the biblical tale of Ya'el and Sisera) the fate of the community rests in the hands of courageous women who use their femininity and sexuality to save it. The tale of Ptolemy and the elephants reflects another branch of this narrtive type, "the *miraculous* rescue of the Jewish community," and it is the main road travelled by Jewish folk narrative thereafter. Here the prayer of the community representative (or of the community as a whole) is answered, and its holy force—an angel, Elijah the Prophet, one of the Thirty-Six Righteous Men, or one of the Ten Tribes—performs an act of magic that brings salvation and acknowledgement by the nations of the greatness of its God. Another important motif appearing in this tale is the inauguration of a special festival to commemorate the rescue. Here the similarity to the *Scroll* is more salient. Indeed, all the tales of this type—describing events for whose commemoration special days of remembrance were celebrated—came under the rubric of "Second Purim" in the folk traditions. These stories perpetuated the memory of local incidences of the rescue of Jewish communities in their various locales. The first "Second Purim" tale we know of is found thus in Maccabees III, and it became one of the central themes of folk narrative in the following generations.[7]

Some scholars have argued that the tale of Judith and that of Ptolemy and the elephants are actual historical accounts, whereas others view them as fictional. The former point to the historically credible background of the tales, and to reliable evidence of these events, while the latter emphasize inconsistencies with historical facts, and the tales' lack of authenticity and fictional or allegorical nature. From the folkloristic perspective, such debate is irrelevant: these tales are consummate historical legends. They fulfill the basic conditions of folk narrative, and conform to its construction and atmosphere. Even if the tales enfold a kernel of historical "fact," the many years that passed between the time the events took place (for example, the edicts against Egyptian Jewry in the time of Ptolemy Philopator) and the time they were set down in writing indicates that the tales long existed in the oral tradition and underwent the process of "folklorization" that we described above in connection with the legend in the Hebrew Bible. Another outstanding example of such a process is the tale of the three bodyguards of Darius in *Apocryphal Esdras*.[8]

In this tale, Darius lays a great feast for his officers and servants in the style of Ahasuerus's revels in the *Scroll of Esther* (the opening scene). Afterwards, as the king sleeps in his bed, his three bodyguards engage in a contest wherein each man must name "the strongest thing" (the confrontation scene). The king will dress the winner in royal garments, and the winner will drink from a golden goblet, sleep in a bed of gold, and be carried in a golden chariot. Each bodyguard writes down his suggestion, and lays the note beneath the king's pillow. After assembling the high and mighty of his kingdom, the king opens the bodyguards' notes and reads their contents aloud: the first proposed wine; the second, the king; and the third, who is Zerubavel the Jew, woman, and stronger than her, the truth (the contest scene). In an episode reminiscent of Plato's *symposium* (wherein a contest concerning the theme of love is waged by means of orations), the king calls upon each contestant to explain his answer in oration. The court unanimously declares Zerubavel the victor. For his prize, he asks permission for the Jews to return to Zion and rebuild the Temple (the resolution scene). The Jews hold a great festival with songs and instruments for seven days (concluding scene, the triumph). The folk character of the tale needs no special proof: the pattern and course of the plot described here, the many folkloric motifs from which the tale is composed (the contest, superlative questions ["what is the strongest of all"], the power of wine and woman, revelation before the royal court, the victory of the unpromising hero [the Jew]), and the etiological character as explanation for an existing phenomenon (the return to Zion and the construction of the Second Temple), are crystal clear. In the present version, the tale is not a folktale: its "high" and sublime style, the insertion of long descriptive and rhetorical sections, and its position within a more encompassing historical composition (*Apocryphal Esdras*), indicate the familiar process we discussed earlier—the transition from folktale to written literary composition.

A similar process is reflected in yet another work from this period, *The Letter of Aristeas*. The letter recounts the act of translation of the Torah by seventy elders brought from Jerusalem to Alexandria by Ptolemy for the purpose of translating for him the teaching of the Jews. The translation is so marvelous that only God's intervention can explain its beauty and precision. In other versions of the tale, in both Jewish and Christian traditions, the miracle is even greater, for Ptolemy sits the translators in separate, isolated rooms, yet their translations emerge identical. The tale of the Septuagint can serve as an outstanding example of historical legend with a social function. It explains an existing phenomenon: the sanctity and centrality of the Septuagint among Egyptian Jewry during the Second Temple period. The divine origin of the translation can serve simultaneously as reason and justification for the Jews of Hellenistic Egypt to read the Torah in Greek, and proof that they held it equal in holiness to the Hebrew Torah handed down to Moses at Sinai. It is clear to us that the struggle for position and authority of the spiritual center of Alexandria is reflected even more so here. In *The Letter of Aristeas*, the familiar folkloric motif of divinely inspired writing of holy books became the kernel of an encompassing work with historical and theological ramifications.[9]

The stories of "Darius's Three Bodyguards," the *Scroll of Esther*, and the *Book of Judith* can be compared in many respects, in that they are realistic tales featuring protagonists whose wisdom and resourcefulness lead to rescue of the community or generate a decisive event in its history. Yet the main similarity between them converges on a single point—the generic distinction. All three are, from a generic perspective, novellae. They take place on the realistic plane, their flesh-and-blood protagonists experience adventures and undergo sharp reversals of status during the course of the story, and they shape their fate through the use of wisdom, cleverness, and resourcefulness. In the first two tales (Esther and Judith), clear use is also made of erotic motification, which is a central feature of the novella. In the tale of Zerubavel, it is only alluded to indirectly, in Zerubavel's speech describing woman's erotic power as stronger than anything (a motif much emphasized in Plato's *symposium*, similar in its literary construction as well).

In their present form, these tales should not be seen as novellae, but as historical legends. They are anchored in a precise historical context (true or fictional); they are told not to amuse but to commemorate a hallowed historical event of the community or to explain an existing phenomenon such as an important holiday (Purim), or a central event in the life of the people (the Return to Zion). We are witnesses here to the important literary process of *transformation from novella to historical legend*. The folk origin of the tale of "Darius's

Three Bodyguards" is clear: this tale features a contest of superlative riddles (who is the strongest, richest, most beautiful of all), in whose course the youngest of the participants, the youngest brother, or the lowliest of the contestants, is the victor and winner of the princess' hand. The single most significant historical event of the Second Temple Period was the Return to Zion and the rebuilding of the Temple. The question as to what it was that persuaded the Persian sovereign to consent to and encourage this process intrigued not only the sages and leaders, but also the folk, which filters historical events through its own unique perspective. Scholars of folk legend, and lately historians as well, have stressed that it was not historical accuracy that engaged the imagination of the folk, but the question of how historical events reflect the folk's spirit and worldview. Therefore, the Return to Zion takes place under Darius, not Cyrus. The custom of the folk is to attribute memories of its past to figures more familiar (therefore Holofernes is Nebuchadnezzar's military commander in the *Book of Judith*). Here the folk (in the broad sense of the term, which includes writers and the learned, who were active participants in the crystallization of these traditions) took up an available wisdom novella, altered it in accordance with its needs, and changed it into a historical-etiological legend that explains the origin of the central historical event of the period. It does so not through use of strategic and political concepts, but through the conventional notions of folk literature—folk wisdom and the triumph of the hero over his Gentile rivals. The historical legend is not interested in social processes, political factors, or historical development, but in the figure of the protagonist who generates the history (or the holy force that stands behind him). Thus the legend of the Return to Zion was told in the Second Temple Period, and the tale of "Darius's Three Bodyguards" is undoubtedly only one example of many tales concerning this theme then in circulation.[10]

[C] The Expanded Biblical Tale

The retelling of the biblical tale (I prefer "retelling" and the term "expanded" to the more popular one—rewritten—as an essential part of these texts was orally narrated, not created in writing) began as early as the Bible itself, and some tales are told a second and third time in various contexts. In examining some such examples in the previous chapter, what we found was more in the category of different versions of a single tale type than the retelling of a biblical tale as a full literary genre. This cultural phenomenon appears fully formed for the first time in the apocryphal literature. Most of the literature which retells the biblical story is constructed upon it as pseudepigraphal literature or relates to the biblical literature in various and diverse ways. Essentially, the expanded tale does not belong to the realm of folk literature. It is usually the creation of a writer or preacher who takes biblical text and relates to it in different ways—commentarial, theological, or rhetorical. The narrative medium is only one among them. The expanded tale is generally a purposeful work, created at a given point in time. It does not appear in multiple versions and does not meet the basic conditions of folk literature. It does not stand as an independent tale, but rather always depends on associations and composite allusions to the original biblical version.[11]

Nonetheless, there is evidence that the expanded biblical tale, in the Second Temple Period and thereafter in the rabbinic period, became one of the most widespread narrative categories among Hebrew folktales. Books such as *The Book of Jubilees* or *Biblical Antiquities* (attributed to Philo), recount the biblical story anew, each in its own way. Neither one can be viewed as a folk book. They include halachic, theological, or historical material of no interest to the folk. Yet certain stories included therein, such as the tale of the binding of Isaac in *The Book of Jubilees* or the tale of Qenaz in *Biblical Antiquities*, have an independent existence, appear in multiple versions, and exhibit discernible formal and thematic qualities of the folktale. It may be surmised that such biblical tales made their way as folk traditions told and retold, and authors saw fit to weave them into their works after revision and adjustment.

For the sake of substantiating questions connected to the expanded biblical tale as a folk narrative genre, let us look closely at the following excerpt from *The Book of Jubilees*:

> And at the end of the nineteenth jubilee in the seventh week, in the sixth year, Adam died. And all of his children buried him in the land of his creation. And he was the first who was buried[p] in the earth. •And he lacked seventy years from one thousand years, for a thousand years are like one day in the testimony of heaven and therefore it was written concerning the tree of knowledge, "In the day you eat from it you will die." Therefore he did not complete the years of this day because he died in it.
>
> At the end of that jubilee Cain was killed one year after him. And his house fell upon him, and he died in the midst of his house. And he was killed by its stones because he killed Abel with a stone, and with a stone he was killed by righteous judgment. Therefore it is ordained in the heavenly tablets:
>> "With the weapons with which a man kills his fellow
>> he shall be killed
>> just as he wounded him,
>> thus shall they do to him."
>
> (*Jubilees* 4:29–31)

The excerpt contains an interesting mix of homiletic and folkloric elements. It has a firm link to biblical verses such as "and all the days that Adam lived were nine hundred and thirty years: and he died" (Gen. 5:5), and "For a thousand years in thy sight are but like yesterday when it is past" (Pss. 90:4); as well as to the stories of the Garden of Eden and of Cain and Abel. The tale is worked into the *Book of Jubilees'* unique perception of historical time, divided into jubilees and "weeks" (that is, periods of seven years). Nonetheless, it basically tells a complete tale with a folkloric hue, into which distinct folkloric motifs are woven: the dual meaning of the divine voice ("day" in the meaning of that same day, "day" in the meaning of one thousand years) the formulaic numbers one thousand and seventy, the folk concept of the punishment meted out to the sinner ("measure for measure"). These are motifs that seem part of a more encompassing and complete tale that described in detail the sin and punishment of Cain (for example, the killing of Abel with the stone). The text's point of departure is the biblical story and additional verses, combined in a new narrative plot. We must understand that in a society where books were extremely scarce, nearly the only way to tell a biblical tale (outside of the ritual public reading of the Torah) was to tell it aloud to various audiences and at various performance events. Once the biblical tale is severed from its fixed, written version, the rules, pattern, and motification that are characteristic of folk narrative apply. Yet it is distinct from the independent folktale, in that expanded biblical tales cannot exist without a continued associative link to the scriptural source.

The tale that is perhaps told and expanded more than any other biblical story is that of the binding of Isaac. The version preserved in *The Book of Jubilees* basically parallels that in Genesis 22. Without relating the theological and literary meaning of the differences between them, it should be noted that the main difference from the viewpoint of folk literature is found in the tale's opening: after Isaac's birth, voices are heard in heaven praising Abraham's loyalty to and faith in God. The Prince of Hatred, Satan, appears before God and proposes to test Abraham by sacrificing his son before his eyes. At the tale's close, the Prince of Hatred appears again before God, this time to be demeaned and to bear his punishment publicly. The importance of this beginning (and conclusion) lies not in that it suggests a motive for God's testing of Abraham, a motive reminiscent of that in the book of Job. The fundamental importance from our perspective is inherent in that it turns the biblical tale of the binding into a folktale. As told in Genesis, the tale lacks the essential characteristic of the folktale, namely, conflict, the confrontation between rival forces. Abraham receives instructions from on high, and carries them out without question. Any hesitation is strictly within the reader's imagination, for the biblical text itself offers no such intimation. The lack of an opposing force, the negative narrative pole, takes from this story the ability to be a folktale. The character of Satan in the tale in the *Book of Jubilees* comes not only to explain in a theological manner the stimulus for the testing of Abraham, it also supplies the chief narrative character without which the story cannot exist as an independent folktale. The tale's conclusion in a tangible and unmistakable victory over the Prince of Hatred is also typical of folk literature: were Satan brought in solely to provide theological cause, there would be no need for him to reappear in the conclusion. Conversely, from the perspective of narrative logic and pattern, a folktale's resolution must be clear and tangible. Thus, the tale of the binding in *Jubilees* ends with the routing of the antagonist (the Prince of Hatred), and with the triumph of the force that represents the narrating society (God, Abraham). This is proof that the binding was told in this period as an independent folktale constructed according to the essential characteristics of the folktale: hero and antagonist, opening situation in balance between the forces active in the tale, conflict (Satan's indictment) and its resolution (Abraham's withstanding of the test), and restoration of the initial, balanced situation after victory over the challenger (the charge against him disproved, Abraham's status in the heavenly kingdom is wholly preserved).[12]

Another tale with a clear link to the tale of the binding reflects a similar process. The pseudepigraphal *Testament of Job* recounts that Job wanted to shatter a graven image that had been erected in his city. God warns him in a dream that Satan, whose image it is, will punish him if he dares harm it. If, however, Job remains steadfast in his righteousness, God will reward him sevenfold. Job demolishes the idol, whereupon the curtain rises on his troubles. The tale of the righteous man confronted with a fateful religious decision and the caveat that the correct path leads to harsh afflictions is surprisingly reminiscent of the spiritual birth of the Christian saint Placidus (Eustacius). The hero in this tale is a commander in the Roman army who is hunting in the forest. Suddenly, his quarry turns to face him. Jesus speaks out of the animal's throat, instructing Placidus to abandon idol worship and become a Christian, but cautions him that Satan lies in wait to harm him and his family. Placidus nonetheless does Jesus' bidding, and consequently his suffering begins, similar in its general lines to that of Job. The parallel between the two tales does not come to claim dependence between them, but to prove the existence of tales parallel in pattern and ideational perspective to that of the expanded tale of Job. Indeed, as we saw in the previous chapter, the biblical tale of Job was also apparently an independent folktale. The addition of the opening episode in the expanded apocryphal tale deepens the dramatic dimension of the story, the protagonist's awareness of his actions, and shears him of the biblical attributes of skeptic and thinker: in the expanded tale, Job no longer need wonder at the meaning of his afflictions, as God revealed it to him explicitly at the start! Thus the center of gravity of the expanded tale is shifted from the philosophical-theological focus of the biblical story, where it is the basis, to the narrative-dramatic aspect that is the basis of the tale in the narrative framework.[13]

The tale of Joseph in expanded form is extant in two books from the Second Temple: *The Testaments of the Twelve Patriarchs* and *Joseph and Asenath*. The latter was written, it seems, early in the second century C.E. in Greek, and thus is beyond the framework of our discussion. Nevertheless, the motifs it comprises bear on our description of the folktale of the period. It tells the great love story of Joseph and Asenath (daughter of the Egyptian high priest), Asenath's conversion, and Joseph's war against Egyptian idolatry. The work employs romantic folk motifs (the love of Joseph and Asenath) and the image of the believer struggling with his pagan environment (widespread also in rabbinic and Christian literature—for example, Abraham's campaign against idols, Daniel in the lions' den, the tales of tortured saints in Christianity). Extant versions of the work are patently formulated as Hellenistic romances. Romance serves here as a narrative framework for the Judeo-Christian worldview: monotheism, war against idolatry, movement to conversion to Judaism or Christianity, the central religious standing of prayer, and so on. The author of the book made use of the tradition of Joseph tales, fused them together by using a narrative genre widespread in his time and place (the romance), and used them as a framework for ideas and conflicts that engaged him and his audience.[14]

The tale of Joseph and Potiphar's wife recounted in "The Testament of Joseph" in *The Testaments of the Twelve Patriarchs* represents another direction in the evolution of the expanded biblical tale in this period. It should be seen as a narrative development of a particular verse: "And it came to pass, as she spoke to [Joseph] day by day" (Gen. 39:10). Scripture never drew upon the tremendous narrative and erotic potential stored in this verse. In the pseudepigraphal story, Potiphar's wife, desiring Joseph, makes daily desperate attempts to seduce him: she threatens to kill him, promises to poison her husband and make Joseph master of her house, treats him as a stepson to get closer to him, flatters him and his religious faith, and even offers to abandon her idols and convert. She showers him with countless gifts and tries to slip aphrodisiacs into his food. She goes so far as to threaten suicide if he does not respond to her favorably.

The basic narrative situation—the wife of a highly placed man falls in love with a young man in her household and does everything she can to seduce him—is surprisingly similar to the Greek tale of Phaedra and Hippolytus. Therein, Phaedra, wife of the valiant Theseus, king of Athens, has designs on her stepson, and uses the same means as Potiphar's wife in "The Testament of Joseph." The Phaedra story, preserved in Euripedes's *Hippolytus*, was, in the period dealt with here, a widely known folk cycle of novellae in the Hellenistic east. The vast similarity, down to the very details, between the plots of these novellae and the tale of Joseph in the *Testaments*, leaves no room for doubt that this literary cycle was a main source of the tale. For example: the claim of Potiphar's wife that Joseph is like a son to her is meaningless in the tale of Joseph because he was purchased for a slave, and there is no way to present him as a son, yet this claim is real in the Phaedra story, where the young man is indeed Phaedra's stepson. The use of love potions is not known to us from Jewish narrative, but is a prevalent folk motif in the Hellenistic culture of the age. In this tale, the framework of the biblical Joseph story is interestingly merged with the details and content of a widespread Hellenistic story. The result is the creation of an expanded biblical tale loaded with the erotic power characteristic of the Hellenistic tale (and almost entirely absent from the biblical tale). This sort of literary syncretism—manifested in the union of motifs and narrative patterns from the foreign literature with biblical narrative—was not, apparently, a phenomenon restricted to the "Testament of Joseph," and it represents an interesting route in the development of the expanded biblical tale as folk narrative.[15]

The second book of Josephus's *Antiquities of the Jews* includes the story known as "Moses in Ethiopia." Moses, prince of Egypt, is sent by Pharoah to fight the Ethiopians who have invaded his land. He surprises the invaders "for he did not march by the river, but by land," employing a serpent-devouring bird—the ibe—to protect his troops from the numerous serpents they encountered on that march. He routed the Ethiopians, who fled to their capitol, Saba. The city could not be captured, but Tharbis, daughter of the Ethiopian king, is smitten with Moses and delivers the city into his hands after he promises to marry her. The tale reflects the trends we described until this point in connection to the expanded biblical tale as a folktale: the welding of homiletic elements, referring to a verse or verses from the Bible, with narrative elements of the folktale. The text can be viewed as a narrative commentary on Numbers 12:1: "And Miryam and Aharon spoke against [Moses] because of the Kushite woman whom he had taken, for he had taken a Kushite woman." In the narrative expansion, clear use is made of the elements of the folk novella: the protagonist is sent by his rival (Pharoah) to execute a task likely to end in his death; use of means requiring wiliness and daring in order to overcome the obstacles in the hero's path; and the basic romantic element—marriage to the princess. In earlier instances, we saw just such a tendency to merge homiletic techniques with motifs of folk narrative. Another tendency to which the tale attests is the adoption of foreign narrative patterns and their grafting onto both the biblical tale and the Jewish world of faith and thought.

The Jewish-Hellenist author Artapanus, who lived in Alexandria in the second century B.C.E., also tells the story of Moses in Ethiopia: Moses, who was adopted by the daughter of the king of Egypt, is credited with teaching the Egyptians the arts of sailing, mechanized stonemasonry, weaponry, and irrigation; he is even said to have invented writing. Since the masses so admired Moses, they called him Hermes, after the Greco-Egyptian god. The king of Egypt, jealous of Moses's popularity, sent him away, at the head of an army of farmers, to war against the Ethiopians. Moses defeated them in battle and established his camp in the city of Hermopolis, where the ibe was held sacred.

The Ethiopians and Egyptian priests adopted the rite of circumcision in emulation of Moses.

Artapanus's tale is an odd mixture of Moses, the biblical hero, with Egyptian and Hellenistic mythological elements: the protagonist son of the gods who steals divine wisdom and gives it to mortals, the etiological tale of the establishment of Hermopolis (city of Hermes) and the origin of the cult of the ibe, and the explanation of how the Ethiopians and Egyptian priests came to circumcise their sons. This unique textual union characterizes the syncretic perspective of Egyptian Jewry in the Second Temple period, and it matters not at all for our purposes if the responsible party was Artapanus himself, or if he made use of folk traditions that circulated among Egyptian Jewry of his day. In any case, this process of creating an expanded biblical tale by fusing narrative elements from non-Jewish folklore together with the biblical tale is plainly manifested here.

It may be that Josephus borrowed directly from Artapanus, and it may be that he had other sources. In any case, a comparison of the versions of Artapanus and Josephus fleshes out the development of the expanded biblical tale: what for Artapanus was a rather unrefined mixture of mythological elements with biblical narrative, became for Josephus a historical novella. In the latter, the mythological elements vanish almost entirely (the ibe, for example, which for Artapanus was a pagan, ritualistic artifact, is war material for Josephus). Had not Artapanus's text survived (by chance, in the writings of the Church Father Eusebius, a resident of third-century Caesaria), it would be difficult to outline this evolution. But Artapanus's testimony gives us important proof of the line of development of the folktale in the Second Temple period. The fact that the tale of "Moses in Ethiopia" was widespread as an independent folktale is also borne out by its later versions, specifically in the translation attributed to Jonathan ben Uzziel and in the medieval works, *The Chronicles of Moses* and *Sefer ha-Yashar*, which also attest that other traditions of the tale must have circulated even if they are no longer available.[16]

[D] The Martyrological Narrative as Folktale

Tales about saints who in their suffering and death "testify" to the truth of their faith (martyrology) are among the most prevalent in the Christian narrative of Late Antiquity and the Middle Ages. Forming the basis of the adoration of legendary Christian saints are tales of their suffering and death in the course of following "in the footsteps of Jesus," in other words, their imitation of his suffering and death (*Imitatio Christi*). The theological significance and functions of these tales are so widely known as to render superfluous their examination here. For our purposes, the fact that martyrological narrative is, in part, folk narrative is important. Its protagonists are members of the folk who later merited the Church's official recognition; the tales of their agonies and death circulate in many versions and are constructed according to the conventions of the folktale. We must not forget that even the story of the death of Jesus of Nazareth himself is a Jewish tale from the period under discussion. It meets the basic conditions that characterize folk narrative: multiple versions, supernatural motification, and an explicitly legendary character. Therefore, the story of Jesus should be seen not only as the prototype of subsequent Christian martyrological narrative, but also as definitive testimony of the nature of such tales circulating in Palestine during the Second Temple period.

One principal difference between folk literature and the martyrological tale should be noted here: the latter concludes in the tragic death of the protagonist, in contrast to the fundamental epic law of the "happy ending." It is nonetheless clear that in the eyes of the narrating society, the hero truly triumphs over his adversaries in death, for by surrendering his life he proves the superiority of his faith. More than a few martyrological tales confirm this via a divine voice, or an appearance of Jesus himself or one of his disciples, who declares the hero a saint—the highest status to which man can aspire.[17]

One of the Second Temple period's most salient contributions to folk narrative comes to the fore in this context. Martyrological narrative can be traced to tales of the apocryphal literature. The most famous is that of "The Mother and her Seven Sons" in Maccabees II and IV. The former also includes the story of the elderly Eleazar, who chose torture and death rather than eat forbidden meat. The tale of the death of the prophet Isaiah in the work known as *The Martyrdom of Isaiah* also belongs to this category. "The Mother and her Seven Sons" is one of the most famous and far-flung tales in Jewish (and Christian) culture. After its two basic versions in the books of the Maccabees, dozens more appear in rabbinic literature, in the Middle Ages, and in the modern period. Some are consummate folk versions, excelling in their brevity and simple language; others underwent literary adaptation in poetry, short story, and drama.

The versions of the tale in the books of the Maccabees are not folktales, but long, complex stories with theological, historical, and philosophical orientations. Hellenistic-Jewish authors were responsible for the tales' broad narrative adaptations here. (Especially important, it seems, is the contribution of the second-century B.C.E. Jewish-Hellenist historian, Jason of Cyrene, some of whose remarks are transmitted in Maccabees II. This makes him the first author we can name to press the martyrological tale into literary and historical service.) The versions of the tale in the books of the Maccabees employ diverse means of Greek rhetoric, ornate language bursting with pathos, and lengthy and cumbersome discourse. Maccabees IV, for example, concentrates wholly on the tale of the mother and her sons. It is long and labyrinthine, and the tale itself is subordinate to exceptionally drawn-out and detailed theological and psychological arguments.

Still, the features of the folktale are clearly visible beneath the literary polish coating the tale in these two versions. These are the formulaic number seven; the intensive use of dialogue, a feature characteristic of the oral tale (or of drama, also an oral medium); the epic law of "two to a scene," such that the sons appear one at a time as the tale progresses (along with the imperial inquisitor), participating in the action only when the previous one has exited. We know that Jason of Cyrene made use of narrative-historic traditions on the period of the Maccabean Revolt that reached him from Palestine. Among them was, it can be assumed, the tale of "The Mother and her Sons" and others detailing the tortures suffered by Jews for the sake of their faith. There is further evidence of this in Maccabees II, which says after the tales of the elderly Eleazar and the mother and her seven sons: "and it is enough in these things about the abuse of the sacrifices and the great tortures" (7:42). This indicates that additional tales of torments circulated, and that the author was content with a sample of two. This in turn leads to the supposition that, in the wake of the Hasmonean Revolt, the Jews of Palestine told and retold stories of the marvelous death by harsh tortures of men, women, and children who sacrificed themselves for their faith in the Torah. Such widespread tales were characteristically told at various opportunities (for example, on the day designated to commemorate the event, i.e., Hanukkah), and circulated over the course of many years in oral traditions. Collecting these traditions, a contemporary historian (Jason of Cyrene, for one) wove in the tale of the martyrdom of the mother and her sons within the historical framework reconstructed in his writings. It is nevertheless clear that setting down the tale in writing did not stop its oral recitation. It was from these oral traditions that the tale worked its way into the aggadic traditions of the rabbinic period, after its historical backdrop of the Maccabean period gave way to that of the destruction of the Temple and the Hadrianic edicts, as we shall see in the next chapter.[18]

The story of the killing of the Prophet Isaiah is another typical martyrological tale that preserved the features of folk narrative: Manasseh sentences Isaiah to death for claiming to have seen God (Isa. 6:1). The prophet flees and hides inside a tree trunk, after Belchira the Samaritan, instigated by Satan, informs against him. Manasseh dispatches his soldiers, who hew the tree. Before his death, Isaiah refuses to accede to Belchira's demand that he take back his prophecy of the fall of Manasseh's kingdom. He dies in torment inside the tree, while Belchira and the rest of the false prophets watch in amusement. This tale has variants in both Jewish and Christian literature of the period, as well as in eastern literature. It is mentioned in the first-century non-canonical *Vitae*

Prophetaram discussed below, and alluded to in the New Testament (Heb. 11:38) and other sources from the early Christian literature. Folk narratives of India and Persia tell of a prophet who fled his persecutors into the desert. When they caught up with him, God caused an opening to form in the trunk of a tree and he hid himself inside. But Iblis (Satan) shows his pursuers the hiding place, and they hew him to death inside the tree. The story of Isaiah's death appears in additional versions in rabbinic literature—in the Babylonian and Palestinian Talmud, in midrash, and in the Aramaic translations. Traces of its existence in multiple versions fulfill the basic condition of the definition of a folktale. Even if originally devised as historical or religious literature, it can still be proven that the tale passed the societal "censorship," that is, became a folktale that circulated in multiple versions that society cared to tell and retell. The eastern variants of the tale perhaps indicate that the tale was not originally Jewish, and had to undergo an alteration process before Jewish culture could accept it.

A number of scholars saw the tale of the Prophet Isaiah's death as a sort of allegory for the life and fate of the Judean Desert sects. The true prophet flees Jerusalem fearing death at the hands of the wicked priests who took over the Temple (Belchira in the tale), and the wicked regime (Zechariah). His students join him, and they live a life of purity in their desert refuge. The forces of darkness, not content to leave them in peace, pursue and execute them with harsh and brutal tortures. Such a literary model reflected, according to this interpretation of the tale, the rivalry between the Judean Desert sects and the Jerusalem establishment that reigned in the ritual center of the Temple, the necessity they felt to escape to the desert, and their fear that the long arm of the wicked establishment would follow them even there. If there is anything to such an interpretation of the tale, it reinforces well-recognized phenomena in the study of the folktale. It reflects, whether consciously or not, the social situation, existential anxieties, and hidden desires of the individual. It is difficult to imagine that this tale, found in so many versions among Jews and Christians in this period, was told and retold with no purpose whatsoever or without constituting an expression of spiritual or social conditions. One possible explanation of the social function of the story is as commemoration of the prophet-saint's act of sacrifice, encouraging others to follow in his footsteps (the martyrological narrative). Another is that the legend of the death of the prophet seeks to reflect (or symbolize) the historical and psychic situation of the narrating society. Thus, we cannot deny the possibility that the tale was indeed devised and told among Jewish sects hiding in the Judean desert, and that it reflected both their ideology (the conscious, martyrological level) and their existential anxieties (the unconscious, existential level).[19]

Vitae Prophetarum, a short work that scholars estimate was written in Hebrew in Palestine in the first century c.e., is replete with folkloric traditions of the Second Temple period. According to the author's introduction, the purpose of the book is to convey "the names of the prophets and where they acted, where did they die, and how and where were they buried." And indeed, the work lists biblical prophets, the places of their birth and death, and the miracles done for the Jews on the graves of the saints. In certain instances, such as the description of the prophets' graves surrounding Jerusalem and Bet Guvrin, the work resembles a kind of "handbook" or travel guide for Jewish pilgrims to the saints' final resting places in Palestine, and this may well have been one of its aims. Such guidebooks and travelogues have always been a most important source of folkloric traditions of Palestine. Extant in the *Vitae Prophetarum* is a story detailing the martyric death of the Prophet Isaiah, alongside tales of the martyrdom of other prophets including Jeremiah, Ezekiel, and Zechariah. Particularly important are the folk traditions of the miracles done on the prophet's graves.

According to the *Vitae Prophetarum*, water flows continuously from the Shiloah Spring because of Isaiah's grave, but only when Jews draw from it. When non-Jews approach it, it dries up forthwith. Jeremiah was buried where the Pharaoh's palace once stood in Egypt, and even the Egyptians hold the site in awe and respect, as Jeremiah's bones forced out the venomous snakes that once infested the palace grounds. Ezekiel was murdered by the Exilarch, whom he had admonished for idol worship. Pilgrimage to the grave site was customary for many. Once, when a large number of Jews were gathered there, the Chaldeans conspired to attack and decimate them. The saint-prophet halted the flow of the river passing by the grave, so that all the Jews could escape to the other side. When the Gentiles attempted the crossing in pursuit, the torrent was renewed, drowning them. Ezekiel's grave performed many other miracles in the sight of Gentile military commanders, so that they would allow the Jews to live in peace. Similar traditions based on miracles with a geographical nature are recounted here about the other prophets.

This small composition preserved an important treasury of folk traditions that the author collected from Jews in first-century Palestine. One of a kind, it attests to an almost folkloristic process of gathering folk traditions "from the field" and committing them to the page. In any case, this important folkloric phenomenon—folk traditions about miracles done near the graves of martyrs—was, according to the testimony of *Vitae Prophetarum*, widespread in Palestine as early as this period. This partially explains the phenomenon's centrality in Jewish folk literature of the generations that followed.[20]

Martyrological tales in the Hebrew literature of the Second Temple period established a new literary form that, in later periods, became a cornerstone of Judaism's stock of folk traditions. Tales of the martyrdom of sages in the talmudic-midrashic literature (known as "The Ten Martyrs") and martyrological tales in the periods of the crusades and the Chmielnicki massacres of 1648–1649 originate here, in the narrative creativity of the Second Temple period.

[E] The Hagiographical Cycle

Unlike the Bible and the talmudic-midrashic literature, the literature of the Second Temple period left behind no clear evidence of the existence of a cycle of tales. Compositions from this time are fashioned as historical chronicles, either in the form of a series of events following Scripture (the *Book of Jubilees*) or the full story of a single event (Judith, Maccabees), but no cycle or grouping of tales. Nonetheless, it seems possible to reconstruct the existence of one hagiographical cycle of the period, surrounding the figure of Daniel. There are four principal sources of Daniel tales: the first part of the biblical Book of Daniel, the Book of Susannah, and the apocryphal Additions to the Book of Daniel. To these should be added three isolated tales: one from the aforementioned *Vitae Prophetarum*, another from a Qumran text that, according to scholarly assessment, also has as its protagonist Daniel, and the third that survived in a post–Second Temple text, Midrash *Song of Songs Rabbah*. From these sources it is possible to reconstruct the existence of eleven tales that survived, it seems, from a more encompassing cycle of legends surrounding the Daniel figure:

(1) Daniel and his companions, Hananiah, Mishael, and Azariah, do not partake of the heathen sacrifices presented them in Nebuchadnezzar's court, eating instead only seeds. A miracle happens, and they appear to be healthier and more satisfied than all the other youths.

(2) Daniel and the Priests of Babylonia: Nebuchadnezzar has a dream and demands of his wise men that they recount to him the dream and its meaning, or be executed. Daniel alone succeeds at both recounting and interpreting the dream. The king appoints him chief over all his ministers, and raises his companions to the office of district prefects.

(3) Nebuchadnezzar erects a golden statue and orders everyone to bow down before it. He is told that the Jews refuse to comply. His soldiers cast Daniel's companions, Hananiah, Mishael, and Azariah, into a blazing furnace and leave them there for seven days, but they are not consumed. Nebuchadnezzar acknowledges the greatness of the God of the Jews.

(4) Driven by jealousy, Darius's ministers search for a way to bring about Daniel's downfall. They persuade Darius to issue an order that anyone refusing to prostrate himself before the king, as before a god, is to be cast into the lions' den. Daniel, after refusing to comply, is

duly sent to this gory death, but the lions leave him unharmed. When the king throws his evil advisors into the cave, they are immediately torn to pieces. Darius again professes the greatness of the God of Daniel.

(5) The story of Susannah: Two elders of the community, judges of the people in Babylonia, lust after the beautiful Susannah, wife of the wealthy Jew, Joakim. While she is bathing in her garden, left alone briefly by her attendants, they demand that she submit to their advances. She rebuffs them, and they bear witness before the court that she committed adultery with a youth in the garden of her home. As "at the mouth of two witnesses . . . shall the matter be established" (Deut. 19:15), she is sentenced to death. The young Daniel calls out from among the assemblage that justice is not being served and demands leave to question the witnesses. He asks them separately under which tree they saw Susannah committing her crime, and each gives a different answer. After detailed discussion, Susannah is exonerated, and the elders are punished in her stead.

(6) Daniel and Bel: Each day enormous quantities of food are brought before the image of Bel, who apparently consumes it all. Daniel claims before the king that it is not the idol who eats the food. Seventy of Bel's priests consent that if Daniel proves Bel is not eating the food laid down before it, they will be executed. Conversely, if he cannot prove his claim, he will be killed. Daniel seals all openings in the hall and scatters ashes on the floor of the temple. When the sealed hall is opened the next day, it becomes clear that while the food has indeed been consumed, footprints in the ashes lead to a hidden passageway to the quarters of the priests who, with their families, themselves consumed the food brought to the image. They are sentenced to death.

(7) Daniel and the dragon (or the crocodile): The king orders Daniel to worship a live crocodile, as opposed to a graven image like Bel. Daniel prepares a mixture of pitch, rye, and hair (skins, apparently), which the crocodile devours, until its insides burst.

(8) The masses charge that the king has complied with all of Daniel's whims because he has himself become a Jew (under Daniel's influence). Pressured by the crowd, the king throws Daniel into the lions' den. He remains there for six days, nourished by food brought miraculously by the Prophet Habbakuk. Since he has stayed alive, the king takes him out and throws his denouncers into the lions' den in his stead.

(9) As punishment for his sins, Nebuchadnezzar was periodically transformed into a beast of the field: his head and forelimbs like those of

an ox, his legs and backside like those of a lion. He eats grass like a beast and after digesting it is transformed back into a man. Daniel prays and asks forgiveness for him, saving him from the awful fate. As reward, the king changes his name from Daniel to Belshazzar, with the intention of raising him to royal status, but Daniel/Belshazzar declines.

(10) Nabonidus, king of Babylonia, falls seriously ill. He turns to his gods, but to no avail. A Jewish saint (Daniel, apparently) heals him through his wisdom.

(11) Nebuchadnezzar tries again and again to seduce Daniel into worshiping an idol. To convince Daniel of the idol's power, he places "the diadem of the High Priest" into its mouth, and when his priests and ministers came to sing its praises, the image speaks the words, "I am the Lord thy God." Daniel, divining the ruse, asks to kiss the idol, professing his love for it. He removes the diadem from the image's mouth, and when the believers assemble to praise it, it is silent. Subsequently, the spirit of God shatters it.

Tales (1) through (4) are found in the biblical Book of Daniel (1:8–17; 2:3,6); (5) is the Book of Susannah; (6) through (8) are in the Additions to the Book of Daniel; (9) comes from the *Vitae Prophetarum*; (10) from the *Prayer of Nabonidus*, found in fragmentary form in the Qumran texts; (11) *Song of Songs Rabbah* 7:9.

We can discern in the "Danielic Cycle," as it were, a kind of chronological development: in the Susannah tale, Daniel is still a boy, as yet unknown to the community; in the first tale in the Book of Daniel, he is revealed before Nebuchadnezzar's servants; in the second tale there, Daniel interprets the king's dream and is revealed before the king and his court, until his ultimate triumph over the denouncers and the king's admission of his superiority. The *Septuagint*'s ordering of the tales backs up such a chronological conception of the story cycle: It puts Susannah first, then the biblical book of Daniel and, finally, the tales of the Additions to the Book of Daniel. Daniel's anonymous childhood thus gives way to renown within the Jewish community, followed by his precipitous rise in the ruler's court (a court tale *par excellence*) accompanied by his rigid campaign against paganism, and culminating with his ultimate victory over it.

In addition to the continuity stemming from the cycle pattern, each of these tales has the standing of an independent tale told on its own without any connection to the other stories. Each of the tales included here fulfills the basic conditions of the folktale: opening situation and conclusion (each tale begins with a situation of balance between the tale's active forces, Daniel and the priests, Daniel and the king, Daniel and the haters of the Jews from the crowd);

it emphasizes the confrontation which sets off the plot (Daniel is told to partake of the pagan sacrifices, to worship idols or the king, to take part in the execution of an innocent woman); the resolution of the conflict and restoration of the initial balanced situation (the pagan priests are executed, the king acknowledges the greatness of the God of the Jews, justice triumphs over injustice). Variants of the tales reinforce the evidence that they are independent folktales: the Susannah story has many variants (the clever child who demonstrates true justice to judges or the king, such as the boy Solomon, or Ali Hodja in Arabic folk narrative); the faithful and besmirched wife whose various names include Christiana and Genofeva, and the Samaritan tale about the daughter of Amram the High Priest whom two monks sought to seduce. Origen, a third-century Church Father, conducted his own research among Jewish scholars in Palestine on the tale of Susannah. He discovered that the tale was not only known and told among them, they could even identify the two elders by name: Ahab, the son of Kolaiah, and Zedekiah, the son of Maaseiah (as told in Jer. 29: 21–23). Tales about saints who were cast into a blazing furnace or lions' den, yet survived, are an inalienable property of Christian tales of saints in the ancient world and the Middle Ages. The tales of Daniel and Bel, or Daniel and the Crocodile, have interesting variants in rabbinic literature, to which we will return later on. All these indicate that the tales were familiar and widespread as independent tales as well.

We have no evidence whatsoever of a complete and organized hagiographical cycle on Daniel. There is sufficient evidence that, in Palestine and Babylonia, Daniel was the hero of many saints' legends, whose main theme revolved around the struggle against idolatry. This period, spanning the final two centuries before the Common Era and a hundred years thereafter, approximately, saw the Middle Eastern cultures struggle with the radical processes of the shift from idolatry to monotheism. Thus, it comes as no surprise that the underlying conflicts engaged society in general, not just its theologians. Folktales like Daniel's hagiographa were almost certainly the primary medium through which themes like the struggle against idolatry reached the broad strata of the society.[21]

In seven of the eleven tales included in the hagiographical cycle, resolution of the conflict is accomplished through divine might (Daniel and his companions are supernaturally nourished, Daniel sees in a vision the interpretation of the king's dream, Daniel's companions survive the furnace, Daniel emerges unharmed from the lions' den—twice, Daniel succeeds in healing the Babylonian kings with God's help). In four tales, the resolution comes via the protagonist's wisdom (getting at the truth in the Susannah story, exposing the ruse of Bel's priests, killing the crocodile, curing the king). These differences in the nature of the force that resolves the tale's plot divide the tales of the cycle into two categories: sacred legends, in which the conflict is resolved via the sacred power of the narrating society; and wisdom tales, in which no supernatural power is involved and the protagonist instead uses means based on wisdom or wiliness to overcome the obstacles set before him. Unlike the tales of Elisha and Elijah in the biblical hagiographical cycles, the image of Daniel is not that of a miracle worker. He makes no use whatsoever of supernatural forces. In most of those stories that involve divine might, Daniel does nothing—he is a passive hero. His activity in these tales is limited to his steadfast devotion to the God of the Jews and his refusal to worship idols. He does not even effect his own rescue—rather, it is God's hand that saves him. Daniel is an active figure only in the wisdom-realistic tales, where he sets the course and determines the outcome by virtue of his own actions. In these tales, he judges righteously, uncovers deceit, and demonstrates his rectitude. From this perspective, there is a fundamental difference between the Hagiography of Daniel and the hagiographical cycles in The Hebrew Bible or in the Jewish narratives of the Middle Ages and the modern period. The protagonists of the latter are always performers of miracles and folk miracle workers. Somewhat similar to the realistic hagiographical tales of Daniel is the cycle of King Solomon tales, *The Parables of King Solomon.* Therein the hero does not act as a folk miracle-worker but as a judge–wise man, and the tales are resolved by dint of wisdom, in a realistic manner.

[F] The Novella and Wisdom Tale

The tale of Susannah is exceptional among the tales of the hagiographical cycle of Daniel in its length, narrative complexity, the detailed descriptions of the community customs and legal practices, the description of Susannah's garden, and so on. The hand of an author-artist is visible here. He took up the first hagiographical tale of the folk hero Daniel, describing his revelation before the community, and turned it into an encompassing and complex literary work. The story of Susannah reached us in two principal versions: that of the *Septuagint* and that of Theodotion, both in Greek, although most scholars agree that the work was originally written in Hebrew. They differ not only literally and orthographically (common for manuscripts of the same work), but also in a manner far more essential, that being the different variants of a given tale-type.

They follow a divergent ideational orientation and literary pattern: the version in the *Septuagint* details the actions of the elders, their conversations, consultations regarding the false accusation against Susannah, and so on. There is no episode of Susannah bathing in her courtyard; the elders ask her to comply with their wishes, and when she refuses they resolve together to accuse her in court. Theodotion's version includes a detailed and rather erotic description of her bathing in her garden: she sends her maids to fetch oil for her skin, whereupon the two elders, who had been watching, emerge from their hiding place and demand that she submit to their advances, else they will denounce her before the community. When she bursts out laughing, they respond with vociferous accusations against her. In Theodotion's version, the elders happen to be in the garden because they sit in judgement over the people in the courtyard belonging to Joakim, Susannah's husband. In the *Septuagint* version, after Susannah's fate is decided, a heavenly angel descends to let its presence rest on the young Daniel. According to Theodotion, Daniel cries out immediately after her sentencing that he is free of this woman's blood, but not so the rest of the community, before whom a travesty of justice is being played out. The community turns to him, and after some discussion, the same council of elders invites him to sit among them and question the witnesses. Theodotion's version recounts that Susannah and her husband go back to living their life of peace and tranquility after their harsh trial, but the *Septuagint* version makes no such suggestion, although it does provide a kind of epilogue in which the narrator demands, as the moral stemming from the tale, that the youth be educated to be God-fearing and knowledgeable in Torah.[22]

The differences between these two versions conform to thematic analysis of the tale according to the law of polarization of folk narrative. One possible polarization in the tale is as follows (Theodotion's version):

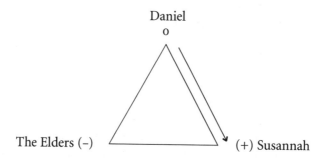

Daniel
o

The Elders (–)   (+) Susannah

The other possibility is as below (the *Septuagint* version):

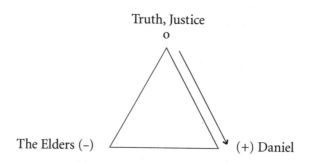

Truth, Justice
o

The Elders (–)   (+) Daniel

According to the first polarization pattern, the tale is a novella; it pits the faithful woman, suffering for a wrong not of her own doing, against her tormenters and accusers. The second pattern portrays a typical wisdom legend, in which the youth in his wisdom reveals the truth (as in the tales of the young Solomon). Analysis of the tale according to the polarization between its active forces (or the binary opposition) conforms precisely to our findings from the comparison between the two versions of the tale: Theodotion's version is a novella. It stresses and details the erotic and dramatic elements, while the judicial and legal aspect is secondary (though existent). The version in the *Septuagint* approximates the legal (or wisdom) tale in that it makes salient the actions of the criminals and almost ignores such juicy details as the elders peeping at the bathing Susannah as utterly irrelevant to the legal proceedings. Nonetheless, the *Septuagint* version emphasizes the divine provenance of Daniel's ruling, and hence, naturally, the obligation to behave accordingly in future as regards the questioning of witnesses. The claim that the Susannah story carries a clear message regarding the legal obligation (that was, for example, accepted by the Pharisees but opposed by the Sadducees) to question witnesses separately to ascertain their credibility, is one possible interpretation of the version in the *Septuagint*. This contrasts with the novelistic character of Theodotion's version, which stresses the personal aspect of the woman's return to her husband—in the manner of the novella. The two versions should be viewed as directed to different audiences: the *Septuagint* version, the judgement-wisdom version, is directed perhaps to a more learned audience, and was likely to serve as a *casus*, or legal precedent, that would obligate judges to investigate witnesses similarly. The novelistic versions targeted more of a folk audience, perhaps composed mainly of women, and their orientation was primarily romantic, their moral in the realm of maintaining one's modesty and the purity of the family.

A similar phenomenon of bifurcation comes to light in two other works mentioned earlier, *The Book of Ahikar* and the *Apocryphal Esdras* (the story of "Darius's Three Bodyguards"). Both *Ahikar* and the tale of "Darius's Three Bodyguards" are constructed as framework tales. The narrative frameworks absorb secondary units (tales, parables, sayings, riddles) that serve as means to resolve the conflict exposed in the framework tale. Thus, the *Book of Ahikar* recounts Nadan's betrayal of his uncle and adoptive father, Ahikar the Wise, chief administrator to the king. Ahikar hides from the king, who has sentenced him to execution, but when the monarch needs a wise man to compete in the contest of riddles with the king of Egypt, Ahikar comes out of hiding, leads Babylonia to victory over Egypt, and regains his lofty status. Into this simple narrative framework are woven many secondary units: two groups of proverbs voiced by Ahikar to his nephew to teach him morals, and a web of riddles and tasks put to him by the king of Egypt in the contest. The network of secondary units that is woven into the framework tale leads to the tale's resolution in favor of the protagonist. The tale of Zerubavel is constructed in the same way, although less apparently so. Here we have a contest of riddles of the superlative type (what is the greatest, the strongest of all) combined with interconnected speeches as secondary literary units, and a resolution of the plot of the framework tale that stems from the most correct solution of the riddle. Other versions of the tale may have substituted secondary anecdotes on the power of wine, or the king and his wife, for orations on the same. This is suggested by Zerubavel's speech, wherein he tells how Darius, the mighty king, submitted to his concubine, as proof of his argument that woman is "the strongest."[23]

The pattern described here leads naturally in two directions—towards the novella and the wisdom tale. The framework tale of the courtier's (Zerubavel, Ahikar) rise to greatness, is typical of the folk novella: it is realistic, and it determines the hero's fate as a function of his qualities—cunning and shrewdness. In the novella, the hero's fate unfolds via sharp turns of the plot (Zerubavel the servant becomes Exilarch, Ahikar the chief administrator becomes a fugitive under sentence of death, and is restored to his former glory). Yet the literary units woven into the framework as secondary texts characterize folk wisdom literature: sayings, parables, riddles, and other rhetorical patterns. We find both directions, that of novella and of the wisdom tale, both as independent tales and as various lines of development within a single tale. The union of didactic-wisdom orientations with the novelistic tale is a dominant trait of the Hebrew tale of the period. It almost certainly grew out of the desire to transmit didactic messages in an interesting and entertaining fashion, and thus turned the novelistic tale into a leading tool of moral edification.

[G] The Fairytale

One main category was missing among the folktales in the Bible: the magic fairytale. It might have existed during the biblical period without leaving its imprint on the biblical books, or perhaps its magic elements underwent changes and were muted in the transition from the folk medium to the canonical biblical text. The tale of David's rise, for example, could be considered a consummate fairytale, in view of its construction: the youngest son is the only one who dares stand up to the giant or monster who turns up periodically to harm the kingdom or demand sacrifices. The hero triumphs, earning the coveted hand of the princess. But the king is not satisfied, and charges him with additional tasks meant to end in his failure. In this way, the king hopes to get rid of him, to distance him from the kingdom. The protagonist accomplishes all the tasks set before him, and finally ascends to the throne. This tale is spread over several chapters in the book of Samuel, woven into a complex network of events of historical significance, and is highly developed from a literary standpoint. It is, furthermore, wholly realistic, ruling out any possibility of its being a magic (fairy) tale. Can it be that the tale of David, and perhaps other stories in the Bible, were told originally as magic fairytales? The structure of the David story reinforces this possibility, but until real evidence is found to support it (for example, variants from the ancient Near East), it is no more than a supposition.

We find the first real manifestation of the magic fairytale only in the Hebrew narrative of the Second Temple period—it is the work known as the *Book of Tobit*. The original definition of the magic fairytale is a tale that takes place out of time and in no specific location, is dense with magic motifs, and is not meant to be believed. The story of Tobit does not fit the definition; the apocryphal version indicates expressly both time and place (Nineveh and Media in the reign of Shalmaneser, king of Assyria, immediately after the exile of the Ten Tribes). But historical adaptation of anonymous independent tales is among the salient characteristics of the tales as they are set in writing. Its literary structure, the main motifs that build the plot, its variants in world literature, and the place set aside for it in the standard classification of international folk narrative establish the *Book of Tobit* as one of the first examples in world literature of a fairytale in its classic sense.[24]

Tobit the father hears that the corpse of a Jew lies abandoned in the marketplace. Heedless of warnings that he will be punished for his practice of burying the dead, he hastens to lay the body to rest. While he is sleeping in the courtyard of his home, bird droppings fall into his eyes, blinding him. Concurrently, and in storytelling's grand tradition of constructing a complex net of tensions, a new narrative direction is developed. This concerns Sarah, daughter of Reuel, in the city of Ecbatana. Her father married her off seven times, but each bridegroom was killed in turn by Ashmedai ("King of the Demons") on their wedding night, before the marriage was consummated. When a servant (or her mother) takes her to task for this, she shuts herself in her room and tries to take her own life (in two offshoots of the plot, the protagonists are here at the lowest point in the narrative development). Tobit the father sends his son Tobias to Media to claim a large sum of money owed him by relatives there. He is joined by the angel Raphael, sent by God in answer to the prayers of Tobit and Sarah. Tobias is nearly rent to pieces by a large fish in the Tigris River, and Raphael instructs him to catch it and preserve its heart, liver, and gall. They reach the home of Reuel, father of Sarah and brother of Tobit, in Ecbatana. Following the angel's advice, Tobias claims Sarah for his wife by law as next of kin. On their wedding night, he again follows Raphael's counsel, burning the fish's heart and liver on whispering coals in the room. The demon exits Sarah's body and flees to the land of the demons (Upper Egypt). Tobias, receiving from his uncle half of his property, returns to his father, spreads the fish's gall on his eyes, and restores his sight.

The general structure of the fairytale and the tale of Tobit have much in common. The initial, balanced state of affairs within the family framework gives way to a situation of loss: the father goes blind, the son leaves home and hearth in search of a cure for his father. A "dispatcher" (the angel) accompanies him, his advice and supernatural powers enabling the protagonist to overcome all obstacles in his path. He confronts a task of magic—struggle with a demonic force. If successful, he will win the hand of the princess and half the kingdom. He does this with the dispatcher's aid, obtains the remedy for his father's ailment, and cures him. The fairytale and the story of Tobit also share many narrative motifs. Scholars have already indicated the vast similarity between the tale type "the grateful dead" and the Tobit story, which they viewed as the first manifestation in world literature of the widely found narrative type (and motif). According to the international tale type, which is found in multiple versions in nearly all cultures, a man fulfills the precept of burying the dead. The dead man's creditors do not allow his burial until his debt is paid; the hero pays the dead man's debt and, now penniless, sets out wandering. A mysterious man accompanies him—it is the dead man, grateful to him—who helps him overcome all the obstacles in his path, teaches him how to chase away the serpent or the demon inhabiting the princess, and raises him to greatness. As in the tale of Tobias, the dead man reveals his identity to the protagonist at the tale's conclusion. The differences between the Tobias tale and the general tale type do not alter the basic picture: The *Book of Tobit* is the first manifestation of one of the most widely found tale types in international folk narrative.[25]

"The grateful dead" is neither the only nor the main magic motif in the *Book of Tobit*. The motif of possession, also among the more widespread folkloric motifs, appears here in expanded form, attesting to lengthy development prior to its appearance here. Indeed, this motif predates Second Temple literature, and is found as early as the *khons* tale of ancient Egyptian literature. In it, the princess is possessed by a demon and *khons*, messenger from god, exorcises it, making her well again. In the tale of Tobias, the sexual-erotic element of the motif comes to the fore in the jealousy of the demon (or of the dead spirit) of the young woman. This motif became known as a cornerstone of *dybbuk* tales.

The tale of Tobias itself offers no reason for the elder Tobit's blindness. From a narrative perspective, it is untenable that such a central event as this lacks a causal connection with the development of the plot as a whole. The father's sightlessness is the situation of loss that causes the protagonist to embark on his journey. In fairytales, this loss comes as a result of the initial clash or offense of the adversary against the hero or his family. Tobit's blinding should therefore be attributed to Ashmedai, whose confrontation with the hero follows in the course of the tale. Nor does the demonic injury to the father come without its own cause, and that is linked to the father's custom of burying abandoned corpses (against which activity he is duly warned). According to such an interpretation of the tale, the angel Raphael is sent by God not only to help the hero of the story, but also to fight against Satan, who harms God's faithful on earth.[26]

Another central motif in the tale is that of the "match made in heaven" or "the predestined bride." This motif is twice made explicit in the tale: first, when the angel Raphael is sent by God to Tobias, the narrator stresses that he, not one of the seven bridegrooms who died in her bed, was her predestined husband. Later (6:18), Raphael seeks to convince Tobias to claim Sarah for his own. He explains to him the law "in accord with Moses' teachings": he is her closest kinsman. The motif appears a second time when she is said to have been "destined for him since the six days of Creation." This notion, arising out of the tale itself, indeed necessitated by it, sheds new light on the development of the plot: the seven husbands died not because of Ashmedai's jealousy, but because Sarah's destiny was to wed Tobias. The father's blindness is part of the same development that leads the two to each other "from one corner of the world to the other," as their union is "predicted in Heaven." Thus, the tale contains the basic theme of another of the most widely distributed tale types in Jewish folklore, as we shall see below.

An analysis of the relationship between the motifs and tale types that make up the *Book of Tobit* indicates that its core tale type is that of "the predestined bride," not "the grateful dead." Additional motifs were intertwined in this fundamental pattern, including the possessing demon, the reward for fulfilling the precept of burying the dead, the hero who sets out to find a cure for his father's illness, and the death of the bridegrooms on their wedding night. All these were meshed into the historical framework of the life of the Jewish community in Assyrian exile. The description presented here illuminates the full complexity of the literary composition created by the author of the book from the raw folk materials at his disposal, as well as the themes, literary character, and orientations of the magic fairytale in this period.[27]

[H] The Contribution to the History of Hebrew Narrative

Folk literature of the Second Temple period contributed to the historical development of the Hebrew folktale both in the formulaic-generic sphere and thematically. Four classic genres of folk narrative make their debut in Hebrew literature in this period: the magic fairytale, the framework narrative, the martyrological legend, and the expanded biblical tale. The first two are known to have existed earlier still in the literature of the ancient Near East, and they are international genres in all respects. Not so the other two genres;

they originated in the Jewish world of belief and thought, and grew out of its particular circumstances and culture. The martyrological narrative and the expanded biblical tale were indeed later adopted by Christian and Islamic literature, but their Jewish derivation and character in this period are in no doubt.

In the realm of the magic fairytale, there was an interesting development that points at a more general direction: the anti-hero, the protagonist's adversary, is not a man with magic or merely supernatural powers, but Ashmedai himself—the primal adversary of God. Satan, head of the group of rebel angels whom God "cast out" of heaven, is the chief figure in the mythologies of the ancient Near East and, as we have seen, also in the mythological tales whose traces remain in the Bible. The transition from Satan's mythological image to his image as antagonist in the fairytale expresses very clearly the "decline" of the myth to the fairytale mode. What was in mythology a central theological element of the pagan and dualistic religions became, in the fairytale, a narrative-entertainment element. The transition from biblical myth (for example, the framework of the book of Job) to fairytale in the Second Temple period indicates an important development in the history of the folktale. Such a change in the images of gods who become heroes of fairytales is familiar from other cultural and periodic expanses. In the history of the Hebrew folktale, this process can be dated with relative precision—it took place during the transition from biblical literature to that of the Second Temple and can thus be regarded as one of the earliest manifestations of this development in the history of world literature.[28]

Three principal themes of the Hebrew folktale of the Second Temple period that were described separately above are tightly bound together: "the rise of the wise courtier," "the defiler of the sacred is punished," and the "miraculous rescue of the Jewish community." The story of the rise of the Jewish courtier at the ruler's court is found as early as Scripture, in the *Scroll of Esther*, and already there is connected to the theme of rescue of the Jewish community in distress. The main innovation of the theme in the Second Temple period was its construction as a cycle of hagiographical tales (Daniel), where each such narrative unit propels the hero one step further in his ascent to greatness. This narrative pattern is apparently what influenced the story cycles of the Jewish courtiers in the later folk narrative, such as those concerning Maimonides, R. Paltiel the Patriarch, and Rabbi Judah Loew of Prague.

The tales of Daniel and Zerubavel are typical courtier tales, and the deeds of the protagonists are revealed therein primarily via the actions they take to rescue the Jewish community or to prevent injury to what it holds sacred. The tale of Judith and the attempts of the foreign kings to enter the Temple or destroy the Jewish community underscore the same adversarial relationship with the Hellenistic world. The main themes in legends of the Second Temple period are the rise of a Jew in the Gentile ruler's court and his struggle with officials who hate the Jews; the Jewish community rescued by a miracle or via the foresight and courage of one of its representatives; injury by a foreign and violent force to Jewish holy sites. These themes can be defined by way of generalization as *tales of survival*. The Second Temple period is the first in Jewish history wherein the Jewish people faced the full intensity of the diaspora. The basic form of the period's tales and the primary message they seek to broadcast should be understood fundamentally in light of the diaspora experience, with which the people were learning to live for the first time. The solutions alluded to via the stories are: (1) irrational faith in sacred, divine might (tales of miraculous rescue); (2) confidence in the intellectual strength of Jews to overcome, via wisdom and foresight, the dangers with which they had to struggle in a hostile world (tales of wisdom and the rise of the Jewish courtier); (3) firm and uncompromising preservation of the Jewish faith even at the cost of life itself (the martyrological tale). Jewish folk narratives in the Second Temple period created and developed narrative themes and forms that constituted bridgeheads to the folk narrative of the periods to come, and thereby also established a most important psychological and social impetus for coping with the diaspora experience.

4 The Folktale in the Rabbinic Period

Between Folk Culture and Rabbinic Literature

[A] Introduction

We must take into account several fundamental difficulties regarding which compositions to include in the framework of a description of the folktale in the rabbinic period. Some texts are not at all problematic; the period of the Palestinian Talmud, Babylonian Talmud, and ancient aggadic and halakhic Midrash is clear enough, it being generally agreed that these works were compiled before the conquest of Palestine by the Arabs (632 C.E.)—the date seen as the end of the "rabbinic period." The other compositions were apparently written down and compiled later on, as late as the thirteenth and fourteenth centuries, among them *Yalkut Shimoni* and the Yemenite *Midrash ha-Gadol*, although most of the material contained in them appears to have originated in the rabbinic period. The task of identifying ancient lore in the later compositions is one of the most formidable and complicated in the study of rabbinic literature.[1]

No less difficult is the determination of just what constitutes folktales in the body of complex talmudic deliberations (*sugia*) or within the stylized framework of homiletic interpretation (*drasha*). Sages and preachers (*darshanim*) employed folktales for an array of purposes: to strengthen halakhic reasoning, to explain biblical verses, to reinforce ethical and political views, and to disseminate theological arguments. The many stories (and parables) pressed into such sacred service are not necessarily "popular" in the sense intended by our description: they were written to serve a clear purpose and reflect the storytelling manner of a single author. They did not exist independently of the specific context they were designed to serve, and they were not "received by the society" in the sense that they did not circulate among the people in different versions reflecting independent processes of creation. From this perspective, a large portion of the stories included in the Talmud and Midrash should be seen as "literature" and not "folktales," and as such, they go beyond the boundaries of our discussion. The distinction becomes still more complex as we note that many folktales underwent the sages' ideological and literary reworking, as is generally the case when folktales are revised by authors and poets. However, even if it is proven by means of interpretive literary analysis that the stories found in rabbinic literature are in fact "literature," there is no refuting the fact that they are a form of literary tradition which circulated orally in Jewish society over a period of a great many years.[2]

Cultural activity during the rabbinic period was concentrated in the *Beit ha-Midrash* and the synagogue. Elite intellectual activity, including the production of the principal compositions of the period—the Talmud and the Midrash—took place in the *Beit ha-Midrash*, a combined academy and legislature. The synagogue served as a spiritual center for the various strata of society, including women and children, and was by its very nature more "popular." The Babylonian Talmud has preserved evidence of this: "R. Ishmael b. Eleazar said: On account of two sins *'amme ha-arez* ["the simple, unlearned"] die: because they call the holy ark a chest, and because they call a synagogue *beth-'am*" (*Shabbat* 32a). That is, the synagogue was regarded, by the people if not by the sages, as more than a house of ritual; it filled a clear social function as well, as the "house of the people" (*beth-'am*); in addition to prayer and Torah reading, sermons were delivered there by community rabbis or itinerant preachers and, also in the framework of oral homily, translators rendered the Torah portion into Aramaic, the lingua franca of the time, almost verbatim, interspersed with exegesis, aggadic elaborations, and homiletic interpretation.[3]

Another sphere of social activity was the marketplace, or street, where the routine activities of daily life were carried out: trade, travel, work, and private and public events of various kinds. While we have no direct evidence of these kinds of social activity, they are alluded to in the discussions of the academy and in the sermons delivered to the public. The literary material of the rabbinic period seems to paint a clear picture of day-to-day life. Before reaching our eyes, however, this picture passed through the dual lens of how the sages viewed and understood daily life, and how they put their remarks in writing in a later period. Hence it can be assumed that the image of the folktale as reflected by this lens is sometimes true to life, and at other times completely distorted.

We should avoid the prevalent, if erroneous, view which regards the spiritual activity of the academy and the daily life of the marketplace as oppositional, attributing folk literature creations only to the latter. It has already been stated in the general introduction, and it bears restating now, that participants in the spiritual life of the academy were a social group just like any other. The stories, parables, and proverbs created there, retold and refashioned in various formulae and contexts, were folk creations. The argument that the story of Rabbi Akiva and Kalba Savua's daughter, or the story *"Kania de-Rava"* are "academy stories" does not in any way alter the fact that they are folktales. They are found in different versions, told in various contexts, determined by means of folk literature's "epic laws," and have been accepted by later generations as part of the folk tradition. Even if they were told only by the sages, and only in the academy, they would still belong to the category of folklore, for the sages were part and parcel of "the people" and the academy most surely one of the places where the spirit of the people lived.

In all three of the period's locales of social and spiritual activity, the marketplace, the synagogue, and the academy, folktales were devised, passed on, and developed both orally and in writing. This chapter describes the Rabbinic period's great treasure trove of traditional stories.[4]

The abundant material from the period has been generically classified, but this classification was not in any way imposed on the literary material. The division was made after analysis of the texts based on their structural and thematic traits and with an eye toward the functions they filled in Jewish society of the period. As such, it does not always coincide with the accepted genre categories in folkloristics. Neither myth, fairytale, nor novella, but rather expanded biblical story, biographical legend, or exemplum provide the focus for discussion. I let the stories themselves fall into groups and categories according to their characters and functions, although an analytical classification would have divided them differently. Any literary typology not based on the worldview of the culture that created these stories, which seeks instead to impose on them analytic-generic principles—correct as they may be—will fail to grasp the unique nature of the material in question. Therefore it seems to me that a synthesis of the aggadic literature's unique world view with the principles of genre classification developed in the study of world folklore is likely to be the most helpful approach to the description of the folktale of the period.[5]

[B] Performance Events

Almost all of this period's folk prose (as well as its other cultural and spiritual expressions) has come down to us in the literary sources born of the academy. It is possible to try and reconstruct the variety of performance events in which folktales were told before an audience of listeners during this period only on the basis of chance remarks, as surviving evidence of them in the aggadic literature is limited and incidental.[6]

Once when R. Manyumi b. Helkiah and R. Helkiah b. Tobiah and R. Huna b. Hiyya were sitting together they said: If anyone knows anything about Kefar Sekania of Egypt, let him say. *One of them thereupon said:* Once a betrothed couple [from there] were carried off by heathens who married them to one another. . . . *The next then began and said:* On one occasion forty bushels [of corn] were selling for a *denar* and the number went down one, and they investigated and found that a man. . . . *The third then began and said:* There was a man who wanted to divorce his wife, but hesitated because she had a big marriage settlement. . . . (BT *Gittin*, 57a)

This cycle of stories is an example of a type of "story chain" in which a subject is first introduced, and then those present each recite a tale in turn dealing with the subject. Where such performance events appeared in general medieval literature, it was in the format of a contest, complete with a victor, but these elements do not appear in this talmudic passage. The erotic subject which unified the three stories included in the above grouping will engage us later on. In any case, while the exposition of the occasion and the transition from one raconteur to another are provided by the text, no details regarding the site of the event are related—we do not know if it took place at the academy, at a meal, or at a festive occasion of some kind—nor is there any description of an audience or its response. An example of a similar performance event has survived in the Babylonian Talmud:

> Raba said to Rafram b. Papa: Tell [us] some of the good deeds which R. Huna had done. He replied: Of his childhood I do not recollect anything, but of his old age I do. On cloudy [stormy] days they used to drive him about in a golden carriage. . . . (BT *Ta'anit*, 20b)

Here Rafram bar Papa tells Raba some stories about the deeds of Rav Huna. It can be assumed that other people were present beside the two whose names are mentioned (Raba asks, "Tell [us]", on behalf of an audience of multiple listeners). The narrator claims to have personally witnessed the deeds. This is another typical performance event, in which someone who was associated in some way with a public figure of note—as a servant or student perhaps—is asked to tell a story about him. During the gap between the actual events and their retelling (usually after the hero's demise) the stories undergo a process of crystallization. As such, it is clear that they do not constitute a reliable account of the hero's life, but rather of the manner in which his image was fashioned by later generations. Rafram bar Papa emphasized in his stories of Rav Huna the latter's exceptional customs regarding the giving of charity. From this it can be presumed that the crystallization of legends of Rav Huna in this vein are more reflective of the ideological and ethical bent of the Jewish community in Babylonia at the time they were told than of the actual figure and deeds of Rav Huna himself.

Another kind of performance event within whose framework folkloric material is brought forth in rabbinic literature is the description by the sages of the folk informants from whom they drew their folkloristic material. A typical example is Abbaye's account of folk beliefs and cures: "Mother told me . . . " (*Shabbat* 66b–67a). It has been speculated that "Mother" was Abbaye's nursemaid, but for our purposes the actual connection between the sage and his informant matters little. What is important is that the sage has reported, almost certainly in the academy, things told to him by a prime example of folk culture—a woman expert in folk medicine and the folkloric traditions then current in Jewish society. In Roman culture, too, there is ample evidence of nursemaids and governesses of the lower classes from whom pundits and men of letters learned of folk customs and traditions. Such lore was ridiculed in Latin as "grandmother tales." These women were among the most important disseminators of folklore in ancient Rome, and were instrumental, as well, in the transmission of folkloric customs to the elite culture. The following passage from the Palestinian Talmud provides another example:

> Said R. Yannai: I was going along the road in Sepphoris, and I saw a min,
> who took a pebble and threw it up into the sky, and it came down and was
> turned into a calf... Said R. Hinena b. R. Hananiah: I was walking in the
> turf (?) of Sepphoris, and I saw a min take a skull and throw it up into the
> air, and when it came down, it had turned into a calf. (PT, *Sanhedrin* 7, 13, J.
> Neusner's translation, pp. 260–261)

In these passages, sages report to their academy colleagues their encounters with folk culture in the street or marketplace. This reportage is not for the purpose of mere entertainment, but rather to strengthen halakhic arguments with the aid of "true-life tales" witnessed by them or that they heard from the people (in the above example—clarifying the difference between sorcery and sleight of hand for the purpose of entertainment).

The following passage indicates other milieu of folk literature in the rabbinic period:

> R. Hiyya b. Abin said in the name of R. Joshua b. Korhah: An old man
> from the inhabitants of Jerusalem told me that in this valley Nebuzaradan
> the captain of the guard killed two hundred and eleven myriads... until
> their blood went and joined that of Zechariah ... He noticed the blood of
> Zechariah bubbling up warm.... (BT *Gittin*, 57b)

This passage may simply be a description of Rabbi Hiyya's pilgrimage to Jerusalem, escorted by one of the city's elders, who is an expert on the local traditions concerning the holy places. During the course of the tour, the elder-as-guide tells Jerusalem's legends, indicating the holy sites where they took place according to the local traditions. Here we have what was almost certainly a prime source of the dissemination of narrative traditions in the rabbinic period. It was commonplace even then for Jews of both Palestine and the Diaspora to tour the holy land, with an itinerary based on the holy places. An essential feature of such tours was the telling of stories about events that took place at the various sites. We know that this sort of folk literature was in vogue as early as the Second Temple period (as evidenced by the *Vitae Prophetaram*, discussed in the previous chapter, which included a tradition of the burial place of the prophet Zechariah), but the phenomenon reached its peak only during the Middle Ages, and we will discuss it further below.[7]

These examples clearly prove that the academy–marketplace dichotomy is artificial. Sages brought folk traditions into the academy after hearing them from folk healers and storytellers. This is so even if they did not explicitly report the source. Additional folk beliefs appear in that section of the Babylonian Talmud and in others as well (*Eruvin* 64b–65A; *Gittin* 68b; *Avodah Zarah* 27a–29a). On various occasions Rav Huna, Rabbi Yohanan, Rabbi Yannai, Rabbi Hiyya, Bar Abin and many others relate the practices of the people and the traditions described by them. It is reasonable to assume that the numerous rumors, folk cures, and magical practices were somewhat revised with their passage from the marketplace to the academy. Hence, for example, we find in these reports extensive use of biblical verses and homiletic techniques that were unlikely to have occupied such a central place in their source among the people.

The well-known story of Bar Kappara at the wedding of Rabbi Judah the Patriarch's son offers another glimpse at a performance event from the rabbinic period:

> R. Simeon son of Rabbi took a wife. Rabbi invited all the Rabbis, but omitted to invite Bar Kappara. The latter wrote upon the gate of Rabbi's house: "After your rejoicing you will die; what profit is there in your joy?" Rabbi went out and noticed it. "Who is it" he asked, "whom we have not invited and who has written these words?" They told him it was Bar Kappara. He said: "Tomorrow I shall make a dinner specially on his account." He made a dinner and invited him. The guests having arrived, they sat down to dine. When a dish arrived he related, as it stood there, three hundred fables about a fox, and so the dishes went cold and the guests did not taste anything. Rabbi asked his attendants: "Why do the dishes come away without being tasted?" They told him: "There is a certain old man present and when the dishes arrived he related three hundred fables about a fox, and so the dishes went cold." Rabbi went to him and said to him: "For what reason do you not let the guests dine?" He replied: "So you should not think that I came to dine, but that my action was due to the fact that you did not invite me together with my colleagues." (*Leviticus Rabbah* 28, 2)

It is difficult to believe that the narrative tradition preserved the event in such precise detail over the hundreds of years that passed between the actual event and its being set down in writing in the Midrash. Still, it seems reasonable to attribute credibility to the outline of the story, as we know of the friction between Judah the Patriarch and Bar Kappara from other sources as well. Bar Kappara is known from other sources to have been a folk storyteller, a rhymerjester, and witty satirist, and this is precisely how he comes across in this story. It bears telling in this context that, among the sages themselves, and certainly beyond their circle, folk storytellers were known to entertain the guests at festive events such as large weddings. Celebrations like these drew guests not only for the abundant food, but also for the tales of the jester or folk storyteller. These *fabulatores* were part of the culture of ancient Rome as well, where they were summoned before rulers at social events to entertain the guests. Jewish culture of the rabbinic period had this in common with the general culture.[8]

Another important kind of performance event is the well-known fable of "The Lion and the Egyptian Partridge," told by Rabbi Joshua Ben Hananiah in the Beit Rimmon Valley. The Roman Empire has decided to break its promise to rebuild the Temple. When the news reaches the Jewish crowd, gathered in the plain of Beit Rimmon,

> . . . they burst out weeping, and wanted to revolt against the [Roman] power. Thereupon they [the Sages] decided: Let a wise man go and pacify the congregation. Then let R. Joshua b. Hananiah go, as he is a master of Scripture. So he went and harangued them: A wild lion killed [an animal], and a bone stuck in his throat . . . Even so let us be satisfied that we entered into dealings with this people in peace and have emerged in peace. (*Genesis Rabbah* 54, 10)

Unlike the preceding examples, the political and historical ramifications of this story make it difficult to regard it as unbiased evidence, uninfluenced by external factors. In all the examples seen thus far it has not been the event that was important but its content—the story told, the message it carried. In this instance, however, it is the historical event itself, of which the folk fable is only one component, that is central to the story. As such, there is a high probability that it does not describe an actual performance event, what is known as "true performance," but a fictive one. That is, the circumstances described therein should not be construed as indicative of the actual manner in which folktales were told. Regardless of whether or not we question the historical accuracy of the account, as in Jotham's fable, discussed above in the chapter on the biblical period, it is clear that the preachers viewed the folk parable as a rhetorical means, whose use at tension-loaded events was likely to influence the outcome of those events. The parable of the fox and the fish, told by Rabbi Akiva to Pappus ben Judah when the latter urged him to forgo teaching Torah in public as decreed by the Roman Empire (*Berakhot* 61b), can be viewed in a similar manner. In this case, too, it is difficult to accept the story as an accurate reflection of an actual performance event, and for the same reasons. Nonetheless, it is clear from this example that the sages viewed the folktale as having an important role in the examination or solution of weighty problems. This indicates that the narrative uses of folktales went beyond mere entertainment, as in the case of Bar Kappara, or the "academic" function of the sages' reports in

the academy. Folktales had a place even in political events with historical ramifications such as public meetings, social organizations, and the like.[9]

Sermons were another outstanding means of folktale transmission. We have
evidence of one such occasion, which constituted a framework for the presentation of a cycle of well-known folktales:

> Raba expounded: What is meant by the verse, In the dark they dig through
> the house, which they had marked for themselves in the daytime: they know
> not the light? (Job 24:16), This teaches that they used to cast [envious] eyes
> at wealthy men, and enthrust balsamum into their keeping, which they
> placed in their storerooms. In the evening they would come and smell it out
> like dogs, as it is written, They return at evening: they make a noise like a
> dog, and go round about the city (Ps. 59:7). Then they would go, burrow in,
> and steal the money . . . R. Jose taught this in Sepphoris. That night [after his
> lecture] three hundred [houses] were broken into in Sepphoris. So they came
> and harassed him. Said they to him, "Thou hast shown a way to thieves!" He
> replied, "Could I have known that thieves would come?" (*Sanhedrin* 109a)

The sermon is cited in the framework of stories about the wickedness of the
Sodomites. It can be assumed that the one story about the people of Sodom
told as part of this sermon led to the telling of additional stories by the
preacher himself or by others among the audience afterwards. These stories
were collected by the editor and set down in the Talmud immediately after the
passage quoted. In any case, such a homiletic performance event took place
before a varied audience comprised of both the wealthy members of the Jewish
community, whose property was stolen afterwards, and the thieves, members
of the underworld, who made use of the story to rob the rich.[10]

Additional aggadic evidence has survived concerning the prohibition against
the interpreters (and preachers) "who raise their voices in sing-song style to
make the people hear" (*Ecclesiastes Rabbah* 7, 5), who turned the sermon into
something of an entertainment. The sages' opposition to this practice is clear
proof that the preachers and professional storytellers used homiletic interpretation and Aramaic translations of the Torah in dramatic presentations of folktales. An unambiguous instance of this comes down to us in the story of the
rivalry between Rabbi Judah the Patriarch and Yose of Maon. The latter
preached, in the synagogue of Maon, against the avarice and pride of the
Patriarch's dynasty. R. Judah was enraged upon hearing of it and Yose fled for
his life. Resh Lakish, in trying to assuage the Patriarch's anger, equated Yose
of Maon's function to that of "clowns in theaters and circuses [of heathens
who] amuse themselves with them" (*Genesis Rabbah* 80, 1; PT *Sanhedrin* 2, 6).
Whereas Yose committed this indiscretion while engaging in words of Torah,
it is clear that Resh Lakish drew a parallel between the preacher and the come-
dians or actors of the gentiles. Further proof is that Resh Lakish's words of

explanation were well received by Rabbi Judah, who calmed down after hearing them.

On this subject it is worth noting another type of public performance or street theater, in which various stories were dramatized. Regrettably, the only such phenomena described in the talmudic and midrashic literature, and hence the only surviving evidence of such, were anti-Semitic entertainments. There is the address of Rabbi Abbahu in Caesaria, concerning the anti-Jewish satires in which the actors mocked Jewish poverty. They would bring a camel into the theater, draped in robes as a sign of mourning. When the actor asked what the camel was mourning, a second actor would reply that the Jews, then in their Sabbatical year (i.e., *Shemittah*, a rest of the soil: every seventh year the Jews were obligated by religious law to leave their fields fallow), had eaten all the camel's thistles and he was left with nothing to eat. Or a bald actor would come on stage and, when asked why he had shaved his head, answered that no oil was to be had in the market, and he could not anoint his head. When questioned further, he explained that the Jews had bought up all the oil to anoint their flesh in honor of their Sabbath (*Lamentations Rabbah*, introduction 17; and another version: *Avodah Zarah* 11b). Jews must have attended such "dramatic" performances (as otherwise they could not have been described in such detail). Various types of street performances, including skits, storytelling, songs, and magic practices were undoubtedly one of the contact points between general folk culture and Jewish culture, and the main place where the sages of the academy encountered the various types of folk culture.[11]

In this chapter, only those performance events described directly in the rabbinic literature have been mentioned. Halakhic discussion in the academy, homilies delivered there and especially in the synagogue (the religious and social gathering place of members of the community), festive occasions, such as wedding feasts and public appearances in the street or marketplace, the transmission of the tradition from rabbi to student or from father to son, and political events with many participants, are typical examples of the performance events described in detail in the aggadic literature. At the same time most of the literary texts are cited there in literary contexts far removed from the actual, "real-life" performance events. It can be presumed on the strength of the direct evidence presented in this section that other folktales were told or presented at these performance events, although this is nowhere explicitly stated. The aim of the editors of the aggadic literature was not to reflect folk performance events as they actually happened. The stories served the halakhic, didactic, and exegetical purposes of rabbinic literature in general. Incidental mention of the events described here was, rather, unbiased evidence, with no clear intent to describe them. This evidence proves that in the rabbinic period, as in any other, folktales served the purposes of recreation and entertainment because the sages knew their power to influence and instruct. They used them as a rhetorical and didactic tool. The description that follows will prove that the role of the folktale in the rabbinic period was rich and extremely varied, and that it was considered important by both the tellers of the tales and those who set them down in writing.

[C] The Expanded Biblical Story

By far the greatest part of aggadic literature is comprised of expanded biblical stories. These expansions, based on the biblical text—word, verse, and story—comprise the vast majority of the material found in the rabbinic midrashic literature and in the deliberations of the Babylonian Talmud and the Palestinian Talmud. Most of this material has nothing to do with folk literature. It is essentially an exegetic and homiletic creation in the service of talmudic learning. Nonetheless, independent folktales were undoubtedly joined to biblical verses either to Judaize stories of foreign origin by means of the verses, or as an aid to understanding the meaning of the verses. Such texts do not belong to the genre of the expanded biblical story, even though they are referred to in a biblical context, as it were. Most of the stories of this type were not developed out of the biblical text or in relation to it. They were independently created, and were linked to verses or incidental events out of a variety of motives. To qualify as a folktale, the expanded biblical story should develop the biblical story itself, or delve into the biographies of biblical heroes. It should also evince the basic characteristics of folktales as stated above. Most of the expanded biblical stories found in the aggadah do not meet these conditions. Out of the countless legends which elaborate on the story of the binding of Isaac, for example, only a handful can be considered folktales. That is to say, these legends were received by society as part of its repertoire of tales, to be told and retold in different versions, orally and in writing.

Nevertheless, it is not surprising that the expanded biblical stories have become folktales. The centrality of Scripture in the day-to-day Jewish life of the period made cultural dependence on Scripture second nature. This dependence augmented the creative dimension, which was based on Scripture, and manifested itself in the activity of the two primary cultural centers of Jewish life of the period, the synagogue and the academy. As stated above, sermons and both halakhic and aggadic exegeses, all grounded in Scripture, were the products of these two centers. It is therefore no wonder that they influenced the third locale where people interacted—the marketplace, or daily life—and here some of them developed into folktales.

The expanded biblical story of the rabbinic period shares a generic and thematic basis with that of the preceding Second Temple period. But the phenomena described above in the context of the expanded biblical story of the Second Temple period are much more developed in the rabbinic period. This is due to differences in the social reality of the two periods, and the nature of the material itself. In the time of the Second Temple, the chief concern of those who studied Scripture was Temple ritual, a preoccupation crystallized in the independent creations of individual writers (who may have belonged to independent sects, breakaways from the established authority of the period). In contrast, the interpretation of Scripture in all its varied forms was the focus in every academy and synagogue in the rabbinic period. Hence the intensity and quantity of material and its development in the rabbinic age reached a plateau unequalled in the preceding period. Moreover, the expanded biblical story in the Second Temple period appears primarily as an entire book encompassing a given story: *The Book of Adam and Eve, The Book of Jubilees, Biblical Antiquities,* and *Testaments of the Twelve Patriarchs,* to name but a few. These compositions are not discourses on the interpretation of verses, but a retelling of books or encompassing events, written by authors and scholars whose connection to the world of the common folk was marginal. In the rabbinic period, however, contemplation of Scripture was widespread, if fragmented. On the Sabbath or holidays, the preacher would deal with only one verse or portion of the Torah, and develop it. The sages seized or expounded on a specific verse to strengthen a point of law, or an ethical or theological question. This isolation of verses and their independent elaboration through narrative or homiletic means led to the accumulation of an enormous quantity of material, as indeed evidenced by the Talmud and the Midrash. The more popular nature of Bible-based cultural invention in this period led to the fashioning of many more Bible-based stories along the lines of folk literature. During this timespan, many more biblical stories underwent a process of "folklorization," and after their first telling, in the format of a sermon or deliberations in the academy, they were absorbed as folk traditions and retold again and again by the people. The reverse process, that is, the absorption of foreign folktales by reorganizing them around biblical subjects or heroes, also took place, as we shall see below.[12]

Folk culture had little interest in the exegesis of verses or in Scripture's philological aspects. Only events of high drama, with the potential for fresh, independent narrative development could provide a point of departure for the re-creation of biblical stories as folktales. The stories of Cain and Abel, the Flood, the binding of Isaac, Joseph and his brothers, episodes from the life of Moses, and various tales from the lives of David and Solomon are satisfactory examples of such material. The basic condition required for inclusion in this genre is self-containment. The plot of the expanded biblical story does not rely on biblical verses, as the scholarly hue of scriptural interpretation has little in common with the world of the folktale. A typical example of a self-contained story is that of Cain and Abel in its manifold versions. Here an entire story is told of the first tiller of the soil and the first shepherd, who did not realize that they could not exist without each other.

About what did they quarrel? "Come," said they, "let us divide the world." One took the land and the other the moveables. The former said, "The land you stand on is mine," while the latter retorted, "What you are wearing is mine." One said: "Strip"; the other retorted: "Fly." Out of this quarrel, Cain rose up against his brother Abel etc. (*Genesis Rabbah* 22, 7)

Cain did not initially succeed in killing Abel, as he did not know where to direct his blows, "he wounded him through and through with a stone on his hands and legs . . . until he arrived to his neck" (*Tanhuma*, Gen. 9). Cain tries to flee, but the Almighty punishes him with eternal wandering (the *Tanhuma* version features another typical folk motif: "it is said a horn he [the Almighty] had fixed in his forehead").

This story obviously presupposes familiarity with the biblical story of Cain and Abel, and with the events which preceded and followed it. Nonetheless, it stands on its own as an independent tale with its own internal plot developments. Its point of departure provides complete narrative information with no need of the scriptural original to complete it. The story before us has numerous midrashic variations, and clearly exhibits the basic rules of the folktale: it begins with a balance between the two forces—Cain and Abel—active in the first part of the story; it sets up a conflict between them; and develops it until the opening balance is restored: God punishes Cain and casts him out of the land from which he dispatched his brother Abel. The story strictly maintains the law of "two to the scene": in the first part, the active characters are Cain and Abel, and in the second, Cain and the Almighty. The law of the three is similarly upheld: the number of functioning heroes is three, the story is built on three episodes (conflict between Cain and Abel, the murder, and the punishment). The story focuses on plot alone, while the descriptive elements—including the few biblical verses quoted within it—serve the story's development. Even the oral elements, such as the relatively compact dialogues, exclamations, and rhetorical questions, indicate that this story served in its various forms as a folktale. Two principal messages emerge from an analysis of the two binary oppositions fashioned in the story: one between the farmer and the shepherd, and the second between the sinner and God. In the former, the common understanding that man cannot exist apart from his society is manifested. There is a complementarity among individuals who serve different functions in a society, and a concomitant interdependence. The second system of polarization gives form for the first time to the relationship between the murderer and society (whose conscience is represented by God). He seeks to hide his deed, and later to escape its consequences, but "the mark of Cain" was upon him forever. As in every folktale, these messages are not explicit. The story itself (and this is surely one reason it became a folktale) brings to life the story of the first murder in a dramatic and fascinating form. The implications we have indicated here exist in the story *potentially*, they are not revealed as the moral in an ethical tale or epimythium in a fable. The story's appeal and power to influence are in its successfully intermeshed narrative content and plot tension, even though the tale's conclusion is known in advance owing to its scriptural origin.[13]

The biblical story of the Flood has always been a magnet for homiletic interpretation and various types of narrative expansion. The folktales woven around the biblical story did not focus on its cosmic and moral features, but on the fate of its principals: Noah, his family, and the animals who lived together for the period of the Flood. Most of the plentiful narrative material on this topic came into being after the rabbinic period. But the extant aggadic stories bear witness to the interest in the subject even then. One such story concerns Noah's drunkenness: Upon leaving the ark, he planted a vineyard. The Devil came and began helping him. He slaughtered a sheep, a lion, a pig, and a monkey beneath the vines, which he irrigated with the blood. When Noah drank the wine produced from those vines, he became "as innocent as that sheep," after "he drank aplenty," he became as mighty as the lion, "since he drank too much he became a filthy pig," and later he became a dancing, swearing ape (*Tanhuma* 58, 13). We shall see below that stories of the besotted were much beloved by audiences in the rabbinic period. Noah's story was typical of these, with two differences: first, Noah's is an expanded biblical story. It deals with a well-known story from the Bible, and there is a presumed knowledge of the events which preceded and especially those which followed (in which Ham discovered his father naked). It is also unique in that it is constructed primarily as an etiological story, that is, as explaining the origin of things, in this case, the reason wine leads to drunkenness and the four levels of degradation aforementioned. The confrontation between Noah and the Devil, the three-part construction of the story (Noah plants the vineyard, the sacrifice of four animals, and how the animals' characteristics emerge in the human world), similar in its construction to the animal parable, the minimal use of biblical verses as support for the story, and its focus on plot development all are patent evidence of the tale's folk nature. Additionally, there are the echoes of folk similes and proverbs within the story: "Wine is the Devil's work" (or, "wine is from the Devil"), "the drunkard cavorts like an ape," "the drunkard as a filthy pig." These notions and sayings, and possibly more no longer known to us, were linked to drinking, and they underlay the formation of the story. The biblical incident of Noah's inebriation, the tales about intoxication then prevalent, the attitude towards the drunkard during the rabbinic period, and the proverbs and similes on the subject, were among the prime factors behind the creation of this expanded biblical story—as a folktale.[14]

The story of Abraham and Nimrod is an example of another type of Bible-based tale. It seeks to fill in the details of the period of Abraham's life not accounted for in Scripture: before God commanded him to "Get thee out." Except for the figures of the main heroes, Abraham, Nimrod, Terah, and Haran, the tale has no basis in the Bible. Terah supported his household by the manufacture and sale of idols. Instead of selling them in the marketplace, his son Abraham persuades prospective buyers that the images are merely ephemeral, ordinary objects, devoid of any Divine force. One day, he smashes them all, and then offers the explanation that, after arguing amongst themselves, the idols destroyed each other. Terah hands him over to Nimrod, who, after a theological debate on the nature of divinity, casts him into the furnace. The Almighty himself descends to rescue Abraham. Afterwards, when his brother, Haran, takes credit for Abraham's deed, *he* is cast into the flames and consumed in Abraham's stead (*Seder Eliyahu Rabbah* 6, Ish Shalom edition, p. 27; *Genesis Rabbah* 38, 28, Theodore-Albeck edition, pp. 361–364).

Apart from the plot's independence, requiring no external knowledge for its understanding, the characteristics of the expanded biblical story as folktale are prominent here as well: minimal use of biblical verses; conformity to the epic laws of folk literature; use of oral narrative characteristics such as the numerous dialogues between Abraham and the shoppers in the marketplace and between Abraham, Nimrod, and Terah, the frequent use of folk idioms such as "why do you make sport of me?"; "should not your ears listen to what your mouth is saying?"; "you are just bandying words." (*Genesis Rabbah* 38, 13). Here, even more than in the previous examples, the story's link to general folk literature is obvious. First, there is the structural basis of the story, that of "the youngest and least promising of sons makes good" (the basis of the David and Goliath story, as well, as may be recalled). Abraham is sent to market to sell his father's wares. When he fails, he is brought before the ruler, where his greatness is revealed. This narrative structure is expanded and developed even further in the medieval composition known as "The Tale of Abraham and Nimrod" (*Ma'aseh Avraham ve Nimrod*), in which it is prophesied to Nimrod that the son born to Terah will usurp his throne. Apart from this structure, it is not difficult to identify additional narrative motifs and types within the narrative weave. The *reductio ad absurdum*: Abraham claims that the idols themselves smashed each other. When Terah argues that statues can do no such thing, Abraham retorts that, such being the case, they certainly could not be gods.

This narrative motif, in which a clever folk hero proves something to a master by means of an extreme example which shows up the latter's folly, is widespread in folk literature throughout the world. This is especially the case in the *novellae*, in which much weight is accorded to folk wisdom and cleverness. Another typical motif is the rescue from the flames. The hero who is cast into a furnace or lion's den and emerges unscathed is familiar to us from the literature of the Second Temple period, from the stories of Daniel and his companions. In Christianity, the motif became a widely used narrative and ideological foundation in the literature of martyrdom. The narrative genre of martyrology resonates in other parts of the story: the saint puts an end to the worship of false gods in his family. He is brought before the regime, and a public debate or investigation of his heresy ensues. He is sentenced to death but is unharmed by the fire or the lions. This is one of the most prevalent patterns in the stories of the tortured Christian saints.

Another traditional structure reflected in our story is that of "the unsuccessful repetition." This is the well-known tale type about the good girl who gives charity, helps animals in trouble and old ladies, and therefore merits rescue and great wealth. The wicked sister who wants the treasure for herself, but does not prove herself worthy, is harshly punished. This narrative structure, to which we will return in the chapter on folktales in the modern period, is clearly reflected in the conclusion of the tale currently under our consideration. Haran does not encourage his brother Abraham when the latter is in distress, but when Abraham is rescued from the furnace, Haran publicly displays his pride of association with him. When Haran is cast into the furnace, he is consumed by the flames and dies. Another well-known motif is that of the contest of (superlative) riddles. Nimrod demands that Abraham prostrate himself before the fire, but Abraham proposes to Nimrod that water, which douses the flames, is more worthy of adoration, and continues in this vein in turn to the clouds, which bring the water; the wind, which disperses the clouds; and to man, who "suffers the wind." We saw such a contest of superlatives earlier in the story of Zerubavel and Darius in the contest between the former and two of the king's bodyguards. The best known example in Jewish tradition is the Passover folk song *"Had Gadya"* ("One Little Goat"), which makes use of the same folk motif. The story of Abraham and Nimrod thus is built according to the fundamental laws of the expanded biblical story as a folktale: its ambivalent connection to the Bible, its narrative independence, the folktale characteristics which inform it, the identifying marks of the oral tale, and especially the intensive use it makes of traditional narrative motifs and tale types.[15]

Stories of the wars of Jacob and his sons comprise a narrative tradition known from the apocryphal literature and are included in the framework of stories of the war against the Canaanite tribes and neighboring peoples in *The Testaments of the Twelve Patriarchs*. We found no direct evidence of these stories in the aggadah, except for that of Joseph in Egypt. Some aggadic sources (*Tanhuma Vayiggash* 3, 5; *Genesis Rabbah* 93, 6) preserve for us the story of Joseph's revelation of his identity to his brothers. Judah, and following him, the rest of the brothers, threaten to lay waste to Egypt as they did earlier to Shechem. Signs of Judah's anger are revealed to Joseph: tears of blood drop from his right eye, his chest hair stiffens and protrudes through his armor, he chews up balls of bronze and spits them out as dust. When Joseph realizes the enormous danger, he identifies himself to his brothers. There is hardly any need here of a biblical context. Scripture contains no indication of this tale, which does not solve any difficulties of interpretation of the biblical account, and citation of biblical verses is almost nil. The story does make clear use of the folk beliefs and stories concerning mighty giants, whose strength is exaggerated and whose behavior is crude and arrogant. Such a figure was Hercules of Greek mythology, as was the Old Testament's Samson. Similar personality traits were attributed to Joab, son of Zeruya, and other heroes. The high and mighty dialogues between Judah and Joseph, fraught with curses, boasts, and grotesque acts, facilitate a vivid dramatization of the story through a reenactment of their voices, gestures, and tone of speech. And the unique intertwining of the humorous atmosphere, resulting from exaggeration and vulgar behavior, with the popular fear of threatening, monstrous creatures, enables us to view it as another expanded biblical story which became a folktale.[16]

This story, moreover, enables us to discern another feature of the Hebrew folktale of the period. In the period under discussion, after the destruction of the Temple and the Bar Kokhba Revolt (C.E. 132–135), the Jewish people no longer maintained an army, nor did it participate in any battles. Hence no tales of combat and conquering heroes can develop here. The heroes nearest this period in time, such as the Maccabees, the zealots, or Bar-Kokhba, are not regaled in story owing to their negative image (Bar Kokhba is always depicted as an antagonist by the sages, for example, in *Midrash Lamentations Rabbah* 2, 4; *Gittin*, 57a). It may be that tales of their valor existed in the *oral* tradition (as it is not clear if the sages' negative view of them was accepted by the broad strata of Jewish society), but if so they did not survive in the Talmud and Midrash. The innate need for battle stories, and perhaps the imitation of such stories then widespread in the Hellenistic and Persian literature, led to the creation of Jewish heroic tales which focused on biblical characters, not contemporary figures. This tendency of the heroic tale to revert to the biblical period becomes still more pronounced in the folktale of the Middle Ages.

One tale of heroism prevalent among the tales of the period is that of David and Yishbi. This is an outstanding example of the way in which the post-biblical expanded tale was connected to Scripture. The latter offers the following account:

> Moreover the Pelishtim had yet war again with Yisra'el; and David went down, and his servants with him, and fought against the Pelishtim: and David became weary. And Yishbi-benov, who was of the sons of the Rafa, the weight of whose spear was three hundred shekels; (this was the weight of its brass) he being girded with a new sword, thought to have slain David. But Avishay the son of Zeruya came to his help, and smote the Pelishtian, and killed him. (2 Sam. 21:15–17)

According to the aggadic story (*Sanhedrin* 95, 1; *Genesis Rabbah* 59, 11), David set out hunting, and the Devil, in the guise of a stag, drew him to the land of the Pelishtim. Yishbi, eager to avenge his brother Goliath, captured and bound him and put him into an oil press. A miracle took place wherein the earth sank below David so that he was not crushed beneath the weight of the press. As it was Friday, the day preceding the Sabbath, Avishay ben Zeruya was washing his hair, when he discovered drops of blood in the water. He understood this to be an omen that the king was in dire peril. After searching for David to no avail, Avishay mounted the king's mule, and his journey was miraculously shortened. Yishbi's mother, Orpa, tried to kill him, but he succeeded in killing her first. When Yishbi saw Avishay, he planted his spear in the earth and threw David into the air so as to impale him on his descent. Avishay pronounced the Divine Name, and David was suspended in mid-air. Avishay spoke the Name a second time, and David safely descended to the ground. Yishbi chased them, but when they told him of his mother's death, he was weakened, and they were able to dispatch him.

There is little here to connect this tale to the biblical account. On the contrary, this expanded tale changes the course of the story even in those particulars which Scripture made explicit. The Bible describes the confrontation between David and Yishbi as taking place in the course of a great battle between Israel and the Pelishtim. In the talmudic tale, the encounter takes place after David sets out on a hunting trip, and is isolated completely, to the point where his men do not even know his location. Hence the biblical story clearly cannot be the origin of the expanded tale. All the signs indicate that this was an independent tale whose connection to David's war with Yishbi in Scripture is not essential. The tale displays an abundance of elements from folk literature, as we saw in other stories: the epic laws of folk literature are clearly identifiable. The same is true of folk sayings such as "a captive cannot free himself," "the son of your son will sell wax and you won't mind," "two curs killed the lion." Particularly prominent is the extensive use of motifs prevalent in general folk literature: the Devil in the guise of a stag who leads the hero astray; the king who goes hunting, loses his way, and finds himself far from his retinue; the giant who does as he pleases with the hero of the story and torments him when he is bound; the motif of the "life token"—where various signs indicate that a close individual is in danger or has died in a distant place; the motif of the miraculously abridged journey; the use of the Divine Name for magic purposes; the suspension of a person or object in mid-air by magical means; the revelation of bad news mysteriously deprives an individual of his physical strength. There is no way of knowing whether the process of Judaization of a pagan myth took place by means of replacing the original heroes with biblical characters, or whether the storytellers wove the plot of the story around biblical characters while making use of widespread folk motifs. The pertinent fact as far as we are concerned is that the heroic folktale of the period is generally attributed to Scripture (and as such belongs to the genre of the expanded biblical tale), makes ample use of folk motifs, and satisfies the natural need of the Jews of the period for tales of valor by means of retreat into the biblical period.[17]

Further evidence of the connection between the expanded biblical tale and general folk literature lies in the well-known myths of Androgenous and Pandora's box. The former crops up in *Midrash Genesis Rabbah* (8, 10, Theodore-Albeck edition, p. 55, and variants cited there). It tells how the first human being was created male *and* female united in one creature: "When the Lord created Adam He created him double-faced, then He split him and made him of two backs, one back on this side and one back on the other side" (*Genesis Rabbah* 8, 1). The second appears as a parable of R. Shimon Bar Yohai, concerning the man who gave his wife all his belongings, but forbade her to open one particular barrel. Naturally, the wife opened it, and the scorpion within stung her. Eve did the same in the Garden of Eden, thereby bringing down upon all humanity the great disaster (*Avot de-Rabbi Nathan* version A, Shechter's edition, 51,1, p. 6; *Pirkei de-Rabbi Eliezer* ch. 13). The plot was not fully developed in either of these stories, which survived only as motifs of which the sages made exegetical or didactic use (on the verses "male and female he created them" and "Thou hast beset me behind and before"). In any case, they prove that folktales and myths prevalent among the peoples with whom the Jews had contact in the rabbinic period were known to them, and that, although they originated in pagan cultures, they were used as materials for the expansion of biblical stories and were thus made a part of Jewish culture.[18]

King Solomon is one of the most popular Jewish folk heroes. The Bible does not tell us why Solomon became so accepted a figure in traditional Jewish literature, more so than any other biblical hero with the exception of Elijah the Prophet. Perhaps the answer lies in the biographical detail supplied by Scripture, which ascribes to Solomon wisdom, wealth, and the love of women, all traits with great narrative potential. The sayings and stories in the Bible which emphasize his extraordinary wisdom and mastery over *shidot*, interpreted as demonic forces, can explain some of the glory which clung to him for generations after the biblical period. The beginning of these traditions surrounding Solomon, which developed over time into one of the central themes of Jewish folk literature, is the expanded biblical tale of the rabbinic period.[19]

The tale of Solomon and Ashmedai in the Babylonian Talmud (*Gittin* 68a-b, and variants) is significant to our discussion in several regards. First, it fully exemplifies all the principles enumerated thus far in connection with the expanded biblical story as folktale. Second, it is the start of the folk tradition concerning Solomon. Third, it is one of the longest, most encompassing, and complete stories found in the aggadic literature. This complex tale is built upon several episodes, at least some of which can stand on their own as independent stories:

(a) Solomon wants to build the Temple but is forbidden to use iron. He learns from the demons that Ashmedai knows the secret of splitting stones without using iron.

(b) Benaiah, Solomon's attendant, is sent to fetch Ashmedai, and uses cunning and the Divine Name to overpower him.

(c) On their way to Solomon's palace, Ashmedai performs a number of strange acts which perplex Benaiah.

(d) In the palace, Ashmedai asks riddles of Solomon, who solves them. Solomon then poses riddles to Ashmedai. Among them he asks Ashmedai to solve the problem of cutting stone for the Temple without using iron. Ashmedai reveals the secret of the *shamir*.

(e) At Benaiah's request, Ashmedai explains his peculiar actions of the journey.

(f) Ashmedai shrewdly overpowers Solomon (by means of stealing his ring), casts him away to a remote location, and takes his place. The Sanhedrin are eventually convinced that the pauper on their doorstep claiming to be Solomon is indeed the king, and once again the Divine Name is invoked to banish Ashmedai and restore Solomon's throne.

It is difficult to know what form the story took when it was told orally, as distinct from its written context in the Talmud. It can be conjectured that it was not always (if ever at all) told in its most complete form, owing to its unusual length, and that this complex form is the work of the literary compilation of an author or editor who joined several separate tales together. Thus the story of the journey to get the *shamir* can stand alone as an independent tale without the other parts of the story. So, too, the episode dealing with the peculiar actions of the supernatural creature as he is escorted by a human being who wonders at their meaning (Benaiah and Ashmedai), or the demon disguising himself in the clothes of a man bathing in the sea or bath house, and assuming his identity (Solomon and Ashmedai). These episodes are found in the repertoire of international folk literature as independent tales and in numerous versions, and they are not an essential condition for the existence of the basic story of the quest to attain the *shamir*. It seems the way in which this important story was woven can be reconstructed along general lines: the story of the quest for the *shamir* is apparently a Jewish application of the tale type of acquiring a therapeutic herb or wondrous flower (AT 467). The hero of this type is usually the youngest son of a king sent to perform the difficult task of bringing the healing herb to the aged king. In the talmudic story, the task is assigned to David's trusted attendant, Benaiah. After the crystallization of this basic narrative framework, many widespread narrative motifs and types were attached to it, which also lacked any previous connection to either the figure of Solomon or to the biblical stories. Thus the supernatural creature's human escort, Benaiah, became the hero of the previous narrative episode, and thus the man or king impersonated by the demon became King Solomon.

To the above should be added one more factor: the separate messages of each of the narrative components which comprise the story. Each of them "pulls" the story in another direction: the first component, about the mission to obtain the *shamir*, belongs to the fairytale or novella genre, in which the hero of the tale (in this case, Benaiah) triumphs over the monster and succeeds in bringing home the wondrous herb. The second grouping, concerning the astonishing deeds of the supernatural creature (Ashmedai, who behaved strangely on the journey to Solomon, accompanied by Benaiah), is of the tale type which characterizes the theodicy theme: the supernatural creature (a god or saint) commits peculiar acts which seem contrary to logic or ethics, but are ultimately revealed to be just and right. The third component, in which Solomon and Ashmedai switch places, is characterized by a different message: pride is laid low. This tale type generally deals with a hero whose pride causes his transformation into a pauper or leads to another punishment so that he who was high and mighty is brought to the lowest depths. This is precisely what befalls Solomon in our tale. These three distinct messages or ideological directions are not co-reconciled during the course of the story, rather they exist side by side. The sole unifying factor is the figure of King Solomon. This strengthens the hypothesis that these episodes were originally individual tales.[20]

Our investigation has proposed that the principal traits of the expanded biblical story as folk literature are as follows:

(a) A tenuous connection to the biblical account. The expanded biblical story does not require a scriptural context for its understanding, but stands alone as a self-contained, independent tale. Relatively few biblical verses are cited in the story. At the same time, some recognition of the main biblical events (as we might expect from the general Jewish public), is presumed.
(b) The tales are built and styled in accordance with the epic laws of folk narrative.
(c) Prominent use of oral literature's conventional rhetorical means.
(d) The stories make wide use of folk motifs from general folk literature, and are comprised of episodes which exist in the living traditions as independent tales.

[D] Narrative Traditions from the Second Temple Period

This section, like the previous one, looks at the dimension of continuity which is reflected in the folktale of the rabbinic period. Yet while the biblical story and its expansions are the greater part of rabbinic aggadah, tales from the

Second Temple period are barely represented. The sages' antagonism towards the literature of the Second Temple stemmed from religious, social, and nationalist reasons. The opposition to the works of this period was so sharp as to produce claims such as the following: "And these are they that have no share in the world to come . . . R. Akiva says: Also he that reads the external books (*sefarim ha-hitzonim*)" (Mishna, *Sanhedrin* 10, 1; Babylonian Talmud (BT) *Sanhedrin* 100b). In any case, it is precisely this prohibition which proves that the noncanonical texts were being read, as otherwise there would hardly be any need for such strong language in banning them. But our interest here is not in a description of the complex structure of relations between the apocryphal literature and that of the rabbis, but rather in an examination of the folk traditions from the Second Temple period that carried over into the period of the Talmud and Midrash. What was the nature of these literary materials in the rabbinic period? Did the folk traditions, which were passed down primarily through oral means and in an uninstitutionalized fashion, succeed in overcoming the prohibitions imposed on them by the sages and in passing on parts of Second Temple literature to the talmudic period? What message did they bear, and what function were they to serve in the new reality?[21]

The expanded biblical story is the literary type we most expect to find in the transition from one period to another, as it manifests the continuity of literary traditions anchored in the books of Scripture. Indeed, numerous were the biblical topics in common to the literature of the Second Temple and that of the sages. The subjects and interests of such compositions as the *Book of Jubilees*, which retells the chronicles of the Jewish people in the biblical period; the *Book of Adam and Eve; Joseph and Asenath*, the pseudoepigraphic work about biblical heroes; *The Testaments of the Twelve Patriarchs; The Biblical Antiquities*, which recounts the history of the wars fought by the Hebrews in their conquest of Canaan; and the various books of revelations are told and retold in the Talmud and Midrash. The question of whether the expansions of biblical stories came to the aggadic literature by way of the literature of the Second Temple, or whether they were created as independent homiletic interpretation of verses without reliance on apocryphal literature, is a difficult one yet to be fully investigated. In the realm of the folk traditions, in any case, these are examples of both processes; that is to say, of the creation of expanded biblical stories in both periods independently, and of the passage of such traditions from the Second Temple period to that of the sages.

The story of Joseph and Potiphar's wife is found in the literature of the Second Temple in the version known as "The Testament of Joseph" in *The Testaments of the Twelve Patriarchs*. This is an expanded tale which dramatically describes the means by which Potiphar's wife tried to seduce Joseph. The resemblance of this tale to Hellenistic erotic literature, especially the story known as the romance of Phaedra and Hippolytus, was discussed above in the chapter on the Second Temple period. The story appears in the aggadic literature in several versions (among them *Yoma* 35b; *Tanhuma va-Yeshev*, 8–9; *Genesis Rabbah*, portion 87). The Babylonian version, for example, describes in detail the means used by Potiphar's wife to seduce him: she offers him a large sum of money and fine clothes, she assures his rise to greatness, she threatens him with imprisonment and execution, she physically tries to overpower him, and so on. A comparison of this version of the story with that of "The Testament of Joseph" reveals a striking similarity of construction, that is, in the daily attempts and revised means to seduce Joseph. The details themselves bear no resemblance to the earlier version (in *The Testaments of the Twelve Patriarchs*, she strokes and caresses him as if he were her son, tries to give him a love potion, and so on, just as in the Greek Phaedra story, descriptions absent from the aggadic versions of the tale). The structural similarity of the two tales stems from the fact that they were both created to expand on the verse "And it came to pass, as she spoke to Yosef *day by day*, that he hearkened not to her, to lie by her, or to be with her" (Gen. 39:10). The narrative and erotic potential in this verse led to what seem to be mutually independent homiletic elaborations. The resemblance between them stems from their shared dependence on a single verse.[22]

Another borderline instance is the story of the binding of Isaac. The first expansions of the story are found as early as the apocryphal *Book of Jubilees*, in Josephus Flavius and other compositions dating from the Second Temple period. While there are some parallels between these traditions and the rabbinic period's aggadic expansions, it seems that here, too, the general similarity of motifs, or of various narrative units, stems from their being expansions of the same verses, and not necessarily from any influence or passage of folk traditions from the earlier period to the later one. One motif worthy of emphasis is that of Satan, who first appears as a main character in the story of the binding of Isaac in the *Book of Jubilees*. There Satan is portrayed as instigating the Almighty against Abraham, similarly to his role in the Book of Job, and thereby inducing God to test Abraham. In the aggadah, Satan plays a much more active role. He accompanies Abraham and Isaac on their journey to the place of binding, attempts to prevent them from passing the test, and even appears to Sarah and tries to harm her, among other things. In both the non-canonical literature and in the sages' aggadah, the Devil serves the function of antagonist, otherwise so lacking in the fashioning of the story of the binding as a folktale. The complex, yet silent tension underlying the biblical account of the binding, between Abraham and himself and between him and his God, cannot take the place of a true antagonist. This gap (from the perspective of folk literature) was filled by the storytellers with the figure of Satan. Satan certainly has a theological function in the story of the binding as well; it was not purely narrative motivation that brought him into the tale. As an indicator of the passage of traditions between the two periods, the Satan motif is ambiguous. It is possible that the story of the binding as a folktale, in which the Devil functions as the antagonist, passed from the folk tradition of the Second Temple period to the rabbinic period, where it was reinforced and developed along new lines. It is also conceivable that the storytellers and aggadists were entirely unfamiliar with this motif of the Second Temple traditions, yet the need for an antagonist, along the lines of Satan in the Book of Job, and various theological motivations, led them to weave him into the tale of the binding.[23]

A third instance reflects most clearly the passage of the narrative tradition between the two periods. Here we come to the story of Moses in Ethiopia. According to the narrative, Moses was sent by Pharaoh to lead an army against the Ethiopians, who had invaded Egypt. After a lengthy military campaign, Moses succeeded in outflanking the enemy, capturing their capital, and establishing a city of his own in its place; there he fell in love with and married the king's daughter. The event is told as an episode of love and betrayal. This tale first appears in the writings of the Hellenistic Jewish author Artapanus of the 2nd century B.C.E., in a syncretic version which attempted to graft Hellenistic-mythological beliefs onto Jewish cultural norms. The tale later appears in a long and important version in Josephus's *The Antiquities of the Jews*, shorn of its pagan foundations and in a revised historical war account. The story is condensed in the ancient Aramaic translation attributed to Jonathan ben Uziel in the following form:

> And Miriam and Aaron spoke about Moses indecent words about the affair of his Cushite wife that the Cushites had married him to her when he fled from Pharaoh and abandoned her. They married him to the Queen of Cush and he abandoned her. (*Targum Pseudo-Jonathan* to Num. 12, 1)

The concise version of the tale here may be a result of translation, which by nature must be short as the translator, who is confined to the verses read from the Torah, cannot fully flesh out all the details of a story. But it may also be that behind the laconic style lay a familiarity with the story among the audience, so that there was no need to reiterate all its details. One thing may be said for certain: the story of Moses in Ethiopia did not arise from original exegesis of the verse. Here there is no possibility of explaining the existence of the tale both in the literature of the Second Temple and in aggadah as a result of independent exegesis of verses. This is a literary tradition which passed, in writing or orally, from the literature of the Second Temple to the traditions of the rabbinic period. While it is true that only one bit of evidence has survived of the existence of the tale in the rabbinic period, the *Targum Jonathan*, it can be assumed that the tale was told often and not written down in the various Midrash on account of the sages' opposition to its "novelistic" content.[24]

The means by which narrative traditions passed from the one period to the next are hinted at in the story of the death of the prophet Isaiah:

[A Tannaitic source] recounted: Simon b. 'Azzai said, I found a roll of genealogical records [*megillat yuhasin*] in Jerusalem and therein was written . . .
"Manasseh slew Isaiah." Raba said: He brought him to trial and then slew
him. He said to him: Your teacher Moses said: 'for men shall not see me and
live' (Exod. 33:20), and you said: "I saw the Lord sitting on a throne, high
and lifted up" (Isa. 6:1) . . . I know, thought Isaiah, that whatever I may say
he will not accept, and should I reply at all, I would only cause him to be a
willful [homicide]. He thereupon pronounced [the Divine] name and was
swallowed up by a cedar. The cedar, however, was brought and sawn asunder.
When the saw reached his mouth, he died [and this was his penalty] for having said, "And I dwell in the midst of a people of unclean lips." (Isa. 6:5),
(*Yebamoth* 49b)

The story of Isaiah's execution by King Manasseh is recounted in the apocryphal literature in the book known as the *Martyrdom of Isaiah,* devoted to this
topic, alluded to in the New Testament (Heb. 11:38), and in the book *Vitae
Prophetarum,* in the short chapter dedicated to the prophet Isaiah. The dissemination of the story among the first Christians and in various Jewish traditions
as early as the start of the first century C.E. suggests that the tale was accepted
as a widely-known folk tradition in the Second Temple period.

The story is also found in various versions in the rabbinic aggadah. In addition to the Babylonian version already cited, it is recounted in the Palestinian
Talmud (*Sanhedrin* 10, 2), in the BT (*Sanhedrin* 103b), *Pesikta Rabbati* (ch. 4)
and in the Aramaic *Targum ha-Toseftah* (Vatican manuscript to Isa. 66:1). The
fundamental lines of the tale are similar in all rabbinic versions of the text;
variations exist in the details, such as the pretext for Isaiah's execution. In the
Babylonian version we looked at, Manasseh finds contradictions between
Isaiah's words and those of Moses, the foremost of the prophets, and so sentences him to death. In the Palestinian version, no pretext is directly offered,
but from the course of events it is clear that Manasseh persecutes Isaiah for
prophesying the destruction of Jerusalem. According to the version of *Targum
ha-Tosefta,* Isaiah prophesies on the seventeenth of *Tamuz,* when Manasseh introduced an idol into the Temple. The story in the *Targum* is told in connection
with Isaiah 66, the last chapter of the book. It is intimated in this final chapter
that, following this prophecy, the prophet was killed. The *Targum* identifies the
tree that swallowed the prophet as a carob, while in the talmudic versions it
was a cedar tree. In the Babylonian Talmud, Isaiah utters the ineffable name
and is swallowed by the cedar tree, a motif which does not figure in the other
renderings. In the Palestinian Talmud, after being swallowed by the tree, the
prophet's *tzitzit* (ritual fringes) remain unconcealed against the outer part of
the tree that swallowed his body, and thus his whereabouts are revealed to
his persecutors. In the Babylonian version, the narrator justifies Isaiah's fate by

referring to Isaiah's slandering of the Jewish people, as a result of which he died when the saw reached his mouth, an element absent from the other versions.[25]

These seemingly insignificant differences between the versions of the tale in fact provide proof that this story circulated as a folktale in the rabbinic period. A comparison of the sages' versions to that of the Second Temple period shows a clear transition from a written, literary format to folk versions whose basis was oral. The tale as told in the apocryphal literature is long and greatly detailed. It is replete with dialogues and long and winding speeches, and is constructed according to the literary conventions of the Hellenistic rhetoric of the age. The versions of the tale from the rabbinic period are brief and concise. This is due to the explanatory or interpretive framework to which they belong, one which does not allow for full narrative development, and to the brief, concentrated, and purposeful nature of folk legend. Instead of the long dialogues between the prophet and other characters in the story, between Manasseh and his wicked counsellors, the detailed descriptions of the prophet's agonies— where the onlookers delight in watching his torture—the sages recount the tale in a direct and purposeful discourse: "then Manasseh *came . . . wanted* to kill him . . . and he *fled* from him and *came* to a cedar, and the cedar *swallowed* him . . . they came and *told* him [to Manasseh] . . . he *said* to them . . . they *went* and *sawed* the cedar and his blood *flowed . . .* " (Palestinian Talmud [PT] *Sanhedrin* 10b). The tale is narrated by means of action-bound verbs which follow in rapid succession, making dialogical and descriptive elaboration unnecessary to the development of the narrative plot. This trait generally characterizes the style of the folktale, and indicates the oral nature of the medium of the story's transmission.

The primary thematic difference between the apocryphal version and that of the sages is the role of the Samaritan false prophet Belchira: he is the central antagonist in the apocryphal version, yet the sages make no mention of him. In the non-canonical tale, Belchira reveals the prophet's hiding place in a cave in the Judean desert, incites Manasseh against him, and he and his gang of false prophets surround the prophet while Manasseh's men subject him to the saw. In the apocryphal story, King Manasseh does not serve an especially negative narrative function. He complies with Belchira's wishes; it is the false prophet who is the antagonist. In the sages' versions of the tale, the primary antagonist is Manasseh, persecutor of the prophet, who falsely accuses him and then orders his execution.

Researchers of the apocryphon, the *Martyrdom of Isaiah*, emphasize that it reflects in one manner or another the lives and outlooks of the Jewish sects who fled to the Judean desert, primarily to escape the heavy hand of the period's Jewish establishment. The flight of Isaiah and his followers to the desert, their hiding in caves, and way of life apparently reflect the actions of these groups. Perhaps here lies the reason for the false prophet Belchira's portrayal as the anti-hero in the tale: he represents those perceived by the Judean desert people as the false priests who, with their lies, managed to incite the (Greek) regime against the sect. When this narrative tradition passed to the rabbinic period, this issue no longer engaged the people. The sects once scattered in the Judean desert no longer existed, and other pressing matters now occupied the nation. Belchira's replacement by Manasseh may be a manifestation of this shift. The enemy was no longer the false prophet, but the regime which persecuted the believers, decreed harsh edicts against them, and martyred them. And indeed, in all the martyr tales of the Talmud and Midrash, as we shall see below, the torturer or investigator is an emperor or king—the character representing the evil regime. So it is in the versions of the story of the mother and her seven sons in rabbinic literature, and in the stories of the Ten Martyrs— Rabbi Akiva, Rabbi Hananiah ben Teradyon, and others. The narrative tension was instigated within Jewish society, from the confrontation between sects and sub-sects, against the cruel and oppressive Roman regime. These transitions in the nature of folk traditions thus manifest the differences, in a historical and ideological context, between the two periods.[26]

The transformations of the tale of Isaiah's death raise another question: how in fact did the traditions pass from one period to the next? In this case, we have a clear indication: "[A Tannaitic source] recounted: Simon b. 'Azzai said, "I found a roll of genealogical records [*megillat yuhasin*] in Jerusalem and therein was written . . . ". The exact nature of that scroll is difficult to ascertain. The story of Isaiah's death itself is not directly passed from ben 'Azzai but from Raba, who interprets the *baraita*. That is, ben 'Azzai found in the scroll only that which he related directly, and the full story is from a later amoraic source. What is clear is that this tradition was transmitted to the rabbinic traditions *from* a written version, *by* oral means. That is, whereas ben 'Azzai found it in a scroll, he told it (as did Raba) in the academy. When the tale passed from the written to the oral tradition, it was shaped and recounted in the manner of a folktale: the style is short and concise, its focus on development of the plot alone, it exists in multiple versions and uses typical folk motifs that storytellers make much use of, such as the ineffable name, the tree which swallows human beings, hiding within a tree trunk, exposure to persecutors by means of a small identifying detail (*tzitzit*), and even the motif of "measure for measure"—the prophet remains unharmed until the saw reaches his mouth, the organ through which he sinned; since he spoke against the Jewish people, he died only when the saw reached his mouth.[27]

Similar questions present themselves to us in connection with another story of martyrdom—that of the mother and her seven sons. Both versions of the tale from the Second Temple period (II and IV Maccabees) have been described above. Its wide dissemination in the rabbinic literature and its status as one of the first martyrological tales known to the Judeo-Christian tradition gained it wide attention by scholars. They concentrated on the salient differences between versions of the tale in the non-canonical books and those before us in the rabbinic literature. The differences—the abundant rhetoric and detailed description of tortures in the apocryphal literature, and the absence of these foundations from the sages' versions—were attributed principally to ideological differences, to a change in the audience to whom the tales were addressed and, mostly, to differences in the realities of the two periods. According to this perception, the sages' versions were created in the atmosphere which produced the Christian martyrology as well. The striking similarity of martyrological motifs prevalent in the Christian stories of the period and the legend of the mother and her seven sons is a result of the mutual influence or of the reflection of the reality of the period, during which such events were all too common.

To the principal differences between the two groups of versions of the tale of the mother and her seven sons should be added one more consideration, previously overlooked, and that is the literary-aesthetic one. The versions in the apocryphal literature were written in accordance with the aesthetic perception that informed Hellenistic literature. Hence the numerous, polished dialogues in the finest Hellenistic rhetorical tradition, the central place occupied by the voice of the narrator, who lays out the principal lines of the plot, goes over the heads of his dramatis personae to address the readers, and turns their attention to the significance of the events about which he tells, the polished nature of the high and ornate style, and so on. The versions in the rabbinic literature, almost without exception, scarcely contain any descriptive passages at all. They focus on the plot alone, and not on the details, as was the convention in Greek and Roman literature. The figure of the narrator is almost unfelt in the tale, apart from intervention by means of quoting biblical verses. Nor do the seven sons offer polished speeches. Rather, they quote the pertinent verse. There seems to be no better example of the principal differences between the concept of Hellenistic literary artistry and the sages' story-craft than that of the tale of the mother and her seven sons. The difference in the literary—not merely ideological or historical—perception is the reason for the differences between the two groups of versions of the story.[28]

We have no direct evidence of the mode of transmission of this story to the rabbinic age. Did it happen when one of the sages read the Books of the Maccabees and retold the story to his colleagues, as in the story of Isaiah's death? Or was the story of the mother and her seven sons originally a folktale widely told among the Jewish community as far back as the period of the Hasmonean Revolt, and with the new age and its rebellions and travails, was it the object of renewed attention, as is and always was the nature of the folktale? Both possibilities exist and are valid, as is a combination of the two: the story may have passed from the literature of the Second Temple to the period of the sages via both means of transmission.

For a description of the folktale in the rabbinic period, it does not matter whether we take the literary or ethnological approach. The multitude of versions of the story of the mother and her sons in the aggadic literature, and the nature of the versions, prove beyond any doubt that this was an inalienable property of Jewish folk literature of the period. From the vantage point of folk literature, these versions can be divided into two groups: those which are a product of literary creation in writing, such as those found in *Midrash Lamentations Rabbah* and *Seder Eliyahu Rabbah*, and those versions nearer to the way the story was told at various, primarily oral, storytelling events (Babylonian Talmud: *Gittin, Lamentations Zuta*, and *Pesikta Rabbati*). In the versions of *Lamentations Rabbah* and *Seder Eliyahu*, there is a clear tendency to elaborate: there are longer and more complex dialogues between the emperor and the sons and their mother; citation of biblical verses by each of the seven sons, and even by the emperor himself; more detailed characterization of the mother and her seventh son; and even a precise description of the mother's fate. All these are laconically written, with the stylistic restraint characteristic of the sages' storytelling manner. An outstanding example of the artistic force of this emotional restraint is the conclusion of the tale in the version of *Midrash Lamentations Rabbah*: "After [a few] days the woman became demented and fell from a roof and died, to fulfill that which is said, 'She that has borne seven languisheth joyful mother of children' (Pss. 113:9), and the Holy Spirit cried out: for these things I weep" (*Lamentations Rabbah* 1, 50). The narrator does not describe the fate of the woman in emotive terms, but solely by means of neutral expressions of action: "became demented . . . and fell . . . and died . . . ," where each such expression carries within it poignant tragic force, hidden between the words, in the latent, connotative ties between them, to be played out only in the reader's consciousness.[29]

As opposed to these "literary" versions, most of the other rabbinic versions are found in a form closer to that of the story told aloud. One version, for instance, does not cover all the sons, but is satisfied with three or four. It is difficult to imagine that at oral performance events the audience had the patience to listen to such a monotonic repetition of the story of all seven of the sons, in addition to the biblical citations the narrator attributed to them. They must have made cuts, as they were accustomed to doing in other stories with a string of repetitive episodes. Also much reduced was the place of their monologues, whose content was theological, as it was not necessarily the religious significance that engaged the people, but rather the wondrous act of sacrifice itself, which lost none of its dramatic force if the sons were not presented as great theological dissidents. Nevertheless, there is no doubt that when the tale was told among the sages or the more educated on occasions such as the Ninth of Av (the day commemorating the destruction of the Temple), the artistry of the story stemmed not necessarily from the plot, which was certainly familiar enough, but from the virtuosity in citation of verse and the sharpness of theological controversy. The legacy of the folktale of the Second Temple period was turned in this case to events of the rabbinic period, and thus penetrated, in a more subtle and complex manner, to the level of the sages, and, in a more popular fashion, to the broad strata of the people. Either way, as regards the story of the mother and her seven sons, it is difficult not to see the connection between the two periods.

The sanctity of the Septuagint as legitimate for ritual use among Egyptian Jewry was based on the legend crystallized in the apocryphal *Letter of Aristeas*. But while it is no surprise to find the story among the Jews of Alexandria, where the Septuagint's sanctity was upheld, it is rather astonishing to find this legendary tradition in the rabbinic writings. While the legal controversies concerning the permission for use (or ban thereof) of the Greek translations of holy writings for synagogue services are well-known, the use of this legend in the very different contexts and atmospheres of the academies of Palestine and Babylonia is of particular interest. The legend in the rabbinic tradition is characteristic of the way in which other Second Temple period traditions were handled. One of many versions of this story that survived among the sages follows:

> R. Judah said: When our teachers permitted (the use of) Greek, they permitted it only for a scroll of the Torah. This was on account of the incident related in connection with King Ptolemy, as it has been taught, "It is related of King Ptolemy that he brought together seventy-two elders and placed them in seventy-two [separate] rooms, without telling them why he had brought them together, and he went into each one of them and said to him, 'translate for me the Torah of Moses your master.' God then prompted each one of them and they all conceived the same idea and wrote for him: God created in the beginning, I shall make man in image and likeness, and he finished on the sixth day, and rested on the seventh day, male and female he created him but they did not write 'created them' . . . They also wrote for him 'the beast with small legs' and they did not write 'the hare' because the name of Ptolemy's wife was Hare ['Arnevet], lest he should say, the Jews have jibed at me and put the name of my wife in the Torah." (*Megilla* 9a–b)

The formal, stylized character of the text reflects the manner in which the legend was orally told. It may be that this was the result of the story's abridgement by one of the sages who read the *Letter of Aristeas* and used it to strengthen the position of those who argued in favor of allowing the use of the Greek translation for ritual. It may also be that the folk tradition itself, as it was told among Egyptian Jewry, reached as far as Palestine and, as is often the case with folk narratives, was told there anew and in accordance with its unique context and atmosphere. In the talmudic version, the story revolves primarily around examples of how enigmatic biblical verses were translated. These verses were at the core of the various religious debates between the sages and learned Hellenists or Christians. The shifting of the narrative core from the plot to exegetical and theological problems connected with interpretation of biblical verses proves that the version of the story before us was not that told to the general population. The folk versions certainly emphasized the *development* of the narrative plot, the means of translation, Ptolemy's making certain there would be no contact between the translating rabbis, the comparison of versions, the king's wonder at the miracle that took place among the translators, and his admission of the greatness of the God of Israel (as indeed evidenced by the story preserved in the *Letter of Aristeas* itself). The Babylonian version can also be regarded as a folk version in that it almost certainly circulated in various versions among the sages and served as an example (*exemplum*) on various occasions: on the question of using the Greek language in ritual, or in controversies over the interpretation of verses laden with theological difficulties.

A closer look at the versions of the story of the Septuagint in the literature of the Second Temple, as opposed to the aggadic literature, shows the principal difference between them to be in the perception of the nature of the miracle. In the apocryphal book, the miracle is perceived as the astonishingly precise and exemplary translation. The king and his counsellors extol the beauty of the translation and its marvelous fidelity to the Hebrew original. In the talmudic story, the wondrous thing is, conversely, the *changes* made to the original text in the process of translation, and the identical interpretation given theologically problematic biblical verses by the rabbis. That is to say, the hand of Providence is visible in the apocryphal account in the preciseness and beauty of the *translation*, whereas the miracle as revealed in the talmudic story is the correct *interpretation* of the biblical text. Hence the ideological variations between the two versions of the story stem from their different functions and purposes: among Egyptian Jewry, the function of the story was to give the Septuagint legitimacy as a composition whose sanctity was no less than the Hebrew version. And yet the apologetic tendency is not absent from this story in its Greek version: the nations of the world, their wise men (Demetrius of Phaleron), and their kings (Ptolemy) stand in awe of the greatness of the Law and its Greek equivalent. The function of the story among the sages was to sanctify their interpretation of biblical verses, that is, to present the "Oral Law" that developed in the academies as a product of Divine Providence itself. Such a perception reinforced the status of the sages as the sole legitimate interpreters of the word of God.[30]

We have already seen in the previous chapter that the cycle of stories concerning Daniel stands out among the hagiographic stories of the Second

Temple period. The first part of the cycle is found in the Bible and is accepted by the sages as belonging to the biblical period. As such, it belongs to the genre of the expanded biblical tale. Only one story from the Daniel cycle became a folk tradition in the rabbinic period, as evidenced by aggadic literature. Interestingly enough, it is not the *Book of Susannah*, the most famous story of the cycle, but rather the story of Daniel, Bel, and the dragon (or the crocodile). Aggadah did not preserve the story in its complete form, but merely alluded to it: "'And behold the Angels of God' (Gen. 28:12)—alludes to Daniel, 'ascending and desending on it'—he went up and brought forth what it had swallowed from its mouth. Thus it is written, 'And I will punish Bel in Babylon, and I will bring forth out of his mouth that which he hath swallowed up' (Jer. 51:44), (*Genesis Rabbah* 68, 12). In the full story, Darius took great pride in the giant statue of Bel as it devoured enormous quantities of food every day. Daniel exposed the ruse of the priests of Bel, who would sneak into the temple of the statue, steal the food, and feast with their families.

In several versions of *Midrash Genesis Rabbah*, there follows an added detail concerning a dragon (crocodile) belonging to Nebuchadnezzar which devoured everything thrown to it. Daniel proved that the crocodile was not a god by means of a trick. He inserted nails into piles of straw, wrapped them in animal skins and threw them one after the other to the crocodile, which swelled up until the nails tore at his insides. In these versions, the story of Daniel and the crocodile is mistakenly identified with the tale of Daniel and Bel. Since this variation is found in a minority of the versions, and in the later of them, it should perhaps be seen as the addition of a later copier who knew the tale of Daniel and the crocodile and slipped it in here because he thought it was the story of Daniel and Bel alluded to in the aggadic version.[31]

In any case, the trick by which Daniel killed the crocodile was a familiar device in the rabbinic period. It was not exclusive to the character of Daniel, and in fact became a commonplace narrative folk motif. The two versions below indicate the manner in which the tale was told in the rabbinic period, and how it was set down in writing in the sources of the period:

> And the snake of King Shevur devoured camels, it devoured wagons. [He] wanted to kill it. They stuffed camels with straw and gave them to it. And it swallowed them and died. (PT *Nedarim* 3, 2; PT *Shevuoth* 3, 1)

It is hard to imagine a more concise, terse style to transcribe a story known from the oral tradition. The author recognized a folk tradition with a mythological character, concerning the battle between the king-hero and the desert monster. He does not relate the tradition in its entirety, perhaps because it was so widely known, or simply because it is characteristic of the Palestinian Talmud to shorten and condense narrative traditions which appear in their broader form elsewhere. In contrast, the *Tanhuma* version preserves the features of the complete tale, closely following the folk version: it sketches the geographical location; obeys the epic laws of three (the three caravans), repetition, "two to the scene," develops the concentrated dialogue which appears at the story's denouement; emphasizes the plot, and includes descriptive elements (the desert and the serpent, for example) which serve the narrative plot:

> R. Jose bar Hanina said: There were in [the desert] snakes as thick as the pillar of the house and scorpions as the full span. A story is told of King Shevur, who travelled through here. His wagon [or caravan] passed there and was swallowed by a snake. The second passed and was swallowed. The third was swallowed. King Shevur was dismayed and did not know what to do. His sages said to him: Bring ten heroes and let them fill ten sacks [or skins] of straw. He brought them and so they did. And they gave [them] to it and it swallowed them until its stomach exploded and they killed it. Thus "who let thee through the great and dreadful wilderness, wherein were serpents, fiery serpents, and scorpions, and thirsty ground where was no water" (Deut. 8:15). (*Midrash Tanhuma, Beshalach* 18, Buber edition 32a–b)

It is reasonable to assume that the storytellers of the rabbinic period were not aware of the connection between this tale and that of Daniel, as, had they known, they would have certainly wasted no time in attributing it to him. It may be that the stories of slaying the monster in the tale of King Shahpur and the tale of Daniel are not connected, but simply made use of a common motif which originated in general folk literature. The fact that all the talmudic variations of the story revolve around Shahpur I, the foreign king (who reigned in Persia in the years 240–270 C.E.) strengthens this hypothesis. Tales of the marvelous travels and deeds of the hero-king made their way to Palestine from Persian folk traditions. There they were woven into the rabbinic literature from stories widely told among Jews in various places (Babylonia and Persia, for example). Tales of extraordinary journeys to far-away lands, desert monsters, and the folk heroes' victory over them were also popular in the rabbinic age. The cycle of stories about Alexander the Great, for example, is of a similar type.[32]

Another example of borrowing from the wealth of eastern folktales and motifs is provided by two important, comprehensive story cycles in the aggadic literature. The first is known as the "Wisdom of the Jerusalemites" (*Midrash Lamentations Rabbah*, portion 1, 4); the second is the story of the contest between Rabbi Joshua ben Hananiah and the elders of Athens (*Bekhorot* 8b). I do not wish to enter here into the details of these two important story cycles, as we will examine them at a later stage. The first is a collection of tales around the leading words in the verse which opens the Book of Lamentations. The second cycle is constructed in the framework of the story chain. In it the emperor commands Rabbi Joshua ben Hananiah to bring him the sixty elders of Athens, a task involving a contest of wits replete with perilous tasks. In the first story in *Midrash Lamentations*, the son who wishes to win his father's inheritance must carry out three acts of *wisdom*. He cannot find the house where his late father lived, as the townspeople had resolved not to show the place to any stranger from out of town. Similarly, in the story cycle in Tractate *Berakhot*, the Athenians are afraid to show Rabbi Joshua ben Hananiah where the elders of Athens live. Rabbi Joshua utilizes the same device as the son in *Midrash Lamentations*: the hero hires a porter to carry a load of kindling to the required address, and follows him there. In the contest between Rabbi Joshua and the elders of Athens, as told in the Babylonian Talmud, it is determined that the victor will be permitted to do as he pleases with the vanquished. In *Lamentations Rabbah* a contest of riddles is arranged between an Athenian who came to Jerusalem and the students of Rabbi Johanan, and the winner "will take everything." In the Babylonian Talmud, two eggs are brought to Rabbi Joshua and he is asked which came from a white chicken and which from a black. In response he brings cheeses and asks which came from a white goat and which from a black. The confrontation in *Lamentations Rabbah*, between the Jerusalem child and the Athenian, is waged in precisely the same manner. The Athenian brings a broken mortar to a Jerusalem tailor and commands him to sew it together. The tailor produces a pinch of dust and asks the Athenian to weave of it the thread with which he will mend the stone. Similarly, the elders of Athens enjoin Rabbi Joshua to mend broken grindstones; in response he instructs them to weave threads of the sand in his hand. Both cycles answer an absurd proposal with an opposing, equally ludicrous demand—it is thus characteristic of both cycles that an absurd question is matched by another of the same type. The connection between the two cycles seems satisfactorily proven.[33]

The unique problems of *The Book of Ahikar* and its connection to the world of Jewish folk literature were discussed above in chapter 3. Its structure is as that of a typical framework tale which combines disparate literary forms (particularly riddles and proverbs). This clearly connects *The Book of Ahikar* to the story cycle of Rabbi Joshua ben Hananiah and the elders of Athens. Ahikar is commanded by the king to go to Egypt, there to match wits with Pharaoh and his magicians. The victor will be rewarded with royal revenues for several years. The personal fate of Ahikar depends on his victory over the Pharaoh, just as Rabbi Joshua's fate hangs in the balance in the talmudic story. But *The Book of Ahikar*'s similarity to the two story cycles goes deeper than its overall framework structure and its nature as a typical quest narrative. It also exhibits the same shared motifs as the two aggadic story cycles. The demand to distinguish between the eggs laid by white and black chickens, the task of sewing together broken grindstones, the device of answering a question with an opposing question which points up the absurdity of the first, all these appear in each of the three texts. *Ahikar* shares another motif with the talmudic cycle: that of building a castle in the air. Ahikar orders eagles to be brought to him and ties to them a basket containing masons. He then commands Pharaoh's slaves to bring building materials to his masons so that they can start building the palace. They confess that they cannot do this, and are thus defeated. So it is in the BT story:

> "Build a house in the the sky." He [R. Joshua b. Hananiah] pronounced the Name and hung between heaven and earth. He then said to them: "Bring me up bricks and clay from down there." They asked: "And is it possible to do this?" He replied: "And is it possible to build a house between heaven and earth?"

The narrative traditions of *The Book of Ahikar* clearly left traces in the aggadic literature. These traces survived in the general literary perception of the quest, in which a king charges the hero to carry out a task which is fundamentally a contest against superior forces. No less significant is the similarity of narrative motifs found in the earlier composition and in at least two places in the aggadic literature. The obvious similarity of the different traditions again raises the question mentioned above: We know that *The Book of Ahikar* was widely circulated among the Jews in Aramaic, perhaps in Hebrew as well, as early as the fifth century B.C.E. Some versions of the composition may have still been around during the period of the sages, who availed themselves of its motifs and traditional narrative structures. Another possibility is that various narrative portions of *The Book of Ahikar* became widespread folk traditions in the east. Jewish storytellers borrowed from this treasury of eastern folk traditions, and their tales were documented (with some emendations) in the two story cycles under discussion. Either way, it is clear to us now that the narrative traditions of the Second Temple period passed to the storytellers of the rabbinic period and were there rewoven into the period's literary contexts.[34]

The last example of the existence of Second Temple period narrative traditions in the rabbinic period is of suspect chronology. This is the version of the tale of Tobit found in *Midrash Tanhumah* (portion *Ha'azinu*, 8). The tale does not appear in the manuscripts examined and published by Solomon Buber in his edition of the *Tanhuma*, but only in the editions of the printed *Tanhuma*. It is suspect in my view as a tale which found its way into the *Tanhuma* only in the Middle Ages, and thus does not belong to the period under review. Certain elements of the story lead to the same conclusion: the Hebrew is full of errors, indicating that the folktale was told in a period when Hebrew was no longer the vernacular; and the weaving of another tale into the fabric of the Tobit story, as we shall see below. This is the tale of Rabbi Reuven's bride and the angel of death, known in the Hebrew literature only since the Middle Ages. In spite of these reservations, the tale in the *Tanhuma* can also be seen as one offshoot of ancient narrative traditions, at the end of the rabbinic period or the start of the Jewish Middle Ages.[35]

The Lord Blessed Be He protects his believers as a man protects his eyeball. And it is told of a man, very rich and respected [*mekubal*—a mystic?]. He had one daughter, beautiful and righteous, and she married three times to three men, and after each wedding night, in the morning, they found her husband dead. (*Tanhuma, Ha'azinu* 8)

Here too, as in the apocryphal *Tobit*, the young woman resolves not to remarry, and remains "widowed and deserted." Her rich father has a poor brother in another country with ten children. When they reach the point where they no longer have bread to feed their children, the eldest son decides to go to his uncle's home. There he demands the hand of the daughter, in spite of the uncle's refusal out of concern for his nephew. He even offers the young man a portion of his wealth if that will satisfy him. Before the wedding feast,

An old man came to him, and he was Elijah blessed be his memory, and said to him in private: My son, I will give you advice, and do not move from it. When you sit down to eat, a poor man will come to you, wearing black and torn clothes, his hair like nails, and no man in the whole world poorer than he . . .

Elijah advises him to accord special honor to this individual. After the feast, the pauper informs him that he is the angel sent by God to take his soul. The young man goes to take leave of his wife, but she confronts the angel of death in his stead and triumphs over him with the halakhic argument that "When a man has taken a new wife . . . he shall be free at home one year, and shall cheer his wife whom he has taken" (Deut. 24:5). The Almighty scolds the angel of death and sends him away. As in the *Book of Tobit*, the young woman's mother and father awake in the dead of night to dig a grave for their son-in-law, only to overhear the newlyweds laughing and joyous.

This is a typical narrative conglomerate, that is to say, a story whose plot is comprised of several narrative types. This is an interesting combination of two tales: the story of Tobit, as stated, and that of the bride of Rabbi Reuven. This is a well-known folktale that goes by the name of Alcestis in world literature, after the heroine of Euripides's play. This part of the story in *Midrash Tanhuma* clearly belongs to the Jewish branch (the oicotype) of the international narrative type, wherein a righteous man has no children (or they die in childhood). When he asks God's grace, he is given a choice between remaining childless and being given a son who will die on his wedding night. He chooses the latter, and when the wedding approaches, Elijah reveals himself to the father and warns him against the awful pauper (who is in fact the angel of death); the rest is exactly as in the *Tanhuma* version. The "seam" joining the two separate plots is visible mostly in the disparity between the young woman's behavior on the three prior occasions when her bridegrooms were taken, and her conduct now.

Why didn't she use the same argument of "he shall be free at home one year" before? Apart from this, the combination of the two narrative plots seems well crafted, and the narrator succeeded in creating a complete, homogeneous tale. It is not difficult to zero in on the primary motivation for the change made in the text. The storyteller took from the tale of Tobit its central motif, that of "the grateful dead"; the angel who accompanies Tobias shows him how to exorcise the demon residing in the body of his bride, Sarah, and cures his father's blindness. This narrative type, and all that goes with it, is unquestionably magical and demonological. By means of weaving the narrative plot of "the bride of R. Reuven" into the story of Tobias, it uses Jewish narrative elements to resolve the narrative conflict in the *Book of Tobit*: the angel of death, God's emissary, not a demon or devil, is the antagonist; Elijah the Prophet functions as the donor or magical helper; and especially, the denouement with the young woman's argument grounded in the Torah. These refinements moderate the demonological character of the *Book of Tobit* and, after smoothing out the rough edges of the Tobias story, create a Jewish folktale par excellence.[36]

This description of the traces of Second Temple period traditions in rabbinic literature leads to several principal conclusions:

a) Few traces of Second Temple period narrative traditions survived in rabbinic literature. Since it is the nature of folk traditions to receive little and sporadic documentation, it is possible that many more narrative traditions were told in the rabbinic age but not preserved in its literature.[37]

b) The vestiges of Second Temple literature, including folk traditions, in the Talmud and Midrash, support our knowledge of the sages' disregard for Second Temple literature. Even well-known compositions such as the *Book of Susannah*, the various Daniel tales, the *Book of Judith* and the historical tales of salvation in the *Books of the Maccabees* did not become folk traditions in the rabbinic period.

c) The folk traditions that passed into the rabbinic period can be divided into two categories: First there are those tales of the Second Temple period which were granted significance and a role once absorbed in the new period (the death of Isaiah, the mother and her seven sons, the story of the *Septuagint*). The second branch is composed of the motifs from general folklore that permeated the fabric of aggadic tales without direct reliance on the preceding traditions from the Second Temple period. This is characteristic of the dissemination of folktales in general, and is not unique to the literary period under discussion here.

d) The means by which the traditions of Second Temple tales were carried over to the rabbinic period were written (and so we have hard evidence) and oral. International folk motifs (as in *The Book of Ahikar*), presumably made their way into the rabbinic period principally through oral transmission.

e) In passing from one period to the next, these traditions underwent formative, thematic, and functional changes. These changes can be explained against the background of the different context in which the traditions were told anew.

f) The analysis and findings of literary and folkloristic processes described up to this point reconfirm the unequivocal reliance of oral folk traditions on those in writing. It can be assumed with a great degree of certainty that, had the sages not banned the reading of the non-canonical books, the other traditions they contained would also have become folktales. The fact that there was a prohibition against reading and copying the non-canonical books, and that they did indeed disappear from the Hebrew literature of the rabbinic period, precipitated the disappearance of their narrative traditions as well. The revival of Second Temple tales during the Middle Ages is, as we now know for certain, connected to the translations into Hebrew of the books of *Tobit, Judith, Susannah, Esdras*, and others. The *literary* reappearance of Second Temple tales, via their translation into Hebrew during the Middle Ages, is what led to their restoration as Jewish folk traditions.[38]

[E] The Biographical Legend

After the expanded biblical tale, the second most important and prevalent genre is the biographical legend. It centers on the persona of a sage, leader, or folk saint around whose various stages of life the people wove legends. Natural human admiration for a charismatic figure and widespread belief in such an individual's supernatural abilities to ease the daily travails of the faithful, account for the preponderance of the biographical legend in Talmudic literature. Certainly this was the case with the general public; yet, even among the learned, biographical legends played an important role. They provided a sterling example of ethical behavior and decision-making according to the desired norms, and thus served as the guidelines for a religious way of life.[39]

Rabbinic literature contains hundreds of biographical legends; their fabula span the full range from a short sentence reporting on a sage's exceptional behavior to a long and elaborate biographical tale. The biographical legends in the Talmud and Midrash fall naturally into one or the other of the two acknowledged categories, according to their source and function: There are those biographical legends that originated in the folk admiration for the figure of a pious individual, and those that serve to strengthen social, ethical, and religious principles. A significant number of these highlight the conflict and rivalry between folk miracle-workers and the sages of the academy. It appears that rabbinic literature came by these legends via folk traditions. Other biographical legends, offered as a basis for a legal ruling (*halakha*) or hagiographical-homiletic interpretation (as in the story of Hillel the Elder and the Sons of Bathyra, for example), emerged from scholars in the academy. Scholarly inclinations and stylistic features are patently evident in these cases.[40]

Even given the acknowledged differences between rabbinic and general folk literature, the designations developed in the research of biographical legend—based on stages in the hero's biography—are likely to be useful in classifying the legends scattered throughout the Talmud and Midrash. Research dating from the end of the nineteenth century formulated the accepted biographical model: "the legendary biography of the hero." This reached its final form in the model proposed by Lord Raglan in the 1940s. This model, which proposes a division of the hero's life into twenty-two to twenty-four stages, suits elaborate myths, or romances of the Middle Ages, but not rabbinic aggadah, which are much shorter and more condensed (although Raglan himself applied the system to the Bible's stories about Moses). On the other hand, Dov Noy proposed the following division, which better accommodates the Jewish biographical legend:

(A) events which took place before the hero's birth—the prenatal legend.
(B) events from the life of the hero—the biographical legend.
(C) events that happened after the hero's death—the posthumous legend.
(D) events connected with the hero's descendants.
(E) events connected with the hero's belongings.

Activity in (B) and (C) centers on the hero himself during his lifetime or after his death; in (A) the active figures are his parents, and in (D) and (E), his descendants or belongings (the saint's grave, for instance) are imbued in some way with his holiness.[41]

Applying this model to rabbinic literature's biographical legend emphasizes its unique character. Hardly any legends belonging to groups (A), (D), and (E) have survived (except for the tales of the descendants of Honi the Circle-Drawer, Abba Hilkiah, and Hanan ha-Nehba, or a few traditions of the graves of saints). The overwhelming majority of the legends belong to classification (B). Furthermore, few subsets of this classification (which include (B1) the miraculous birth, (B2) exceptional childhood, (B3) family life, and (B7) demise) are represented in the rabbinic biographical legend.

Some examples of the prenatal legend have survived, although their purpose is not unambiguously biographical:

> There was a woman with child who had smelled [a dish]. People came before Rabbi [questioning him what should be done]. He said to them: Go and whisper to her that it is the Day of Atonement. They whispered to her and

she accepted the whispered suggestion, whereupon he [Rabbi] cited about her the verse: "Before I formed thee in the belly I knew thee" (Jer. 1:5). From her came forth R. Johanan. [Again] there was a woman with child who had smelled [a dish]. The people came to R. Hanina, who said to them: Whisper to her [that it is the Day of Atonement]. She did not accept the whispered suggestion. He cited with regard to her: "The wicked are estranged from the womb" (Pss. 58:4). From her came forth Shabbetai, the hoarder of provisions [for speculation]. (Yoma 82^b)

The hero of this prenatal legend is the mother; the story centers on an exceptional action of hers as an explanation—or prediction—of the saint's birth. Typical of rabbinic literature, the tale is woven into a halakhic discussion on the issue of 'a woman with child who had smelt.' It comes to praise pregnant women who revere the Day of Atonement (exemplum). But the story is also offered as proof, by means of example, that a woman who cannot bear the temptation is permitted to taste the dish—as was in fact the custom of Rabbi Hanina according to the Mishnah (casus—a type of legal precedent). In any case, it is clear from the tale's context and style that it did not serve as a biographical legend about the birth of Rabbi Johanan. We cannot reject the possibility that the tale originated in the folk literature beyond the walls of the academy, and that it underwent essential changes as it passed into the sphere of legal decision.

Few tales corresponding to the other stages of biographical legend are to be found in the sages' aggadah. Conversely, stories of the "origins" of the sages hold an extremely prominent place. The tales of Hillel studying Torah, of R. Eliezer ben Hyrcanus, and R. Akiva are among the most famous in aggadah. The tales have various formulas in rabbinic and post-Talmudic literature, which proves, for our purposes, that the tale "passed" the societal barrier, and should be seen as a folktale in every sense. The common denominator of the stories of the emergence of these and other sages is their ignorance until a relatively advanced age, and the commencement of Torah study despite the obstacles society placed before the hero. The social and didactic significance of this narrative pattern is obvious. The tales serve the function of birth tales of the heroes in folk literature outside of the Talmudic literature. From the perspective of this literature, the significant births of Hillel the Elder, R. Eliezer ben Hyrcanus, or R. Akiva were not the biological events, but their spiritual rebirths. Stories that so overtly replace biological processes (which figure in general folklore) with spiritual ones, and value Torah study above all else, plainly seem to have originated in the learned culture of the academy. I consider this a typical example of the transformation of tales originating in the academy into folktales. They were created to serve the interests of the learned, but became folktales nonetheless, owing either to the fame of their heroes, or to the narrative framework and its particular message: The lowly hero, whose origins and personality as initially revealed are hardly promising, succeeds by sheer willpower in reaching the social ideal. In this fashion, the academy sages mobilize the very widespread narrative model (the unpromising youngest son rises to greatness) to illustrate the ethical and ideological goals whose dissemination they seek.[42]

Tales of the "emergence" of R. Akiva provide a good example of the complexity of these biographical legends. Rabbinic literature preserved three different tales, each with several versions. One is the story of the well: "When he was forty years of age he had not yet studied a thing," when he noticed how the stone of the well was grooved and marked by the water. "Thereupon Rabbi Akiva drew the inference with regard to himself: "If what is soft wears down the hard, all the more shall the words of Torah, which are as hard as iron, hollow out my heart, which is flesh and blood! . . . He went together with his son and they appeared before an elementary teacher," and so he advanced until he became the first and foremost wise man of all of Israel. The second is the most celebrated of the three tales. It concerns the daughter of Kalba Savua, who married R. Akiva though her father disowned her as a result—that is, until he returned with twenty-four thousand pairs of students (*Nedarim* 50a; *Ketubot* 62b–63a). In the third tale, R. Akiva himself talks about his rebirth as a learned man:

> Said R. Akiva: Thus was the beginning of my labor of learning before the sages. One time I was walking along the way, and I found a neglected corpse, and I attended to him for about four mils, until I brought him to the graveyard, and I buried him there. Now when I came to R. Eliezer and to R. Joshua, I told them what I had done. They said to me: For every step you took, you were credited as if you had shed blood [for taking the neglected corpse away from the spot in which he should have been buried]. Now I said: If when I intended to acquire merit I suffered blame [for not doing things right], when I do not intend to acquire merit, how much the more so [do I suffer blame]. From that time I have not ceased to serve [and study with] sages. (PT, *Nazir* 7, 1, J. Neusner's translation, pp. 181–182)

It must first be remarked that various traditions of these stories survived in different periods and in different places. The first tale, about the well which precipitated Rabbi Akiva's Torah study, survived in Palestinian tannaitic sources (*Avot de-Rabbi Nathan*); Palestinian sources of the amoraic period (the Palestinian Talmud) preserved the third tale, about the deserted corpse, while the tale of Kalba Savua appears in the traditions of the Babylonian Talmud. The diversity of tales and their versions suggests that Rabbi Akiva became a folk hero as early as the tannaitic period, a status which apparently intensified with time. The abundance of extant stories indicates the talmudic editors' keen interest in them, as well as the ample supply of such traditions from which they could draw the different versions.[43]

A closer reading of the three stories and their variations shows that, notwithstanding their common subject—R. Akiva's emergence—each tale constitutes an independent tradition of a particular stripe and bias. In the story of the well, the hero explicitly states [Schechter, version B]: "Is my heart stronger than the stone?—I shall go and study a portion," and the narrator concludes: "They [the angels after death] say to a man: why did not you study Torah in this world? He says: Because I was poor. R. Akiva as well was a poor man . . . Perhaps your fathers were not worthy of it [that they will have a learned ancestor]? R. Akiva as well did not have worthy fathers. That is why our Rabbis, blessed is their memory, said: R. Akiva will shame many people who did not study Torah." In other words, through this story the sages preach that Torah study is an unconditional duty, and that there can be no justification for avoiding it. The tale as a whole seems, on the face of it, a composition constructed on an analogy widespread in Jewish culture since biblical times, between water and the Torah: as water etches stone, so the Torah engraves man's heart. Who better to embody this idea than Rabbi Akiva, who was alleged by many ancient traditions (apparently reliable) to have begun his studies as an adult and to have become the greatest luminary of his generation. The aim of this tale was patently didactic.[44]

The second tale, that concerning the daughter of Kalba Savua, is distinctly novelistic. It is the story of a great love which proves stronger than family and material possessions; the hero sets out for distant parts, where his wisdom and diligence reward him with both wealth and greatness. The protagonist in all versions of the tale is not R. Akiva but Kalba Savua's daughter. She is the active character who renounces wealth and parentage, urges her husband to go off and study in remote lands, and willingly chooses a life of poverty and hunger. The tale's conclusion with the common figure of speech, "mine and yours [learning] is hers," indicates the status of the heroine as central to the unfolding of the plot. There is a latent social message to this tale: the husband's studies depend on the will and spiritual strength of the wife: Rabbi Akiva himself would not have reached his potential if not for the wife who encouraged him at every step. This message also explains the tale's novelistic construction; since it was directed mainly toward female society, the literary mode chosen to carry the message was the novella.[45]

The third tale focuses on a typical halakhic issue (the deserted corpse) and exposes, through use of the autobiographical tale, the conflict between the am-ha'aretz ("the simple folk, the unlearned") and the scholars of the Law (the following statement was attributed to Rabbi Akiva: "When I was an am ha'aretz, I said: I would that I had a scholar [before me], and I would maul him like an ass" [*Pesahim* 49b]) Rabbi Akiva committed a grave religious sin in this story, as he was ignorant of the law. The thrust of the story, in other words, is that knowledge of the halakha, and its application according to the rabbinic interpretation, is an essential condition of living correctly according to Judaism ('whoever did not serve the Rabbis deserves to die' [PT *Nazir* 7a]). Consequently, it is clear that the sages of the academy created this story too, to serve their needs and bolster their position in the sometimes acrimonious confrontation with the uneducated common folk.[46]

We have seen how three stories dealing with the emergence of a single figure make use of three distinct genres with different social functions and implications. As regards their subject and overall objective, they belong to the category of biographical legend through which people across the social spectrum, simple folk and scholars, express their admiration for the hero of the story. Yet we also saw that each version of the tale has its particular bias and significance. Therefore, the biographical aggadah should not be seen strictly as hero admiration. Its form and meaning were crafted to serve additional functions in the social or religious context.

In the legends of Rabbi Akiva's wealth, we see the passage of these biographical legends from the educated society of the academy to the broader public. Of the three legends, only in the distinctly folk novella about the daughter of Kalba Savua does Rabbi Akiva inherit his father-in-law's wealth. In the other two legends, his eminence in Torah study is sufficient reward for his toil, certainly not a surprising position for scholars.

Besides the legend of his marriage, another tradition concerning the sources of Rabbi Akiva's wealth survives:

> From six incidents did R. Akiva become rich: From Kalba Savu'a. From a ship's ram. For every ship is provided with the figurehead of an animal. Once this [a wooden ram] was forgotten on the sea shore, and R. Akiva found it. From a hollowed out trunk. For he once gave four zuz to sailors, and told them to bring him something [that he needed]. But they found only a hollow log on the seashore, which they brought to him, saying, "Sit on this and wait." It was found to be full of denarii. For it once happened that a ship sunk and all the treasures thereof were placed in that log, and it was found at that time. From the serokita [Ishmaelite traders]. From a matron, the wife of Turnus Rufus [the Roman governor of Judea, that after his death, his widow married R. Akiva after converting to Judaism, and brought him great wealth]. From Keti'a b. Shalom. (*Nedarim* 50a-b)

These stories confirm what we already know: when scholarly narrative traditions are borrowed by broader layers of society, they undergo changes in accordance with the folk's perception of the world. And indeed, the biographical legend told in the folk traditions cannot end only with a rise to greatness in

Torah. It must add possessions and wealth, which are the essential hallmarks of success in the common perception.

Another stage in the life of the talmudic hero around whom biographical legends were concentrated is death. Here too we find numerous legends concerning the death of sages, and the typical example is again that of R. Akiva. There are two extant versions of the story of his demise: one in *Berakhot* 61b, which relates his death by torture following the controversy with Pappus Ben Yehuda (in which he uses the famous parable of the fox and the fish); the second is in *Midrash Mishlei* (chapter 9, Wissotsky edition, pp. 67–69), which tells of his death in prison and burial thereafter by Elijah and R. Joshua ha-Garsi. The latter brought him "to the four-arched gateway of Caesarea, [and] they went down some descents and up three ascents. There they found a bier spread out, a bench, a table, and a lamp. They placed R. Akiva's corpse upon the bier, and immediately the lamp was lit up and the table was set [of their own accord]." These versions of the legend of Rabbi Akiva's death illustrate the different objectives of the biographical tale: the first emphasizes R. Akiva's martyrdom as a personal example of the principle of "And thou shalt love the Lord thy God with all thy heart, and with all thy soul . . . even if he takes your soul away." In other words, another deviation from mere biographical description. In contrast to this, the second version describes the holy man's just deserts upon his death: the Prophet Elijah himself tends to him, and a wondrous grave is prepared for him in advance. This is the natural concluding stage in the legendary biography of a saint.[47]

In the second version of the legend of Rabbi Akiva's death, there are two supernatural motifs: The appearance of the Prophet Elijah, who notifies Rabbi Joshua ha-Garsi of Akiva's passing, and the opening of the miraculous cave. The rabbinic literature preserved evidence of widespread traditions on such unusual phenomena accompanying the death of a saint. Both the Babylonian Talmud and the Palestinian Talmud contain a concentration of such traditions with vast folkloric importance:

> When the soul of R. Abbahu went into repose the columns at Caesarea ran with tears. At [the death of] R. Jose, the roof gutters at Sepphoris ran with blood. At that of R. Jacob [b. Aha], stars were visible in daytime. At that of R. Assi, [all cedars] were uprooted. At that of R. Hiyya [b. Abba], fiery stones came down from the sky; at that of R. Menahem [b. Simai], all images [of idolatory] were effaced and came to be [used] as stone rollers; at that of Tanhum son of R. Hiyya [of Kefar Acco], all human statues were torn out of their position; at that of [R. Isaac, son of R.] Eliashiv, seventy houses were broken into [by thieves] at Tiberias; at that of R. Hamnuna, hail stones came down from the sky; at that of Rabbah and R. Joseph, the rocks of the Euphrates kissed each other; at that of Abaye and Raba, the rocks of the

Tigris kissed each other. When the soul of R. Mesharsheya went into repose, the palms were laden with thorns (*Mo'ed Katan* 25b).

On the day that he [Rabbah b. Nahmani] died, a hurricane lifted an Arab who was riding a camel, and transported him from one bank of the River Papa to the other. "What does this portend?" he exclaimed, "Rabbah b. Nahmani had died" he was told. "Sovereign of the Universe!" he cried out, "The whole world is Thine, and Rabbah b. Nahmani too is Thine . . . why do you destroy the world on his account?" Thereupon the storm subsided. (*Baba Mezi'a* 86b, and compare also: PT *Kil'ayim* 9c; PT *Kethubot* 12c; PT *Pe'ah* 81a)

Narrative motifs or traditions describing the participation of natural forces in worldly events are very widespread in folk fiction beginning with ancient mythology. The traditions extant in rabbinic literature underwent a typical process of demythologization: the natural forces which participate in the mourning for a saint are no longer mythic, rather they serve as symbols, or as an embodiment of Divine grief over the passing of one of His chosen. Nor is the hero any longer a mythic hero whose relatives, the gods, mourn for him— rather he is a scholar of the Torah, whose teaching is his pedigree and strength. Nonetheless, there are remnants of the features of mythic power in these traditions. Forces of nature share men's feelings and, as in the work of later authors and playwrights, here too mythological motifs are mobilized to give expression to larger-than-life emotions. A description of nature mourning the death of a sage is therefore a technique of externalizing emotions and projecting them onto the world beyond the human spirit. Cosmic grief over the death of prominent sages is a vivid use of this technique.[48]

These traditions, which very briefly describe the final stage in the legendary biography of many sages, testify to the existence of legends dealing with other stages of their biographies. The nature and subjects of these legendary traditions are extremely diverse. There are, for example, the legends of the miracles surrounding the corpses of the sages Rabbah bar Huna and Rav Hamnuna, who died abroad and whose bodies were brought to Palestine on camelback. When the camels halted at a narrow bridge, the escorts explained to the Ishmaelite driver that each beast wished to honor the other with the first crossing of the bridge. The Ishmaelite crossed the camel carrying the body of Rabbah bar Huna first, and his cheeks and teeth fell off as punishment for the offense to R. Hamnuna (*Mo'ed Katan* 25a–b). Rabbi Eleazar, son of Rabbi Simeon (Bar Yohai), instructed that he was not to be buried, but laid out in the attic of his house, where he lay for at least eighteen years without decomposing, even deciding questions of law that were brought before him (*Baba Metziah* 84b; *Pesiktah de-Rav Kahanah* 11, *Vayehi Beshelach*). Additionally, there are the legends of unusual burials or burial sites, such as the cave where Rabbi Akiva was laid to rest; the snakes entwined around the mouths of the burial caves of Rabbi Shimon bar Yohai, his son, Rabbi Eleazar, and his grandson (*Baba Metziah* 84b); or the serpent which guarded the mouth of the tomb of Rav Kahanah, barring Rabbi Johanan from entering (*Baba Kama* 117a-b). These legends and motifs concerning the corpses or graves of holy men who perform posthumous miracles are very widespread among folk traditions across many cultures. The importance of these traditions as they figure among the Jewish sages lies primarily in their concentration and diversity, and secondarily in their antiquity. They are apparently among the most ancient folk traditions of this kind known to us.[49]

No less interesting is the group of legends describing the moment of death itself (*memento mori*). Around this subject too, a range of traditions were concentrated in tractate *Mo'ed Katan* 28a, which tell of dying moments and encounters with the angel of death. Rava asks his brother to tell the angel of death not to hurt him too much; R. Nahman asks the same of Rava. R. Eleazar eats *Terumah* (priestly tithe on produce) and the angel of death must wait until he is finished; Rav Sheshet is not ready for the angel of death to take his soul like a beast to market, and Rav Ashi puts off the angel of death thirty days until he completes his studies; even Rabbi Hiyya only gives himself over to the angel of death when the latter entreats him not to make him go back and forth anymore. R. Hisda studies Torah and the angel of death cannot approach him. Only when the angel of death sits down on a cedar tree and it breaks, momentarily distracting Rav Hisda, can he be taken.

The last tale is particularly intriguing because of the relatively large number of versions in which it has been preserved in the aggadic literature. One version is found in Tractate *Makot* 10a: Rav Hisda is learning Torah in the academy and the angel of death sits on one of the building's pillars and breaks it, thus distracting Rav Hisda and enabling the angel to take his soul. Of particular importance are the other two versions of the legend: one concerning Rabbah bar Nahmani, for whom the angel of death was sent, but since he did not cease his studying, he was untouchable. When wind blew through the room, Rabbah mistakenly thought the cavalry was after him (perhaps someone had informed on him), feared capture, and decided it would be better to die than fall into the hands of the regime. He stopped studying—and died. When his friends and students looked for him, after a note fell from the sky announcing his death, they found him by means of the birds who sheltered his corpse from the sun with their wings (*Baba Metziah* 86a). A close parallel to this version is the well-known tale in which the angel of death is sent for King David, whose mouth never stops moving in Torah study. The angel of death blew through the trees in the garden, and when David stepped out to see what the noise was, a wooden step broke beneath his foot and he fell. This moment was enough for the angel of death. Here too, since it was the Sabbath, the corpse could not be attended to. Solomon called on the eagles, who sheltered the corpse against the sun with their wings (*Sabbath* 30a–b; *Kohelleth Rabbah* 5, 10; *Rut Rabbah* 3, 2).[50]

The relatively numerous versions of the death legend indicate the great interest of people of the period in these stories, as well as the wealth of folk traditions from which the editors of rabbinic literature could borrow. All the death legends suggest a connection between the greatness of the figure and its ability to bear the difficult moment—the encounter with death. The primary means of delay, albeit temporary, was Torah study. Involvement in the Torah was the only effective defense. In this collection of legends, too, we witness that the tales were not necessarily brought forth to sketch out the final stage in the sages' lives, but to crystallize and transmit a clear message; they came to flesh out an idea that was important to the society that told it, and certainly to the sages, who lost no time integrating these folk traditions into the compositions that emerged from the academy. At the same time, the traditions portray in faithful fashion Jewish society's perception of death at the time: death was no abstract entity, but a concrete personality that mortals could talk to and reason with. The pains attendant on the moment of death were fierce. Fear of death was common to all strata of society, as was the belief in the possibility of postponing it, or of attaining an unusually easy end. On the subject of death too, the folktale serves as a principal means of expression and revelation of the modes of folk thought.

Another branch of the biographical legend of the sages is comprised of the tales of folk saints. Apart from those anonymous figures called "a pious man" (*hasid*) or "one pious man," the names of Honi the Circle-Drawer and his descendants, Abba Hilkiah and Hanan ha-Nehba, R. Pinhas ben Yair, and R. Hanina ben Dosa have remained. In chapter 3 of the Babylonian Talmud tractate *Ta'anit*, known to later generations as "the chapter of piety," the names and stories of more sages appear, including R. Zerah, Nahum of Gimzo, and the wealthy Nakdimon ben Guryon, and additional figures such as Abba Umana, Yose of Yokrat, and Eleazar ben Judah of Birta, who belong to that group of individuals named "hasidim."[51]

In the main, in seems that at issue are individuals who gained renown by virtue of their extreme religious and ethical behavior and the punctiliousness with which they performed religious precepts beyond society's accepted norms. The first of these figures—and the most celebrated—belong to the early tannaitic period. Their stories passed into the amoraic period, and are scattered throughout both the Palestinian Talmud and the Babylonian Talmud. In the amoraic period, individual tales of the deeds of amoraim themselves were added. These deal principally with rain-making, and most are concentrated in that large collection of tales in Babylonian tractate *Ta'anit* (23a–25b).

These tales are typical of holy man legends. Honi the Circle-Drawer and his descendants bring rain; Pinhas ben Yair meticulously tithes *demai* (that is, "doubtfully tithed crops") to the point where his donkey refuses to eat untithed corn; he saves the harvest in a place plagued by vermin; sows barley belonging to the poor in his own fields, and when they come to ask for it—he gives them all the crops yielded; he returns to the king a pearl swallowed by a mouse; supplies water to a dried-up spring; miraculously parts a river in order to cross it. R. Hanina ben Dosa treads on a snake and is unharmed; his goats capture bears with their horns; he magically extends the rafters of his house to fit; miraculously supplies food and, like Pinhas ben Yair, brings back to life a girl who drowned in the river, and much more. While these tales generally appear in story cycles, and in a terse and concentrated style, clearly such was not the case originally. Within the cycles of tales, there is no connection between one story and the next—except the character of the hero who figures in each. Therefore it is clear that they were generally told as independent tales at various performance events. Nor was their literary nature originally so laconic—they became so as a consequence of their literary insertion into rabbinic sources.[52]

It has already been pointed out that little of the halakhic statements of Honi the Circle-Drawer, Pinhas ben Yair, R. Hanina ben Dosa, and others were preserved. On the contrary, the tales indicate unequivocally the antagonism between them and the sages of the academy. Simeon ben Shetah's sharp reprimands of Honi the Circle-Drawer after his "public display" in Jerusalem in time of drought are only one example. R. Hanina ben Dosa brought rain where the sages of the academy failed; Abba Umana and other, anonymous, folk figures excel in deeds of God-fearingness and piety superior to those of the sages; when all accepted means of bringing rain failed, two sages were sent to Abba Hilkiah, son of Honi the Circle-Drawer, who proves his superiority over them in God-fearingness and practical piety. It seems that beyond folk literature's great affection for legends of holy men, here is manifested folk reaction against the sages' outspoken belittling of the am ha'aretz ("ignorant, common people"). Each individual tale preaches the practice of a precept or some behavioral norm—caring for the poor, tithing, extreme honesty and fairness, and so on. Altogether they clearly express the sentiment that God-fearingness and greatness in the study of Torah are not mutually inclusive. There are exemplary figures among the uneducated whose deeds and qualities surpass those of the sages. Perhaps even more importantly, they are favored by the Creator Himself above those engaged in Torah. The miraculous deeds with which they are associated, especially making rain in times of drought, are unequivocal proof as far as the people are concerned of the Almighty's preference for common piety over greatness in Torah. (It should be noted that this position is the reverse of that of the scholars of the Law, who claim true God-fearingness cannot exist without greatness in Torah, or at least not without upholding it according to the sages' interpretation, as we have seen.) It is clear to us that the people sensed a certain "haughtiness" on the part of the Torah scholars, in spite of the various efforts to blur it. Once again we are witnesses to the important function served by folktales as almost the sole tangible expression of the sentiments of the "mute" strata of society.[53]

This dichotomy between scholars and folk pious men is not always clear and unambiguous. The tales were told and put into writing within the ivory tower of the academy; that is, the sages themselves did not generally regard them as stories of protest or as a threat to their status as national leaders. There can be many reasons for this. It may be that they did not always sense the protesting nature of the tales; the moral they bore may have been more important to them—especially as they certainly did have a sense of the tales' power to influence broad strata of society. It may even be that there was some reservation within the academy against considering exaggerated Torah study an end in itself, and not just one path to God-fearingness. These folktales of pious men and men of good deeds could serve as proof that Torah study is not an essential condition for God-fearingness, and the miracles associated with these individuals were clear proof of it.

At least one tale illustrates that a prominent holy man, R. Pinhas ben Yair, was a Torah scholar as well. When Rabbi (that is, Judah the Patriarch) seeks to annul the sabbatical year, R. Pinhas ben Yair intervenes. He is adamantly opposed to such a step. Rabbi, hoping to bring him around in a private conversation, invites him to his home, but R. Pinhas ben Yair, after seeing a team of mules in Rabbi's courtyard, which demonstrates the Patriarch's pride, utilizes all kinds of devices to avoid the meeting. When each of them fails, "Fire descended from heaven and surrounded him [so that Rabbi's attendants could not reach him]. They went back and told Rabbi [what had happened]. He said: Since I did not merit to have my fill of him in this world, may I merit having my fill of him in the world to come (PT *Demai* 1, 3, J. Neusner's translation, pp. 45–46). That is, there is more than a hint here that R. Pinhas ben Yair was taken to the next world by the heavenly fire, as was Elijah. According to this tale, R. Pinhas ben Yair was a worthy opponent of the Patriarch in the halakhic arena, and the tale is not alone in bringing forth the harsh rivalry between Rabbi and several other sages against the background of halakhic and social controversies.[54]

Of special interest is the nature of the miracles performed by the holy men of the age. The tale of Honi comes close to a magic deed: He drew a circle around himself—a commonplace magical device in various cultures (and one whose purpose is to place a barrier between the two realms—that within and that without), and swears a kind of conditional oath: "I swear by Thy great name that I will not move from here until Thou hast mercy upon Thy children" (*Ta'anit* 23a). The use of the "great name of God" is another indicator of outright magic. By contrast, his descendants, Abba Hilkiah and Hanan ha-Nehba, merely pray, and none of their actions can be construed as making use of supernatural forces. The other holy men reason their actions as ethical and normative in purpose, even if the actions are fundamentally magical. A certain village was plagued by vermin because its residents were not meticulous in the tithing of their crops; R. Pinhas ben Yair gathers all the mice together and understands their language—typical magic actions; similarly in the tale of the well which dried up when the villagers did not properly tithe their crops. The quintessential tale in which religious-normative argument is grafted onto a fundamentally magical tale is the story of Pinhas ben Yair and the River Ginnai:

> [Once] R. Pinhas b. Yair was on his way to the academy, and the river Ginnai was swollen. He said to it: Ginnai! Ginnai! Why do you hook me back from attending the academy? It split before him and he crossed it. His disciples said to him: May we [also] cross it? He said to them: Whoever [among you] knows within himself that he never has treated a Jew improperly, let him cross and he will not be harmed. (PT *Demai* 1, 3, J. Neusner's translation, p. 45)

The way the hero addresses the river—twice calling it by name—and the stipulation ("if . . . then")—as in the tale of Honi—are characteristic magical formulations. In his explanation to his students, Pinhas ben Yair attributes the miraculous parting of the waters to a simple religious-social precept. The miracle happened for him, and will happen for anyone else who never demeaned another Jew. The foundation of the tale is a magic story about a holy man who makes use of the forces at his disposal to change the surrounding reality. But in the sages' stories of pious men and men of action, the tale underwent a generic transformation from a magical tale to an ethical tale, in which moral distinction, not magic, is the focus.

In another well-known legend, an Ishmaelite king asks R. Pinhas ben Yair to find a pearl swallowed by a mouse. Our hero, in all innocence, responds: "Who am I, a magician?" (PT *Demai* 1, 3). Immediately thereafter, he casts a spell over the mice and commands the one who swallowed the gem to cough it up. That is, the tale seeks to emphasize that, while seeming to practice sorcery, the *hassidim* are of another sort altogether, as their actions are supported by ethical norms and Divine force. The hero's supernatural powers are not due to his birth or the inspiration of a supernatural power, but are precipitated by his deeds, his moral choice. We do not know when this transformation of the magical tale into a moral one took place, but it is difficult to believe that they were told in this manner across the social spectrum. It is more reasonable to presume that this was one of the changes which informed the holy man legend when it was inserted into the new contexts of rabbinic literature.[55]

It seems appropriate to conclude the discussion of the biographical legend with an exceptional literary phenomenon, the "negative" biography of Elisha ben Avuyah. These stories were certainly not created by the society in its broad sense, but by the sages, and came to serve the goals and polemics of the academy. At the same time, they are important to an understanding of the period's folk literature in that they show how the sages made use of biographical legend for the reverse objective: not to praise a folk hero, but to denounce and demonstrate the negative and the peril inherent in every stage of his life story. The legends of Elisha ben Avuyah are a biographical legend of an anti-saint, which utilizes the foundations of biographical folk legend, and whose ultimate purpose is to make known the types of behavior negated by society.

In the "legends" of Elisha ben Avuyah that survived in the rabbinic literature, his skepticism and heresy are particularly stressed, yet an interesting picture emerges from the fragments of the "biography": Smoke rises from his grave for a long period of time, which symbolizes punishment and agonies after death (beating by evil spirits). This is his fate until Rabbi Johanan passes away, and brings Elisha ben Avuyah along with him to the next world (*Midrash Ecclesiastes Rabbah* 7, 8). As we have seen above, the grave and the miracles associated with it are one of the proofs of the greatness of a saint. The tradition of Elisha ben Avuyah's grave inverts the legends of saints' graves: it uses society's deeply ingrained folk beliefs in the deeds of a saint after his death to argue that this logic works in the opposite direction as well. His grave produces no miracles or marvelous plants. Instead, it gives off a foul smoke.

An interesting tradition regarding Elisha ben Avuyah's "emergence" was also recorded: (PT *Hagigah* 2, 1):

[Elisha] said . . . "The end of a thing is better than its beginning" so long as it is good from its beginning. And so it happened to me. My father, Avuya, was one of the important people in Jerusalem. When the day of my circumcision came, he invited all the important people of Jerusalem and sat them down in one room, with R. Eliezer and R. Joshua in another room. When they had eaten and drunk they began stamping their feet and dancing. R. Eliezer said to R. Joshua: While they are occupying themselves in their way we will occupy ourselves in our way. So they sat down and engaged in the study of the Torah, from the Pentateuch to the Prophets, and from the Prophets to the Writings. And fire fell from heaven and surrounded them. Avuya said to them: My masters, have you come to burn my house down around me? They said: God forbid . . . and the words [of the Torah] were as alive as when they were given from Mount Sinai. And the fire shone around us as it shone from Mount Sinai . . . Avuya, my father, said to them: My masters, if this is the power of the Torah, if this son of mine lives I will dedicate this son of mine to the Torah. Because his [original] intention was not for the sake of heaven, therefore it was not realized in this man. (PT *Hagigah* 2, 1, J. Neusner's translation, pp. 46–47)

According to another version of his birth,

> Still others say that it happened because when his mother was pregnant with
> him, she passed by idolatrous temples and smelled [the offerings]. They gave
> her some of that kind [of food] and she ate it, and it burned in her stomach
> like the venom of a serpent [and infected him]. (*Ecclesiastes Rabbah* 7, 8)

In these legends, as in the other birth legends, the biography begins with events
in the lives of the hero's parents, which set the tone for the hero's destiny and
deeds. But while in all the other birth legends, the parents perform exceptional
deeds, such as withstanding temptation or giving charity, Elisha ben Avuyah's
parents sin against society's norms (in this case, those of the sages), and this
sin is an omen (or cause) of the birth of the anti-saint. Here too, a "learned"
legend made brilliant use of structures and motifs of the biographical folk legend in order to create an anti-legend. Its power indeed stems from the traditional associations of the tale—folk motifs familiar to the audience of listeners
from other traditions, but its moral significance and psychological effect are
based on the breaking of these traditional narrative norms. These legends were
intended to set Elisha ben Avuyah apart from other holy men and present him
in all his negativity by means of reverse signs of the same narrative-traditional
structures particular to the "true" saints.[56]

[F] The Exemplum

Tales of the rabbinic period have come down to us in a broad array of
contexts—halakhic, exegetical, or ethical. They were intended to serve functions connected with the perception of the world of the sages. The purpose of
the tales as far as the sages were concerned—as in any other religious literature—was to offer concrete guidelines for following religious and ethical principles. Therefore, they should all be viewed as exemplary tales. A particularly
revealing and precise expression of the sages' perception of the exemplary tale
can be found in the parable of Rabbi Eleazar ben Azaryah:

> Speak to Aharon thy brother, that he come not at all times. We do not know
> what was said to him [initially]. Rabbi Eleazar ben Azaryah says: To what
> can this be compared? To a doctor who goes in to a sick man. He says to
> him: Don't drink cold water and don't lie in dampness. Another comes and
> says to him: Don't drink cold water and don't lie in dampness *lest you die in*
> *the manner that so-and-so died.* This has a stronger effect than the former.
> (*Sifra*, Aharei Mot, Ch. 1; *Yalkut Shimoni*, Aharei Mot, no. 571)

A warning couched in logic does not have the same influence on the person
warned as that to which a practical example is attached. R. Eleazar ben

Azaryah's statements explain the wide use made by the sages of stories to illustrate and exemplify their points on every issue.

The beginning of the genre of the exemplum comes as early as the classical Hellenistic literature, where it served as an important foundation in the construction of rhetoric. Its function was to elucidate and exemplify the ideas presented in oration, so that listeners would understand and accept them. This perception of the function of the tale inserted into a theoretical text passed into the New Testament and the early Church Fathers, and reached its peak in the rich exemplary literature of the Middle Ages. The exemplum is a short tale presented as a report of an actual event. The element of authenticity is important to this genre, owing to its purpose: to persuade the listeners (or readers) to behave according to the religious-moral principles which it comes to illustrate. The exemplum is thus a narrative which makes tangible an abstract idea, seeking to convince that the tale should be viewed as an example to be emulated.[57]

The definition of most talmudic and midrashic stories as "exemplary" stems from their context and function, but it blurs the great differences between those that should properly be viewed as exempla and the rest. If we could ask the editors of the rabbinic literature questions as to the generic nature of the tales included, they would define the vast majority, if not all, as exempla. They almost always had in view the function the tale was to serve in the given context, not its artistic nature. This is certainly the reason they themselves regarded most of the aggadic tales as "factual tales," that is, as stories of events that actually took place. Nevertheless, we must point out the differences between the exemplum and other tales in order to understand its nature and special status in the folk literature of the period. In the previous section we saw how biographical legends serve as a model for Torah study, maintaining desirable behavioral norms. From this perspective, the biographical legends serve an outstanding exemplary function, although they should not be considered true exempla. Since the exemplum is directed at broad sectors of the folk, its purpose being to influence and persuade, its ethical orientation must be spelled out. It is not to be expected that members of the broad audience would conclude for themselves the desired behavioral norms from the story they heard.

Three fundamental components manifest the didactic aim of the exemplary tales: the structure of the tale itself, the moral conclusion which appears at the end of the tale (coda), and the context (halakhic or homiletic) in which it appears. In most of the biographical legends discussed above, we had to analyze the story in order to reveal its significance. Since they do not explicitly state their educational message or function, they do not belong to the genre of the exemplum, although they too, like all aggadic tales, have a clear normative function.[58]

One example among many of the broad incidence of the concept of exemplum is provided by the story in *Midrash Leviticus Rabbah* (portion 38, 2), about the man who delighted in philanthropy. He sold his home and all his possessions and donated the proceeds to charity. Once, on the festival of *Hoshana Rabba*, his wife gave him money to go to market and buy his children a gift. On the way, he met alms collectors raising money to clothe an orphan girl. He gave them the money. Embarrassed to return home, he went to the synagogue, where he filled a sack with *etrog*s (citrons, used on the festival of Sukkot) left there by the children, and set out to sea. In the foreign country where he found himself, the king was suffering a stomach ailment, for which his doctors prescribed the *etrog*s of the Jews, but none could be found anywhere in his kingdom. Enter our hero with his sack of *etrog*s. After the king ate of them and was cured, he refilled the sack with dinars and sent the hero home. A generic analysis of the tale shows it to be a typical novella: the tale is realistic, it brings its hero to adventures in distant lands, where, by virtue of his wisdom or integrity, he makes his fortune and returns home. In other tales of this type, the hero finds a miraculous herb with which he saves the king from leprosy or some other disease and thus rises to greatness. This novella clearly underwent a process of Judaization, so that the cure in the international type became the etrog over which a blessing was made on the eve of the festival (*Hoshana Rabba*). But the more significant Jewish coloring of the tale is in the beginning of the story, in his motivation to set out—the hero's extreme observance of the precept of giving charity. In this regard, and owing to the context in which the tale figures in *Midrash Leviticus Rabbah* (the giving of charity), it belongs to the exemplary genre, which seeks to make plain and prove that he who gives charity merits a great reward. It is as we said: functionally, this tale is an exemplum, although its literary nature, structure, and atmosphere are novelistic. Since it does not seek to influence by means of direct statements but rather by the significance of the tale, we cannot view it and many other similar tales as belonging to the exemplary genre. The stories we will examine below are brief, told in a matter-of-fact, precise style, and seek to *directly* influence the broad strata of society as regards day-to-day matters such as the Sabbath, honoring one's parents, returning a lost object, charity, ritual hand-washing, adultery, and so on.[59]

It was taught: R. Nathan said, There is not a single precept in the Torah, even the lightest, whose reward is not enjoyed in this world; and as to its reward in the future world I know not how great it is. Go and learn this from the precept of tzitzit. Once a man, who was very scrupulous about the precept of tzitzit, heard of a certain harlot in one of the towns by the sea who accepted four hundred gold [denars] for her hire. He sent for her four hundred gold [denars] and appointed a day with her. When the day arrived he came and waited at her door . . . [when he was about to lay with her] all of a sudden the four fringes [of his tzitzit] struck him across the face; whereupon he slipped off and sat upon the ground . . . [he explained to her that the four fringes reminded him of the sin he is committing. She took his name and that of his school, sold all her properties, converted to Judaism, and married him]. Those very bed-clothes which she had spread for him for an illicit purpose she now spread out for him lawfully. This is the reward [of the precept] in this world; and as for its reward in the future world I know not how great it is. (*Menahot* 44a)

The immediate framework in which the tale is inserted, the statement of a religious norm at the outset, and the promise of reward—which is repeated at the story's end—are clear evidence of the role played by the story in society. Although this tale too must be defined as a novella, as we shall see at once, its social-religious function, likewise its stylistic formulation, turn it in this context into an exemplary tale. In another version of the tale (*Avodah Zarah* 17a), the hero is R. Eleazar ben Dordaya "that he did not leave out any harlot in the world without coming to her." It was the prostitute who claimed that, on account of his sins, his repentance would never be accepted; he went and settled in the mountains and begged mercy of them, the sky, the sun and the moon, and the other natural forces, but was not answered. "Said he: The matter then depends upon me alone! Having placed his head between his knees, he wept aloud until his soul departed. Then a heavenly voice was heard proclaiming: 'Rabbi Eleazar b. Dordaya is destined for the life of the world to come!' "

The two versions of the tale differ in their plot and their import as well. While the first version has a novelistic character—a love story between a Torah scholar and a prostitute—and ends in marriage, in the manner of the novella, the second story has a tragic cast. In this version, much use is made of biblical verses—in the hero's appeal to the various forces of nature, the mountains and hills, the sky and the earth, the stars and the constellations (in a manner reminiscent of Moses's appeal to them to help him reach the land of Canaan, *Midrash Tanhuma Va-Ethanan*, 6)—and therefore does not seem like a version that in this form could have served as a folktale. Even the message—the power of repentance to endow life in the world to come even to the greatest of sinners, does not correspond to folk modes of thought.

The folktale always seeks to provide an immediate tangible reward or punishment; just deserts are not postponed until the end of days or the next world. The first version deals with a commonplace precept—the wearing of the ritual four-fringed garment; its significance is practical and derived from a) the context, b) the moral conclusion, and c) the course of the tale itself. Most important is the fact that the reward for fulfilling the precept brings the hero real and immediate profit, something of a latent societal wish—wealth and honorable marriage. Hence this version should be seen as a typical folk exemplum, while the second version, in which the hero is Eleazar ben Dordaya, is a scholarly, stylized narrative which apparently served the sages in their deliberations on the thorny issue of repentance.[60]

The topics typical of exempla in the rabbinic period are connected to the simple prohibitions and precepts related to daily life and the general public. The sanctity of the Sabbath naturally belongs in this grouping. In tractate *Shabbat* of the Babylonian Talmud, stories of the exceptional preparations customarily performed by the sages for the Sabbath were collected:

> R. Hanina robed himself and stood at sunset of Sabbath eve [and] exclaimed, "Come and let us go forth to welcome the queen Sabbath." R. Jannai donned his robes on Sabbath eve and exclaimed: "Come, O bride, Come, O bride!" . . . R. Abba bought meat for thirteen half zuz from thirteen butchers . . . R. Abbahu used to sit on an ivory stool and fan the fire. R. 'Anan used to wear an overall . . . R. Safra would singe the head [of an animal]; Raba salted fish; R. Huna lit the lamp. R. Papa plaited the wicks. R. Hisda cut up the beetroots. Rabbah and R. Joseph chopped wood. R. Zerah kindled the fire. R. Nahman b. Isaac carried [the goods for Sabbath] in and out.
> (*Shabbat* 119a)

Immediately after this passage comes the famous tale of Joseph-who-honors-Sabbaths, which concludes, "He who lends to the Sabbath, the Sabbath repays him."

This collection of tales displays two types of exempla: the exemplary behavior and the narrative. The cited examples of the sages' practices come to provide a model for the listeners in similar situations; they present a range of possibilities from which one may choose in order to fully participate in the Sabbath preparations. Yet only the tale of Joseph-who-honors-Sabbaths is a true exemplum: it uses an entertaining story—the pratfall of a non-Jew—to demonstrate by means of a concrete event the reward for keeping the Sabbath. As in the previous example, the exemplum of Joseph-who-honors-Sabbaths presents the fruits of obeying the precept as being of this world, as opposed to projecting the just reward to an intangible future. This is not the case in the cluster of anecdotes of exemplary behavior. No tangible reward comes to the sages who behave in a particular manner on Sabbath eve. This feature is a requirement of the tale, as it could not be complete without a real and *immediate* reward.

Another interesting difference between the descriptions of exemplary conduct and the tale is the identity of the protagonists. In the first part of the passage, the heroes are famous sages. The tale of Joseph-who-honors-Sabbaths, on the other hand, concerns a rather anonymous figure. It seems that the reason is once again the folk nature of the exemplum: the hero's anonymity suggests that every man, every Jew can reach that level of virtue in honoring the Sabbath. There is no need here for exceptional spiritual faculties. This is not the case in the description of the sages' conduct, which is beyond the scope of ordinary individuals. It is the name and fame of the sages which endows this passage with its force. Each is upheld as a paragon of virtue that should be looked up to, even emulated, although few will succeed.[61]

Another type of exemplary tale concerned with the keeping of the Sabbath is the animal tale. We have already encountered animals who observe certain precepts, such as the donkeys belonging to R. Hanina ben Dosa (*Avot de-Rabbi Nathan* 8), Pinhas ben Yair (PT *Demai*, 1, 3), and R. Yose of Yokrat (*Ta'anit* 24a). The lesson of these tales was worked via inference from minor to major: if a beast of burden can observe the precept of tithing, one should certainly expect at least as much from a Jew. When an individual faces the actual ethical choice—between tithing or not—one of these stories might come to mind and sway him to make the desired decision. The following well-known tale on this theme is found in *Pesikta Rabbati* (portion 14, Ish Shalom edition 56, 2–57, 1): A Jew sells his cow to a non-Jew, and she plowed for him during the six days of the week. On the Sabbath, the cow lay down and would not budge, even when her new owner beat her. When the Jew came and whispered in her ear that she was no longer obligated to keep the Sabbath, she rose and began plowing. When the non-Jew learned the truth of the matter, he immediately converted to Judaism, and was renamed R. Johanan ben Torta (son of the bull). The same typical "exemplary apparatus" is at work here: at the core stands the problem of the confrontation between Jews and non-Jews and the motives of those who choose to convert to Judaism. Yet these questions are shunted to the side in this version of the tale in order to focus on the primary subject—the keeping of the Sabbath. The basic picture etched into the memory of the listener is that of the cow who refuses to get up from her Sabbath rest, and it is likely to crop up in his consciousness anytime he vacillates before an ethical choice.[62]

The power of the exemplum comes from its presentation as daily reality, recognized and plausible, from its dealing with the problems likely to be encountered in the course of routine affairs, and the activation of the powerful apparatus of reward and punishment which is operative in this familiar world. Death, disease, impoverishment, sterility, and so on are the punishments awaiting one who does not act in accordance with the norms reinforced by the exemplum; meanwhile wealth, social advancement, greatness in the Torah, and life in the afterworld are the reward for upholding them: "Will our master teach us: One who ate and did not (ritually) wash his hands, how will he be punished?" Two tales follow immediately: one concerns a Jewish shopkeeper in the time of persecutions, who would cook and sell pork to non-Jews, so that they would not identify him as a Jew, while he would serve kosher meat to Jews who entered, ritually washed their hands, and made the blessings over food. Once a Jew entered but neither washed his hands nor uttered the blessings; he was served pork and hence was punished unknowingly. The second tale is as follows:

> It happened once that a man ate beans and did not wash his hands (afterwards). [He] went to the market and his hands were dirty from the beans. His friend saw him, and went and said to [the former's] wife: your husband told to give me that [precious] ring, and he gave you this sign, that he ate beans just before. After a time her husband came [home] and asked her: Where is the ring? She told him: That man came, and gave me the sign, and I gave it to him. He became very angry, and killed her. Thus, a man who does not wash his hands after food is like a murderer. (*Tanhuma*, Buber edition, *Balak* ch. 24, pp. 3a–b, BT *Hullin* 106a)

The open, pronounced context in which these stories are presented is noteworthy, both in the opening, in which a question of halakha is presented, and in the moral conclusion. This context is manifested clearly within the structure of the text, where ritual hand-washing is the main foundation of the story, driving the plot and bringing it to resolution. The narrative reality is also, as we have stated, one of daily routine and familiar to all: the shop, the market, the home, buying food, and trading in jewelry. All these are intended to show how an individual must be conscious of his actions, precisely and especially in his daily, familiar, and routine conduct. And after hearing these "examples," anytime an individual sets out to purchase food, or after a satisfying meal, he will know what is expected of him. This is how the exemplary apparatus functions: by presenting a correct behavioral model alongside a warning of the consequences should one not conform.

An example which indicates another direction can be found in *Seder Eliyahu Rabbah*: "A man has to keep his thoughts in his own heart, and not to be engaged in a lot of laughter, gossip, and frivolity, as laughter, gossip, and frivolity are no more than incest [or: uncovering of nakedness]." Special emphasis is given to conduct in the synagogue. Here a routine event from daily life is presented, which serves to sharpen the individual's sensitivity to his behavior:

> A tale of a man who would stand with his son in the synagogue, and while all the people responded, "Hallelujah" to the prayer leader, his son responded with frivolous words. They said to him: See that your son is responding with frivolous words. He said to them: "What shall I do to him? He is a child, let him play." On the morrow he behaved in the same manner. All the people responded, "Hallelujah" to the prayer leader. He responded with frivolous words. They said to him: See how he is responding with frivolous words. He said to them: "What shall I do? He is a child, let him play." Each of those

eight days of the festival, his son responded with frivolous words, and he said not a word to him. It was said: the year had not passed, nor two, nor three, before that same man died and his wife died and his son died and his son's son died. Fifteen souls departed from his house. He had none remaining save only two sons, one lame and blind and the other wicked and foolish.

Another tale of a man who felt remorse for not having studied the Bible and not having learned. One time he and I [the speaker is Elijah] were standing in the synagogue. When the prayer leader came to the "Sanctification of the Name" [*Kedushat ha-Shem*], he raised his voice and responded loudly. They said to him: "Why did you raise your voice?" He said to them: "Is it not enough that I did not study the Bible and did not learn, now that I have permission should I not raise my voice and my soul bow down within me?" They said: "The year had not passed, nor two, nor three, before that same man went up from Babylonia to the Land of Israel. They made him the emperor's appointee, and put him in charge of all the castles in the Land of Israel, and gave him a place, and he built himself a city and dwelled there all the days of his life, and he left it for his sons and the sons of his sons until the end of all the generations." (*Seder Eliyahu Rabbah*, 14, Ish-Shalom edition, pp. 65–66)

Children misbehaving at synagogue must certainly have been as common a sight then as it is now. Worshippers objected to it and the exemplum, apart from reflecting a vibrant day-to-day reality, serves as a powerful tool for the prevention of the phenomenon by working in the natural fear of death. The second tale works in reverse, although its action and apparatus are similar. It presents a positive course of action and its reward, and the reward, as stated above, is tangible and tied in with the success of the protagonist and his descendants, just as in the first tale the punishment involves death and the loss of family. The tales also preserved in an exceptional manner the oral style of the story: the formal repetitions of the worshippers' complaints and the father's reply, "All the people responded, 'Hallelujah' to the prayer leader, his son responded with frivolous words. They said to him: See that your son is responding with frivolous words. He said to them: 'What shall I do to him? He is a child, let him play.' On the morrow he behaved in the same manner. All the people responded, 'Hallelujah' to the prayer leader. He responded with frivolous words. They said to him: See how he is responding with frivolous words. He said to them: 'What shall I do? He is a child, let him play.'" Idioms relating to the passage of time on the part of the narrator repeated word for word in both stories, at the stage of the passage from the deed itself to its reward or punishment: "the year had not passed, nor two, nor three"; and the increased use of dialogue, which makes real the oral conversational style. It seems that before us are two tales for which we can reconstruct the performance events: the synagogue during a break from the service, and its purpose: to urge the fathers to curb their children's naughty behavior in the synagogue, and to encourage the worshippers to pray loudly and with sincerity. The threat of death and other punishments, and the promise of wealth and property make up the psychological apparatus that turns the tale into an active social force for change.[63]

There is an important difference between the anonymous exemplum and that whose hero is a familiar and sacred figure. The protagonist in each of the two tales is a simple human figure with whom it is easy to identify, and therefore the apparatus of exemplary persuasion is likely to be more effective. By contrast, the tales of sacred figures, dealing with the same topic, propose an extreme example, idealized to the point where ordinary individuals cannot aspire to it:

> Even if a serpent is coiled to strike at his heel, he should not interrupt . . .
> They said concerning R. Hanina b. Dosa that while he was standing and praying, a poisonous lizard bit him, but he did not interrupt his prayer. They went and found the lizard dead at the entrance to its hole. They said: woe to the person who is bitten by the lizard. Woe to the lizard who bit R. Hanina b. Dosa . . . His students said to him: Master, didn't you feel anything? He said to them: I swear! I was concentrating on my prayer and felt nothing. (PT *Berakhot* 5, 2, J. Neusner's translation pp. 199–200)

Following this passage are further tales of sages who would not interrupt their prayers no matter what, even if the king passed through. These are superlative examples of paragons of virtue that ordinary individuals cannot hope to emulate, but that they can acknowledge and admire from afar. It seems that, in these tales of the marvelous deeds of the greats, there is no explicit demand to conduct oneself according to the story. Rather, they sketch the extreme boundaries of the ideal, while the norm is "stretched" here to its highest limit. In contrast to these, the tales which feature anonymous heroes are more forceful, as they present the consequences to ordinary individuals—for better or worse—of maintaining or breaking the norms within everyone's reach.

This distinction between the anonymous exemplum and that whose protagonist is a known figure is interestingly expressed in the divisions according to topic. In tales of honoring one's parents and restoring a lost possession, for example, the heroes are always known figures, and the tales deal with extraordinary deeds. The group of tales on the subject of parental honor in the Palestinian Talmud (*Pe'ah* 1, 1) begins as follows: "They asked R. Eliezer: How much can [one] honor his father and mother? He said to them: Are you asking me? Go and ask Dama, son of Netinah . . . ." Then follow two tales about the Gentile military commander from Ashkelon. His mother struck his face with her sandal before his men. When she dropped the sandal, he bent down to retrieve it so that she could continue her tirade uninterrupted. The second tale concerns a pearl whose owner would not sell it, although the buyers offered a huge sum for it, as his father was sleeping with his leg propped up on the crate in which it was stored. In the Palestinian Talmud, tractate *Bava Mezia* (2,5) there are five stories of sages who returned lost possessions belonging to non-Jews: a donkey was purchased for R. Simeon ben Shetah, after which a pearl was found hanging from its neck; he returned it to its owner; Rabbi Samuel ben Sosarty who found the queen's jewels and returned them with no expectation of reward.

Although these are realistic tales, anchored in known figures and places, they seem to border on the imaginary; it is difficult to construe them as having any normative demand to behave as their protagonists. The fact that none of them explicitly state the hero's reward also proves that they do not present a behavioral model for the listener to emulate. It may be that the reasons for this are connected to the nature of the topics to which the exempla belong: honoring one's parents, for example, is a basic, unarguable precept, but on the other hand, it is very personal and individual. The tales present the ideal of honoring one's father and mother through the extreme conduct of their exceptional heroes. Within the broad confines delineated by the tales, an individual can select the extent of honor to his parents appropriate to his personal situation and his personality. The same is true with regard to returning lost property: the structure of relations between Jews and non-Jews was so complex it would have been impossible to make demands and threaten punishments against one who behaved in one manner or another vis-à-vis non-Jews. The tales showcase the ideal, but do not demand adherence to the model. Once the listeners know the limits of conduct on this issue, they can choose an appropriate means of behavior, according to the conditions and structure of relations they maintain with the non-Jews with whom they come in contact. And again—it is impossible to promise rewards and threaten punishment in these tales, as the bounds of permissible conduct are very flexible within the norms proposed in the tale.

We have seen that there is a distinction in the talmudic literature itself between the "tale in context," to which belong all the tales included in the Talmud and Midrash, and the exemplary tale, which presents a behavioral model and demands that the listeners follow suit. These stories are united not only in their function, but also in their topics. They tend not to be used to make complex theological or ethical topics comprehensible—their domain is everyday issues. The exemplary system of influence works primarily on the psychological level: the threat of harsh punishments and the promise of tangible reward. But not all the exemplary tales we examined include a demand to behave according to the description, or a presentation of the appropriate reward and punishment. In a large portion of the tales whose heroes are exemplary figures, the conduct described is so extreme and exceptional that the tale cannot threaten punishment against anyone who does not behave similarly. These are actually "praise stories," wherein ideal behavior is so extreme that ordinary individuals are not expected to follow suit.

Some see a connection between the exemplum and another ancient literary form, the *casus*. These are tales cited in legal controversies, meant to constitute proof of judgement in previous instances. It is similar to today's legal "precedent," but in ancient literature, a *casus* was primarily a traditional tale, received as a real event even in courts of law. The rabbinic literature also contains not a few examples of stories used as a legal *casus*. The most famous is the tale known as "Rava's Reed":

> When an oath is administered, he [the man swearing] is admonished: 'Know that we do not adjure you according to your own mind, but according to our mind and the mind of the Court. . . . It excludes such an incident as Rava's cane. . . . (*Nedarim* 25a)

A man who borrowed money from another was brought for judgement before Rava. The lender demanded his money back, but the borrower claimed he had already returned it. Rava said he must swear that he had already returned the money. Before swearing his oath, the borrower fashioned a cane out of a reed in which he stashed the money. When the time came for him to swear his oath, he handed the cane to the lender to hold while he prayed. He swore on the Book of the Law that he had returned his debt in full. The loaner, enraged, broke the cane, and the money inside spilled out onto the floor. Therefore, one must swear on the knowledge of the court, and not on the intent of the swearer. In the version of the tale which appears in *Pesikta Rabbati*, and in *Leviticus Rabbah* (6,3) the subject of the judgement is "Thou shalt not take the name of the Lord thy God in vain," and the sages ask why the word *lashav* (in vain) is emphasized. The explanation given is that, "taking an oath even when affirming something which is true is taking God's name in vain . . . A story told of Bar Telamyon justifies the Rabbis . . . It happened that a man who had deposited a hundred denar . . . " In other words, the story of the money in the staff strengthens the opinion of the sages in a halakhic controversy, and so halakha was determined according to the *casus* related here.[64]

The plot of the story itself, as distinct from the contexts in which it is inserted in the rabbinic literature, is doubtlessly a folktale: it is known in many versions and in many cultures; it is built on the folktale's three-part structure (on the level of the plot as well as the characters operating in it), and the characteristic contrast between good and evil. Neutral authority brings the tale to its resolution in favor of the positive element—according to the standards of the society telling the tale. The tale's topical connection also places it in the category of rich legal folklore prevalent in many cultures. Another example follows:

> Let our master teach us: At the time when it was the practice to prepare a red heifer for the rite of purification, was it permitted for a Jew to purchase one from a heathen? Our Masters of the Mishna taught as follows: Though in the opinion of R. Eliezer a Red Heifer may not be purchased from a heathen, the Sages say that it may be purchased. (*Pesikta Rabbati*, *Piska* 14, Braude's translation, pp. 259–260)

Here R. Phinehas ben Hama ha-Kohen tells a *ma'aseh* ("factual tale"), in which the Jewish community needed a red heifer and learned that the only one available belonged to an idolater. After lengthy haggling, during which the latter was abusive towards the emissaries, and after raising the cow's price from three gold pieces to a thousand, he agrees to sell it to them. They leave to fetch the money, and the cow's owner, enjoying his joke at the expense of the Jews, yokes the beast. Little did he know that there were two signs to ascertain that a heifer had never been yoked: two erect hairs on her neck, and eyes squinting and aimed in the direction of the yoke. When the Jews returned and discovered these signs absent, they laughed at him: "Take your heifer. We can do without her. Fool around with your own mother." When the owner realized he had just lost a thousand gold pieces,

> his mouth which had said "I will have some fun at their expense," proceeded to say "Blessed is He who chose this people." Then he went into his house, strung up a rope and hanged himself. So perish all Thine enemies, O Lord [Judg. 5, 31]. Thus you know that a heifer may be purchased anywhere, either from a Jew or from a heathen. You should not say, "It is written in the Torah that a heifer may be purchased only from a Jew," since it may be purchased from a heathen as well. (ibid.)

If we remove the tale from its halakhic context, it seems that we once again have a typical folktale. Its subject is the friction between Jews and non-Jews, where the latter's strength is in violence and vulgarity, while the Jews' edge comes from their acuity, born of Torah study. The superiority of the Jews' wisdom, in a world where they were ever the underdog, is a latent wish particularly characteristic of the Jewish folktale. The story's folk nature comes through in its style as well, which is an attempt to imitate the haggling, crude speech, and humor of the animal market. Clearly, this tale was not produced to decide a halakhic issue—whether or not it is permissible to purchase a red heifer from a non-Jew—but as a story of the confrontation between Jews and non-Jews. The sages who dealt with the halakhic issue viewed it as unbiased evidence that the custom was to buy a red heifer even from a non-Jew, and used the tale as a *casus* for halakhic decision. Since the bulk of rabbinic literature is halakhic literature of a special nature—it exposes the processes of the creation of the Jewish codex of laws—the extensive use of the folktale is not surprising.[65]

[G] The Historical Legend

Historians have always lamented that only historical legend, not real historiography, survived in the rabbinic literature. Just as the sages were not philosophers, scientists, or poets, nor were they historians. They drew on the accumulated knowledge of all these branches, but their purpose was ever didactic: to use all the means at their disposal to improve the ethical-religious values of their society. Aggadah contains more than a little history, but it is fragmented, stylized, and unreliable from a "factual" perspective. A close examination of the historical issues in rabbinic literature shows that, from a literary perspective, most, if not all, belong to the genre of the historical legend.[66]

The question of the preservation of historical elements in the folk legend and how to identify them has been much discussed in folkloristics, as well as in earlier sections of this book. The starting point in any discussion of historical legend must be its claim to credibility. Legend mobilizes all the artistic means at its disposal (recognizable and identifiable time and place, authentic background and heroes, intensive use of conventional folk beliefs and the collective social memory) to attain the main goal: belief that the events related therein "really happened." Nevertheless, analysis by historians and folklorists alike has shown the kernel of historical truth in most of the legends to be very small indeed, and quite difficult to identify and define. The difficulty stems primarily from the fact that most historical legends concern events for which we have no evidence from any other source, and it is very hard, therefore, to verify the information presented. These problems in the study of history via legend do not belong to our discussion. The pertinent fact as far as we are concerned is that historical legend is the principal component of the historical consciousness of the people. It is a product of that historical consciousness, and preserves the manner in which that consciousness grasps the past; it furthermore mobilizes this past in order to better understand the present and shape hopes for the future.[67]

One of the most famous historical legends in rabbinic literature concerns Raban Johanan ben Zakkai's escape from Jerusalem when the city was besieged by Vespasian's troops. Several versions of this story have survived. Two of them (*Midrash Lamentations Rabbah* 1, 31 and tractate *Gittin* 56a–b) begin with a description of three (four in *Midrash Lamentations Rabbah*) wealthy Jerusalemites, whose fortunes were so great they could have supported all the denizens of the city for twenty-one years. When the sages sought to negotiate with the Romans to save the city, zealots burned the vast stores of grain and timber in order to impel the besieged citizenry to fight more fiercely out of hunger. This opening of the legend of Raban Johanan ben Zakkai is typical of the blend of fact and fiction in the historical legend. The nucleus of the tale is certainly reliable, and is supported by Josephus Flavius: the civil war that raged within the besieged city led to a scarcity of food and equipment and a visible weakening of the fighting strength of the inhabitants. The same is true of the violence and terror instigated by the zealots. But the detailed descriptions of the wealthy men and their legendary fortunes are certainly fictive folkloric elements, added to a fundamentally authentic historical tradition. We shall shortly see how, with the continuation of the legend of Raban Johanan's escape from Jerusalem, this trend is intensified.[68]

The sages were well aware of the lack of credibility of historical legend. One tale displays both approaches: in the story of the destruction of Tur Malka ("the King's Mountain") in tractate *Gittin* (57a), a detailed description is given of the horrific destruction: three hundred thousand Roman soldiers with swords drawn enter Tur Malka and slaughter its citizens for three days and three nights. Tur Malka was so large that while the slaughter was taking place on one side of the mountain, those on the other side danced and made merry in their ignorance. According to this legend, the villages belonging to Tur Malka numbered sixty myriads, each populated by as many inhabitants as individuals who left Egypt. There were three more villages, each with double the number of the Exodus:

> 'Ulla said: I have seen that place, and it would not hold even sixty myriads of reeds. A certain Min said to R. Hanina: You tell a lot of lies [referring to the exaggerated statements about that place]. He replied: Palestine is called "land of the deer" (Jer. 3:19). Just as the skin of the hind cannot hold its flesh [because after the hind is killed the skin shrinks], so the Land of Israel when it is inhabited can find room, but when it is not inhabited it contracts.
> (*Gittin* 57a)

'Ulla and the Zadokite had the temerity to apply the geographical reality to the legendary tale, and reached the conclusion that the storytellers were lying. R. Hanina, on the other hand, expresses the folk approach (or the "organic" approach as it was defined by some scholars) to the historical legend. This approach does not see the truth of the historical legend as "factual," but as social and cultural: historical truth is as flexible as the hind's skin. This truth, claims R. Hanina, has many faces, most important of which is the intrinsic meaning of the legend. The fact that the place itself was much smaller than described in the legend is of no significance. What is essential is that, in the wake of the destruction, the glorious past of the nation was gone, never to return. It does not matter that the past was not all that glorious (in reality, Tur Malka was a small place). According to the collective consciousness of the people, its fate was as the hind's skin: once destroyed and banished, it can no longer reclaim its past glory. This is the truth reflected in the legend of Tur Malka, not whether or not three hundred thousand soldiers really invaded the city.

Indeed, the first part of the Tur Malka legend is more problematic from a historical perspective, yet the disputants hardly refer to it at all:

> Through a cock and a hen Tur Malka was destroyed. How?—It was the custom that when a bride and bridegroom were being escorted a cock and a hen were carried before them, as if to say, Be fruitful and multiply like fowls. One day a band of Roman soldiers passed by and took the animals from them, so the Jews fell on them and beat them. So they went and reported to the Emperor that the Jews were rebelling, and he marched against them. There came against them one Bar Daroma who was able to jump a mile, and slaughtered them. The Emperor took his crown and placed it on the ground, saying: Sovereign of all the world, may it please thee not to deliver me my kingdom into the hands of one man. Bar Daroma was tripped up by his own utterance, as he said: "Hast not thou, O God, cast us off, and thou goest not forth, O God, with our hosts" (Pss. 60:12) [meaning: we do not need your help] . . . He went into a privy and a snake came and he dropped his gut [out] and died. The Emperor said: Since a miracle has been wrought for me, I will let them off this time. So he left them alone and went away. They began to dance about and eat and drink and they lit so many lamps that the impress of a seal could be discerned by their light a mile away from the place. Said the Emperor: Are the Jews making merry over me? And he again invaded them. (*Gittin* 57a)

According to the tale, the custom of the place was to approach the bride and groom with a rooster and a hen, as ritual fertility symbols. Once, during a wedding, Roman soldiers snatched the birds. The Jews assaulted them. The emperor regarded it as sedition, and sent in his troops. Among the Jews lived a man by the name of Bar Daroma, who was so strong he could traverse an entire *mil* (1000 strides) in a single bound. He killed many of the enemy soldiers, until he became so prideful of his strength he said: "Hast thou not rejected us, O God? so that thou goest not forth, O God, with our hosts" (Pss. 60:12). When that same Bar Daroma went to the latrine, a snake came and disemboweled him. Consequently, Tur Malka was delivered into the hands of the Romans. The "factual" veracity of this tale is naturally open to question. Tur Malka was not destroyed because of a rooster and a hen, but as a result of the Bar Kokhba Revolt. Nevertheless, two important historical truths are revealed in this legend: one, that according to the social consciousness, the reason for the Jews' revolt against the Romans was the latter's belittling of Jewish custom and tradition. It is immaterial how strange and "barbaric" these customs seemed to the Romans, their crude insult to this tradition was the direct and immediate cause of the rebellion. The second truth has to do with the tale of Bar Daroma. Again, according to the perception of Jewish historical consciousness (and it does not matter if it is "factually" true), the Jews were brave enough and mighty enough to withstand the Roman legionnaires. Their defeat resulted not from any physical weakness, but from the loss of faith that led to the Almighty's abandonment of them. The snake that killed Bar Daroma often serves as God's messenger in rabbinic legend; Bar Daroma was killed by the Almighty himself, not by any human force. These two penetrating truths of folk historical consciousness are manifested not by means of theoretical or historical deliberations, but through historical legends crystallized over the course of many years. Between the event itself, which perhaps took place during the time of the Great Revolt (or during the Bar Kokhba Revolt) and the written account, at least two to three hundred years passed. During this long period, layers of folkloric motifs and folk narrative episodes settled onto the "factual" historical kernel of truth, shaping the final contours of the legend. This is precisely the meaning of folk legend's "collective creation": each generation and social group which absorbs the tale adds to it and molds it in accordance with its character and worldview. The legend of Tur Malka reflects not the historical facts, but the way the folk historical consciousness crystallized the truth of its past.[69]

The legend of Bar Daroma as a folk legend belongs to the narrative type whose subject is "pride laid low." Bar Daroma himself is fashioned as a somewhat mythological hero with supernatural strength and bravery. When, in his pride, he offends the Almighty, to the point of rebellion, God sends one of his little messengers to kill him in a humiliating way, demonstrating Bar Daroma's insignificance when compared to the Creator.

Within this legend we can see the kernel of another, more important and complex legend, that of Bar Kokhba. The legend of Bar Kokhba reached us in the Palestinian sources (PT *Ta'anit* 1, 8; *Lamentations Rabbah* 2, 4). The great similarity between the two legends again proves the flexibility of folk legend, which replaces heroes to fit the interest and needs of the society which tells the tales: "Through the shaft of a litter Bethar was destroyed" (*Gittin* 57a). The tale as told in here and in *Lamentations Rabbah* opens similarly to the story of Tur Malka: It was customary to chop down the cedar and acacia trees planted upon the birth of (respectively) the groom and bride, and use them to build the wedding canopy. Once, when the daughter of the emperor passed through, the axle of her chariot broke. The Romans chopped down a cedar to make a new axle. The Jews attacked them; the emperor regarded it as a sign of revolt. Then it is told how Bar Kokhba would select his soldiers—by their having a finger severed and uprooting a cedar tree—and how Hadrian's troops could not overpower them. And when they went forth to battle they cried: O God, neither help us nor discourage us! That is what is written: "Hast thou not rejected us, O God?

so that thou goest not forth, O God, with our hosts" (Pss. 60:12). Similarly, Bar Kokhba is depicted as a mythological hero who could wield catapult stones with one hand and kill hordes of enemy soldiers. Hadrian besieged the city of Bethar for three and a half years, and was considering giving it up when a Samaritan realized that the city would hold out only so long as Rabbi Eleazar of Modi'in remained within and continued to entreat the Almighty to protect them. That same Samaritan penetrated the city and whispered a few words in R. Eleazar's ear, so that Bar Kokhba would suspect him of treason. Bar Kokhba kicked the sage, killing him, sealing Bethar's fate of destruction and his own death warrant. When Bar Kokhba's corpse was brought out, a snake was found wrapped around his neck, and Hadrian himself announced that Heaven alone could harm him.[70]

Which foundations of the tale can withstand the test of historical veracity? One detail of note concerns the forceful and cruel personality of Bar Kokhba himself. We know from other sources (such as Bar Kokhba's letters, found in "The Cave of the Letters" in the Judean Desert) that he inspired dread in his subjects and threatened anyone who did not obey his orders with harsh punishments. It is interesting to see how folk consciousness preserved this memory. But Bar Kokhba's characterization is built principally as a real mythological figure: no mere mortal he, rather the "son of a star" (his name's Hebrew meaning). No less than Rabbi Akiva alludes to his divine origin. He puts his men through inhuman tests of cruelty and endurance (motifs taken from international folklore as well). He himself is attributed supernatural strength, and his death can only be brought about by Divine might (another allusion to his divine origin). Such a description comes to prove that Bar Kokhba and his men had the potential to triumph in their revolt, but the sin of pride led them to rebel not only against Hadrian, but against the Almighty himself. The episode concerning R. Eleazar of Modi'in is the main addition to the story as it exists in the Bar Daroma tale. It incorporates the special significance of the tale: the secret of Bar Kokhba's strength had nothing to do with his physical attributes, as he and his soldiers believed. It was, rather, R. Eleazar's presence within the besieged city of Bethar that preserved them. The sage's spiritual fortitude endowed the revolt with its real strength; the moment he was brutally killed, Bar Kokhba lost his ability to withstand the Romans. The import is that it was the spiritual support of the Jewish sages in the revolt that was the secret of Bar Kokhba's might. Once mere brute force was left to defend against brute force, it was defeated forthwith.

In historiographic theory, there is a growing perception that the point of historical writing is the isolation and identification of certain events which took place in the past, and their arrangement in such a way that they will fashion a narrative plot. All historical writing tells a story in such a manner as to crystallize the order of events and the causal context between them according to the historiographer's perception. Therefore there is no point in seeking out the facts as presented in the historical tale. It is rather their narrative organization, as shaped by the historiographer, and the worldview that this organization represents, that are essential. Indeed, the legend of Bar Kokhba, in its different versions, organizes the known events of the revolt according to a narrative structure with clear meaning. This is the familiar structure of the sin and its punishment, where the sin is pride, and downfall its wages. This is the pride which characterizes mythological figures who sinned against heaven (the Greek *hubris*), for which the gods reduced them to dust. The legend of Bar Kokhba was not told by a historian, but created in folk consciousness over many years, and crystallized in a literary format which gives it meaning. The true balance of powers between the rebels and the Roman forces, and the political and economic conditions of the time, were meaningless to Jewish society when this legend was told. As far as this society was concerned, the revolt might have succeeded had it not been for Bar Kokhba's arrogance against the Lord and his sages. It is not possible today to estimate how much was truly known about the Bar Kokhba Revolt in the rabbinic period. Folk consciousness chose certain details from the collective memories of the Revolt, and they were arranged in a meaningful literary structure. This process certainly did not happen all at once, but stretched over the two to three hundred years between the events themselves and their crystallization as oral and written legend.[71]

The tale of Raban Johanan ben Zakkai's escape from Jerusalem is built similarly, by means of organizing the facts preserved in the various traditions into a meaningful plot:

> For three and a half years Vespasian surrounded Jerusalem, having four generals with him: the generals of Arabia, of Africa, of Alexandria, and of Palestine. With regard to the general of Arabia, two sages differ as to his name, one declaring that it was Killus, and the other Pangar. (*Lamentations Rabbah* 1, 31)

At the outset of the tale the narrator dwells on the name of the Arab officer. It is not yet clear at this stage why the focus is on him, while the other officers are ignored. Later, before the city was breached, Vespasian asks his advisors (joined now by Raban Johanan ben Zakkai after his escape from Jerusalem) to solve two parables which he puts to them: A snake has settled into a barrel—what should be done? Raban Johanan answered—bring a snake charmer to mesmerize the snake, and leave the barrel undisturbed. In contrast, Pangar, the Arab officer, answers that the snake should be killed and the barrel (which concealed it) smashed. Similar responses followed the second riddle, in which the snake hid in a tower. Raban Johanan advised removing the snake and leaving the tower standing, while Pangar suggested burning it down altogether. When Raban Johanan ben Zakkai becomes enraged at the destructive counsel of the

Arab officer (as concerns Jerusalem's fate), Pangar claims to be acting in the Jews' best interests, as "so long as the Temple exists, the heathen kingdoms will attack you, but if it is destroyed they will not attack you." Raban Johanan proves to him the hypocrisy of this position, that in his heart he certainly intends the worst for the Jews. The Arab officer appears in the tale a third time with the capture of the city. It was his assignment to capture and destroy the western portion of the Temple Mount. The other officers destroyed the sections assigned them, as commanded by the emperor. He did not, justifying his action by saying it would show future generations Vespasian's greatness. The emperor punished him with a "trial by ordeal": he was to climb to the roof and throw himself off: if he survived, he would live; if he died, so be it. Pangar went up to the roof and threw himself off; "Thus the curse of R. Johanan b. Zakkai alighted upon him," and he died.

The figure of Pangar the Arab accompanies that of Raban Johanan ben Zakkai in the main stages of the plot, and serves the narrative function of the antagonist. The tale begins and ends with this anti-hero, who seems to be the center of the plot. In order to understand the real function of this figure, the figure of the protagonist, Raban Johanan ben Zakkai, must first be defined. With his arrival at the Roman camp, he prophesies Vespasian will one day become emperor. Later, the commander puts him through a series of wisdom tests, and even asks him to heal his aches and advise him in matters of government after he learns he is to be emperor. As emperor, he seeks Raban Johanan ben Zakkai's counsel on matters connected to the Jews, that is, how to deal with the besieged city, and asks him to name his price for service to the crown. All these shape the figure of Raban Johanan ben Zakkai as "the wise Jewish courtier," who rises to a position of prominence at court, has the ruler's ear and advises him on matters of vital importance. The Jewish courtier sees himself as the Jews' representative at court, responsible for their security and well-being. The main political struggles at court involve a Gentile counselor, a hater of Jews who always seeks to bring down the Jewish courtier and, especially, to harm the Jewish society he represents. Earlier we saw a typical model for tales of the Jewish courtier in the stories of the Scroll of Esther and the Second Temple literature. But it seems that the tale of Raban Johanan ben Zakkai has a more important status in the Jewish culture, as it delineates the objective of the Jewish courtier: not revenge, as in the Scroll of Esther, or rebuilding the Temple, as in the Second Temple literature (the tale of Zerubavel), but *the preservation of the spiritual tradition*. Raban Johanan ben Zakkai fought for Yavneh at court, that is, to preserve the spiritual heritage. And again: it does not matter, as the historians claim, that this is not the way it really happened. What is crucial to our understanding of the historical legend is how the historical kernel crystallized over the course of many generations into a meaningful narrative model.[72]

The plot of the story develops in parallel lines around the figure of Raban Johanan, the hero of the society which tells the tale, and that of Pangar, the Arab officer and anti-hero. On one hand, we have the Jewish courtier, whose star rises at court by virtue of his knowledge of the Torah. He has an astonishing ability to interpret and apply biblical verses to the circumstances at hand (by means of biblical verses he knows Vespasian will become emperor, by Torah study he knows what hour of the day or night it is, other verses reveal to him how to cure the emperor). Alongside him, the Gentile courtier acts deceitfully; he is a hypocrite, and wicked. Pangar's death by the hand of God is the legend's promise for the future. The construction of the tale of Raban Johanan ben Zakkai's escape along the lines of the "Jewish courtier" model may not accurately reflect events "as they truly were," but it does unveil the historical significance which folk consciousness, and those who sought to fashion it, sought to give the past by means of the legend.

One important aspect of the legend as social genre is its etiological element. As etiological myth aspires to afford simple, comprehensible explanations of the origin of phenomena central to human reality and nature, so historical legend strives to reveal that which led to pivotal events in the history of the society. This revelation is always achieved through narrative. The tales never serve as theoretical historical, social, or political analyses that contain an explanation of the structure of active forces that brought about historic occurrences. Instead, they are generally tales which endow great historical events with a human and moral dimension, as social consciousness understands them. Etiological explanations such as these use various folktale devices: plot tension, the confrontation between stereotypical heroes who represent extremes, continuous and functional dialogue, the simple, purposeful style, the magical denouement of the narrative conflict. These various devices may have been utilized by the sages to make the stories attractive to many more people than would otherwise be interested. The stories were slowly shaped over the course of years, in the process of the development of folk traditions:

> Rav Judah said in the name of Rav: What is signified by the verse: 'And they oppress a man and his house, even a man and his heritage (*Michah* 2, 2)?' A certain man once conceived a desire for the wife of his master, he being a carpenter's apprentice. Once his master wanted to borrow some money from him. He said to him: Send your wife to me and I will lend her the money. So he sent his wife to him, and she stayed three days with him. He then went to him for her. Where is my wife whom I sent to you? he asked. He replied: I sent her away at once, but I heard that the youngsters played with her on the road. What shall I do? he said. If you listen to my advice, he replied, divorce her. But, he said, she has a large marriage settlement. Said the other: I will lend you money to give her for her Kethubah. So he went and divorced her

and the other went and married her. When the time for payment arrived and he was not able to pay him, he said: Come and work off your debt with me. So they used to sit and eat and drink while he waited on them, and tears used to fall from his eyes and drop into their cups. From that hour the doom was sealed. (*Gittin* 58a)

This tale is an outstanding example of the etiological nature of the historical legend. It starts out from the assumption that the destruction of the Second Temple is an existing fact with which all the audience of listeners live and by which they are influenced. They do not think in abstract historical or political terms; behind the events function people of flesh and blood, whose actions are the reasoned explanation for the tragic events. The legend implies that moral decay was the real reason for the destruction, but it translates such abstract formulations as these into the language of the tale. And the tale, in the manner of legend, uses a narrative model that was extremely widespread in folk literature: a rich man lusts after another man's wife, and is willing to help him financially if he sends the wife to receive the money. From this point, the tale can unfold in one of two directions: in one the wife refuses, but her husband's distress forces her to go to the wealthy man. When the latter demands that she yield to him, she convinces him that it would be a sin, he restrains himself and loans her the money with no strings attached (the tale of Nathan de-Tzutzita). The other possible outcome is the substance of our story, in which the husband, wife, and rich man participate in the transgression. This goes to show that in the historical-etiological explanation as well, the legend mobilizes traditional narrative structures, and uses them to shape the society's historical worldview.[73]

The stories of Tur Malka and Bethar used the same etiological elements: on account of a rooster and hen, Tur Malka was razed, for want of an axle, Bethar fell; the historical legends concerning the destruction of the Temple follow suit: "The destruction of Jerusalem came through a Kamza and Bar Kamza." As in the tale of the carpenter's apprentice, we are shown a web of relations among real people: Bar Kamza's enemy shamed him publicly by ordering him to leave his feast. Bar Kamza sought revenge against the host and the sages who did nothing to stop the humiliation, and informed the emperor that the Jews were plotting rebellion. As proof, he inflicted a blemish on the sacrificial calf sent by the emperor to the Jews. Although some of the sages wanted to offer the calf anyway, so as not to offend the throne, R. Zechariah ben Abkulas objected firmly. When the emperor was told how the Jews rejected his gift, he dispatched his troops. This famous legend is another typical example of the etiological nature of historical legend. It portrays the worst disaster to befall the Jewish people in the ancient world as the result of human emotions: hatred, jealousy, revenge, and religious extremism. Rabbi Johanan is explicit in laying blame:

on account of "the scrupulousness of R. Zecharia b. Abkulas our House has been destroyed, our Temple burnt and we ourselves exiled from our land." The structure of the legend hints at two stages in the process of its formation: first, the tale of Kamza and Bar Kamza is built according to the folktale's typical formula: the invitation to the feast, mistaken identity, dialogue between the host and Bar Kamza, the informing, and the additional dialogue with the emperor. The second stage—including Rabbi Johanan's reaction—almost certainly reflects how the tale was absorbed in the academy. This part, which includes halakhic questions of permission and prohibition, the influence of political reality on religious law and the sages' arguments among themselves, does not enter into the folk tradition, and therefore could not have been part of the folktale.[74]

An example of a similar literary process is found in the legend of Herod (*Bava Batra* 3b–4a): Herod heard a voice telling him to rebel against the regime at once and he would rise to greatness, from slave to king. He killed off all members of the Hasmonean dynasty, except for one young woman whom he wished to marry, but she leapt off the roof and died. He kept her body immersed in honey for seven years, during which time he periodically lay with the corpse. When he realized the sages would not support his sovereignty, as he was not of the Davidic dynasty, he put them to death too, leaving only Bava ben-Buta alive, though he blinded him. Herod, incognito, tried to get the blind sage to curse him—to prove rabbinic hatred of him—but Bava ben-Buta would not be coerced. Herod, realizing how cautious the sages were, regretted their murder and sought means of redress. Bava ben-Buta advises him to rebuild the Temple, which he does despite Roman objections.

This legend is a typical mixture of three elements: a historical grain of truth (shored up by other sources: Josephus, Roman historians), in Herod's persecution of the Hasmoneans, his marriage to a daughter of that family and her suicide, and his massive renovations on the Temple Mount. The second component is the folk narrative motifs, such as the immersion of corpses in honey, necrophilia, and the king who conceals his identity from the blind man. The third element at work in this legend is connected with the sages' worldview: the sages were always the first to come to harm, as they were the people's representatives. But the sages were extremely cautious in their political considerations, never doing anything that might endanger the safety of the people (to wit: Bava ben-Buta's discretion in not cursing Herod). The principal motif in this version of the tale is that which claims that the sages' deaths and Bava ben-Buta's discretion were the direct motivation for the rebuilding of the Temple by Herod. There is no doubt that various legends were told among the people concerning Herod and the building of the Temple (such as the one which told how rain did not fall during daylight all the while construction was underway—*Ta'anit* 23a). These legends, like all historical legend, preserved the historical details that had meaning to the society which told them. Folk motifs were added and they were emplotted in such a way as to create a meaningful narrative model. When these traditions were brought to the academy, whether to set them down in writing or discuss them for whatever reason, they underwent further changes in order to express the sages' perception of the events and their significance. The texts as they appear in the rabbinic literature—the aggadic tales surrounding Herod, Kamza, and Bar Kamza, among others—underwent full literary reworking. A careful analysis can, nonetheless, isolate the three layers which compose them—the history, the folk tradition, and the thought of the sages—and their complex interrelationship.[75]

Two traumatic national events, the destruction of the Temple and the Bar Kokhba Revolt, left indelible traces on the historical legend of the rabbinic period. The tremendous significance of these two events to the Jewish society that followed them is borne out not only by their great influence on the worlds of art and of rabbinic thought, but also and in particular by their dramatic force in the folk legend of the period. The yardstick by which we measure the depth of a historic event's influence on society is not its expression in the thought of some author or sage. The crux is whether or not folk legends were created to give the event significance in the long run. These two events certainly pass this test. The power of their influence on folk consciousness has been discussed above. There is yet another aspect to the legends created around these events: the tales of suffering and martyrology. While the etiologic legends discussed deal with the ethical aspects which preceded the destructions, the tales of suffering and martyrdom cover their tragic human consequences.

The first tales of martyrdom known to us belong to the Second Temple Period. They are the tales of Eleazar and the mother and her seven sons in the *Books of the Maccabees* II and IV. The latter passed into the rabbinic period, as was discussed above (in section D of this chapter). In tales of this sort we must distinguish clearly between descriptions of the suffering that followed the military defeats and the original tales of martyrology. The groupings of tales concentrated in *Gittin* 57b–58b and *Midrash Lamentations Rabbah* portion 1, are collections of stories of the suffering endured by individual members of the Jewish people in the wake of the disasters. They constitute extreme examples of the great tragedy: the four hundred boys and girls abducted to indulge their captor's depraved purposes, who drowned themselves; the captured son and daughter of Ishmael (or Zadok) the Priest who, when ordered to mate with each other, died of sorrow; Zofnat bat Peniel the High Priest, whose captor beat her through the night and in the end sold her like an animal at market; Doeg ben Joseph whose mother measured his weight in gold and ultimately, in the time of the siege, slaughtered and ate him; the daughter of Nakdimon ben Gurion, the richest man in Jerusalem, who picked barley from horse manure in Acre. These tales are constructed according to the model of "the fall from high to low": the bigger they are, the harder they fall, and the deeper their degradation. Each of these figures enjoyed a high social position before the destruction; they were the richest people in Jerusalem, the children of the High Priest, and so on. The destruction precipitated their fate: humiliating death, abasement, abject poverty. These legends seek to make real, through the fate of individuals, the true meaning of the destruction: the pain was not merely general, but a personal tragedy for each and every individual. These tales establish a special category of folktale; folk fiction in general likes to set up opposing, extreme situations in which, in general, the lowly hero—the youngest of the brothers, the swineherd, the farmer's daughter—suddenly rises to the top of the social ladder, and becomes royal or extremely wealthy. The model of the fall generally treats an anti-hero, a wicked individual (for example, the Gentile who sold all his property and purchased the pearl found by Joseph-who-honors-Sabbaths.

The group of tales concerning the destruction proposes a reverse model, in which the heroes themselves are the injured, the "fall" is final, and there is no recovery. It seems they should not be viewed as folktales in the simplest sense, as they only fit a specific structure and context: events commemorating the destruction. The concentration of these tales in *Midrash Lamentations Rabbah*, for instance, shows the fixed ritual format—the reading of the Scroll of Lamentations each year on the Ninth of Av and the customs of mourning—in which such tales could be inserted. When on such an occasion they are told (or read from the Midrash), they are considered folktales not by virtue of the typical construction of folk literature (to which, as stated, they do not conform), but on account of the fixed context of "the day of the destruction" in which they are referred to and to which they belong.

The second category of tales we mentioned was that of original martyrdom stories. These establish a literary category whose structure and consistent nature are unique to the Jewish and Christian world. In order for the tale to be a martyrological one in the original sense of the term, there must be an act of choice in the related event: not every killing or slaughter of Jews is a tale of martyrdom. The story generally takes the form of a sort of legal discussion: the accused stands before a representative of the regime, before an audience, and the regime's representative tries to persuade him to give up or deny his faith. The martyr publicly proclaims the truth of his faith, withstands cruel tortures but does not yield, and ultimately is executed. Many tales of martyrdom are accompanied by a supernatural event attendant on the saint's death: his corpse disappears, a voice proclaims his holiness, his body remains unharmed by torture, and so on. Such supernatural motifs which conclude the martyrological tale give evidence of Divine confirmation of the event, and provide a parallel, despite the hero's death, of the happy ending which is one of the basic rules of the folktale. From this perspective, martyrological tales, in spite of their character and special position as religious literature, are folktales in every sense.

In old Christian literature, martyrological tales bear no connection to specific historical events, and therefore should not be seen as historical legends but as legends of saints. In contrast, the Jewish martyrological tales are always connected to given historical events: the stories of Eleazar and the mother and her seven sons in the *Books of the Maccabees* are tied in with the edicts of Antiochus and the Maccabean Revolt; the tale of Miriam, daughter of Boetius, and her seven sons in rabbinic literature is connected to the Great Revolt and the destruction of the Temple; and the tales of The Ten Martyrs (which do not appear contiguously in the rabbinic literature) have to do with the decrees following the Bar Kokhba Revolt. It seems that while the martyrological tales of Christianity come to reinforce the truth of the religion in the eyes of its followers, serving a clear missionary function, the Jewish martyrological tales in the rabbinic period are historical, rather than theological, tales. The tale of the mother and her sons as told by the sages is almost always inserted among other stories relating to the destruction, and not necessarily in theological or didactic contexts. It may perhaps be concluded from this that it does not come to strengthen Jewish faith, an apparently unnecessary goal in this period, but to make tangible the extent of the tragedy brought on by the destruction. The tales of the Ten Martyrs—Rabbi Akiva, Rabbi Hananiah ben Teradyon, Rabbi Judah ben Bava, and their colleagues—come to show that with the close of the hostilities of the Bar Kokhba Revolt, the sages' war for the preservation of the embers of the Torah began. They are not killed because they are Jews (as Christians are killed because of their faith in the Christian tales, for instance), but because they persist in teaching the Torah en masse so as to establish the next generation of religiously observant Jews. From this perspective as well, the martyr tales of the rabbinic period should be seen as historical legends, as they depict how, by means of the sages' self-sacrifice, the nation succeeded in maintaining its integrity even after the horrific devastation. And again: this is spiritual, not "factual," historiography. These legends carry the explanation and reasoning for the historical phenomena so central to the lives of the society that told them. The significance of this "historicity" is not that the legends report in any manner on events that took place, but that they reflect the perception of Jewish society in the rabbinic period of the tragic events of the past and their meaning for their lives in the present.[76]

[H] Tales of Magic and Demonology

In principle, the sages opposed demonological beliefs and practices. This hardly comes as a surprise, as the Bible banned witches and magicians, as well as any appeals to them for advice or assistance. Judaism's development, since Old Testament times, toward a purer and firmer monotheism was supposed to completely rid the people of beliefs in the existence of those dark powers not directly controlled by the Almighty. Still, the sages' attitude towards the demonic world was, if not fully accepting, ambivalent at the very least. That broad sectors of society believed in demons and spirits, in witches and other supernatural phenomena, is neither suspect nor surprising. What is astonishing, perhaps, is that the sages included so many tales of demons, spirits, and demonic folk beliefs in the Talmud and Midrash. Moreover, many sages actually figure in these tales as protagonists or as lesser figures who perform various sorts of magic practices. Research into the sages' thought has focused on topics connected to magic in the rabbinic period, mainly on the legal approach to magical beliefs, the question of the sages' belief in supernatural phenomena described in the talmudic literature, and the connection between these beliefs and magic in other cultures of the period, particularly Greek and Christian. The following discussion aims to distinguish between the beliefs and magic practices scattered in the rabbinic literature and magic tales. The connection between them is clear and understandable, although the tales always have the additional complex artistic aspect which sets them apart from direct reports of magical beliefs, until now the primary focus.

Magic tales in rabbinic aggadah are unique in form and content. Their profusion and diversity constitute some of the earliest, most important evidence of this genre in folklore. These tales significantly enhance our understanding of how Jews of the period perceived magic. The sages define the many magic beliefs scattered in the rabbinic literature as pagan rites; their attitude towards them is always critical and disapproving. Here again we have the familiar dichotomy between "the folk" who, believing in the world of magic and demonology, act accordingly, and the sages who report, rationally analyze, and criticize these beliefs. In the tales, however, magic exploits feature the sages themselves as heroes who profess unqualified belief in the power of magic. One weakness of the research into this question seems to be the lack of a basic distinction between magic beliefs and the tales as two different manifestations of a single phenomenon. They should be treated with tools appropriate to their nature and societal function.[77]

The sages share the fundamental notions of magic and demons evinced by folk beliefs and tales of magic:

> It has been taught: Abba Benjamin says, If the eye had the power to see them, no creature could endure the demons. Abbaye says: They are more numerous than we are and they surround us like the ridge round a field. R. Huna says: Every one among us has a thousand on his left hand and ten thousand on his right hand. Rava says: The crushing in the Kallah [the as-

semblies of Babylonian students] lectures comes from them. Fatigue in the knees comes from them. The wearing out of the clothes of the scholars is due to their rubbing against them. The bruising of the feet comes from them. (*Berakhot*, 6a)

This was how reality was perceived at the time: beyond the visible lies the occult—teeming with threatening demonic creatures. They swarm about mere mortals, just waiting for one to stumble so that they can attack. As we can well see from the rabbis' statements above, the demonological tale, in one respect, serves the etiological function—a kind of "pseudo-science," a methodological explanation of some kinds of social calamities. The solution to all those familiar little mysteries, such as what causes the crushing of crowds, fatigue in the knees, or frayed clothing, is in the "world full of demons" which surrounds us. Abbaye, Rav Huna, and Rabbah, some of the most quoted personalities in rabbinic literature, delivered these statements concerning these hordes of menacing demons. If they were not made in a humorous vein, mocking fools who believe anything, they testify to the depth of penetration of such beliefs even among the educated elite. Similarly, Greek and Roman sources attest to members of the educated class espousing magic beliefs. They may ridicule the "fools" who believe in them, yet their statements betray a deep belief in the existence of and danger presented by demons, spirits, and sorcerers. Such an ambivalent attitude of the educated toward the world of magic is hence the legacy of all Late Antiquity.

In most of the period's magic tales, demons constitute a menace to the human world, and can be countered only with defined magical means and actions. Proof of the currency of this notion can be found in the impressive array of such measures (incantations, amulets, and spells) whose descriptions are scattered throughout the rabbinic literature. The fuller expression of demonic beliefs of the period survived in them, and not necessarily in the magic tales, whose number is relatively small. In any case, the importance of the tales is that they reflect, in a masterful and unbiased manner, the beliefs, practices, and modes of thought that could not have been openly expressed in any other format.[78]

A complex text with typical magic aspects appears in tractate *Pesahim* (111a–b): Therein is cited a collection of various magic beliefs having to do with trees: "R. Isaac said: What is meant by the verse, Yea, though I walk through the valley of the shadow of death, I will fear not evil, for Thou art with me (Pss. 23:4)? This refers to him who sleeps in the shadow of a single palm-tree or in the shadow of the moon." After that five specific trees are listed. According to folk belief, harmful spirits beset anyone who rests in their shade. The most fearsome locale is described below:

[The demons] of sorb-bushes are [called] Shide. A sorb-bush which is near a town has not less than sixty Shide [demons, haunting it]. How does this matter? In respect of writing an amulet. A certain town-officer went and stood by a sorb-bush near a town, whereupon he was set upon by sixty demons and his life was in danger. He then went to a scholar who did not know that it was a sorb-bush haunted by sixty demons, and so he wrote a one-demon amulet for it. Then he heard how they suspended a hinga [musical instrument] on it [the tree] and sing thus: "The man's turban is like a scholar's, [yet] we have examined the man [and find] that he does not know 'Blessed art Thou' [ridiculing his pretensions to scholarship]." Then a certain scholar came who knew that it was a sorb-tree of sixty demons and wrote a sixty-demon amulet for it. Then he heard them saying: Clear away your vessels from here.

The tale's structure is distinctly exemplary: it elucidates the efficacy of the rule obligating the sage to know the number and type of harmful spirits in every such perilous location, so that he can thwart them. However, the tale's target audience is not limited to sages or writers of amulets; it aims to reach the broader public, whom it cautions to avoid the shade of such dangerous trees. Shade, as the vehicle of the magic or demonical inspiration, is a familiar motif in rabbinic literature and international folklore. This tale takes the premise a step further: Demonic strength and human weakness have an ebb and flow governed by time and place; demons lie in wait for people to stumble, then they attack. A widely accepted form of demonic attack in folk belief is possession. Beliefs in spirits (dybbuk) which possess or attack an individual developed from this notion. The visible effect on an individual of this form of demonic attack is strange behavior or signs of illness, generally unusual mental disturbances. The explanation for it (as we have seen in the "pseudo-scientific" phenomenon) is that demons attacked because the individual was not properly warned.[79]

No less important is how the sages referred to the 'scholar.' The intention is certainly to a folk healer or witch-doctor, expert in the writing of amulets. The Talmud does not distinguish here between this type of folk healer and Torah scholars. Instead it ridicules, through the demons' statements, the scholar who is inexpert in the secrets of demonology! As in conventional medicine, the correct "prescription" for a patient depends on a precise diagnosis of the cause and origin of the disease: whosoever does not recognize the malady in all its details cannot cure a poor soul afflicted by demons. It is important to note that the Talmudic tale treats the demonic world, and the means of fighting it, with utmost seriousness and in a "scientific" manner.

Other encounters between humans and demons and harmful spirits take place in the street, or on a journey. Thus Rabbi Hanina ben Dosa and Abbaye, walking at night, chance to meet a she-demon named Agrat bat Mahlath, who is accompanied by her retinue of destructive angels. The sages command her to keep out of populated areas, and she submits, except for Wednesday and Sabbath nights, when she is permitted (*Pesahim* 112b). These two tales concerning Hanina ben Dosa and Abbaye can be viewed, as the previous story, either as a demonological tale or as an exemplum. On the one hand, this is a typical tale of demons. It describes the demons "Igrath the daughter of Mahalath, she and 180,000 destroying angels go forth, and each has permission to wreak destruction independently." It also describes their habits, particularly the days on which they lurk about, when it is hazardous to venture outside. Essentially, it describes a demonic phenomenon and prescribes how to protect oneself from it. On the other hand, the tale emphasizes that Hanina ben Dosa and Abbaye were not harmed by the demons: "On one occasion she met R. Hanina b. Dosa [and] said to him, 'Had they not made an announcement concerning you in Heaven, "Take heed of Hanina and his learning," I would have put you in danger. . . . On another occasion she met Abbaye. Said she to him: 'Had they not made an announcement about you in Heaven, "Take heed of Nahmani and his learning," I would have put you in danger.'" In other words, the Torah is the true shield against injury by demons. Knowing the habits of the demons, the times when one must be wary of them, and the like are limited, "technical" means of grappling with them. To be a Torah scholar, however, is to guarantee one's safety in this demon-infested world. Thus, among the sages, the demonological tale became an exemplum whose objective was to reinforce the practical value of Torah study. The following text serves to illustrate the same. It is one of several depictions in the rabbinic literature of another demon who endangers walkers, Ketev Meriri:

> Our Rabbis explain that Ketev is a demon. And why is he called Ketev? R. Abba, son of Kahana, said: Because he breaks into the daily studies from the beginning of four hours of the day to the end of nine. R. Levi said: Because he robs pupils of their noonday lessons from the end of four hours to the beginning of nine hours. He holds sway neither in the shade nor in the sun but between the shade and the sun. His head is like that of a calf and a horn grows out from the center of his forehead, and he rolls like a pitcher. R. Huna in the name of R. Joseph said: Ketev Meriri is in form covered with scales, hairy all over, and full of eyes. And, said R. Simeon b. Lakish, he has one eye set in his heart, and anyone who sees him can never survive, whether it be man or beast. Anyone who sees him drops dead. Meriri holds sway during the period between the seventeenth of Tammuz and the ninth of Av. Hezekiah saw him and dropped down on his face and died. R. Pinehas the priest said: It is related that one saw him and was stricken with epilepsy.

They reported that Judah b. Samuel saw him and did not drop down. Nevertheless, it is reported that he died. (*Numbers Rabbah* 12, 3)

This remarkable text includes an interesting assortment of demonological attributes, edifying in several respects with regard to the demonic tale in the rabbinic period. We begin with the many messengers who transmit the folk tradition. The most eminent sages participate here in relaying information on the form and demonic character of the "Ketev Meriri." Each messenger adds a folk motif or detail, which taken together create a fearsome demonic figure. Secondly, the descriptions of the demon are not unique, rather they were borrowed from general folklore's treasury of motifs: his head typifies the familiar motif of the unicorn, which is a horse or a bull (or even a calf) from whose forehead protrudes a single horn. The demon's body, overlaid with "scales, hairy all over, and full of eyes," is the motif of the many-eyed dragon whose body is covered with impenetrable scales, making it invincible against weapons. The tradition recounted by Resh Lakish, about the single eye fixed in his heart, is another motif, that of the Cyclops, grafted onto the folk belief in the so-called "evil eye" possessed by some individuals and creatures. A mere glance is enough to kill. All these show the firm bond between the Jewish demonological world and general folklore of the period.[80]

Also significant is that, after the description of the Ketev Meriri and how he endangers anyone who encounters him, two illustrations are offered. One concerns Hezekiah, who was killed, the second, told by R. Phinehas ha-Kohen and other bearers of tradition, deals with actual reality. These tales offer no suggestions as to how one might avoid harm at the hands of the demon, except perhaps the definition of the period between the seventeenth of Tamuz and the ninth of Av as the most perilous. The following tale belongs to the same grouping of traditions, and puts forward a means of defense against the demon:

> Abbaye was walking along, with R. Papa on his right and R. Huna, son of R. Joshua, on his left. Seeing a Ketev Meriri approaching him on the left, he transferred R. Papa to his left and R. Huna, son of R. Joshua, to his right. Said R. Papa to him: Am I different that you were not afraid on my behalf? "The time is in your favor," replied he. (*Pesahim* 111b)

This tale is indeed more developed than the previous one, in that it details the names of its heroes and the conversation between them, yet it sets up the same narrative situation: sages walking in the street encounter Ketev Meriri, whose glance is lethal. The principal difference is in that here the hero, Abbaye, knows how to defend himself: he puts up a barrier between himself and the demon. While the conventional barrier in folk belief is an amulet or mirror (the protagonist reflects the "evil eye" back at its owner with the aid of the mirror, killing him), Abbaye opts for an ethical solution: he puts Rav Papa between himself and the demon. Rav Papa's numerous merits are the reason that "the time is in your favor." This is yet another text which reflects the belief that the Torah is the surest defense against demonic malevolence. Indeed, this outlook is made plain by the sages:

> What is the exposition of the text: "He will cover thee with His pinions [evrato]" (Pss. 91:4)? It implies that He will protect you for the sake of the Torah which was given with the right hand of the Holy One, blessed be He . . . If one comes to take refuge beneath His wings the Holy One, blessed be He, will be unto him "A shield and a buckler" (ibid.) of truth. . . . R. Simeon b. Lakish explained: The Holy One, blessed be He, says: "I shall forge a weapon for all who trade in the truth of the Torah." R. Simeon b. Yohai said: The truth of the Torah is the weapon of him who possesses it . . . "Thou shalt not be afraid of the terror by night" (Pss. 91:5), namely of Igrath, daughter of Mahlat [the demoness] and her chariot, and of any of the demons who hold sway at night. (*Numbers Rabbah* 12, 3)

This view, which was styled by prominent sages, in addition to the heroes of the tales quoted above, who belong to the same esteemed circle, show us that it almost certainly originated within the educated culture of the period, as opposed to the common people. Here we witness a phenomenon well recognized in other cultures as well: the representatives of the religious establishment employ society's basic fears (death, the world of demons, hunger, disease, and so on) to impart their perceptions to the masses. A most effective means to this end is to accept exemplary tales as true reports of actual events, magnifying their influence. It can be surmised that the didactic-exemplary foundations of these stories did not appear in the versions told among the broad strata of the people. The tales originally expressed society's deeply ingrained dread of the various sorts of demons and harmful spirits, against whom human beings can defend themselves, as we know from other cultures, by avoiding any encounter with them and with the use of defensive magic measures such as amulets and chants. The sages used these tales to disseminate their view of the centrality of the Torah—which can protect the people against one of the most fundamental existential fears—and to concomitantly entrench their own position in society.

Agrat bat Mahlath and Ketev Meriri are demons active in populated areas. One might encounter them while out walking one's hometown streets during the day (Ketev Meriri) or night (Agrat bat Mahlath). The beliefs and tales concerning them are not merely traditional tales anchored in the distant past. On the contrary, they are relevant to daily urban life in the rabbinic period in Palestine and Babylonia. Demons and harmful spirits are not confined to remote forests and deserts. They are a part of everyday reality with which each individual must come to terms:

Abbaye also said, at first I thought the reason why one does not sit under a drain pipe was that there was waste water there, but my Master has told me, it is because demons are to be found there. Certain carriers were once carrying a barrel of wine. Wishing to take a rest they put it down under a drain pipe, wherupon the barrel burst, so they came to Mar, son of R. Ashi. He brought forth trumpets and exorcised the demon who now stood before him. Said he to the devil, "Why did you do such a thing?" He replied, "What else could I do, seeing that they put it down on my ear?" The other [Mar, son of R. Ashi] retorted, "What business had you in a public place? It is you that are in the wrong, you must therefore pay for the damage." Said the devil, "Will the Master give me a time wherein to pay?" A date was fixed. When the day arrived he defaulted. He came to court and [Mar b. R. Ashi] said to him, "Why did you not keep your time?" He replied, "We have no right to take away anything that is tied up, sealed, measured, or counted; but only if we find something that has been abandoned." (*Hullin* 105b)

This tale and others like it are proof of the development of "urban legends" in the rabbinic period. In contrast to romantic cultural notions, in recent generations the study of folklore has increasingly emphasized the development of folk traditions within large urban population centers: in neighborhoods, city centers, the workplace, and marketplace, and not only in remote agricultural settlements, where ethnographers tended to "go out and collect" folklore. These legends revolve around the simplest day-to-day activities—walking in the street, work, shopping, prayer, eating, and the like. The supernatural element penetrates this "trivial" reality, although on the surface it seems inappropriate as a venue for the creation of a tale as it is so ordinary. This alien element shakes it up, demonstrating that behind the mundane routine of everyday life lurk occult powers with the propensity to catapult that routine into chaos. Such tales are credible to the society which tells them, as they integrate well into the practical reality so familiar to each of the listeners: they take place in the listeners' own environment. When a supernatural element invades this reality, it too instantly becomes a part of it, and the listeners accept it as they did other details of the story. The psychological effect created by a single supernatural element appearing amidst the weave of the realistic tale is always stronger than if that same element were to appear in a magical fairytale, for instance. Fairytales are set in an imaginary time and place and make no claim of authenticity. The multitude of supernatural motifs is not disconcerting and is perceived as part of the artistic convention of the genre. On the other hand, the invasion of the supernatural element into the urban tale seems to creep into our real lives as well, causing a psychological jolt by threatening our daily reality.[81]

The text is laid out as a legal tale: it presents the events themselves; the suit before the court; the summons of the accused and how the court forces him to appear by virtue of its power of excommunication. Then there is the litigation itself, the verdict and its arguments, and, ultimately, the execution of the sentence. The commonplace activity described in the tale—of porters carrying a cask of wine and sitting down to rest in the shade of a house—belongs to the same urban reality of work, street life, and everyday routine. Even the bursting of the cask does not, on the surface, seem particularly unusual. At the same time, it is clear to the porters, and to the judge to whom they turned, that a cask does not just burst unless one of the hidden forces surrounding humanity has a hand in it. The claim against the demon is that he strayed beyond his realm. Yet the statements preceding the tale warn against sitting beneath rain gutters, as doing so is just asking for trouble. The intent appears to be that while demons have their prescribed domains, they can be anywhere—primarily certain predictable hot spots, where one should be doubly wary.

Like most demon tales, this one appears in an exemplary context. Its purpose is not to entertain but to prove a principal argument, and warn against undesirable behavior. Abbaye is of the opinion that one should not leave belongings or sit beneath rain gutters because of the refuse that might be tossed from the upper floors or from the roof. But the tale of Mar (son of Rav Ashi) convinces him that the rational explanation is not the true one. In the demon's words of explanation at the story's end we find yet another admonition: one should not leave property in a public place if it is not clearly marked in some way as belonging to somebody. Such an unmarked item falls prey to the demons. This demon tale is thus intended to substantiate two demands regarding desirable behavior in daily life. Additionally, it illustrates the demons' subservience to the court. The demon is under the spell of the Rabbinic court and accepts the court's verdict. These beliefs mitigate the anxiety of individuals living in the period regarding the menacing spirit world. If demons, too, are subject to the order of the Jewish court and established rules of behavior, then the demonic world is not entirely irrational, and there are ways to protect oneself from its depredations.

One might expect to be invulnerable to demons in the synagogue or academy, at whose doors one was supposed to leave behind the material concerns of daily life. Once inside, one was presumably closer to the Almighty than anywhere else. The academy was by definition a shield against the demons. Nonetheless, at least one important text has survived among the tales of the period featuring demons in the academy:

> . . . R. Jacob, son of R. Aha b. Jacob, was once sent by his father [to study] under Abbaye. On his return he [his father] saw that his learning was dull. "I am better than you," said he to him; "do you [now] remain here, so that I

can go." Abbaye heard that he was coming. Now, a certain demon haunted Abbaye's schoolhouse, so that when [only] two entered, even by day, they were injured. He [Abbaye] ordered, "Let no man afford him hospitality; perhaps a miracle will happen [in his merit]." So he [R. Aha] entered and spent the night in that schoolhouse, during which it [the demon] appeared to him in the guise of a seven-headed dragon. Every time he [R. Aha] fell on his knees [in prayer] one head fell off. The next day he reproached them: "Had not a miracle occurred, you would have endangered my life." (*Kiddushin* 29b)

This is one of the fiercest demon tales extant in rabbinic literature. It belongs to the category of rescue tales in which a dragon takes over a place and harms its inhabitants. A mythic hero (or Christian saint) who happens to come on the scene, or who is summoned, fights it, cuts off all seven heads, and saves the people.[82]

The Talmudic tale had undergone a process of Judaization: R. Aha Ben Jacob came to the academy to study Torah; he does not vanquish his dragon with a sword or with any overtly magical means, but prays sincerely and bows as was his custom during the prayer (in some Christian versions of the legend of Saint George, the hero does not strike the dragon with his sword but brandishes the cross at him). He is not a figure of a warrior or exorcist who knowingly volunteers to fight the dragon, but is manipulated to behave in such a way by Abbaye, and he acts to save himself. The site of the miracle is strikingly different in the Jewish version as well. In the Christian legends of saints, the site of the event is the shore of a lake or a great forest, near a capital, and so on. In the Jewish tale, the action happens in the most sacred of places, where a Jew is closest to his God. The narrative milieu in the Christian versions is open nature, and therefore the saint acts as a mythological hero for whom the forces of nature are the backdrop. The milieu of the Jewish tale is a room or the academy—a space enclosed by four walls in which the hero acts as a scholar, not as a mythological hero. Moreover, the triumph of the Christian saint takes place in full view of the residents of the town, a vast audience so taken by his great valor that they agree to convert to Christianity afterwards. Not so in the Jewish tale, wherein victory over the dragon takes place in absolute isolation. The internalizing dimension of the Jewish tale, as opposed to the externalization in the Christian one, is not unique to this story, and is repeated in other examples as well. Hence it is clear that before us lies a Jewish demon tale which underwent an extreme process of Judaization regarding location, the heroes and their motives, and the magic practice itself. Furthermore, the story of R. Aha Ben Jacob is replete with motifs connected to the study of the Torah: his son is sent to study the Law with Abbaye, the father tests the son upon his return, the father himself goes off to study the Torah, the dialogues between Abbaye and his colleagues take place in his academy, R. Aha Ben Jacob stays in the same academy, he uses prayer to save himself from the dragon. This density of motifs of the realm of Torah study and divine worship indicates both the process of the story's transformation from a distinctly demonological text to an ethical tale, as aforementioned, and its intended function—an example of the power of the Torah and of prayer—in Jewish society.[83]

In the tales we have dealt with thus far, demons are negative forces, encounters with whom are fearsome and perilous. This is not, however, always the case. There are stories wherein the demons are not unequivocally malevolent: after some sort of pressure is exerted upon them, they become cooperative and even emulate human behavior. In the tale of the porters and the broken cask, the demon is a menace only until Mar Bar Rav Ashi subjugates him by blowing the *shofar*. The demon then obeys the court's order, tells how his ear aches when a cask is set down on it, asks for a deferral of his fine and explains why he failed to appear at the appointed hour. In the famous tale of Solomon and Ashmedai (*Gittin* 68a–b), the latter resists until the moment Benaiah produces Solomon's ring, engraved with the Ineffable Name. Thereafter he accompanies Benaiah, answers his questions, demonstrates a well-developed sense of humor, advises the king how to attain the *shamir*, and even pursues the King's wives as might any man. There is also "*Joseph Shiddah*" ("Joseph the Demon"), a favorable character who helps people in various matters, who is mentioned in the rabbinic literature.[84]

Another amiable demon serves a similar function: Bar Themalyon. When once the regime issued decrees against the Jewish people, Rabbi Simeon bar Yohai and Rabbi Eleazar, son of Yose, were dispatched to the Roman emperor in a bid to have the decrees rescinded. On the way, they chanced to meet the demon Bar Themalyon coming toward them. He asked to come along and assist them in their mission. He went on ahead, entered the body of the princess—and she went mad. The demon screamed from her mouth that R. Simeon bar Yohai must be brought. When in due course he arrived, he proclaimed "Bar Themalyon, get out! Bar Themalyon, get out!" and the demon promptly vacated his host. As a reward, the emperor permitted the rabbis to enter his treasury and take what they wished. They entered, found the writs of the decrees, and tore them up (*Me'ilah* 17a).

This tale belongs to the tale type "miraculous rescue of the Jewish community," one of the most prevalent in the stories of the Jewish people. It opens with a rupture of the balance which existed between the Jews and the Roman overlord—the issuing of the decrees. The hero—holy man, miracle worker, or spiritual leader—is sent to the ruler in search of salvation. There he uses his magic power to cure the emperor or a member of his family. In return, he is rewarded with treasure, a cancellation of the decrees, and a return home in great honor. This narrative framework is well-known and widely scattered through both Jewish and Christian folk literature. The motif of the ploy makes the tale of Bar Themalyon unique: The emperor's daughter is not truly ill, her ravings are merely the result of our friendly demon invading her body as part of a ruse he planned with the sages. This tale is something of a parody on the dybbuk and possession tales already in circulation (especially among the young Christian culture, as evinced in the New Testament). The exorcism itself is conducted in a humorous vein, with R. Simeon bar Yohai and his contingent knowing full well that the princess is not ill at all. He uses the accepted formula for chasing out spirits: "[demon's name] Out!" mimicking the ritual then widely used by the Christian saints to banish spirits.[85]

Sometimes the harmful spirits themselves need the assistance of mankind. Such is the tale (in *Tanhuma*, Buber edition, *Kedoshim* 9, 1; *Lamentations Rabbah* 24, 3) of a spirit of a spring who revealed himself to R. Abba Jose of Zaythor. He told him he had been living in the spring for several years, never harming anyone. Now he was trying to fight off an evil spirit who intended to take his place and harm anyone who came to draw water. He offered specific instructions for helping him: "Go and warn the townspeople and say to them: Whoever has a hoe, whoever has a shovel, and whoever has a spade should all come out here tomorrow at the break of day and watch the surface of the water, and when they notice a disturbance of the water let them strike the irons together and cry: 'Ours wins!' And let them not go away from this place until such time as they notice a clot of blood on the surface of the water." They did so, banishing the evil spirit. In this tale, the spirit or demon of the well is perceived as part of the community; he and the human inhabitants were dependent on each other. The pact between humans and the "good" demons is likely to aid humans in their struggle against the malevolent world of the demons. This positive aspect of the demonic world crops up in other tales as well, in which the demons and spirits serve as messengers to test the hero by virtue of their ability to change their form. Such is the well-known tale of Matya ben Harash, tempted by the devil in the guise of a beautiful woman (*Tanhuma*, Buber edition, supplement to *Hukkat*, p. 131; *Yalkut Shimoni*, no. 161; and in medieval sources such as *Midrash of the Ten Commandments*, ch. 7). The following tale, from the Palestinian Talmud (*Shabbat* 1, 3) also belongs to this type:

> There we have learned: Do not trust yourself until the day of your death. There was the story of a certain pious man, who was sitting and repeating the tradition as follows: Do not trust yourself until the days of your old age. He thought: for example, me! A spirit came to him in the form of a woman and tested him [and he was not able to withstand the temptation], and then

he began to regret it and [the spirit] said to him: Do not be troubled. I am a spirit. Now go and conform to [the version of] your fellows. (PT *Shabbat* 1, 3, J. Neusner's translation, pp. 54–55)

This story is especially important as it highlights a critical phenomenon in the history of the Jewish tale—the transformation of the folktale as it was absorbed into the rabbinic literature. The tale itself belongs to a narrative type widespread in general folklore: marriage between a man and a she-demon, known in Hebrew literature since the Middle Ages as "The Story of the Jerusalemite." In it, a married man desires a she-demon, marries her, and even produces children with her, yet none of this is considered a moral transgression, as she is not regarded as a flesh-and-blood woman.[86]

The version before us is patterned just as an exemplum, brought forth to substantiate a familiar moral perception or idea. The tale, in its folk origin a distinctly demonic story describing the structure of relations between the human and demonic worlds in the sexual realm, recasts the spirit as the advocate of one side of the scholarly debate on ethical principle and man's tendency to pride. What in the folktale was a fast belief in the existence of the spirit and its relationship with the man, became in the talmudic tale a kind of parable offered as evidence in the legal debate.

Until now we have dealt with the magical tales whose heroes are supernatural creatures, mostly demons and spirits. Another class of tales of the period treats human heroes with supernatural attributes—witches and sorcerers. These figures are always portrayed as having negative supernatural power, while representatives of the narrating society—generally the figures of famous sages—engage them in battle, and prevail. As in the demon tales, and perhaps even more so, these stories embody R. Johanan's statement: "Why are they [the sorcerers] called Kashafim?—because they deny [makh'khishin—a pun on Kashafim—the existence of the] Divine agencies" (*Sanhedrin* 67b). According to folk beliefs of the period, these practitioners of sorcery had real power deriving from negative sources (i.e., the devil, the world of demons), and their goal was to perpetrate evil. They function, according to R. Johanan's statement, in spite of, and in opposition to, legitimate Divine powers, and as such it was obligatory to fight them and neutralize their power. Among the most influential and well-known tales of this sort is that of Rabban Simeon ben Shetah and the witches of Ashkelon (PT, *Sanhedrin* 6, 6 and *Hagigah* 2, 2):

When R. Simeon ben Shetah became Patriarch, he pledged to kill all the witches, and kept his promise. Someone informed him that there were eighty witches in a cave in Ashkelon. As proof of his trustworthiness, the informant plucked out his eye—and restored it. One cold and rainy day, R. Simeon gathered together eighty tall young men, then gave each a vessel with a dry *tallit* (prayer shawl) folded up inside. He hid them outside the cave and instructed them that when he whistled they were each to take their *tallit* out of the vessel and put it on. When he whistled a second time, they were to enter the witches' cave and lift one witch each into the air, as their power waned when their feet could not touch the ground. He then approached the cave alone, introducing himself as a magician. They decided to hold a contest of magic. The witches displayed their talents first, then asked him what he could do. He replied that, with a whistle, he could make eighty men appear before the cave in dry garments despite the rain. So he did, following which each hoisted aloft the witch of his choice. Once out of the cave, R. Simeon hanged the lot.

This tale of war against magic is built as a military operation in every detail: the intelligence report, the selection of the day of battle for its weather, the logistic preparations (the vessels and ritual shawls), formation outside the cave, the deception, the set of orders with emphasis on two points: the enemy's weak spot and the means of communication between the vanguard (R. Simeon ben Shetah) and the main camp. All these indicate a story carefully planned according to the conventions of the war tale. In this manner the analogy between military battle and that against witchcraft could be created for the audience of listeners. For obvious reasons, the erotic element of the tale is blurred, although it does not vanish completely. Eighty witches together in one cave certainly do not stay there solely for purposes of sorcery—they probably made their living by ritual prostitution. R. Simeon ben Shetah's selection of eighty tall young men, his suggestion to the witches that they have a good time with them, and their choice of a partner each, all indicate the sage's exploitation of their licentious ways. There is nothing surprising in the erotic aspect of the tale, as prostitution and witchcraft have always been perceived as two sides of a single coin, in non-Jewish culture as well. It can also be assumed that when this tale was told aloud, it included fuller erotic description and detail, which were a component of folk versions but omitted, most probably, when set down in writing in the talmudic framework.[87]

The erotic aspect of witchcraft in the rabbinic period was also manifested in other actions ascribed to witches in stories—they were able to stall labor and childbirth and render men impotent. One of the only witches called here by name is Yokhani Bat Retivi, but only her name is mentioned here (*Sotah* 22a). Rashi, however tells her story: She was a widow-witch who would hold up childbirth with her magic. Only after much suffering on the part of the woman did she say she would go to ask for mercy—in the hope, as it were, that her prayers to God would be accepted. She would then return home and lift the spell, whereupon the infant could be born (it can be presumed that the intent here is that she received payment for her services, otherwise her actions are meaningless). Once a passing laborer happened to hear her magic spells. They made a sound like the cry of a fetus still in the womb. He opened the lid of the vessel from where the sounds emanated, whereupon the spells escaped, the mother's womb was opened, and she delivered her child. In this manner everyone learned that Yokhani Bat Retivi was, in fact, a witch. (The possibility that this version of the demonological tale is medieval is discussed in the following chapter.)

One of the impressive magic tales that survived from this period deals with the same subject: R. Eleazar, R. Joshua ben Hananiah, and Rabban Gamaliel were guests of a Jew in Rome.

> When they sat down to eat, [they noticed] that each dish which they brought in to them would first be brought into a small room, and then would be brought to them, and they wondered whether they might be eating sacrifices offered to the dead [e.g., brought before an idol]. They said to [their host]: what is your purpose in the fact that as to every dish which you bring before us, if you do not bring it first into a small room, you do not bring it in to us? He said to them: I have a very old father, and he has made a decree for himself that he will never go out of that small room until he will see the sages of Israel. They said to him: Go and tell him, come out here to them for they are here. He came out to them. They said to him: Why do you do this? He said to them: Pray for my son, for he has not produced a child. Said R. Eleazar to R. Joshua: Now, Joshua b. Hananiah, let us see what you will do. He said to them: Bring me flax seeds, and they brought him seeds. He appeared to sow the seed on the table; he appeared to scatter the seed; he appeared to bring the seed up; he appeared to take hold of it, until he drew a woman, holding on to her tresses. He said to her: Release whatever [magic] you have done [to this man]. She said to him: I am not going to release [my spell]. He said to her: If you don't do it, I shall publicize you. She said to him: I cannot do it, for [the magical materials] have been cast into the sea. R. Joshua made a decree that the sea release [it] and they came up. They prayed for [the host], and he had the merit of producing a son, R. Judah b. Bathera. They said: If we came up here only for the purpose of producing that righteous man, it would have been enough for us. (PT *Sanhedrin* 7, 13, J. Neusner's translation, pp. 259–260)

Here we have a mystery tale: the sages arrive at precisely this house when they reach Rome, the mysterious room into which each dish disappears before being served to the guests, the strange oath of the old father, the mystery of the host's sterility and the means of its solution, via the recall of the spells—all these establish a plot built on a series of mysteries. The special structure is one reason for the narrative tension which dominates the tale from start to finish. The old father's oath certainly indicates a lengthy stay in the room. Why was his exit conditional on seeing Jewish sages? Perhaps it was because the son had already turned to others who dealt with such matters—folk healers, various sorts of magicians—but they could not help him. The success of the Jewish sages after the efforts of those others is intended to illustrate that in the contest between magic and the Torah, the Torah is superior.

From a generic perspective, this tale can be classified with the biographical legends dealt with above. This is a typical pre-natal legend, concerning supernatural, prolonged sterility before the birth, and the appearance of an angel or holy man who prophesies the birth of a hero, after removing the obstacles which had prevented it thus far.

Another matter needing clarification is why the witch cast her spell precisely in that manner. The tale does not explain this, but it may have been the revenge of a woman scorned, or perhaps another woman paid the witch for her services. In any case it is clear that this deliberate sexual incapacitation was vengeance for some prior sexual event. Noteworthy, too, are the stages of R. Joshua ben Hananiah's magic, which simulate the processes of conception, gestation, and childbirth: sowing, watering, growth, and emergence. This suggests the technique of sympathetic magic, that is, enabling procreation by means of mimicking it magically.[88]

Also characteristic of the description of the witch is her fear of exposure. Such was the case in the tale of Yokhani Bat Retivi, who was rendered powerless once unveiled. Witches, according to these tales, are respected women in society, perhaps even members of the elite, who secretly practice witchcraft, and as such are dangerous. There is the tale of Rav Hisda and Rabbah bar Huna (*Hullin* 110b; *Shabbat* 81b) who were journeying over water. A certain lady asked to sit with them. When they refused her, she stopped the ship with a single word. They countered, releasing the boat with a single word. Much the same is the tale (*Gittin* 39b) of Rabbi Hanina bar Pappi, in which a lady of standing attempts to seduce him. He spoke—and immediately leprous sores and boils covered his body (so as to distract himself from temptation). Then she spoke—and he was healed. He fled to a bath house where harmful spirits lurked, a place so fraught with peril that even those who entered there during daylight fell prey to their mischief. The next day he was asked how he had managed to survive an entire night in such a place. The answer is that he survived because he resisted temptation and did not sin. These stories show that the period's folk beliefs held witches to be esteemed women of established social position and upright reputation who, once unmasked, lost their powers.

An interesting point in the tale of the witch in Rome is that R. Eleazar—the senior of the three sages—asks R. Joshua to handle the task before them. R. Joshua ben Hananiah was known as a staunch opponent of witches—particularly non-Jewish ones. We have already discussed the cycle of wisdom-magic tales concerning R. Joshua ben Hananiah and the Elders of Athens (*Bekhorot* 8b)—one of the most important contest tales to survive in the rabbinic literature. Of special importance is the tale recounted in the same location of the Palestinian Talmud, preceding the story of the three wise men in Rome: Rabbi Eleazar, Rabbi Joshua, and Rabbi Akiva entered the Tiberias bath house. A min (Christian-Jew), who was a magician besides, saw them and uttered an incantation to make the walls of the bath house close in on them, so that they could not move. Here too, R. Eleazar ask R. Joshua to do something to release them. When the magician rose to leave, R. Joshua spoke—and the gate to the bath house caught and trapped him, so that no one could pass in or out. People started pushing and pummeling him from both sides, until he asked R. Joshua to let him go. In exchange, the latter demanded his and his companions' release; all were freed. As they left, R. Joshua taunted the min, asking him if that was all he knew how to do. The heretic took them to the sea and magically split it before him, proving to them that he can do not less than "Moses their Master." The sages said that Moses did not stop there, but walked across the dry land bared by the parted sea. When the heretic did just that, R. Joshua called upon the angel of the sea, and the min was swallowed up by the waters.[89]

This tale sets up a situation characteristic of magic contests, as the tale of the Elders of Athens was a contest of wisdom. It describes a kind of encounter, undoubtedly commonplace in urban public places, between sages and their Christian rivals. Such encounters in the early second century sizzled with vitriolic one-upmanship and hostility. As the tale of the Elders of Athens expresses the rivalry between Judaism and Hellenism, so the tale of R. Joshua and the magician reflects the conflict with the Christians. This is borne out principally by the final episode, in which the min seeks to prove to the sages that "Moses their Master" was nothing but a trickster, regarding both the staff which he transformed into a serpent, and the splitting of the sea. This may have been one of the many subjects of debate between Jews and Christians (it should be noted in this context that the Jews considered Jesus to have been a magician, and perhaps this is why the heretic sought to demonstrate to the sages that Moses, teacher of the Jews, was nothing more). The theological polemics of Judaism versus Christianity was conducted among the upper strata of educated society—sages versus the first Christian teachers and the Church Fathers. But the theological dispute in all its complexity and detail could hardly supply a response to the challenge of Christianity among the broader sectors of the Jewish population. As the tales of miracles of Jesus and his disciples reflected the spirit of Christianity as far as the Christian masses of the period were concerned, so tales like that of R. Joshua ben Hananiah served the Jews. In their view, this tale proves the sages' strength greater than any magic powers of the new Christians; in particular, when individuals of their historical period

(Jesus, for example) dare to compare themselves with the great deeds of the biblical forefathers, they make utter fools of themselves. The story, in the true fashion of the folktale, does not come to put forward a theological argument, but to show how that argument resonated in the folk consciousness. Such an analysis of the tale of the magicians indicates that it can be read on several levels: indeed it reflects the belief of the generation in magicians, but is perhaps likely to express, on a deeper level, the historical background of the great religious crisis of the period. Folktales—magic tales included—clearly and sharply express some of the period's religious, historical, and social tensions as reflected by the folk consciousness. My reading of the texts completely contradicts the allegoristical approach, which seeks to nullify their demonological aspects, viewing them as mere expressions of other ideological or historical truths.[90]

"R. Nathan said: If all the magicians of the world will gather together and will want to turn the morning into evening, they will not be able to do it." (*Tanhuma*, Buber edition, *parashat Korah*, 6) This approach seems to contradict everything we have seen so far, expressing a perception invalidating magic practices. It is not clear if R. Nathan's intention was to rule out sorcery or only to maintain that magic is ineffective against the basic forces of nature. The sages' ambivalence toward this subject is manifested in tales that contradict each other:

> Raba said: If the righteous desired it, they could [by living a life of absolute purity] be creators, for it is written: "But your iniquities have distinguished between etc." (Isa. 59, 2). Rabbah created a man, and he sent him to R. Zerah. R. Zerah spoke to him, but received no answer. Thereupon he said to him: 'Thou art a creature of the magicians, return to thy dust.'
>
> R. Hanina and R. Oshaia spent every Sabbath eve in studying the 'Book of Creation' by means of which they created a third grown calf and ate it. (*Sanhedrin* 65b)

Compare with the following:

> Said R. Yannai: I was going along in the road in Sepphoris, and I saw a min, who took a pebble and threw it up into the sky, and it came down and was turned into a calf. And did not R. Eleazar say in the name of R. Yose bar Zimra: If everyone in the world got together, they could not create a single mosquito and put breath into it. But we must say that that min did not take a pebble and throw it up into the air, so when it came down it was turned into a calf, but he ordered his servent to steal a calf from the herd and bring it to him. Said R. Hinena b. R. Hananiah: I was walking in the turf of Sepphoris, and I saw a min take a skull and throw it up into the air, and when it came down, it had turned into a calf. And I came and I told father,

and he said to me: If you actually ate of the calf meat, it really happened, and if not, it was a mere illusion. (PT *Sanhedrin* 7, 13, J. Neusner's translation, pp. 260–261)

The distinction between magic and deception engaged folk thinking from time immemorial, and the sages were not exempt. These tales contradict each other not only in the question of whether or not it is possible to create a calf, but also in the test of authenticity: R. Hanina and R. Oshaya went so far as to eat the meat of the calf created for them, a motif seen as irrefutable proof that the calf was real.[91]

Even R. Joshua ben Hananiah (again!) is prepared to put his own magic practices to a real test: "Said R. Joshua ben Hananiah: I could take cucumbers and watermelons and make of them rams and deers and they will breed rams and deers"; and, again, the remarks attributed to Rabbi Joshua: "the magician who does a deed is guilty, but not the one of deceives [as entertainment] (PT *Sanhedrin* 7, 11; BT *Sanhedrin* 68a). In other words, contrary to the extreme claims that all magic is deception, R. Joshua presents the following position: there is trickery for the sake of entertainment, upon which there is no ban and from which there is no danger, and then there is actual sorcery, which is perilous and halakhically prohibited. How could R. Joshua ben Hananiah's view of magic be reconciled with the tales of magic in which he serves as a central hero with magic powers? The tales of the magicians in Rome and the drowning of the magician in Tiberias showcased a kind of "white magic," that is, the use of magic means to bring about ends beneficial to the narrating society. Hence such tales were received more favorably than others displaying magic abilities with no clearly defined social or religious purpose. The tales of magic were undoubtedly told after R. Joshua's death, and do not accurately reflect his view of sorcery. This is similar to the many magic tales which clung to Maimonides in the folk traditions widespread to this day, although Maimonides himself was a staunch opponent of anything connected with magic. Still, it was not without cause that magic tales were associated with R. Joshua ben Hananiah. That he had an abiding interest in the subject is clear from the traditions of his students and the statements attributed to him, whose authenticity we have no cause to doubt. The examination of the stories of R. Joshua ben Hananiah showed us that one must clearly distinguish between the statements of the sage himself, which apparently express his views on the subject, and tales about the sage, reflecting the beliefs and opinions of society many years after his death.[92]

One reasonable explanation for the dual approach to magic is that the sages, like others of their time, believed in the possibility of sorcery, yet feared lest society confuse it with the central orientation of the Jewish faith. One way of overcoming this difficulty was to claim that the stars have no power over Jews: matters of magic, astrology, fortune telling, and so forth are valid in general, but not for Jews. According to the Torah of the Jewish people, Providence, and the reward and punishment it dictates, determine the fates of individuals: Two astrologers in Tiberias are sitting near the gate to the city and notice two Jews leaving. One said to the other: "Those two men are going out but will not come back as the snake will burn them." When they returned safely, the astrologers asked them to tell what happened on the way, "they told them: We did not do any [special] thing, only what we used to do, we read the *shema* and prayed. They said to them: You are Jews. The prophecies of the astrologers do not realize in you as you are Jews." A similar tale is found in the Palestinian Talmud (*Shabbat* 6, 9), concerning two disciples of Rabbi Hanina who set out to cut wood. An astrologer saw in the stars that they would not return. On their way they generously gave an old man half of their loaf of bread. On their return, as they looked over the load of wood, they found a dead snake among the logs. The most famous tale of this type concerns Rabbi Akiva's daughter (*Shabbat* 156a–b): The sages are deliberating whether or not, as Rabbi Hanina puts it, "Israel stands under planetary influence," or, as Rabbi Johanan states: "Israel is immune from planetary influence." Then comes the story of Samuel sitting with the astrologer Ablat. They observed people going out to cut hay. Ablat pointed one out, saying he would return home no more, as a snake would strike him in the field. Samuel replied that if the man was a Jew, he would return safely. When he did just that, Ablat examined the hay on the harvester's shoulder and found a dead snake within. The Jew told how one of the workers had had nothing to contribute that day to their common meal. To save his fellow worker from embarrassment, he pretended to have shared with him. Thereupon the following story is offered:

> From R. Akiva too [we learn that] Israel is free from planetary influence. For R. Akiva had a daughter. Now, astrologers told him, On the day she enters the bridal chamber a snake will bite her and she will die. He was very worried about this. On that day [of her marriage] she took a brooch [and] stuck it into the wall and by chance it penetrated [sank] into the eye of a serpent. The following morning, when she took it out, the snake came trailing after it. "What did you do?" asked her father. She replied, "A poor man came to our door in the evening, and everybody was busy with the banquet, and there was no one to attend to him. So I took the portion which was given to me and gave it to him." "You have done a good deed," said he to her. Thereupon R. Akiva went out and lectured: "But charity delivereth from death," and not [merely] from an unnatural death, but from death itself.

The tale of Rabbi Akiva's daughter is a typical example of a tale of fate: It is predicted at (or before) someone's birth that he will die on the day of his Bar Mitzvah or wedding (in Jewish tales there is some overlap between these two life stages). The father tries to prevent this fate. In Jewish folktales, he succeeds, although in general folklore the destiny foreseen is most often unavoidable. The story of Rabbi Akiva's daughter is one of the first tales of fate we know of in Jewish folk literature, and serves as an archetype for dozens of tales with a similar structure in the Middle Ages and the modern period. What is of interest to us here is the fact that the sages do not use it as a tale of fate or charity, but as proof that "Israel is free from planetary influence." The prediction, according to the tale, is entirely valid, and circumstances occur precisely as predetermined. But it neglected to consider one factor: Rabbi Akiva's daughter is a Jew, and is therefore outside the realm of the astrologers and magic. Her destiny is determined by Judaism's internal structure of values.

It is important to note that, in all of the tales seen thus far, it is not the Jewishness of the heroes which saves them from death, but their individual deeds. It may be that the tales seek to emphasize in the didactic manner characteristic of the sages that one's actions, namely, one's daily conduct according to the principles of Judaism (charity, prayer), have the power to lift the Jew from the circle of influence of astrology and magic. It can be assumed that the story of Rabbi Akiva's daughter was employed in the campaign against belief in magic only in the Talmud and Midrash, whereas in its folk origin it was simply and wholly a legend of fate.[93]

The sages' deprecation of magic and idolatry was also manifested in the enumeration of dozens of incantations, amulets, folk cures and various spells which they define as 'idolatry customs.' All are prohibited, not because they are false or ineffective, but because the sages view their use as idolatry.[94]

In addition to these halakhic and aggadic deliberations on the ban of magic practices, tales of rabbis—R. Johanan, R. Joshua ben Levi, R. Aha, and R. Eleazar ben Damma, to name some—who adamantly refused to accept cures tainted by idolatry emerged from the circles of sages (PT, *Shabbat* 14, 4). This was so important to them that it even outweighed a paramount principle—the saving of a life:

> No man should have any dealings with Minim [heathens], nor is it allowed to be healed by them even [in risking] an hour's life [another hour or two of life]. It once happened to Ben Dama, the son of R. Ishmael's sister, that he was bitten by a serpent and Jacob, a native of Kefar Sekaniah [a disciple of Jesus] came to heal him but R. Ishmael did not let him; whereupon Ben Dama said, "My brother R. Ishmael, let him, so that I may be healed by him; I will even cite a verse from the Torah that he is to be permitted"; but he did not manage to complete his saying, when his soul departed and he died. Whereupon R. Ishmael exclaimed, Happy art thou Ben Dama for thou wert pure in body and thy soul likewise left thee in purity; nor hast thou transgressed the words of thy colleagues. (*Avoda Zarah* 27b; *Tosephta, Hullin* chapter 2, Lieberman's edition, p. 503; PT *Shabbat* 14, 4)

The didactic orientation of such tales is clear: Jews, wherever they may live, be it in Palestine or one of the lands of the Exile, sometimes needed the services of various folk healers, who made no distinction between medicine and magic. The religious leadership feared, and rightly so, a blurring of the boundaries between the various forms of folk belief (or folk religion) and normative religion. The need of folk medicine was the most dangerous manifestation of this tendency, as people required it as a matter of course. When someone is critically ill, neither he nor his relatives are likely to be particularly discerning about what is and what is not permissible. The tale above is very interesting from this perspective: Even R. Eleazar ben Damma, feeling the venom spreading through his veins, sought the means which would allow him to accept the "medicine of Jesus." This set of tales of sages who refused to be cured by idolatry well illustrates how they themselves utilized the folktale. It can be assumed that these stories were created among the sages and even spread by them. They were designed to sway opinion, like the exemplum, by way of practical example, to accept the ban on the use of magic with regard to a highly sensitive subject: curing diseases and preventing death. It was clear to them that a direct injunction against such practices would have little impact on the broad sectors of society. On the other hand, tales of sages who even on their deathbeds rejected any magic tainted by idolatry were more powerful and effective than overt preaching or demands could ever be.[95]

The multitude of magic practices found in the rabbinic literature indicates that their rejection was accompanied by a recognition of their specifics. The collection and formulation in writing of these beliefs, customs, incantations, and spells correspond to a similar process in folkloristic field research: Instead of mentioning them in passing, the Talmud describes them in detail, using the jargon of the practitioners of magic "in the field." Halachic discussion accompanies these descriptions, defining them as pagan rites. It is limited to the academy and the circles of sages, and comes to establish what may be termed "oppositional" narrative traditions about famous sages who refused to use magical practices to save their own lives. The existence of these tales in folk traditions indicates the sages' understanding that harmful folk beliefs could only be countered by other folk traditions. The success of this campaign is another question altogether, and one for which no direct evidence has survived. In any case, even after the sages' prolonged and hopeless struggle against folk beliefs in magic, they did not cease to exist. Our concern here is the cultural phenomenon of creation and the use of folk traditions among the educated class to fight the folk manifestations they opposed.

The current discussion of the magic tale has not sought to describe or analyze the sages' attitude to the belief in magic and demons. Many such descriptions already exist. Instead we have sought to examine those tales that can be construed as "magic." While our selection was not exhaustive, it represents the different types of magic tale to appear in this rich literature. There are other examples of each of the topics covered. The tales do not reflect the established approach to magic, but the manner in which many societal levels of the folk viewed the supernatural world and its influence on their own daily lives. Hence the difficulty: all the folktales we dealt with reached us through the filtering medium of the sages, and therefore we must consider their attitude toward magic, as well, at every step of the way.

Juxtaposing the popular approach against that of the sages in the matter of magic and the supernatural shows that the dichotomy and sharp opposition are expressed primarily in direct, overt statements. Conversely, the tales themselves indicate the sages' involvement in magic practices, just like other folk healers and magicians. It can be reasonably concluded that the explicit statements of disapproval of pagan rites and magic in all its various forms (such as those of R. Joshua ben Hananiah), were indeed made by the sages. In contrast, the tales of the same sages engaged in magical activity are narrative traditions created by the folk after their deaths. We chose to deal mainly with the second type in order to arrive at the tales and traditions scattered among the people in this period, before they were crystallized into the form given them in rabbinic literature.

The picture which emerged—representing but a tiny component of the full collection of magic tales prevalent among the people in this period, most of which did not reach us—is one of a developed and diversified narrative world which makes much use of non-Jewish demonological motifs, and puts them through processes of transformation, turning them into Jewish traditions. The stories of magic prove that among the broad strata of society, magical manifestations were viewed as a part of commonplace reality in the street, workplace, and even places of worship. The tales, in the manner of folk literature, crystallize in artistic fashion the beliefs current in the narrating society, and so externalize the dread and anxiety produced by the darker side of reality. The different categories of magic tale (among them the contest of magic as a struggle between Jews and Gentiles, the witches as part of Jewish society, the demons who behave as human beings, purification of haunted locations, and Judaism and its precepts as a shield against injury by demons) recur in Jewish magic narratives in the history of Jewish folklore. It seems they were first crystallized into this form in the rabbinic period, thereafter decisively influencing the Jewish folklore of the generations to come.

[I] The Comic Tale

Little of the rich humor of Jewish society during the rabbinic period has survived in writing, as is also the case for other cultures of the time. It may be surmised that folk humor, including erotic jokes, foul language, and descriptions of bawdy situations, could not be integrated, for the most part, into the Talmud and Midrash. Therefore, only a few, doubtlessly expurgated, remnants can be found in the literature of the period. These are the only extant examples of the character, subjects, and meaning of Jewish folk humor of the time. The comic forms and subjects which survived in the Talmud and Midrash may represent only that material which interested the sages, while other subjects, perhaps more popular among the people at large, are entirely unknown to us. The picture we get from the available material is rich and variegated, its characteristics within the parameters of the classification of humor in general folklore. The main subjects discerned in other cultures, including confrontation between religions and races, gender relations, humorous characterizations, the clever figure outwitting fools, and various tall tales, appear in aggadic humor tales. So do the principal formal distinctions of international humor: the division between verbal and situational humor is evident in the formulation of humor in rabbinic literature.[96]

The study of humor seeks to prove that the joke and the comic tale are more than mere entertainment or vulgarity. These folkloric forms fulfill an important social function in shaping the structure of relations between society's different components. Their role is to offer release to the individual or social grouping from the anxieties and pressures born of traumatic events. The joke enables the observer or researcher to understand the tensions and the structure of relations between the various components of a given culture at a certain time. While the surviving humor of the rabbinic period does not paint a complete picture of comedy's context and function in this period, it does offer flashes of insight into different aspects of life of the time. The comic tales illuminate what people of the day found objectionable and ridiculous, as well as their fears and rivalries.

One question of enduring interest to scholars and researchers of humor is, "What is funny?" What is there about humor that causes the psychological and physiological reaction called laughter? Without entering too deeply into this complex issue dealt with by many disciplines, it can be said that the theory of incongruity is the most likely explanation. Humor, according to this theory, is the effect of a clash of its fundamental components: the expected, accepted, and normative, as opposed to what actually takes place in the plot of the joke. This collision of what the listener expects to hear, based on the reality and the norms to which he or she is accustomed, with what is said as the joke unfolds, creates a situation akin to psychological "shock" in the consciousness of the listeners, which is the primary cause of laughter. The clash, the incongruity, of the expected and the events as told, is the source of the stimulus we call "laughter." This distinction is of great importance to researchers of the folk joke, as it indicates how it can be used to understand the individual, societal, or national system of tensions which produce the comic phenomenon. Since the joke is the product of clashing values, we can examine the latter by analyzing the workings of the former. For this reason I have chosen to present most of the material from the wealth of comic tales of the sages according to the types of conflict they manifest. This makes it possible to identify the topics which engaged the humor of the period via its basic structure, that is, polarization of individuals, principles, types, and so on.[97]

"Blessed is the man that walketh not in the counsel of the wicked" refers to the sons of Korah . . . "Nor sitteth in the seat of the scornful" like Korah, who spoke in scorn against Moses and Aaron. What did Korah do? He assembled all the congregation against Moses and Aaron, as is said "Korah assembled all the congregation against them unto the door of the Tent of Meeting (Num. 16:19), and in their presence he began to speak words of scorn, saying: In my neighborhood there was a widow, and with her two fatherless daughters. The widow had only one field, and when she was about to plow, Moses said to her: Thou shalt not plow with an ox and an ass together (Deut. 22:10). When she was about to sow, Moses said to her: "Thou shalt not sow thy field with two kinds of seed" (Lev. 19:19). When she was about to reap the harvest and to stack the sheaves, Moses said to her: "Thou shalt not harvest the gleanings, the overlooked sheaves, and the corners of the field' (Lev. 19:9; Deut. 24:19). When she was about to bring the harvest into the granary, Moses said to her: "Give me the heave-offering, the first tithe, and the second tithe." She submitted to God's decree and gave them to him. What did the poor woman do then? She sold the field and bought two sheep, so that she might clothe herself in the wool shorn from them, and so that she might profit out of the lambs. As soon as the sheep brought forth their young, Aaron came and said to the widow: "Give me the firstling males, for this is what the Holy One, blessed be He, said to me: 'All the firstling males that are born of thy herd and of thy flock thou shalt sanctify unto the Lord thy God' (Deut. 15:19)." Again she submitted to God's decree, and gave the young of her sheep to Aaron. When the time for shearing arrived, she sheared her two sheep. Then Aaron came again and said to the widow: "Give me the first portion of the shearing." She said: "There is no strength in me to withstand this man; behold, I will slaughter the sheep and eat them." After she slaughtered them, Aaron came again and said to her: "Give me the shoulder, the jaws, and the maw." The widow said: "Though I have slaughtered my sheep, I am still not free of thy demands: behold, I devote my sheep to the uses of the Temple." But Aaron said to her: "If the sheep are to be devoted to the uses of the Temple, they belong entirely to me, for it was said to me: 'Everything devoted in Israel shall be mine' (Num. 18:14)." Thereupon Aaron lifted up the sheep, went on his way, and left her weeping with her two daughters. Is such a thing right? Oh, the despoiled woman! the hapless woman! Moses and

Aaron have done all these things to her, but hang the blame on the Holy One, blessed be He! (*The Midrash on Psalms*, 1, 15)

This tale is constructed as a sort of dramatic sketch featuring Aaron (or Moses) and the widow. It can be dramatized as it stands, with one voice that of the authority figure, tyrannical, quoting the relevant Scripture with skill and pathos, and the other, the hesitant, submissive voice of the poor widow. Korah, "the jester," is brought to life by the popular clowns who appeared on market day, weddings, and other occasions. They used mimicry and voice changes to produce these "one man shows." On the level of meaning, the tale is built on the polarization between representatives of the regime and the moneyless, powerless strata of the people. The expectation—and this is the norm mentioned earlier—is that the leadership support and defend fate's beleaguered victims. This normative perception furthermore maintains that the Torah itself was given to the Jewish people in order to protect its weakest individuals, as the powerful do not need protection. The "jesting" in this instance stems from stressing the laws of the Torah *ad absurdum*, putting them to the most extreme test. Under this scrutiny, they have the opposite effect. In this way that same incongruity is produced, whose result is the comic stimulus mentioned above: the flaw is revealed in what seemed to be laws of justice of Divine origin as the leaders manipulate them to exploit the indigent. The story in fact ends as follows: "Moses and Aaron have done all these things to her, but hang the blame on the Holy One, blessed be He!" In another place Korah's wife says, "See what Moses has done. He himself has become king; his brother he appointed High Priest; his brother's sons he hath made the vice High Priests. If teruma is brought, he decrees, Let it be for the priest; if the tithe is brought, which belongs to you [the Levites], he orders, Give a tenth part thereof to the priest" (*Sanhedrin* 110a). The social protest in these statements is unmistakable. Putting the story in a biblical context, and featuring the figure of Korah (controversial in any case), shows that the storytellers did not intend—at least not consciously—to relate directly to the events of their own time. It is difficult to discern today what perceptible social situation these stories relate to, if at all. What is important is that the basic hypocrisy (and corruption) of the regime is exposed through definite comic means. No less important is that the creator (or creators) of a tale such as this demonstrates a highly developed comic flair, as illustrated by the parodical polish on the exposition, the virtuoso use of the sources, the diverse interplay of meanings between the biblical past and the storyteller's present, and the complex establishment of the theatrical situation. Humor, then, was plainly an important facet of the period's cultural activity, as yet not accorded its due significance.[98]

Social protest against the misuse and exploitation of power are apparent in another grouping of tales, also hearkening back to the biblical period, this time to the people of Sodom. This fascinating cycle of tales, preserved in the tractate *Sanhedrin* (109a–b), comprises some ten stories of the iniquity of the inhabitants of Sodom (we will return to them in section J, in the discussion of story cycles). Some are comical, their humor based on the polarization between social classes:

> They ruled: He who has [only] one ox must tend [all the oxen of the town] for one day; but he who has none must tend [them] two days [poorer should be most oppressed]. Now a certain orphan, the son of a widow, was given oxen to tend. He went and killed them and [then] said to them [the Sodomites]: He who has an ox, let him take one hide; he who has none, let him take two hides. "What is the meaning of this?" they exclaimed. Said he: "The final usage [i.e., the disposal of the ox when dead] must be as the initial one; just as the initial usage is that he who possesses one ox must tend for one day, and he who has none must tend two days; so should be the final usage: he who has one ox should take one hide, and he who has none should take two."

The tale opens with a statement formulated as a "city ordinance," legal in every respect: whosoever owns one bull grazes his flocks one day, and so on. It is deliberately structured and styled in the manner of actual ordinances. Their imitation is at the heart of the parodic effect, which is bolstered by the orphan's explanation of his subsequent "ordinance": it too is structured and based on the original city bylaw; as the original was "just," so must his be. His reasoning resembles legal argument in style: "The final usage must be as the initial one." The parodic effect is quite pronounced. This tale is similar to that of Korah in two more respects: first, in taking the ordinance or the law to its absurd extreme. The orphan "tests," as it were, the justness of the ordinance by applying it to a new situation never considered by the framers of the original: How are the hides of dead bulls to be disposed of? This application of ordinances or laws *ad absurdum* is a perfect example of the expression of folk thought or logic. The same logical principle stands at the core of many folktales, according to which the unjust rule is tested in a new situation and its hitherto concealed iniquity and absurdity are brought to light. Second, the similarity of the protagonists—in both tales the bearer of social protest is a representative of the weakest members of society: widows and orphans. In the tale of Sodom, as in that of Korah, those rules intended to strengthen the interests and profits of the wealthy and aggressive at the expense of the town's poor, are cloaked in "legalistic" garb designed to hide their true purpose. The orphan's deed is intended to unveil their villainy.[99]

A similar comic device underlies still more parodic "ordinances" in the tales of the inhabitants of Sodom: ferryboat passage is one *zuz* while someone who wades across (for lack of the fare) pays two *zuzim*; if someone strikes another's pregnant wife, causing her to miscarry, her husband must turn her over to the assailant so that he can impregnate her as compensation; if one cuts off the ear of another's donkey, the animal's owner must deliver the beast to its attacker, who keeps it until such time as the donkey grows a new ear; if one individual injures another, the injured party must pay the aggressor a bloodletting fee. Like the earlier tales, here, too, the absurdity of the law is revealed. Eliezer, Abraham's manservant or anonymous launderers (once again, members of the lowest classes), are the typical protagonists of these stories. When the judge orders that Eliezer pay his assailant the bloodletting fee, Eliezer takes a stone, strikes the judge, and demands his own bloodletting fee. As any social or historical description taken to an extreme, the tales illuminate a more interesting social reality. The humor may seem, on the surface, mere entertainment, but it sends a message that the existing laws and regulations were created to serve the wealthy and the powerful, and in order to deprive the poor and weak of what little they have. The stories belie the image of social harmony fostered by the "official" texts; beneath the sugar coating seethed sharp resentment of social injustice. Such sentiments undoubtedly have existed among the weaker segments of all societies in all times; what is significant here is the manner in which they surface: in the vehicle provided by seemingly innocent, amusing jokes.

Another type of comic tale of the period revolves around the polarization of the sexes. These stories should not be presented, as is usually the case, solely as misogynist humor. A closer reading shows them to be much more complex than a mere torrent of satirical barbs against women:

> A certain Babylonian went up to the Land of Israel and took a wife [there]. "Boil me two [cows'] feet," he ordered and she boiled him two lentils [misunderstanding his Babylonian pronunciation, or taking him literally: he said two lentils, meaning, some, and she boiled him exactly two lentils], which infuriated him. The next day he said: "Boil me a griwa" [a large quantity, to test her, if she intentionally mocked at him yesterday], so she boiled him a griwa. "Go and bring me two bezuni" [he meant melons] so she went and brought him two candles [another meaning of the Aramaic word]. "Go and break them on the head of the baba [threshold]." Now, Baba b. Buta [the Rabbi] was sitting on the threshold [of the town], engaged in judging a lawsuit. So she went and broke them on his head. Said he to her: "What is the meaning of this that thou has done?"—She replied: "Thus my husband did order me." "Thou hast performed thy husband's will," he rejoined; "may the Almighty bring forth from thee two sons like Baba b. Buta." (*Nedarim* 66b)

Wordplay drives the tale; a series of comic situations derived from puns unfolds as the husband's instructions (understood by the audience of listeners according to linguistic conventions) give way to the wife's actions. The collision of these two plot extremes creates the comic effect. Here, the humor is essentially based on words, rather than on descriptions or actions, as the results of the plot stem from a given linguistic situation. The incongruity here is based on the different meanings of words and expressions in Babylonian Aramaic (as spoken by the husband) and Palestinian Aramaic (native to the wife), a situation indicative, perhaps, of a cultural gap between the Babylonian center and Palestine. At the same time, it is clear that linguistic ambiguity alone cannot account for the humor of the situations; the woman's stupidity is indispensable. She behaves like a robot: hearing her husband's orders, she carries them out literally, making no attempt to deduce their intent. However we must, in my opinion, look beyond her stupidity to find the challenge to the deeply-rooted wifely norm of blind obedience to the husband. Indeed, Bava ben Buta's response expresses precisely this normative stance: he forgives the slight to his honor in favor of what he regards as the more important principle—a wife's dutifulness to her husband. According to him, heaven's blessing is a woman's reward for unhesitating compliance with her husband's wishes. Thus, in juxtaposition to the normative stand which demands blind obedience to her husband's will, stands a test of the norm under extreme circumstances (what we have defined as application *ad absurdum*): The story seeks to portray the consequences of this norm upheld where the woman is utterly lacking in common sense. In other words, Bava ben Buta's position in the tale—representing the social norm—is pitted against incisive criticism seeking to overturn it. The two demands made on the woman—to blindly obey her husband and, at the same time, use her own judgement and common sense—are irreconcilable, as shown by the absurd developments described in the tale. Of course, the tale can be read in a straightforward manner; we can laugh at her foolishness and marvel at the sage's magnanimity. Yet analysis of the incongruity at the core of the tale indicates an additional meaning, deeper and perhaps unconscious.

In the same context, in tractate *Nedarim* (ibid.), appears the well-known tale of the Jew who swore not to approach his wife until she proved some part of herself attractive to R. Ishmael. When R. Ishmael bar Yose endeavors to find in her even one appealing feature, the husband enumerates her numerous physical flaws:

> Perhaps her head is beautiful?—It is round, they replied. "Perhaps her hair is beautiful?"—"It is like stalks of flax." "Perhaps her eyes are beautiful?"—"They are bleared." "Perhaps her nose is beautiful?"—"It is swollen." "Perhaps her lips are beautiful?"—"They are thick." "Perhaps her neck is beautiful?"—"It is squat." "Perhaps her abdomen is beautiful?"—"It protrudes." "Perhaps her feet are beautiful?"—"They are as broad as those of a duck." "Perhaps her name is beautiful?"—"It is Likhlukhit [which means: the dirty

one, repulsive]." Said he to them: "She is fittingly called Likhlukhit, since she is repulsive through her defects." (*Nedarim* 66b)

The tale is styled with all the virtuosity of an impressive richness of language in the various descriptions of ugliness. It is difficult to believe that the story was told at this level of virtuosity in the folk tradition. In any case, the primary similes—hair like bundles of flax stalks, feet as broad as a duck's, and so on, are undoubtedly folk expressions for homely women, which exist in the folklore of all nations. Particular attention should be paid to the wife's name, "the ugly one" (literally, "the dirty one"), which creates a kind of folk "etymology" for the identification of an individual's characteristics with his or her name. The same is true of the names of the judges of Sodom: "There were four judges in Sodom [named]: Shakrai, Shakurai, Zayyafi, and Maztley Dina [Liar, Awful Liar, Forger, and Perverter of Justice] (*Sanhedrin*, 109b).

At each stage of the tale, while the husband (or his representative) enumerates his wife's flaws, she remains silent. Only the sage, who seeks to be the champion of right, seeks a point in her favor. He finally does find "a beautiful thing," her name, and so releases the husband from his vow. The cruel humor of the story stems from the expectation of being able to find at least one attractive feature in any woman. The elimination of one feature after another in this woman's case contradicts that expectation. Step by step, the humor builds until, finally, her name (the only non-physical trait considered), which expresses all her physical faults, and is thus befitting, is pronounced seemly. What a woman of the period felt upon hearing this tale we can only surmise. It treats the woman like a material object, whose worth is dependent on the physical attributes which determine her fate and society's treatment of her.

The woman does not always take a passive stand in response to insults. The following tale can be seen as an interesting antithesis to the story of "the ugly one":

A woman came to Rabbi and said to him: "I have been violated." Said he to her: "But was not the experience pleasant to you?" She retorted: "If a man dipped his finger in honey and put it into your mouth on the Day of Atonement, would not the act displease you, yet after all it would be toothsome?" He accepted her argument. (*Numbers Rabbah* 9, 10)

The tale is constructed as a series of two sharp retorts, by which the protagonists respond to the statements of the other. It opens with the woman's claim of rape; Judah the Patriarch's response is surprising and antagonistic. The woman's retort is longer and more complex because she chooses to use an analogy to something comprehensible to the Patriarch and the other men in his court, who could not otherwise fathom the feelings of a woman who had been raped. The allegory figuratively parallels its referent. Poking the finger into the mouth of a devout Jew on the Day of Atonement is likened to the act of penetration in a rape; accomplishing either requires violent force. The Day of Atonement itself, the holiest of days, parallels the purity and chastity of the violated woman. Even the honey (incidentally, a euphemism for sexual intercourse), which initially tastes bitter on account of being forced into the mouth, eventually produces physiological sensations that are beyond an individual's control. The comic device at work here is, at first glance, similar to that in the previous tale. The expectation, based on the accepted norm, is that a woman should not complain of a rape, as ultimately, she enjoyed it; the Patriarch responds in accordance with this norm. The woman's response counters this norm, the clash (or "incongruity") is sharp and immediate, as is the manner of the retort in jokes, and creates the effect of psychological stimulation called laughter.

But this anecdote is still more complex, as the woman confronts none other than Rabbi Judah the Patriarch. After his reply, instead of defending herself, the woman attacks him head on, demanding that he admit the comparison of what befell her to a hypothetical situation to which he can relate. On another level the humor here is based on the expectation that the sage, the man of the Law, always has the upper hand. Smashing this expectation adds another aspect to the confrontation between man and woman at the heart of the tale. But most significant is the attempt to shatter the conventional male perception of woman as a sexual object, and to emphasize that her physical integrity is every bit as sacrosanct as is the holiness of the Day of Atonement to Rabbi Judah the Patriarch. Indeed, such an idea could not have been overtly expressed in the rabbinic period, nor in later periods. The joke, as an amusing, non-binding folkloric element, discreetly expresses this idea and thus gives vent to the protest otherwise silenced.[100]

Folklore the world over reserves a special place for tales of drunkards. These tales always belong to the realm of the joke and folk humor, in which the drunk's addiction to wine is seen as grotesque and ridiculous. Such addiction violates the accepted social norms of self-respect, property, family, and honest labor. In these tales or jokes the opposition between that which society deems acceptable behavior, and the drunk wallowing in his own vomit, ignoring his family and property, and his unresponsiveness to every attempt to persuade him to change his ways, is what creates the comic effect. In folk narrative, society does not view alcoholism as a disease, or the sufferer as an object of pity. Rather, he is an incomprehensible and ludicrous figure. In the rabbinic literature, discussion of drunkenness and drunks is bound up with the figure of the biblical Noah. Most of the material on this topic appears in the various Midrash in the portions dealing with him. Indeed, the drunk tale that stands out here is in fact an expanded biblical tale, which portrays Noah as the root of all drunkenness:

> When Noah came to plant a vineyard, Satan came and stood before him. He said to him: "What are you planting?" He said to him: "A vineyard" . . . What did Satan do? He brought a sheep and killed it beneath the vine. After that he brought a lion and killed it, after that he brought a pig and killed it, after that he brought a monkey and killed it beneath the vineyard and sprinkled their blood in that same vineyard and they irrigated it with their blood. God indicated [by these] that before a man drinks of wine, behold he is as innocent as that sheep that does not know anything and as a ewe is dumbstruck before those who [come to] shear her. When he has drunk aplenty, behold he is as bold as the lion and says: "There is none like me in the world." When he has drunk too much, he becomes like a pig, dirtying himself in his own urine and excrement. When he has gotten drunk, he becomes like the monkey: standing and dancing and uttering obscenities before all and unaware of what he is doing. (*Tanhuma, Noah*, 13)

This story is an excellent example of an etiological tale. It is anchored in an "etiological focal point" so that every event that takes place in the tale leaves its mark on the generations to follow (such are the seven days of creation and the forty days of flood as well). It attributes the demonic origins of drunkenness to the pact struck between Satan and Noah. Such a pact is always a source of harm and disaster. But the tale is primarily concerned with the analogy between the drunk and various animals. This motif is prevalent in general folklore, wherein each stage of man's life is symbolized by a different creature. Hence aging and physical decline take the form of progressively "lesser" animals. The tale of Noah and the devil demonstrates that the defining human characteristic—namely, preeminence over beasts—does not apply to the drunk; beyond degradation, he has shed his humanity. This is perhaps not such a humorous story, although it reveals society's attitude toward drunkenness: a phenomenon of demonic origins and calamitous consequences.[101]

In the Midrash, beneath the directive, "Do not drink wine or strong drink" (Lev. 10:9), comes forceful condemnation of liquor and its consequences. It usually takes the form of homiletic interpretation, parables, scriptural exegesis, and etymologies denigrating drunkenness in no uncertain terms. Among them are three typical folktales, two in *Midrash Leviticus Rabbah* (12, 1, Margolies edition, p. 245), and one in *Midrash Tanhuma* (Shmini, 11). The first is as follows: An old man sold all the contents of his home to buy wine. He was about to sell the house itself when his sons, fearing he would pass away without leaving them anything, got him well and truly drunk and laid him out in a cemetery. Passing wine merchants, who had heard of a royal tax levied in the city, decided to cache their goods in the cemetery while they went on ahead to investigate the rumor. They set down their wineskins near the old man—who lay as still as a corpse. Awakening later, he helped himself to some of the wine and began to sing. Three days later the sons returned to see what had become of their father—would they find him alive or dead? When they came upon him drinking and singing alongside a pile of provisions, they understood that the Creator had not abandoned their father even among the dead. They took him home and agreed to take turns making sure their father was supplied with wine.

The second tale tells of a man who was accustomed to drinking twelve servings of wine a day. One day he drank only eleven, and could not fall asleep. He rose and went to the tavern in search of his customary twelfth, but the bartender feared the city guards on patrol. He did, however, agree to squirt some wine into the man's mouth via the keyhole in the door. There crouched the customer, mouth to keyhole, when along came the guards. Thinking him a thief, they beat him—but he felt nothing; they wounded him—but he was unaware, so engrossed was he in capturing the drops of wine coming through the door.

The third tale concerns a pious man whose father was a drunk. The father would leave the tavern stinking, and street toughs would ridicule him in the marketplace, throw stones at him, and beat him. The son convinced him not to go to the tavern anymore, promising to bring him wine so that he could drink at home and not endure public scorn and abuse anymore. And so it went until one rainy day the pious man, on his way to the marketplace, saw a drunk lying in the mud, drunk as Lot. The urchins were mocking him. The son ran home and brought his father to witness the scene, in the hope of curing his addiction once and for all. But upon his arrival, "What did the old father do? He went and asked the drunk which tavern he drank in."

The three stories are typical, universal tales of drunks, containing nothing distinctively Jewish (except for the description of the son in the last tale as a "pious man," which is not in any case germane to the body of the tale); they might take place in any society, in any place and at any time. The humor of the tales is based on comic situations and on the surprising reactions or conclusions stemming from the drunks' behavior: each of the tales presents one dominant image as the climax of the story: the old man among the graves in the first, wineskin in hand, merrily singing; in the second tale—the drunk crouching at the tavern door, mouth to keyhole, wine flowing into his mouth, and oblivious to the blows of the patrolmen; in the third tale—the anonymous drunk lying in the mud in the rain, street urchins hurling stones at him, and the second drunk (the pious man's father) leans down to ask where he bought wine so fine it rendered him insensate. The humor of these situations is based on the extreme opposition between them and every social norm of the audience: a graveyard is a place of mourning and grief, hardly the appropriate backdrop for drunken revelry; a man drinks not from a cup but via a hole in a door, and so on. The second comic foundation is the surprise—the conclusion arising from the drunk's response to the given situation: The sons, who expected to find their father dead, discovered that even a stay in the cemetery (and the natural dread of death) could not make him change his ways. Neither the late hour, the closed tavern, nor even the blows of the patrolmen could keep the drunk from his customary twelve daily servings. The pious man's father had so great an appetite for wine he could not be cured by the sight of the bum lying in his own vomit and mud or by his son's words of moral reproach. All three tales confront the drunkard with a threat to his existence—death, physical pain, scorn, and abuse—yet his response flies in the face of our expectations. The conclusion? No matter what you do, you cannot cure the drunkard. As aforesaid, in folk culture this conclusion is humorous, not tragic, as drunkenness is not considered a self-destructive disease but a shameful human frailty.

It is, however, also possible to read these tales as a challenge to the social order: the drunks built themselves their own internal world, which they alone understand. All means of persuasion taken by the dominant society's representatives to rehabilitate them, that is, bring them around to accepting "proper" social norms, fail. The drunks are the winners in all three tales, and efforts to penetrate their world with logic or violence are utterly fruitless. These tales may reflect, not only in the rabbinic period, the attitude of exceptional figures who do not wish or are unable to fit into the accepted social order, who build their own world and who are unprepared to surrender it despite the dominant society's position.[102]

It has already been stated that the unique historical and social circumstances of the Jewish people gave rise to a wealth of tales of confrontation between the Jews and other nations in our folk literature. Indeed, as regards the comic tale as well, folk narrative of the period is replete with tales praising Jewish cleverness and ridiculing members of other religious and social groups. Such jokes generally serve two functions: they sharpen the rivalry with other societal groups, and intensify the sense of identity and social belonging of the members of the narrating society. The largest group of these tales is known as the tales of "Wisdom of the Jerusalemites," preserved in *Midrash Lamentations Rabbah* (1, 4–19). Tales of confrontation with Athenians are concentrated in the first part of the cycle; the second part features stories of confrontation with the *minim* (Jewish-Christians) who interpreted dreams. The tales in both groupings pit Jew against non-Jew, the former exposing the latter by wit and cunning as an utter fool:

> A Jerusalemite went to see a merchant in Athens. On his arrival there he put up at an inn where he found several persons sitting and drinking wine. After he had eaten and drunk he wished to sleep there. They said to him: "We

have agreed among ourselves not to accept a guest until he has made three jumps." He replied to them: "I do not know how you jump. You do it before me and I will copy you." One of them stood up and jumped, and found himself in the middle of the inn; a second jumped [from where the first finished] and found himself by the door at the entrance of the inn; The third jumped and found himself outside. He got up and bolted the door in their faces and said to them: "By your lives, what you intended to do to me I have done to you." (*Lamentations Rabbah* 1, 5)

The comic structure of several of the tales in this cycle is similar: the Athenian who habitually ridiculed Jews, until they tricked him into standing in the Jerusalem marketplace with a shaven head and soot-blackened face, hawking sandals at such exorbitant prices that passing shoppers laughed and scorned him. These stories build active comic situations on continuous plot action, leading step by step to a situation completely opposite to the tale's opening: the Jew who was the underdog or object of ridicule at the outset trades places with the non-Jew by story's end. In contrast to these, the same chain contains other tales whose comic technique is language-based. Instead of a series of images, the audience is treated to puns and wordplay, sharp verbal repartee, and clever replies to complex questions:

An Athenian came to Jerusalem; he found a mortar which had been thrown away [because it was cracked]. He picked it up and took it to a tailor, saying: "Sew this broken mortar for me." The tailor produced a handful of sand and said: "Twist this into threads for me and I will sew it."

An Athenian came to Jerusalem where he met a child to whom he gave some money, saying: "Bring me eggs and cheese." On his return, the man said to him: "Show me which cheese is from a white goat and which from a black goat." He replied: "You are a grown-up man, so show me which egg is from a white hen and which from a black." (*Lamentations Rabbah* 1, 8–9)

All the tales of this grouping match Athenians—representatives of the period's dominant Hellenistic culture—against merchants, shopkeepers, cobblers and tailors, and especially children. Passing children reveal to the Athenian, their "better," the source of the meat and wine he offered them, and that he was illegitimately conceived; they pose him a riddle that he cannot solve, gain possession of his property, and so on. In addition to the cultural polarization between Jew and Greek, these tales also juxtapose children with elders and simple folk with representatives of Hellenism. These additional polarizations add depth to the narrative confrontation, and so strengthen the tales as a tool of social, nationalistic struggle.

The anecdotes and witticisms herein collected present another interesting facet of the confrontation between the Jews and Hellenism in the rabbinic period. The better-known disputes are political, cultural, and philosophical, whereas the comic tales reflect how the confrontation played out on the popular level. The broad strata of society did not bother with the theological or philosophical aspects of the clash of the two cultures, and the political and social tension was manifested among them, naturally, on the popular level. The protagonists of these tales (many of which must have been lost over time) are simple laborers and schoolchildren, the locale is the marketplace, tavern, shop, or schoolhouse. Once again we witness the phenomenon wherein folktales illuminate important social and psychological aspects of society, yet are almost completely ignored by the educated culture of the period.[103]

Among the tales of magic treated in the previous section are many confrontational stories. Some are categorically humorous, differing from "the Jerusalemites'" tales of confrontation only in the supernatural foundations woven into them. For example, the tale cited earlier wherein Rabbi Joshua ben Hananiah drowns in the Sea of Galilee the apostate magician who tried to prove he could split the sea like Moses, the Jews' teacher. The following tale of magic is similar:

> Jannai came to an inn. He said to them: "Give me a drink of water," and they offered him shattitta [a drink of water and flour]. Seeing the lips of the woman [who brought this] moving, he [covertly] spilled a little thereof, which turned to snakes. Then he said: "As I have drunk yours, now do you come and drink mine." So he gave her to drink, and she was turned into an ass. He then rode upon her into the market. But her friend came and broke the charm [changing her back into a human being], and so he was seen riding upon a woman in public. (*Sanhedrin* 67b)

These two magic tales are similarly constructed: both open with a situation in which the apostate or magician traps or endangers the Jewish hero. The latter proves, magically, that his own powers are stronger than those of the apostate. In the tale of Yannai and the innkeeper, the reversal is fashioned in an unquestionably comical manner; the symbolic imagery is not easily ignored: Yannai rides to market on the witch's back. The reversal by which the rival goes from rider to ridden is the comic mechanism which creates the feeling of social strength and unity for the Jewish listeners of this anecdote.

The peak of Jewish folk satire of other ethnic and religious groups comes through in the following tale:

> Our Rabbis taught: Sabta, a townsman of Ablas, once hired an ass to a Gentile woman. When she came to Pe'or [where moving one's bowels was the preferred method of idol worship], she said to him, "Wait till I enter and come out again." On her issuing, he said to her: "Now do you wait for me too until I go in and come out again." "But," she said, "are you not a Jew?"

He replied, "What does it concern you?" He then entered, uncovered himself before it, and wiped himself on the idol's nose, whilst the acolytes praised him, saying, "No man has ever served this idol thus." (*Sanhedrin* 64a)

Folk humor does not turn its nose up at vulgarity, of that there can be no question. Folk humor's indulgent interest in genitalia, and its use of non-normative expressions and descriptions, serve a recognized function of psychological externalization; that which is forbidden to think, and certainly to say aloud in polite company, is permissible when done in a humorous atmosphere. Very few such anecdotes survived in the rabbinic literature, for reasons easily understood. This tale belongs to the category of debates between Jews and other nations that take place on the popular level. As aforementioned, the rivalry expressed in these tales is not reflected along ideological or cultural lines, but on the level of biting, caustic action. The members of other religions are accused here not only of filthy rites, but of idiocy as well. The principal humorous aspect of this tale is not defecation as a religious ritual, but the manner in which the Jewish hero ridicules its practitioners. This protagonist fits in well with those of the other tales we have examined: a donkey driver for hire, he, too, comes from the working class of Jewish society. The confrontation is once again waged between a simple Jew and a member of the non-Jewish spiritual elite. Here we have a tale, originally no more than a crude joke told among the people, that made its way into the aggadic literature. The redactor of this topic in tractate *Sanhedrin*, for example, which deals with the ritual worship of the deity *Ba'al Peor*, must have known of the folk tradition, and, despite its vulgarity, decided to include it in the present discussion on account of its relevance to the subject, and especially for its denigration of the members of other faiths.[104]

Jewish society's attitude to adherents of other religions is clear. The question which logically follows is, how did other cultures regard the Jews? We have much evidence of anti-Jewish humor in the Greek and Roman literature of the period, reflecting mostly the attitude of the Roman writers and intellectuals, and some folk humor. Ironically enough, the evidence of such humor comes to us through the rabbinic literature. Two such examples in particular merit our attention:

[a] R. Abbahu opened his discourse with the text, "They that sit in the gate talk of me" (Pss. 69, 13). This refers to the nations of the world who sit in theaters and circuses. "And I am the song of the drunkards": after they have sat eating and drinking and become intoxicated, they sit and talk of me, scoffing at me and saying: "We have no need to eat carobs [the food of the poorest] like the Jews!" They ask one another: "How long do you wish to live?" To which they reply, "As long as the shirt of a Jew which is worn on the Sabbath! [used only on Sabbath, it lasts a long while]." They then take a camel into their theatres, put their shirts upon it, and ask one another, "Why

is it in mourning?" To which they reply, "The Jews observe the law of the Sabbatical year [when the land lies fallow and its produce is not gathered] and they have no vegetables, so they eat this camel's thorns, and that is why it is in mourning!" Next they bring a clown with shaven head into the theatre and ask one another, "Why is his head shaven?" to which they reply, "The Jews observe the Sabbath, and whatever they earn during the week they eat on the Sabbath. Since they have no wood to cook with, they break their bedsteads and use them as fuel; consequently they sleep on the ground and get covered with dust, and anoint themselves with oil which is very expensive for that reason!" (*Lamentations Rabbah*, proem 12)

[b] Said Rab Judah in the name of Samuel: They have yet another [ritual, in addition to those already mentioned here in the Mishna] in Rome [which occurs] once every seventy years. Then a healthy man [symbolising Esau= Rome] is brought and made to ride on a lame man [symbolising Jacob= Jews]; he is dressed in the attire of Adam [either naked, or with legendary fancy clothes], on his head is placed the scalp of R. Ishmael [one of the Ten Martyrs executed by Hadrian, who was flayed before his execution], and on his neck are hung pieces of fine gold to the weight of four zuzim, the market-places [through which these pass] are paved with onyx stones, and the proclamation is made before him: "The reckoning of the ruler is wrong. The brother of our lord [Jacob], the imposter! Let him who will see it see it; he who will not see it now will never see it. Of what avail is the treason to the traitor or deceit to the deceiver!" [considering the condition of the Jews nowadays]. And they concluded thus: Woe unto the one when the other will arise. (*'Avodah Zarah* 11b)

These two texts appear in their specific contexts in the Midrash and the Talmud for well-known reasons: *Midrash Lamentations Rabbah* describes the destruction of the Temple and its grievous repercussions. The image of the Jew, as reflected in this text, is one consequence of that tragic event, and its description serves to augment the sense of pain and degradation befitting the day of mourning. The second text, from tractate *Avodah Zarah*, is related as one of the descriptions of Rome's pagan rites. The text in *Lamentations Rabbah* has an additional explicit purpose: to indicate the types of entertainments indulged in by other peoples, and thereby to prevent Jews from frequenting "theatre houses and circuses," when they should be spending their time in the study hall and the synagogue in praise of the Creator. Indeed, these two texts, which portray in great detail the non-Jews' public appearances and rites, show that the sages' concern was not without cause. The fact that Jews could describe them in such detail proves that they were in fact spectators—by design or happenstance—of such performances.

The first text describes two different situations: the first, boisterous feasting and drinking in a tavern followed by anecdotes at the Jews' expense. The type of mockery is also interesting: not for their religion or history are the Jews ridiculed, but for their indigence: after sating gluttonous appetites the revellers jest, now we won't have to eat carob like the Jews (who have nothing else to eat). Likewise, the Jews' festive Sabbath garb is so timeworn, the revellers hope they live so long. This portrayal is significant for the unbiased evidence it offers of the Jews' social image among the non-Jewish residents of Palestine in the period following the destruction of the Temple: hunger, rags, and abject poverty were the Jews' distinguishing characteristics.

The second part of this text describes two short humorous "sketches" in which the principals are a camel dressed for mourning and a bald jester. The sketches take the form of dialogues between the "innocent" interviewer, who wonders at their odd appearance (a camel in mourning and a bald jester)—and the reply, which connects the phenomenon to Jewish customs. Here the satire is aimed at typical Jewish customs, which seemed very strange indeed to the non-Jews: the year of *shemittah* ("rest of the soil") and Sabbath observance. It stands to reason that such satirical sketches lampooned other Jewish customs as well, particularly circumcision, which the Romans considered a barbaric castration ritual.

Text [b], which describes Esau riding Jacob in the marketplace, seems to be the reverse of the magic tale above cited of Yannai, who changed a woman into a donkey and rode it to market. This tale is a description of a type of street theater with an added cult or carnival dimension: it takes place at precise intervals of seventy years; uses symbols (the cripple and the healthy individual, the fine clothes "of the first man," the scalp, the chain of gold coins); and ritualistic language ("Let him who will see it see it; he who will not see it now will never see it," for example). In contrast to the theater of Caesaria, Roman ritual has a distinct historical orientation: it utilizes current figures to illustrate the past. In other words, Jacob symbolizes the nation brought low, and Esau the Roman (or perhaps Christian), riding him as a beast. The point of this ritualistic drama is that the present situation has its roots deep in the past: Jacob was a cheat who stole the birthright, yet Esau emerged triumphant—despite all the biblical prophecies of the End of Days. This ritualistic drama presents, by visual-symbolic means, the popular Roman (or Christian) response to the Jewish polemic against the pagan world. The pain and degradation Jewish spectators felt at such satirical performances certainly did not stop the audience from cheering and applauding the jesters' mimicry, the spectacle of colorful costumes, and the portrayal of the Jews' reduced circumstances.[105]

Of all the types of comic tales in rabbinic literature one in particular stands apart: the tall tale. This comic genre is widespread in almost all the cultures known to us, yet despite its wide distribution it is always marked as a strange and unique phenomenon. Moreover, its categorization as humor is not always self-evident. As opposed to other types of humor, the comic effect of tall tales does not always take—the audience does not always laugh—and neither is it clear to us that they were always designed to provoke laughter. Folklorists have classified such stories in international indexes of motifs and story types as "tales of lying" or as "comic legends," indicating the confusion in the categorization of tales of this type as a clear-cut genre.[106]

A quantitative comparison of the tall tale to other types of humor appearing in the rabbinic literature shows it to be predominant. This indicates either a great affection for this literary type during the rabbinic period (and the multitude of tales reflects their frequency in the social reality of the time), or that the sages themselves had a preference for this genre, as evidenced by the many examples that have survived in writing, while in reality they appeared and were told infrequently, compared to other types of humor. In either case, it can be concluded that, while for every other period in the history of Jewish folk literature only solitary clues remain to indicate the existence of the genre (except for the *chizbats* [Arabic: tales of lies] of the Palmah period), in the rabbinic period it was widespread and accepted even by sages, thanks to whom we have much surviving written evidence.

This popularity of the genre in the Jewish world matches its appeal for the Greco-Roman culture. The Roman authors, particularly Lucian, cite examples of sailors' tales, space travel, encounters with mythological monsters, and other tall tales prevalent among the folk culture of their time. It seems that, in this realm as well, Jewish folk culture developed along parallel lines and under the influence of the period's general culture. Similarly parallel are the learned classes: the sages' interest in these tales, as we shall see below, resembles in large part that of the Greco-Roman writers in the same genres.[107]

The largest, but by no means only, concentration of tall tales among the sages appears in the fifth chapter of tractate *Bava Batra* in the Babylonian Talmud (73a–74b)—the cycle attributed to Rabbah bar Bar Hana. Many other tales of this ethnopoetic genre appear in the Babylonian Talmud, the Palestinian Talmud, and in the Midrash. The wide distribution in the talmudic literature indicates that interest in the tall tale was not incidental or given to considerations of taste of a single narrator or editor alone, but was prevalent in different places and periods. Nonetheless, before embarking on a discussion of this genre among the sages we must first examine the tales of Rabbah bar Bar Hana. While these talmudic tales are not the earliest known to us in world literature, they are certainly among the most important on account of their scope, literary quality, and significance. Here the redactors of the Talmud concentrated twenty-two tales, all belonging to one genre. The tales have uniform structural and stylistic features, and content, revealing well-developed and exceptional folkloristic talents. My intention here is not to individually analyze each of the twenty-two tales, their interconnectedness, or their parallels to world literature. Our interest here is rather the manner in which these tall tales characterize the comic tale in the rabbinic period.

> Rabbah bar Bar Hana further stated: I saw a frog the size of the Fort of Hagronia. What is the size of the Fort of Hagronia?—Sixty houses. There came a snake and swallowed the frog. Then came a raven and swallowed the snake, and perched on a tree. Imagine how strong was the tree. R. Papa b. Samuel said: Had I not been there I would not have believed it. (*Baba Bathra* 73b)

As in the analysis of previous comic tales, here too we must seek the tale's comic mechanism. In other words, precisely what in the text makes us laugh? It seems that here, too, the same system of looking for incongruous elements within the tale applies. There is a pronounced incongruity between the tale's realistic and fantastic characteristics. On the one hand, the tale contains elements intended to inspire a sense of reliability: the narrator is present at the performance event and declares in the style of "had I not been there"—he himself saw the events in question, and the comparison to the Hagronia (Agranam) Fortress, recognized as an actual place by the audience of listeners. Even the "heroes" of the tale—the frog, the crocodile, the crow, and the tree—are recognizable, commonplace elements, in and of themselves nothing out of the ordinary, and finally, the conclusion of the tale features the reinforcing declaration by another famous sage. All these are rhetorical elements of verisimilitude whose purpose is to impart credibility to the tale. On the other hand, non-realistic elements figure here as well: there is the monstrous size of the characters, a description which jeopardizes the credibility built by the verisimilitude. It is the clash between credible and fantastic elements that creates the tall tale's mechanism of incongruity, and constitutes the tale's primary comic stimulus.

When reading (or listening to) this tale and others of its type, there is no escaping the feeling that the narrator is lying and that the audience knows it, therefore it is not to be construed as a lie, but as something else. But if we assume that Rabbah bar Bar Hana was known and recognized as a "professional" fabricator, how is it that sages such as Joshua ben Hananiah, R. Papa bar Samuel, Rav Dimi, Rabbi Yohanan, and Rav Ashi were willing to tell or be connected with such "lies"? There appears to be only one answer: we must conclude that the invention of such tales was considered a skill, a test of the cleverness or sharpness of folk storytellers or sages as tall tales in this period were a widespread, legitimate literary type:

> They [the Athenian Sages] said to him: "Tell us some *milei de-bdiei* [literally: words of lying]." He said to them: "There was a mule which gave birth, and round its neck was a document in which was written: 'there is a claim

against my father's house of [one hundred] thousand zuz.'" They asked him: "Can a mule give birth?" He answered them: "This is one of these *milei de-bdiei.*" (*Bekhorot* 8b)

One test of R. Joshua ben Hananiah's wisdom in the famous contest of wits with the Elders of Athens was his skill in spinning fictitious yarns ("tales of lying"), here named and explicitly defined as a conventional literary genre. Indeed, when Rav Papa bar Samuel backs up Rabbah bar Bar Hana's words, personally attesting to having been there and witnessing the events with his own eyes, (Rav Papa lived several generations after Rabbah bar Bar Hana), it is not his credibility being scrutinized but his comic wit and ability to weave that yarn (*milei de-bdiei*). We must view his words in their context—in the comic or ironic tone in which they were offered, namely: "of course it is true, I myself was there and witnessed it." What makes the tale of lies ("lie" is the term used by Rabbenu Gershom and Rashi in their commentaries on this text) unique is the special technique of exposing the comic device: the fictional descriptions are so exaggerated and far-fetched that the audience of listeners readily "catches on" that no "serious" portrayal of true details is on display, rather they are being taken along on an imaginary flight in pursuit of the comic stimulus. The realistic reinforcements added to the tale (such as the sages' corroboration) are another device to authenticate, as it were, the truth of the matter, whose true purpose is, in fact, just the opposite: to make plain to the listeners that the tale is a tissue of lies. What we have here is a double deception, whose aim is to expose the comic mechanism by means of presenting the entire tale as a sort of *Fata Morgana*; all are amazed by the tale, despite—or perhaps, perversely, on account of—the fact that all know it to be delusion.

The following homiletic interpretation proves the sages' interest in this genre:

"And the frog came up, and covered the land of Egypt" (Exod. 8, 6). R. Eleazar said: It was one frog, which bred prolifically and filled the land. This is a matter disputed by Tannaim. R. Akiva said: There was one frog which filled the whole of Egypt. But R. Eleazar b. Azariah said to him: "Akiva, what hast thou to do with Haggadah [narrative, legend]? Cease thy words and devote thyself to 'leprosies' and 'tents' [the Halakha—legal discussions]. One frog croaked for the others, and they came." (*Sanhedrin* 67b)

In order to interpret the Scripture's use of the singular, R. Akiva mobilizes the folk genre of the tall tale. It may be that he was indeed alluding to a tall tale like that of Rabbah bar Bar Hana about the giant frog. In other words, this literary type was so well-known and accepted that a sage of Rabbi Akiva's stature did not hesitate to press it into exegetical service. The fact that this technique of homiletic interpretation did not sit well with other sages, who preferred realistic exegesis to wild imagination, does little to diminish the centrality of the genre in either the folk literature of the period or among the sages themselves.

We have thus far used the term "tale," although few narrative foundations figure in the texts we have reviewed. The story of Rabbah bar Bar Hana, for instance, is constructed as a series of sentences which, with three exceptions, are all descriptive. The first sentence is the opening formula, "Rabbah bar Bar Hana stated," the concluding sentence is Rav Papa's authentication, and in the middle, when the size of the frog is compared to the Hagronia Fortress, the narrator offers the image of sixty houses as the measure of the creature's massive size. In sum, the tale contains no narrative sentences whatsoever. Other tales in this grouping recount how Rabbah bar Bar Hana arrived at the objects which he describes, whether by sea or desert caravan, what transpired in the course of his encounter with the marvelous phenomena of nature, and so on. But the rule is that in the tall tale as told by the sages (as opposed to folktales), description (not plot) is the essence of the text. Since the tall tale is meant to describe exceptional phenomena, it is only natural that the narrators focus their attention on the description of such, and not on the detailing of what happened to the hero during his encounter with them.

The twenty-two tales included in the grouping of stories of Rabbah bar Bar Hana have been defined by scholars as travel tales. They convey what Rabbah heard from mariners or desert people, and especially what marvelous things he saw with his own eyes in the fabulous places to which he wandered. Yet this definition fails to take into account the tension woven into these tales between the strange, distant reaches of the earth and the world of the academy to which the wanderer always returned to report on his comings and goings:

> He [the Arab merchant] said unto me: "Come and I will show you the Dead of the Wilderness [those who died in the Sinai desert during the forty years of wandering]." I went [with him] and saw them; and they looked as if in a state of exhilaration. They slept on their backs; and the knee of one of them was raised, and the Arab merchant passed under the knee, riding on a camel with spear erect, and did not touch it. I cut off one corner of the purple-blue shawl of one of them; and we could not move away. He said to me: "[If] you have taken something from them, return it; for we have a tradition that he who takes anything from them cannot move away." I went and returned it; and then we were able to move away. When I came before the Rabbis they said unto me: "Every Abba [the narrator's original name] is an ass and every bar Bar Hana is a fool. For what purpose did you do that? Was it in order to ascertain whether [the Law] is in accordance with the [decision of] Beth Shammai or Beth Hillel [for the dispute of these two schools over this matter]. You should have counted the threads and counted the joints."

He said unto me: "Come and I will show you Mount Sinai." [When] I arrived I saw that scorpions surrounded it and they stood like white asses. I heard a heavenly voice saying: "Woe is me that I have made an oath [to send Israel into exile] and now that I have made the oath, who will release me?" When I came before the Rabbis, they said unto me: "Every Abba is an ass, and every bar Bar Hana is a fool. You should have said: 'Thy oath is void!'" He, however, thought that perhaps it was the oath in connection with the Flood [and so he could have destroyed the whole world again]. (*Baba Bathra* 73b–74a)

Each of these two texts is constructed as a two-stage report of Rabbah bar Bar Hana; one part describes his experiences in distant, wondrous places, and the second describes the performance event itself, in which he stands before the sages of the study hall. In each text Rabbah encounters mythological entities: legendary desert corpses in one and the *Shekhinah* (holy spirit) exiled to the desert, in the other. Either encounter could have had far-reaching ramifications for Jewish destiny—a resolution to the schism between the houses of Shammai and Hillel over the matter of the *tallit*, and perhaps even the coming of the End of Days. The magical and historical significance of Rabbah bar Bar Hana's encounter with mythological phenomena becomes clear only when they are recounted in the study hall. Until that point not even the hero of the tales understood. The sages of the study hall, in their wisdom, do indeed comprehend the significance of the matters, but they do not set out to investigate for themselves. They analyze and direct the course of life, but do not choose to experience it personally. Conversely, Rabbah bar Bar Hana, here representing the simple wanderer, the man of the people, meets things head on, but their understanding and application is beyond him. Since the narrators and stylists of these tales were the sages themselves, the ultimate criticism is for the wanderer, who is denigrated. It may be that when these fantastic tales were told in other circles, the image of the sages was ridiculed no less. In any case, the tension created in these tales between home and what lies beyond, between experience and the academy, where it undergoes scrutiny, is an important ideological theme of the genre of the tall tale among the sages.

In the examples quoted thus far we could see how the creation of the tall tale included the participation of more than just the narrator. The next example will illustrate that this literary type was among the few in folk literature that can be proven, by direct evidence, to be a "social" rather than an individual creation, in the sense that the contributions of several participants to the tale's various layers develop and crystallize the tale:

Rabbah bar Bar Hana further stated: We traveled once on board a ship, and the ship sailed between one fin of the fish and the other for three days and three nights; it [swimming] upwards and we [floating] downwards. And if you think the ship did not sail fast enough, R. Dimi, when he came, stated that it covered sixty parasangs in the time it takes to warm a kettle of water. When a horseman shot an arrow [the ship] outstripped it. And R. Ashi said: That was one of the small sea monsters which have [only] two fins. (*Baba Bathra* 73b)

The names of the sages mentioned here do not only shore up the realistic foundations of the tale, they indicate its process of creation. One sage offers a narrative tradition which serves as the basis of the process and, later, other sages add layers to the tale, either from familiar traditions or their own imaginations. In any case, the tales attest to the process of joint creation in which various narrators contribute to the creation of the text.

The two tales considered in the previous example indicate another important phenomenon in the sages' tall tales—corroboration and authentication of religious myths. In them, the hero purportedly sees the desert dead as the former slaves who left Egypt behind in search of the promised land, as described by earlier Jewish traditions, and hears the voice of the *Shekhinah* unceasingly mourning the Destruction. The exodus and the *Shekhinah*'s grief are two traditions deeply rooted in Judaism's collective consciousness, as they are bound up with the fundamental theme of exile and redemption. Tales of Rabbah bar Bar Hana's contacts with them are intended to impart to these traditions an added dimension of credibility and substantiality: a human being actually saw them and testified as such before the sages of the study hall, who accepted his testimony. Jewish myths are the subject of other fantasy tales as well: Rabbah bar Bar Hana sees the place where Korah and his followers were engulfed and hears their voices, he sees Ziz Shaddai, the mythical bird, he reaches the end of the earth and sees the "wheel of heaven," which regulates the day's transition to night. He and other seafarers encounter the Leviathan of Genesis which will one day strain the banquet table of the righteous, and see the geese, dripping with fat, to be eaten in the world to come. Rabbi Johanan tells of seafarers who saw the chest of precious stones belonging to the wife of Rabbi Hanina ben Dosa, who, it is said, will one day weave them with the blue thread of the ritual fringes of the righteous in the world to come (ibid.). In another cycle of tall tales, the narrators testify to their journeys in Palestine, where they saw milk flowing from the full udders of goats, dripping and mixing with the date honey and, "and these mingled with each other. 'This is indeed,' they remarked, '[a land] flowing with milk and honey'" (*Ketubbot* 111b), that is, first-hand evidence of the authenticity of another foundation myth—that of the land flowing with milk and honey.

Jewish myths join the typical features of the international tall tale as an integral part of rabbinic tall tales. Since these myths deal primarily with the world to come, their proof could only be found in distant places, and the narrators encounter them in far off, mysterious locales. These typical subjects of Jewish tall tales constitute proof of their social and religious function, and the reason why the sages so freely employed them. The travelers' and seafarers' face-to-face encounters with the basic themes of Jewish mythology supply proof of their existence. The Leviathan and the wild geese, the desert dead, the punishments of Korah and his followers, the *Shekhinah* weeping over the Destruction, and the fertility of the Land of Israel, come across not as fictitious traditions, but as factual and real, according to the personal testimony of travelers and sages. Here we see how a folk genre was recruited to substantiate and fortify the national and religious consciousness of the period.

These tales are also a perfect example of early "Jewish humor." While they utilize general comic techniques, the comic mechanism which drives them is based on an understanding of Jewish heritage and tradition, and therefore most could not function in any context outside of Jewish society.

Rabbinic literature contains tall tales other than the large cycle of tales attributed to Rabbah bar Bar Hana. In addition to his "travelogue," another type stands out among the tales of lies spread about the sources: the agricultural tall tale.

> R. Hiyya b. Adda was the Scriptural tutor of the young children of Resh Lakish. [On one occasion] he took a three days' holiday and did not come [to teach the children]. "Why," the other asked him when he returned, "did you take a holiday?"—"My father," he replied, "left me one espalier and on the first day, I cut from it three hundred clusters [of grapes], each cluster yielding one keg. On the second day, I cut three hundred clusters, each two of which yielded one keg. On the third day, I cut three hundred clusters, each three of which yielded one keg, and so I renounced my ownership of more than one half of it." "If you had not taken a holiday [from the Torah]," the other said to him, "it would have yielded more."
>
> Rami b. Ezekiel one day paid a visit to Bene-Barak where he saw goats grazing under fig trees, while honey was flowing from the figs, and milk ran from them, and these mingled with each other. "This is indeed," he remarked, "[a land] flowing with milk and honey."
>
> R. Jacob b. Dostai related: From Lod to Ono [is a distance of about] three miles. Once I rose up early in the morning and waded [all that way] up to my ankles in honey of the figs.
>
> Resh Lakish said: I myself saw the flow of the milk and honey of Sepphoris and it extended [over an area of] sixteen by sixteen miles. (*Kethuboth* 111b–112a)

The text goes on to describe the sages' discovery of a peach as large as a village cooking pot with a five-*seah* capacity—"One third [of the fruit] they ate, one third they declared free of all, and one third they put before their beasts." A year later, R. Eleazar found himself in the same place, and saw it as well. In Gabla, R. Joshua ben Levi saw grapes as large as calves. In another cycle of agricultural tall tales (PT *Pe'ah* 7,3) agricultural produce of gargantuan proportions is described, such as a turnip upon whose upper leaves nestled a fox, or a cluster of mustard, one leaf of which was large enough to cover an entire hut, and even the tall Rabbi Simeon ben Halafta "climbed it as if he climbs on top of a fig tree." Here there are more tales of honey so plentiful that whole houses were coated with it. And another tale (*Menahot* 85b) of the people of Lydia (Laodicea) who "were in need of oil; they appointed an agent and instructed him, 'Go and purchase for us a hundred myriad worth of oil.'" They found it neither in Jerusalem nor Tyre, but with a man from Gush Halav, "It is said that he hired every horse, mule, camel, and ass that he could find in all the Land of Israel," and loaded them all with the pots of oil—all produced by one lone farmer. Also:

> [Rabbi testified:] The lettuces in our place have six hundred thousand peelings [of small leaves] around their core.
>
> Once a certain cedar tree fell in our place and sixteen wagons alongside each other passed its width. Once the egg of Bar Yokhani [a fabulous bird] fell and its contents swamped sixteen cities and destroyed three hundred cedar trees. (*Bekhoroth* 57b)

Beyond the sages' interest in such tales, their abundance shows how very widespread they were among the agricultural societies of Palestine in this period. As demon tales surfaced in urban or semi-urban environments, so agricultural tall tales take place in a rural milieu. It is natural, and familiar enough from other cultures, that agriculture-based societies develop stories around their source of livelihood. The numerous tales of rainmaking in the folk literature of the rabbinic period also fall within this category. Of particular interest is the agricultural tall tale, which displays the two principal elements of the tall tale in general: the first is the comic-entertainment aspect. Experienced farmers can only laugh upon hearing fantastic tales of giant produce. But there is a more serious aspect too, namely, the psychological one. These tales build on the secret desire for great success which, in the case of farmers whose agricultural output is their livelihood, would be fruits of extraordinary size. As the tall tale of travelers to distant parts oversteps the boundaries of imagination to vistas beyond the reality familiar to the audience of listeners, so the agricultural tall tales involve a leap of the imagination, in this case inward, into the familiar, day-to-day reality of the narrating society. The tales are at once a bit of comic relief in a life filled with hard work, and a faint hope that even some small part of the fantasy could come true.

Anecdotes, and the tall tale in particular, generally seem like nonsense tales whose power lies in the immediate laughter they provoke. We sought to show here that at least two basic types of tall tales in the rabbinic period—the travel tale and the agricultural tall tale—have significant and interesting social and psychological functions. As with any folktale, they would not have had such currency, they would not have appeared in so many versions and survived for so long, had they not fulfilled a deep need of the narrating society. Substantiating sacred Jewish myths, the secret hope of financial success to ease the hardship of daily life and, in general, the release of the imagination to soar above the gray, all-too-familiar reality, were basic human needs, manifested in the wide circulation of the tall tale during this period.

[J] Parables and Fables

Talmudic literature abounds in fables and parables, generically called *mashal*. They generally serve a rhetorical function, exemplifying or elucidating the topic of discussion. Most fall formally and thematically into the sub-genre of "parable," a literary-rhetorical form used to analogize the idea put forward by the text. This type of *mashal* presents a familiar, perceptible representation or picture as an aid to understanding or fleshing out a complex idea. These "pictures" generally lack a literary plot, and they are not designed to exist as independent tales; they are literary units contextually dependent upon the preacher's analogy to the idea he is developing. This being the case, I do not intend to treat these hundreds of parables as folktales of the rabbinic period. They were generally devised for one-time use, and were not told beyond the confines of homiletic interpretation or legal discussion. Therefore they in no way meet the criteria of folktale.[108]

The distinction between fable (narrative mashal) and parable in rabbinic literature, for all its fundamental importance, is not unequivocal, and it is sometimes difficult to tell the two forms apart. Below we see a typical example:

> ["After the doings of the Land of Egypt . . . Ye shall not do" (Lev. 18:3). This bears on the text, "As a lily among the thorns, so is my love among the daughters" (Canticles 2:2)]. R. 'Azariah in the name of R. Judah, son of R. Simon, says: The matter may be compared to the case of a king who had an orchard planted with one row of fig trees, one of vines, one of pomegranates, and one of apples. He entrusted it to a tenant and went away. After a time he came and looked in at the orchard to ascertain what it had yielded. He found it full of thorns and briars, so he brought wood-cutters to raze it. He looked closely at the thorns and noticed among them a single rose-colored flower. He smelled it and his spirits calmed down. The king said: "The whole orchard shall be saved because of this flower." In a similar manner the whole world was created only for the sake of the Torah. After twenty-six generations the Holy One, blessed be He, looked closely at His world to

ascertain what it had yielded, and found it full of water in water [wicked people in wicked environment] . . . So he brought cutters to cut it down; as it says: "The Lord sat enthroned at the Flood" (Pss. 29:10). He saw a single rose-colored flower, to wit, Israel. He took it and smelled it when He gave them the Ten Commandments, and His spirits were calmed . . . Said the Holy One, blessed be He: "The orchard shall be saved on account of this flower. For the sake of the Torah and of Israel the world shall be saved." (*Leviticus Rabbah* 23, 3)

The literary structure, stylistic character, introductory statement, and the linking of this parable to its epimythium, epitomize the talmudic parables as example. Yet it also includes features which enable us to view it as a fable based on an independent tale. The sequential development of the plot, the conflict between the active elements of the story, the increasing complexity of the plot, and its resolution according to the values and expectations of the narrating society all characterize a narrative structure. In addition, the tale is built upon the commonplace folk image (or motif) of "the rose among the thorns." It unfolds into a plot complete with narrative development and tension. In this case, it is especially difficult to evaluate the derivation of the tale: did it originate in folk tradition or was it inspired by the image from the Song of Songs (Canticles 2:2), to bolster the interpretation presented immediately thereafter? The second possibility seems more plausible, as the mashal is so extraordinarily suited to the interpretation. Complementarity this precise is most likely the product of custom manufacturing. In any case, this example shows that the foundations of folk literature and the constellation of folk beliefs and customs were mined for use in the many parables scattered through the literature of the period. It is clear that the borders between the period's popular and educated cultures are not easily defined. The sages habitually made sophisticated, imaginative use of the contents and forms of folk literature.

The parable is one of the most ancient literary forms known. Many parables and remnants of animal tales have been found in the writings of ancient Sumer, Babylonia, and Egypt, indicative of intensive activity in these areas both as regards elite literary creativity and folklore. Some would attribute this creativity to the anthropomorphic worldview of the ancient cultures, according to which animals were graced with human thoughts and attributes, and lived in kingdoms analogous to those of humanity, in which they interacted with each other in human ways. The anthropomorphic perspective, paired with the will to comprehend animals' ways of life on account of their proximity to and interdependence with people, was responsible for the many myths and tales on the origins of animal traits and the complex relationship between the animal kingdom and the human world.[109]

The ancient Babylonian myth of Etana is our starting point to describe the connection between an animal tale and a parable. The tale opens with a pact between the serpent and the eagle: they agree not to harm each other, with the sun as witness. The eagle breaks the pact: he swoops down and devours the serpent's offspring. When the serpent returns and discovers his loss, he demands vengeance. The sun instructs the serpent to lie in ambush for the eagle, who is then captured. After pulling off his wings, the serpent hurls his foe into a pit to die of hunger. The extant versions of this ancient myth are few, fragmented, and incomplete. Fortunately, the continuation of the myth of the shepherd Etana, who rescued the eagle and became king, is of less interest to us than the revisions wrought by Aesop (sixth–fifth centuries B.C.E.), who turned this ancient animal myth, dating from 1800–1500 B.C.E., into a full fable:

> An eagle and a fox who had struck up a friendship decided to live close to one another and made their living together a pledge of the friendship. The eagle flew up to a very tall tree and had its brood there, while the fox went into the thicket below and bore her young. Once when the fox went out to hunt, the eagle, having no food, flew down to the thicket, snatched up the young foxes, and helped its nestlings to devour them. When the fox returned and realized what had been done, she was not so much troubled at the death of her young as she was concerned with revenge. As an earthbound creature she could not pursue her winged neighbor and therefore stood and cursed her enemy from a distance, which is the only resort of those who are weak and impotent. But it turned out before long that the eagle paid the penalty for her violation of the friendship. Some men were making a sacrifice in the country, and the eagle flew down and carried of a piece of burning entrail from the altar. When she brought this to the nest, which was made of old dry sticks, a strong wind caught it and started a bright fire. The nestlings, who were still unfledged, were caught in the fire and fell to the ground. The fox ran up and ate them all before the eagle's very eyes. (*Aesop without Morals*, translated by Lloyd W. Daly, New York and London 1961, p. 93)

The connection between Aesop's fables and the literature of the ancient Near East is a familiar and as yet unresolved question, but more pertinent to our discussion is the allusion to this tale in rabbinic literature:

> "And he [Jacob said to Isaac his father]: Because the Lord thy God sent me good speed" (Gen. 27:20). R. Yohanan said: He was like a raven bringing fire to his nest. (*Genesis Rabbah* 65, 19)

While it is conceivable that the image of a raven bringing fire to its own nest was based on reality, it is hardly likely. Far more feasible is the deduction that Rabbi Yohanan was referring to the story of Etana, especially because he is interpreting here the classical story of betrayal—Jacob betrayed his brother, Esau—equivalent to the betrayal of the eagle and the fox. Perhaps he reasoned that the tale was so well-known he did not have to tell it in full, that a hint by way of a familiar adage would suffice. This happens often in rabbinic literature. What path did the ancient myth travel in its migration to the rabbinic period? Perhaps it seeped in much earlier by way of the ancient eastern stock of narrative types and motifs, and perhaps R. Yohanan had in mind Aesop's famous fable. The second possibility is the more likely in view of the vast evidence that Aesop's fables were well known in the Palestine of the rabbinic age, and as the two tales are similar.[110]

The concise, pithy form of the mashal is also significant. Study of the ancient parable has indicated that one typical form was epigrammatic, condensing the tale's plot into a single utterance, and summing up the tale's didactic significance: "The smith's dog could not turn on the heavy sledge, so he turned on the pot of water." This proverb encapsulates an entire narrative plot. The narrator in this instance was not interested in conveying the tale (already well-known), but its ethical lesson. This ancient Babylonian parable has a close parallel in the aggadic literature as well: " . . . the nations of the world . . . want to incite The Holy Blessed Be He but cannot, so they come and incite Israel . . . It is similar to one who cannot beat the ass, so he beats the saddle" (*Tanhuma, Pekudei*, 4).

The ideological orientation of this epigrammatic parable is plain, for in the rabbinic literature, as opposed to that of the ancient east and Aesop, all parables are quoted in their literary context, and their function is easily defined. Clearly, this literary context reflects not the actual situations in which the parables were told, but the manner in which the sages chose to include them in their literary work. Nonetheless, it does offer clues as to how people of the period perceived such parables. Another pair of examples takes the argument a step further:

> Mar Zutra b. Tobiah remarked in Rab's name: This is what men say, "When the camel went to demand horns, they cut off the ears he had." (*Sanhedrin* 106a)

According to Aesop, the parable is as follows:

> The camel saw a bull with a fine set of horns. She was envious of them and decided to try to get a pair just like them. So she went to Zeus and asked him to give her horns. Zeus lost his temper with her for not being satisfied with her size and strength, but wanting something more, and not only didn't give her horns but even reduced the size of her ears. (*Aesop without Morals*, translated by Lloyd W. Daly, p. 143)

In these texts the connection between Aesopian fable and rabbinic proverb cannot be attributed to coincidence. The proverb is the essence of the tale. It may omit the ox, the camel's envy, the appeal, and the dialogue with god, but it retains the essential narrative elements, which convey the tale's significance. The sages used this mashal to analogize Bil'am, the son of Be'or, who sought reward for harming the Israelites, and was instead himself punished and killed. The interpreter in this instance chose not to recount the tale in full; he laid out only the essential elements. In so doing, he focused the listeners' attention on the message of the animal tale, offered not for entertainment but for edification. Here we find important proof that the transformation from parable to aphorism was not rabbinically steered, but the result of the folkloric process in action: Mar Zutra quotes Rav, evidence that the proverb was already in circulation, and in the vernacular—Aramaic. In other words, the compression of the tale into an epigrammatic formula was a folkloric process, not a deliberate action in the service of homiletics. Whether in ordinary conversation or during a performance event, speakers prefer allusion to circumlocution. Another, similar example is Aesop's celebrated fable of the shepherd boy who cried wolf. The sages reduced this fable as well to a proverb: "It is the penalty of a liar, that should he even tell the truth, he is not listened to" (*Sanhedrin* 89b).

The following example provides us with two forms (the proverb and the narrative parable) found in the sages' writings (as well as Aesop):

> R. Samuel b. Nahmani said in R. Jonathan's name: What is meant by the verse, "Faithful are the wounds of a friend; but the kisses of an enemy are deceitful?" (Prov. 27:6)—Better is the curse wherewith Ahijah the Shilonite cursed Israel than the blessing wherewith the wicked Balaam blessed them. Ahijah the Shilonite cursed Israel by a reed as it is said: "For the Lord shall smite Israel, as a reed is shaken in water" (1 Kings 14:15); Just as a reed grows in well-watered soil and its stem is renewed and its roots are numerous, and even if all the winds of the world come and blow upon it they cannot dislodge it from its place, but it sways in unison with them, and as soon as the winds subside, the reed still stands in its place, [so may Israel be]. But the wicked Balaam blessed them by the cedar: just as the cedar does not stand in a watery place, and its roots are few and its stock is not renewed, and even if all the winds of the world come and blow upon it they cannot stir it from its place, but immediately the South wind blows upon it it uproots and overturns it on its face [so may Israel be]. Nay, more, it was the reed's privilege that a quill thereof should be taken from the writing of the Scroll of the Torah, Prophets and Hagiography. (*Sanhedrin* 105b–106a)

And the proverb: "Our Rabbis taught: A man should always be gentle as the reed and never unyielding as the cedar" (*Ta'anith* 20a).

This example reinforces the two points under discussion: first, the generic transformation undergone by parables from story format to proverbial expression; and second, the dependence of rabbinic parables on Greek and Roman fables, particularly those attributed to Aesop. The condensed proverbial fable does away with such narrative elements as plot development, dialogue among the tale's protagonists, and so on, imbuing the remainder with expressional character, turning it into a proverb. Still, the pre-existence of the fable's narrative basis is essential, as, without it, the proverb, appearing independently and without associative dependency on the fable, would be unfathomable. Why indeed should man be flexible as the reed but not rigid as the cedar? Only prior knowledge of the tale could give the proverb meaning.[111]

Especially interesting is the manner in which the fable is woven into the commentary on the scriptural verse, so that Bil'am's words, "cedar trees beside the waters" (Num. 24:6), are construed as a curse, not a blessing. The cedar's strength is seen as a weakness, not an advantage. The sages employ the famous fable to illustrate why this is so. As we shall see below, the folk parable, woven into rabbinical literature, functions principally in the service of hermeneutics, as do the hundreds of instances of parable-type mashal already mentioned. The parable in the last example, like the proverb to which it was reduced, preaches moderation and adaptation, as opposed to the intransigence and zealotry which ultimately lead to ruin. It seems to me that we cannot ignore this parable's practical significance for the time. The sharp contrast offered by R. Samuel bar Nahmani between the cedar and the reed refers not only to events of the biblical age, but also to events and figures of his time. It may be assumed that he was referring to, among others, those zealots of the preceding period (the Destruction and the Bar Kokhba revolt) whose excesses had had such cataclysmic consequences—the fall of the entire "cedar." The way of the reed, namely, adaptation to changing circumstances and lying low to weather the storm, was more likely, according to this view, to preserve the core.

One way, then, of interpreting this type of mashal is as a hermeneutical tool, fleshing out or clarifying complex issues of Scripture. A second avenue is ideological, with practical implications. Both typify the function generally filled by folk parables in rabbinic literature.

The following versions of a famous fable display another link between Aesopian fable and mashal:

> A hungry fox spied some bread and meat left in a hollow tree by some shepherds. He crawled in and ate it, but his belly swelled so that he could not get out again. As he moaned and groaned, another fox passing by came up and asked what was the matter. When he heard what had happened, he said to the first fox: "I guess you'll just have to wait until you get back to the size you were when you went in, and then you won't have any trouble getting out."
>
> The story shows that time overcomes difficulties. (*Aesop*, translated by L. Daly, ibid. pp. 103–104)

"As he came forth of his mother's womb [naked shall he go back as he came, and shall take nothing for his labor]" (Eccles. 5:14). Geniva said: It is like a fox who found a vineyard which was fenced in on all sides. There was one hole through which he wanted to enter, but he was unable to do so. What did he do? He fasted for three days until he became lean and frail, and so got through the hole. Then he ate [of the grapes] and became fat again, so that when he wished to go out he could not pass through at all. He again fasted another three days until he became lean and frail, returning to his former condition, and went out. When he was outside, he turned his face and gazing at the vineyard said: "O vineyard, O vineyard, how good are you and the fruits inside! All that is inside is beautiful and commendable, but what enjoyment has one from you? As one enters you, so he comes out." Such is this world. (*Ecclesiastes Rabbah* 5, 14)

Differences between the two versions are apparent on several levels: Setting—while both are set against a backdrop of Mediterranean agriculture, their respective visual images (a hollow tree trunk versus a fenced vineyard; eating meat and bread as opposed to gorging on grapes) show a different emphasis, stemming perhaps from a different reality. On the level of plot, Aesop's fable employs another protagonist—the second fox— to function as the "donor," who guides the protagonist to a resolution of the conflict. The mashal leaves the protagonist isolated throughout, and left to his own devices he solves his predicament. The principal difference is in the way they are respectively characterized. Aesop's fable puts forth a whiny hero, helpless and oblivious of what is happening to him. The mashal, conversely, offers an independent protagonist who reacts philosophically to his plight and (not waiting for the fabulist to do it, as usual) gives the event an overall meaning.

Another difference, along the same lines, lies in the styles of epimythium offered by the fabulists—Aesop (or a redactor of his fables) and Geniva (the name or nickname of a sage). Aesop emphasizes practical significance, the lesson to be learned for the sake of a better, easier life. The sages' epimythium is philosophical, existential, and suits the overall context of the Book of Ecclesiastes. The stylistic differences between the two versions follow the same pattern. While the Aesopian version is terse, in simple language (these are features of the Greek original), the mashal displays a polished style. Its use of short, concentrated, and measured sentences creates a sense of balance between the separate parts. More distinctive still are the transitions between different, complex modes of expression: the shift from Hebrew to Aramaic, from indirect to direct speech, from declarative statements to the formulation of rhetorical questions, from concrete expression of specific events (the description of the fox's exploits) to a system of generalized, abstract formulations (which resemble the style of the folk proverb).

The Folktale in the Rabbinic Period 197

These differences between the two versions rule out a reading of the mashal as a copy or reworking of Aesop's fable. The fabulist of rabbinic literature did indeed use the central motif of the Aesopian fable—the fox who must regain his former proportions in order to extricate himself—but he wove an original mashal around it, with artistic features appropriate to its conceptual context in the midrash. It is difficult to believe that the teller of the mashal was familiar with the fable in its original form, attributed to Aesop. It, and dozens more, presumably melted into the general stock of folktales over hundreds of years of Hellenistic rule in Palestine, and so was told in numerous versions and contexts by Jewish storytellers, in Greek, Hebrew, and Aramaic. One such version was worked into the midrash on the Book of Ecclesiastes, because it suited the interpretation desired for a particular verse. Indeed, it seems that the principal variations in the rabbinic, as opposed to the Greek, version stem from the different spin given it in the midrashic context, namely as an existential allegory. The fox in the midrashic parable does not fatten himself on bread and meat, as in the Greek version, but on grapes, conjuring up a clear association with wine and indulgence. In keeping with the perception of human existence in Ecclesiastes, the fox is a solitary figure, alone in the face of the consequences of his actions and omissions in this world. Indeed, it is only after the events have transpired that the fox turns back to view what has gone before in a generalized, philosophical manner. This outlook is in the spirit of Ecclesiastes, and diametrically opposed to the utilitarian view of the Aesopian fable.[112]

Alongside such explicit parallels between the mashal and Aesop's fables, there are others sharing a common motif. In such cases it is clear that the sages drew not from Aesop's fables but from the reservoir of Near Eastern motifs that supplied both cultures. Here is one example:

> "And the elders of Moab and the elders of Midian departed" (Num. 22:7). A. Tanna taught: There was never peace between Midian and Moab. The matter may be compared to two dogs in one kennel which were always enraged at each other. Then a wolf attacked one, whereupon the other said: If I do not help him, he will kill him today, and attack me tomorrow. So they both went and killed the wolf. R. Papa observed: Thus people say: 'The weasel and cat [when at peace with each other] had a feast on the fat of the luckless. (Sanhedrin 105a)

This parable has counterparts among Aesop's fables. One concerns the lion and the boar who quarreled over who would drink first at the watering hole. As words gave way to blows, they caught sight of a hovering flock of vultures and decided it was better to remain friends than become prey for the vultures (no. 11). Another tells of a snake trading blows with a cat. Nearby mice, usually prey to both, observed the fight and came out of their holes. When the contenders caught sight of their customary quarry, they stopped scuffling and turned on the mice (no. 122). Despite their basic similarities, the differences in detail rule out a view of such Jewish fables as "copies" or "imitations" of the Greek fables. They are, instead, the product of typical folkloric use of the stock of Greek folk culture, which during the course of hundreds of years had taken root in the folk culture of the eastern Mediterranean.

The mashal serves a twofold hermeneutical function: it exposes the inherent difficulty of the biblical verse, and in solving it, sheds new light on its meaning. Moab and Midian were like two dogs who must share their food. Given that friendship and loyalty are unlikely to grace such a relationship, it is perplexing to read of them walking together. The mashal resolves this incongruity by explaining their pact as a defensive strategy in the face of mutual peril. The biblical story is now shown to have another aspect, its significance made clearer and sharper with the aid of the mashal. Rabbinical literature has many varied examples of folk parables in hermeneutical service. Some representative examples follow:

> "After these things did king Ahasuerus promote Haman the son of Hammedatha etc." (Esther 3:1). This account bears out what Scripture says: "For the wicked shall perish, and the enemies of the Lord shall be as the fat of lambs" (Pss. 37:20), which are fattened not for their own benefit but for slaughter. So the wicked Haman was raised to greatness only to make his fall greater. It was like the case of a man who had a sow, a she-ass, and a filly, and he let the sow eat as much as it wanted, but strictly rationed the ass and the filly. Said the filly to the ass: "What is this lunatic doing? To us who do the work of the master he gives food by measure, but to the sow which does nothing he gives as much as she wants." The ass answered: "The hour will come when you will see her downfall, for they are feeding her up not out of respect for her but to her own hurt." When the Calends [the first day of the Roman month—observed as a feast day] came round, they took the sow and stuck it. When afterwards they set barley before the filly, it began sniffing at it instead of eating. The mother then said to it: "My daughter, it is not the eating which leads to slaughter but the idleness." So, because it says, "And set his seat above all the princes that were with him," therefore later, "They hanged Haman." (*Esther Rabbah* 7, 1)

The text leads to a new angle on the biblical text. In a simple reading of the events as told in the Scroll of Esther, Haman's rise to greatness at court is perceived as part of a historical chain of events. The same text read in light of the mashal, however, exposes a previously unnoticed irritant. As the foal questioned her master's motives, so will the reader wonder why the Almighty raised Haman up so high. This is one version of the eternal theodicean question: why are the wicked crowned with success? The problem now exposed, the mashal proceeds to propose another way of understanding the text. Haman's rise, like his fall, was part of the Divine plan, just as the sow's extravagant rations were part of the farmer's. The solution to the theodicean puzzle is that injustice is merely a misconception stemming from a limited view; justice does prevail, but is apparent only if one can obtain a full picture of reality as a unified whole originating in Divine plan. This is a characteristic example of a mashal expertly wielded to analyze the scriptural text, laying bare the loose ends for scrutiny and then neatly tying them up.

The vast gap between the object of analysis (the Divine plan revealed in the Scroll of Esther) and the subject of the fable (the fattening of a pig for the pagan new year) indicates that the latter was not an original creation devised by sages or preachers to illuminate the scriptural verse. It was apparently a folk fable cited by the preacher (or by an editor of the portion in the Midrash on the Scroll of Esther) for the stated exegetical purpose. Had the preacher intended to create a new mashal to this end, he would almost certainly have chosen parable form, which is more congenial to the subject and its sacred nature (for example, a fable about "a king of flesh and blood"). This was in fact the case for hundreds of other parables. Additional proof that the parable was not authored here is the conclusion of the tale of the donkey's daughter, who refused to eat after seeing what befell the sow. The concluding moral has no bearing on the scriptural issue of Haman's rise. The ending shows us that the point of the original fable had less to do with the fattening of the pig for slaughter than with its idleness as the reason it met such an end. Any beast who did not prove himself useful might suffer the same fate (which was precisely the moral of the Aesopian parallel of the fable [no. 145], in which the calf was allowed to remain idle as she was destined for the slaughter). It seems that even the point of the original fable was altered to suit the scriptural verse. Still, in other respects, the fable as it appears in the midrash is probably quite similar to the form it took in the folk tradition. Its protagonists and earthy, somewhat vulgar subject, and its narrative qualities—the trio of heroes, repeated dialogues, and the simplistic message, in praise of work and scornful of idleness—indicate the manner in which it was probably told orally. With the transformation to scholarly literature, it took on hermeneutical trappings and became the key brought forth to elucidate a theological problem (divine justice). The same literary process overtook other fables which found a home in Midrash Esther Rabbah. There are, for example, two similar folk fables concerning Haman, one likening him to a chicken who tried to vanquish the sea by bringing all its waters from the source to dry land (*Esther Rabbah* 7, 10), and the other comparing Haman to the lion who invited the other animals to dine with him, and covered his home with the skins of animals on whom he had preyed (ibid., 7, 3).[113]

> "Abraham begot Isaac." Do I not know that Abraham begot Isaac?! R.
> Hananiah Rabbah said: 'This can be compared to a dove that was chased

by hawks and ravens. She fled from them and went in and sat on her nest. People said: "These eggs are from the hawk," and another said, "From the raven." Another said to them: "As long as they are eggs we do not know if they are from the raven or the hawk, but leave them until she [hatches them] and they become chicks, and you will know from whom they are." Thus Sarah was often moved about, [she was] with Pharoah, with Avimelekh. Thus [people] began to say: "She conceived by Pharoah," and others said, "She conceived by Avimelekh." The Almighty said to them: "The mouth of those who speak lies shall be stopped" (Pss. 63:12). Wait until she births, and you will see whom he resembles. At once the Almighty instructed the angel in charge of the newborn's form, he said to him: "Do not fashion him to resemble his mother, rather his father, so that all will know that he is none other than his father's." He came out forthwith resembling his father. Hence it is said, "These are the generations of Isaac, Abraham's son. Abraham begot Isaac."' (*Aggadat Bereshit* 37)

Once again there is a fundamental discrepancy between the fable and its epimythium. Neither Pharaoh nor Avimelekh pursued Sarah; she was, on the contrary, delivered to them almost willingly. Moreover, these events transpired many years before Sarah conceived at the age of ninety, when she was still young and beautiful, hence they could hardly be suspected of Isaac's paternity. Perhaps most surprisingly, Sarah is likened to a dove who would allow the other birds to do with her as they would, and whose offspring's paternity is in question. This suggestion of infidelity is presented as by "those who speak lies," but the basic analogy proposed by the preacher between the dove in flight and Sarah is no less perplexing. This could not have been the preacher's intention. These implications are the result of the tale's "excess meaning"—details extraneous to its exegetical implementation: the animal tale itself suggests many more ramifications than the preacher intended in his effort to expound on the text. This disparity generally stems from the attempt to yoke together two essentially different literary units. Had the preacher devised a new mashal expressly for the exegetical purpose here, no such difficulty would have arisen. This was the case in the fables discussed earlier of the biblical Yotam, and the donkey, her foal, and the sow. The sages tended to make analogies between independent folk fables and exegetical notions on a single level, without considering other possible colorings the tale might bestow on the text they undertook to interpret.

Up to this point we have found the mashal to be an exegetical tool. It has yet another purpose, and that is in the service of debate—nationalist, religious, and political:

> R. Simeon b. Jose b. Lakunia said: In this world Israel is likened to rocks, as it says, "For from the top of the rocks I see him" (Num. 23:9); "Look unto

the rock whence ye were hewn" (Isa. 51:1). They are compared to stones, as it says, "From thence the shepherd of the stone of Israel" (Gen. 49:24); "The stone which the builders rejected" (Pss. 118:22). But the other nations are likened to potsherds, as it said, "And He shall break it as a potter's vessel is broken" (Isa. 30:14). If a stone falls on a pot, woe to the pot! If a pot falls on a stone, woe to the pot! In either case, woe to the pot! So whoever ventures to attack them receives his deserts on their account. (*Esther Rabbah* 7, 10)

The proverbial fable, condensing an entire story into a single sentence, is cited for exegetical purposes—to explain the fact that it was the peoples of Persia, not the Jews, who were disadvantaged by Haman's plans. It is nonetheless clear that the implication is not time-specific. It has implications for the rabbinic period no less than for the period of the Scroll of Esther. The mashal's function in this homiletic interpretation is to have the past speak for the present, to emphasize the positive outcome of a long-ago clash with other peoples and thereby inspire confidence for the present in the listeners. Of particular interest is the manner in which the popular form of the fable was modified for use in the sermon. The Aesopian parallel follows:

> The clay pot said to the copper one: "Do your bouncing away from me, for if you so much as touch me, I'll break even though I touch you unintentionally."
>
> That life is uncertain for a poor man when a grasping man of power lives close by. (*Aesop*, translated by L. Daly, p. 218)

In the Aesopian version, as in all the many other versions of the parable, sympathies lie with the fragile clay boat, at the mercy of the copper boat. It certainly bears more than a passing similarity to the situation of the Jewish people, the inevitable loser in any conflict with the other, strong nations. Yet the fabulist of the midrash gives the fable an entirely new spin. For the sake of allusion to the appropriate verses, he had to replace the copper craft with one of stone, with the aim of imbuing his Jewish audience with a sense of security in their power to survive clashes with other peoples of the world. He perversely identifies the weak and vulnerable party with the copper (or stone) boat, and in so doing seeks to underscore Jewish fortitude and endurance. Clearly, this fable was refashioned to suit the exegetical aim—the story of the Jews' salvation in the Scroll of Esther. Yet the main purpose of the modifications was polemical-political. In their numerous skirmishes with the other nations of the world, in the time of the fable's telling no less than in the past, the survival of the Jewish people was assured. The ones to suffer any such conflict would be the rival nations, as past experience showed.

One type of mashal designed as a polemic is the controversy-parable. Here the plot revolves around an argument or debate, and the victory of one protagonist over the others is the main subject of the tale and its messages. One example of this type was presented above in the fable of the she-ass, the filly, and the sow, where the first two debate the justice of fattening the third. Two typical fables belonging to this category survived in the rabbinic literature, and deserve our attention:

[1] The wheat, the straw, and the stubble engaged in a controversy. The wheat said: "For my sake has the field been sown"; and the stubble maintained, "For my sake was the field sown"; Said the wheat to them, "When the hour comes, you will see." When harvest time came, the farmer took the stubble and burnt it, scattered the straw, and piled up the wheat into a stack, and everybody kissed it. In like manner Israel and the nations have a controversy, each asserting: "For our sake was the world created." Says Israel, "The hour will come in the Messianic future and you will see. . . . " (*Genesis Rabbah* 83, 5)

[2] R. Joshua b. Levi said: Moses said to Israel: "If you will not obey the judges, then sin will be on your head." This may be illustrated as follows. The tail of the serpent said to the head, "How much longer will you walk first? Let me go first." The head replied: "Go." The tail went and came onto a ditch of water and dragged the head into it; it encountered a fire and pulled [the head into it]; and coming to thorns, dragged it amongst them. What was the cause of all this? Because the head followed the tail. So when the rank and file follow the guidance of the leaders, the latter entreat God and He answers their prayer; but when the leaders permit themselves to be let by the rank and file, they perforce must share in the visitation that follows. (*Deuteronomy Rabbah* 1, 10)

The latter mashal is typical of the blending of exegesis and polemics. The text opens with a verse and its explication, in a manner characteristic of aggadic commentary. The preacher argues here that Mose's statement upon the appointment of judges carried with it a veiled warning of the consequences of disobedience. At this point, R. Joshua ben Levi brings in the fable to give weight to Moses's words. The text's conclusion, which functions as an epimythium, indicates that it was in fact told for the purpose of influencing contemporary behavior, not as commentary. Obedience to contemporary leaders and luminaries was an issue in every period, but the fact that R. Joshua ben Levi chooses to interpret the biblical verse in precisely this manner shows that he was referring to an issue of practical concern to his listeners. The traditional nature of interpreting Scripture and the folk wisdom of the fable reinforce each other in this text, and are used to further an actual social-political struggle, whose precise details are beyond our reach.[114]

The first fable, unlike the second, indicates directly the target of the polemic, namely the nations of the world engaged in theological debates with the Jews. The epimythium deals with the sages' response to competing religious and cultic perceptions on a question of great import, namely, which nation is "God's people," or which is the chosen religion, and how can it be proven so. Easily understood and featuring elements from the daily life of the period, a typical agricultural fable is employed. As in the fable concerning the quarrel between the snake's head and tail, initially there is no objective means of knowing which of the three types of produce is preferred; only the results will tell. Indeed, as the end of the agricultural process—sorting at the threshing floor—shows which of the three is truly the most valuable to man, so too the Almighty will make clear in the End of Days which is truly the chosen people. In both the fables quoted here, and in others mentioned above, the preachers display extraordinary artistic ability in using folk fables for rhetorical purposes. Tailoring an independent folk fable, with its baggage of characteristics and meanings, to the subject of the homily requires the use of precise techniques of artistic and ideational transformation. The flawless application of these rhetorical techniques is responsible for the difficulty in ascertaining where lies the "seam" between "original" parts of the folk fable and the new homiletic foundations which turn it into an integral part of rabbinic commentary.

The actual performance event at which a mashal was told is very rarely in evidence. Given that the depiction of an event is fictional, and not a reflection of an actual performance event (as in the fable of Yotam), we gain a glimpse of the sages' view of the fable's ideal venue and the role they assigned it in the historical and social reality of their time.

> Antoninus [the Roman emperor or local governor] said to Rabbi: "The body and the soul can both free themselves from judgment. Thus, the body can plead: The soul has sinned [the proof being] that from the day it left me I lie like a dumb stone in the grave [powerless to do ought]. Whilst the soul can say: The body has sinned, [the proof being] that from the day I departed from it I fly about the air like a bird [and commit no sin]." He replied: "I will tell thee a fable. To what may this be compared? To a human king who owned a beautiful orchard which contained splendid figs. Now, he appointed two watchmen therein, one lame and the other blind. [One day] the lame man said to the blind, 'I see beautiful figs in the orchard. Come and take me upon thy shoulder, that we may procure and eat them.' So the lame bestrode the blind, procured the figs, and ate them. Some time after, the owner of the orchard came and inquired of them, 'Where are those beautiful figs?' The lame man replied, 'Have I then feet to walk with?' The blind man replied, 'Have I then eyes to see it?' What did he do? He placed the lame upon the blind and judged them together. So will the Holy One, blessed be He, bring the soul, place it in the body, and judge then together." (*Sanhedrin* 91a–b)

The tale belongs to the well-known cycle of the friendship between the Roman Emperor Antoninus Pius (137–161 C.E.) and Rabbi Judah the Patriarch. The question of the historicity of these tales has hardly lacked for attention. The same can be said for the mysterious individual for whom Antoninus spoke and for the reflected relationship between the Jewish leadership and the Roman rulers. In this tale, Antoninus turns to Rabbi as to his own spiritual teacher with a theological-ethical question—the separation of body and soul and its ramifications for the doctrine of reward and punishment. Such questions intrigued Greek philosophers as well, and it can perhaps be assumed that the matter-of-fact formulation, different from the sages' customary manner of presenting such questions, indicates an external-Hellenistic source. The mashal is recounted by Rabbi in the very popular parable form: "a king of flesh and blood," but thematically it belongs to the category of narrative parables with a folk origin, as can be seen from its continuity of plot, its parallels, structure (the triad of protagonists), and the use of such "folk" types as the handicapped and thieves.[115]

The narrative situation reflected here is one of a ruler or philosopher who turns to Jewish sages for answers to theological questions. The latter customarily turned to the broad strata of society in an effort to simplify and concretize a philosophical problem. They would draw an example from everyday life to turn the philosophical problem into something basic and easily understood. Hence Rabbi Judah the Patriarch (assuming, for the moment, that the tale reflects an actual encounter) employs a typical folk parable to illustrate his response to the theological problem. The situation described here is of a meeting between two intellectuals, and the parable serves as proof in the philosophical discussion (as was often the case in Greek philosophy). Perhaps the discussion was public—before Rabbi Judah the Patriarch's students, for example—or maybe it was a private conversation between a Jewish sage and a Greek scholar, or maybe it never actually transpired outside the imagination of the sages, who fashioned it according to the accepted literary conventions of their time. This parable is one example of dozens of parables with similar opening statements, and they do not enable us to firmly define the event at which they were told.

The two most famous fables in rabbinic literature are included in the tales of R. Joshua ben Hananiah and Rabbi Akiva. R. Joshua told the fable of the Lion and the Egyptian partridge to calm the rebellion brewing in the Beit Rimon valley after the Romans reneged on their commitment to rebuild the Temple (*Genesis Rabbah* 64, 10); the fable of the fox and the fishes appears in Rabbi Akiva's tale of the death of the martyrs (*Berakhot* 61b). These two stories lay out public performance situations in which the fabulists (in these instances, two of the foremost tannaim) seek to influence the politics of their audiences. In the first tale, R. Joshua ben Hananiah uses the famous Aesopian fable ("The Wolf and the Heron") to persuade the raging Jewish crowd to accept the sages' dictum not to revolt against the Romans. It is difficult to ascertain definitively whether or not the story truly reflects an actual historical event. It does, however, indicate the sages' view of the fable's function.

The fabulist made no essential changes to the tale to make it fit the situation he sought to reflect. The parallel between Rome's refusal to live up to its commitment to rebuild the Temple and the bone caught in the lion's throat is neither simple nor obvious. Perhaps the fabulist was under pressure, as the story implies, and he retrieved the fable from memory without the luxury of time to rework or match it to the situation at hand. In this case it can be stated that the fable worked (and worked well, if we are to take the tale at face value) not only because of its logical match to the epimythium, but primarily on account of its humor: the audience laughed at the naive partridge who believed the lion's promise, and in so doing recognized its own naivete in trusting Rome's assurances. Furthermore, the audience grasped the futility of the bird's desire to take revenge on the lion, analogous to a revolt against Rome. The fable's success hinges on the use of rhetorical means verging on demagoguery— that is, playing to the audience's emotions, as opposed to an attempt to persuade it by logic, on an intellectual level. The story argues that R. Joshua and the sages, who dispatched him to the task, never intended to sway the crowd with an analogy—the primary mechanism of the mashal—rather they set out to move them with humor and emotion.[116]

Rabbi Akiva was known for "publicly bringing gatherings together and engaging in the study of Torah." He replies to Pappus ben Judah's entreaty not to disobey royal decree with his fable of the fox and the fishes. This performance event, too, was public, and Rabbi Akiva, in answering Pappus, was in fact addressing his many students who, according to the story, were present. Researchers' attempts to unearth parallels to this fable in Aesop's writings and beyond have turned up nothing. The fable's character, style, and structure notwithstanding, it was not taken from Aesopian literature, but apparently created originally as a Jewish fable. One proof of this is that, in response to the fox's suggestion to the fish that they come and live with him on dry land, where they would be safe from the fishermen, the fish answer: "Art thou the one that they call the cleverest of animals? Thou art not clever but foolish . . . " This statement indicates that the fabulist was quite familiar with the Aesopian stock of fables in which the fox is the archetype of wiliness and cleverness, an archetype he sought to belie. In other words, the fabulist functions here within the literary conventions of the Aesopian fable (hence the striking similarity to them), yet attempts to create a fable of antithetical content and message. As a result, the creatures do not behave predictably: the fox, so admired by the Greeks for his cunning, turns out not to be the truly clever character, whereas the meek and silent fishes are the archetype of the Jewish people. Here the process of Hebrew fable creation seems to peak with regard to the Greek parable: no more retooling of readily available fables, but invention of new ones which fully reflect the sages' religious and social perceptions, with a clear connection to the form and character of the Aesopian fable.[117]

The traditional categorization of the mashal has generally been according to the type of protagonists: animal, vegetable, mineral, or human. Each of these categories is represented in the fables and parables presented herein: fewest in number are the fables of (normally) inanimate objects. Among these we saw the parable of the stone and the clay pot, and that of the creation of iron (the trees are apprehensive about iron's creation, as it will one day be used to chop them down, but God assures them that unless they join with the iron [as in an ax], it will be unable to harm them). Fables of plants are more numerous. The examples from this category presented earlier are the reed and the cedar; the straw, the stubble, and the wheat; and the rose among the thorns. Parables with human heroes are less well-represented, but to them we must add the hundreds of king-parables, whose protagonists are always human. But the most prevalent type of mashal in rabbinic literature features animals. Most of the examples discussed so far belong to that category, in direct proportion to their numbers among the narrative fables of the rabbinic period. However, this division of fables according to their protagonists is no longer justified. Those featuring human beings or animals may very well serve the same function, while others with like protagonists often serve entirely different functions. This said, it should also be mentioned that the division according to the protagonist can illuminate a central feature of the parable—its stereotypical character. The heroes of mashal always embody some trait, idea, or human type. Frequent use of stereotypical images facilitates brevity, condensation, and immediate absorption. Every reader or listener knows what the lion, the fox, or the sheep represents, and so the fabulist can use this common "code" to send home the fable's message. Closer examination of the mashal's categorization according to protagonist type does not reveal creation or use of stereotypes in the manner of Aesopian fables. The straw, the stubble, and the wheat, for example, represent traits or types only within the confines of a single mashal. Before their function in that mashal is revealed, the audience of listeners could not divine what they stood for. The same holds true for the donkey, the foal, and the sow, and the camel and the dogs. The snake, for example, a protagonist of several fables, represents the Jewish people on one occasion, commanded by Moses to obey the elders and judges, yet another time the snake appears as a traitorous creature, and then elsewhere as faithful and appreciative. The figure of the lion is an exception. It always symbolizes a powerful and self-centered ruler (see the parables of the lion and the Egyptian partridge, and the lion who invited the beasts to a feast). The last example we looked at, Rabbi Akiva's fable of the fox and the fishes, is salient precisely for its awareness of its protagonists' stereotypes. In fact, the meaning of the fable arises from this awareness: we have a reversal of the traits as shaped by Hellenistic culture. The fable meshes well into the orientation we identify with others from the rabbinic period—ignoring the stereotypes fashioned by Hellenistic literature or in opposition to them. It seems that alongside the ideological rejection of other values of Hellenistic culture, the stereotypes characteristic of its primary didactic genre were also rejected, and with them their attendant meanings and ideas. This is a prime example of matching literary means to an ideological orientation.

Rabbinic literature is full of animal tales that are not fables. They describe the world of animals without an allegorical-symbolic orientation. They reflect the manner in which people of the day viewed the animal kingdom or explained its unusual phenomena, but without a clear intent to discover a moral or make an analogy between them and the human world. The story with which we opened this section, the myth of Etana, is an animal tale, not a fable. It exhibits an anthropomorphic perception of the world. Historical studies show that animal tales preceded fables in the literature of the cultures that arose in the cradle of humanity. The fable is a literary form requiring of the narrator and audience a measure of abstraction and ability to analogize, in order to learn some lesson from the world of animals or inanimate objects. Such complex thought indicates a higher level of development than anthropomorphism, which tries to understand the world of animals within a humanity-based frame of reference. And it is, in fact, generally accepted that only after the primitive belief in the humanity of animals faded was the ethical conclusion, the epimythium, added to the tale, thereby transforming the tale and the animal myth from a simple belief into an ethical wisdom tale.[118]

Whether or not this theory of development is correct, rabbinic literature preserved animal tales alongside the many animal fables. These tales generally deal with unusual phenomena in the animal kingdom: the monstrous size of the beasts, the whale and the ram, the strength and roar of the mighty lion, the doe's miraculous foaling in spite of her narrow womb, or the wondrous way the ibex finds water in the parched desert. A typical animal tale follows:

> [It is written, "When a man's ways please the Lord, He maketh even his enemies to be at peace with" (Prov. 16:7)] . . . R. Samuel b. Nahman said: The verse refers to the serpent. The school of Halafta b. Saul taught: A serpent is very fond of garlic. It once happened that a serpent went down into a house, where he found a dish of garlic, of which he ate and he then spat [his poison] into it. Now there was a snake in the house, which could not fight against it; but as soon as the first departed, it went and filled the dish with earth. (*Genesis Rabbah* 54a; *Tanhuma*, Buber edition, *Beshalach* 3, PT *Terumot* 8, 3)

The tale describes the world of animals in human terms: the dichotomy between the good hero and the bad, the concept of loyalty as perceived in the human world, the saving of a man's life as the embodiment of good. While here the snakes do not speak as humans as in other tales (that of the Garden of Eden, for example), typical human characteristics are overtly assigned to them. Another characteristic feature of the animal tale is the attribution of their behavior and traits to Divine will. Indeed, in common to all the animal tales thus far mentioned is their pronounced conviction of God's greatness revealed through the wondrous traits of the animals—encapsulated by religious thinkers of the Middle Ages in the verse, "He has made his wonderful works to be remembered." (Pss. 111:4) The interest in the traits and deeds of animals in rabbinic literature is not presented as an end in itself, but because that way lies evidence of the Almighty's guidance of the world:

> When Rabbi Akiva came to this verse he said: "O Lord, how manifold are thy works, etc. You have creatures living in the sea and living on land. Those that live in the sea would die if they were to go onto the land. And those that live on land would die if they were to go into the sea. [There are] those that live in flame and those that live in air. Those that live in flame would die if they went out into the air. And those that live in the air would die if they went into the flame. The place where one lives is the death of the other, and the place where the other lives is the death of [the first] and I say: O Lord, how manifold are thy works and them all, etc." (*Sifra shmini* 5, 52, 2, Finkelstein edition, p. 218)[119]

Here we can indicate the dividing line between folk and learned culture of the rabbinic period, a line discernible in most of the examples of mashal cited above. Animal tales are among the most numerous in every culture's stock of folk literature; certainly the rabbinic period is no exception. The tales and fables which survived in the canonical literature reflect numerous and varied types which were part of the period's reservoir of tales. But when these animal tales appear in the rabbinic literature, they no longer serve (with a few exceptions) the folk culture which seeks to describe the animal world by means of human relationships and terms, to satisfy natural human curiosity about the world of these near-yet-different creatures. In the rabbinic literature, they and the natural world serve as a theological tool for the understanding of God's will.

[K] The Story Cycle

One particularly striking, albeit often ignored, literary phenomenon is the frequent appearance in the Talmud and Midrash of clusters of tales sequentially told. Although this phenomenon is overt, aggadic research has always focused on individual tales. Hardly any attention has been spared for the story cycle, yet, as a literary medium, it is crucial to understanding the art of storytelling in rabbinic literature. This neglect probably stems from the misconception that the cycle, in and of itself, is of no importance, that it was merely a technical, artificial means of presenting more than one tale at a time. Even if this were so, we can hardly ignore a phenomenon of such wide scope: over forty story cycles containing over three hundred and fifty tales; each grouping comprising between three and forty tales. The redactors of rabbinic literature thus displayed a clear tendency to present the tales they wished to tell in narrative clusters. This begs a number of questions: What were the origins of the story cycles? Should we view them as collections of tales recorded as they were told orally by folk storytellers, or as the literary creation of those who put them in writing? In what manner were the groupings organized and edited, and by what artistic and ideological motivations were they inspired? Below I attempt to answer these questions in the course of examining the more prominent story cycles.[120]

First we must define the story cycle as it exists in the Talmud or Midrash, where tales do not exist independently, but are woven into a legal or aggadic context. It can be exceedingly difficult to determine the boundaries between the tale and its immediate context, and the difficulty is magnified when it comes to the story cycles. The usual method of presentation for tales has one brought in the context of legal or aggadic deliberations, after which the deliberations continue at length (or not, as the case may be), then another tale is offered, and the debate resumes once more. This pattern may repeat itself any number of times. Most of the tales in rabbinic literature appear in these acknowledged contexts, and they should not be confused with "story cycles." The literary phenomenon I wish to discuss here is an unbroken sequence of tales. On occasion, a biblical verse or rabbinic saying comes between two tales, as we shall see below, but these fall within accepted norms in almost all story groupings, including those outside rabbinic literature.

The quantity of non-narrative material separating the tales is important in distinguishing between a story cycle and an encompassing aggadic *piska* (section) which also comprises numerous tales. Such a distinction is necessary to ascertain both the compiler's narrative conception and how the text was received by the readers (or listeners). "*Perek khelek*" (*Sanhedrin* 90[a] and ff.) epitomizes the aggadic *piska*. It is peppered liberally with tales, sages' remarks, commentary and homily, expanded biblical tales, sermons, and so on. The compiler of this wide-ranging tractate was clearly less interested in the tale and its narrative character than in the ethical idea or ideas developed in the course of the discussion. He does not engage in telling tales for the sake of the narrative world constructed within them—rather, he uses the tales to flesh out and develop his ideas. The reader is not treated to broad canvasses of independent tales, is not swept away by a growing narrative tension, does not eagerly anticipate the next tale. After each story the reader is instead jolted anew, almost forcefully, by the compiler, who provides a reminder of the tale's ideological significance and its bearing on the problem at hand.

Conversely, in all the story cycles discussed hereafter, the tales follow one another uninterrupted (or nearly so), the compiler clearly not intending to break their continuity or intervene with a moral or with didactic sermonizing. Before the reader's eyes passes a sequence of diverse narrative worlds, each with distinct figures and/or narrative reality, but linked firmly by a clear structural and compilerial conception. In the course of reading (or listening) to a story cycle comprised of ten, twenty, or thirty tales, the reader is immersed for a relatively long period in an imaginary world, attention focused on the tales' narrative qualities as opposed to their ideological significance. The story cycle thus differs from the solitary tale, which usually acts on the reader for a much shorter period and which generally attempts, in a roundabout way, to complement the message or meaning with which it opened. Within a story cycle, the conclusion of a tale is the occasion for the start of another, predisposing the reader to anticipate the next story. We have recognized this literary phenomenon in the Middle Ages and later, yet overlooked it as regards the rabbinic period.

Did comprehensive, independent collections of tales exist in the rabbinic period, from which the compilers of talmudic and midrashic story groupings drew their tales? Moses Gaster made just such a tenuous assumption many years ago, but most scholars rejected it out of hand. We have no historical evidence of self-contained works in any branch of Jewish culture of the rabbinic period; the process known as the "separation of the disciplines" began only with the advent of the Middle Ages.[121]

Some story cycles have tales in common with others. Similar versions, particularly when several tales appear in the same order in more than one cycle, seem to suggest that the compilers had before them a ready-made collection of tales from which to draw. Yet evidence intrinsic to the cycles themselves belies that argument. The large grouping of tales known as "The Wisdom of the Jerusalemites" (*Lamentations Rabbah*, 1, 4), for instance, has two tales in common with *Sanhedrin* 104a–b. One concerns the blind slave and the other, four Jerusalemites who apprised their innkeeper of his true parentage—he was the offspring of fornicators. The texts present these tales in different order and in entirely dissimilar forms, indicating distinct versions of a single narrative type, as opposed to textual borrowing from a common source (outside of the cultural folk tradition shared by the compilers of both compositions). The story cycles concerning the Destruction in *Gittin* (55b–58a) and in *Midrash Lamentations Rabbah* also have tales in common. Here too, the differences in their order of presentation and, in particular, their versions are so pronounced as to rule out the possibility of a story grouping from which both could have drawn.

Of the story groupings I examined, I found only two whose versions and order of presentation were so similar as to be nearly identical. These are the story cycles on animals in God's service in *Genesis Rabbah* (10, 7), and in *Leviticus Rabbah* (22, 4, Margolies edition, p. 503 ff.). The cycle in the former comprises six tales; in the latter, ten. The first five tales in *Leviticus Rabbah* correspond to the first five of the cycle in *Genesis Rabbah*, but then it offers five more. The sixth tale in the cycle of *Genesis Rabbah*, concerning Titus and the gnat, was not inserted into the story cycle in *Leviticus Rabbah* as it appears in an earlier *piska* (22, 3, Margolies edition, pp. 499–502). It is difficult to conclude other than that the compiler of *Leviticus Rabbah* took the tales from *Genesis Rabbah*, and appended a group of five tales on the same topic. This is the only example (except for the biographical story cycles on R. Judah the Patriarch and R. Eleazar ben Simeon, which I will discuss later) of codependent groupings of tales, and it is more a question of chronological relationship between the two midrash than of the existence of independent collections of tales from which material could be taken.[122]

Let us analyze the story cycle compilers' relationship to their sources. Our first example is taken from the grouping of tales on the wickedness of the Sodomites (*Sanhedrin* 109a–b). The central active figure, that of Eliezer, servant of Abraham, fits cleanly into the category of protagonist known as the "trickster." Yet of the ten tales in the cycle, Eliezer is the hero of only three. The second tale in the cycle concerns "an orphan son of a widow," caught in the vise of Sodom's legal system. The law states that anyone owning a single ox must graze the city's flocks one day, while those who own no livestock at all (i.e., the indigent)—are obligated to twice take them to pasture. The orphan killed and skinned all the oxen, and when the time came to distribute them he determined that whosoever owned a single ox would receive one skin, while anyone who owned none, would receive two. This tale belongs to the category of stories of the folk scoundrels who expose society's flaws and hypocrisy—a role given to Eliezer in this story cycle. But the compiler did not attribute this tale to Eliezer, a variation which would have enriched the corpus of Eliezer tales and one which any folk storyteller dealing with this type of tale would have instituted without hesitation. The compiler of this grouping was faithful to the version as he received it from his sources. He set it down in writing without the modification we might expect—attribution to Eliezer. The sixth tale in the cycle reinforces this orientation. It concerns the poor tailor who must pay the Sodomites an exorbitant sum to comply with their law that whoever rides the ferry must pay four *zuzim*, while whoever wades across the water (for lack of fare), must pay eight. The same tale is retold immediately thereafter—with Eliezer as the protagonist. Again, one might have expected the compiler to follow storyteller convention and attribute the tale to the better-known figure, but instead, having heard two versions of the tale, one featuring the anonymous tailor and the other Eliezer, he faithfully transmits both.[123]

Another example of the same phenomenon appears in the cycle of tales of the Destruction of Jerusalem in tractate *Gittin* (57a). Among the stories detailing the slaughter of Jews appears the following: "Once when R. Manyumi b. Helkiah and R. Helkiah b. Tobiah and R. Huna b. Hiyya were sitting together they said, If anyone knows anything about Kefar Sekania of Egypt, let him say. One of them thereupon said: Once a betrothed couple [from there] were carried off by heathens who married them to one another. . . . The next then began and said: On one occasion forty bushels [of corn] were selling for a denar. . . . The third then began and said: There was a man who wanted to divorce his wife. . . . " After this follow four tales not directly related to the Destruction, some with a pronounced erotic character. This conspicuous incongruity (to which we will return later) between the atmosphere of the cycle as a whole and that of the group of tales on Kefar Sekania shows that the compiler did not bother to adapt the tales to the overall tone of the grouping. Instead he presented the performance event in its entirety, precisely as had learned it. I assume that this story cycle (of Kefar Sekania) was not the work of the compiler of the topic treated here, but a story cycle told orally at some authentic performance event, and thus it was preserved—together with a description of the event itself.

While these are individual examples, we can extrapolate from them the manner in which compilers of rabbinic story groupings related to their narrative sources and how, at least sometimes, they chose fidelity to those sources over literary and thematic unity of the grouping. This distinction shows that a not-insignificant portion of the tales in rabbinic literature are the written versions of the tales as they were told in the oral tradition, and that they should not be automatically perceived as extreme literary reworkings done at the final stage of their formulation.

The key to the story cycle, the core question of our inquiry, is to identify its organizing principle. How can we describe the literary or ideational rationale which led the compiler to collect in one place a given set of tales and none other, in a particular order? The effort to describe this organizing principle is likely to illuminate the attitude of the redactors of talmudic-midrashic literature to the story, as well as the cultural role they intended for it. The method used to define this principle is to identify the links in a sequence of tales: each tale's moorings to the stories immediately before and afterward, and its orientation to the common idea or unified literary structure at the foundation of the grouping.

Of course, the compilers of the groupings did not use definitions or analytical distinctions to justify the inclusion of a given tale in a cycle. Rather, they relied on aesthetic or intellectual intuition to guide them in the process. In other words, they viewed their organizing principles as ethnic rather than analytical categories; their consideration was for how the social group for whom the tales were intended would understand the connections between the tales and their significance. With this in mind, and in order to stay as close as possible to the roots of the logic that guided the compilation of the groupings, we will also attempt to describe the principles mainly in ethnological, not analytical terms. Furthermore, we will use analytical categories only in cases where the ethnological principle is neither understood nor definable otherwise. It should be noted that the forthcoming categories do not cancel each other out. More than one organizing principle may operate in a single grouping, generic and associative, for example, or ideological and biographical, or any other combination. The more numerous and complex the organizing principles of a story grouping, the greater the sense of its unity, and we can presume that such was the compilers' aim. The division below is therefore methodological in the main, intended to make salient the basic principles of compilation, although hardly any story cycles comprise only one such category. In reality, they are intertwined in various ways.

[1] The Framework Grouping

The framework tale as a superstructure housing other stories is one of the oldest unifying principles for groupings of tales. We have seen it in the literature of the Ancient East—*The Book of Ahikar*, the Biblical Joseph narrative, and the biblical story cycles concerning Elijah and Elisha, among others. I have only been able to locate one story cycle in aggadic literature which uses a paradigmatic framework structure. This is the narrative of R. Joshua ben Hananiah and the Elders of Athens (*Bekhorot*, 8b–9a). We have already discussed the thematic and formal connections of this story cycle with *The Book of Ahikar* (chapter 4, section D). It is conceivable that the use of this literary form, so rarely seen in rabbinic literature, originated in *The Book of Ahikar*, which circulated widely in Aramaic versions among Jews as early as the fifth century B.C.E.[124]

The cycle begins with a dispute between the emperor and R. Joshua ben Hananiah. The emperor claims that the wisdom of "the Elders of Athens" is greater than that of the Jewish sages. R. Joshua ben Hananiah undertakes to best them and deliver them to the emperor. The cycle thus begins as a typical task tale: a king challenges a hero to accomplish some impossible task, the hero sets out and performs a series of acts of heroism and wisdom in order to accomplish it. The fate of the protagonist (or of the community he represents) rests on his success or failure. This is another significant parallel to *The Book of Ahikar*, in that Ahikar's life depends on his ability to prevail over the Egyptian king's magicians in a contest of wisdom. R. Joshua pits himself against the Elders of Athens, and in the course of the competition he prevails seventeen times against them—sometimes by carrying out a task and other times by answering shrewd questions. "The Elders of Athens" are defeated. He brings them to the emperor in a ship, then kills them with further acts of wisdom.

A diverse sampling of tales was gathered into this framework. We are familiar with many of them as independent tales, included in other sources (such as, for example, in the story cycle, "The Wisdom of the Jerusalemites"). These tales describe such tasks as overcoming the defenses which the "Elders of Athens" erected to protect their dwelling; the building of a palace in the air; delivering the Athenians to the emperor; the ability to tell tales so tall as to render speechless even the Athenian Elders, emerging victorious from a contest of riddles, where the riddles included: "How does one mend broken grindstones, or identify a hen's color from the appearance of its eggs?" In other words, the narrative framework of a protagonist setting out to accomplish the task set him by the king serves the cycle's compiler as a means of collecting diverse tales together. The framework has considerable influence on the character of its component tales, as the emperor's esteem for the Jews hinges on the execution of each task in the contest between R. Joshua and the Elders of Athens. The light, entertaining character of the tales in their original form is at least partially replaced by a sense of anxiety and tension, stemming from their location and role within the structural framework. The narrative grouping thus creates a special relationship between the organizing principle of the cycle and the tales it comprises, where the ties linking secondary tales to each other and to the framework tale are stronger and more taut than in other types of groupings. The sages did not favor this principle of compilation, and it seems that this isolated example was borrowed from an ancient literary form.[125]

[2] The Generic Principle

The generic conception of the groupings' compilers is ethnic, not analytical. It is a mixture of narrative themes and ideas with basic, simplistic structural distinctions. The unifying principle of several story cycles can be defined by a general, vague sense of the tales' belonging to one literary category. A cycle of three magic tales appears in the Babylonian Talmud (*Sanhedrin* 67b). All three propose a method of distinguishing between true magic and sleight of hand according to the principle determined in the legal discussion preceding the tales. The first tells of an Arab merchant who chopped up a camel into pieces. He then rang a bell, and the camel rose to its feet. The second concerns a small-time farmer who went to Alexandria to buy a donkey. Later, when he gave the beast water, it turned into a bridge plank, for the farmer had been tricked. The third tells of a bartender who tries to serve a wine merchant a potion which would turn him into scorpions. The intended victim becomes wise to her machinations, turns her into a donkey and rides her to market. The tales are connected both thematically—all are stories of sorcerers and magic—

and by a common structure: The protagonist realizes that overt reality is a deception, perilous unless one can discern the true, hidden reality. In each of the tales the hero encounters a simple, seemingly innocent and familiar phenomenon that is revealed, in the second part of the tale, as fraudulent and illusory. This particular choice of tales from the large store of magic tales known in the rabbinic age can be explained only by merging theme and structure. What can today be defined as generic selection guided the hand that picked these tales.

A similar example exists in a grouping of tales about the Destruction in *Midrash Lamentations Rabbah* (1, 45–51). This grouping comprises ten stories that, formally speaking, are interconnected through the agency of the formula: "Then the Holy Spirit cried out, For these things I weep," which is repeated at the end of most tales in the grouping. The tales share a theme of the killing of martyrs, the slaughter, and the depiction of bloodshed. In other words, thematically, all ten tales of the grouping belong to the genre of the martyrological tale. However, the requisite pattern of the martyrological tale—presenting the protagonist with the opportunity to choose between breaking the principles of his faith and dying, and the protagonist's opting for death—exists in only two of them, the first (Jerusalem luminaries, on board a ship transporting them to captivity, deliberately leap into the sea rather than fall into disgrace), and the ninth (Miriam, daughter of Boetius, and her seven sons). The heroes in the other tales are not given the choice; they are tortured or brutally executed. In any case, most of the tales in the grouping conform to a different literary pattern, the model of the fall from zenith to nadir. The tales are divided into two parts, the first describing the high social status, standing, and wealth of the protagonists, and the second, their miserable situation after the Destruction: the two children of Zadok the Priest enslaved; Miriam, daughter of Boetius, wife of the High Priest, once so pampered rugs were spread before her as she walked to the Temple to hear her husband read on the Day of Atonement, after the Destruction is tied to horses' tails and dragged through the streets of Jerusalem; Miriam, daughter of Nakdimon, to whom the sages once awarded huge sums of money just for her perfume (based on what she had been accustomed to), was in the end seen "collecting barley under the horses' hoofs in Acre"; in another story, the same Miriam, daughter of Boetius, was redeemed out of slavery in Acre, without a shred of clothing to cover herself; the mother of Doeg, son of Joseph, who "used to measure [her son] by handbreadths and give his weight in gold to the Temple every year," during the siege slaughtered and ate him. The clearest confirmation of the pattern of the "model of the fall" appears in the first tale, which concerns the captives on board ship who jumped into the sea. In a parallel in the Talmud (*Gittin* 55b), the captives are children; in *Lamentations Rabbah*, they are Jerusalem sages, a modification undoubtedly introduced to play up the fall from greatness to degradation and scorn. This example shows that the grouping was the product of a generic conception, a blending of theme and pattern. The intention was not to define in analytical terms the model of the fall, but to use that fall to reflect and express the social and psychological devastation caused by the Destruction. This may be the generic-ethnic distinction at its best, and was the basis for the grouping's organization.

There are two large aggadic cycles of humoristic tales: those of Sodom (*Sanhedrin* 109a–b) and the tales of Rabbah bar Bar Hana (*Bava Batra* 73a–74b). The first comprises ten stories, mostly belonging to the narrative genre of the folk trickster who circumvents the official institutions of society and exposes their wickedness and hypocrisy. The protagonists include Rabbi Yose of [Zippori], the orphan son of the widow, the launderer, and Eliezer, servant of Abraham, in Sodom. Each of these belongs to that same category of folk hero who is at once a part of society and detached from it, and whose actions take society's laws to the brink of absurdity, and in so doing lay bare its hypocrisy. Hence the generic conception of this story cycle rests on a three-part distinction: the shared theme (the wickedness of the Sodomites), the protagonist type, and the narrative pattern which repeats itself in most of the cycle's tales.

A similar literary phenomenon appears in the second story cycle. It is more complex than the first in that it comprises some twenty-two tales, but the organizing principles are basically the same. The cycle appears in the Talmud in the chapter "He who sells a ship," in the framework of a discussion of the names of various fishing craft. The problem deals with seafarers, so it is their stories that are presented here. The mariners' tales are presented as reports of faraway and exotic places, and of unusual creatures and natural phenomena, hence the inclusion here of the tales of Rabbah bar Bar Hana and his desert travels. The fixed, recurring model in these stories includes the hero's journey to distant, wondrous lands, his report, a description of the phenomenon he encountered and, finally, an attempt to define and establish the truth of the matter. This story cycle exhibits the same generic selection of tales, relying on a common subject (sailors' or wanderers' tales), the figure of the hero—the rabbi-wanderer (Rabbah bar Bar Hana, Rabbi Johanan, Rav Judah of India, to name some) and the narrative pattern which characterizes travel literature. The humorous atmosphere of the tales does not necessarily stem from the comic situation in which the hero outwits the wicked, characteristic of the cycle of tales of the Sodomites, but from the chronic tension in all the cycle's tales between truth and lie, fiction and reality. The protagonists of most of the stories claim to have seen it with their own eyes ("I saw it myself"), and since they are esteemed sages, it is difficult to doubt even their most far-fetched exaggerations. Consequently, we should add the scope and atmosphere of the tall tale to the three core components of this generic conception.[126]

[3] The Biographical Cycle

We found no biographical story cycle in rabbinic literature that could be categorized as hagiography. Nor is there even a single story cycle that orders biographical legends chronologically and reflects a continuous progression of the hero's life. For example, the story cycle of Hillel the Elder (*Shabbat* 30b–31a; *Avot de-Rabbi Nathan* version A 15, version B 29 [Schechter edition, pp. 60–62]) contains four tales (except for that in *Avot de-Rabbi Nathan*, which has three), yet none recall the main biographical story of his prominence in Torah study or how the Shabbat was desecrated in the study hall of Shemaiah and Avtalyon (*Yoma* 35b). R. Akiva is the protagonist of numerous sage stories, yet in all of rabbinic literature not one story cycle focuses on him. A contemporary researcher can, of course, collect the many biographical legends of the life of R. Akiva, from the onset of his studies to his demise, and so construct a complete biographical story cycle almost entirely based on aggadah. But no such biographical composition exists in the literature of the rabbinic period.

Two short story cycles characterize the attitude of the grouping's compilers to their protagonists' biographies. Their main interest lies not in the stories of those heroes' lives, nor even in emphasizing their greatness, exceptional qualities, or miraculous feats. The tales reach beyond the figures themselves to attain the cycle's didactic goals.

The story cycle of Hillel the Elder, and that of Geviha, son of Pesisa, (*Sanhedrin* 91a) each comprise four tales. Only the first part of each cycle is clearly biographical, focusing on an event that actually took place during the protagonist's life: the pranksters who placed bets on which of them could provoke Hillel the Elder, and then hounded him on, of all days, Sabbath eve. The second cycle opens with a tale of an apostate attacking Geviha, son of Pesisa, over the Jewish claim that the dead will one day come back to life. When Geviha responds with a winning argument, the vexed apostate threatens to kick Geviha continuously until his hump is straightened. Geviha, unmoved, replies that if successful, he will be hailed as a great healer.

The remaining three tales in each cycle have a uniform and exemplary construction: in the first cycle (according to the Babylonian Talmud), a non-Jew turns to Hillel the Elder's rival, Shammai, and says he will convert to Judaism. In each of the three tales he has a different stipulation: in the first, that he study only the written Torah; in the second, that Shammai teach him the entire Torah standing on only one foot; and in the third, the non-Jew is prepared to convert only if he is made High Priest. Shammai aggressively rejects the prospective convert in all three, while Hillel, in his modesty, draws him nearer the sheltering wings of Providence. All three tales consider Gentiles' skewed perception of Judaism. Hillel's tolerance, which brings them closer to first-hand understanding of the foundations of Judaism, leads to their unqualified acceptance.

The three tales of the cycle are alike not only in their hero figure, but also in the character of the antagonist, their literary structure (the initial appeal to Shammai, the manner of Hillel's reception, the Gentile's reaction to Hillel's instruction), and their ideational significance.

A very similar phenomenon is discernable in the second story cycle: in the latter three stories, people of other countries—Africa, Egypt, and the sons of Keturah and Ishmael—present legal claims against the Jewish people before Alexander the Great. The sons of Africa claim the Land of Canaan belongs to them, the Egyptians demand back the property stolen by the Hebrews at the time of the Exodus, and the sons of Keturah and Ishmael demand dominion over part of the land of Canaan. In each of the three tales, Geviha, son of Pesisa, volunteers to represent the Jewish people in court. His testimony is so convincing that the litigants abandon their fields and homes in a flight for their lives for fear of Alexander's judgement against them. Protagonist and construction do not unite the three exclusively; style, too, binds them: Geviha's petition to the sages that he be permitted to represent the Jewish people, the address to the plaintiffs, the nature of his arguments, and the manner of flight, are styled almost identically in each of the tales, indicating that they were composed by a single author. All three stories are in Hebrew, whereas the opening tale of the cycle is in Aramaic. For our purposes, the important point is that in these story cycles woven around a familiar central character, the hero and his deeds are not the connecting factor of the constituent tales. In addition to the figure of the hero, there is a clear ideational literary perception manifested in the conceptual construction of the cycles. The cycles' form—the first tale being biographical and the three which follow similar to each other and different from the first— seems to hint at the manner in which they were created. The compiler or author of the cycle was familiar with one folktale which characterized the image of the protagonist in folk culture: Hillel the patient and the modest in the story of the jokers who tried to provoke him, and Geviha ben Pesisa the ugly, to all appearances good-for-nothing, revealed to be clever and capable of delivering fiery words to great effect. On the basis of each of the two tales the authors knew from folk literary tradition, they composed three additional tales (nor is the choice of this formulaic number surprising) that bear the stamp of the same author. These "scholarly" tales (that is, penned by an author) seek to imitate the folktale that served as their basis, yet depart conspicuously from their source in their literary pattern, style, and message.

In contrast to the literary-learned nature of these two cycles, there are two biographical cycles of broader scope, the character of whose tales indicate that they were culled from folk tradition. The tales in both of these cycles revolve solely around the protagonist, and in each are preserved its qualities as an independent tale. The compiler's hand is barely visible; he did not try to make them fit together in any way, nor did he try to imbue them with a unified literary construction and significance. From this perspective we witness the work of a typical compiler-collector, who gathered the tales according to the most basic of editorial principles—the image of the hero, without any attempt to order them chronologically.

The story cycle concerning Rabbi Pinhas ben Yair (PT, *Demai* 1, 3) is such a biographical cycle. It opens with a tale of R. Pinhas' donkey, who refused to eat fodder of doubtful tithing—the legal issue discussed in this portion of the text—and continues on to tales unconnected to the first, except for their common hero. There were the needy, who left two *seah*s (a measure of volume) worth of barley with Pinhas ben Yair; he sowed and harvested the grain, and when the poor returned to collect, they had to heap their shares upon camels and donkeys. In another story, R. Pinhas ben Yair orders the vermin plaguing a village to depart, and hears in their squeals that the plague was punitive, for the villagers had not properly tithed their crops. He returns a pearl swallowed by a mouse to its owner, the king; restores a well to a village that had not properly separated their tithes; commands the River Ginnai to cease flowing and allow him to pass, and so on, ten tales clearly belonging to the saint legends genre, and probably transmitted unmodified in the cycle.

The cycle of R. Bena'ah (*Bava Batra* 58a) compositionally resembles the cycle concerning Pinhas ben Yair, but the character of the tales differs somewhat owing to the hero's different personality. R. Bena'ah marks the burial grounds of saints, that is, he measures them inside and out so that passersby will know where lie ritually unclean places. In the Cave of the Patriarchs, he meets Eliezer, who describes how Abraham lies there in Sarah's arms; he comes to the burial cave of Adam and describes his beauty, "his two heels . . . were like two orbs of the sun." Afterward follow four tales of Rabbi Bena'ah's wisdom: he explains to orphans the perplexing will of their late father, in a case brought before him he reveals which is the true son of the deceased, and that the other nine were born of their mother's harlotry (by means of the psychological test wherein he beat the father's grave). The final two tales are connected chronologically and via their plots. Together with the tale detailing the true son's identity, they can perhaps be viewed as a single ongoing story composed of several episodes, each of which could exist as an independent tale: The nine sons who did not inherit inform the king that Rabbi Bena'ah considers cases without witnesses. Rabbi Bena'ah is imprisoned, but according to his instructions, his wife poses a riddle to the king that only Rabbi Bena'ah can solve, and the king is amazed at the depth of wisdom which informs the Rabbi's legal rulings. The last tale tells how Rabbi Bena'ah, sitting as a judge at the city gate, sees the writings of the judges who preceded him in that place. While the connection between the cycle's constituent tales is more easily recognized than in the cycle of R. Pinhas ben Yair, it is clear that the compiler did not arrange the stories in chronological-biographical order, but was satisfied with the common protagonist as the unifying principle of the entire cycle.

The only two biographical cycles to come very close to being edited according to biographical logic are those concerning Rabbi Judah the Patriarch (PT, *Kilayim* 9, 3) and the tales of R. Eleazar ben Simeon (*Bava Mezia* 83b–84b). The latter is the largest biographical grouping of tales in rabbinic literature, and comprises twenty-two tales (excluding five interspersed tales about Rabbi Johanan and Resh Lakish). Each cycle emphasizes a single traumatic event in the life of its protagonist. The cycle on Rabbi is constructed in a digressive form: it begins with his demise, recalls the toothache that plagued him for years before his death, recounts the event billed as the cause of the trouble—a calf fleeing slaughter sought refuge with Rabbi, but Rabbi turned it over to the butcher, claiming that the calf had been created for that very purpose. This momentary cruelty tormented Rabbi for the rest of his days. The following tale concerns Rabbi Hiyya, who overheard Rabbi say he would give up his seat—as did the sons of Bathyra for Hillel the Elder—for Rav Huna Resh Galuta [head of Diaspora] if he came from Babylonia. When Rav Huna died, and his coffin was brought to Palestine for burial, Rabbi Hiyya teased Rabbi, saying that Rav Huna had come from Babylonia (without mentioning that he is dead), and look how Rabbi trembled. At this point comes the tale of Rabbi's anger at R. Hiyya, lasting until the latter's dying day and burial. In other versions of the story cycle (PT *Ketubot* 13, 3; *Genesis Rabbah* 33, 3), the order of the tales is somewhat different, and two are switched: Elijah the Prophet (appearing in the guise of R. Hiyya) lays his finger on Rabbi's aching tooth and heals it, and the tale of R. Hiyya, who did not rise before R. Ishmael in the bathhouse because he was absorbed in *Aggadat Tehillim* [Midrash on Psalms]. Rabbi then appointed two students to accompany him, lest his absent-mindedness that came of his involvement in Torah lead him into harm on his way. As we said above, many tales about Rabbi, which could make of this story cycle a complete legendary biography of the hero, are scattered in rabbinic sources (such as the well-known story grouping of Antoninus and Rabbi), yet the compiler did not gather them together and he did not organize them as a biography. In any case, what we have before us in the cycle is something of an attempt to show the connection and causal relationship between various events in the life of the hero. Yet it seems that here too, emphasizing the causality of transgression and punishment, of pride and its due, is the essence of the compiler's interest in the cycle, not telling about the life of the hero.

The story cycle concerning Rabbi Eleazar ben Simeon is more comprehensive and complex than that of Rabbi, but it is grounded in a similar literary conception. The cycle begins *in medias res*, with the recounting of the formative event in the hero's life, one whose influence did not wane even after the hero died. The Roman authorities hire R. Eleazar as a sort of detective or informant (*parhaguna*), to apprehend Jewish thieves and robbers. Some sages fault him for taking this position, calling him "vinegar, son of wine"—meaning a son unworthy of his great father. The question of the tale's historical background has drawn considerable attention from scholars of the rabbinic period, but from a literary perspective we view it as the motivation and principal cause for the development of the grouping of tales. In the second story, an anonymous launderer is disrespectful to R. Eleazar, who informs on him, and consequently the authorities find and execute him. Although it does turn out later that that very same launderer "and his son laid with a betrothed young woman on the day of atonement," and despite R. Eleazar's initial sense of relief, he felt remorseful ever after for this action. In the third tale he takes upon himself the mortification of body and soul; in the tale which follows that one, sixty cups of blood and pus are removed from beneath him every day, the result of his torments morning and night; his wife leaves him on this account and he lives in solitude and poverty (though his wife's family was affluent, he had no resources of his own). Yet a miracle occurs, and sailors saved from drowning for having uttered his name during a storm bring him vast wealth.[127]

The harsh confrontation between R. Eleazar and other sages is also linked to these acts of informing. The irregular rulings he makes before them are miraculously revealed to have been just (all the women he pronounced ritually clean bore male children, as he had foretold to the sages, and so each of the sixty sons bore Eleazar's name). But when he died, the angry sages would have nothing to do with his burial. Knowing this, before his death he instructed his wife to lay out his corpse in the attic, where it lay "there no less than eighteen years and not more than twenty-two years" without decomposing or giving off any odor whatsoever. Legal petitioners would come and make their cases from the doorway, and he would rule on them. Only when Rabbi Simeon bar Yohai (his father) himself appeared to the sages in a dream and instructed them to carry out his son's burial, did they see to it, and with great ceremony: they put the casket in the burial cave of Rabbi Simeon bar Yohai after convincing the snake coiled at the opening that they were bringing the son to the father. Rabbi, who wanted to marry R. Eleazar ben Simeon's wife, was rebuffed. To prove that R. Eleazar was the greater in Torah and in deeds than Rabbi, another story is immediately brought in, the last in the grouping, concerning the period of their youth, when they studied Torah before Raban Simeon ben Gamaliel and R. Joshua ben Korha.

The story cycle's presentation as a nearly continuous tale, according to chronological order, indicates that it is closer to the biographical story cycle than any of the others. Its importance lies not only in its scope and sequential pattern, but in the complexity of the protagonist's characterization. R. Eleazar ben Simeon is portrayed as vulgar and gluttonous and as a sage for whom Divine

Providence performs miracles proving his greatness, yet also as one suspiciously close to the Roman regime. This mixture of realistic-historical stories with tall tales (the nearly Rabelaisian description of Rabbi Simeon: his huge proportions, obesity, gluttony, crude speech, and gestures), and of tragic remorse over his actions with coarse humor, establish a story cycle exceptional not only for its scope and construction, but also for its artistic complexity.

[4] The Biblical Verse as a Unifying Principle

The exegetical quality of aggadah, which develops out of biblical verses or is illustrated by them, is reflected in several story cycles. The methodological question which arises in the study of both halakha and aggadah—should the biblical verses be regarded as their source, or did they serve merely to strengthen the legitimacy of the material which developed independently— is irrelevant in regard to the story cycles. While it can be shown how an individual tale developed from a given verse, a similar relationship held by a large group of tales is unlikely. An author or storyteller would not compose an entire system of tales on the basis of a single verse. We shall see that the writer-compiler *collected* stories on the basis of their compatibility with a particular verse.[128]

The first characteristic of the relationship between story cycle and biblical verse that merits our attention is the conclusion of tales with the verse that served as the starting point for the unfurling of the story cycle. In the cycle in BT tractate *Shabbat* (156b), the discussion revolves around the verse, "charity delivers from death" (Prov. 10:2 and 11:4), and the first two of three tales in the grouping close with this verse. In the story grouping on martyrdom in *Midrash Lamentations Rabbah* (1, 45), more than half the tales conclude with the opening verse: "For these things I weep" (Lam. 1:16). In a third grouping, in the Palestinian Talmud (*Shabbat* 6, 9), relating to the verse, "therefore will I give men for thee" (Isa. 43:4), the first three of nine tales end with the verse, while the remainder do not conclude with any verse at all. The explanation, perhaps, is simply that the compiler was unwilling to so monotonously repeat the same expression, as he already imprinted it on the readers' consciousness by earlier repetitions. Yet it seems more likely that the reason is linked to an important phenomenon, one of a more general incidence, which I describe below:

In the story cycle in *Midrash Lamentations*, the first tale deals with the three shiploads of Jerusalem sages who leapt into the sea to escape captivity, and the second with Hadrian, who gathered the Jews in the Beit Rimon Valley and massacred them. Both end with the verse, "For these things I weep." The third tale tells of Jews who hid in caves and, for want of food, would sneak out under cover of darkness and bring back the flesh of the fallen to eat. One of them discovered his father's corpse among the gruesome provisions. The concluding sentence here reads: "Therefore the fathers shall eat the sons and the sons shall eat their fathers" (Ezek. 5:10). Of the tales which follow, the fourth and fifth conclude again with the verse, "For these things I weep." The sixth, seventh, and eighth conclude without any verse, the ninth, concerning Miriam, daughter of Boetius, and her seven sons, ends with the opening verse, and the tenth tale has no concluding verse.

What can we deduce from this? First, that the compiler was not satisfied with two or three tales ending with the same verse, but continued to cite it at stories' ends, until the ninth tale. Second, as early as the third tale in the cycle he switches the concluding verse. It therefore seems probable that the compiler of the cycle opted to conclude with the verse only when he judged the tale to perfectly reflect the idea expressed therein. Finding a more apt verse for the third story ("Therefore the fathers shall eat the sons"), he uses it instead of the opening verse, but returns to the former in the very next tale. In the sixth, seventh, eighth, and tenth tales, he does not conclude with the verse, "For these things I weep." These are the tales which belong to the narrative pattern of "the fall," namely, tales of the pampered wives of the wealthy Jerusalemites, who, following the Destruction, were reduced to the humblest of circumstances: Miriam, daughter of Boetius, for whom, earlier, rugs had to be spread between her house and the Temple before she would deign to attend; Miriam, daughter of Nakdimon, who cursed the sages who ruled legendary sums for her perfumes, because she felt they were not enough for her; the mother of Doeg ben Joseph, who measured her son's weight in gold. The absence of the verse, "For these things I weep," after each of these tales is a covert message from the compiler, that for such individuals he does not weep. They had set themselves apart from the people in time of plenty; they deserved no one's tears in their time of need. In contrast, the ninth tale, concerning Miriam, daughter of Tanhum, who sacrificed her seven sons for the glory of God, does end with that verse, despite its distance from the first tale in the cycle, as the compiler felt the verse fit the meaning he sought to give the tale.

We can easily locate a similar phenomenon in the other story groupings. The first two tales in the cycle in BT *Shabbat* suit the verse, "righteousness delivers from death." The first tells of the Chaldean who envisioned that a man setting out to work in the field would be struck by a snake and not return home. When the laborer did return, with pieces of the snake lying atop his load of firewood, he told of the kindness he had done for another worker in the forest. The second tale, about Rabbi Akiva's daughter whose charitable act toward a poor man on the day of her wedding saved her from her anticipated death, is also perfectly suited to the opening verse. The third tale, however, tells of the woman whose son, according to the astrologers' predictions, would be a thief. She ordered him never to leave the house with his head bare, and on the one occasion when his head covering fell off, he nearly succumbed to the sin of theft. This tale has nothing to do with the verse, and hence the compiler chose not to conclude this tale with it. Why then was the third tale included here, if it did not fit the topic of the cycle? The answer lies in the principle of "associative accumulation" one of the main unifying means in rabbinic story cycles, to which we will return below.

In the story cycle revolving around the topic of "therefore will I give men for thee" (Isaiah 43:4), the same phenomenon recurs: only the first three tales, which suit the opening verse of the cycle, conclude with the verse; it is missing from all the other six which do not touch at all on the subject (PT, *Shabbat* 6, 9). Yet alongside this curiosity is another interesting phenomenon: the closing verse, "therefore will I give men for thee," does not truly fit the tales describing how Jews were saved from perils, while the non-Jews suffered injury. The last part of the verse: "and people for thy life," according to the traditional biblical commentary, refers to the Gentiles. Therein lies the link to the tales. In other words, it happens that a story cycle depends not on the verse, but on its traditional interpretation.

A striking example of this phenomenon is found in the story cycle of the "Wisdom of the Jerusalemites" (*Lamentations Rabbah* 1, 4): "She that was great among the nations" (Lam. 1:1). But has it not just been mentioned "that was full of people" (ibid.)? Why, then, is it stated "She that was great among the nations?" The meaning is that she was great in intellect. R. Huna said in the name of R. Jose: "Wherever a Jerusalemite went in the provinces, they arranged a seat of honor for him to sit upon in order to listen to his wisdom." Indeed, none of the tales in the first part of the large cycle boast Jerusalem's greatness among the nations, rather they treat the Jerusalemite hero who travels abroad among the nations of the world, where he triumphs over them with words of wisdom. The tales, then, do not reflect the simple meaning of the verse, but its very specific explication.

Our last observation on the connection between verse and story cycle merits an additional comment. The tales do not relate solely to the general spirit of the verse, rather they seek to flesh out narratively that which is said in it (or in its interpretation). Indeed, the interpretation describing the Jerusalemite competing with the wise men of all the nations in the Gentile world, and emerging victorious, is transposed nearly word for word to a narrative plot. In the first tale, for example, the Jerusalemite sets out for a town to collect an inheritance left him by his father who died there in his employer's home. The son carries out three acts of wisdom (in accordance with the conditions set by his father), and returns to Jerusalem with his inheritance as well as the Gentiles' admiration for his wisdom. The second and third tales present the same narrative pattern of Jerusalemites who go to Athens, where they carry out impressive acts of wisdom and earn the Gentiles' recognition of their intellectual superiority, just as was written in the exegetical interpretation with which the story cycle opened.

None of the three tales in the first part of the cycle were included in order to suit that opening interpretation. They were culled from a wide stock of folktales because they fit the narrative pattern for which it called. There are two bits of evidence of this: first, each of the three tales belongs to clear-cut tale types, found in the general folk literature in forms similar to that in which they are told in *Midrash Lamentations Rabbah*. The second proof that the tales were not appended to suit the opening interpretation is that only the first three actually do suit it. From the fourth tale onward, the pattern of tales is altogether different. Had these tales been created solely for the sake of the interpretation, it is difficult to believe that the author would have been satisfied custom tailoring only three.[129]

Another outstanding example of the link between the story cycle and opening verse can be found in *Midrash Ecclesiastes Rabbah* (11:1), in the story cycle on the verse, "Cast thy bread upon the waters: for thou shalt find it after many days" (Eccles. 11:1). This cycle exhibits most of the phenomena described up to this point. Most of its constituent tales relate not to the simple, literal meaning of the verse, but to the manner in which it was interpreted, with the help of a second verse from Isaiah (55:1): "Ho, every one that thirsts, come to the water." The meaning of "water" in this instance is not the usual "Torah," but "charity." Indeed, the first story tells of Rabbi Akiva, who saw a boat sink at sea and grieved for one of his students who was aboard. But when he arrived at Cappadocia, his student was there. Rabbi Akiva asked how it could be so, and the student replied that he had been tossed from wave to wave until he reached the shore, meriting rescue by having given charity to a pauper on board the ship. The third, fourth, and sixth tales of the cycle also tell of people who helped non-Jews who had escaped from drowning, giving them food and clothing. By virtue of this deed, all the Jews of the place were later saved from a decree, indeed they were rewarded with gifts and great wealth. In contrast to these tales, which relate to the verse in accordance with its interpretation, that is, the giving of charity, there are two tales here which do not depend on the verse's content (or commentary) but on the tangible-figurative picture arising from it. The second tale concerns a large ship, stuck, immobile on a windless sea, until a miraculous solution was designed: those on board roasted a young goat and hung it out in front of the ship. The bait stuck in the throat of a big fish who towed the ship after him until they reached a place where the winds picked up and the ship could continue alone. This tale, in its own words, illustrates the picture of "cast thy bread," namely the "casting" of food from the boat and the seafarers' ensuing salvation from a bitter fate. The tale does not depend for its meaning on the verse or its perceived content, but on the tangible-literal picture the verse suggests, and which it translates into the language of narrative plot.

Tales of seafarers such as these are widespread; the sight of a large fish, hooked on the bait and speeding away with the vessel in tow, was not uncommon. Thus we cannot say for certain that the story was "custom made" by the compiler to suit the verse. Yet the fifth tale in the cycle is apparently exceptional in this regard. It concerns a man who would toss bread into the great sea every day. One day while fishing, he found a pearl inside the catch, and he was thereafter called "Cast thy bread upon the waters." But what purpose could be served by tossing bread into the sea? It seems that this episode, which opens the tale, should be viewed as a plot unit which "was custom made," or devised, to make it fit the opening formula of the verse. A seminal study has already proposed that this tale, and especially later and more developed versions of it from the Middle Ages, is constructed in such a way as to nearly match the literal meaning of the biblical verse. Tossing the bread into the sea, use of the word root, "found" in the sense of treasure, and "most of the days" to mean the long period of time between action and result, the play on the Hebrew words for "sea" and "days"—all these indicate an attempt to link the tale to the verse, an attempt that has no exclusively narrative pretext, only a logical argument: the wish to create a tale which would most closely suit the associations arising from the given verse. It seems this tale is an exceptional example of the connection between verse and story, and it suggests the verse as the direct source of its narrative pattern. Such examples are few in the aggadic literature, but the identification of this phenomenon is important for the understanding of one method of creating tales in the rabbinic period.[130]

[5] The principle of "associative accumulation"

One factor unifying most of the story groupings in rabbinic literature is association. Even in those cycles with another central unifying principle, tales are occasionally combined on the sole basis of some element they have in common. This is so even if the other literary foundations (theme, pattern, and genre) are disparate. The basis of literary association is metonymy: a representative object or concept conveys the sense of the whole. Thus a motif, or any other narrative element drawn from one tale, appearing in another story, recalls the former tale in full. This is the case even if the motif is of minor importance, and even if it is the only literary element shared by the two stories. In this way a tale can "drag" another, and that can pull along a third, until there is a large cluster of tales whose grouping is motivated almost solely by this associative "dragging."[131]

The story cycle concerning R. Bena'ah (*Bava Batra* 58a) is, as we have already seen, biographical. Its first two tales tell how R. Bena'ah customarily marked the locations and borders of saints' burial caves. The third tells of Rav Kahana's shofar, which had belonged to Jacob and, before him, to Adam. Even Rashi (commenting on this location) wonders why that third tale follows the first two, and offers the explanation that, since the first two dealt with the burial places of the forefathers, Jacob's shofar was mentioned, and the description of Adam's beauty ("his two heels . . . were like two orbs of the sun"), and his shofar, described in the third tale, were natural additions. In any case it is clear, as Rashi sensed, that the motivation for the third tale has nothing to do with the theme or construction of the earlier tales, rather it hangs on the link between Adam and Jacob, thus the second "drags" the third. The fourth tale is still more astonishing. Here we have a tale of a Magus who would poke about the cemetery (apparently a grave robber, or one who used the limbs of corpses in magic practices). In the cave of Rabbi Tobi bar Matanah, the corpse reached up and grabbed him by the beard. Abbaye was merciful and released him. The Magus tried again, but this time Abbaye did not consent to free him. His beard had to be cut to free him from the dead man's grasp. Here again, the Magus' action is the exact opposite of R. Bena'ah's; the former sought to do harm to the graves while the latter tried to protect them. One motif—the involvement with graves—is shared by both the tale of R. Bena'ah and that of the Magus. Although in all else the tales are completely dissimilar, this one motif in common caused the inclusion of the tale in a group concerning another matter.

The humorous story cycle concerning Rabbah bar Bar Hana (*Bava Batra* 73a–74b), whose chief unifying principle is generic, nonetheless bases the connections between many of its tales on the principle of "associative accumulation." The starting point of the cycle is the chapter of the "one who sells a boat," hence the chief unifying principle is typological—seafarers' tales. Indeed, the first two tales describe huge waves reported by seafarers. But the third tale tells of the mischievous demon Hormiz, son of Lilith, who cast marvelous enchantments in Babylonia on the River Ravg'nag: he ran along the merlons on the wall surrounding the city Mahoza, and a mounted rider racing along the ground below could not catch up with him; he leapt onto the saddles of two mules standing on either side of the river's bridge, two glasses of wine in hand, and poured the contents from one into the other, never spilling a drop to the earth. And to magnify the impact of the marvelous trick, the narrator goes on to say that it was a stormy day, and the waves of the Ravg'nag raged. What does this tale have to do with the others in the grouping, concerning seafarers' tales? It seems the answer is twofold: the narrator, Rabbah bar Bar Hana, figures in each of the tales and always says, in his characteristic style: "I myself saw it." Since the compiler began collecting seafarers' tales told by Rabbah bar Bar Hana, he went one step further and added a tale that did not belong with them topically or categorically. But a second element this tale has in common with its predecessors is the tempest motif. Since the two earlier tales dealt with the reports of great waves and fierce storms encountered by the seafarers, the compiler includes another story with mention of a storm and waves, even though they figure marginally at best, as mere asides of the narrator.

The accretion of tales by association, by virtue of the commonality of a single narrative element, gathers steam as the cycle continues. The fourth through ninth tales present seafarers' accounts of the monstrous sea creatures they beheld (or from whom they escaped). In the tenth tale, Rabbah bar Bar Hana recounts his journey through the desert, where he saw giant geese, dripping with fat, flying overhead, and perceived that they were the intended repast for the righteous in paradise. The eleventh story concerns an Arab caravan merchant (tay'a) who, upon being shown a handful of desert dust, would know immediately where it came from, and how far that place was from water. The twelfth is the famous tale of the dead sons of Israel whose huge bodies were left in the Sinai desert during the exodus from Egypt, and in the thirteenth, Rabbah bar Bar Hana tells of his journey to Mount Sinai. In the fourteenth, he relates that the Arab merchant showed him the place where Korah and his followers were swallowed up by the earth during their rebellion against Moses; in the fifteenth, of having seen the wheel of heaven and testing its rotation by laying his pack upon it and finding it the next day in the same place. The sixteenth through nineteenth tales are, once again, consummate seafarers' tales.

The associative trail here is complex and torturous, but to understand the thinking of the cycle's compiler, it must be followed: since he dealt with the monstrous creatures of the sea, he opted to add another tale of giant beasts— the geese destined for the groaning board of Eden. The setting of that tale was the desert (remote from the geographical starting point on the high seas!), so he told of a means of finding water in that parched terrain; in the following tale, having dealt with a desert and mentioned the Arab trader, he relates Rabbah bar Bar Hana's visit with the desert dead. Having broached the world of Jewish myth, he tells in the tales that follow of Rabbah bar Bar Hana's visit to Mount Sinai and with Korah and his followers. Thus, by degrees, the tales move to cover thematic ground far beyond the original orientation of the cycle, rolling on with the force of narrative momentum.

Didn't the compiler of the story cycle sense what we do today? Why didn't he reduce the scope of the cycle to those tales that suited, at least somewhat, the declared subject with which he opened? Were this curiosity limited to but a few story cycles, we could consider it an insignificant deviation from the norm. But, as stated, rare is the rabbinic story cycle which does not exhibit this tendency to some extent. Its most likely impetus is narrative momentum, which, as it gathered speed, had the power to stand against the ideological, purposeful character of rabbinic literature. Thus a tale could be included for the sake of its narrative interest, irrespective of its contribution to the surrounding context of halachic or ideological discussion. We probably have no better example of narrative momentum in the rabbinic period than the associative accumulation revealed in these story cycles.

As aforementioned, this phenomenon shows up in most of the story cycles, and outstanding examples could have been brought from the story cycles on magicians (as in *Sanhedrin* 67b), or on the giving of charity to the poor "as much as he needs" (as in *Ketubbot* 67b). Its fullest expression, however, comes in the largest story grouping in rabbinic literature, about rain-bringing (*Ta'anit* 23a–25b), which comprises thirty-eight stories. Associative accumulation leads to frequent deviations to subjects completely unrelated to the main theme of rain-making, and back again, only to go off again at the very next opportunity on a new, unrelated track, and so on. This is the main reason, it seems, for the sense of structural weakness in this large story grouping. I will list a few salient examples: the first through fifth tales are famous tales of rain-bringing, featuring Honi, his sons, and grandsons. The sixth tale tells of Rabbi Mani who, tormented by the men of the patriarchal dynasty, lay across the grave of his father (R. Jonah) and prayed for relief. When one day they passed near the father's grave, he reached up and grabbed their horses' hooves, and did not release them until they promised not to trouble his son any longer. What does this tale have to do with the preceding ones of rain-making? The fifth tale mentions "Rabbi Jonah, the father of Rabbi Mani" in a list of rain-makers in Babylonia. The compiler lingered here over an auxiliary figure of the preceding tale, and, on its account, offered another story he knew. The seventh tale relates how Rabbi Mani came before R. Isaac ben Elyashiv to complain that his wealthy in-laws were causing him grief. R. Isaac said they would soon become impoverished. Some time later, Rabbi Mani returned, saying, now that his in-laws were poor, they gave him even more trouble, and R. Issac replied that they would become rich once again. Another time he came to complain about his wife's ugliness. True to R. Isaac's word, she soon turned beautiful, yet Rabbi Mani returned to complain that now she rejected him. R. Isaac ben Elyashiv said, "Shall Hana return to her ugliness [lit. blackness]," and Hana returned to her ugliness. A splendid tale in its own right, it has nothing to do with the surrounding tales of rain-making. It is only here because of the principle of "accumulation" or associative "drift." Since the preceding tale (which doesn't belong here either), treated Rabbi Mani's complaints, the compiler offered another tale sharing the same motif and protagonist.

The eighth story tells of Rabbi Isaac ben Elyashiv's students, who want him to make of them great Torah scholars. This is yet another story added on account of its motif in common with its predecessor: exaggerated appeals to Rabbi Isaac. The ninth tale concerns Rabbi Yose bar Avin, who leaves Rabbi Yose of Yokrat to study with Rav Ashi, on account of his former teacher's cruelty. How did this tale come to be included here? The associative element at work in this case is not the figure of the protagonist, but the theme of student-teacher relations, in common to both tales. Since the last story dealt with the figure of Yose of Yokrat, three more concerning him follow. The twelfth tale deals with Yose of Yokrat's mule, who refused to move on account of a pair of sandals forgotten on his back. The thirteenth story moves on to R. Eleazar of Birta, who gives his daughter's dowry to a charitable donations collector, and refuses to enjoy the harvest from an entire wheat field which he himself had sowed, as the field belonged no more to him than to all the poor of the Jewish people. Here, too, the story of R. Eleazar was "dragged" by its associative link to the motif of extreme ethical behavior evinced by both him and R. Yose of Yokrat (and his mule). Tales fourteen through nineteen are again straightforward tales of rain-making, and after them there is more "associative accumulation," it seems, and round and round until the end of the large story cycle.

The twenty-sixth tale of the grouping, following a series of rain-making stories, deals with Rabbi Hanina ben Dosa's power to start and stop the rain. After that follow six more tales concerning the same protagonist. A narrative element in a tale (here, the figure of the protagonist) has associatively dragged not just one tale, as in the earlier examples (wherein each tale may have in turn dragged another), but a whole story grouping, which is nested as a secondary story cycle within the main one. The result is a biographical cycle situated within a grouping of rain-making tales. Nor is this phenomenon unique to this cycle; it is repeated often in other story groupings.

We examined a splendid example of this earlier, in the story grouping of the Destruction (*Gittin* 55b and ff.). Wedged into this series of tales was the story of the performance event featuring sages who sat together and decided to tell tales of "Kefar Sekania of Egypt," including erotic and ethical tales with very little in common with the surrounding story cycle. The connection is made only in the final tale of this secondary story grouping, which tells of Kefar Sekania's ruin, awakening the associative link to the story cycle of the Destruction. The important story grouping in the BT tractate *Ta'anit* (20b) harbors a similar phenomenon: the grouping opens with a series of three tales about Rabbi Adda bar Ahavah, one of which tells how Rav Huna tricked him, used him to extricate his wine from a house about to collapse, because he knew that as long as Rabbi Adda was there, the house would stand. Then the compiler adds: "Rava said to Rafram b. Papa: Tell me some of the good deeds which R. Huna had done. He replied: Of his childhood I do not recollect anything, but of his old age I do. On cloudy days they used to drive him about in a golden carriage . . ." Three tales about Rav Huna follow, in which the compiler presents, as in the earlier example of Kefar Sekania, not only the tales but also the performance event at which they were told. He also states that he did not gather them himself, rather he relayed the story cycle as it was told at that event. Further on in this story grouping, the compiler again travels the characteristic associative path to the motif of walls and rickety structures that do not collapse so long as holy people are within. Thus the fifth tale recounts the tale of Nahum of Gimzo, who lay blind and crippled in his bed. When his bed was removed, the dilapidated building collapsed forthwith. Then, since the last tale dealt with Nahum of Gimzo, the compiler completes a short story cycle about him.

The nesting of story clusters as secondary cycles within primary groupings is repeated in several other places: in the story cycle on snakes befouling food (PT *Terumot* 8, 3); the tales of the moment of death and encounter with the angel of death (*Mo'ed Katan* 28a); in the cycle surrounding the verse, "therefore will I give men for thee" (PT, *Shabbat* 6, 9); in the story cycle on animals in the Almighty's service (*Leviticus Rabbah* 22, 4), and in the large biographical story grouping on R. Eleazar ben Simeon (*Bava Mezia* 83b–84b).

This last contains a somewhat exceptional phenomenon that proves once again the importance of the process of associative accumulation. In the sixth tale of the story cycle, a Roman matron questions the paternity of the children of R. Eleazar, son of Rabbi Simeon, and R. Ishmael, son of Rabbi Yose. Her argument is that they are too fat to have had sexual intercourse: their paunches were so huge, the text holds, that when they stood belly to belly a yoke of oxen could pass beneath. In the next tale R. Johanan comments on the size of the waist (or member) of Rabbi Ishmael, son of Rabbi Yose; it was as big "as a bottle of nine kabs capacity." Rav Papa then notes in return that R. Johanan himself was also generously endowed: "R. Johanan's was as a bottle containing five kabs . . . that of R. Papa himself was as the wicker-work baskets of Harpania [a town in Babylonia where baskets were manufactured]." The five tales which follow describe Rabbi Johanan's physical beauty, his famous encounter with Resh Lakish at the Jordan River, Resh Lakish's demise, and Rabbi Johanan's subsequent grief. Later, the cycle returns to tales about R. Eleazar, son of Rabbi Simeon. The interesting phenomenon is that at the core of a biographical story cycle, "associative drift" causes an additional biographical story cycle, concerning another protagonist, to be "dragged in." This tangent diverts the listeners' attention from the figure of R. Eleazar, son of Rabbi Simeon, to the other protagonist (although the pronounced sensualism of the tales on Eleazar, son of Rabbi Simeon, also exists in the stories of Rabbi Johanan and Resh Lakish). In this cycle, as well as the earlier examples, the compiler preferred narrative variety and richness over the thematic or ideological uniformity of the cycle. This is probably one of the clearest proofs of the great narrative richness of and affinity for the tale, which was an important and interesting feature of Jewish culture in the rabbinic period.[132]

One means of consolidation featured in all the story groupings, which is so obvious we haven't treated it directly until now, is the idea or theme. Rainmaking, the Destruction, the wisdom of the Jerusalemites, and the wonders of nature (as revealed, for example in the seafarers's tales), are subjects which serve as the basic pretext for the joining together of dozens of stories. All the other means of organization presented until now for the story cycle have generally been more complex or obscure, at times functioning below the conscious level. Were we to ask one of the compilers of the story cycles why he combined these tales together, his reply would indicate the subject or common idea despite the fact that the tales deviating from the declared subject in each of the many story groupings outnumber by far those stories which truly fit the given theme.

The true importance of the conceptual link between the various stories of the cycle is in the accumulation of meanings arising from the totality of the tales. This accumulation helps shape the grouping's general atmosphere, and influences the meaning of each of its constituent tales. Here lies the fundamental importance of the story grouping: the reader is influenced not only by the individual tale, but by the sum of meanings of all the grouping's tales, which imbue it with their own distinct character and atmosphere. The atmosphere of the grouping influences the manner of reading of each of the stories contained therein; the tale read as an independent unit would convey an altogether different impression.

This distinction holds for any story grouping, but I want to prove its validity with the aid of four examples:

[a] One of the smaller story groupings treats the subject "He who judges his neighbor in the scale of merit is himself judged favorably" (*Shabbat* 127b), with three tales. The first describes a hired laborer who, having worked three days for a house owner, requested his pay before returning home on the eve of the Day of Atonement. The house owner claimed he had nothing, that he could give his employee neither coins, nor fruit, nor land, nor beast. After the holiday, the owner "took his wages in his hand together with three laden asses, one bearing food, another drink, and the third various sweetmeats, and went to his house. After they had eaten and drank," the house owner inquired as to the laborer's suspicions as to why he had not paid him, and the laborer responded that he had suspected nothing, believing sincerely that the house owner had had a valid reason for not paying him earlier. Such was indeed the case. The second tale concerns the righteous man who, after ransoming a young woman from captivity, had her lie next to him at the inn while his students spent the night outside the locked door. In the morning he went to bathe (for ritual purification). When he asked the students their suspicions, they responded that they suspected nothing untoward, for they knew he had kept the young woman close to prevent his students from sinning with her, and that he had gone to bathe in the morning because, owing to fatigue from the journey, he had had a nocturnal pollution.

The third tale tells of the dispatch of R. Joshua to Rome, to a particular lady. He entered, locked the door and, after leaving, bathed. Here too, his students claimed not to suspect ill doing, rather they knew he bathed in order to purify himself after the lady, during their conversation, sprayed him with saliva.

The three tales are constructed as riddles: enigmatic actions of great individuals, which lend themselves to misinterpretation as serious transgressions. Once explained, it becomes clear in each case that the hero acted as he did for lofty purpose (the house owner in the first tale is Hyrcanus, father of Rabbi Eliezer the Great, whose property did not in fact belong to him that day as he had repudiated all his wealth). In each of the tales, a sharp tension develops between reality and fiction, between truth and falsehood. Appearances are not necessarily clear markers of sin, as opposed to good deeds. The hint of suspicion replacing nearly blind faith in the actions of men of merit is especially pronounced in the erotic atmosphere arising from the latter two tales. The atmosphere of the cycle crystallizes from the accumulation of meanings and tones of each of the three tales, not just from those of one. The story cycle is preferable (in the eyes of the compiler, at least) to the individual tale not only because it strengthens the meaning that the compiler seeks to promote (in this case, the rightness of giving everyone the benefit of the doubt). The accumulation of tales, in and of itself, spawns auxilliary implications which amount to more than merely the sum of meanings of the individual tales. While reading or hearing a single story may determine the attitude toward a specific occurrence or others similar to it, the purport arising from the accumulated meaning of all the cycle is the manner in which one should relate to reality in general: how one should apprehend and interpret the riddles and challenges which confront one daily.

[b] Another grouping in the Babylonian Talmud (*Ketubbot* 62b) was edited in the wake of the discussion of the question, "If a man forbade himself by vow to have intercourse with his wife." The Mishnah (ibid. 61b) states that the "Students may go away to study the Torah, without permission [of their wives for a period of] thirty days." The Talmud adds, "but the sages ruled: Students may go away to study Torah without the permission [of their wives even for] two or three years," and brings forth seven tales of scholars who left their wives for protracted periods. This parting was traumatic in all the stories but one, the famous tale of Rabbi Akiva and the daughter of Kalba Savua. In the first tales, the scholars are punished; they die for having aggrieved their wives. Others focus on the risks of returning home af-

ter a long absence, the wife's death, quarrels with other family members, and so on. The accumulation of meanings and impressions arising from a reading of all the cycle's tales points to the tension between the study hall and the home (and family) in the lives of Torah scholars. A scholar for whom the study of the Law is his life's purpose, is juxtaposed with the outcry and distress of his family. The stories do not attempt (except for the one on Rabbi Akiva) to superimpose a harmonious picture on the harsh reality of such a life, and a large portion of the tales do not even propose a solution—rather they end with the destruction of the family and the death of a spouse. And here, the story cycle achieves what an individual story never could: each such tale exposes an isolated instance, a private and unique situation of a man or woman bound by the reality of their lives. The story cycle, on the other hand, raises the individual cases to the level of sweeping abstraction. The totality of the tales lays open to view the toll of intensive Torah study on the family; the wife, neglected in favor of ideals considered greater and more important than she, cries out in loneliness. Thus the grouping of tales constructs its meaning, one broader than that of any of its constituent tales.[133]

[c] A similar example is the story grouping concerned with the Sodomites (*Sanhedrin* 109a–b). Here too it seems that there is no direct relationship between the subject of the discussion and the cycle's overall meaning. The Talmud uses stories here to flesh out the words of the Mishnah that "The men of Sodom have no portion in the future world" (ibid. 107b). Individually, most of the tales are humorous—the exploits of the clever wanderer Eliezer, and of other heroes. Yet a continuous and overall reading of the tales commands consideration of those tales which are not humorous, as well, such as the tragic story of the maiden who was cruelly tortured by the Sodomites in punishment for having given food to a pauper, or the "rules of misdeed" legislated by the men of Sodom, and the names of their judges, "Liar, Awful Liar, Forger, and Perverter of Justice." Together, these tales create a sharp sense of satire against the regime, which seeks to cloak itself in legalistic mantle while pitilessly exploiting the weak and tormenting the vulnerable. The accumulation of tales precipitates a new atmosphere which would not have existed so powerfully by virtue of the individual tales. This is an atmosphere of fierce social protest, heard not only through the voices of the tales' protagonists, but also through that of the cycle's compiler himself, who conveys his messages by means of the selection and ordering of the tales.

[d] The story cycle on the Wisdom of the Jerusalemites provides another good example of this phenomenon. Jewish culture of the rabbinic

period existed to some extent in the shadow of its conflict with Greek and Hellenistic culture. This conflict was manifested on all levels of Jewish culture of the period: in law, philosophy, custom, religious thought, and art. Reciprocal influence and rivalry between the Hellenistic and Jewish cultures played out in the realm of folk culture of the period as well. The debates in the world of art and thought were generally waged between Jewish sages and Greek *philosophos*, that is, at the highest level of the educated class. As for the conflict or tension between Hellenism and Judaism on the folk level, in daily contacts between the broad strata of the people, we have little evidence to go on. The large story grouping concerning the Wisdom of the Jerusalemites provides us with one of the few testimonies. Unfurled here is a panorama of situations taking place in the lives of members of the broad masses of the two societies: agents, travelers, and merchants in Athens, are ridiculed by the townspeople, and respond by performing acts of wisdom, earning the esteem of the denizens of "the city of wisdom"; Athenians in Jerusalem encounter cobblers, tailors, schoolchildren, and slaves, and, again, each of the tales deals with a contest of wit and cunning between the protagonists. Each tale in the cycle, individually, belongs to the widespread narrative type, "confrontation between Jews and Gentiles." As a whole, they illuminate the Hellenistic–Jewish tension on the folk level—not on the elitist level of sages versus philosophers, but in the arena of daily relationships and encounters. Thus we again have proof that the meaning of the story cycle is not shaped by separate consideration of its individual tales, but by the accrued impressions and the variety of images laid before the reader. The tales of the Wisdom of the Jerusalemites are no longer individual tales of confrontation, outlining single, happenstance events in which Greek and Jew meet in the street. Taken together, they offer a full and intricately detailed picture of Jewish society's position on its relationship with the Greek world.[134]

These examples were offered in order to show how the story grouping builds its accumulated meaning. Now it remains for us to clarify how the atmosphere or overall meaning of the grouping returns to influence the individual tale. In many of the story groupings, one or more tales are found which are exceptional in subject, literary type, or meaning. The question of how the compilers included these tales in story cycles with such a different character was explained above by means of presenting the cycle's unifying means, especially the technique of "associative accumulation," which enabled the insertion of anomalous tales. How did the cycle's atmosphere influence the individual tale, and does a continuous reading of the story cycle, causing the accrual of meanings in the course of passing from one story to the next, also influence the reading and significance of the individual tales? We will try to answer this question by means of several characteristic examples.

The story cycle on animals in God's service (*Genesis Rabbah* 10, 7) includes six tales on the theme of animals, perceived as useless and unnecessary in the world, yet dispatched by the Creator to do His work. In the first tale a man watches as a frog ferries a scorpion across the river. Once across, the scorpion stings and kills a man. The frog then returns to transport his passenger back across the river. Contrast with this the second tale, which concerns a man harvesting in the field, who took some of the cuttings and made a wreath for his head. In the course of his labor he killed a snake. Along came another man, (a magician) who, seeing the snake, knew it was not the type of snake a man was capable of killing. He asked the laborer to remove the wreath of thorns from his head, and with his staff touch the dead snake, whereupon all the man's limbs fell off. The tale is typical of many of this sort, which tell of marvelous herbal medicines. What has this tale to do with the surrounding stories of animals carrying out assigned tasks? The tale deals with a central and prevalent subject of literature and folk thought in general—"He has made his wonderful works to be remembered," that is, the wonders and oddities of nature are proof of God's greatness, therefore the multitude of stories of this type are meant to strengthen religious faith. But the tale is not received this way when it appears elsewhere, without other tales before and after (*Nedarim* 41a). The subject and mood of the story cycle "impart" the subject and mood of the individual tale. Within the framework of the cycle, the tale is read as if even the snake, or the grass of life, are messengers of the Almighty on earth, and they are the creatures who do his will, even though according to the letter of the story they were not sent by God to perform any task whatsoever.[135]

The same cycle offers another example: its sixth tale is the well-known story of Titus and the flea. On the surface, we have no more typical tale of a small creature doing the Creator's bidding than that of this gnat who entered Titus's nose. But this and other versions of the tale indicate that this is not the key or original meaning here. The tale effusively describes the insults Titus heaps on the Almighty; his intrusion into the Holy of Holies, the tearing of the curtain covering the Ark of the Law, the admission of a prostitute to the most sacred of places and, still worse, how he bedded her there, and later on his insolence toward heaven during his voyage back to Rome. These narrative elements make up the bulk of the tale, therefore its meaning must be sought there, not in the final episode concerning the gnat. The tale undoubtedly belongs to the narrative types of "the blasphemer is punished" and "pride before the fall"—the protagonist crudely offends the sacred foundation of the narrating society, or is pridefully insolent before God, and is accordingly punished. But a continuous

The Folktale in the Rabbinic Period 237

reading of the five tales which precede this in the cycle, all dealing with animals fulfilling tasks set them by the Almighty, imbues this tale with the general mood of the grouping, and the emphasis thus shifts from punishment of the blasphemer to the story of the smallest of animals carrying out the will of God.[136]

Another example of the same phenomenon appears in the story cycle in the Palestinian Talmud (Pe'ah 8, 8). The cycle deals with tales of disrespectable paupers that flaunt their defects or who are really wealthy men in disguise. There is, for example, the tale of Samuel, who sat among the paupers and heard that they eat out of bowls of gold and silver, or the tale of Rabbi Johanan and Resh Lakish who went to the springs of Tiberias, where a pauper begged of them alms, and then died, whereupon they found his pockets full of dinars, and so on. The fifth tale tells of Rabbi Hanina bar Papa, who did good deeds by night. In one place, the leader of the spirits wanted to do him harm, arguing that he had overstepped his boundaries, but by virtue of the charity he had done for the poor, Rabbi Hanina managed to escape. Clearly, this tale has nothing to do with disreputable paupers, or with the indigent at all; it is a typical demonical tale, which belongs to the narrative type, "charity delivers from death," mentioned above. In any case, the general atmosphere of the grouping as a whole, which deals with giving charity to various sorts of paupers, infuses even this exceptional tale. It is not read here as a demonic tale focusing on the evil spirits who rule the streets after dark (or on the good deeds that can save a man from their clutches). Instead, it questions whether good deeds ought to be done for paupers at a dangerous hour, and suggests, in the air of suspicion lingering from the preceding tales, that paupers might not merit the charitable acts of one who jeopardizes himself to help them. The meaning and general orientation of the grouping influence the way the individual tale is read, bending it to a meaning conforming to that of the whole. Therefore, when the reader moves on to the sixth tale, and those that follow, he naturally "catalogs" the fifth tale, which belongs to an entirely different category, to the same mood as the other stories.[137]

The following example is similar: In the group of stories about food left unsupervised, which dangerous animals, particularly snakes, then render unfit for eating (PT Terumot 8, 3), is the tale of a man who fed ten people from a cucumber upon which a snake had secreted venom—and they all died. In another, a woman hid a pauper, to whom she had given charity, from her husband, who had forbidden her to do so; the pauper saw a snake poisoning the husband's meal—and saved his life. Eight such tales are found in the grouping. The second tells of a cook in Sepphoris who served meat from animals not slaughtered ritually, and from forbidden animals, to Jews. One Sabbath eve he got drunk, climbed to the roof of his home, fell off, and died, whereafter dogs ate his flesh (as his corpse could not be seen to on the Sabbath). This typical tale of sin and punishment differs from the rest of the story cycle housing it. Yet only an analysis of the tale indicates such a difference. There is hardly any doubt that the reader to whom this story cycle was intended did not see anything in the tale to set it apart from the message and mood of the cycle as a whole—which was not to eat food left unsupervised. In other words, it is the meaning of the story cycle which emphasized a particular aspect of the tale: the Jews of that neighborhood in Sepphoris ate prohibited flesh because they did not properly supervise the food sold them by the cook. The original intention of the tale was clearly other than to caution people about careful observance of the laws of *kashrut*, even if it cost them money. The overall meaning of the story cycle is what colors the individual tale with its "accumulated" meaning, so that one previously marginal element of the tale (the supervision of the cook's actions) becomes the foundation upon which the story's meaning rests.

In the story cycle on the Wisdom of the Jerusalemites, the eighth tale deals with an Athenian who, having arrived in Jerusalem, meets a *cohen* ("priest"), and asks him how much smoke is likely to issue from the burning of a known quantity of firewood. The priest gives him a precise answer, having arrived at it via the biblical description of the burning of the wood from the table of the shewbread. The tale is similar to many others in which wise men of other nations meet and vie with a Jewish sage in matters of wisdom and acumen. The Jewish wise man's response is based on a biblical verse, and is the correct one. This tale is characteristic of all those stories in which wise men fathom the heart of reality and foresee the future, on the basis of scriptural interpretation. It is out of place in this story cycle on the Wisdom of the Jerusalemites, which presents folktales on the confrontation between the Jews and the Gentiles in a humorous vein. This tale, in contrast to its immediate neighbors, uses the exegetical technique of analogizing reality to a verse, and falls into the domain of the benchwarmers of the study house; it is therefore difficult to believe it was told in any context beyond the society of the learned. Nonetheless, this tale went the way of other anomalous tales within the ancient story cycles: the story cycle's humorous, folk-entertaining mood is imparted to this tale as well, and as such, it is no longer read as a tale whose purpose is to praise the power of Torah study and the institution of exegetical interpretation, but as a humorous tale of confrontation, whose center of gravity lies not in the study and interpretation of the Law, but in the manner in which the Jerusalemite mocks Greek wisdom. This was not the original intention of the tale, but its very presentation in the context of the story cycle paints it with the same brush as colored the other tales in the cycle. The tale has been transformed from a consummately "learned" tale to a folktale, by sole virtue of the context into which it is inserted.

This engrossing literary phenomenon has an important methodological ramification. It illustrates the futility of studying a tale that is part of a story

The Folktale in the Rabbinic Period 239

cycle as if it stands alone. The general mood of the cycle must be considered as a determining factor of its meaning. Scholarship to date has not done so. Considerable attention has been devoted to the contexts of the tales, but only in aggadic or halachic contexts. The versions of tales that fill the story cycles have been removed from context for study; they have always been treated as freestanding tales, as if they were not part of a larger fabric. The cycle is not merely an indeterminate grouping of self-contained tales. On the contrary, it constitutes a dynamic, creative context which imparts its own overall meaning to each of the narrative units it comprises. From here on, we must define the meaning of the tale not only on the basis of an analysis of its various components, but must also consider the manner in which the accumulated meanings of the totality of tales in the grouping influence the tale under scrutiny.

A number of times in the course of this chapter, the question arose as to whether the story grouping in rabbinic literature is folk literature or artistic literary creation. This question can be answered by means of a look at the construction of three encompassing story cycles: the tales of rain-bringing; the tales of the Wisdom of the Jerusalemites; and the tales of the Destruction in BT tractate *Gittin*. The cycle on rain-making (*Ta'anit* 23a–25b) is the most comprehensive of the rabbinic story cycles, if the most amorphous. Here there is a constant tension between two means of aggregation of tales. One is thematic: all the tales strive for harmony with the central theme of rain-making, which, from a formal perspective, at least, is the direct pretext for the collection of these tales in one place. At the same time, as we have seen above, a large portion of the tales do not belong to the narrative type, rain-making, yet they were included in the grouping as a result of the technique of "associative accumulation" discussed above. This technique creates a local aggregation of tales within a larger series that are related by at least one literary element (motif, genre, protagonist), although they have no link to the general subject of the grouping. After the compiler concludes the presentation of these tales, he returns to those which belong to the key subject, rain-making. This kind of tension between the techniques of local organization (association) and the overall, topical organization is especially prominent in this grouping because of its scope, but it characterizes other groupings as well.

The compilerial hand is more conspicuous in the story grouping about the Wisdom of the Jerusalemites (*Lamentations Rabbah* 1, 4). The cycle opens with the verse from Lamentations 1, 1, followed by commentary that when a Jerusalemite set out for a foreign town, he was put upon a throne so that all could hear his wisdom. The narrative construction of the first tale is nearly identical to the situation described in the commentary at the start of the cycle: it describes the Jerusalemite youth who set out for a town to reclaim his inheritance after his father died far from home. There his wisdom is revealed before the nations. At the end of this story it is said, "This is to fulfil what is said,

She that was great among the nations, i.e. great in intellect." This concludes, in the circular fashion typical of aggadah, a complete exegetical unit composed of verse, commentary, tale, and return to the commentary and conclusion with the same verse. Here the whole matter should have come to a close. But on the heels of these concluding words come another sixteen tales, constituting the well-known story cycle. What happened here from a compilerial perspective can be described as follows: One commentator put together a unit expounding the homily on, "She that was great among the nations," which included the tale of the son who set out to retrieve his inheritance. Another compiler knew more tales dealing with the travels of Jerusalemites to foreign lands, particularly Athens, and decided to append them to that original discourse. And again, in the spirit of the original discourse, after the cycle is completely over, he once again returns to the original homily: "This is to fulfil what is said, She that was great. . . ." It is conceivable that a similar process took place in the creation of other story cycles.

From the second story onward, an interesting literary process is reflected, bolstering the sense of the presence of the compilerial hand: In the second and third tales, we once again read of Jerusalemites setting out for Athens and there performing acts of wisdom. It should be noted that the first tale describes the departure of a Jerusalemite for a town, precisely as stated in the opening commentary, whereas the two tales following concern Jerusalemites heading for Athens. The fourth through the eleventh tales reverse the pattern: Athenians visit Jerusalem, where they encounter various Jerusalem types—slaves, craftsmen, schoolchildren—who best the visitors in contests of wits. From the twelfth story on, the tales are no longer of confrontation between Athenians and Jerusalemites, but of dream-solving, in which the Jewish sages expose the Cuthites, interpreters of dreams, as charlatans, deceiving those who turned to them. From the fourteenth through sixteenth tales, the grouping continues with dream tales, but with the interpretation given by Jewish sages to Jewish inquirers, in the framework of a general discussion of dreams and their function. The grouping's final tale describes a confrontation between Rabbi Joshua ben Hananiah and children who outwit him. In spite of the apparently amorphous feeling, the story cycle is built in a precise and planned manner: the first group of tales, concerning the Jerusalemites in Athens, substantiates the statements made in the opening commentary. Having run out of this type of tale, the compiler collected stories about the Jerusalemites and Athenians crossing verbal swords in Jerusalem. In other words, the compiler here gives up one element of the commentary (the departure of Jerusalemites for other lands), while preserving the central element—the contest of wits between Jerusalemites and Athenians. This group of tales ended, the compiler gathers tales of confrontation between Jews and the foreigners closest to the Jews—the Cuthites. Here the compiler chooses another unifying element, generic this time, to consolidate this sub-group: these tales of confrontation are stories of dream interpretation. And again, the distinct use of the technique of "associative accumulation"; when this group of tales is concluded, he offers yet more tales of dream solving, without a trace of any confrontation at all, and they take place within the confines of the Jewish society. The final tale, about Rabbi Joshua ben Hananiah's encounter with the children, returns to the element of polarization of children and adults (which appeared several times in the preceding tales of the cycle), but this time the confrontation takes place within Jewish society. The development of the story cycle is now clear: the compiler moves further and further away from the basic structure established in the opening commentary, but preserves at every step (that is, in each sub-group of tales) the unity of structure and of theme. The transition between one story group and another within the cycle is gradual and uniform. By degrees, the compiler gives up the elements of the opening commentary, thus enlarging the story cycle's boundaries beyond those he himself demarcated with his opening. It appears that here, too, the presence of an intentioned compilerial hand is proven. This hand gathered the tales together not merely for the sake of plenty; energy was invested in their organization and ordering.

The third story cycle, also betraying a compiler's consciousness, is that of the tales of the Destruction in BT tractate *Gittin* (55b–58a). Here, too, the pattern of the cycle is set in the introduction: "R. Johanan said: What is illustrative of the verse, Happy is the man that feareth always, but he that hardeneth his heart shall fall into michief (Prov. 28, 14)? The destruction of Jerusalem came through a Kamza and Bar Kamza; The destruction of Tur Malka came through a cock and a hen; The destruction of Bethar came through the shaft of a leather." Indeed, the entire story cycle is built as three story groups: one dealing with the causes of Jerusalem's ruin; the second with the destruction of Tur Malka; and the third with the fall of Bethar. But the logical construction of the cycle is realized not only in its overall organization, but also within each of its three constituent groups of tales. Here, the organizing principle is one of cause and effect: each group opens with a list of the causes and factors behind the destruction of, respectively, Jerusalem, Tur Malka, or Bethar, followed by depictions of the results: the conquest, the killing, the captivity. It can be said at this juncture that the compiler of this story grouping had in his mind's eye the overall construction of the cycle together with the modes of organization of the secondary units. This cycle, perhaps more than any other in aggadah, is constructed in a consolidated and integrated manner, such that the compiler's hand, and artistic and ideational conception, are obvious. In contrast to the two earlier groupings, not even one tale could be added to this story cycle without marring the conceptual edifice built by its compiler. The tales are interlocked by locality (Jerusalem, Tur Malka, Bethar) and causality (sin and punishment), and thus only the stories chosen by the compiler of the cycle can fit into the framework. In contrast, tales could be added to the two earlier cycles, by being "joined" associatively to the concluding stories. In the tales of the Destruction, a "closed" story cycle was fashioned, constituting a structured literary unit that stands alone, not as a group of "accumulated" tales, but as a unified literary text, planned from start to finish.[138]

The shift in emphasis in tales of rabbinic aggadah from the individual tale to the story cycle may indicate a more general artistic phenomenon, namely, the transition from folktale to literary work. Examination of the aggadic story cycles reveals that they constitute a transitional stage between these two modes of expression. As in later periods, the Middle Ages, for example, there is still no true conception of literary originality or authority. For this reason, the sages do not hesitate to tell most of the central tales in aggadah many times over. They see in nearly all of them true traditions, as opposed to the creation of the fictional art whose strength lies in its originality. This is one of the foremost intersections of the aggadic tale with folk literature. The breakthrough from folk literature to belles lettres began with the story cycle. Here, as shown by the above discussion, the writer or compiler of the grouping no longer sees the individual tale as an independent and isolated tradition, but as one component of an inclusive literary unit, with a unique literary pattern, atmosphere, and significance. The overall view of the grouping's compiler is almost epic: it encompasses dozens of events, characters, locales, and human experiences, which follow one another and interact, creating that same accumulation of images, narrative situations, and meanings—similar to the manner in which secondary tales melt into the epic plot. Ch. N. Bialik once lamented that rabbinic aggadah bequeathed us no great epic plot or song, doubtless having in mind such epics as the *Iliad* and the *Odyssey*. It may be that the encompassing sets of tales found in rabbinic literature, for people of the period, took the place of those epics. Yet as was customary for the sages, even in the realm of science and philosophy, they did not create an overall, systematic context. Rather, they preferred to deal with the problems that cropped up in the course of their juridical deliberations. The same seems to have held in the literary world: instead of all-inclusive, epic creation, they preferred the hundreds of tales dealing with people and events close by and meaningful to the daily life of the community over the epic pathos, which, in the words of the poet R. Judah ha-Levi regarding Greek wisdom, "has no fruits, only flowers."[139]

The sages regarded most of the tales as factual, not fictional. Therefore, in their view, the myriad facets of the tales reflected the manifold aspects of reality. In the large story cycle on rain-making, for example, the first tale of Honi the Circle-Drawer would have sufficed to substantiate the notion of the power of prayer for bringing rain—in which the commentator was interested. But the grouping's compiler was not satisfied with just one tale; he gathered dozens more, each thematically equivalent, but setting forth new and different worlds from the ones preceding; various means of bringing rain, different types of people, the variety of needs of the individual and the public connected to rain-bringing. This is a narrative perception deviating from the boundaries of the individual tale, sliding from the world of one tale to the next, and shaping a narrative reality which has unity of subject and orientation with an impressive variety of events and types. The story grouping was no epic, but it was the sages' primary vehicle for the characterization of the sweeping, multifaceted images fashioned in other societies by means of the epic.

5   The Middle Ages

External Perils and Internal Tensions

[A] Introduction

The notion of a "Middle Ages" in Jewish history is controversial. For some, it corresponds to Christian Europe's medieval period; others demarcate an era to apply exclusively to Jewish history. Still other scholars reject altogether such a classification for Jewish history, on the grounds that they do not find the markers of transition between eras that would justify its definition as a distinct historical epoch. Instead of the conventional delineation between the ancient period and the Middle Ages, they suggest viewing the evolution of Jewish cultural history, from the ancient period to the modern age, as a gradual shifting of elements as each "picture" gradually replaced its predecessor.[1]

It appears that a description of the history of the folktale is less in need of a time line than are other cultural spheres of inquiry. Needs, basic human anxieties, even internal social tensions and conflict with other peoples, generally remain static through the progression of historical periods. It has been proven, for example, that folktales from the period of the ancient East underwent few changes before being told by the storytellers of today's Israeli ethnic communities. Basic genres, the pattern of narrative motifs, plot construction, and ideational contents have remained nearly intact, in spite of the intervening thousands of years. Yet in examining Hebrew folk tales of the period designated "the Middle Ages," we see that they deviate significantly, and on several levels, from the folktales of the preceding rabbinic period. The socio-historical and literary contexts of the tales changed drastically. A portion of the narrative types widespread in the earlier periods no longer exist in this time, and others, marginal in the rabbinic age, now take center stage. Some of the themes treated by folktales in this period are found in the previous period, but many others reflect systems of interpersonal relationships characteristic of the new age. Taken together, and notwithstanding the aforementioned reservations, these contrasting features obligate us to examine the Hebrew folktale in this period as a cultural phenomenon in its own right.

According to modern Jewish historiography, the Jewish Middle Ages begin with the Muslim conquests and expansion in the second half of the seventh century. This demarcation has great significance in the history of Jewish culture. For the first time, there is a clear division between those sectors of the

Jewish people located in Christian Europe, and the larger and more important communities (at least in the early part of the period) in the lands under Islamic rule, from Yemen in the east to Spain in the west. This division is essential to understanding medieval Jewish culture, and yet more important as regards the folk literature of the period. As a result of this division, Jews absorbed the surrounding Muslim or Christian culture, and links were forged between elite Jewish and folk cultures. The people's position astride two cultures gave rise to new narrative genres and social tensions. Because of these factors' greater sensitivity to the influence of the dominant cultures, they have a greater impact upon folk traditions.

Another phenomenon with important ramifications for understanding the nature of the folktale of the period is known as the "separation of disciplines." The talmudic literature central to the earlier period was a holistic, or encyclopedic, creation. This one composition integrated all components of the period's Jewish culture: biblical exegesis and medicine, halacha alongside astronomy, prayer and liturgy side-by-side with linguistics. By the height of the geonic period (eighth–ninth centuries C.E.), there was a noticeable trend toward the creation of special works of halacha and Hebrew grammar, biblical commentary and Jewish philosophy, sacred poetry and Jewish history. The earliest works of Hebrew narrative literature almost certainly belong to this time and place, as well. Although the vast majority of Hebrew narrative compositions of the Middle Ages were anonymous, scholarship has shown that at least two of them—*Midrash of the Ten Commandments* and *The Alphabet of Ben Sira*—were produced in the cultural expanse of Babylonia and Persia during these centuries. These are the first texts in the history of Hebrew literature with an unreservedly literary orientation, and which can be defined as groupings of artistic-fictional tales, almost entirely devoid of overt ideational-didactic objectives. We can surmise that two main factors influenced the creation of these story groupings: first, the numerous story groupings of a similar nature that were scattered throughout the talmudic literature. The intensity of this phenomenon, described in detail in the previous chapter, was not overlooked by the storytellers and compilers of the new period. But the phenomenon would not have unfolded, it seems, if not for the second factor: the existence of story groupings in Arabic in the same cultural region. *Kalila we-Dimnah*, *The Tales of Sendebar*, and early versions of *The Arabian Nights* were widespread in Babylonia and Persia at the time; Jews were also familiar with them. The combination of the two influences, namely, the internal legitimization by means of borrowing literary models from the talmudic literature, and the inclination to adopt literary models from the Arab culture, apparently led to the barrier-breaking new phenomenon in Jewish culture.[2]

The narrative compositions of the Middle Ages are critical to understanding the history of Hebrew literature. Their versions, literary construction, and thematic orientations have already been outlined in a series of studies, but the picture is not yet complete. As in the earlier chapters, we will not deal with the construction and nature of the compositions themselves, but with their constituent tales. A substantial portion of medieval folktales are included in historiographical compositions, commentaries to Scripture and the Talmud, geonic responsa, and the various midrash produced during this period. Our interest lies in the testimony they offer of the day's folk traditions, not in the compositions per se. The groupings of tales are indeed of greater importance to us, as they comprise only—or primarily—tales, and in broad ranges. Nevertheless, the story groupings themselves were collected from the folk traditions by writers or compilers who wrote them in order to be read (especially aloud). The absorption and transcription of the folk traditions involved reworking, editing, and organizing the material. These were, in other words, full-fledged literary creations (in medieval terms). In works such as *The Alphabet of Ben Sira*, the author shortened tales to make them fit the framework of the new composition, and rewrote them to express his own ideational or narrative proclivities; in the family chronicle, *Megillat Ahimaaz* (the Scroll of Ahimaaz), the chronicler collected his family's surviving traditions, worked them into a chronological framework of his own, styled them in the medieval mosaic style, and set them in rhyme. And the same was done in most of the other compositions. In all of these, the folk traditions are identifiable, but the compositions themselves must be treated with different tools. We should distinguish between the folktales that constituted the basis or the raw materials for the narrative compositions of the Middle Ages, and the cultural process that turned these folk traditions into literature. The narrative compositions of the Middle Ages constitute only one context in which testimony survived of the medieval Hebrew folktale, and we will relate to it thus below.[3]

The vexing question of language arises in regard to any treatment of the medieval Hebrew folktale. Hebrew was not the spoken tongue of the people at any time during this period, though it was assuredly its written language. Jews in the lands of Islam spoke Aramaic at the dawn of the period, and Arabic shortly thereafter. In Christian Europe, the local languages and dialects used by Jews gave way to Yiddish. Thus, medieval Jewish folk literature never existed in Hebrew; it was, rather, a polyglot of other languages. Hebrew, however, was the language of the literature's preservation, in a manner similar to the relationship between local tongues and Latin in Christian Europe. Nevertheless, we have considerable data attesting to the fact that Hebrew did serve as a spoken language, and as the vehicle for the transfer of folk traditions, as did other "living" tongues. It is known, for example, that, in several Jewish centers, the business of daily life was conducted in Hebrew, as well as in the vernacular, for the duration of the Middle Ages. We know that emissaries, who left Palestine for the lands of the diaspora to collect donations for indigent communities at home, customarily recounted the marvels of the holy land, miracles that took place on the graves of saints in the Galilee, and so on, in Hebrew. They would wander among the Jewish communities in Europe, their only language in common with their hosts being Hebrew. We also know that Torah scholars from the east studied in the academies of the German lands and France; and that merchants and captive Jews were brought from afar and ransomed by local communities. All of these individuals enjoyed robust communication in the Hebrew language. Even the narrative compositions of Jewish communities in the lands of Islam—*Midrash of the Ten Commandments*, *The Alphabet of Ben Sira*, Hibbur Yafeh me-ha-Yeshu'ah—make the westward journey in Hebrew, and they were evidently even read aloud at various social opportunities. All these prove that, although Hebrew was not a vernacular in the Middle Ages, it was decidedly a living language, not merely a written tongue and, moreover, the principal medium of creation and dissemination of the Hebrew folktale.[4]

There was, at the same time, a parallel phenomenon of translation of tales from the Jews' spoken languages into Hebrew. The authors of *Midrash of the Ten Commandments* and *The Alphabet of Ben Sira* took many of the stories included therein from Jewish folk traditions told orally in Arabic, which they then translated and adapted into Hebrew. It is similarly clear that a large portion of the stories included in the Hebrew story groupings of the late Middle Ages (such as the legends of R. Samuel and Rabbi Judah the Pious) were told in Yiddish and recorded in Hebrew. The intensive transitions of the narrative traditions from the spoken languages into Hebrew was an important characteristic of the period's folk narrative.[5]

At what performance events were folktales told during this period? First, the distinction must be drawn between fictive models and authentic performance events. By "fictive models" I mean those contexts in which tales are presented within literary compositions. In the *Alphabet of Ben Sira*, King Nebuchadnezzar summons Ben Sira, the child prodigy, to whom he poses twenty-two questions. Ben Sira replies by means of stories. In *The Tales of Sendebar*, the King's wise men and his faithless wife engage in a contest of tales concerning wifely and filial fidelity. The rich literature of the rhymed narrative (*maqama*) is replete with descriptions of the situations at which people told tales: on a journey, at a banquet table, at work in the field, and so on. None of these are evidence of authentic performance events. They are, rather, fictive creations based on the author as he is imagined, or on widespread literary models.

In contrast to these, we have instances of "unbiased" (and therefore more valuable) evidence. In the opening of *The Scroll of Ahimaaz*, the author, Ahimaaz ben Paltiel of Capua, Italy (in the year 1054), outlines his intentions in writing, saying that he wants to start a dialogue and an exchange of traditions with the elders and learned of the community. He intends for his composition to be told and read aloud among the intellectual members of the Jewish community. It seems that he means that these narrative events will take place where the learned elite of Jewish society gathered—the study hall or synagogue. These were among the conventional locations for the telling of folk traditions: during breaks in study or prayer, or at other community events at which people assembled for various purposes. Incidentally, we learn from this yet again that folk traditions were not the exclusive preserve of the unlearned classes of the community.

Another reliable testimony among the few that survived is that of the traveler Menahem ben Peretz ha-Hevroni, who toured Palestine in the year 1215, and whose stories were set down in writing. In the first part of the work, Menahem describes, in first person, his experiences as a traveller:

> And this is how I heard [the tales] from the children of the land of Israel. As I, Menahem ha-Hevroni, wrote them, so they are, from beginning to end . . . No one should suspect me and no one should say in their hearts that I wrote [them] to find favor and in order to extract money from them. It is revealed and known to the Creator that this is how I heard [the tales] from the natives of *ma'arava* [The land of Israel].

In the second section of the travelogue, another author continues:

> R. Menahem ben Peretz, who saw a great beast, told us more . . . and R. Menahem ha-Hevroni saw that beast . . . and told us further of a tree of metal and copper . . . and also told us what the captain recounted to him on board his ship during his return [journey] to the land of his birth, . . . So told us R. Menahem bar Peretz ha-Hevroni. . . . He also told us of a dream dreamt by a widow. . . . (Oxford-Bodleian manuscript Or. 135, p. 363a–b)

This passage indicates that the writer heard the remarks straight from R. Menahem's mouth, not too long after his return from the holy land. That would be sometime in 1215–1216 (as it is difficult to believe that "now," referring to the time of the traveler's return to France, could have encompassed a period longer than a year or two). In other words, Menahem ben Peretz, by his own testimony, earns a living from stories of the holy land, and it was the copyist of the manuscript who put his tales in writing in a style similar to that of oral storytelling. It was an accepted practice for travellers and visitors from the east to tell tales they heard there for profit or to raise money for charity. The example above is direct evidence of this.[6]

The question of genres, that greatly occupied us in the preceding chapters, also receives a new twist in the medieval period. Traditional genres, such as myth, animal tales, and fables, nearly vanish from the repertoire of folktales. R. Berechiah ha-Nakdan did compose his *Mishlei Shu'alim* ("Fox Fables") in the thirteenth century, but this work belongs to the literary creative sphere (like the books of *maqamot*), even if individual fables in his collection (and this is rather doubtful) were culled from the oral traditions. Another genre that was very widespread as a folk tradition in all the earlier periods was the expanded biblical tale. We have seen how folk raconteurs take familiar scriptural stories and expand them to serve not only as historical or theological tales, but also as consummate folktales. In the medieval period, the creation of expanded biblical tales continues. Medieval midrash, such as *Pirkei de-Rabbi Eliezer* and *Genesis Rabbati*, biographical midrash, such as *Ma'aseh Avraham Avinu* and *The Chronicles of Moses*; and novelistic midrash, such as *Midrash va-Yissa'u* ("The Book of Wars of the Sons of Jacob") and *Sefer ha-Yashar*, utilize narrative techniques similar (if not identical) to the expanded biblical tales of the earlier periods. Yet these compositions do not tell folktales, and they should be seen as literary works in every respect, although folk traditions are occasionally woven into them.[7]

The emergence of some genres in the Middle Ages stands out in contrast to the waning of those that had been central in the preceding periods. The religious exemplum, the cycle of praises (hagiography) of luminaries, and the novella are the narrative genres that in this period constitute the lion's share of the narrative repertoire. Most prominent of all, it seems, are the aggadic tales retold. For each of the period's great story groupings—*Hibbur Yafeh min-ha-Yeshu'ah*, *Sefer ha-Ma'asim* Oxford manuscript, *Sefer ha-Ma'asiyyot* Gaster edition (and the Yiddish *Mayse-Bukh*)—approximately two-thirds of the constituent tales are retold aggadic narratives. This phenomenon has deeper implications than the mere copying of talmudic literature, for the medieval variations are often substantially different from their rabbinic sources, indicating that the aggadic tales were told orally in the period's folk traditions. Their high rate of representation in every story grouping shows the vigorous demand and great popularity enjoyed by tales from this source in medieval Jewish society. It can thus be stated that the renovated aggadic tale inherited the position once held by the expanded biblical tale. It is not as familiar in this period as the biblical text, and thus its aesthetic effect of renewal and surprise is still powerful. And its great variety in the rabbinic sources available to the medieval writers and storytellers affords a plentiful supply of new material, which they adapted to the tastes and orientations of the denizens of the period.[8]

[B] Rabbinic Aggadah as Folk Narrative

In the Middle Ages, the stock of tales of the preceding cultural period was a wellspring of literary inspiration. This need not surprise us, as the fruits of each fading epoch continue to nourish the emergent age even after new cultural patterns crystallize. Such is the classic Jewish perception of the "chain of tradition," according to which each generation transmits its teachings to the generation ahead. The venerable teachers of the past rise in stature as the years go by and the first link in the chain, "the source," slips back ever farther in time. One ramification of this fundamental concept was that cultural materials inherited from generations past were more highly valued than any contemporary creation. For this reason, rabbinic tales rebound to be told in the Middle Ages in many forms. Some are copied verbatim or read aloud from the rabbinic sources; others are reworked on various levels, transformed by combination with others into a developed tale, or lifted out of their original context to serve as a nucleus for the development of a new and independent tale. They are found in all types of medieval literature: commentary, responsa and historiographical literature, compilations, and mystical writings.

The viability of rabbinic tales in the Middle Ages was quite impressive. They entered into nearly all types of Jewish creation of the period, whether as legal and intellectual illustrations, sources of information, a means of moral guidance and edification, or as historical evidence. This confirms that they were told and retold, in writing and orally, by and to diverse strata of Jewish society. Tales of rabbinic aggadah were also woven into medieval homilies. These were delivered to assorted audiences, the tales serving ideational, as well as aesthetic-rhetorical, purposes. We find rabbinic aggadah in the period's important story collections—*Midrash of the Ten Commandments, The Alphabet of Ben Sira, An Elegant Composition Concerning Relief After Adversity, Sefer ha-Ma'asim (The Book of Deeds)* Oxford manuscript—where they are intertwined with unadulterated folk traditions borrowed from international folklore. This blending proves that the compilers of the collections, together with the target audience, regarded rabbinic aggadah as folk traditions as well, designed for performance events like those of the other tales.

Further corroboration of rabbinic aggadah's folk nature in the Middle Ages comes from the variants that crop up in the sources of the period. The aggadic narratives to be treated in this chapter took various forms in the medieval sources. Whether they were told at various events, and therefrom taken down in writing in the manuscripts and compositions of the Middle Ages, or copied from one composition to another—they underwent pronounced changes in the process. These changes corroborate their absorption by the medieval Jewish society—in other words, they became folk traditions. This point deserves special emphasis, as the erroneous view of "authentic" folk literature as strictly oral still holds sway. Yet the folk—in the broader sense that includes the scholars and the learned—saw fit to uproot these tales from the literature of the preceding period and use, alter, and recreate them. This demonstrates the proprietary attitude of the folk and folk culture toward the traditions of its past. We can most clearly apprehend and describe the following material through this lens.

Micha Josef Bin-Gorion (Berdyczewski), in his extensive collection of folktales, *Mimekor Yisrael* (originally in German, *Der Born Judas*, 6 vols., Leipzig 1916–1923, Hebrew version edited and supplemented by Emmanuel Bin-Gorion, 1938), devotes a comprehensive chapter to "Talmudic Tales Retold." Here the writer and scholar amassed scores of legends of rabbinic origin which surfaced to be retold again and again in medieval sources. This chapter offers a good representative sampling of the types of stories, in their many variations (upon which he elaborates in the appended notes). Particularly noteworthy are those appearing in numerous versions. For example, the tales of Rabbi Hanina ben Dosa (*Ta'anit* 24b–25a, and elsewhere) are copied in *Hibbur Yafeh min ha-Yeshu'ah*, *Sefer ha-Ma'asiyyot*, Gaster edition, Elijah de Vidas' *Reshit Hokhmah*, and the Yiddish *Mayse-Bukh*. The famous tale of one of three sisters who slanders others, and thereby causes the deaths of several people (*Leviticus Rabbah* 26, 2), is again recounted in Elijah de Vidas' *Reshit Hokhmah*, the Yiddish *Mayse-Bukh*, *Sefer ha-Ma'asiyyot*, Gaster edition, the smaller Midrash in Jellinek's *Beit ha-Midrash*, and in *Hibbur ha-Ma'asiyyot ve-ha-Midrashot ve-ha-Haggadot* (The Collection of Tales, Midrash and Aggadah). The rabbinic aggadah of the student who meticulously observed the precept of *tsitsit* (the wearing of "ritual fringes") (*Menahot* 44a), reappears in *Hibbur Yafeh min ha-Yeshu'ah*, *Sefer ha-Ma'asiyyot ve-ha-Midrashot ve-ha-Haggadot*, al-Nakawa's *Sefer Menorat ha-Ma'or*, Elijah ha-Kohen's *Sefer Me'il Tsedaka*, Gaster's *Sefer ha-Ma'asiyyot*, and the Yemenite *Midrash ha-Gadol*. The rabbinic aggadah of the pious man and the tax collector's son (Palestinian Talmud, *Hagigah*, chapter 2, paragraph 2 [7d], Babylonian Talmud, *Sanhedrin* 44b), is retold in the Middle Ages in *Hibbur Yafeh min ha-Yeshu'ah*, Jellinek's *Beit ha-Midrash*, by Rashi in his commentary to the passage and in al-Nakawa's *Menorat ha-Ma'or*, in the *Arukh* dictionary, in the *Tosefta Atikta*, in *Sefer ha-Ma'asiyyot*, Gaster edition, and in the Yiddish *Mayse-Bukh*. The tale of Rabbi Joshua ben Levi, who tricked the Angel of Death, made away with his sword, and leapt with it into the Garden of Eden (*Ketubbot* 77b), is retold in *Hibbur Yafeh min ha-Yeshu'ah*, *Sefer Likkutei ha-Ma'asim*, in the smaller Midrash in Jellinek's *Beit ha-Midrash*, *Sefer ha-Ma'asiyyot*, Gaster edition, *The Alphabet of Ben Sira*, and *Eshkol ha-Kofer*, and other versions turn up in a number of as yet unpublished manuscripts. These examples, and more, confirm that which we sought to prove—in the Middle Ages the rabbinic aggadah culled from the Talmuds and Midrash became living folk traditions appearing in diverse sources and in varied, independent forms.[9]

Further examination of the last three tales can illuminate the modifications they underwent. The first tale is the familiar story of Eleazar ben Dordiyya and the commandment of the fringes (*Sifrei Numbers*, the end of portion *Shelach*, Ish Shalom edition, p. 35, 2; *Menahot* 44a). It is told in two forms: the one in the Babylonian Talmud, tractate *Menahot*, tells of the prostitute hired by R. Eleazar ben Dordiyya. Before he approached her, she ridiculed him, for, on account of his transgression, he would not merit life in the world to come. In this case, it is the woman who saves the scholar from sin. When ben Dordiyya fathoms the seriousness of his misdeed, he sets out for the mountains to beg forgiveness of the forces of nature: the sun, the moon, the mountains, and the hills. They refuse him, he rests his head upon his knees, weeps bitterly, and dies. The second version, which appears in the *Sifrei*, is narrated as a novella. According to this version, the scholar's *tzitzit* (fringes), about which he was fastidious (this point is emphasized in contrast to other precepts which he did not observe strictly), kept him on the straight and narrow. As he undressed, the *tzitzit*, which he wore under his clothes, caught his eye. When the prostitute understood what lay behind his sudden restraint, she sold all her property, donating most of it to charity, and repented. She went to the study hall of that same Torah scholar with a third of her wealth, where R. Hiyya converted her and then wed the couple. Only one of these talmudic versions is retold in the Middle Ages. The medieval version, told by R. Nissim of Kairouan in *An Elegant Composition Concerning Relief after Adversity*, and in other medieval sources, is the novelistic one, which concludes with the Torah scholar's reward in the form of wealth and seemly marriage, and not the tragic-moralistic tale of the Babylonian version. This preference is further proof of the folk nature of the medieval versions. The one passed over is a moralistic tale with an ascetic tinge: a sinner in self-imposed seclusion dies of remorse. This is not a tale given to absorption by the broad strata of the folk and transformation into a folk tradition. In contrast, the version of the tale that was selected was constructed as a love story, erotic in every respect. The protagonists are ultimately joined in happiness and wealth, an optimistic resolution of the plot in keeping with folktales' customary "happy ending."[10]

The lines of the plot as sketched by R. Nissim of Kairouan are similar to those of the *Sifrei* version. Yet it is clearly not identical: the details—the description of the prostitute waiting for him, the behavior of the Torah scholar, their conversation, and so on—parallel the corresponding details of the rabbinical tale, but are different. Even in language the tales differ (R. Nissim's book was originally written in Arabic). One detail in particular deserves elaboration: in the *Sifrei* version, the woman arrives at R. Hiyya's study hall and presents the note left her by the scholar with his name and address. R. Hiyya reads it and weds them after converting her. This episode bears a halachic thorn, as conversion for the sake of marriage is controversial. The tale seems to prove that some sages, among them R. Hiyya, dismissed this restriction, and were customarily lenient in matters of conversion. R. Nissim of Kairouan recounts the episode as follows:

> She then said to [R. Hiyya]: "my lord, I would like you to order someone to administer a ritual ablution to me, for I wish to enter into your faith." R. Hiyya replied: "Begone from me! No doubt you lust after one of my disciples

and desire to marry him." So she indited a letter [to him], informing him of all that had happened between her and [his] disciple. When R. Hiyya learned these [facts], he said to the disciple: "Arise, my son, and marry her, for God has rewarded you for your fear of His punishment, and you deserve to attain her in accordance with the requirements of the holy law." (Brinner's translation, p. 42)

In other words, R. Nissim, who already knew that the (later) halachic ruling in this controversy was stringent, revises the episode somewhat in order not to disconcert those familiar with the law. In any case, it is clear that the tale of the prostitute and the Torah scholar was retold in the Middle Ages—not copied from the written source. It was selected from the rabbinic versions, and revamped to function as a folk narrative tradition and suit the character of the new period both as regarded its plot and its details. We can observe a similar process of taking up the more "folk" version—that is, the one more likely to be absorbed into medieval traditions—in the tale of Beruriah's children. While her husband, Rabbi Meir, was away at the synagogue, their two sons died. Beruriah laid them out in their beds, but said nothing to her husband upon his return. Only when the Sabbath had ended did she show him their bodies, upon which he uttered the blessing: "The Lord gives, and the Lord takes away." This version was indeed copied from the midrash (*Midrash Proverbs* 31,10) into other medieval compositions, such as *Yalkut Shimoni* and *Sefer ha-Ma'asiyyot* Gaster edition, but the main medieval literary sources, such as *Midrash of the Ten Commandments* (fourth commandment) and *An Elegant Composition*, present another version: the father sets out with his sons to synagogue. On the way, a wall collapses on them, burying the sons beneath rubble. The father continues to the synagogue; he does not desecrate the Sabbath. Later, he returns home and tells his wife that he left their children in another's care. When he returns again, later that evening, and still does not tell her the whereabouts of their sons, she understands what has happened, and justifies their fate:

> When Evening came, the wall was cleared from over the two boys, and they were found alive and were taken to their parents. As the parents were conversing with each other, behold, their two sons approached. They fell upon them, weeping copiously, and asked them, "What was it that saved you?" The boy replied, "The wooden beam of the wall formed a roof over us and made a brace between us and the stones and earth, and when [all] this was removed from over us, we came out safely." (Brinner's translation, p. 91)

The medieval versions diverge from the midrash in two respects: first, it is not the mother (the controversial Beruriah, wife of Rabbi Meir) who is the protagonist, but the father. To this end the narrator had to rebuild the tale. This point was apparently so important to him that he did so unreservedly. The midrashic version's depiction of the woman as superior in righteousness and wisdom to her husband appears to have been unacceptable to medieval story-tellers, hence their far-reaching changes in the tale's construction. The second respect is, of course, the story's conclusion. The midrashic version portrays the faithful's full and final acceptance of the judgement, the reward for which is the virtue of acceptance itself. A tale that ends thus could only be told among moralists and the learned, who sought no immediate reward for their actions, and who truly believed that "virtue is its own reward." In the folk traditions, such a conclusion is untenable. Indeed, the version from *An Elegant Composition* and *Midrash of the Ten Commandments* tells of a practical and immediate reward—the children lived on account of their parent's piety—as well as a reward in the hereafter. This is a quintessential modification to a learned literary tradition, prerequisite to its becoming a folk tradition.[11]

The tale of "The Righteous Man and the Tax-Collector's Son," as told in *An Elegant Composition* and in the versions based on it, belongs to the same group of versions as the tale in its rabbinic original. Differences between the rabbinic versions and the medieval traditions, such as those in the tale of the children who died on the Sabbath, are prominent here, too. They include the narrative style and the adaptation of details to the new reality (the tax collector of the talmudic tale is in *An Elegant Composition*, the individual who collected the tax from non-Muslims [the *kharaj*] in the lands of Islam). But in its general flow and meaning, the tale is basically the same as its rabbinic source. In contrast, Rashi, in his commentary on this in the Babylonian Talmud (*Sanhedrin* 44b), and the *Arukh* dictionary (Kohut edition, vol. 2, p. 145), both offer an interesting version. Rashi and the author of the *Arukh* were evidently quite familiar with the rabbinic version of the tale, yet both prefer to tell it according to another version, as if to emphasize their access to other traditions of the same story. According to this version, the wicked tax collector died on the same day as one of the pillars of the community. Most of the townspeople flocked to accompany the great Torah scholar to his resting place, while only a few showed up for the tax collector's funeral. Enemies attacking the town that very day caused everyone to flee for their lives. When the townspeople returned later, the biers had been switched; the wicked tax-collector was consequently buried with great honor, while the scholar's final journey was a lonely and ignominious one. A student of the great rabbi was a perplexed witness to these events. His teacher appeared to him in a vision, showed him that the wicked man was in Gehenna while he himself was honored highly in the Garden of Eden. The Rabbi explained to him that he had been punished for not protesting when once he overheard slander against the sages. The wealthy man, ironically, received his due in this world for one unpremeditated good deed: he had prepared a great feast for a city dignitary and, when his guest did not come, he distributed it to people in need.

This version is connected to the ancient rabbinic version; it might even be a derivative. But the dissimilar construction of the plot implies more than a different tale. More importantly, it indicates ideational modification: the rabbinic version carries a sharp tone of social protest—the privileged and the wealthy, wicked as they may be, are venerated by society, while those of more humble means, righteous and erudite in Torah as they may be, are disdained, even in death. While the tale ultimately reveals the hand of Providence and a moral-theological logic underlying the events, the offense to the humble Zaddik is never redressed, and his promised reward in the world to come is but little consolation. Contrastingly, the medieval versions offer a correspondence between a man's measure and his social status: the illustrious rabbi merits great honor, and all the town attends his burial, while the wicked tax collector is to be interred in disgrace. The wrongful act in this case is the astonishing switching of the biers, for which Providence, not society, is responsible. In other words, this version of the tale does not belong to the category of social protest (as society behaved irreproachably), but rather is a theodicean story: it dramatizes the limited vision of mortals observing God's actions and deeming them unjust. Jewish society conducted itself according to the correct ethical norms, and God's jarring of the social hierarchy came only to consummate and reinforce that hierarchy, not to derail it. One widespread tale in folk narrative of the period, concerning Rabbi Joshua ben Levi and Elijah the Prophet, deals with the same theme. It tells how Rabbi Joshua accompanied Elijah, and observed his unethical behavior. It was ultimately revealed to him that Elijah's actions were truly grounded in wisdom and justice, and that Rabbi Joshua had misconstrued them because of his limited human capacity to understand. This period apparently saw a great deal of interest in tales of this type, and therefore both the *Arukh* and Rashi cited this version rather than the earlier rabbinic one.[12]

The tale of R. Joshua ben Levi and the Angel of Death offers further evidence of this same phenomenon. It originates in the Babylonian Talmud (*Ketubbot* 77b):

> R. Joshua b. Levi, however, attached himself to these [sufferers afflicted with *ra'athan*—a contagious skin disease causing nervous trembling] and studies the Torah [as a protection]; for he said: a lovely hind and a graceful doe (Proverbs 5, 19) if [the Torah] bestows grace upon those who study it, would it not also protect them?

Compare this to the version of the tale's opening in *An Elegant Composition* (appendix):

> The rabbis said that R. Joshua ben Levi was a completely righteous man. When his time to die came, the Blessed be He said to the Angel of Death: Accept whatever he asks from you. (Hirschberg edition, p. 106)

In the Talmud, the tale of Joshua ben Levi is set among a cycle of tales about the moment of death of great sages, describing how Torah delays or eases this moment. The tale about R. Joshua ben Levi opens with a verse-based homily and, in the manner of rabbinic aggadah, comes to fill out and substantiate that homily. The medieval version opens with a portrayal of R. Joshua ben Levi. Such was unthinkable in talmudic literature, but in the eleventh century it was essential for an audience unfamiliar with rabbinic literature, who neither knew nor studied Torah. The medieval tale does not even mention death's deferral on account of Torah study, only its easing, as R. Joshua ben Levi in this version "was a completely righteous man"—not a great Torah scholar. Here too, it seems the tale was targeted at the broad audience beyond Torah scholars. The storyteller's intention was to emphasize the *fine qualities* of his protagonist, not the life of Torah study, so central to rabbinic literature and so far removed from the medieval audience. The talmudic tale was assuredly a prevalent one among erudite circles, its purpose being to underscore the benefit of studying the Torah. The medieval tale, however, was aimed at an uneducated audience, and it is this departure that underlies the tale's revision.

The medieval tale also dramatizes the tale's core event—R. Joshua ben Levi's leap into the Garden of Eden after leading astray the Angel of Death, and his refusal to submit to this Angel's dreadful ministrations. What in the Talmud was encapsulated in two terse sentences,

> He [the Angel of Death] held him by the edge of his gown. He [R. Joshua] said to him: I swear that I will not get out.

became significantly longer in the Middle Ages:

> He said to him: get out from there! R. Joshua swore in the name of God that he will not get out, and the Angel of Death was not allowed to enter there. The Ministering Angels said to The Holy One Blessed Be He: Master of the Universe! See what Ben Levi did: by force he took his portion in the Garden of Eden.

And so it continues: Before giving back the Angel of Death's slaughtering knife, R. Joshua ben Levi extracts from him a promise not to show it to people when he takes their soul, so as not to terrify them. And a new episode is added at the end, in which the Angel of Death complains about R. Joshua's conduct to Rabban Gamaliel. Rabban Gamaliel justifies R. Joshua's actions, and instructs the Angel of Death to ask R. Joshua to describe in writing Gan Eden and Gehenna:

> After that R. Joshua ben Levi returned to the Garden of Eden and wrote these things and sent them to the Patriarch Rabban Gamaliel and to the elders of Israel and told them all he saw in the Garden of Eden and in

Gehenna. (*An Elegant Composition*, Hirshberg edition, appendix, p. 107, and a close variant in Gaster, *Exempla of the Rabbis*, pp. 96–97)[13]

The narrative expansions and the construction of dramatic dialogues, the network of conflicts between the Angel of Death and R. Joshua ben Levi, the ministering angels and the Almighty, the Angel of Death and Rabban Gamaliel, all these reconfirm that the tale in this format was targeted at a broad audience of listeners, with the emphasis on its literary, not ideational features. In addition, this tale contains hallmarks of the medieval period: the intensive preoccupation with and anxiety over death. In the tale's version from *The Exempla of the Rabbis* (Gaster edition), the Angel of Death is described:

> The Holy One blessed be He said to [the Angel of Death]: Go and adorn yourself with signs of death. It was said of the Angel of Death: he stretches from one end of the world to the other, he is full of eyes from the sole of his foot to the crown of his head, his attire is fire, his covering is fire, all of him is fire and in his hand, the knife; and from it is suspended a drop of bile, from which man dies, from which he reeks and from which his face turns pallid. (Ibid., p. 96)

Folk beliefs, folk art, and the narrative traditions of the Middle Ages often portray the Angel of Death as a fearful, menacing figure brandishing his slaughtering knife or scythe above the heads of people of all ages and occupations. Such, for example, are the series of paintings depicting "the dance of death" (*totentanz*) that expressed the deep anxieties dogging medieval man all his days. Indeed, this version of the story appears to be designed as a barricade against these widespread folk beliefs and the anxieties they produced. It emphatically claims that mortals can see neither the Angel nor his blade before death—thanks to R. Joshua ben Levi. R. Joshua's tour through Paradise and Gehenna, and their precise description which he sent to Rabban Gamaliel and the sages, introduces another common medieval literary genre into the tale—journeys through Paradise and Hell. This genre peaked in the fourteenth century, with the pinnacle of medieval poetry, Dante's *Divine Comedy*.[14]

The famous legend of Rabbi Akiva's first steps toward becoming a luminary is also told in several versions in medieval Hebrew letters. Most of these (*An Elegant Composition, Rav Pe'alim*, the Yiddish *Mayse-Bukh, Likuttei ha-Ma'asim*), retell it, according to the various forms of the tale in rabbinic aggadah—and with the typical modifications discussed at the start of this section. One group of versions from the Middle Ages, as represented in *The Exempla of Rabbis* Gaster edition, steers us to another important phenomenon: the eclectic versions. Here the storyteller takes up four aggadic versions of R. Akiva's beginning of biography on the road to sagehood: his marriage to Rachel, daughter of Kalba Savua; the water-etched stone that he and his son saw in the city of

Lod, on account of which he embarked upon a life of Torah study; the account of R. Akiva lighting his home with bundles of straw; and that of his great wealth later in life, and the great honor with which he treated his wife. In rabbinic sources, these are four separate and independent narrative traditions, transmitted in different contexts. The medieval storyteller links them by adding connective episodes and omitting contradictory details. He strives to build a continuous, logical plot. The storyteller's objective here is twofold: to overcome the fragmentation of the sages' biographical legends, and to construct a more complete biographical tale that spans the protagonist's lifetime, from the start of his studies until his demise. Yet the storyteller does not incorporate the aggadic tales of his martyr's death, or other biographical aggadah found in rabbinic sources, only those with a novelistic nature—whose themes are romance and wisdom, R. Akiva's complex, enduring relationship with his wife, and his career as a Torah scholar. Therein lies the second objective behind the changes made to the story: to play up the woman's role in her spouse's successful Torah scholarship, and to provide an exemplar of the gratitude and appreciation a scholar owes such a wife (" . . . [he] made for his wife all kinds of jewelry such as are in the world, and he made for her a great tiara of gold inlaid with large, fine precious stones and pearls, and in it a figure of the sun and the moon, stars, and constellations," *The Exampla*, Gaster edition, p. 601). When the notion is transmitted in the concise narrative sections of rabbinic aggadah, they seem to the medieval storyteller insufficient, especially as these sections are fragmented and spread among different sources. Such an arrangement of the versions portrays a relationship based on the wife's self-sacrifice, and her husband's ensuing respect, in all its complexity. This is not merely a mechanical cutting and pasting of different texts, rather it is an artful retelling of a tale, with aesthetic and ideational purpose.[15]

A humorous story cycle on drunkards appears in *Midrash Leviticus Rabbah* (12, 1). These are typical folk tales of drunkards which the preachers in the rabbinic period put to purely rhetorical use, as part of a comprehensive homily. Some of the tales resurface in new versions in the Middle Ages as well. Of particular interest is one version (from *Kaftor va-Ferah*) in which the storyteller creates a synthesis of three such tales of drunkards. The first concerns the sons who abandoned their father in the cemetery, to keep him from wasting their inheritance on wine. Crooks, intending to smuggle wine into the nearby city, cached their store in the cemetery, unwittingly supplying the forsaken father with a long-term supply. The second tells of the drunken father who, instead of learning a lesson from another inebriate lying in the mud and filth of the gutter, asks where he purchased such fine wine. The last describes the drunkard who put his mouth to the keyhole of the closed tavern door so that wine could be poured through it directly into his mouth. He never felt the blows of the city watchmen, who thought him a robber. There seems to be no motive for the synthesis of these three tales beyond the narrative objective: the composition is designed to magnify the narrative and humorous effect by means of knitting up several separate tales into a single narrative framework.[16]

Another typical instance of this technique of narrative synthesis can be found in the tales of R. Hanina ben Dosa in *An Elegant Composition*. Most of the versions of the biographical legends concerning R. Hanina, both in the rabbinic literature and in the medieval story cycles, are offered as single tales woven into various contexts. R. Nissim of Kairouan, author of *An Elegant Composition*, sensed that the tales could deliver their maximum ethical effect only if they were presented together. He pursued this course, but instead of preserving the tales' original form as a biographical story cycle—as in the rabbinic source—he synthesized several different tales. One way that R. Nissim realizes this goal is by omitting those details which singularize the various tales, and by adding episodes and connective matter. But his primary means of synthesis is the emphasis on the righteousness of R. Hanina ben Dosa's wife. She is behind the saint's deeds. This theme recurs in and connects each episode of the new story, functioning both as a narrative technique and as an ideational element. In this manner, he realizes two goals: first, the compression of the hero's actions and ethical characteristics into one powerful, didactic-ethical text. Second, the emphasis on the place and role of the wife who, according to the medieval model of the tale, is the driving force behind the saint's actions. Although such notions of a wifely role in the success of a sage or saint already exist in the rabbinic literature, R. Nissim was interested in stressing this point. To this end, he chose the technique of synthesizing separate sources.[17]

These examples of the recurrent model of synthesizing different rabbinic versions of tales show this phenomenon to be neither unique nor exceptional. The storytellers of the Middle Ages sought to "overcome" by this means the fragmentation and diffusion of rabbinic aggadah, and thereby to magnify their narrative effect and drive home their social and ideational messages.

Another interesting link between rabbinic literature and the medieval tale is the dilation of a rabbinic terse statement—an enigmatic saying or verse—into a complete Hebrew tale in the Middle Ages. Scholarship has extensively analyzed one such tale, that of "the language of animals" motif, based on the verse: "Cast thy bread upon the waters: for thou shalt find it after many days" (Eccles. 11:1). The fully developed tale first appears in *Midrash of the Ten Commandments*, but it is copied and retold in other medieval sources. It has been proven, on the basis of the verse and of additional texts found in the story cycle on this verse in the midrash *Ecclesiastes Rabbah*, that medieval storytellers developed the complex tale of the son whose father instructed him to toss a loaf of bread into the sea each day. In reward for obeying his father, the Leviathan carries the son away and, after marvelous exploits, he becomes tremendously wealthy. The storytellers made varied use here of "homiletical" literary means, with whose aid they developed the "anchor words" (upon which the text is built) of the biblical verse (water, days, bread and salt, finding, treasure), into narrative episodes. They also utilized motifs of international folk literature: the father's bidding, standing in trial before the Leviathan, the study of the tongue of the animals, deception of the birds who sought to harm him, the finding of great treasure. All these indicate the growing tendency of medieval storytellers to create tales of greater scope and complexity, different fundamentally from the conciseness and fragmentation of rabbinic aggadah.[18]

Other excellent examples of the same phenomenon are the legend of "the weasel and the well," and the fable of "the fox and the wolf at the well." Both appear in the work of medieval talmudic commentators as explications of enigmatic sayings in the Talmud. The tale of the "weasel and the well" survives in two basic versions—one in Geonic responsa and in the *Arukh* dictionary (eleventh century), and the other in Rashi's commentary to the Babylonian Talmud. Both refer to the perplexing passage: "R. Ammi further said: Come and see how great the Men of Faith are as is evidenced from the episode of the weasel and the well. If this is the case with one who trusts in the weasel and the well, how much more so if one trusts in the Holy One blessed be He!" (*Ta'anit*, 8a). The version in Rashi known as "the short version," while that in the *Arukh* is known as "the broad version." The important differences between them do not necessarily lie in their relative length, as both are quite brief relative to other tales. Rather, their narrative character and worldview are significant. Rashi's version is characteristic of his style in commentary and in the other tales therein, namely, laconic, clear, and concentrated. Rashi's versions in these tales are a perfect example of narrative density: each narrative sentence carries an entire episode; the narrator concentrates only on what is necessary for narrative development, completely ignoring anything that does not serve the commentarial objective. The version in *He-Arukh* (identical to the version in *Teshuvot* [responsa of] *ha-Ge'onim*), is, for all intents and purposes, a tale. It appears to have been crystallized and polished in the hands of generations of preceding storytellers. Yet the most significant difference is the tragic cast of Rashi's version, which concludes with the death of the sons and the young man's confession of guilt, as opposed to the novelistic, optimistic hue of the tale in its broad version—which concludes with his marriage to the young woman who remained faithful despite suffering and anguish. Perhaps these differences arise from the pessimistic nature of Rashi stories in general, or maybe the exegetical context of the tales did not permit Rashi to conclude the tale appropriately. In any case it is clear that only "the broad version" would work as a folktale.[19]

An important question arising in connection with the legend of "the weasel and the well" is whether the medieval storytellers were telling an ancient tradition of rabbinic origin, or were they taking a contemporary folktale and applying it as commentary to a rabbinic utterance? We cannot answer this question until supporting evidence is unearthed from either the rabbinic period or medieval European folklore. In any case, the following example is likely to furnish supporting evidence that also lends itself to the legend of "the weasel and the well." This passage comes from the Babylonian Talmud (*Sanhedrin* 38b–39a):

> R. Johanan said: R. Meir had three hundred parables of foxes, and we have only three left: [a] the fathers have eaten sour grapes and the children's teeth are set on edge (Ezek. 18:6). [b] Just balances, just weights (Lev. 19:36). [c] The righteous is delivered out of trouble and the wicked comes in his stead (Prov. 11:8).

The Talmud does not cite the fables here, but their epimythia—biblical verses. Two commentators, close in time, Rav Hai Gaon and Rashi, explain this utterance by means of example. Rashi tells of the hungry wolf with a craving for fox. The fox persuaded the wolf to go to the courtyard of the Jews and feast with them on Friday evening, as there he would dine far better. When the wolf appeared in the Jews' courtyard during their Sabbath Eve repast, they beat him and chased him away. When the wolf recaptured the fox, the quarry convinced him that food aplenty lay at the bottom of a well. The fox descended in one bucket to the water level, and showed the wolf the reflection of the moon, saying it was a slice of cheese. The wolf, fooled, lowered himself in the second bucket, and of course, in so doing, raised the first bucket, freeing the fox. The verses cited in the talmudic text describe the escape. The fable offered by Rav Hai Gaon, in explanation of the words of R. Johanan, also concerns a fox in a wolf's hungry clutches. The fox shows the lion more desirable prey—a man crouched on the far side of a covered pit, which was actually a lion trap. The lion fell for the bait, leapt to pounce on the man, but fell into the trap. The fox stood at the edge of the pit and called out to him, "The righteous is delivered out of trouble and the wicked comes in his stead."

It has been proven that the two fables offered by these commentators were products of the Middle Ages. The environmental details upon which they are built were characteristic of Europe or Iraq, Persia, and India in the period shared by Rashi and Hai Gaon, not of Jewish life in Palestine in the time of R. Meir or R. Johanan. These details include the courtyard of the Jews, where the members of several families gathered for a shared Sabbath eve meal; the particular type of well from which water was drawn via two buckets at either end of a single rope; the round, flat cheese, resembling the shape of the moon; and the lion trap and its bait. Furthermore, variants of this fable have been found in the European fable literature of the period—before Rashi or his contemporaries—among such important fabulists as Marie de France, Petrus Alfonsi, and Odo of Cheriton. We should not discount the possibility that Hai

Gaon and Rashi indeed received their tales from an earlier tradition and changed the details, as was the custom of storytellers past and present. Still, it can be assumed that they preferred to preserve the ancient version as it was, in realistic detail—had they such a version in hand—in order to imbue their commentary with more authenticity, as their aim was, after all, not to tell fables but to explicate ancient texts. The variants in the general folklore of the day and the precise details of the contemporary reality of the storytellers are sufficiently compelling evidence of the claim that neither Rashi nor Hai Gaon had an ancient tradition from the rabbinic period of the fox fables of R. Meir. Instead, they adapted contemporary folklore to the talmudic passage. If this was their modus operandi in telling fables, it may be that they did the same with the legend of "the weasel and the well" and other narrative texts.[20]

We can find more medieval examples of the narrative development of rabbinic utterances in the tales inspired by the following words: "Our Rabbis said: Even those things which you may regard as completely superfluous to the creation of the world, such as fleas, gnats, and flies, even they too are included in the creation of the world, and the Holy one, blessed be He, carries out His purpose through everything, even through a snake, a scorpion, a gnat, or a frog (*Genesis Rabbah* 10, 7). In other versions, the list of such "unnecessary" things includes madness and the insane. Medieval storytellers join three tales about, respectively, insanity, the spider, and the wasp, to illustrate the saying, namely that none of God's creation lacks purpose. They use scriptural motifs, such as David's pretense of insanity to save his life among the Philistines. They also borrow motifs from international folklore: David has fled from Saul and hides in a cave, where a spider weaves its web across the opening. His pursuers, seeing the web, assume the cave is empty, and pass it by. Abner the giant is about to crush David with his knee, after catching him trying to sneak into Saul's camp by night. A wasp stings Abner, causing him to lift his leg, thus saving David. There is no shortage of such tales of giants imprisoning the hero, the youngest son, who escapes with the aid of friendly creatures.

Here we see how tales were culled from various sources and welded together into one narrative text to illustrate a saying from the rabbinic period. A precise reading of the rabbinic utterance, and its comparison to the narrative use made of it in the Middle Ages, shows a significant reversal of roles of the two texts. In the rabbinic period, the utterance was designed as an expression of a specifically theological understanding—Divine justice is always served, even when the purpose of phenomena is beyond men's understanding. The medieval tale is almost entirely devoid of theodicean import, and is told primarily as a collection of animal tales (the spider and the wasp), whose orientation is definitively narrative-recreational.[21]

Just as noteworthy, there is a similar literary phenomenon beginning with an allusion found in rabbinic aggadah. This is not an issue of an enigmatic utterance requiring elucidation, rather a motif or name, with no need of explanation. The mention of some incidental element takes an unexpected twist and evolves into a narrative plot. Two examples will suffice: the first concerns a sage known as "Samuel's father." Out of this appellation (notwithstanding the wide currency of such nomenclature in the rabbinic period) grew a medieval legend which took different forms. Briefly, Samuel's father set out on a business trip to a distant land. There a woman (a witch, apparently), set her sights on sleeping with him, for she had foreseen that that night he would sire a son "unrivalled in wisdom." By means of a miraculous shortening of the journey, he went home to his wife and returned to the distant land all in one night. To avert suspicion of infidelity, for the wife conceived that night, when her husband was known to be out of town, he adopted the name "Samuel's father."

Another widespread narrative tradition in the Middle Ages concerned the birth of Rabbi: At the time, the Roman empire had forbidden the Jews to circumcise their sons. Rabbi's mother was commanded to bring the child before the regime to prove compliance with the ban. The mother of Antoninus, a member of the aristocracy, consented to exchange babies for the day. This narrative tradition clearly grew in the wake of the famous story cycle of Antoninus and Rabbi, of great fascination among the Jewish community even in the Middle Ages. The closeness between the Roman emperor and the Jewish patriarch precipitated a tale utilizing common medieval motifs: the substitution of one child for another, of a different social class, and the mysterious linking of infants from birth, that determines their destiny.[22]

These last examples strongly suggest that rabbinic aggadah was not only a rich source for the retelling of folk traditions, it also inspired the creation of new Jewish cultural traditions in the Middle Ages. Though rooted in rabbinic allusion, these traditions grew out of the folkloric motifs and traditions of the medieval cultures. Rabbinic aggadah was not accorded the same reverence as the biblical tale. It also encompassed a more diverse and contemporary range of themes, themes of practical and vital interest to people in the Middle Ages. It should be remembered that in this time frame, the Talmud and the literature associated with it came to embody the "Torah" of the Jewish people. The concept of "Torah study" meant talmudic scholarship. As the Talmud was the primary subject of inquiry and exploration, it is no wonder that the tales interspersed among its halachic deliberations would return to engage the society, albeit on another level. And indeed, the perpetual, total involvement of Torah scholars with the Talmud caused a social and class rift. On the other side were those strata of the people who could not wholly devote themselves to Torah study as vocation. The objective, *inter alia,* of rabbinic aggadah told in folk traditions—in the diverse forms described in this section—is to somewhat bridge the gap between the class of academy denizens and the rest of the people. It was as if they were saying, we also take part in the Talmud, a different but no less important part. Thus, rabbinic aggadah, as told in folk traditions, also had a significant equalizing function in medieval Jewish society.

Despite the scattering of Jewish communities in the Middle Ages throughout the lands of Islam and Christianity, and among many diverse local cultures, and notwithstanding the differences of custom, language, and community structure in the different lands of dispersion, Jews had a sense of collective belonging to one people. This sense was based on numerous factors, such as national origin and a shared legacy. Common identity in any culture, however, is also based on folk traditions, which belong to the totality of attributes of a given social unit. Most of the narrative traditions of medieval Jewry were not shared by all the communities, as they took shape in the lands of the dispersion and so were unique to each community and its sphere of cultural influence. The folk traditions originating in rabbinic literature constitute nearly the last cultural resource to be shared by all communities. Therefore the wide dissemination of rabbinic aggadah in the Middle Ages should be seen as one means by which broad strata of the people identified with the notion of "a Jewish people" in its general and more basic meaning.

[C] Tales from International Folklore

One of the more salient basic characteristics of folktales is their ability to pass from one society to another and adapt to the absorbing culture. This phenomenon is more pronounced in medieval Jewish culture than among other peoples. The fundamental circumstance of the Jewish people during this period was its dispersal across vast cultural expanses and the ambivalent position of its members as both natives and outsiders. Such was the Jewish condition throughout Christendom as well as the lands of Islam, and in all the local variations of these two great cultures of the Middle Ages. This situation influenced all walks of life, particularly within the sphere of folk culture. Daily contacts with the foreign culture took place primarily at the lower and middle social levels: between merchants on long journeys, among ship-board travelers at the mercy of the weather, hawkers in the market place, and women washing clothes at the local water source. There were contacts at the elite level as well: religious polemics between Christian scholars and rabbis and Christian exegetes who turned to Jewish luminaries for their "reading" of difficult passages. Still, such "opportunities" at the elite cultural level were extremely rare, of defined orientation, and generally fraught with theological tensions that effectively barred any significant transmission of narrative traditions from culture to culture.[23]

During this period, perhaps for the first time in the history of Jewish culture, a large number of narrative compositions were translated into Hebrew from Italian, Arabic, Spanish, and perhaps from other languages as well. *Kalila we-Dimnah*, the fifth book of the great Indian collection of animal tales, *Panchatantra*, was translated from Persian or Arabic into Hebrew as early as the tenth century. *The Tales of Sendebar*, a collection of tales on the theme of female fidelity and deceit, was also translated into Hebrew, and can be found in numerous manuscripts beginning from the twelfth century. Likewise for *The Romance of Alexander the Great*, one of the most widely disseminated works at the end of the ancient period and in the Middle Ages; the collection of animal fables, *Iggeret Ba'alei Hayyim*, the romances of King Arthur and the knights of the round table, and the adventures of Sir Amadis de Gaula. Furthermore, works of Arabian folklore—tales from *The Arabian Nights* and the *Romance of 'Antar*—were transcribed in Arabic and in Hebrew characters, as evidenced by documents that survived in the Cairo Genizah. To these should be added the important translations of various European works—knightly romances in particular—into Yiddish at the end of the Middle Ages. These translations gave their readers a taste of the foreign cultures' literature of adventure, romance, and fantasy. It can be surmised that these narrative works were read aloud before various audiences (as was also done in the European and Muslim cultures), as few written copies were available and as the audiences (of women and children) were not educated to literacy. Thus, many tales were lifted out of their original contexts within the compositions and transferred to oral traditions as independent tales. This was another vehicle by which foreign tales penetrated into Jewish culture.[24]

In the realm of folk narrative, there is usually no way of positively identifying the "source," as opposed to a "copy," where a given tale is found to be widespread in international folklore. The question of the "source," which so enthralled scholars of generations past, is no longer important. Despite the natural or nationalistic curiosity from which it stems, this is a question for which a reliable answer is nearly impossible. The result simply does not warrant the prodigious effort required to solve such a puzzle. The futility of any such quest for "the source" of some narrative tradition is made all the more obvious by its discovery—for then the incessant debate resumes over its inevitable resemblance to some earlier Jewish tale, from which the freshly unearthed "source" itself may or may not have sprung. How the narrative tradition was absorbed by our culture is of far more importance, as are the structural, ideological, and functional differences between the versions of the tale created with their passage from one culture to the next. A prime example of this debate, and of a foreign tradition's process of penetration into Judaism, is the tale of R. Joshua ben Levi and Elijah the Prophet. It first appears in the Jewish sources in R. Nissim of Kairouan's *An Elegant Composition Concerning Relief after Adversity*, in the first half of the eleventh century. The earliest scholars of Jewish studies (*Wissenschaft des Judenthums*) at once discerned this tale's similarity to one well-known in the Koran concerning Moses and the miraculous servant of Allah

(Surah 18, 66–80). In this tale, the hero (R. Joshua ben Levi in the Jewish versions, Moses in the Koran and the later Muslim sources) asks to accompany a wondrous figure (Elijah the Prophet in *An Elegant Composition*; the servant of Allah, according to interpreters of the Koran, is el-Khadr ["the green"] prophet, also identified with Elijah). The miraculous one stipulates that his escort neither question the meaning of his actions nor probe them too closely. After a series of odd behaviors, the hero can no longer contain himself and asks the miraculous one the meaning of this actions. He is answered, after which they part company.

Aside from the substitution of R. Joshua ben Levi for Moses, and the minor difference in the actions taken by the miraculous figures, the tales in the Koran and in *An Elegant Composition* are astonishingly alike. Some scholars have suggested the talmudic tale of Ashmedai and Benaiah, son of Jehoiada, (*Gittin* 68b) as a possible source for the Koranic tale. Ashmedai performs unusual acts in Benaiah's company as they journey to Solomon's palace. Ultimately, the demon reveals their meaning to his puzzled escort. But the great similarity between the Koranic version and that in *An Elegant Composition*, and the centrality of the Koranic text in the culture amid which R. Nissim lived, leave almost no room for doubt as to the "source." Still, it is clear that R. Nissim—or another Jewish storyteller—did not read the tale in the Koran and then translate it into Judeo-Arabic (the language in which *An Elegant Composition* is written). R. Nissim declares in the introduction to his book that he has gathered *Jewish stories*; it is thus clear that he was already familiar with the tale as a Jewish tradition. A process of transferral on the folk level apparently took place here: a Jew heard the Koranic tale from a neighbor, at a place of entertainment, at the marketplace, a desert caravan, or perhaps during a religious debate. He identified Jewish foundations within it: Moses, Elijah the Prophet, the principles of reward and punishment, and God's justice revealed to skeptics (compare, for example, with Job), and so deemed it suitable for telling among his own community. It underwent two not particularly significant changes in the course of passage: Moses occupies such a central and venerable a position in Jewish culture, that it would not do to say that he learns of the ways of God from another. He is replaced here by R. Joshua ben Levi, who appears in the rabbinic literature as one involved in such acts (he accompanies Elijah, the Angel of Death, performs various machinations and asks perplexing questions). In the Koranic tale, the miraculous one kills the young child of honest, righteous parents. In the Jewish story, Elijah kills the cow of a poor man who had graciously hosted them. Instead of boring a hole in a ship belonging to poor people as in the Koran, Elijah in the Jewish version wishes all the wealthy, who had refused to host him, to be "heads," while wishing the hospitable poor only one head between them (because, with one leader, they would prevail).

It may be that such acts as killing a child and sinking a ship seemed too cruel to the Jewish storytellers, so they replaced them, but the changes can be otherwise explained. The tale in the Koranic versions emphasizes the theological nature of the acts: the child's parents, deeply pious believers, would be apostatized by their son should he mature, for he would become a heretic. In contrast, the alternative episode in the Jewish tale, which tells of the killing of the poor (but hospitable) man's cow, deals with *class distinctions*—the ethical distinction between rich and poor: it is the needy who must rely upon and aid each other, while the wealthy are covetous and haughty. Instead of boring a hole in the ship, as in the Koranic tale, the Jewish version recounts that "... and they went on all day long until that night, when they entered a synagogue and found there seats of gold and silver, each person sitting in his own seat. The people asked, 'Who will show honor to these poor men tonight?' to which one of them replied, 'These men, their food is but bread and salt,' and so they paid no attention to the two wayfarers" (*An Elegant Composition*, Brinner's translation, p. 14). In contrast, the poor hosts made Elijah and R. Joshua ben Levi welcome in their home and gladly shared all that they had. In other words, the Koranic version emphasizes the theme of adherence to Islam as the center of an Arab's life—and, indeed, this subject engaged Islamic leaders in the period of the Koran's composition. The Jewish storytellers of the tenth and eleventh centuries, were, however, interested in stressing social aspects: the class gap, community leadership (many heads or one leader), and mutual assistance among members of the community. Despite these important differences, the central theodicean principle upon which the tale is based (divine justice is realized despite mortals' failure to apprehend it), exists in both the Muslim and Jewish versions.[25]

Another example of the absorption of a tale into the Jewish tradition, connected with a central theological principle of Islam, is the tale of Elijah the Prophet and the ox buyer. A wealthy man on his way to purchase oxen encounters Elijah and refuses to say, "God-willing" even after Elijah cautions him to do so. The money is twice stolen from him. Only on his third venture, after uttering those words, does he find the missing money, buy fine oxen, and then sell them to the king at a great profit. This tale is germane to a fundamental Islamic principle: "Do not say of anything: 'I will do it tomorrow,' without adding: 'If God wills'" (Surah 18:23), which of course became one of the foundations of Muslim life from Islam's inception. The theological principle, and the subsequent Islamic custom, assuredly sparked many stories on the theme. Some were exemplary, intended to consolidate and disseminate the custom among the faithful, and some were of a less obligatory nature. Such a tale survived in tenth-century Arabic sources:

> Abu Yalek set out one day from Medinah to purchase a mule. His friend met him and asked: Where are you going? He answered: I am going to market to

buy a mule. His friend said to him: It is appropriate for you to say: *insh'allah* ["God-willing"]. Abu Yalek replied: There is no need to say *insh'allah* now. The money is in the pocket, and the mule is at the market. But along the way, the money disappeared. He sadly retraced his footsteps, and his friend, who met him again, asked him: What have you done? And he replied: My money was stolen—*insh'allah*. (Yassif, *Ben Sira*, p. 167)

This humorous version of the tale well reflects the Muslim religious elite's demand of adherence to the custom of uttering "*insh'allah*" at the appropriate place and under appropriate circumstances. In a society wherein the custom was so widespread, there were undoubtedly those, of the simpler folk, who used it to provoke laughter, if not scorn. Anecdotes such as these were apparently meant to limit, guide, and caution against irreverent, profane use of God's name.

The Jewish version of the tale has a different literary construction and another function. It is built as an exemplary tale—not as an anecdote about the village fool. The plot of the Hebrew version is based on the construction that balances sin against its punishment, and good deed against its reward. The protagonist ignores and violates the societal norm, and is punished forthwith. This is the epitome of the literary construction of the religious exemplum that seeks to establish or propose a new behavioral norm and inculcate society with it. And indeed: the practice of saying "God-willing" before every action does not appear at all in the ancient Jewish sources. There is no doubt that Jews living amid Muslim society and witnessing their neighbors using the expression "*insh'allah*" every now and then, saw this practice as a suitable means of expressing God-fearingness, and the acceptance of absolute, routine dependence upon the will of God. The inculcation of a new behavioral norm into society was generally accomplished through preaching and education, behavioral imitation, and the dissemination of exemplary tales that threatened anyone who did not conduct themselves accordingly while promising great rewards to those who upheld the norm. Now the reason for the differences between the Arab and Jewish versions is clear to us: in Muslim society, wherein the custom was already extremely widespread in the ninth and tenth centuries, the tale comes to review and limit its use, so as not to detract from other sacred principles of the faith; in Jewish society, wherein the custom was not yet entrenched, the tale was propounded in order to encourage its adoption. In any case, two forms of the tale, the humorous and the exemplary, were widespread from the Middle Ages onwards in the traditions of different cultures, and they served similar functions.[26]

One unusual tale in *An Elegant Composition*, and one particularly given to controversy, is the famous story entitled "The Shining Robe" (Brinner's translation, pp. 48–52). Two sages are confronted with an angel holding a shining robe, which is missing a collar. It becomes clear to them that the robe belongs to one Joseph the gardener from Ashkelon. When they tell him of the robe intended for him, Joseph and his wife decide to complete the garment by selling the wife into servitude and donating the money to charity. They did so, and the woman remained chaste, despite all the temptations and suffering that were her lot during the time of her service. She was finally released, and the couple received word from heaven that the robe was now complete. This tale contains a number of elements alien to the Jewish value system: the giving of all a man's property to charity, which is forbidden by halacha; the selling of a women into servitude and her repurchase; material clothing for souls in the world to come. Opposite these foreign elements stand a number of consummately Jewish effects, such as the names of the protagonists, the two sages at the Temple on the Day of Atonement, and the centrality of charity in religious life. The merging of these with elements foreign to Jews caused scholars to ponder the question of this tale's "source" as well. One found the following tale in the Muslim traditions of the ninth century:

> Said the messenger of God . . . in my dream people appeared before me, dressed in robes, some of which reached the chest and some until [a point] just below it. Umar ibn al-Khattab also appeared to me, wearing a robe that trailed along [the ground]. They asked him: And how did you solve [the dream], messenger of God? He replied: Piety.

It is reasonable to assume that itinerant Muslim preachers of the same period, who would rouse the masses with their sermons in the mosques and city squares, made the most of this tale. This version portrays Umar ibn al-Khattab as first and foremost before Allah, and thus serves as a polemic in the political controversies of early Islam. When the tale passed into Jewish society—and it can be assumed that Jews occasionally heard Muslim preachers in the city thoroughfares—it was employed to underscore values of interest to Jewish society. But this tale emphasizes values contradictory to the Jewish system: It was inconceivable that a Jewish man might sell his wife as a maidservant—and later take her back. This tale is thus representative of a group of tales absorbed from foreign cultures, tales whose very foundations run counter to Jewish mores. These tales exhibit a perpetual tension between alien and Jewish elements. Joseph the gardener's concern for the poor contrasts sharply with his disregard for the privations of home and hearth; the spirituality of the Temple on the Day of Atonement is incongruous with the almost garish corporeality of a world to come wherein worthy souls wear silken robes. This internal tension between contradictory elements is evidence of the complex process of the tales' absorption by Jewish society.[27]

Let us model the existence of a similar type of narrative tension with two more tales. The longest and most complex story in the twelfth–thirteenth century cluster of tales copied in the Oxford-Bodleian manuscript (Or. 135) concerns R. Yohanan and the scorpion. As he lay dying, R. Yohanan's father instructed him to buy the first item offered to him at the marketplace. R. Yohanan is offered a goblet at an exorbitant price, and after considerable inner struggle, buys it. Within he finds a small scorpion. The creature devours prodigious quantities of food, in fact eating R. Yohanan's family out of house and home, and so rapidly grows to monstrous proportions. When at last they have nothing left to sell, the scorpion grants them their wish: it teaches R. Yohanan the language of animals, and makes the wife enormously wealthy. In the second part of the tale, a raven drops a strand of hair that glitters like gold at the foot of the king, who until this point has refused to take a wife. He orders a search for the woman to whom it belongs, and it is R. Yohanan who must accomplish this task. On the way, he aids a dog, a raven, and a fish, and eventually reaches a town whose queen is the source of the mysterious strand of hair. She will accompany R. Yohanan and wed the king on condition that he fulfill three tasks. He accomplishes the feats with the aid of the animals he helped earlier. Upon his return, accompanied by the queen, he discovers that his wife has died and his property has been stolen. The king is then killed in a war before he can marry the queen. She converts to Judaism and marries R. Yohanan.[28]

The basic pattern of the tale's plot is the blending of the tale type of the unpromising hero's marriage and rise to greatness with the motif of tasks he accomplishes with the aid of grateful animals (a blending of tale types AT 531 and AT 554). Researchers of this fairy tale pointed to the origin of these types in the eastern cultures and mythologies of India and Persia. In particular, the totemic elements of closeness to animals, aid to them, and their resulting gratitude to their saviours were emphasized. This assistance is especially manifested by their familiarizing the protagonists with the mysteries of nature: they bring him to the bottom of the sea, to paradise or hell, deep into the center of the earth, and so on. Such mythological-pagan motifs, which may have been the legacy of Jewish culture in its very early stages, were completely foreign to it by the Middle Ages. Therefore, for such a tale to be absorbed by medieval Jewish culture, the pagan and mythological elements must either vanish or Jewish elements must be introduced as a counterweight. Instances of the latter display structural and thematic tension between the foreign and Jewish elements. Indeed, such is the case regarding the tale under discussion.

It begins with the father's dying instructions to his son. As we shall see below, this was a preferred means of Judaizing foreign tale types, facilitating their absorption into Jewish tradition. The scorpion, who tells R. Yohanan and his wife the story of his life, is the offspring of Adam, the biblical first man, who cohabited with all the beasts and creatures of the field before the creation of his mate. The scorpion "become[s] ever smaller over the course of a thousand years, until the end of the millennium, and after the millennium I grow for another thousand years, and I was not there at all on the day that thou [ate] of [that from which] thou shalt surely die" (*The Exempla of Rabbis*, Gaster edition, p. 199). The storyteller avails himself of two episodes from earlier rabbinic aggadah: the first human, coupling with the animals, and the myth of the Phoenix, who would not be tempted by Eve, did not eat the fruit of the Tree of Knowledge, and therefore merited immortality. Thus the storyteller turns the gift-bestowing creature (the scorpion) into a prime Jewish protagonist. Additionally, by making certain to always call the hero "Rabbi" components of the familiar Jewish world are meshed with narrative elements inherently alien to Judaism. The forest to which R. Yohanan journeys in search of the golden strand of hair is no ordinary forest, but *ya'ar devei ilaii* (a forest mentioned in the Talmud and known for being full of beasts) (*The Exempla*, p. 201). And each of the creatures therein phrases his arguments in this style:

> And the dog would cry and groan and say: Master of the universe! You made me a huge and strange dog, therefore I could not eat enough to satisfy myself, for the scrap will not satisfy the lion . . . and you are compassionate and gracious over all your deeds . . . R. Yohanan replied and said to him: the Holy One, blessed be He, did not create you to die of hunger because his mercy extends over all his deeds. (*The Exempla*, p. 209)

In this manner, the same episode is reiterated for each of the animals appearing in the tale. The odd blending of a mythological creature (the giant dog) who speaks in rabbinical proverbs and phrases from the prayer book, reflects the aforementioned tension between foreign elements and the Jewish world. It was no mean feat for the storytellers to present as a Jewish story a tale infused by so many foreign mythological elements. Hence they strive to achieve a balance by extensive use of rabbinic aggadah, consummately Jewish adages, traditional idioms, and Jewish titles and customs. This practice was by no means limited to a single author; rather it spread and developed over generations of storytellers (the version of the tale found in the sixteenth-century Yiddish *Mayse-Bukh* corroborates such evolution). In any case, this important tale's structure and style reflect the tension between these polarized elements, which seeped in over the course of time.

A second example of a polarized formation of a tale absorbed by the Jewish tradition from international folklore is the legend of Joshua bin Nun. While the tale is extant only in a seventeenth-century source, it is clear from evidence found within the story itself that it originated much earlier. The tale, according to this version, was intended to explain the origin of Joshua bin Nun's name (meaning, "Son of the Fish"), or the other name by which he was known— "Chief of the Decapitators." Joshua's father was a great zaddik ("righteous man") who had no sons. He prayed for one, yet when his wife conceived, he was not overjoyed. He explained that he had seen in a vision that his son would one day kill him. Fearing the harsh prophesy, the mother lay the newborn child in a basket and set it adrift on the Nile. When he matured, and in his wanderings reached the city of his birth, the king appointed him chief executioner. His father, captured by the regime, was put to death by his son and, as was the regime's custom, the condemned man's wife and property were given to him. As he approached her bed, it filled with milk. His mother at once divined that this was her son, and told him the story of his birth. He repented and lived thereafter as a wholly righteous man.

Scholars discerned that the tale was a mixture of the Oedipus myth, still very popular in the Middle Ages, and the legend of Pope Gregory, one of the most widespread and important folk traditions of Christian Europe. The mythological and pagan elements of these two tales carried over into the tale of Joshua bin Nun: the hero's fate is foreordained; the mature son kills his father to reign in his stead; the protagonist's bedding of his mother. Yet alongside these, Jewish elements are conspicuous: the birth of a son after protracted barrenness; the mother pushing her baby downstream in a pitch-coated basket; and, especially, the mitigation of the final episode: Joshua does not in fact have sexual intercourse with his mother, as did Oedipus and Gregory. The act is forestalled by the use of a particularly impressive narrative motif: the bed upon which mother and son lie fills with mother's milk. The prohibition against intimacy between son and mother in the Torah is linked metaphorically to another ban—that on cooking a kid in its mother's milk. Indeed, the image of Joshua immersed in his mother's milk is an overt symbolic expression of sexual relations between mother and child, one that the mother interprets correctly, and thereby saves them both from committing the heinous sin. The identification of mythological-pagan symbols in the tale, alongside those loaded with Jewish significance, exposes the sharp tension between them. The tension between such disparate elements gives rise to the discomfort attendant on hearing (or reading) the tale in Jewish society. And perhaps this is also the reason that only one medieval version of the tale survived, one that was retold in numerous versions later on in the Hassidic narrative traditions.[29]

Against the background of all the tales discussed thus far stands the question of method in Judaizing foreign tales. Can we identify the special means employed by the storytellers in their desire to tell tales from the outside to a Jewish audience? Scholarship has dealt with this question, and it seems there are grounds for comparing the Judaizing methods in the Middle Ages with those used in later periods. For the purposes of this discussion, we will divide the means of Judaization of international narrative types in the Middle Ages into three levels, in ascending order of importance: the rhetorical-technical level, the structural level, and the functional-societal level. Until now, scholars have focused primarily on the Judaizing methods of the first level: Jewish storytellers make changes mostly to the beginnings and endings of the tales;

they open and close with a biblical verse, link the introduction to famous events or figures from Jewish history—the biblical period, King Solomon, or Elijah the Prophet, to name a few. In the tale of R. Yohanan and the scorpion, we saw diverse methods of Judaization, all belonging to the rhetorical-technical level: the storyteller turns the protagonist into a rabbi and peppers the tale with biblical verses, Jewish proverbs, rabbinic sayings, and liturgical phrases. On this level, the changes do not occur in the pattern or significance of the tale, but in the blending of rhetorical patterns (verses, proverbs, common expressions) and realistic details drawn from Jewish culture. The audience identifies these tales with its own cultural system. Thus, by means of strictly superficial modifications, the foreign tale succeeds in fundamentally blending into Jewish culture's stock of narrative traditions.[30]

Sometimes Judaization at this level is likely to be more complex. The Jewish versions of the tale of Crescentia—"the slandered and banished wife" (AT 712), bear a very similar pattern to the eastern branch of this tale type, widespread in both the east (India, the lands of Islam), and in Europe: A beautiful woman's husband travels far away to trade, and leaves her in his brother's care. The brother tries to seduce her. When she rejects him, he accuses her falsely and she is sentenced to execution by stoning, the prescribed penalty for an adulteress. A Jew rescues her, and takes her in as a governess for his son. But the older brother (or his servant) tries to rape her, in the process killing the younger son, who happens to be nearby. Banished from the home of her benefactor, she boards a ship where, again on account of her allure for the sailors, she is abandoned on a desert island. There she becomes a marvelous healer, and all those who had harmed her in the past, and who were consequently punished with leprosy, congregate around her, including her leprous brother-in-law, accompanied by her husband. They must confess their sins to be cured; the truth comes out, and her husband takes her back. In the European versions, the plot of the tale is strikingly different, but more germane to this discussion are the touches added by storytellers. These stand out when the Jewish versions are compared to the eastern ones, which are identical as regards plot construction. The brother who accuses his sister-in-law of adultery brings her before the Sanhedrin, the man who saves her from stoning brings his son to Jerusalem to study Torah, and employs her as governess to his son. At the tale's conclusion, rabbinic sayings are quoted together with a biblical verse:

> And come and see how great is the punishment for slander and false testimony and defamation, the end of one [who does these things] is to be afflicted with leprosy. And all who fear the Almighty should guard their tongue against evil speech. As it is said: He who guards his mouth and his tongue keeps his soul from troubles (Prov. 21:23). (*The Exempla of the Rabbis*, Gaster edition, p. 197)

These means are part of the same constellation of rhetorical-technical methods enumerated above. In addition to them, this tale showcases another, purely rhetorical, device—the woman's speeches. She delivers ethical orations, in the Jewish spirit, to her wicked brother-in-law, the mariners, and all the sinners who come to her for healing. Such a rhetorical device, which generally weighs down the plot's narrative continuity, was apparently taken up by storytellers who saw themselves as moralists, or as leaders and teachers of the community. Instead of preaching directly, they spoke through the protagonists of the tale, in homilies fashioned to fit the narrative logic. In other words, this means had a twofold purpose, and was accordingly more complex: it was intended to turn an international tradition into a Jewish tale, and simultaneously to press the tale into didactic service.[31]

Another technique wielded by the storytellers on the rhetorical level is the merging of stylistic patterns borrowed from known folktales, and identified with them, with international story traditions. Thus, when a stylistic formulation of a Jewish legend is so well-known and ingrained in society's cultural consciousness, it is borrowed to shape a foreign legend, which new legend will then be received as a part of the Jewish folk traditions. I will offer one lucid example of this phenomenon: the tale of the fox's heart in *The Alphabet of Ben Sira*. The Leviathan, who has heard of the fox's wisdom and cunning, schemes to eat its heart so as to acquire these traits for himself. He sends the fishes to the fox; they tell him they want to make him their king. After luring him in, they tell him the truth. He claims he has left his heart on dry land, and that they must return him there so that he can fetch it. They do so—and the fox escapes. It has already been proven that this tale is based on the tale of the monkey and the crocodile from the Indian *Kalila we-Dimnah*, translated into Persian and Arabic as early as the seventh or eight century. The changes to the Jewish version (substituting the fox for the monkey, the fishes for the crocodile, and the Leviathan for the crocodile's wife), were not enough to turn it into a Jewish tale. But the stylistic formulation of the tale shows the technique of Judaization taken up here by the storyteller:

> And they saw a fox standing there at the water's edge. They all congregated
> at the water's edge, and rejoiced and danced before him. The fox said to
> them: Happy is he who eats his fill of your flesh . . . but if you truly want to
> make me king, I will reign over you from here. They said to him: You of
> whom it is said that you are the most clever of animals. You are nothing but
> a fool. For well you know that humans make traps and nets to hunt us at sea.
> And if we should come onto the land, how much more so? (Yassif, *Ben Sira*,
> p. 251)

The storyteller took the construction of *Kalila we-Dimnah*'s tale of the monkey and the crocodile, and reformulated it along the lines of Rabbi Akiva's mashal of the fox and the fishes in the famous homily in the Babylonian Talmud (*Berakhot*, 60b). Since this rhetorical pattern became an inalienable property of the Jewish traditions (it appears in the most famous story on martyrdom—the death of R. Akiva), such a formulation of the new tale serves as an excellent means to the tale's absorption.[32]

The second level is structural. Here I include all the modifications made by storytellers to the construction of the plot—as a Judaizing device. In Vatican manuscript 285, from the fourteenth century, we find the first known version of the tale of "The Widow and the Pitchers of Honey." The tale appears later in the cycle of tales, *Meshalim shel Shlomo ha-Melekh* (Parables of King Solomon) (fifteenth–sixteenth centuries C.E.), and from there it was copied into other widely circulated story groupings, and is found in abundance in the oral Jewish traditions. The tale seems to have originated in the Arabic cultural expanse, as evidenced by the great collection of tales, *The Arabian Nights*. This is the tale of a rich merchant, Ali Hodja, forced to flee his home. He hid his money in urns, filled them with honey, and left them in the care of a trusted guardian. When he returned years later, he found the urns filled with honey, the money gone. The wise judge to whom he appealed broke the urns of honey and found a few gold coins still stuck to the bottom, proving the merchant's claim.

According to the Jewish traditions, the tale takes place in the days of King Saul. A righteous man, who has no sons, prays for the birth of sons learned in Torah. Later he asks for the wherewithal to support them. Elijah the Prophet appears to show him a hidden treasure. When the righteous man dies, the head of the community attempts to seduce his widow. She hides her wealth in a hundred urns, fills them with honey, and leaves them in the care of her husband's friend. When she returns three years later, she finds the urns contain only honey. She appeals to King Saul, but he rejects her claim for lack of proof. Little David, playing with the other children outside, asks permission to rule in this case. He uses the same trick as the wise judge in the Arab story, and the tale concludes:

> At that moment King Saul rose from his throne . . . and placed the crown on David's head, and said: This one is fit to be king over Israel. (Vatican manuscript, pp. 82a–84a)

Rhetorical-technical modifications (period of Saul and David), are in evidence here, too. But the most important change is that made to the structure of the plot: the storyteller prefaces the main story with a new episode concerning the righteous's sterility, poverty, and prayer to God, the son learned in Torah who was then born, and Elijah's appearance. There can be no explanation for this addition other than that the storyteller viewed it as a consummate Judaizing technique: the tale of the widow can, after all, stand alone as an independent tale requiring no exposition. And indeed, many other Jewish traditions open with this motif of childlessness and prayer for a son—beginning with the stories of the patriarchs in the book of Genesis, Samson in the book of Judges, Hannah in the book of Samuel, and many tales in rabbinic aggadah. Barrenness, prayer for a worthy son, and for the wherewithal necessary, not for a life of permissiveness, but for the sake of Torah study (in later folk traditions)—all these are distinct Jewish mental patterns, that turn the tale into a Jewish tradition well before the figures of Saul and David come into play.[33]

We can spot a similar phenomenon in two very common tales connected to the figure of King Solomon. In the first, the king, in his wisdom, says that "One man among a thousand I have found; but a woman among all those I have not found" (Eccles. 7:28). When the Sanhedrin find this curious, Solomon conducts a kind of experiment. He asks that the most true-hearted husband and wife in his kingdom be found, then commands that the husband be brought to him. Solomon offers him the princess' hand in marriage, on condition that he first kill his wife. The husband, despite his assurance to the king, finds he cannot go through with the murder out of love for his wife and compassion for his children. When the king proposes to the wife that she kill her husband and then marry him, she does not even hesitate. This tale too, in its essential lines, is known in the international folk narrative from ancient Indian narrative, and from medieval European narrative. We have three basic versions of the tale: *An Elegant Composition* (eleventh century C.E.), Joseph ibn Zabara's *Sefer ha-Sha'shu'im* (twelfth century C.E.), and *Parables of Solomon* (fifteenth–sixteenth century C.E.). The main difference between the international traditions and the Jewish versions is in the opening episode. Here, instead of a love story between partners who pledge to remain true even after death, the Jewish traditions present the figure of the Jewish feudal king (Solomon). Sitting upon his throne, surrounded by the elders and judges of the people, in his divine wisdom he makes an unreasonable claim—as expressed in the biblical verse. This episode, which combines a biblical verse, the image of Solomon's reign, and the atmosphere of deliberations over the commentary to a biblical verse, is the product of carefully calculated structural modification to the international tradition in order to adapt it to Jewish culture.[34]

A third example of the structural level of modifications also features the figure of Solomon. Before the start of the Sabbath, three merchants cache their money. The Sabbath over, they go to retrieve it, only to discover it missing. There is no question but that one of the three is the thief. They come before Solomon's court. The king postpones his decision in their case, asking them, in the meanwhile, to assist him in considering another case before the throne. It concerns a young man and a maiden who had, some years earlier, promised to marry each other when the time came. Further, they swore that if they should not wed, neither would marry another until they first shared a bed. After a separation measured in years, she wished to marry another. Together with her fiancee, she went to ask the young man's permission to marry. He released her from her obligation. On their return, a highwayman overtakes them and wants to bed her, but when they tell him all that has happened, he not only releases them, he gives them back the money he had stolen. Solomon asks the merchants which of the three did the noblest thing: the husband-to-be, who consented to his wife returning to her first boyfriend; the boyfriend, who released her, although he could have claimed her; or the robber, who gave up his prey. The merchant who answered that the highwayman had acted the most nobly was the thief. The tale is particularly widespread in international folklore (AT 976–AT 976a), and even merited two marvelous literary reworkings in the Middle Ages—one in a story by Boccaccio and the other in Chaucer's narrative poetry. The medieval versions open with a woman's commitment to have sex with a man who desires her—on condition that he perform the impossible (produce a flowering garden in mid-winter, or duplicate the enormous cliffs along the shore elsewhere, and the like). When he fulfills the task with the aid of a great sorcerer, and after the woman tells her husband what has happened, the husband insists that she keep her promise. The man passes up his reward, and even the sorcerer who performed the task waives his promised fee. Here, too, the question is posed as to which action is the most generous.

Beyond the differences in practical details, in cultural atmosphere, and literary construction—which are self-explanatory—our interest here lies in the differences in the structure of the plot. There are mainly two: first, the opening episode, wherein Jewish merchants seek to hide their money before the onset of the Sabbath; Solomon holds court; and he uses a psychological technique to get to the truth (a method also taken up by the biblical Solomon in the famous "Solomon's Judgment" case). All these build a characteristic opening episode, turning the alien tale from the very start into a Jewish story—as in the preceding examples. In the course of the tale, important modifications serve a similar purpose: the foreign tale usually opens with a scene of passionate longing on the part of the hero for a married woman and she, in order to get rid of him, promises to yield if he performs an impossible task. The Jewish tale opens with "a boy and girl who promised each other." Such an opening scene, in which a man pursues a married woman, suits the European narrative of the Middle Ages (as in the sensual tales of Boccaccio and Chaucer), but it is difficult to imagine it in Jewish society. The opening episode of the internal tale (Solomon's riddle to the merchants) in Jewish terms, parallels that in another rather common Jewish folktale—the legend of "The weasel and the well," which we discussed above. There too, after the young man rescued the maiden from the well, they betrothed themselves to one another, and the betrayal of that promise is the conflict around which the plot develops. Thus the objective of such modifications to the body of the tale is to replace wholly the foreign element with norms of Jewish society, to implant an opening scene borrowed from familiar Jewish traditions, and thereby make it a part of Jewish folklore.[35]

The last example of the structural level leads us in turn to the third level of modifications in the process of Judaizing folktales in the Middle Ages, namely, the functional-social level. The tale known as Placidas (or Eustacius) in international folklore, is "The Man who Never Took an Oath" in the Jewish narrative. In international folklore, this tale merited comprehensive monographs. Numerous studies attempted to ascertain its historical credibility, its eastern origins in India and Persia, and the development of its versions in the Middle Ages and the modern period. The extensive studies enable us to now locate quite precisely the Jewish versions within the overall development of the international type. The first Jewish versions are found in the eighth–ninth-century *Midrash of the Ten Commandments*, which originated in the cultural expanse of Persia-Babylonia. Hence the Jewish versions' first link was to the eastern branch of the tale. Conversely, there is considerable structural similarity between the Jewish and Christian versions (the first written versions emerge from the first half of the eighth century). The main lines of the tale in its eastern versions are as follows: a king of one of the cities in the east attacks neighboring cities, and treats their inhabitants mercilessly. He does not respond to warnings, and when they raise an army and conquer his land, he flees with his wife and two sons. His wife is kidnapped by the captain of the ship; he and his sons are cast into the river. Fishermen rescue one son; farmers the other. The king wanders for ten years as a beggar, until the citizens of one of the big cities appoint him their king. His children, now grown, come to the city in search of work, and the owner of the ship anchored in the port brings the kidnapped wife. The family is reunited and resumes living the good life they had lost. The Jewish traditions of the Middle Ages tell the tale with significant differences: an aged father on his death bed enjoins his son never to swear to anything—even on a matter of truth. Swindlers, knowing of the father's command, claim that he owed them money before his death, and when the son refuses to swear otherwise before a court, they take his money. Ultimately, when he has nothing left to give the plaintiffs, he is imprisoned. His wife is snatched away by the owner of a ship, and after the protagonist's release from prison, he takes his sons and sets off wandering. The sons are swept away trying to cross the river, but saved by fishermen and shepherds, and the father becomes a shepherd in a distant Jewish community. On the verge of suicide, he has a vision of an angel who informs him that the time has come to reward him for obeying his father's dying command. The angel reveals the location of a treasure and guides him in the purchase of a plot of land. There he establishes a city on the shore, and his sons and wife return to him—as in the tale of the international type.

The structural changes made here to the tale, in addition to the self-explanatory rhetorical means, appear in two decisive places in the tale's plot: in the opening episode—the father on his death bed and the instruction to never swear to anything, and in the turning point of the plot, wherein the angel appears to the protagonist and compensates him for his suffering. The attached opening episode, in which the father expresses his dying wish, appeared in many folktales that circulated in Jewish culture. Several of the aforementioned tales open this way: a father instructs his son to cast bread upon the water; R. Yohanan is instructed to buy the first thing offered him at the marketplace; a son's father commands him not to leave the synagogue before the service's conclusion under any circumstances; a young man's teacher directs him to embrace his cousin and lie in bed beside her; a son's father instructs him to wait overnight before acting upon his anger, and so on. It should be noted that all of these paternal directives are enigmatic. The sons do not comprehend their intent, nor does the audience. In truth, it is the upholding of the father's injunction that gets the sons into trouble in the first place, and brings them to the brink of destruction—but ultimately raises them to greatness. If we compare the plot's construction in the eastern branch to the Jewish oicotype, we can discern that the eastern versions are tales of reward and punishment: the protagonist commits a sin of pride and cruelty, and the share of suffering and anguish he endures are on the order of punishment and atonement for his sins. In the Jewish versions, the suffering and anguish that are the lot of the protagonist are perversely the result of strict adherence to the father's will. In other words, no sin brings on the hero's misery, rather it is brought on by obedience to the precept of maintaining the legacy left by preceding generations. If this is the case, then this tale in its Jewish version, like all the tales mentioned that open with this episode, seek to say that patrimony—that is, the Jewish tradition—is bound up with numerous trials and tribulations. It leads to wandering, estrangement, and poverty, yet this is the sole avenue to the hero's rise to "kingship," namely, preservation of his social and historical identity.

The second change to the plot's construction leads in the same direction: in both the eastern and Christian branches of the tale type, the turning point is realistic: the hero is chosen king by the citizens, the protagonist is discovered by the emperor's emissaries and invited to once again lead the Roman army (in Christian versions). In the Jewish branch of the tale, the turning point is always supernatural: an angel or some other supernatural creature is sent to inform the protagonist of the imminent end to his suffering and onset of his redemption. Indeed, on the symbolic level, the subject is no less than true redemption. The great cultures of the Middle Ages, both Arabic and Christian, saw in the hero's altered fate a realistic process transpiring in the realm of historical forces. They believed in the power of their society to guide its own destiny: after all, they wielded the reins of government, military, and property, and so their struggles were social or national. The Jewish outlook in the Middle Ages was another story: Jewish society was not the master of its own destiny, and Heaven alone could stem the suffering that was the Jewish legacy.[36]

In sum, the narrating society's historical standing and perception of personal identity gave rise to the structural modifications to the international tale type. The changes were apparently the outgrowth of a narrative perception shaped by the historical and social consciousness characteristic of Jewish folk mentality in this period. This was that the weighty legacy of generations past was responsible for suffering in the diaspora, and that earthly forces could not provide the solution to their circumstances—relief was the sole prerogative of Providence. These modifications can illuminate a deep layer of the sensitivities and national consciousness of medieval Jewish society.

The last example in this chapter will relate specifically to a tale that does not differ from the non-Jewish versions, yet has an entirely different social and ideational function. I refer to the novella of Solomon and the Queen of Sheba—a tale common to several medieval cultures. Because of its wide dispersal and centrality in Muslim, Christian, and Ethiopian culture, the tale has been the subject of many studies illuminating it from various perspectives. It is useful here in locating Jewish versions within the international tradition. The most ancient texts of this legend survive in the Muslim traditions, from the Koran and later. In brief, they are as follows: Solomon sends a bird to order the mysterious queen to Jerusalem. Alarmed, she sets out at the head of a stately procession to Jerusalem. There, Solomon's advisors (or demons) caution him that the queen is, in fact, a demoness. He welcomes her while seated upon his throne above a glass floor, beneath which water streams past. The queen, who thinks he is sitting in a pool of water, lifts her skirts, and Solomon sees her hairy legs—that is, the legs of a demoness. He prepares a special ointment for her with which she removes the hair from her legs, after which the king sleeps with her. After he solves her riddles, she returns to her kingdom. The digest of the tale offered here is an abstract of the different versions in which the tale appears in many traditions in ancient Islamic literature. The reasons that this tale is of concern in Islam, Christianity, and Ethiopia have been well studied, and do not concern us. Let it suffice to say that scholars emphasized the demonic dimension appearing in the story: the connection between the human and demonic worlds, and the demons' acceptance of the former's authority. This tale also had a definite political dimension, in Ethiopian culture, for example. The son of Solomon and the Queen of Sheba was, according to Ethiopian tradition, Menelik I, the patriarch of the Ethiopian royal dynasty, which received its sovereign authority from the "historical" link to King Solomon.[37]

Of concern to us here is why medieval Jewish society resumed telling a tale that, as far as we know, was rejected by the sages themselves. It is no wonder that Jews in Baghdad, Basra, or Cairo, upon hearing their Arab neighbors telling of Solomon and the Queen of Sheba, connected them at once to these biblical figures, and viewed the tale as a part of their own culture. Nonetheless, the erotic-novelistic elements at the core of the tales hampered any such identification by Jewish society. In spite of this, the tale was well-absorbed into Jewish traditions. The first text proving the tale's absorption by Jewish culture is the seventh- or eighth-century work known as *Targum Sheni* ("Second Translation") of the Scroll of Esther. It is dedicated to describing the grandeur and wonder of King Ahasuerus' kingdom, which reminds the author of the splendor of King Solomon's kingdom—ten times greater. To illustrate this majesty, the tale of Solomon and the Queen of Sheba is told, in fragmented form. The second text, in order of appearance in Jewish literature, is the *Alphabet of Ben Sira*. Here King Nebuchadnezzar asks the child, Ben Sira, how he was able to so completely remove the hair from the rabbit he had sent him. Ben Sira claims to have learned it from Nebuchadnezzar's mother, the Queen of Sheba, who had obtained the secret of the ointment from King Solomon. Thus, the first two proofs of the tale's absorption into Jewish folk tradition are found in polemical contexts of national confrontation with other peoples: in *Targum Sheni*, with Ahasuerus; in the *Alphabet of Ben Sira*, with Nebuchadnezzar. The role of the tale in these contexts is to prove to readers and listeners that Solomon, symbol of the kingdom of Israel, had his way with the greatest queen of the east. Not only did he sleep with her, he first changed her identity, transforming her from a demoness to a cultured woman. Clearly, Jewish storytellers' interest in the tale was not merely to quench the natural thirst for this sort of erotic tale. More importantly, it satisfied the need for a sense of triumph. Solomon, who uncovers the nakedness, literally, of the queen of the desert (symbolizing his neighbors, the Arab nations) apparently answered a latent wish hidden deep in the hearts of medieval Jews.

We must not forget that the Jewish storytellers presented Nebuchadnezzar as the issue of Solomon and the Queen of Sheba. Nebuchadnezzar was infamous for razing Solomon's Temple. Different Jewish versions of the tale conclude with the verse from Isaiah 49:17, "thy destroyers and they that made thee waste go away from thee" (the Hebrew verb for "go away" also translates as "issue"). In other words, the sin of the builder of the Temple produced its destroyer. This international novella was thus given an important ideational element in its Jewish version: Beyond all the actions of the nations lies an internal dimension, that of Jewish guilt for their own fate. Had they not damaged the moral infrastructure of Judaism, history would have unfolded differently. Thus the Jewish storytellers, by modifying the plot, succeeded in employing an erotic novella from general folklore to serve Jewish society's ethical and ideational needs. This last example shows us that even without extensive structural modifications, the storytellers knew how to mobilize international traditions for Jewish society's needs, be they apparent or masked.

[D] The Exemplum

The exemplum held an important position among the other genres as far back as the rabbinic period, as we saw in the preceding chapter. This genre reached its prime during the Middle Ages, as regards both its artistic development and the quantity in which it was produced. Reasons for this lie on several planes. The Middle Ages are defined, and rightly so, as "the age of faith." All spheres of life—public no less than private—were subject to religious rules and sentiments. Religious faith in this period informed all views, constituting the lens through which every facet of life was perceived. As a result, there developed a constant tension between the religious faith and practice of the unlearned society of the Middle Ages ("the folk religion"), and the religious leadership. The latter, in Christianity as in Islam, sought to mold the religious world of the people as it saw fit.

An important vehicle for the transfer of religious values from the religious leadership to the people was the exemplum. Thus it comes as no surprise that, in this period, the exemplum was developed and disseminated extensively. Moreover, the second half of the twelfth century and the first half of the thirteenth are considered "the golden age" of exemplary literature in Christian Europe. The great collections of exempla were written during this period, each comprising hundreds of tales. Yet the European exemplum existed hundreds of years before the written collections, and for many years after the vast majority were set down in writing in those collections, they were still widely told orally. These developments in medieval culture must have had influence over or connection with the Jewish culture of the day. Indeed, it is not by chance that the largest collection of exemplary tales in Hebrew literature, *Sefer Hasidim* (*Book of the Pious*), was born of the same period.[38]

Still, the flourishing of the exemplary genre in Jewish culture should not be attributed solely to external influence. Two prime collections of exempla predate *Sefer Hasidim*. They are *Midrash of the Ten Commandments* and *An Elegant Composition Concerning Relief after Adversity*. Both of these works emerged among the Jewish society living in the region of Arab cultural influence, and both make extensive use of rabbinic aggadah. Internal development—that is, the influences of rabbinic literature on medieval Jewry—laid the foundations for the exemplary genre in medieval Jewish culture, while the possible influences of Muslim culture helped it along. It is known that as early as the eighth and ninth centuries in Islamic culture there developed the literature of the *adab* and the *faraj*—ethics, seemly customs passed along by means of entertaining literature. This literature made much use of tales to instruct and guide, and earned vast popularity in the Muslim world as early as the ninth and tenth centuries. Further evidence of this supposition can be found in the composition historians consider the first exemplary work in Christian culture, the eleventh-century *Disciplina Clericalis* of Petrus Alfonsi. Alfonsi, born Mosé Sefardi, converted from Judaism and became an influential figure in the Christian world of his day. The book of ethics-through-tales he wrote does indeed preach Christian values, but the construction of questions and answers according to which it is arranged, and most of the tales it comprises, originate in Arab culture—Alfonsi's own, prior to his conversion. In other words, as a Jew in Spain, Petrus Alfonsi was influenced by Arab culture, hence his propensity for using tales to spread moral and religious values. The example of Petrus Alfonsi indicates that Jews living amid Islamic culture employed the genre of the exemplum before its broad dispersal in the Christian world could influence them.[39]

In *Sefer Hasidim*, for example, we find approximately four hundred exemplary tales. All but some twenty-three were created by the book's primary author, R. Judah he-Hasid ("the Pious"). Yet they never made their way beyond the work to appear in other contexts. They were not included in various story collections, nor, apparently, were they told orally. In other words, the folk traditions of the Jewish society did not absorb them, and they did not become folktales. Dozens, if not hundreds, of such original exemplary tales were included in books of responsa, the literature of customs and ethics, Jewish mysticism, and more, yet few became folktales. We will focus below only on those exemplary tales that did in fact become folktales, even if they were not included in the principal collections of exempla mentioned above, but scattered as independent tales in various compositions and manuscripts. Discussion of the exemplary collections themselves is a matter better suited for a study of medieval Hebrew literature.[40]

"Therefore *Sefer Hasidim* was written to make known what one should do and of what one should be wary" (*Sefer Hasidim* section 27). This was R. Judah the Pious's rationale for writing his book. It is also perhaps the most concise, precise definition of the orientation and function of the exemplum in the Middle Ages. The roots of the literary genre called "exemplum" extend back into the ancient world, where it constituted one element of Hellenistic rhetoric. Some see in the New Testament and the writings of the Church Fathers the model followed by medieval writers and preachers. Writers of the Middle Ages tended to see exempla in all types of literature—fable and animal tale, legend, fairy tale, myth, and humorous anecdote. Nonetheless, most medieval authors who employed the exemplum made several fundamental assumptions that should be regarded as such for the genre: first, the exemplum is a short tale presented as a factual report of an actual event. The element of authenticity is particularly important here in light of the tale's function, namely, to persuade the listeners (or readers) to accept it at face value, and behave according to its counsel. We see that R. Judah the Pious attributed a similar purpose to the genre: "to make known what one should do and of what one should be wary." No aesthetic elements of pleasure or entertainment informed the medieval authors' conception of exempla. In their view, tales of this sort were created exclusively to serve a preconceived purpose.[41]

The broad functional view of the genre, namely the possibility of seeing in every tale, of every sort, an exemplum, if only it is presented to didactic purpose, robs it of its right to exist as a legitimate genre. The notion that appending some moralistic utterance to a long and entertaining fairytale miraculously changes it into an exemplum, is, to my mind, an utter distortion of any generic conception. For example, one of the most widely found medieval Jewish folktales is that of "The Bride and the Angel of Death" (AT899—Alcestis). This tale deals with the question of life and death; with female independence and aggression, manifested when the family's safety (her domain, in society's view) is threatened; and with the issue of reality's subjection to the laws of the Torah. There is nothing "exemplary" about it. It does not seek to inculcate a behavioral pattern, nor does it constitute an example of desirable conduct. The tale, as it appears in the *Midrash of the Ten Commandments*, concludes:

> And what were her deeds that she merited this [i.e., saving her husband from the Angel of Death]? Her mother used to draw water daily and give it to the schoolchildren [although] she was an old woman. And the daughter [i.e., the bride] would take a staff and put it in her mother's hand and support her, and the daughter would bear the water and say to her mother, "Mother! Do not discontinue this good deed. If you cannot do it, I will do it in your name," and so she did all her days. And on account of this good deed she [could] save her husband from death. And of this it is said, "A woman of valor, who can find. . . . " (*Ozar Midrashim*, p. 458)

The storyteller of this variant has thus tried to reshape the theme of the woman's brave and independent struggle into a normative tale of honoring one's father and mother. But is it in the power of the moralistic addition at the end to make an exemplum of "The Bride and the Angel of Death"? It does not seem so. While the tale's mobilization to fortify some religious or social value can alter the tale's immediate function, its literary structure and fundamental meaning remain unchanged.

I maintain that the definition of exemplum cannot rest solely on function. Not every tale drafted into service automatically becomes an exemplum. The construction of the plot must be preconceived to provide moral guidance. In my opinion, a tale can be regarded as an exemplum only when it leads its protagonist from sin to punishment, from precept to reward, or from sin to precept, and only when the moral imperative is wrought deep in the tale's construction. Reducing the definition of exemplum to its functional component would make of every folktale an exemplum, and in so doing utterly abolish this genre's raison d'être. Preachers, orators, and leaders did indeed customarily draw tales of all sorts to model various modes of behavior and ideas. But there is no justification, to my mind, in viewing these as exemplary tales. They are, rather, examples of folktales' interchanging functions. Conversely, the only tales we can regard as exempla are those created, whether by the religious leadership or other circles, to constitute a paragon of conduct and moral guidance—the conceptual model being anchored in the construction of the tale itself.[42]

Research on the exemplum has distinguished between two basic techniques of conceptual signification in the tale: analogy and metonymy. The former uses parables (*mashal*) in the main, which substantiate a complex idea by means of a story or simple situation drawn from practical, everyday life, or from the classic literature. This technique suffuses medieval Jewish culture; we find it in ethical literature, Jewish philosophy and Kabala, and in the parabolic literature (Berechiah ha-Nakdan, the literature of the *maqama* [i.e., rhymed narrative]). None of these, however, became folk traditions, and therefore they are not germane to the present discussion. The metonymic (or paradigmatic) technique presents a model of behavior for emulation should one find oneself in a similar situation. Rather than equating or likening one thing to another, this exemplary model builds realistic situations, so that, when confronted by such situations, one will have a ready model of behavior. This view of the exemplary mechanism overlaps the definition of the type proposed above: the demand of a given behavioral norm is ingrained *in the structure of the tale*, not tacked on to its end or determined by the tale's context:[43]

> A story of one who saw someone who had died several years earlier. He said to him: "Why is your face black?" He answered: "Because he [I] had been condemned to Gehenna." He asked him: "For what?" He said: "Because I was not scrupulous in reciting the benediction over bread and the benediction over fruit and the grace after meals with devotion." They said to him [in heaven]: "For your own pleasure you had devotion yet you did not want to praise your Creator with devotion?" . . . (*Sefer Hasidim*, # 555)

The plot here is based on the presentation of an enigmatic occurrence: a dead man appears in the world of the living, his face blackened (indicating that the deceased had been sentenced to the flames of Gehenna). The solution to this riddle—the dead man's explanation—constitutes guidance as to the desired behavior: the mandate for correct behavior is part and parcel of the narrative construction. Such a tale has no need of an instructive coda, since the core of the plot is in and of itself a behavioral directive. In this regard the tale is an exemplum par excellence; no other classification could come close.

The tale, like most in *Sefer Hasidim*, is short and succinct. These characteristics of the exempla stem, perhaps, from their insertion of moral instruction and guidance into various sorts of homilies. R. Judah the Pious deliberately avoided long, cumbersome tales. A possible explanation—and one that also suits exempla exclusive of such contexts—is that the storytellers sought to underscore the tales' moral orientation. To keep listeners from being distracted by the tales' entertaining aspects, the storytellers underplayed them. Still, it is clear that the tales that were told aloud were longer, and contained elements typical of the oral traditions:

> And Rabbi Judah the Pious, of blessed and saintly memory, said that he knew a Jew from Worms who was known as R. Binom who was elderly and who buried the dead. And I heard, for certain and true, that once that Jew awoke early to go to synagogue, and he saw a man sitting in front of the synagogue, upon his head a crown of herbs . . . He was frightened for he thought him a demon. And he called and said to him: "Come here to me and do not fear." And R. Binom went to him and said to him: "Are you not the same one who died and whom I buried?" And he said to him: "Yes." He said to him: "How are you in that world?" And he said to him: "Very properly." And he said to him: "What merit have you? Were not you a plain man?" And he said to him: "Only on account of this [I gained this reward], that I would recite the benedictions in a pleasant voice in the synagogue. For this I was brought to the paradise and honored. And as a sign to you that I am [the same one you buried], you can see that the sleeve of my robe is torn in the same place as you made a tear when you wrapped me in shrouds." And he asked him, "What is that on your head?" And he answered him: "Herbs from paradise that I put upon my head to dispel the foul odor of this world." And I, Isaac, son of R. Moses, may his soul be bound in eternal life, wrote down these events so that the God-fearing will [know] of these acts and be careful to speak the Almighty's praises in a pleasant voice, and with devotion, and will merit paradise. (*Sefer Hasidim*, Parma manuscript, marginal note appended to #427)

The tale is delivered in the early 13th century by Isaac ben R. Moses (author of *Or Zaru'a*), one of the greatest Tosafists, as he heard it from R. Judah the Pious (having been one of his students in Regensburg). If this version was indeed told by R. Judah the Pious, and we have no reason to suspect otherwise, it is clear that what was set down in writing is only a pared-down version of the stories he customarily told aloud. This testimony reflects the folktale tradition: the dialogues characteristic of the vital, dramatic interplay between storyteller and audience; the digressions to the vernacular in order to explain to the audience practical details they would only recognize in their everyday language; emphasis on elements of authenticity, whose function is to make the tale credible ("he knew a Jew from Worms. . . . And I heard, for certain and true," etc.).

Though this tale is more developed than the one from *Sefer Hasidim* cited earlier, it is also concise and purposeful: it comprises only those narrative details required for the development of the plot. The only descriptions therein are those vital to it: namely, the wreath and the tear in the shrouds. Each of these pulls the reader along a direct vector to the plot's destination—the dead man's explanation of how and why he merited all good things in the world to come. It is clear that, here too, the storyteller refrained from any narrative development that might slow the tale's rapid momentum toward its resolution.

Another similarity between these two exemplary tales is the constant structure that facilitates the varying message. The narrative pattern wherein a dead man appears, tells of his fate in the world to come, and links it to things he did while among the living, is a constant model reappearing in many tales, including some from the European literature of the day. This fixed pattern enables storytellers to proceed swiftly and without impediment to the moral lesson that warranted their telling of the tale—the import of the dead man's actions. In the first exemplum, this was the purposeful recitation of the grace after meals; and in the second, the melodious recitation of the benedictions in the synagogue. Other tales promote observance of the Sabbath, honoring one's father and mother, and so on. The expediency of such exemplary narrative patterns is apparent. Medieval preachers, sermonizers, and moralists could weave these ready-made "exemplary models" into any homily, and easily inject them with the message they sought to impress upon their congregations. The practice bears comparison with the way that the folk singer-poet could extemporaneously draw upon oral poetry's ready-made epic poem patterns during a live performance. For this reason, a narrative pattern like that of the dead man returning to the domain of the living was widely utilized in the medieval traditions of Christians and Jews alike.[44]

Another narrative tale type, also widely found among the Jewish traditions of the Middle Ages, is that of "The Neighbor in Paradise." In this tale type, a Jewish sage wants to know who his neighbor will be in the place of honor undoubtedly awaiting him in the Paradise. He learns in a vision that it will be a base, disreputable individual: a butcher, a panderer, a tax collector, or the like. The wise man sets out to investigate that individual, and finds him to be a secret zaddik (i.e., a person of exceptional virtue) who has performed one good deed. At this point he is delighted with the company he will keep. This tale offers an "open" plot pattern; the narrative framework is fixed and reappears intact in all the versions, yet it allows for the substitution of various types of good deed that the prospective neighbor might have done, such as honoring his father and mother, redeeming captives, preventing licentiousness, or martyrdom.[45]

The direct messages found in different versions of the tale of "The Neighbor in Paradise" stem from the action of the protagonist. Thus, when the author of

The Midrash of the Ten Commandments sets out to encourage the honoring of one's father and mother in the spirit of the fifth commandment, he writes it into the hero's part. By this conduct, the character merits a place of honor in paradise. When R. Nissim, author of *An Elegant Composition*, is interested in underscoring mutual dependence within the Jewish community as key to the redemption of captives—in a time when threats of kidnapping and the slave trade loomed large—he tells of an exemplary act of ransoming captives. Yet beyond these messages laid into the tale's open structure, the pattern itself carries a clear message. It is unrelated to the type of good deed performed by the protagonist. The hero is a sort of "hidden righteous." His occupation marks him as the dregs of society, and even those nearest to him consider him degenerate to the core. The investigation of the wise man, his future neighbor in paradise, and the revelation of the protagonist's true nature and the tenor of his actions, show him to be more virtuous than all those who held him in contempt. This ideational theme is wrought into the pattern of the plot. It is not given to alteration or substitution as is the internal story. And indeed, the fixed significance of this narrative pattern for its listeners is that the true measure of an individual is determined by the nature of his actions, not by his social image. Appearances can be deceptive, insists the tale—look beyond them before evaluating a person's worth. This is the true meaning of the tale, and the unwavering moral imperative at its core. Preachers and compilers of collections of tales can ceaselessly vary the direct message of the internal tale by "plugging in" the good deed of their choice. They cannot, however, alter the fixed meaning present in every appearance, written or oral, of the tale type.

The exemplary tales we have considered thus far are constructed according to the classic pattern of the religious tale: sin and its punishment, meritorious deed and its reward. In contrast to these, there was a common group of exemplary tales from this period that set forth the consequences of both sin and good deeds. This double pattern allowed the storytellers to present two alternatives at once, in the space of a single narrative framework. The tale of "Elijah and the Ox Buyer," discussed in the previous section, is a good example of this narrative pattern. A man on his way to purchase oxen encounters Elijah, who charges him to say "God-willing." The man ridicules Elijah, and his money is twice stolen. The third time, when he obeys the directive, his money is miraculously restored to him, and he even makes a handsome profit on the oxen. The storytellers who used this exemplum sought to demonstrate both eventualities to their listeners, two paths of development in the tale. The aim in displaying the two resolutions side-by-side is to convince the listener that they are potential occurrences in his own life. The plot, which sets forth the two possibilities and their applicable punishment or reward, aids (or coerces) the listener to choose the path sanctioned by religious norms. Constructed thus, the tale unfurls before the listener or reader the everyday dilemmas that confront him, and steers him to substitute the right path for the wrong in accordance with the norms upheld by the storyteller.

Another example, quite common in the Jewish traditions of the period, is the legend of "R. Akiva and the Wandering Dead." On his way through the forest, R. Akiva meets a spectacularly ugly man carrying a load of wood. Upon questioning, the man tells him that he is a dead Jewish man. On account of his heinous sins, he falls short even of Gehenna's standards, and so he must wander and collect the firewood in which he will burn each day. He goes on to say that he left behind a wife and son, and that only if his son is called up to the Torah (or recites the mourner's *kaddish* for him) will his punishment be mitigated. R. Akiva discovers that the son is an illiterate and savage child. He educates him. After the boy is called up to the reading of the Law, and takes upon himself the observance of Jewish precepts, the dead man appears to R. Akiva and thanks him for delivering him from his horrible torments.

While in this case it is not the protagonist (the dead man) who performs the good deed, in Judaism, and certainly for the purposes of the tale, a man's son is his equivalent and stand-in. Once again, we have a tale that offers listeners two alternatives translated into narrative language by means of two paths of development: the father and the road of sin he represents, and the son and the path of the Torah, which holds the remedy for the sins of the father. In the manner of the folktale, it lays bare two polarized possibilities: the road of sin juxtaposed with the path of Torah; fearful punishment in the world to come as opposed to pardon and eternal life. The choice of a listener confronted with both—and a denizen of the Middle Ages believed that the world shown him by the tale was a true representation of reality—was not in any doubt.[46]

The tale about the prayer of the innocent (the shepherd) first appears in Jewish literature in *Sefer Hasidim*, but thereafter becomes one of the most common of Jewish folktales. True, as early as rabbinic literature the tale of the innocent's prayer bringing rain is found, but the medieval tale belongs to another branch of this type. A wise man discovers in passing that an innocent and simple-minded shepherd prays in a most unusual way to God each day (whistling, playing a flute, prattling crudely). The wise man cautions him against continuing in such an unseemly manner, teaches him a proper prayer, and continues on his way. The shepherd ceases to pray altogether, because he has forgotten "the correct" prayer, and the prayer of his own devising was forbidden him. In a vision, the wise man is rebuked, and told to return at once to bid the shepherd resume his own prayer. In *Sefer Hasidim*, the tale comes to convey that a man must do his best in the service of God, and his best, humble though it may be, is as acceptable to the Almighty as another's more distinguished efforts. Such an interpretation of the tale is correct if the storyteller's intention is to illuminate the naïve shepherd and his actions. But the tale itself tells another story, focusing instead on the wise man. The innocent shepherd is an entirely passive figure, who does nothing unless he is told. The active figure, whose actions determine the course of the story, is that of the wise man. He is also the fixed figure appearing in all stages of the tale. Indeed, the wise man does two things: first, he determines how the shepherd is to pray—for which action he is punished. Second, he instructs the shepherd to resume his former practice—this being the tale's preferred method. It is unthinkable that the preacher or storyteller is directing his message to people like the innocent shepherd, who do not participate at all in the community's religious activity. The appeal is precisely to those who believe they have the authority to enforce their own manner of worship on the members of their community. This tale is, in my opinion, proof that the exemplum was not intended only for the simple classes of the people, but also for the learned elite—in those same matters that were a part of their world. This question, whether unconventional worship of the Almighty was preferable to no worship at all, ever occupied religious leaders and teachers, and it seems that this exemplum targeted them specifically.[47]

In each of the three tales just now presented, the protagonist moves from one situation to its counterpart, from sin and punishment to good deed and its reward. In other words, the hero in these stories demonstrates *moral development.* As is customary for the folktale, the development is anything but gradual; this development does not take place in the psyche of the protagonist, as in a novel, for example. It is complete and immediate: the oxen buyer who twice refuses to say, "God-willing," learns his lesson—and on the third assay does as he was told. The change that came over the protagonist is plain to see: the oxen buyer, after his lesson, will no longer stray in that manner. The son of the dead sinner, representative of his father among the living, is no longer an uncivilized child, but a respectable Jew. Even the wise man, in the tale of the innocent's prayer, has lost his earlier certainty that his way of praying to God is more correct than others'; he will never again presume to coerce others to follow suit.

However, among the medieval exempla there are some tales presenting clear moral-psychological development of their protagonists. These are among the most developed and powerful exemplary tales in the period's narrative traditions. Here, too, I will present only a few examples from the wide selection available. We have already encountered at least one such tale in the discussion of the exemplum in the rabbinic period—that being the tale of R. Eleazar ben Dordaya and the prostitute (*Menakhot* 44a). After realizing the enormity of his sin, he sought forgiveness from the forces of nature (in itself an externalization of the profound, mythic spiritual striving for reparation and repentance). His plea rejected, he put his head between his knees and wept until death. Successive stages in the narrative plot of this tale, ancient as it is, were constructed according to the step-by-step development of the protagonist's conscience.

The first tale of this type is known by the title, "The Tale of the Half Friend" and numbers among the best-loved didactic tales in Jewish literature. True, the tale is not originally Jewish, and is no less common in international traditions, but its absorption into Jewish culture was so complete that it can be viewed as a Jewish tradition in every respect. The tale concerns the only son of a wealthy man who boasted to his father of the many friends with whom he caroused. The father advised him to put them to a test: he should put a slaughtered lamb in a sack and appear at his good friends' homes in the dead of night. Then, continued the father, he should say he had killed a man, and appeal to them for sanctuary. Every last one of his companions chased him from his home. The father then sent him to his own "half friend," a poor tailor who, after some hesitation, agreed to harbor his friend's son. The father explained to his son that the brief hesitation was what made him only half a friend. A second tale generally follows, in which the father tells of an ideal friend, but that is not of interest to us now. The tale reflects a typical process of maturity: the son spends his life in a kind of "bubble," alienated from reality. His father, by means of the experiment, forces a confrontation with real life, with all its rigors and hypocrisy. The plot is constructed of four narrative units: the three times the son appeals to his favorite companions, and the fourth episode in which he turns to his father's friend. The plot develops with the young man's fresh insight into the excesses of his youth, and the development of his moral awareness and ability to cope with reality. The main protagonist of the beginning of the tale is a changed man by story's end. In spite of its schematic construction and one-dimensional characterization of protagonists—some of the folktale's characteristic effects—society views the tale as a reflection of the conscious evolution that every maturing individual must undergo. From this perspective, the tale is unquestionably an exemplum, replicating the simplistic conception of "reward and punishment" as the more complex perception arising from the tale.[48]

A second example of this sort of exemplary tale is similar in content to the aforementioned talmudic tale of R. Eleazar ben Dordaya. A handsome Torah scholar by the name of R. Meir journeyed annually to Jerusalem. He stayed in the home of Judah the cook, where he was welcomed by his host's modest wife. She passed away, and the cook remarried. This young wife passionately desired R. Meir. She got him drunk and he, unawares, spent the night with her. In the morning, after her husband left for work, she affectionately told R. Meir what had taken place the night before. As proof, she mentioned certain physical marks that she had seen on his body. He appealed to his rabbi, prepared to risk his life for forgiveness. The rabbi orders that he be bound to a tree in the forest and left to the mercies of the wild beasts. For two nights, the lions toy with him. They finally pounce on the third day, ripping a bone from his flesh. He limps for the rest of his days, but the fact that they did not tear him limb from limb is interpreted as pardon for the act. This is one version of the tale type, and the most widely seen, found in the *Midrash of the Ten Commandments*, and in a Cairo Genizah manuscript, among many others. A second branch of the tale type appearing in *An Elegant Composition* and the versions similar to it, recounts that R. Meir became convinced that in fact he had not sinned, and that the woman's story was a complete fabrication. He then had a vision that strengthened this conviction that he had not sinned.[49]

If the tale is taken literally, then all that happened to R. Meir, except his decision to confess to the head of the academy, was without his knowledge or initiative. He sleeps with the cook's wife while in a drunken stupor, he is tied fast to a tree and abandoned, helpless, to the mercy of the lions. In this regard, perhaps this is not an exemplary tale, as the protagonist is utterly passive. But then again, perhaps it is this very passivity that is the theme of the tale: passivity in the face of the actions and temptations of mankind is the true sin, while its converse—namely, passivity as acquiescence to God's actions—leads to purification and reparation. The protagonist of the tale, in fact, goes through two stages in his path to acceptance of reality: first, he accepts the affections and services of the cook's wife without resistance, just as he accepts everything, without suspicion or struggle. His sin lies in his lack of suspicion of the advances of a woman he does not know; in his compliance in allowing her to get him drunk; in his inaction as he lets her do as she pleases with his body while he sleeps, oblivious to the dangers surrounding him. In essence, passivity on the level of human affairs is a sin. In the second part of the tale, the protagonist is still passive. Bound to a tree as per his rabbi's order, he is helpless. In between the two parts, the protagonist confesses to the head of the yeshiva, ready to deliver himself to the Almighty—his sole action in the story. With this act he delivers himself into the hands of Divine Providence's representative:

> What did Rabbi Meir of blessed memory do? He went to the head of the Yeshiva and told him all that had happened to him, "For this purpose I have come before you, so that I may happily accept any verdict you decide" . . . He said to him: "I have sought your judgement and have seen it to be within the law that a lion devour you." He said to him: "I accept Heaven's judgement." (Wertheimer, *Battei Midrashot*, p. 185).

The passivity of the hero's actions in the second part of the tale, indicating his absolute relinquishment of self to Divine Providence, is the fullest embodiment of religious activism. Its practical significance is that man should utterly yield his body and soul to what he perceives as God's representatives: the head of the yeshiva and the lions.

The hero thus learns that passivity and naivety cannot be the guiding principle of one's interaction with the human world around him. He should, however, accept divine manifestations in the world with absolute innocence and devotion. At this point, it seems, R. Meir—and with him listeners to the tale—

has his epiphany: man must reserve complete dedication of self to that which is between him and his god, and he must beware lest that attitude edge its way into his stance in practical affairs.

The tale of Nathan de-Tzutzita is one of the most famous ethical tales in medieval narrative traditions, and apparently was so as early as the rabbinic period, and in the Islamic *hadith* literature as well. According to the story, Nathan, known as "de-Tzutzita" ("of the forelocks"), who later became the Babylonian exilarch (identified as Ukban bar Nehemiah—*Shabbat* 56b), had been a very wealthy panderer. He was consumed with passion for one Hannah, another man's wife—but was not permitted even to see her. Unfulfilled desire made him ill. Subsequently her husband, imprisoned as a debtor, charged her to go to Nathan de-Tzutzita to ask for money. Nathan was prepared to give her anything, if only she would give herself over to him. When she tells him that would be a sin, he concedes, overcomes his desperate passion for her and merits becoming so great a zaddik that it was said, "a light shined above his head." R. Nissim of Kairouan concludes the version of the tale in *An Elegant Composition* as follows:

> It is therefore obligatory for the believer to consider the consequences [of things] and not to indulge his fancy, so that he might be saved. On the contrary, he should be eager to do that which endures, and energetic in earning that which neither ceases nor is cut short, namely the reward of the hereafter. He should renounce that which would earn for him great pain and bring upon him distressing punishment. He should reflect that this is like [the case of] a person who eats honey mixed with deadly poison—let him not delight in this sweetness, for it will pass in the shortest time, while the deadly poison will remain. By my life, he who overcomes [his desire] is a mighty man, as the Sages have said: "Who is a mighty man? He who overcomes his Inclination [to evil]" (Brinner's translation, p. 131).

R. Nissim's remarks here truly sound like ethical exhortations made after telling the tale of "Nathan de-Tzutzita" to his students in his academy, or perhaps to a wider audience in the synagogue or some other public gathering. The simple analogies (honey and poison), the rhetorical calls, the personal appeals ('By my life!'), were all apparently some of the effects of his oral style that he attempted to reconstruct when writing his book. We can, then, perhaps view the tale of Nathan de-Tzutzita, and its subsequent moral lesson, as a kind of real performance event at which the tale was delivered for a patently didactic purpose.[50]

R. Nissim speaks here of the heroism of self-restraint. I include it in the group of tales on the development of the protagonist and the crystallization of his moral awareness, as it seems to me that this is the tale's primary focus. Nathan de-Tzutzita's suppression of desire is not a sudden or isolated incident, rather it stemmed, as the plot clearly shows, from a difficult and painful psychological transition. Indeed, the procurer's boisterous hawking of his wares fades slowly into the voice of defeat: he appeals to healers, yields again and yet again, until finally he shuts himself up in his home, utterly crushed and forlorn. It is difficult to imagine Nathan de-Tzutzita successfully overcoming his desire at the outset of the tale. Accompanying his pain and anguish was a process of learning and purification. The panderer, whose entire life had been devoted to the pleasures of the flesh, gradually learns that pangs of the spirit wound more deeply than any physical torment. The process of purification through suffering taught him that his true longing was not for Hannah's flesh, but for Hannah the person. This being the case, his triumph over temptation was an act of choice: he chose to view her as a human being, and out of his consequent respect for her wishes and feelings, he had to frustrate his physical longing for her. At the end of the story, R. Akiva persuades Nathan to study Torah with him, subsequently making of him a great scholar and zaddik. The true development, however, took place earlier, when Nathan learned that losing the body of the woman he loved was correlated with the gain of preserving her honor and person. The external, narrative change, from panderer to Torah scholar, reflects overtly and concretely the internal, *spiritual* process undergone by the protagonist as his moral consciousness took shape.

Scholars of the exemplum in medieval Christian culture view it as an outstanding mediating factor between the elite, educated culture and the broad strata of the people. Early on, Gregory the Great (pope from 590–604 C.E.) emphasized the power of the exemplum to influence through concrete examples and lauded its superior efficacy as compared to a formulation of abstract ethical rules. Jacques de Vitry, a noteworthy Christian preacher of the early thirteenth century (he was appointed bishop of Crusader-held Acre in 1216), argues that "the keen-edged sword of argumentation has no influence on the common man." In his opinion, heartening and entertaining examples were indispensable to the edification of one's audience. Only an inexperienced sermonizer, continues Jacques de Vitry, ignorant of such tales' power to influence, would disdain them. Many other preachers complain that "When God is spoken of, the listeners fall asleep, yet to hear stories, they awake at once." The samples of exemplary tales in Jewish culture of the Middle Ages indicate a similar trend. Experienced educators and moralists, like R. Nissim of Kairouan and R. Judah the Pious, made intensive use of tales. They did so precisely because they recognized that the religious and social truths they sought to inculcate to their congregations could "pass" most efficiently via the tale. In other words, the transfer of values from the religious, educated elite to the masses took place likewise among Jewish scholars by means of stories, and from this perspective it parallels the process in Christian society.[51]

The difference between the largest collection of exempla in medieval Jewish literature, *Sefer Hasidim*, and Christian collections of exempla, is that the latter collected tales from the oral traditions. Not so R. Judah the Pious, who created his own exempla. Indeed, the large majority of tales included in the great Christian collections—Petrus Alfonsi's *Disciplina Clericalis*; Jacques de Vitry's *Sermones Vulgares*; Walter Mapp's *De Nugis Curialium*; Etienne de Bourbone's *Speculum Naturalis*; Jacobus de Voragine's *Legenda Aurea*; and Caesarius of Heisterbach's *Dialogus Miraculorum*, to name some—are consummate folktales. They exist in the folk traditions of the Middle Ages in written and oral form and are copied from one collection of exempla to the next. The situation is reversed in *Sefer Hasidim*: of the more than four hundred tales it comprises, only some thirty can be defined as folktales. In *An Elegant Composition*, R. Nissim offers numerous rabbinic tales in the course of literary copying, tales that never became a part of folk tradition. The reason for this difference, it seems, lies in the Christian preachers' choice of tales already familiar to the populace as folktales. They recognized them as having already crossed society's "barrier," thus they were easily employed to transmit religious messages. Conversely, Jewish religious leaders, like R. Judah the Pious, sought to transmit new messages to their society—such as the system of values of the German Pietism. They had to do this by means of tales that, like the viewpoints they came to express, were unknown previously. For this reason only a few of the tales created by R. Judah the Pious became folk traditions, and only those tales that existed as folk traditions before R. Nissim of Kairouan collected them in his book remained as such thereafter. The reason for the absorption or rejection of an exemplum by folk traditions is connected not only with its narrative character (although this is certainly a basic condition), but also on the nature of the values it seeks to disseminate.[52]

Most of the exemplary tales known to us from the folk traditions, as opposed to doctrinary works such as *Sefer Hasidim*, deal with themes connected to daily life. These include interpersonal and sexual relationships and family purity, the Sabbath, charity and concern for the poor, relations with non-Jews, human attributes such as deceit, hypocrisy, dress, and external appearance, and food. When an exemplum addresses values of a sectarian nature, such as asceticism and extreme purity (as in *Sefer Hasidim*), or a developed theodicean conception, (as in *An Elegant Composition*), then the exemplum does not "pass" the social barrier, and never becomes a folk tradition. The exemplum's power lies in its ability to express society's social and moral outlook, its basic hopes and anxieties, and to utilize them to disseminate and inculcate the values espoused by the religious leadership. An exemplum that promises its hero a fine reward only in the world to come, such as most of the exempla in *Sefer Hasidim*, cannot become a folk tradition and fill a didactic role among the broad strata. Wealth, offspring, lofty social status, greatness in Torah—these are a concrete reward in observable reality, they are the returns promised in the folk exempla to those who fulfill the desired norms. Hunger, disease, death, sterility, bereavement of children, exile, and conversion, are the comeuppance of the sinner. Both punishment and reward assuredly reflect the deep anxieties and overt and secret hopes deep in the consciousness of medieval Jewry. The exemplum made use of both conscious and unconscious elements to serve its religious and social goals.

[E] The Historical Legend

Historical legend is central to the formation of society's collective consciousness. Anthropologists, sociologists, and social historians arrived at this conclusion long ago. Still, historians continue to search for "the facts" in historical legends, and to treat such legends as factual documents. The assumption that developed in nineteenth-century folkloristics that legend contains a "kernel" of factual-historical truth, arose out of the circumstances of historical scholarship specific to that period, and out of folkloristics' then-prevalent romantic notions. One legend, for example, tells how Charlemagne brought R. Kalonymus of Lucca (in Italy) to the Rhine communities in Germany, and of the establishment of the preeminent Torah center in the German lands. What historical "kernel" lies nestled within this legend? There was a historical Charlemagne, who conquered Germany and Italy, as well as a Jew by the name of Kalonymus, who hailed from Italy, and who was a forbear of an illustrious family of the Rhine communities. And what else? Was there any connection whatsoever between these two figures? Were they even contemporaries? The answer to such questions is usually "no," and so efforts to reconstruct the "factual kernel" from which such stories grew usually fail.

Modern historians (primarily of medieval European culture), though they implement historical legend as a valuable tool in their work, acknowledge that its usefulness does not necessarily lie in the "factual" realm. Thus, as regards the historical perception of the Middle Ages, it has come to be understood that "facts" and "truth" are not necessarily one and the same. History is no longer taken as "what actually took place," but as "that which was believed to have taken place." The point where fabula (the historical legend) meets society's perception of its past (its collective memory and consciousness), contains the historical "truth" of the Middle Ages. Indeed, it seems that only such an understanding of the historical mindset can explain the frequent, if not astonishing, use by medieval chroniclers of historical legends, the reliability of whose recounted "facts" was flatly suspect. Ahimaaz ben Paltiel, author of *The Scroll of Ahimaaz*, recounts that a lion devoured R. Aaron of Baghdad's mule, a beast R. Aaron had used to work his millstones. R. Aaron then uttered the Holy Name, thereby harnessing the lion to the millstones. When his father saw him using the lion for such lowly work, he punished R. Aaron with exile. Did

Ahimaaz believe the "facts" as he presented them, that is to say, the tale of be-witching the lion and other such marvelous tales found aplenty in his work? It is difficult to say. He certainly believed in the historical truth reflected in this story. This "truth" can be defined as the tale's accord with the values, the system of norms, the collective memory, and the consciousness of the society to which Ahimaaz belonged at the start of the eleventh century.[53]

Historical legends of the Middle Ages survived in two types of sources: historiographical works, on the order of the *Book of Josippon*, *The Scroll of Ahimaaz*, *Sefer ha-Kabbalah*, *Shevet Yehudah*, and *Shalshelet ha-Kabbalah*, to name some; and in independent form—inserted into commentarial works, cycles, books of ethics and philosophy, or collections of tales. The historiographical works are not, by definition, folk literature, but a receptacle in which folk traditions, *inter alia*, were preserved. These works are not of interest to us here and most have, in any case, already been thoroughly researched. It should be noted that the works were written by and for the educated elite of Jewish society. All authors of historical chronicles were scholars or members of eminent families in Spain or Italy. The historical legends, conversely—those that survived as independent tales and the traditions included in the historiographical compositions—were the property of all of Jewish society, and so they should be regarded as the primary material to shape the historical consciousness of the Jewish communities. It was not the reading of historiographical works that shaped this consciousness, but the spread of the oral historical traditions among all strata of the people.

The historiographical works are not the *source* of these historical legends, but rather their repository. A common error in the study of medieval historical-legendary traditions views *Shevet Yehudah* or *Shalshelet ha-Kabbalah* as the origin of some legend or another. Such a misconception contradicts the oft-repeated claims of the compilers themselves. Some examples from *Shevet Yehudah*, by Solomon ibn Verga (writing at the time of the expulsion from Spain): "I heard this from the mouth of a great sage of Ashkenaz who came as an emissary" (Shohat edition, p. 91); "I also heard from the mouth of a kabbalist sage who had come from France, that in one city, called Boudonne (?) a decree was proclaimed" (ibid.); "From such a pious and wise man as R. Abraham ibn Arama I heard that a miracle was performed by my master, R. Judah ibn Verga of Seville. I will write of it here" (Shohat edition, p. 92); "I heard from elders, emigrants from Spain, that one ship came here because of the plague" (Shohat edition, p. 122). Solomon ibn Verga writes his composition some thirty years after the expulsion. At the time, the great expulsion, as well as those that preceded and heralded it, was an issue of consuming interest to Jewish society. These historical-narrative traditions were very widespread, and made their way among the various communities, yet few merited immortality in Ibn Verga's composition. His testimony proves that the majority of tales included in his work, as well as in other historiographical works, were created, developed and disseminated in the Jewish communities as oral narrative traditions before they were set down in writing. This is the material I wish to describe below. The works themselves, their historiographical and literary qualities, are the subjects of another sort of study.[54]

What are we to understand as "historical," in the historical legend? We have already seen that the concept of "truth" was pivotal to the medieval historical consciousness. Indeed, the historical legend makes every effort to boost its credibility. It does this primarily by the agency of "verisimilitude," which reminds listeners of details familiar from reality and from their society's collective consciousness. Mention is made of events or figures from the Bible and rabbinic literature, which are analogized to landmark events of world history (the conquests of Alexander the Great or Charlemagne, the Crusades or the Black Plague). This limits the recounted action in a legend to a geographical expanse well-known to the listeners, or one that they recognize from the past. To these must always be added a sturdy chain of tradition: we have seen above how Solomon ibn Verga attributes his traditions to reliable sources—a great and wise rabbi, a famous kabbalist, participants in the event who themselves had been expelled from Spain, and so on. The literary form of the historical legend is another factor influencing the measure of faith it inspires in the audience of readers and listeners. Generally speaking, the legend is deliberately a-rhetorical. It is formulated in simple, direct language, without stylistic ornaments and descriptions or developed dialogues. The less "artistically" the legend is crafted, the more credible and accepted by listeners as "truth." Two conflicting interests sometimes confronted the authors of historical chronicles. On the one hand, they recognized the cardinal importance of credibility for the tales, and so sought to deliver them in a simple, non-rhetorical manner. On the other hand, they leaned toward the poetic—ornamented, stylized, florid writing (in imitation of the examplar of classical historiography).

Such tendencies exist primarily in works such as the *Book of Josippon* and *Shevet Yehudah*, wherein the artistic drive prevails over aspirations to credibility. For this reason, Ibn Verga's work has often been defined as "novelistic." It seems fitting to focus on his work to examine the tension between the two orientations. I will try to model this by means of another type of legend: the tales of the blood libels, which occupy so central a place in *Shevet Yehudah*. Some are relatively long tales, whose emphasis is not strictly blood libels, but the debate between the good king—who disbelieves the libel against the Jews— and the slanderers themselves. Thus, in one of the tales ("The Eighth Persecution," Shohat edition, pp. 46–50), three people plant a "corpse in a Jewish home, and [went] to the judges, shouting that they [found] a dead Christian in the home of a Jewish man." Representatives of the Jews are summoned to the royal court, where a debate ensues between the prosecutors, the Jews, and the king over the question of Christian hatred of Jews, the true religion, and God's reasons for punishing his beloved people. This verbal swordplay makes up most of the tale (pp. 46–49). After it concludes, the king proclaims throughout his kingdom that whoever unveils the truth will be handsomely rewarded. A boy who witnessed the plotters cast the corpse into the Jew's yard appears and testifies. The king severely punishes the libelers. From the construction of the tale it is clear that Ibn Verga heard the libel tale from oral sources. He is not especially interested in the blood libel, but rather in emphasizing the religious controversy, the ideological confrontation between Christianity and Judaism, at the learned level of the Middle Ages. The shifting of the tale's focus in this direction weakens its credibility as a historical document. Nonetheless, we will examine another tale of blood libel, told in brief, in the same composition:

> I heard that in Spain there were some libels that a youth had been found in the home of a Jewish man, killed and with his chest torn open, and it was said that [the Jews] had taken his heart for use in a ritual. Don Solomon ha-Levi, a wise man and kabbalist, came and put one name beneath the youth's tongue, and the boy awoke and told who had killed him, and who had removed his heart in order to slander the Jewish poor. And I did not see it in writing, and so I heard it. ("The Sixty-First Persecution," Shohat edition, p. 126)

Herein was preserved a folk tradition in the form closest to the manner in which such legends were told. Solomon ibn Verga apparently only made minor modifications in the process of committing it to print. None of the usual hallmarks of his narrative style are recognizable here: the short, dense quality of the story, its direct, simple style, the concentration of the narrative plot, and the emphasis on location (Spain) and the princely figure (Don Solomon ha-Levi), all contribute to the "verisimilitude" at the foundation of the historical legend. Thus it appears that this legend, despite its supernatural hue, commands more belief, and is better accepted by society as "historical" than the previous legend that, though thoroughly realistic, showed the very obvious markings of artistic-tendentious reworking.[55]

While Ibn Verga offers both tales for the same purpose—to recount the persecutions and blood libels for the sake of future generations—it is clear that each had its own orientation and function. Indeed, it is a rule of thumb that in order to ascertain the meaning and function of historical legends, one may not rely upon their declared objectives, which are styled by the author of the chronicle or the direct narrator. Instead, the legend's narrative character and system of symbols must be analyzed. My aim in this section is to offer representative medieval historical legends, categorized according to the functions and orientations they were intended to serve in the period's Jewish society. The four kinds of orientation discussed below are in no way mutually exclusive.

Each historical legend has more than one orientation or meaning. In classifying them, I aim to underscore the central meaning. In other historical or social contexts, these orientations are given to change, as I will attempt to show below.

[1] The Historical Legend as Collective Memory

At the uncontested forefront of this category are the biblical tales, rabbinic tales of the Hasmonean Revolt and the Destruction of the Temple, the Bar Kochba Revolt and the departure to exile, and so on. The reason that the medieval texts are loaded, as we saw above, with materials drawn from rabbinic aggadah is that, in a society that lacks universal organized education, and whose existence depends upon a commonly-held and robust social consciousness, memories of a common past are a vital foundation of culture. Among the learned social elite, historiographical compositions fit the bill. *Iggeret Rav Sherira Gaon* (the letter of Rabbi Sherira, head of the academy) which recounts the chain of sages and their deeds; *The Book of Josippon*, which tells the history of the Second Temple—a history that had nearly vanished from Jewish historical consciousness before its appearance; R. Abraham Ibn Daud's *Sefer ha-Kabbalah*, which recounted the history of the Jewish sages and the dissemination of the Torah in the diaspora until the twelfth century; the Jewish Chronicles of the Crusades, which tell the dreadful tale of the slaughter of the Jewish communities in the year 1096 C.E.; *Shevet Yehudah*, which intensively enumerates the edicts and riots perpetrated against Jewish communities until the expulsion from Spain; Gedaliah Ibn Yahya's *Shalshelet ha-Kabbalah*, which tells the history of great Jewish figures and their deeds until the sixteenth century; all these were composed in order to shape a common infrastructure for the collective memory. For this reason, some of these works (such as *Josippon*), were so widely available to medieval Jewry, becoming almost the "official" history books of learned Jews.

These compositions did not shape the communal mentality of the broad strata of the people, that is, the uneducated. The historical legends from which the chronicles drew a significant portion of their information, and those rampant in the folk traditions but not included in the chronicles, were largely the components of the historical consciousness of the broad Jewish society. It is clear that the learned and the leaders, who understood the power and importance of common memory for society's stability, told aloud the tales they had read in historiographical works at various opportunities—to youths in the study halls, to women and craftsmen in the synagogue, and to children in schoolhouses. Hence the traditions flowed both to and from the compositions.

The tales of the edicts of the Crusader period are a good example of the position of the historical legend in collective memory:

When the members of the holy covenant saw that the decree had been proclaimed and that the enemies had defeated them, and [the rioters] entered
the courtyard, all shouted together, old and young, men and women, and
children and servants, to their Father who is in heaven, and cried for them
and their lives, and said: Heaven's will is just. And they said to each other . . .
We are glad, if His will is done, and happy is he who is killed and slaughtered and dies professing the unity of God, for he will be summoned to the
world to come and will sit among the righteous, *Rabbi Akiva and his fellows*,
foundations of the world, who died martyrs . . . *and the precious sons of Zion*,
sons of Mainz who underwent the ten trials like *Abraham our forefather*, and
like *Hananiah, Mishael and Azariah.* They too bound their sons as *Abraham
bound Isaac his son* . . . the one bound and was bound; and the other bound
and was bound . . . and they were killed and slaughtered for the sake of the
unity of God the venerated and awe-inspiring. (Habermann, *Gezerot
Ashkenaz ve-Zarfat*, pp. 30–32)

And in another tale:

And it was on the twenty-fifth of Iyyar, and the wanderers and burghers
said: Here are those who remained in the court of the bishop and in his
chambers; we will have revenge upon them as well . . . And there was a
young man, and his name was Rabbi Meshulam ben R. Isaac. And he called
out in a great voice to all who stood there, and to Madam Zippora, his beloved: Listen to me adults and children, God gave me this son, borne by
Zippora, my wife for time of old age, and his name is Isaac. Now I will
sacrifice him as did *Abraham our forefather to Isaac his son* . . . and he bound
Isaac his son, and took in hand the knife to slaughter his son, *and he recited
the benediction for the ritual slaughter*, and the youth answered: Amen. Then
he slaughtered the youth. (Ibid., p. 96)

The tales chronicling the massacres of 1096 make intensive use of the martyrological motifs embedded in Jewish collective historical consciousness. Before
us is a perfect example of how medieval Jewish chroniclers perceived collective
memory as a motive force in history. They were fully cognizant that by having
the protagonists mention Abraham and the binding, Hananiah, Mishael and
Azariah, or the mother and her seven sons, they were awakening common Jewish memories. Likewise for such stylistic formulae as: "The precious sons of
Ziyyon" (Lam. 4:2) or "Lay not thy hand upon the lad" (Gen. 22:12); and the
frequently recurring metaphor of ritual slaughter (checking the *kashrut* [ritual
correctness] of the knife before killing their families, reciting the benediction
for the ritual slaughter of animals). The social and cultural outlook shaped by
these shared memories broadens to incorporate the tales. Once the tales become widespread written and oral traditions among the people and reached the

communities farthest from the location of the dire events, they themselves constitute a collective memory, a point of common reference for future generations. Indeed, the reference to them in later historiography, for example in *Shevet Yehudah*, which deals with events of four hundred years hence, or in the chronicles of the 1648–49 massacres, is unambiguous proof of this process.[56]

[2] The Historical Legend as an Expression of Confrontation with Other Peoples

The reality faced by medieval Jewry—young and old alike—as a social minority amid a ruling society, had a decisive influence on all walks of Jewish life and culture. Folk traditions were no exception. Indeed, the historical legends of the Middle Ages reflect this reality in all its perils and advantages while illuminating it from the viewpoint of the broad strata of the people, different as it was from that of the learned elite.

We find an excellent example of such a cross-section of Jewish society in the blood libel tales. Most of those in *Shevet Yehudah* are realistic; the libelers appeal to the king who, recognizing the Jews' high moral fiber, does not believe the lies and rejects the libel. But the bishop, the priests, and the inflamed masses are not assuaged; they force the king to open an investigation. A debate ensues between the Jews (or the king, representing them) and the libelers. The truth ultimately comes to light, and the libelers are punished. This is the general paradigm according to which most blood libel tales in the composition are constructed. This model reflects Solomon ibn Verga's profound belief (presumably shared by members of his circle) in the basic fairmindedness of the regime: it comports itself rationally and recognizes the worth of the Jews. It is only the pressure of religious zealotry and the inflamed passion of the masses that compel him to act against the Jews. This pattern has a clear social-political function: the tales justify the communities' reliance on the rulers, and suggest that the Jews' sole prospect for security lies in supporting these rulers, financially and politically.

In *Shevet Yehudah*, still other narrative traditions of blood libels survived. One, on the resuscitation of a murdered child with the aid of God's mystical name, we have already seen above. In another (p. 63), the Christians coerce the king into executing eminent Jews who, they claim, conspired to murder a Christian in order to use his blood. The Jews are put into barrels studded with nails, thereafter to be rolled through the streets. But an angel, disguised as a Christian officer, claims that, by law, the king must deliver the first kick. When the king lifts his leg, it is suddenly paralyzed. He realizes his error and repeals the decree. The Jews pray for his health; he is healed. Ibn Verga concludes: "There are [other] versions of this. But that which I saw in the book of the chronicles of the kings of France is true" (p. 66). And in another tale of this type Ibn Verga opens: "From such a pious and wise man as R. Abraham ibn Arama I heard that a miracle was performed by my master, R. Judah ibn Verga of Seville. I will write of it here" (p. 92). According to the tale, Christians falsely stated that Jews had exhumed the body of a Christian who had converted from Judaism and who had been buried in a Christian cemetery. They reinterred the body in a Jewish graveyard, in order to prevent its soul from entering Paradise. The Jews appealed to Judah ibn Verga, who asked the Duke to grasp a clean sheet of paper. R. Judah pronounced the Holy Name, and when they looked at the paper, there appeared a drawing depicting the deceitful actions of the priests, along with their full names. After the Duke apprehended them, they admitted their crimes and were harshly punished.

Ibn Verga emphasizes that he drew these particular three tales from the oral tradition (the declaration concerning "the book of chronicles of the kings of France" is apparently a figure of speech). This comes as no surprise as, indeed, this is precisely where the blood libel tales of the social elite diverge from those of the folk traditions. The latter do not recognize or accord credence to any fairmindedness on the regime's part. Said regime comes to the Jews' aid only after Divine intervention. Ibn Verga's tales of blood libel are realistic, whereas the folk tales are supernatural, but not necessarily because Ibn Verga was an enlightened individual who put no stock in sorcery. Herein are reflected the two different approaches of Jewish society to relations with the overlord: one believed that Jewish society depended for its existence on its ability to appeal to the reason and enlightened attitude of the Gentiles. This approach thus promoted close economic and cultural ties between Jews and Gentiles. The other approach, more characteristic of the folk, it seems, was shared by the broad strata of the people, whose culture was oral. They continued to count on Divine Providence for their existence, and rejected the argument of the regime's decency and the assumption that proximity to the gentile nations could yield any benefit to the Jews.[57]

One of the tale types representing the confrontation between Jews and gentiles is "the miraculous rescue of a Jewish community in distress," whose earliest appearance can be seen as early as the biblical *Scroll of Esther*, and thereafter in the literature of the Second Temple period, as we saw in early chapters of this book. The special circumstances of medieval diasporic communities were certainly fertile ground for the continuation and evolution of this ancient tale type. Indeed, all the blood libel tales mentioned earlier, in which a community is threatened with annihilation in the wake of false accusations, and ultimately saved, whether by miracle or in a realistic manner, belong to this tale type. So too the "Second Purim" tales, wherein communities or families celebrate the miracle of their rescue from various calamities—a kind of private, local Purim. For the purpose of the present discussion one of many possible examples will suffice: Yoseph Sambary tells in his chronicle (late seventeenth century) of a *qadi* (that is, a Muslim judge whose rulings are based on Islamic law) who hated the Jews was all-powerful in Egypt, and oppressed and embittered the lives of the local Jewish community. R. Moses al-Damohi, a pillar of the community, decides to stand in the breach. He purifies himself and visits the graves of the saints, digs a deep pit and stands within it. He demands of the dead that they come to the aid of their living brethren, "just as we pray for you three times a day and say: Blessed art Thou, O Lord, who restores the dead to everlasting life, so you should pray and be to me of assistance [during this time of] trouble for your people, the children of Israel, who are in exile and [who are] as sheep who have no shepherd, and oppressors bear down upon them, and will devour them" (*Sefer Divrei Yosef*, S. Shtober edition, pp. 160–161). R. Moses sends his attendant to see if anything has transpired in town, and discovers that that same *qadi* has suddenly died, "and the land was quiet."[58]

The course of the tale, and in particular the protagonist's remarks cited here, characterize the web of anxieties and fears that were the impetus for the creation of such tales. While the erudite elite interpreted events rationally, and explained them against a background of political or economic events in the non-Jewish world, the folk picture of the world was much simpler and without shades of gray. In the folk view, danger lurked in all places and at all times. Folk traditions put forward no logical or realistic solutions for this ever-present peril. Only the sanctified forces of the people—Providence, Elijah the Prophet, the sainted dead, and the living righteous—could provide a substitute for the practical ruling power that diasporic Jewish communities lacked. In other words, the solution put forward by the folk traditions for the Jewish situation in exile was in the realm of the mind, not of the body; inner action, as opposed to actions taken on the stage of history. Religious symbols, embedded deep in society's collective memory, embodied this solution. The broad strata of the people do not view efforts at intercession with Gentile rulers or attempts to draw closer to them on the cultural level as effective means of rescue. These tales propose internal fortification by means of adherence to religious symbols and common memories. That Jewish society accepted them and turned them into traditions so widespread indicates that they suited society's ideational and psychological perception. The Gentile world was portrayed in these traditions as hostile, one-dimensional, and unappeasable by ordinary means. Only frontal confrontation with the aid of the Jews' sole weapon—their sanctified spiritual power—was effective. The difference between the picture arising from a composition such as *Shevet Yehudah*, and the folk traditions (some of which are reflected therein as well) is explicit. Learned Jews regarded the Gentile world in a wholly different light than their less-educated brethren, the mass consumers of the folk traditions.

A similar tendency to play up the extreme differences between Judaism and Christianity against a backdrop of religious ideology—as opposed to social or economic differences—comes to the fore in three prominent anti-Christian legends of medieval Jewish culture: *Toledot Yeshu* ("The Life of Jesus"), "The Legend of Simon Cephas," and "The Legend of the Jewish Pope." The composition known as *Toledot Yeshu* belongs to the early Middle Ages or to Late Antiquity. This relatively long satirical tale describes various stages in the life of Jesus. It targets fundamental Christian dogmas: the immaculate conception; Jesus as the son of God; the crucifixion and resurrection. As this is not a legend, but a satirical work that has already been comprehensively analyzed, we will not treat it here.

The legends of Simon Cephas and the Jewish pope are somewhat similar: both have a narrative-polemic construction; both portray principal figures of Christian history—St. Peter and an important pope—as Jews who abandoned their heritage in favor of Christianity. The narrative pattern according to which covert Jews preside over the Christian religious establishment naturally puts into question Christian faith *in toto*. The protagonists of the tales, who reached the apex of the Christian hierarchy, yet clung to their Judaism and rejected Christianity, constitute—for the tales' audience—overwhelming proof of the latter's falsity. While a similar ideational pattern underlies both legends, they have different narrative constructions and dissimilar goals.[59]

"The Legend of Simon Cephas" recounts that, following the first Christians' harsh persecutions of the Jews, or as a result of the two communities' proximity, which constituted a religious peril, one of the greatest of the sages, Simon Cephas (i.e., Peter, "stone" in Aramaic), went over to Christianity and succeeded Jesus as head of the Church. He legislated with a view toward keeping Christianity and Judaism apart. Later, he demanded that the Christians build him an isolated tower, where he lived on bread and water, studied Torah in secret—and wrote *piyyutim* ("liturgical hymns")—that were later accepted by all Jewish communities.

This legend is an outstanding example of how folk tradition treats theological controversy. The manner and circumstances of Christianity's split from its Jewish foundations, beginning with Paul, were among the predominant topics to occupy the religious leadership of both Christianity and Judaism. But when this question trickled down to the folk tradition, it shed completely its sociological, historical, and theological arguments and took on the principal form of the folk tradition, namely the concrete narrative plot. According to the folk perception reflected in the legend of Simon Cephas, the break between Christianity and Judaism was engineered by a Jew, not, as history held, a Christian. While the initiative appeared to have been taken by a Christian leader (Peter), he was in truth a Jew in disguise. From here it was a short step to denying the claim that Christianity abhorred Judaism on account of its customs. Truth be told, maintains the legend, were it not for the initiative of the Jewish sages in the period of Christianity's inception, contemporary Christians would be leading a Jewish way of life. This historical view is substantiated metaphorically by means of the figure of a martyr, Simon Cephas, who sacrificed that which was most dear to him—his Jewish way of life—for the sake of Judaism. "The Legend of Simon Cephas" is thus a prime example of the manner in which the folk tradition translates a theological theme into the concrete and artistic language of the narrative plot.

"The Legend of the Jewish Pope" is indeed similar in its use of the motif of the Jew at the apex of the Christian hierarchy, but it differs in its sources and aims. Different versions of the tale also attest to different objectives and emphases. The main lines of the story are that the son of R. Simeon the Great of Mainz was kidnapped by a Gentile woman and raised as a Christian. Owing to his marvelous wisdom, he rose to prominence in the Church, ultimately assuming the papacy. Knowing the identity of his father, he summoned R. Simeon to an audience. Upon learning the truth, R. Simeon counseled his son to publicly sanctify the Holy Name. The Jewish pope assembled all the Church leaders, proved that Jesus and his doctrine were false, and leapt from the tower, becoming a martyr before all. According to another version, he wrote a condemnation of Christianity and fled to his father's home in Mainz, where he lived out his days as a Jew.

The tale uses one of the most common folk motifs of medieval Judaism—"the captured child": a Jewish child, kidnapped and raised among the Gentiles, comes to recognize his Judaism and returns to the embrace of his people. The perils of conversion to Christianity, fear of exposing the younger generation to the temptations of the Christian world, and prospects of success and elevated social status among the Christians, especially for the more talented—all these precipitated and spread the motif of "the captured child." Yet the "Legend of the Jewish Pope" grew from fertile ground in the Christian world itself. It turns out that at the start of the twelfth century, various rumors circulated in Rome, among Church circles, that one Peter of the wealthy Pierleoni family, in line to become pope, was in fact a secret Jew. These rumors took wing among political rivals, who backed another papal candidate. And yet Peter was elected pope, taking the name Anacletus II, in the year 1131. There is evidence that a family forebear was in fact a Jewish banker who had converted. The Jewish legend probably grew out of a combination of the folk motif of the captured child and the rumors, which undoubtedly did not escape the hearing of the Jews in Rome, concerning the Jewish origins of one of the popes. One version of the tale constructs it as a novella, in which the hero circumvents his rivals and returns in peace to his family's embrace. The conclusion of another version turns it into a tale of martyrdom, in the spirit of many tales that circulated widely throughout the medieval communities.

The tale makes two main claims through its multiple versions: by virtue of wisdom a Jew can, if he so chooses, rise unimpeded to the apex of the Christian social hierarchy. The Church in the late Middle Ages—the time frame in which the tale was created and spread—took pride in its schools and splendid institutions of higher learning, and in its sophisticated theological and philosophical literature. As such, it rivalled the Jews' claim of superior spiritual assets. On the level of the educated elite, this conflict was manifested in debates and polemics between the most learned of both religions. "The Legend of the Jewish Pope" is an excellent example of the folk reaction to this rivalry: the protagonist, despite his youth and foreign origins, rises to the summit of the Christian hierarchy.

This tale puts forward a second claim, namely that even a Jew who knows Christian theology and life in depth finds them utterly devoid of substance. The implication is that, if one knowledgable enough to rise to the papacy held this view, it is pointless for anyone else to even toy with the notion of conversion, whether willingly or under coercion. The protagonists of both tales, "Simon Cephas" and "The Jewish Pope," advance to the frontlines of the Christian world, yet they differ in motive. Simon Cephas does so deliberately, for the sake of a defined objective—to ground Christianity upon shaky foundations and render it as separate as possible from its Jewish roots. It therefore comes as no surprise when he disavows Christianity. Elhanan the Pope is thrust there by chance, yet even after understanding all in depth, and after meriting the greatest honor Christianity can bestow on earth—he rejects it just the same.

The tale of Simon Cephas is thus a tale of the past. It accounts for Christianity's vast departure from Judaism, despite their common origins. The tale of the Jewish pope is directed to the future. It has an exemplary orientation, suggesting that in the face of Christianity's sweetest promises of material and spiritual gain, one should remember Elhanan the Jew, who reached the pinnacle, yet gave it all up for the sake of Judaism's truth. By means of these narrative models, the folk traditions substantiate the religious and existential tension between Jews and the Christian society with which they had to cope day after day.

[3] The Legend as a Response to Historical Processes

This section focuses primarily on the question of the "truths"—as distinct from the "facts"—that are reflected in historical legend. Separating one from the other requires a complex decoding of narrative patterns, folk motifs, and cultural symbols, and of the manner in which they reflect historical processes. Most historians who analyzed historical legends had preconceptions about the historical process. They already knew of it from existing documents, from the responsa literature, from demographic research, and the like. Analysis of the historical legend neatly "dovetailed" with historical processes already known. Had the historians interpreted the legends without prior knowledge of the historical processes reflected therein, they certainly would not have relied exclusively upon them to reach historical conclusions. In other words, the historical legend, insofar as it serves as a research tool in the hands of historians, is no more than supplementary evidence of historical processes already known.

My point of departure, as an observer of folk traditions, is different. Historical or cultural processes are expressed in two principal ways; one is through the works of learned Jews: responsa, historiography, letters, commentaries, ethical books, liturgical hymns, and the like. The other is by means of the folk consciousness, through which the historical process is reflected in a different manner and with a different meaning. Folk traditions are the vehicle for this consciousness. Therefore, I do not see the historical legends as yet more documents confirming known historical processes. These legends are, in my view, the principal medium through which these processes are viewed by Jewish society at large, and a fundamental expression of this society's intellectual and psychological response to historical events. Of course, for this to hold true, society must absorb the tale and it must become a folk tradition. If an authored tale is found in some source, and is otherwise unknown to us, it should be presumed not to have become a folk tradition, and thus does not reflect what we term "the folk consciousness."

One example of these distinctions is provided by the foundation legends of the central medieval communities of Mainz and Narbonne. According to them, a Christian ruler (Charlemagne) settled Jews there, granted them special rights, and was thus credited with their flourishing into great centers of Jewish life and learning. Forming one branch of these legends are the traditions concerning Kalonymus of Lucca. They recount that Charlemagne brought him from Italy to Mainz, where he established the greatest Torah center on the Rhine. Another branch shifts the locale to the Provence region, and tells how Charlemagne asked the Arab king in Babylonia to send him a wise Jew. The king sent R. Machir to Charlemagne, who settled him in Narbonne, where R. Machir founded the great Torah center. According to a third branch, Jews participated in Charlemagne's crusades in Provence. They assisted him, from within the city, in capturing Narbonne, and he gave them a third of the city. According to another version, Charlemagne lost his mount in the midst of the battle for the city gate. None of his soldiers, save one, dismounted to help the king, for fear of the terrible fray raging all around. The exception was a brave Jewish soldier who leapt from his horse, helped the emperor onto it, and was then himself killed in the battle. The emperor granted the Jews many privileges in recognition of their valiant countryman who had saved Charlemagne's life.

Scholarship has shown that these legends reflect known historical processes: the shift of the Jewish cultural center from Italy to the German lands, the Jews' acquisition of writs conferring upon them special rights from Charlemagne (whether authentic or counterfeit) to preserve their civic status; the flourishing of the great Torah centers in the German lands and Provence as a result of the political and economic rights that they succeeded in acquiring in these locations. Scholars have discerned that these legends reflect known processes of general history as well: the effort to obtain documents (or forgery thereof) establishing a favorable legal position for various groups; or the establishment and success of the Narbonne academy as the parallel Jewish manifestation of the Carolingian renaissance that renewed the classical studies in Europe. In these cases, the legends served to create an outstanding feudal bond of "covenant and trust" between the Jewish communities and their Christian rulers. Thus the Ashkenazic branch of the legends, as represented by Rashi and R. Eleazar of Worms, holds up the Carolingian empire as an ideal, and promotes a return to the "imperial golden age" where all elements of society could live side by side in peace, Jews included.[60]

Another well-known legend, that of "the four captives," was graced with similar historical regard: four Jewish wise men, captured by a Spanish officer, were sold as slaves in north Africa, Italy, and Spain, where they established the great Torah centers of the Middle Ages. The legend reflects, according to this view, an important cultural process of the break between the European Torah centers and the ancient one of Babylonia, and the "cultural transfer" (*translatio scientiae*) that took place. The legend which opens *The Scroll of Ahimaaz*, according to which R. Aaron of Baghdad is exiled (for harnessing the lion to the millstones after it devoured the mule who had hitherto done the labor), similarly reflects a historical process known for some time, namely the phasing out (as far as Southern Italy was concerned) of the former Palestinian sphere of influence in favor of the Babylonian. As we have said, if the historians did not know in advance of the existence of these processes and events, they certainly would not rely on legends as evidence of such.[61]

Let us now look at a particular version of the Kalonymus legend: In the time of the terrible Mainz persecutions, the community leader entrusted his only daughter and all his property to the care of "a burgher." Thus she alone, of all the town's Jews, survived. The Christian entrusted to care for her upheld the father's wishes, and never baptized her. When Charlemagne and his army reached Mainz, R. Kalonymus of Lucca, the great Jewish sage, was part of his retinue. The emperor stayed in the spacious home of this particular townsman. Fearful lest his guests discover his secret, he hid the girl up in the tower, but imperial soldiers happened to catch sight of her. The emperor demanded to know why his host had hidden her. The householder told the story, whereupon Charlemagne gave her to Kalonymus in marriage, as well as all her late father's property. Kalonymus went on to found the great academy of Mainz, becoming the first in a chain of distinguished luminaries to preside over it. This version of the legend reflects the historical processes mentioned earlier, while its crystallized artistic form indicates that more is hidden within.[62]

How did the folk traditions regard these historical processes? Neither the documents, nor the halachic literature, nor the commentaries of the Middle Ages can tell us. The legend translates the historical processes into concrete concepts. In the realm of legend, these are not processes but individuals, the events of whose private lives turn the wheels of history (we might say, symbolize them). Moreover, the new Mainz community did not sprout from barren soil. It was founded on the ashes of the earlier, more ancient community. The historical legend thus emphasizes the continuity of Jewish history: the destruction of one community leads to the flourishing of another in its wake; suffering and anguish precede rebuilding and new growth. R. Kalonymus marries the Jewish maiden, the sole surviving descendent of the ravaged community. The folk legend stresses that nothing new can come where nothing was before, that the success of the new communities derives from their successful creation of a link to what passed before them, in their standing upon the infrastructure built for them by the ancient communities. In this way, death and life are bound together, old with new, ruin with rebuilding, hatred of the Jews with concern for their lives, in a cycling of opposites that reflects medieval Jewish society's self-image. The historical processes may shed light on one aspect or another of these legendary traditions, but of inestimably greater significance is how the traditions illuminate the independent consciousness of Jewish society, for which such meager evidence has survived. The belief that nothing can come of nothing in the building of a culture; that all the pogroms and massacres will cease, to be followed by relative calm and security; that rebuilding follows every destruction, and death always accompanies rebirth; that alongside the rioters and haters are enlightened and sympathetic rulers. These were fundamental convictions of medieval Jewish life, and the historical legend casts light upon them as the *true* processes (in the deeper sense of the notion of "truth") of the Jewish consciousness of the period.

Such an approach is more productive and correct, as it does not relate to the historical legend as a text that reflects processes already known, but as a means of revealing the Jewish folk consciousness. These legends served not only those with access to all medieval modes of communication, but also those broad strata of Jewish society for whom folk traditions were the sole means of expression.

[4] The Historical Legend as an Expression of Internal Tensions

The numerous messianic tales that circulated throughout the medieval Jewish communities provide a good example of the overlap of all four orientations categorized herein. The tales of messiahs that cropped up at different periods of the Middle Ages in Persia, Kurdistan, Iraq, and Europe constitute a kind of collective memory that welds the various communities to a common historical past. They express the tensions between Jews and Gentile regimes as viewed by the folk consciousness. Well-reflected in these messianic legends are the regimes' fear of the awakening of the messianic movements, their exploitation of these movements to harm the Jews, the contacts between representatives of the Jews and the Gentile regime, and the awakening of the messianic movements in periods when the Jews' status and security were threatened. The tales exhibit the known and important historical processes of medieval Jewish history, as well as the known folk mentality that tended to grasp a charismatic figure as an anchor of hope and salvation. But perhaps above all else, the messianic tales are interesting as an expression of the domestic tensions that rocked the communities.

Alongside tales of the better-known messiahs (David Alroy, David Reuveni, Solomon Molcho, and Shabbetai Zevi), are still others concerning dozens of "local" saviors who emerged in various communities, performed their exploits, and vanished some time thereafter. The narrative patterns of these tales are very similar: a charismatic figure appears and performs public miracles. The pious and faithful folk gather around the messiah; the community leaders impugn and campaign against him; the Gentile regime, seeing in the movement an expression of rebellion, joins forces with the community leaders to bring down the messiah and his movement. The end result is trouble for the Jews; the messianic awakening is directly responsible for the community's weakened status.[63] Below is a version of one such short legend:

> One arose in the year four thousand nine hundred and thirty (1170 C.E.) in
> the lands of the east near the Euphrates River, and said that the Messianic
> era had arrived and that he would gather all the dispersed and bring them in
> a short time to the land of our fathers. Then some fools from these lands in-
> nocently followed him, because he showed them, by means of spells, a num-
> ber of signs and wonders, which in the opinion of the fools, was a sign from
> God and evidence of his being the Messiah. And one of the signs was that
> leprosy rose on his body, and the next day he healed himself. And the crowd
> interpreted in their dreams that this was the leprosy of Moses before the re-
> demption from Egypt, a sign of his being the Messiah. [This continued] un-
> til the wise men of the generation had no power left to prevent them. And
> after he saw that his advice was not carried out and the wise men of the gen-
> eration opposed him, he fled unrecognized to whence he came and where he
> is. (Some say that the wise men of the generation outlawed him and killed
> him secretly.) And following this there continued several foul troubles in the
> lands of the east to Jews until, as a result of so many troubles, more than ten

thousand souls in the area surrounding this Euphrates River converted.
(*Sefer Me'oraot Zvi*, p. 26b)

The harsh style used by the storyteller of this text lays bare his negative attitude toward the event, which stems, apparently, from his opposition to Shabbetai Zevi and the messianic movement he led. But beneath his words we can discern the apprehensions underlying the tale: the messiah promises "that the Messianic era [has] arrived and that he [will] gather all the dispersed and bring them in a short time to the land of our fathers." This promise was absorbed because it fell upon fertile ground—that of a society in dire peril and desperate for a glimmer of hope. The masses did not necessarily flock to him because of the miracles he performed, as it were, but because he promised that for which the community had so long yearned. The tension between the community's objective situation and the messiah's guarantees is merely the first in an array of strained relationships beneath the surface of the tale.

Likewise, this tale emphasizes the tension between "some fools from these lands . . . followed him . . . the crowd" and "the wise men of the generation [who] opposed him." All the messianic tales report the clashing of these sectors of the community. Messianic awakenings undermined the community institutions and internal hierarchy that had been diligently built up over the course of many years. The savior usurped authority from the traditional community leaders. His movement jeopardized the delicate balance between the community and the Gentile regime, also achieved only after long years of effort and sacrifice. There were, furthermore, ideational and theological arguments for opposing any messianic awakening that failed to unfold precisely as promised by the sages of old. In any case, the emerging polarization between the established leadership of the community and "the folk" is more salient in the messianic legend than in any other folk tradition. Feeding this tension was the question of immediate goals for those living in the diaspora: should they continue to maintain and even reinforce the existing structures, or should they aspire to fundamentally alter the situation? The community can be somewhat crudely divided in two: at one pole were those who were not prepared to give up what they had; at the other were those who had nothing to lose.

The aftermath only increases the strain upon the community: "And following this there continued several foul troubles in the lands of the east to Jews until, as a result of so many troubles, more than ten thousand souls in the area surrounding this Euphrates River converted." Or in other messianic tales: "But in any case [the king] said that he wanted to extract revenge against the Jews who followed [the messiah] and asked of all the communities that they hand over to him all those who had followed that accursed one . . . then the King ordered them seized, and from their prison they assessed their means and compromised with the king with a vast sum of money" (*Shevet Yehudah*, p. 76); "[the king] commanded and all the [community] heads were confined in a strong prison. And, in their distress, they were made to give the sum. And many of them sold their sons to meet the sum. And after giving him what he asked, he said that in return for his offense, they too would suffer offense, in that the Jews would walk barefoot, their pants no longer than their thighs" (*Shevet Yehudah*, p. 78), and many others in similar versions. The consequences of messianic awakenings are persecutions and mass conversions, harsh decrees, loss of life and property, humiliation, and abrogation of privileges. It should be noted that most of the messianic legends were documented in compositions whose compilers forcefully opposed the phenomenon, and who belonged to society's elite. We have no way of knowing how messianic legends were told in other circles. In any case, the internal social tension of the messianic tales also comes through in the styling of their conclusions. Description of the disastrous consequences of such awakenings is meant to fill a clear social role, namely, the prevention of further such revivals. Yet they emerged again and again, in spite of their opponents' efforts to inculcate negating legends into collective memory. This indicates that the tensions did not diminish, but cropped up anew in each period. In other words, the messianic legends of past events were not intended merely to describe historical events; rather, they were a response to the domestic tensions that strained the narrating society.

Of particular note in the messianic legends is the argument that the catastrophes to befall the communities did not stem from the Gentiles' initiative. Instead they were caused by the Jews themselves, who put their faith in false messiahs, following them despite the warnings of spiritual leaders. Indeed, this predisposition for self-recrimination is also rampant in historical legends on other themes, and occasionally reaches an extreme. One legend, for example, tells of a wealthy widow in Mainz who complained that, "they made her pay more than the appropriate taxes" (A. David, *Shai le-Heiman*, p. 79). She was in the habit of approaching the holy ark daily, burying her head within and crying to the Almighty. Her tears and complaints caused the Almighty to bring on the massacres of 1096. It is not clear here whether the Almighty's wrath was kindled by the community's overtaxing of the widow, or by the well-heeled woman's taxing of God's patience. In either case, controversies and injustices within the Jewish community are, according to the tale, the direct causes for one of the most terrible calamities to befall medieval Jewry.

The legend is similar in its literary construction and orientation to the legends of the destruction of the Temple, familiar from the rabbinic age. There, too, the destruction was regarded as the result of the fraternal hatred, envy, and disputes that rent Jerusalem. A thorny theological question was clearly the motivation for legends of this type: How could Divine Providence allow His chosen people to suffer such grievous harm at the hand of the Gentiles? These

legends, constructed according to the traditional pattern of reward and punishment, put forward the supposition that the Almighty was Himself the cause
of the dreadful events—just as He is the just and true cause of everything. Second, they imbue the historical events with clearly understandable significance.
Medieval Jewry, not being in a position to apprehend the motivation behind
the Crusades, the social and political forces that spurred them, or the social
makeup of the crusaders that was an important factor in their assaults against
the Jews, expresses its own interpretation of the events via the historical legend.
It sees them as an outgrowth of events that took place within Jewish society so
that the crusaders, for example, are but a tool with which the God of Israel does
his work. Third, the moral lesson: the historical legends seek to edify and guide
by means of uncovering the past. Thus the sense takes shape within the community that these events were not for naught. Indeed, the lesson that the load
upon the various classes within the community must be fairly and properly
distributed, that the community must guard against internal jealousy, causeless
enmity, and strife, is a lesson that many historical legends on the theme of the
destruction of communities tried to transmit.

Another tradition recounts that the community of Worms suffered harsher
decrees than other Jewish communities. The reason proffered hearkens back
to the return to Zion that followed the destruction of the first Temple. Their
brethren in Palestine sent letters inviting them to return from the diaspora—
but they refused, as they had already begun to establish themselves in Worms,
to acquire property, and to gain the respect of the Gentiles. Parallel traditions
told of similar events in Yemen, Persia, and Spain. According to them, Ezra the
Scribe dispatched letters to the Jews in exile, in which he gave them the news
of the return to Zion, and summoned them to return. Jews of these communities, knowing that true redemption had not yet arrived, did not answer the call,
and remain in their exile still.

These traditions also reflect the communities' typical internal divisions.
Various periods within the Middle Ages saw immigration movements to
Palestine. The reasons were varied—messianic yearnings, religious awakening,
the desire to be buried in the holy land, the existential peril of a given community, and so on. It is known that within the communities, controversies arose
in connection with this activity. Some regarded it in a positive light—as an act
likely to hasten the redemption and as a renunciation of the fleshpots of the
diaspora. Others considered anticipation of the Messiah to be premature and
liable to weaken the communities. The various versions of the narrative traditions well reflect these divisions. On the one hand, there is the argument that
the diaspora, with all its travail, is the consequence of the Jews' own hesitation
in answering the summons to Palestine. Beyond these versions lies the understanding that it is still not too late, and that the solution to the troubles of
the diaspora is, after all, immigration to the Land of Israel. Juxtaposing these

claims are other versions that justify remaining in the diaspora and patiently awaiting the true redemption. After all, the history of the Second Temple proved that the call of Ezra the Scribe—and all the subsequent summons to Zion that he symbolized—were fundamentally in error. These folk traditions clearly reflect such divisions that, openly or covertly, arose in the medieval Jewish communities.[64]

The legends were also intended to strengthen medieval Jewry's social structures, to entrench the position of the leadership classes and leading families, and to broaden the influence of the important Torah centers. It was generally the interested parties who "mobilized" these legends, disseminating them for the purpose of furthering their interests. Two such important traditions have already been mentioned: "The Legend of the Four Captives," intended to indicate not only the break between the academies of Babylonia and the new Torah centers around the Mediterranean, but also, and primarily, to establish the latter's position. The traditions emphasize that the Torah greats who settled in Kairouan, in North Africa, in Fustat, Egypt, and in Cordoba, Spain, established in those places important academies that drew their authority from the personages who founded them. When "The Legend of the Four Captives" circulated, from the eleventh century on, these Torah centers were already well-known and established. Yet there existed considerable tension between the various Torah centers, primarily between the new ones and the ancient Babylonian academies. Maimonides, for example, claimed emphatically that the rabbis of Spain were Torah scholars of extraordinary brilliance in and of themselves, and did not require sanction from Babylonia for their authority. Indeed, the traditions of the "Four Captives" grew against the background of the struggles for authority between the various Torah centers. They were spread by factors within or around the academies who were interested in establishing or broadening their authority. This is a well-known, and entrenched, utilization of folktales for political and social ends. It proves that even the learned elite employed them as needed, and as it saw fit.

The second example mentioned above is "The Legend of Charlemagne." These legends surrounding R. Kalonymus's move from Italy to Mainz and the establishment of the Rhine's Jewish communities, or the bestowal of feudal rights to the Narbonne community, are not mere descriptions of historical or demographic processes. They are distinctly functional, designed to strengthen the communal structures within Jewish society. Credit for obtaining special privileges and for maintaining close personal or communal relations with the Gentile regime was always an important factor in determining authority in Jewish society. The communities founded by Charlemagne, or those that obtained writs of privilege with the seal of his administration, were considered by the communities themselves, and perhaps also by others, as more established, stable, and secure. Charlemagne was considered the founder of western

Europe's political and cultural hierarchies for the duration of the Middle Ages. The social and administrative orders he put in place achieved a nearly sacred status, and were rigorously maintained. Therefore, communities that could claim to constitute part of these orders had a distinct advantage vis-à-vis other communities. Indeed, the Jewish traditions about Charlemagne and the Jews of Mainz and Narbonne were intended above all for internal ends: to reinforce the communities' infrastructures and institutions and give them advantages and primacy over rival communities.

Another type of legend spotlights another manner of establishing close ties to the gentile regime. "The Legend of Bustanai," about the Babylonian exilarch, is one of the most widespread of these. According to it, the Babylonian king decreed that all descendants of the Davidic dynasty be killed. By chance, a woman just married to a scion of the family, and carrying his child, escaped. The king dreamt he was hewing down trees in a fruit grove (*bustan*) when a rubicund old man appeared and struck him with mortal blows. An elderly Jew was brought to the king from prison to interpret the dream. The grove, he said, represented the descendants of David, and the old man who appeared therein was King David himself, seeking to punish the man who harmed his issue. The king, endeavoring to rectify his actions, cared for the pregnant woman and raised the child she bore, who now carried the name Bustanai, in remembrance of the grove in the dream. The child grew up to display such wisdom and capability to rule that the king appointed him and his offspring patriarchs over Jews throughout his realm.

The social function of this tale is obvious. It confers double legitimacy upon the dynasty of the Babylonian exilarch: first, as descended from the house of David, such that Divine Providence itself bestowed upon its members the authority to rule. The emphasis on the personal closeness between the local Jewish leader and the gentile ruler is another way to confer authority. These two legitimations are clearly manifested in the construction of the tale. It opens with decrees against the house of David; in this way emphasizing that belonging to a royal house involves more than extra privileges and benefits—leaders also bear the brunt of suffering.

The second part of the tale details the origins of Bustanai's special connection to the king. Therein appears the famous motif of the fly: the insect stings the young Bustanai, drawing blood. Bustanai, standing before the king, lifts nary a finger to swat the pest away. In response to the king's question, he replies, "This tradition we inherited from our fathers . . . in palaces of a king one does not speak, or laugh, or raise a hand before them." At this juncture, the king apprehends the Jewish youth's nobility of character and begins to advance his career. The fly thus became the symbol of the Babylonian exilarchs. This episode—and the symbol of the fly that it engendered, as it were—is the symbolic expression of the closeness between the Gentile regime and the Jewish leaders. It contains a mixture of submission and humbleness of spirit (as expressed in the tale's fly episode), with independence and authoritativeness stemming from the personal relationship with the ruler. The order of events made prominent in the plot also indicates a hierarchy of importance. First there is the Davidic lineage: from here stems the true authority, based on the tradition that determines the Jewish community's internal hierarchy. After this comes the source of authority emanating from proximity to the foreign regime, from the manipulative ability of the Jewish leader to function in the royal court for the benefit of himself and the community he represents. This is, without a doubt, the classic model of the court tale fashioned, as we have seen above, by Mordechai's deeds as chronicled in the Scroll of Esther.[65]

"The Legend of Bustanai" alludes to another connection between the community and the Gentile regime—that precipitated by a representative of the Jews who does a favor for or rescues the ruler, preparing the ground for a personal relationship. In this case, it was the old man who interpreted the king's nightmare, and in so doing saved his life. One version of the aforementioned "Legend of Charlemagne" recounts how, in the battle for the conquest of Narbonne, he fell from his horse at the city gate. Of all his soldiers only one, a Jew, dismounted to reseat the king. By this action, he saved the king's life, at the cost of his own. According to this legend, the emperor granted privileges to Narbonne's Jewish community on account of this sacrifice. Another legendary tradition emphasizing the same motif is that of Shephatiah, who exorcised a demon from the Byzantine emperor's daughter. The legend first appears in the mid-eleventh century in *The Scroll of Ahimaaz*, and spread thereafter in a number of versions. The Byzantine emperor Basil I (ninth century C.E.) had decreed mandatory conversion of all the Jews of his realm. He sends messengers to R. Shephatiah, leader of the community of Oria, situated in southern Italy's Apulia region. Upon his arrival at the court in Constantinople, he prevails over the emperor in a religious dispute. The emperor appeals to him to cure his daughter, who is possessed by a demon. Shephatiah uses the holy names he knows, and after an argument with the demon, imprisons him in a bottle, which he then tosses into the sea. The princess quietly returns to her parents and the grateful king exempts Oria's Jews from the decree.

This tale was set down in writing in the mid-eleventh century by a descendant of R. Shephatiah. This was, in all probability, a family or community tradition passed on orally for generations. According to this tradition, a personal favor done by a patriarch of the Ahimaaz family for the Byzantine emperor saved the communities of southern Italy from ruin. Here too, the innocent tale should not be viewed at mere face value. Ahimaaz, the author of the scroll, hints several times in its course that he has authored it despite the opposition of adversaries. It is difficult today to know precisely which rivalries Ahimaaz was alluding to, but it is clear to us that he wrote the *Scroll of Ahimaaz* as a response to some controversy within the Jewish communities of southern Italy. He regarded the tale of his family's history as a means of reinforcing its position, perhaps to abolish the divisions and rivalries then rife in the community. The claim that emerges from the tale (as from other tales in the scroll), is that an ancestor of the Ahimaaz family was responsible for the forging of ties between the community and the Byzantine regime. Furthermore, according to the tale, it was the Ahimaaz family who struggled for hundreds of years to protect Jewish privileges in the area. This is unquestionably a tendentious claim, motivated by self-interest. In any case, what is significant for our purposes is that this claim is substantiated via the traditional narrative pattern of "exorcising the demon." Tales of demonic possession, deliverance from demons and dybbuks (evil spirits), were accorded many roles in medieval European society, as we shall see below. Here, in the legend of Shephatiah and the Byzantine emperor, the social-political aspect of these tales is revealed.[66]

In our endeavor to understand the ways in which legends reflect historical events, we are prone to forget that the legends were told by and for people. Medieval Jews were not mere historical "factors." First and foremost, they were individuals with commonplace concerns, who needed spiritual reinforcement and support no less than any individual in any age. Our tendency to ignore the motives born of these anxieties causes us to miss an important level of meaning in these legends. Indeed, when we dealt earlier with the legends of blood libels whose resolution was supernatural, we saw in them primarily a narrative pattern representing the approach of the broad social strata to the Gentile world, an approach at odds with that of the educated elite. Likewise when we discussed the tales of the rescue of communities in dire peril. The blood libels, the edicts decreed against the communities for various and sundry reasons that were not at all understood by the individual Jews of the period, represent the harsh anxieties with which they had to deal daily. The spheres of earning a living and economics, preservation of the Jewish identity, the maintenance of the family and community structures, and the fear for their very lives, were a part of daily life—even in periods of relative security and calm. The historical legends that conclude with a miraculous release express above all the basic human need to lower the threshold of anxiety by confronting it again and again (inducing a psychological reaction similar to catharsis), using the tales to take the anxieties to extremes. The miraculous ending affords the narrating society some security—illusory as it may be—that such salvation, having already taken place, may repeat itself in the present. This is the raison d'être for such "therapy" in historical legend. For the stories to successfully lower the threshold of the listeners' anxiety, they must be credible. The historical legend, of all the other genres of folk narrative, is in fact constructed for this purpose.

When savage riots erupted in the city of Halle (Germany), at the urging of King Dagobert (seventh century), members of the community fled the city, led by "our rabbi Benjamin of Halle of blessed and saintly memory" (eleventh century). The rioters, hearing of their escape, pursued them with murderous intent. A miracle occurred, whereby the mob mistook the Jews for a flock of sheep—and passed them by. Another legend tells that in the time of the Black Plague, residents of the city of Mainz were preparing for a pogrom against the Jews. Between the graves of R. Eleazar of Worms (!) and R. Meir Shatz, an enormous pillar of stone grew, extending over the city. It startled the Christians, who understood it to be a warning not to harm the Jews, and they retreated. Part of the stone pillar can still be seen in the Mainz cemetery.

The "facts" that serve in both legends are not only factually baseless, they contradict each other. King Dagobert and R. Benjamin of Halle did not live in the same period, and R. Eleazar of Worms was not buried in Mainz. But it was not these "facts" that imbued the legend with truth. The celebrated sacred figures that function therein, the famous communities in which the events took place, and the lasting proofs (a city atop a mountain, a pillar in the cemetery) create the legends' verisimilitude. Yet the paramount significance of these legends lies in their function, which is to show that Jews may stand in awe only of Divine Providence (in the first tale) or of sacred figures (in the second). I do not argue that the legends of this type—which are among the most common in Jewish folk literature—were created as a means of psychological support by storytellers with this objective in mind. If it can be said of any tales at all that they are an unconscious "creation of society," then these legends number among the most outstanding such examples. The fears, secret desires, and illusions in men's hearts created these legends, and the legends, for their part, are the main vehicle of these intangibles' overt and externalized expression.

Tales offering one of two responses to confrontation with the Gentiles have been presented up to this point: Solomon ibn Verga represents the solution achieved by wisdom, via logic, in the spirit of the enlightened debate; the folk strata preferred a miraculous resolution, in the spirit of the ancient traditions. But the historical legend of the Middle Ages offers yet a third, if extraordinary, solution:

> In one of the cities of Ashkenaz, the Christians rose up and assembled the Jews, and told them if they accepted the faith of Jesus within three days— well and good, and if not—they should know for certain that all would die by the sword, there was no escape. The Jews gathered, and in sackcloth and ashes and fasting cried out to the Almighty. And after the three [days], as they saw that heaven did not reply, they all agreed to die. The young men among them said: We will seek vengeance for our anguish and then we shall die to sanctify the great Name. And in the morning, as all the Gentiles and their judges gathered to wait for the Jews to arrive and convert to Christianity, each of them to take one to his home to teach him their faith and

dogma, the young Jewish men arose, their swords beneath their garments, and walked to the opening of the place of assembly, and left no survivors of the Christians. And before coming they instructed their wives to light a fire in four places in the city. No one put out the blaze, as all were at the place of assembly, thus the entire town burned, the Jews within. I heard this from the mouth of a great sage of Ashkenaz who came as emissary. (*Shevet Yehudah*, "The Thirty-Fourth Persecution," Shohat edition p. 91)

If the tales we examined earlier fed the illusion that salvation came of miracles or wisdom, this tradition reflects the end of the illusion, and in particular, the process of awakening from it. The change is formulated here in a single line: "The Jews gathered, and in sackcloth and ashes and fasting cried out to the Almighty. And after the three [days], *as they saw that heaven did not reply*, they all agreed to die. *The young men among them said: We will seek vengeance for our anguish. . . .* " The first part of the sentence expresses the traditional approach of the Middle Ages: pray for a miracle and Divine intervention. When the miracle did not arrive, they faced martyrs' deaths. These two stages express the dominant Jewish outlook throughout the Middle Ages. Yet this tradition testifies to the existence of revolutionary elements within the community ("the young men"), who rejected both illusion and the martyr's death alike, and adopted a new approach, of active struggle. The notion of responding with force to religious persecution was not entirely unheard of; some earlier medieval Jewish thinkers and leaders had toyed with it. But in the narrative tradition, the various approaches come together here, in a remarkably developed sequence: despairing of the time-honored passive and martyric paths, the protagonists take up arms. For our purposes it matters not whether the event actually took place, and if so what its "factual" nature was. It is enough for us that the medieval narrative traditions accepted or passed it on from one generation to the next. In other words, "the fighting solution" for Jewish existence in this period was accepted by society, alongside the others. It was not, of course, as common as the miraculous and the martyrological, yet it bore the seeds of the consciousness that began to grow in the next period of Jewish history.[67]

[F] The Saint's Legend

Historical and biographical legend are two offshoots of a single branch of folk literature: both deal with familiar historical periods and feature historical celebrities. The striking differences are of emphasis and social function. The plot of the biographical legend revolves around the life events, character traits, and social status of the central figure. Surrounding historical events, and their ramifications, are secondary for this category. Its function is to paint a vivid picture of the figure, using a palette of its deeds. These tales flesh out historical figures familiar to society only in the abstract. Formerly known by name, and famed for their historical contribution or for the compositions they penned, they come to life as real people operating in a well-defined reality. Every biographical legend adds another piece to the mosaic of society's image of the man. As we shall see below, the legend as a component in the biography of a public figure is only one aspect, and not always the most important one, of the various functions that it serves in society. In any case, this difference— the focus on the image of the hero—is the touchstone by which we distinguish between biographical and historical legend, even though it is not possible for all legends, and historical and biographical elements are not always clearly distinguishable.

A principal question for those dealing with biographical legend is that of historical reliability. Here, too, as with the historical legend, the question is not presented correctly. Most legends offer the sole extant biographical details concerning leaders and sages. Apart from the works of these men, hardly any substantial information survived regarding their lives and deeds. The legends were included in works written dozens, if not hundreds of years after their subjects died. At times, the protagonist of legend acts in ways diametrically opposed to the historical figure's thinking as preserved in his own writing. In this regard it should suffice to mention the legends that describe Maimonides dabbling in Kabbalah, specifically its practical aspects, namely, sorcery and demonology. Nothing could be farther removed from the character and world of Maimonides. These legends can in no way be construed as "factually" accurate. Indeed, scholars of the *Wissenschaft des Judentums*, as early as the nineteenth century, railed against the legends and any suggestion of using them as a biographical source for preeminent Jewish historical figures. Leopold Zunz disdained the numerous legends about Rashi that circulated in Jewish society:

> . . . Yet another culture arose of rogues and liars, who deceitfully fabricated [yarns of] amazing things and wonders to embellish that saint [Rashi]. Such things never happened, but folk who would listen to falsehood, who are not intelligent enough to discriminate, will believe anything. One will make of him a worker of great miracles before Duke Godfrey, and another will rouse him from the sleep of the dead, and wake him from eternal rest to fraternize with the living or speak in a vision to a man of his choosing. One will have him wandering at length in various lands to disseminate his booklets in the synagogues and study houses. Another will make of him a scoundrel and schemer of schemes who speaks not in his customary, distinguished manner, but in allusions and riddles, saying, for example, that only a person of eminence, a hundred years old, will clarify and interpret the writings of the Holy One . . . Some will raise his bones from France and dig them a grave in Prague, and some will have him consort with occultists and obscuran-

tists . . . and the compiler of *Shalshelet ha-Kabbalah* has him descending to
Egypt to enjoy Maimonides's company, though the latter was born several
years after [Rashi's] death. Ultimately, all that they say is nonsense and utterly devoid of content; [only] those who crave miracles and believe in amaz-
ing things will look to them. (*Toldot Rashi*, p. 44b)

Attempts to draw any sort of factual conclusions from the legends on the assumption that they held "a kernel of truth" were indeed ludicrous from the
start. That is not to say, however, that they are devoid of historical truths.
While we cannot know whether these legends reflect in some manner the heroes' biographies, we can be certain that they reflect the manner in which the
narrating society sought to perceive these historical figures. The 'folk' invested
in them its anxieties, hidden desires, and worldview. Thus the legends echo important historical truths, if not biographical facts. Reading the medieval biographical legends with this in mind, the disappointment of biographers and
historians gives way to the excitement of discovery. These tales provide unbiased evidence of medieval Jewish society's communal mentality. Further examination of the tales sheds light on how they functioned within that society.[68]

The biographical legends are extant in diverse sources: legal (halachic) and
ethical treatises, commentaries on prayers, and compilations of tales, letters,
and historiographical works. A typical example of the nature of the sources
is the sixteenth-century historiographical composition entitled *Shalshelet ha-
Kabbalah* ("The Chain of Tradition"), by Gedaliah ibn Yahya. This work, which
was derided as *Shalshelet ha-Shekarim* ("The Chain of Lies") on account of the
legendary quality of its material, is perhaps the most important source of medieval Jewish hagiography. Herein Gedaliah ibn Yahya compiled the folk traditions surrounding Rashi, Maimonides, R. Abraham ibn Ezra, R. Yehiel of Paris,
Nahmanides, and many more. Also invaluable is that he generally cites the
sources of his information: "*Some say* that when Maimonides heard so many
words of provocation and contempt" (p. 19b); "*I saw written* in an old booklet (*kuntres*), which said that in the year 4968 (1208 C.E.) Maimonides fled . . . *I
heard it* in another manner . . . " (p. 20a); "[Even] if I could, my son, recount to
you all the awe-inspiring deeds *that I have seen in writing and that I have received
in person* from this rabbi, time would run out before I ran out [of deeds to re-
count]" (p. 20b); "*I received [it] from an old man*, and he told me that he saw this
deed written in an old booklet . . . " (p. 21b); "And more that *I received in person* from the elders and sages of the generation" (p. 22b); "*from the elders of the
generation* and especially in Tessalonica when I was there in the year 5328 (1568
C.E.) [I heard] that when Rashi went . . . " (ibid.); "*I received* from the students
of R. Meir of Padua that when Rashi was an exile . . . " (ibid.); "*before me testified* Jewish merchants from Mantua who were on their way to the imperial
court . . . " (ibid.); "*I saw it written* that there was one officer in France called

Gote Frido (Godfrey) . . . " (p. 23a); "*I also saw written* in a booklet that when Nahmanides was in Barcelona on the seashore . . . " (p. 26a); "*I saw in a booklet* that this saint [R. Yehiel of Paris] was also sage in Kabbalah . . . and similarly, *I heard* that it befell Maimonides and others . . . and I could not copy many other fine things that were in this booklet because the sage who showed it to me did not want [me to]" (p. 28a).[69]

Gedaliah ibn Yahya's saints' legends thus originated in oral traditions that he had heard from "reliable persons," or seen in "booklets" that included various sorts of materials. Several times in the course of his composition, Ibn Yahya testifies that he came upon different versions of the legends, in both oral and written form. From this testimony it becomes apparent that in the first half of the sixteenth century, at the latest, hundreds of biographical legends about medieval Jewry's famous figures were commonplace in the oral and written traditions. The traditions must have existed for generations in order to exist in multiple versions, to spread through the various communities, and reach the degree of narrative development displayed in *Shalshelet ha-Kabbalah*.

Also noteworthy is that R. Gedaliah himself—a member of the community's social elite—accepts the traditions as biographical facts: as a man of the Middle Ages he adopts his sources, both oral and written, at face value; he is ready to include the information therein as authentic episodes in the biographies of national figures. If Gedaliah ibn Yahya and the sages from whom he received the tales related to them thus, then the broader strata of society assuredly did no less. As generations of storytellers told and retold the legends over the course of scores and hundreds of years, and as the communities accepted them as part of their historical and cultural consciousness, they should be seen as an unerring expression of medieval Jewish society's views, hopes, and fears.[70]

Some see Jewish hagiography as beginning with R. Gedaliah ibn Yahya's composition of *Shalshelet ha-Kabbalah* in the early sixteenth century, and the creation of the other important hagiographical cycles, on R. Samuel and R. Judah the Pious, and R. Isaac Luria (the 'Ari of Safed). From the perspective of folklore, however, compilation and writing are the concluding stage of prior development and crystallization of the legends of the saints. The legends almost certainly evolved over the course of the Middle Ages, and only toward their close did compilers such as Gedaliah ibn Yahya surface to gather and set them down in writing. Hagiographical groupings undoubtedly existed before *Shalshelet ha-Kabbalah*. Gedaliah testifies that he copied some traditions about Maimonides, Rabbi Abraham ibn Ezra, R. Yehiel of Paris, Nahmanides, and others, from "old booklets." Gedaliah ibn Yahya, like those who penned the "booklets" before him, drew most of his tales from the oral traditions that developed over time.

Below we will treat these traditions as independent folktales that testify to the central place held by biographical legends in medieval Jewish folk culture.

As for the legends' coverage of the protagonist's life span, they do not differ from other biographical story cycles. It is not too great a leap to suggest that legends of the sages in the Talmud and in the Midrash were the primary source of inspiration for the biographical legends of medieval personalities. The famous legends surrounding Hillel the elder and Rabbi Akiva, Nahum of Gamzu and Hanina ben Dosa, were the templates for the legends of medieval Jews.

The Vitae of the period's Christian culture offer an interesting parallel. Since the dawn of Christianity, and particularly since the end of Late Antiquity, a body of oral and written hagiographical literature of enormous scope and importance developed. It is difficult to imagine that medieval Jews in Europe and in the Byzantine Empire were beyond this development's circle of influence. They no doubt witnessed the great adoration of saints that manifested in the rites and tales of saints, in pilgrimages to their burial sites, and in the collection of reliquia and worship thereof, and they certainly did not view their own holy men as less deserving of veneration and immortality.

Nonetheless, it seems that the immediate impulse to create biographical legends was internal. Prima facie evidence to this effect is the lack of saints' rites among Jews in the medieval period. Although they witnessed vast throngs of their Christian neighbors flocking to the burial sites of saints that were scattered throughout Europe, medieval Jews did not devise parallel rites and pilgrimages. We have no evidence of organized expeditions to the graves of Rashi, R. Samuel, or Judah the Pious (although Jews assuredly visited the graves of renowned Jewish figures). I have not mentioned Maimonides here, as pilgrimage to his grave is part of a different phenomenon—one that was perhaps influenced by Christian culture—namely, pilgrimages to holy graves in Palestine, a practice that should in no way be considered exclusive to the Middle Ages. This is the traditional Jewish framework for pilgrimage—to holy places, graves of the patriarchs, the prophets, the *tannaim*, and the *amoraim*—a practice that began, as we saw in an earlier chapter, in the time of the Second Temple. In the medieval traditions, there was a tendency to "move" graves (R. Judah ha-Levi, Maimonides) to Palestine and then visit these sites (generally fictive) in the framework of pilgrimage to other graves.[71]

The narrative structure of medieval biographical legends provides further proof that their formation and function were driven from within the bounds of Jewish culture. They can be divided into four categories, corresponding to four stages in the life of the saint: birth, maturation, adulthood, and death. From this perspective, there is perhaps no fundamental difference between them and Christian hagiographical tales. However, the narrative quality and significance of each of these stages sets the Jewish tales apart from their Christian counterparts. In the legend of the birth of Maimonides, it is told that Maimon, his father, had not wanted to take a wife at all. In a dream, he was commanded to marry the daughter of a butcher from another town. He ignored the message, though the vision returned repeatedly. Eventually he married this woman, who died giving birth to Maimonides. Maimon later remarried and fathered more children, who scornfully nicknamed their step-brother "son of the butcher." The birth legend of R. Judah the Pious includes an unusual act of his father, R. Samuel: He had made improper use of the Holy Name—specifically, to load sacks of flour onto a lion so that they would not get soaked in the rain—and his father's punishment was that he would father no sons. But R. Samuel's departure into lengthy exile mitigated this sentence, hence, when his exile was over, R. Judah the Pious was born. Perhaps the most famous birth legend is that of Rashi. His father possessed a rare pearl of great value. Christians, wanting it to adorn their church, offered him a large sum. Rashi's father could not refuse the Christian ruler's demand, but on his way to the bishop he cast the pearl into the river—by accident, as it were—and thus merited the son "who enlightened the world with his wisdom, like a pearl."

These birth legends attest to the link between medieval traditions and the birth legends of the Patriarchs in the Bible, and of various figures in rabbinic aggadah. The birth of the saint is bound up with an exceptional act of the father; it is determined and proclaimed by no less a figure than Divine Providence—and generally a consequence of the father's action. Jewish legend does not depict sainthood as the result of a personal resolve, as in Christian hagiography (wherein the saint decides to abandon his forebears' path of idol worship and cling to Jesus), but as stemming from his forebears' meritorious conduct, and as preordained. Thus the Jewish biographical legend portrays the saint's life as a continuation and development of his father's actions, and the very fact of his life as decreed by heaven. As Providence itself orchestrated his birth, his teaching—the contribution he made to Jewish culture—must stem from that same Divine authority. Hence both the religious power of the teaching and its social influence.[72]

Jewish legend contrasts most sharply against the background of the Christian saints' legends at the saint's maturation stage. It is at this point that the protagonist begins to study Torah. R. Judah the Pious, as a child, is an utter savage. While his two older brothers study with their father and the other students in the study hall, he wanders about with bow and arrow, shooting at passers-by (*Mayse-Bukh*, #166). His father resolves, under pressure from his students, to persuade him to assume the burden of the Torah. He quickly discovers that his son's talent is so vast that it could only have come from the Almighty. Maimonides too, who was mocked as the "son of the butcher," "was very slow of understanding" (*Shalshelet ha-Kabbalah*, p. 21b), and had no desire whatsoever to study. His father would beat him, until one day he ran away from home and fell asleep, still weeping, in the synagogue. He awoke a new man, and went to study Torah with Joseph ibn Migash. Years later he returned to his home town, where he delivered a marvelous sermon, and his father and brothers received him with great honor. According to another version of the legend (J. Berger, *Ha-Rambam*, p. 220), his father locked him in a room with nothing to eat or drink. An august old man (Elijah the Prophet) appeared before him, and offered him a vessel with water. After drinking from it he saw the light, and began his lifelong study of the Torah. Interesting in several respects is another version of the same legend, also told by Gedaliah ibn Yahya in *Shalshelet ha-Kabbalah* (p. 28b):

> R. Menahem de-Recanati, who wrote a kabbalistic commentary on the Torah and a book of law. I [learned] from my teacher, Rabbi Jacob de-Recanati, who was a descendent of his, that it had been passed down in his family that this great scholar (*ha-gaon*) loved the Torah, but in fact was quite thick-witted. He would often fast, and pray that Heaven would expand his intelligence and his heart so that he could fathom the Torah. Once when he was praying and fasting in the synagogue, he fell asleep, and there was a man, and in his hand a vessel filled with water. He woke him and said to him: "Drink." He rose and drank and did not finish all the water, and suddenly the man left him. He then went to the study hall, as was his custom, and found that his mind was clear. He realized that he had been transformed into another man. Then he wrote the commentary on the Torah and a treatise on *Ta'amei ha-Mitzvot*.

This tradition attests to the manner in which biographical legends were transmitted and preserved: From father to son, this tale was handed down from generation to generation as a family tradition. A scion of the family, when teaching one of the works of his forebear, the protagonist, takes it beyond the bounds of the family circle to the broader society. This tradition, along with dozens more like it, takes its final, written form in the historiographical composition of Ibn Yahya—a student who heard it from a teacher/descendant of the protagonist, and turned it into a non-exclusive Jewish tradition.

As we have seen in the biographical legends of the sages, the protagonist's life *of consequence* begins only with his first steps on the path of Torah study. Until this stage, he was "good for nothing," that is to say, from the perspective of Jewish culture, non-existent. This need, typical of Jewish legend, to portray the hero as one not *born* with scholarly talent, but who instead *acquired* it at a later stage of his life, deserves special attention. Despite the structural similarity of medieval and rabbinic legends, we can pinpoint a fundamental difference between them: Hillel the Elder, Rabbi Akiva, Eliezer ben Hyrcanus, and others begin to study Torah, at an advanced age, of their own accord. They resolve to overcome social limitations and advanced age out of personal conviction in their path. The decision to study Torah is theirs alone (except, perhaps, in the famous version of the Rabbi Akiva legend wherein his wife pushes him to do so), and they press forward despite vigorous opposition from the surrounding society. By contrast, no less than Divine Providence inspires the medieval protagonists—Maimonides, R. Judah the Pious, R. Menahem Recanati, and others—to study Torah. In their case, the surrounding society (friends, family) encourages their study, and in fact deprecates them until they do begin. The pure water with which Elijah quenches the thirst of Maimonides and Recanati is a traditional Jewish symbol of the Law of Moses. They do not actively set out to acquire it (as did the Talmudic sages), they receive it from God Himself.

The reason for this difference should be seen in the social function intended for the legends: In the rabbinic period, the tales' paramount function was exemplary; to preach to society that even at a late age one could study Torah, and the greatest of the sages prove it by virtue of their own life stories. In the medieval period, these legends are essentially biographical, not exemplary. They showcase wisdom derived of Heaven, but do not necessarily advocate emulation of its mortal repository. In the Middle Ages, the legends had a propagandizing function: to effect broad acceptance of the writings of controversial scholars—Maimonides and R. Judah the Pious, for example. Their teaching, which was "channelled" (remember the water!) to them directly by Providence, thus radiated Divine endorsement. Legends of maturation of the Talmudic sages were intended to serve as a didactic model, to lead others to follow in their footsteps. Legends of the maturation of the medieval scholars—specifically, those whose teaching was hotly debated—were intended to disseminate their writings and augment the basis of their authority.

Most of the saints' legends concern the maturation stage of the protagonist. He wanders the streets of the Jewish world, composes his books in an exceptional manner, and performs wondrous, miraculous deeds. Most of the discussion below is dedicated to these tales. The fourth stage, death, is not fundamentally different from the saints' legends of earlier Jewish traditions or those of the Christian world. The saint, for example, performs miracles posthumously: Before dying, R. Judah the Pious tells his students that he will cause harm to befall the Christian gatekeeper who humiliated the Jews by ringing his bells whenever a Jewish funeral passed. When R. Judah the Pious' funeral procession nears the gate, the tower collapses, burying the villain. Maimonides appears to his disciples prior to his funeral, and reveals the location of his missing toe, so that it can be buried together with the rest of him. Robbers try to snatch Maimonides' coffin on its way to burial in Palestine, but thirty men cannot budge it. Nahmanides, who departs for Palestine an old man, tells his students, "By this you will know [the day of my death, for] on [that day] the gravestone of my mother, who is buried in this town, will split lengthwise (?), and in the rift you will see the image of a painted lamp (*menorah*) . . ." and so it happened.[73]

Wandering was a central theme of medieval Jewish biographical legends concerning the stage of maturation and activity. Protagonists of these traditions were perpetual wanderers: Rashi, for one, sets out to roam at length after composing the bulk of his biblical and talmudic commentaries. He treks from one study hall to the next, through all reaches of the diaspora, strewing across the reading tables pages of his commentaries, in an effort to ascertain whether others wrote similar commentaries, and to gauge their acceptance. Not until he was convinced of their value did he return to his hometown to conclude and publish them. According to another version of the legend, Rashi's father, after casting the pearl into the water to keep it out of Christian rites, regrets his action and weeps over his loss. As he did not embrace wholeheartedly this sacrifice, it fell to his son to atone for him. To this end, Rashi embarks upon the path of exile and wandering. Nor did Maimonides remain in one place; he migrated often, to Fez, Algiers, and Egypt, and finally to Palestine. Sometimes he moved, according to these legendary traditions, to escape religious persecution, other times he moved in search of a suitable Jewish community into which to settle. R. Samuel the Pious, R. Judah's father, was no less the nomad. After improperly using the holy name, as aforementioned, and his father's consequent punishment in the matter of not fathering any children, he was given the opportunity to atone for his actions by taking to the road—but he was forbidden to remain anywhere for longer than one night. Foremost of all the Jewish wanderers of the Middle Ages was R. Abraham ibn Ezra—wandering became his hallmark. He visited all the Jewish communities of east and west. The most distinguished figures of the day (and some not of his day) hosted him, among them Rashi and Maimonides. He wandered in destitution, hiding his identity behind rags and crude behavior.

The multitude of legends concerning these itinerant medieval Jews can be explained in a number of ways. They are a means to describe numerous and diverse communities (mostly fictitious); the wanderer-saint is a means to uncover them. Legends of wandering enable the narrative traditions to bring together people who lived in distant places—or in different periods, time being as easily traversable as geography. More importantly, these legends of wandering expose society's self-image as a body perpetually on the move. Medieval Jewry had a high migration rate, relative to the non-Jewish communities: wandering in search of sources of livelihood following expulsions; in the wake of undermined security; and for the sake of Torah study (a phenomenon with parallels in the Christian world). For our purposes, it does not matter whether or not this phenomenon was a part of "factual" reality; the legends reveal that medieval Jewry regarded wandering as part and parcel of its existence. Medieval traditions ascribe the practice to nearly all their protagonists, indicating that the society that created and disseminated these traditions regarded it as an integral phase of its reality. Even if these journeys did not occur (and there were communities that lived in one place for hundreds of years), they were deeply imprinted—as a potential or impending threat—upon the social consciousness of the period's Jews.[74]

A primary impetus for the peregrinations of the biographical legends' heroes is confrontation with antisemites. Thus Maimonides and Nahmanides had to evade their pursuers with the aid of the Ineffable Name: Maimonides issued halachic rulings that humiliated the Muslims, hence he had to flee the Qadi's wrath. He stepped onto a boat, lay upon it a note bearing the Holy Name, and traveled, in the wink of an eye, from Algeria to Egypt. He gave the boat's owner a second note, also bearing that magic formula, so that the boat would immediately return to whence it came. The same motif is utilized in a legend of Nahmanides, who, with his students in Barcelona, observed the launching of a new ship. When the shipwrights could not budge it, Nahmanides boasted to his pupils that he would move it "with the breath of his lips." The king compelled him to make good his boast, and fearing accusations of sorcery, he made his escape, as did Maimonides, in a small boat. The sailor, returning in the same boat, fell asleep, and the craft, by virtue of the sacred Name it bore, breached the shore and reached the middle of the city before the sailor awoke, destroyed the note upon which the formula was written, and "there the townspeople built a tower to commemorate this day" (*Shalshelet ha-Kabbalah*, 26a).

Other traditions have Maimonides and R. Abraham ibn Ezra making use of the Divine Name to resurrect Muhammad, Jesus, and Mary. Muhammad revived is ugly and foul to behold, and declares before the king that he set Maimonides to this task to prove that he was not worthy of humanity's belief. Jesus and Mary take up swords and kill the Gentiles who had sought to harm the Jewish community. Tales of confrontation in which the protagonist uses the Name are especially numerous among the legends of R. Judah the Pious: he resurrects a dead man for whose murder the Gentiles had accused the Jews; he levitates a building so that a court Jew can see where his enemies hid the treasure that they had stolen from the king, so as to implicate him and thereby harm all the Jews; he traps the head of the Bishop of Salzburg in his window after the latter attempts to do him injury. The Bishop, recognizing the caliber of R. Judah the Pious, converts. R. Judah's father, R. Samuel the Pious, similarly resurrects the priests who had tried to best him in a contest of sorcery. The tales present a generally uniform model of sacred action: danger hovers over the individual or the community, and the saint takes up medieval Jewry's principal magic tool—the Ineffable Name—to resolve the conflict powerfully and immediately. These tales reveal nothing unique in the actions of their heroes: R. Judah the Pious, Maimonides, and others adopt identical means. For this reason, so many motifs are common to the hagiographical tales of several protagonists, having passed from one to the next.

The fact that these tales, in which the protagonists make such pronounced and sensational use of God's name and other magic means, are told about figures such as Maimonides, R. Abraham ibn Ezra, and Nahmanides, who are renowned for their rationalist approach (each one in a different degree), deserves special attention, and we will return to it below.[75]

As opposed to the legends of confrontation between Jews and Gentiles, whose resolution is magic and that are of a general nature—that is, their protagonists evince no unique characteristics—other legends dealing with this confrontation feature heroes who behave according to what is known of them from their actual biographies. Here the transfer of motifs is nearly impossible; figures in the tale must somehow represent the actual personalities. Maimonides, for example, functions in these tales of confrontation as a physician. He responds to the challenge of the king's other doctors, who envy his success, and consents to drink the deadly potion that they concocted for him. His disciples treat him with an antidote that he prepared in advance—and he lives. After partaking of their own lethal concoction, it is the doctors who breathe no more. Court advisers scheme to frame Maimonides for attempting to poison the king. They taint the medicine that Maimonides offers the king and the king consequently condemns him to execution. Maimonides chooses death by bloodletting, but instructs his students how to save him. Afterwards he hides in a cave for twelve years, where he writes the *Mishneh Torah* (The Code of the Law). Nahmanides's disciple, Abner the Apostate (*ha-Mumar*, the intention apparently being Abner of Burgos), rises to prominence in the Church. He appears before his teacher on the Day of Atonement, slaughters a pig, and consumes its blood. When Nahmanides asks him the reason for his apostasy, he claims that Nahmanides once insisted that the world in its entirety was to be found within the Torah portion, *Haazinu*, and as he believed no such thing, he rejected Judaism altogether. He demands of Nahmanides proof that his very own name is written within that portion. This accomplished, he does not return home again, but sets out to sea and disappears. Such traditions concerning the confrontation between Jews and Gentiles employ knowledge of characteristics unique to the tales' protagonists, or of their creations. They are fundamentally different from the magic legends in that they are realistic in spirit; the resolution of the plot is intellectual, rather than magical. Traditions of this type indicate that those tales connected to the spiritual legacy of the protagonist—his books, his students, his particular conduct—are more personally and exclusively connected to the historical figure than to the magical motifs.[76]

The most famous legend of confrontation in the medieval traditions is that of Rashi and Duke Godfrey of Bouillon, the crusader conqueror of Jerusalem. This tradition is exceptional in its extensive distribution, and as it exhibits both types of the confrontation legend presented above. Within the legend of Rashi and Godfrey, magic confrontation legends, of the first category, and realistic, wisdom confrontation legends, of the second, overlap. The gist of the tale is as follows: Duke Godfrey of Bouillon sets out at the head of his soldiers to capture the Holy Land in the [first] Crusade. He passes by Troyes, Rashi's city, and wishes to know how the wisest of the Jews envisions the Crusade's success. Rashi refuses to appear before him. When Godfrey arrives at Rashi's school in person, Rashi makes himself invisible. In response to Godfrey's question, he replies that he will conquer Jerusalem, but reign over it for only three days. On the fourth day, the Arabs would rout him, and he would return to France with only two soldiers remaining of all his enormous army. Godfrey, enraged, vows that if Rashi's prophesy should prove untrue in even the slightest detail, he would bring great injury upon Rashi and the Jews of the city. Rashi's prophesy comes true, but Godfrey returns to Troyes with three soldiers, instead of Rashi's predicted two. As they pass the city gate, a heavy stone falls on one of the soldiers, killing him. Godfrey goes to Rashi's school to admit that he was right, only to discover that Rashi has meanwhile passed away.[77]

The tale's plot is constructed of three sequential episodes: Godfrey's visit to Rashi, the capture and loss of Jerusalem, and the final visit to Rashi. The three narrative units are arranged in ascending order: the first, in which Rashi speaks with Godfrey while invisible, is a common folkloric motif, often found in international folklore. In the second episode, Godfrey conquers Jerusalem and is himself soon vanquished—just as Rashi predicted. These are historical events that Rashi correctly foretold, which proves the involvement of Rashi's God in such universal events. At the same time it is conceivable to understand these events—as indeed all do—as realistic processes whose explanation is merely historical-strategic, and not necessarily connected with some divine decree or plan. The third episode, wherein the stone falls on the head of the third horseman, and Rashi's prophesy comes true in its last detail, can only be seen as the hand of Providence. This is the climax of the tale not only because it is the most surprising, but as it "explains" the two earlier episodes: If here there is no doubt of Divine involvement, then the two earlier events must be interpreted accordingly. Such an interpretation is of greatest import with regard to the second episode, as here lies the essence of the tale—proof that the God of Israel is the master of even the weightiest of world events, and that all that happened in the tale, from start to finish, is to be seen as the execution of a precise Divine plan. The graduated organization of the three narrative units—from least to most significant—cannot be incidental. The pattern of this legend, manifested in all versions, both oral and written, indicates artistic crystallization of clarity and significance.

This legend is the most widespread of those concerning Rashi, although Rashi himself barely appears in it. His part in the tale concludes in the first episode. This suggests that the essence of the confrontation-biographical legend is not inherent in its hagiographical quality, as a stage in the saint's life, but in the nature of the confrontation between Jews and Gentiles as described in the tale. From this perspective, the legend of Rashi and Godfrey of Bouillon is constructed as a paradigmatic confrontation legend. Polarization in the tale is not restricted to the active figures (Rashi versus Godfrey), it is also discernible in the narrative structure and the fabric of its world. The structure evinces a distinct polarization between Godfrey's brash and robust appearance in the story's opening episode, and his submissive, humiliated mien in the conclusion. The stylistic level reinforces this dramatic polarity. Harsh and violent terms describe details relating to the Christian world: the rampaging army, the mob congregating at Rashi's school and the city wall, vast geographical expanses (from Troyes to Jerusalem), battles, conquests, and threats. Juxtaposing these is the stylistic portrayal of the Jewish environment, which is depicted in spiritual terms: Rashi becomes invisible, thus incorporeal; his status as "sage" (as opposed to Godfrey, the military commander and mass-murderer); Rashi's power of prophesy; Godfrey's two approaches to Rashi, take place at the Torah study hall—a consummate spiritual symbol.

Thus the legend's dramatic construction, not its hagiographical quality, is the bearer of its fundamental meaning. Until now, the general consensus was that the purpose of this legend was to denigrate the leader of the First Crusade, even if only in narrative, in return for what his minions did to the Jewish communities along their way. Such a vengeful sentiment no doubt tinges each and every appearance, oral or written, of the legend in Jewish society. Evidence to this effect exists in the Jewish chronicles of the Crusades, wherein the Crusades are described according to the same pattern as in the legend of Rashi and Godfrey: the crusaders set out, attack, and abuse Jews along the way, reach the holy land where, after a brief victory, the Almighty punishes them, they ultimately return, diminished, disgraced, and defeated (Oxford Bodleian manuscript Heb.d.11, p. 242a, early 14th century). The legend, however, is more complex than the chronicle, and constructed of several layers of meaning.

The tale's narrative structure proves that it reflects above all the manner in which medieval Jewish society perceived the difference between itself and the Christian world. This difference is manifested in terms of spirituality as opposed to physicality; wisdom versus brutality; security that stems from the bond with Providence juxtaposed with a confidence based on the physical, violent strength of those who wield the reins of power. The graduated construction of the narrative expresses the sense that the God of Israel is involved in historical events of the highest magnitude, which unfold according to His preordained plan. Thus the tale lays bare the psychological and social components by means of which medieval Jews defined their niche in the composite world of their age.

The biographical legends uncover yet another focus of tension in medieval Jewish society: internal controversy. As in the historical legends we examined in the previous section, so too, the legends of Jewish personalities unveil planes of disharmony characterizing Jewish life of the period. We are quite familiar with some of them from other evidence that survived from this period. An excellent example of one such plane of discord is well known from many other sources of the Middle Ages, namely, that between the rationalist-philosophers and the conservative scholars of the law, and that between both these groups together and the kabbalists. Tensions erupted with the famous controversy surrounding the books and philosophy of Maimonides. R. Abraham ben David of Posquierres was among the first to impugn Maimonides's *Mishneh Torah*. An interesting echo of this clash that took the Jewish world by storm in the thirteenth century reverberates in the following tradition preserved by the author of *Shalshelet ha-Kabbalah*:

> Some say that when Maimonides heard so many words of provocation and contempt in Rabbi Abraham ben David's critique [of his work], he said: Tell the Rabbi that is in Posquierres that he will not finish what he started. [It is also] said that Rabbi Abraham ben David did not complete his year [of life]. (p. 19b)

When Gedaliah ibn Yahya composed *Shalshelet ha-Kabbalah* (mid-sixteenth century), Maimonides's status as the preeminent halachic authority of medieval Jewry was already well established. The legend recognizes a given situation and suggests that a leader of Maimonides' status had to stand on his dignity. It is possible, if this tradition indeed dated back to the time of the great controversy, that it served as a weapon in the hands of those who sided with Maimonides, by virtue of its emphasis of his superiority over his rivals. Of even farther reaching ramifications are the legends that turn Maimonides into a kabbalist:

> I saw in the *Iggeret Hamudot* of R. Eliah Haim, that he says in his introduction: "I saw the letter Maimonides wrote from Jerusalem to Egypt to his student, wherein he said: 'After arriving from the Holy Land I found an old man who enlighted my eyes with the paths of the Kabbalah [and had I] known then what I accomplished now, I would not have written many of the things I have'" . . . and know that Maimonides, in his last days, knew the wisdom of the Kabbalah. (*Shalshelet ha-Kabbalah* 20b)

The hundreds of years that had passed since the great controversy apparently quelled some of the initial vitriol. Many scholars studied halacha, philosophy, and kabbalah (for example, the sixteenth and seventeenth centuries' mystics of Safed; the sages in Yemen and the Magreb) without seeing any contradiction between them. But the echoes of clashes past were not easily silenced. By now, the outlook prevailed that the pursuit of wisdom necessarily entailed study of the kabbalah. Maimonides's stature as first and foremost of the Jewish sages was already so entrenched in the period of these legends' crystallization (the fifteenth and sixteenth centuries), that Jewish society could not conceive that the crown of his teachings might be complete without the gem of mysticism. Another argument holds that the legend sprouted from the midst of the kabbalists, who were loathe to exclude Maimonides from the circle of supporters of mysticism. It may even be that the harmonizing tendency of the folk strata of Jewish society, who did not fully understand the import of the caustic debates, and viewed both approaches as words of the Living God, influenced the creation of this legend. In any case, it shows us in an interesting form the folk reaction to the ideological strains of the spiritual elite. When these strains trickled to the larger circles of folk strata, the response was to create traditions that nullified them, and to heal the breach between rival camps.[78]

In discussing the centrality of the motif of wandering in these biographical legends, mention was made of the fact that their protagonists hid behind a facade of poverty and boorishness. This is especially true in the legends of R. Abraham ibn Ezra, but Rashi and R. Samuel the Pious behaved in a similar manner. R. Samuel the Pious approached the community of Cologne for help in collecting donations. A wealthy miser tossed a single coin in front of the young man sent to assist who, taking offense, would not pick it up. When R. Samuel heard tell of this incident, he went to the home of the miser and picked it up himself, explaining that there is no shame in accepting charity, if it is God's will that one live off of others. Upon witnessing R. Samuel's humility, the miser gave generously. According to another tale, R. Samuel the Pious knew that a harsh edict was about to be decreed against the community of Speyer. He prayed—and the decree was annulled, with no one in the community any the wiser. He slaughtered a chicken in honor of the rescue. One of his students arrived at his home by chance and was astonished, as he knew that R. Samuel was so poor that he could not allow himself the pleasure of eating so well on weekdays. R. Samuel revealed to him the reason for the celebration, but forbade him to tell the others. The folk motif of the destitute saint who flaunts rather than conceals his poverty is even more pronounced in the legends of Abraham ibn Ezra. This protagonist reached the home of two other eminent people— Rashi and Rabbi Judah Halevy. He behaved in a demonstratively crude way—he wore filthy clothes, refused to wash, spoke crudely, and refused to participate in any religious ritual. His identity ultimately comes to light by means of a riddle that he writes upon the gate to the house, or a line of poetry that he supplies when Judah Halevy falters.[79]

It is difficult to overlook the class tension that bubbles up through these legends, which feature distinguished Jewish personalities as paupers, behaving in non-normative fashion, their outward appearance that of any itinerant Jewish beggar. Such people were not ashamed of their poverty, as they knew their true worth. The legends put into high relief their confrontation with the wealthy homeowners, who rejected them for their appearance, but ultimately recognized their spiritual nobility. The legends reflect the folk point of view on class polarization within Jewish society, and they seek to send clear messages to both the poor and the established. These messages carry more weight and sting more deeply when conveyed via the actions of distinguished personalities such as of Samuel the Pious and Abraham ibn Ezra.

A class confrontation of a different sort is manifested in one of the most intriguing biographical legends to reach us from the Middle Ages, and is connected with the figure of R. Judah the Pious:

> When I studied in Speyer before Rabbi Yedidiah of blessed memory, I found in his school the manuscript of Rabbi Zalman [son of R. Judah the Pious]. This is [what it said]: My father and teacher, the Pious, told me that in his time there was an incident involving a wealthy man in Speyer who used scissors to shave his beard. My father and teacher would approach him and protest against [this practice]. The wealthy man did not heed his words, saying, "a refined person (istenis) am I, and I cannot suffer the beard." My father and teacher told him: "You should know that you will know a bitter end, for after your death, demons resembling cows [will] trample your beard. This is the lot of those who cut their beards. And you will know the truth of the verse, 'You shall not round the corners of your heads, neither shalt thou mar' (Lev. 19:27), which is an acrostic for [the Hebrew word for] 'cows' (parot)." And when that man of means passed away, all the great men of Speyer sat near [the corpse], and my father and teacher was there. He wrote a name and threw it on that man of means, and he [the dead man] stood up. And all those who had been sitting there fled [in fear of the dead]. Then the dead man began to pluck at his head and pull his hair. My father and teacher said to him: "What [is happening] to you?" He said to him, "Woe is me that I did not heed you." My father and teacher said to him: "Please tell what is happening to your soul?" He said to him: "When my soul left [my body], a demon, looking like a great cow, came with a vessel full of pitch, sulfur, and salt, and imprisoned it in it, so that [the soul] could not get out. The harsh justice ensued and took the vessel with the spirit [within] from the demon and brought it before the Creator of Souls. A divine voice sounded, and said to me: 'Have you studied and repeated?' I said to him: 'I have studied and repeated.' At once he ordered that a Humash (Pentateuch) be brought and said to me: 'Read it.' As soon as I opened the book I found written, 'neither shalt thou mar the corners of thy beard' (Lev. 19:27) and I did not know what to answer. Than I heard a voice declaring: 'Put this one's soul on the bottommost level.' As they were bearing [my] soul to the bottommost level, a divine

voice sounded: 'Wait. My son Judah is more righteous than us (the angels) and has now asked mercy. Your soul will not descend to *She'ol* [netherworld]." Until this point, in his own words. (*Sefer ha-Gan*, attributed to R. Isaac ben R. Eleazar of Worms, Venice 1606, pp. 9b–10a)

This legend was preserved in a family tradition begun by the son of R. Judah the Pious, R. Zaltman. According to his testimony, and there is no reason to doubt it, it was told by R. Judah the Pious himself. R. Judah the Pious sought to impose his ethical path on one of the city's wealthy men. The growing of a beard is indeed an act of religious significance, but the rich man considered it a social label: "[he said,] a refined person am I, and I cannot suffer the beard." The rich man set himself apart from the community by means of the symbolic act of shaving his beard. In this way he asserted his membership among another chosen group of people, the moneyed nobility who tried, perhaps, to resemble their Christian counterparts. It is difficult for us today to ascertain the actual social background that led to this clash between R. Judah the Pious and the affluent man. In any case, it is clear to both of them that his act symbolically set apart "the refined" from all the rest. We can assume that the legend was told for a social purpose: to caution a growing circle of prosperous Jews, who felt the ungainly outward appearance of the Jew no longer suited men of their stature. Joining the class tension in this legend is that between the community's financial mainstay and its scholar. Judah the Pious, as portrayed by all the testimony of his day, saw himself as a moral guide whose duty it was to involve himself in all details concerning members of the community, and, by virtue of his religious authority, to equalize society. It is not difficult to surmise that such a perception led to clashes with the other leadership—the financial pillars and the communal institutions. The tale undoubtedly also reflects the strain that arose between the extremist moral teacher, motivated by unambiguous ethical considerations, and the "bourgeois" elements, with more complex financial and societal considerations. Such a strain certainly existed, in different degrees, in other communities, as well, during this period.[80]

The tradition according to which Rashi set out to wander in order to ascertain the true importance of his commentaries across the breadth of the Jewish world (*Shalshelet ha-Kabbalah*, p. 22b) has already been mentioned above. Whom might this legend have interested? What lies beneath its surface, and to whom was it addressed? The issue of originality in a Torah commentary and its acceptance by the community of Torah scholars certainly did not concern Jewish society at large. If we were to take a similar question, as to the originality of the book you are reading at this moment, to a cab driver, a physician, a grocer, and a computer expert, it would not engage them in the least, whereas the same question posed to a university faculty and research staff would generate scrutiny. Questions of originality and acceptance are the concern, primarily, of those whose business it is to write and read such works. Hence this tradition's emphasis on Rashi's wandering among the various study halls and Torah centers, where he lay the pages of his scholarly efforts on the tables for the perusal of other scholars.

The earliest evidence of this tradition dates to the mid-sixteenth century (*Shalshelet ha-Kabbalah*), but the tradition is assuredly older by far, having developed in the period between the generation of Rashi's disciples (the early twelfth century) and its delivery to Gedaliah ibn Yahya by "the sages of the generation," namely, the elderly scholars who had received it at the end of the fifteenth century. During the period of Rashi's students, the great Torah centers of the *tosafists* developed. This was a fruitful period for commentaries and commentaries to the commentaries—following the path laid down by Rashi. Every student in the tosafist academies of France and the German lands wrote commentaries for himself, whether as study drills or for other purposes, and undoubtedly contemplated publishing them one day. This was a period of tremendous productivity, although the vast supply of such material threatened to bring down the level and importance of the commentaries. It stands to reason that the legend of Rashi's wanderings to test his work would flourish in precisely this cultural context.

The why and wherefore of publishing the greatest scholars' works interests primarily those whose vocation (or avocation) lies there, just as today we are interested in the circumstances of publication of the books of the greatest of contemporary generations. Such tales about Rashi undoubtedly provoked interest in the academies of his grandsons, their students, and their students' students—the tosafists. Such a legend carries within a caveat to students: one should not be overly hasty to publish one's works. The tradition concerning Rashi must serve as an example to us: if the great Rashi himself checked a thousand and one times, and finally sat back down and emended his work on the basis of what he had heard—then it falls upon us to be at least as prudent and painstaking in our efforts. This tradition may reflect tension or controversy within the world of those who studied Torah, between those who viewed with a critical eye the flood of commentarial works of a certain sort, and others who perhaps regarded such publications—even if they did not always contain an original contribution—as beneficial, as something that strengthened the Torah world, and so gave them their blessing.[81]

Narrative traditions on such topics are likely to interest one Jewish social class in particular—the circle of those who studied the Torah and its broad periphery. The same can be said of the legends outlining the circumstances of the composition of many books—how Rashi himself wrote *Sefer ha-Parnas* during a visit to the home of a great Jewish leader in Spain (*Shalshelet ha-Kabbalah*, p.

22b); how Maimonides wrote his *Mishneh Torah*, over the course of twelve years of isolation in a cave (*Shalshelet ha-Kabbalah*, p. 20b); how Abraham ibn Ezra composed some of his poems, and how Divine inspiration was what guided Menahem Recanati to write his commentary on the Torah and *Sefer Ta'amei ha-Mitzvot* (*Shalshelet ha-Kabbalah*, p. 28b).

Scholars of medieval Christian hagiography distinguish between "popular" and "learned" hagiography. The former, directed to and told by the masses, makes use of numerous supernatural motifs and deals with subjects of interest to the broad strata of society. Learned hagiography uses elevated language, often cites the classic literature, and deals with subjects of concern to the literati. The tales of Rashi's wanderings, of the circumstances surrounding the composition and acceptance of important works in Jewish culture, alongside the numerous magical legends of saints, indicate that similar trends should be discerned in medieval Jewish hagiography as well.[82]

For example, the multitude of traditions that Gedaliah ibn Yahya heard from wise men and study hall scholars should be noted, among them: "I [learned] from my teacher, Rabbi Jacob de-Recanati, who was a descendent of his, that it had been passed down in his family . . . " (p. 28b); "And more that I heard in person from the elders and sages of the generation" (p. 22b); "I received it from the sages of the generation" (ibid.); "I [learned] from the students of R. Meir of Padua" (ibid.); "I received it from the students of the teacher, Rabbi Leon de-Muriel, who had received it from his teachers . . . " (ibid.) The traditions that Ibn Yahya recorded from the Torah scholars generally deal with the topics mentioned here: the circumstances of composing books, the origins of the wisdom of the tales' protagonists, exceptional commentarial methods, and the like.

"Folklore of the Academe" holds a special place in this treasury of Jewish culture's "learned hagiography." By this I mean tales told within the educational institutions about the exceptional behavior of teachers, and events connected to the lives of the students there. A great many rabbinic tales were apparently created in such contexts, as memoirs of the sages about their time with their teachers in the study halls, or the intensive way of life led within those halls. Such also were the Christian traditions, transferred from one generation of students to the next in every educational institution in the world, schools, universities, and the like. We will dwell only on one relevant example, namely the tales of R. Jacob ben Yakar, Rashi's teacher. Rashi himself, and other students who studied at the Worms academy, customarily told anecdotes about the eccentric behavior of their teacher; when they turned to him with a question about wine sold by a Christian to a Jew, he simply ran away rather than deliver a restrictive ruling—Rashi and his colleagues chased him and brought him home; how he would customarily appear before the Christian authorities barefoot; how in his humility he likened himself to a worm, and more. Such anecdotes generally survived one or two generations of students, and if not set down in writing, disappeared with the passing of generations who no longer knew the teacher or his students personally. Some anecdotes, however, successfully surmount the barrier of time and become developed and crystallized legendary traditions. Such an anecdote survived in *Sefer Hasidim*:

> "And thou shalt love the Lord thy God with all thy heart, and with all thy soul, and with all thy might," with all the depth of your thoughts as it is said (Pss. 92:6): "thy thoughts are very deep." For our Rabbi Jacob, son of Rabbi Yakar, [his soul] rest in Eden, would sweep [the floor] in front of the Holy Ark with his beard. And when the congregation would pass before the king or before the regime he would remove his shoes. He said: I am poor, they with their money and I with compassion and supplications. And so, they with theirs, and I with mine. (section 991)

In one of the birth legends of Rashi, extant only in a late version though it is much older, it is told that Rashi's father was a pauper. Since he could not honor the Torah with money, he did so with his body. He would sweep the floor in front of the Holy Ark with his beard. As a reward, Elijah the Prophet informed him that he would father a son who would enlighten the world with his wisdom. The prophet even asked to be the child's godfather. At Rashi's circumcision ceremony, the father waited for Elijah's arrival for a long time, despite the protests of those present, this being a further test of his faith.[83]

The differences between the two versions of the legend are essentially on the narrative and moral-ideational levels. From a narrative perspective, the first version is a short anecdote, one of many that R. Jacob ben Yakar's students would habitually tell of their teacher and mentor's eccentric behavior. It is nothing more than the kernel of an undeveloped tale. The tale of Rashi's birth is a developed legend, which includes all the narrative elements of this genre: narrative development, confrontation between the active characters, developed dialogues, tension, and the happy ending. The anecdote concerning R. Jacob ben Yakar is, in truth, the first episode of a developed legend. The differences between the two tales are likely to fill in the gaps of our knowledge of what happened during the hundreds of years that passed between the version in *Sefer Hasidim* and the legend on Rashi. R. Jacob ben Yakar's students, among them Rashi himself, were in the habit of telling (to their students, perhaps) various anecdotes about their mentor. The students of their students remembered the tale—because of the unusual image well-engraved on their memories, of the great and esteemed rabbi crouching on all fours before the Holy Ark and sweeping the floor with his beard, and so remembered that the tale was somehow connected with Rashi. The true protagonist has already been forgotten. With the passing of the generations Rashi—the better-known figure and apparently one teller of the anecdote—became the protagonist of his own tale.

Such a transfer of tales from a lesser-known figure to a more famous one is a well-recognized folkloric process.

The second difference between the two versions of the legend lies in its ethical significance. R. Jacob ben Yakar demonstrated exceptional pious conduct, and with that the tale ends. Of particular importance is the fact that he did not accept any sort of payment for his actions. Conversely, Rashi's father, in the developed version, merits a practical and immediate reward for the same act. The ethical idea expressed in the anecdote of R. Jacob ben Yakar is that "virtue is its own reward." No one should expect a reward for doing a good deed. The second version, on the other hand, reflects the belief that for doing a good deed the doer may expect practical and immediate reward—and such was the birth of a son like Rashi, who enhanced his father's social status. Folk thinking is not satisfied in delayed reward or punishment, or with spiritual gratification alone. The developed legend crystallized over the course of hundreds of years in accordance with the modes of folk thinking, and became quite remote—not only in time, but in perception as well—from the principles guiding learned thinking. The anecdote on Jacob ben Yakar undeniably belongs to the category of learned hagiography, and reflects the worldview of the elite of Torah scholars. The legend about the birth of Rashi is a perfect example of folk hagiography that developed out of the folk's ethical perceptions and thought.[84]

> The manner of [Nahmanides's] study of the wisdom of the Kabbalah was that when he was an outstanding physician and philosopher, he almost disdained this wisdom, until an old man, a great sage of the wisdom of the Kabbalah, came to him. And when he saw that Nahmanides so loved learning and was a great wise man, he tried to teach him the Kabbalah. But Nahmanides did not heed him. And then one day the [old] sage circumvented the law by going to a brothel, and when he came to the courtyard he was arrested and sentenced to [execution by] burning on the holy Sabbath day. The thing was made known to Nahmanides, who did not wish to come to [the sage's] defense. The captive sage sent word to Nahmanides on that Sabbath, demanding to know why he would not defend him. Nahmanides admonished him for the act of prostitution. [The sage] apologized, saying it was a lie, and that he trusted that God would save him. Therefore [Nahmanides] should prepare the three [customary Sabbath] meals for him. And it came to pass on the holy Sabbath, they took the sage to the marketplace to be burned, and threw him onto the fire. But the sage, with the practical wisdom of the Kabbalah that he knew, substituted a donkey instead, and he went to Nahmanides's house after the afternoon prayer, found him reciting the blessing over the wine, and answered, Amen. Nahmanides was astonished, and the sage replied: Have you not seen with your own eyes the power of this wisdom. Then Nahmanides was enthusiastic to learn it, and woke

early and stayed up late for it, until he emerged head of the sages of his generation in this wisdom. (*Shalshelet ha-Kabbalah*, p. 25b)

This narrative tradition corroborates most of what we have said about the biographical legend. It reflects details already known from the protagonist's factual biography, in this case, Nahmanides wavering between rationalist philosophy and kabbalah, and his involvement in the latter at a relatively late stage of his spiritual development. Nevertheless, we would never dare rely only on the legend if we did not know these biographical facts from more reliable sources. The importance of the legend therefore lies elsewhere, not in the biographical information it offers concerning the hero. In the eyes of later generations—and certainly in the eyes of the broad strata of the folk—halacha, philosophy, and kabbalah were three integral aspects of their sacred heritage, the Torah of Israel. One could not exist without the others, and surely the eminence of a Jewish religious scholar could not be established unless he was expert in all three. For this reason, among others, the legends turned Maimonides into a kabbalist, and this is the "historical truth" reflected in the legend of Nahmanides as well. It also expresses clearly the difference between "folk hagiography" and the world of the learned elite in Jewish society. In the eyes of the folk traditions, kabbalah is 'applied kabbalah' (*kabbalah ma'asit*), that is, the utilization of supernatural forces—magic. In order to prove to Nahmanides the greatness of the kabbalah, that same old man (R. Eleazar of Worms?) had to employ it to perform a supernatural act. Kabbalah is without a doubt an elitist tier of Jewish culture: it is abstruse and esoteric, by its very nature the province of the very few who would devote to it their entire existence. The broad folk public sees only the tangible spectrum of the kabbalah; its theoretical underpinnings are not visible to untrained eyes. This is clearly symbolized in the tale of Nahmanides's apprenticeship: The old man fails to engage Nahmanides's interest when he approaches him on an intellectual level. However, when confronted with its practical manifestations, Nahmanides is "enthusiastic to learn it." Nahmanides here is the protagonist of a folk tradition, and as such he embodies the outlook and perception of the society that created and told the tale. This audience has no interest in the meditative aspects of kabbalah, only in its applications, in the practical benefits to the reality of their lives.

Such was the path of the biographical legend in Jewish culture of the Middle Ages: it took elements from the learned culture—the figures of the preeminent scholars, their works, and their spiritual development, and translated them into the language of folk thinking. Here the elitist elements become tangible motifs in a narrative plot that emphasizes their place not in the spiritual world, but in practical reality: blood libels and confrontation with the Gentiles, wandering and the wherewithal for existence, class and financial polarization within the community, and the thorny controversies within the Torah world.

[G] The Novella and Gender Stories

The novella is one of the oldest genres in Hebrew literature, as earlier chapters in this book attest. Jewish storytellers preferred it to the fairytale for its realistic quality, and for its ready accommodation of Jewish effects and values. Like the fairytale, it satisfied the basic need for an entertaining story, full of adventures and flights of imagination; religious-historical legend and didactic exempla could not ordinarily satisfy this need.

The folk novella (as distinct from the literary novella, whose world is fundamentally different) is a realistic tale that takes place in a defined time and locale. Its protagonists are ordinary people—not heroes or dignitaries—who seek their fortune among mortals, in a realistic landscape. Chance, or appetite for adventure, leads them far from home along a path strewn with difficult trials. The novella tends to emphasize human traits—cleverness, loyalty, passion, cunning—as the driving force of the narrative plot. The event recounted in the novella is uncommon, but always within the confines of the possible (as perceived by the narrating society). The novella highlights wisdom and romantic love above all else as the driving force of the plot, and as the means to its resolution. Supernatural motifs might be employed in the folk novella, but always within the bounds of the society's accepted beliefs and understanding.[85]

The novella occupies a kind of middle ground between fairytale and legend. As a borderline genre, it fills the vacuum between these two poles, as such satisfying a societal need as well as a literary gap. As opposed to the supernatural magic fairytale, the novella is realistic; it takes place in the realm of what the narrating society considers possible. It differs from legend—whose strength is in verisimilitude—in that it is stylized; the novella does not try to imitate or reflect a well-known reality. Unlike legend, the novella is neither didactic nor theological. Its central folk wisdom elements set it apart from the fairytale, which exists solely to entertain and amuse. The listener (or reader) is not distanced from the novella, as from the magical fairytale, by a profusion of magic motifs, which would most likely brand it as naive and intended for children. Nor does the novella demand, as does the religious legend or exemplum, that the listener believe what is told and accept its practical directions. The atmosphere of adventure, the powerful emotions, and the journey to marvelous, yet familiar locations, distances the listener sufficiently from the contents for him to enjoy the tale without the obligation that legend imposes. At the same time, the (occasionally quite vivid) erotic motifs found in the tale are counterbalanced by rhetorical expressions, citations from the sacred sources, and the like. The listener can allow himself to be swept away by the atmosphere of adventure and eroticism, because it is circumscribed by a clear framework of social restrictions and traditional wisdom.

The boundaries of the novella are best defined by means of its extreme examples, namely, those that most closely approximate fairy tale or legend. Thus
we can more clearly ascertain the middle region. Two tales will serve this purpose; the first is found in an important grouping of tales from the first half
of the thirteenth century—*Sefer ha-Ma'asim*. The tale (Ms. Oxford, Bodleian
library, Heb.d.11, #51 in the grouping) belongs to the tale type of the contest of
suitors, rivals for the hand of the maiden (AT 653). The poor Torah scholar,
whose prosperous uncle wants him for his daughter's bridegroom, competes
against the mother's choice, her nephew, who is an ignorant boor. The head of
the academy at which the poor suitor studies advises him to embrace and caress
the maiden—who prefers him—and even to lie beside her in her bed. When the
pair is discovered, the young man must beat a hasty retreat to save his skin. He
boards a ship to distant lands. The mariners cast him onto an abandoned island; he subsequently discovers a marvelous healing herb, which he later uses
in the capital city to cure the leprous king. As a reward, the king grants him a
parcel of land that includes the town of his birth. He arrives there as the new
governor, just in time for the maiden's wedding to his rival. He reveals his identity before one and all, and marries her.

The second part of the tale—the protagonist's wanderings and the finding
of the healing herb—is a typical fairytale. It is not defined in terms of time and
location, it is heavily laden with supernatural motification, and it concludes
with the protagonist's rise to power and his marriage to a "princess." This unit
of the plot has variants in international folk literature (AT 653). The first part
of the story takes place within the Jewish sphere: the community, the family
structure, the academy, the relationship between the rabbi and his students,
and the ethical-normative infrastructure of Jewish society. Such elements of
time and place are utterly foreign to the nature of the fairytale—that which is
fashioned in the second part of the tale. Such a combination of lifelike realism,
wisdom, and romance in the first part of the tale, and the wandering in a marvelous space where the protagonist experiences supernatural events, is that
which shapes the hybrid genre called *Novellenmärchen*.[86]

This example is likely to delineate very clearly the boundaries of the novella
and its aesthetic function. The second part of the tale—the fairytale—serves
to dismantle and break out of the framework of social reality described in the
first part. When storytellers seek to deviate from the day-to-day limitations of
concrete reality and the social norms entailed therein, they mobilize the effects
of the fairytale—wandering, adventures, strange and marvelous landscapes,
and supernatural occurrences. The converse is equally true: when the fairytale
gives vent to an uncontrolled burst of imagination, with the capacity to undermine the universe of Jewish beliefs and views—sometimes touching on the pagan beliefs whose traces in fairytales in general are still recognized—the Jewish

storytellers rein it in by means of the realistic elements of place, time, and Jewish values.

The tale known as "Solomon's Daughter in the Tower" can serve as an example to distinguish another type: that in the historical dimension. Setting the tale in the remote past of King Solomon has the same effect as setting it in a distant locale; both alienate listeners from the narrative action. Yet the king's authoritative image, as a master of others' fates, and haughty with the pride of the mighty, evinces values characteristic of the contemporary medieval feudalistic atmosphere. This blending of the remote with the near, the alien with the familiar, exists on the tale's ideational plane as well: belief in fate, as seen in the stars by the king, contradicts the Jewish worldview, as Maimonides, for example, had contended. On the other hand, belief in the notion of "a match made in heaven," determined forty days before the birth, is assuredly a deep Jewish belief. These transitions between the foreign and the familiar, the permitted and the prohibited, between the broadened perspectives of medieval folk consciousness and the rigorous norms of Jewish culture, are fundamental characteristics of the "Jewish novella." They enable medieval listeners to broaden the horizons of their imagination, while at the same time keeping them within bounds by shaping content to fit the spirit of Jewish culture. The novella is thus a borderline genre that grew out of social and psychological needs, and these contradicting orientations. Its great popularity, beginning with the folk narrative of the Middle Ages, patently indicates its success at staking out the middle ground between orientations.[87]

The cycle of tales, *Sefer ha-Ma'asim*, in the Oxford manuscript mentioned earlier, can apprise us of the novella's importance in medieval folk narrative. More than half of its sixty-one tales belong to the genre of the religious legend. The tales of R. Akiva, Nahum of Gamzu, R. Joshua ben Levi, and Hanina ben Dosa, on the sanctity of the Sabbath, on prayer, charity, and guarding against idolatry, came to reinforce the faith of the listeners (or readers), to encourage fastidious observance of the precepts and prohibitions, and to drive home these lessons through the portrayal of exemplary individuals from the past. It is the preponderance of religious legends in this grouping that imbues it with its normative-obligatory atmosphere. Some sixteen tales (nearly a quarter of the whole) have to be categorized as novellas, according to the above definition. (Another important story grouping—*Midrash of the Ten Commandments*—contains the same percentage of novellas, which demonstrates that this division should not be viewed as incidental.) If we want to compare this relative share to the novella's standing in international folk literature, we find that of the twenty-five hundred tale types included in the Aarne-Thompson standard classification, one hundred and fifty (AT 850–999) are defined as novellas, that is to say, only 6 percent. To round out the picture of the novella's relative weight in the grouping, one further distinction is worthwhile: the entire grouping of tales was copied on eighty pages of the manuscript (300a–340b). Of these, the sixteen novellas included therein cover some forty-five pages, or more than half the total space, which necessarily implies that it would have taken as long to read (or tell aloud) the novellas as the remaining tales! This is chiefly due to the relative length of the novellas as compared to the legends. This brief mathematical exercise shows that the novellas' true importance vastly outweighs their number in the grouping, and that, in the eyes of the medieval copyist and anthologist, novelistic tales had a weight equal to sacred religious legend.

The romantic quality of the novella, its treatment of matters of the heart and sexual propriety (or lack thereof) as determined by Jewish norms, all revolve around the figure of the woman. Indeed, in contrast to the religious legend, all of whose protagonists are male exemplary figures, the protagonists of the novellas are principally women. This genre is thus one of the few in folk literature (in addition to the fairytale, which treats this theme on another level) that contends with society's image of women. As folk narrative in general is an expressive mode, it consolidates its attitude toward the subject in extreme terms of positive and negative, good and bad. Indeed, the key novellas of the period can be divided into two groups, according to the polarized view they take of women. The expressive character of the folktale leads to extremism, to disproportional amplification of whichever element it seeks to emphasize. Such are the modes of expression of the tale, for it does not *reflect* reality so much as it *expresses* attitudes toward its theme.[88]

Many of the medieval novellas, among them those that merited literary treatment in such works as *The Arabian Nights, The Decameron,* or *The Canterbury Tales,* take a harsh misogynic tone. The social, psychological, and religious motivations for negative attitudes toward women in medieval literature have already been discussed in detail, and there is no reason to reiterate them here. In the Jewish world of the Middle Ages, the subject also received a certain amount of attention, especially as formulated in works of *maqama*—in Joseph ibn Zabara's *Sefer ha-Sha'shu'im,* and in Judah ibn Shabbetai's *Minhat Yehuda Sone Nashim* (Judah's Gift, The One Who Hates Women), for example.[89]

Since most texts on this theme were created in the region of Arab influence, and but few misogynic tales are known to us from the rabbinic period, and also as a significant portion of narrative material of this sort has known variants in the non-Jewish cultures, it appears that the bulk of such material reached Jewish narrative of the Middle Ages from without. A story cycle that represents this misogynistic attitude is *Meshalim shel Shlomo ha-Melekh* (Parables of King Solomon), created at the end of the Middle Ages. All five tales of the cycle belong to the genre of novella; four of them are patently misogynic. The tale of "The Woman and the Robber," for example, tells of a woman who desired a particular young man and persuaded her father to marry her off to him. Later, on the way to visit her parents, a robber captured the newlyweds. Bound to a tree, the husband watched his bride merrily couple with the robber. After they fell asleep, a snake drank from the bottle of wine, leaving behind some of its venom. The robber drank from it and died immediately. The woman agreed to untie her husband only if he promised not to harm her. He kept his promise, but recounted the entire tale to her father, who killed her.

The second tale is known as "One Man Among a Thousand I Have Found; But a Woman Among All Those I Have Not Found" (Eccles. 7:28). In it, the Sanhedrin (assembly of the supreme judges) object to Solomon's statement. He commands them to find the most faithful husband and wife in all of the Land of Israel, and bring him the husband. Solomon directs the man to kill his wife, after which he will give him his daughter's hand in marriage and raise him to greatness. The faithful husband refuses to harm his wife. When Solomon puts the wife to the same test, she is ready and willing to carry out the plan (Solomon, who knew this would be the case, had given her a tin sword and thus prevented her husband's otherwise certain death).

The third tale, "Solomon's Three Counsels," tells of three brothers who served the king many years, after which the elder two preferred payment in money while the youngest chose words of wisdom. The king's advice saves the youngest from the disasters that overtook the elder two, and he alone arrives home safely, with all his brothers' property. But he ignores the king's third piece of advice—to never reveal a secret to a woman—and tells his wife the secret of his wealth. She tells her friends, and he is consequently accused of fratricide. Solomon, before whom the case is brought, recognizes him at the last minute and saves him from death. In one version of the fourth tale, "The Paternity Test," an adulterous woman boasts to her daughter that, of her ten children, only one was her husband's. The dying husband left all his property to his true son, and a wise judge succeeded in determining his identity.

Each of the four tales has ancient origins in the Jewish traditions or in international folklore. The second and fourth mentioned here appear in earlier sources: in the rabbinic literature, in the tale of R. Bena'ah ("The Paternity Test"); and in the twelfth-century *Sefer ha-Sha'shu'im* of Joseph ibn Zabara ("One Man Among a Thousand"). All four of the tales are well known in the international folklore as tale types widespread in the Middle Ages in both the Persian-Arab traditions and in Europe. All underwent definite modifications to bring them in line with Jewish culture, a literary process described above. In any case, the fact that the tales reached Hebrew folk literature from without does not nullify the significance of the misogynic theme in the period's Jewish culture. Since the tales were absorbed and accepted into Jewish culture after undergoing a complex process of adaptation, and also circulated in multiple versions, it is clear that they must be seen as Jewish tales in every respect.[90]

Two of these tales feature female sexual promiscuity: the adulterous women in "The Woman and the Robber" and "The Paternity Test" lust after every man they meet. One tale ("One Man Among a Thousand") concerns the woman's indefatigable efforts to advance her social station in life, where all means are acceptable, including the use of her body and the betrayal of those nearest her—her husband in particular. One tale deals with her garrulousness and insatiable appetite for gossip, which ultimately bring about the ruin of her family.

The division of tales according to the "sins" of the woman offers an impressive catalogue of the accusations against her in medieval culture: she was power-hungry or preoccupied solely with life's vanities; marriage to such a creature was hazardous and brought calamity down upon men's heads. These arguments were already prevalent in the Christian world. Direct attacks on the institution of marriage emanated chiefly from those Christian authors and thinkers who spent most of their lives as monks or priests, and who were thus denied emotional bonds with women. Contrastingly, the Jewish religion viewed marriage as a central precept and a religious value. In other words, while the misogynistic tales in Jewish and Christian folk culture are indeed similar, their respective practical implications as construed by the religious leadership were at odds: In Judaism, marriage was an obligation, according to the ancient principle "In the west [Palestine] they used to ask a man who married a wife thus: Matza or motze? 'Matza' for it is written: Whoso findeth [matza] a wife findeth great good (Prov. 18:22). 'Motze,' for it is written: 'And I find [motze] more than death the woman'" (Eccles. 7:26) (*Berakhot* 8a). A successful marriage, or its failure, was seen as the hand of destiny or of Divine Providence. Conversely, in medieval Christianity, the most extreme conclusion was sought from the image of woman as reflected in folk culture—separation of the sexes. Marriage was only sanctioned out of necessity.[91]

The misogynic stories, according to their literary construction and social function, belong to the genre of the novella as described above. Nonetheless, there is a steep contradiction between the themes of the misogynic tales and the themes of the novella. The novella describes the adventures of its hero or heroine. With the aid of wisdom or by force of destiny they merit the fulfillment of their romantic aspirations—to marry their beloved. All the misogynic tales that we have just seen *begin* at this stage, and present what happens *after the wedding*. During the marriage, the true time of trial, the woman's hidden nature is exposed; she is revealed to be captive to her desires, disloyal, and reckless. The misogynic tales thus turn the narrative model of the novella upside down: they choose to pick up the narrative where the "original" novella left off, and turn the model of romantic love into a pattern of betrayal and disillusionment. It is difficult to avoid the conclusion here that the misogynic tales can be seen as a kind of parody of the romantic novella. This is a tale that takes a model of romantic love and knocks it down to expose its insincerity. It claims that a woman's integrity is a sham that crumbles after the concluding stage of the novella, i.e., marriage, which she views as a mere stepping stone in her headlong rush to satisfy her appetites; the continuation in the misogynic tale reveals her true colors. The conclusion of the tale "Solomon's Three Counsels" expresses the parodic quality of the tale in an unambiguous manner: after King Solomon revokes the death sentence of his former servant, who almost died on account of his wife's witlessness, the King says to him: "The wisdom you acquired saved you from death, and from the hand of this woman; Now go and rejoice with your wife." In other words, the vast wisdom he acquired was recognition of woman's nature. How could he now maintain a marital life? Or, perhaps now that he was aware of her true nature, he could resume his married life with the appropriate caution. The contradiction between Judaism's imperative to marry, and women's presumed wicked nature, manifests vividly the deep strains etched on the Jewish versions (oicotypes) of misogynic tales from general folklore.

Presenting folk literature—and the novella in particular—as anti-woman is not entirely justified. Alongside the novellas discussed above are others that come to praise womanly traits. In the famous tale known in international folk literature as the tale of Genofeva or, "The Slandered and Banished Wife," a merchant leaves his wife in the care of his brother. The brother tries to seduce her and, failing that, to rape her. She manages to ward him off, he accuses her of adultery, and she is stoned (until this point it is similar to the ancient novella belonging to the same type—Susannah and the Elders). A father, who brought his son to Jerusalem to study Torah, finds her beneath the heap of stones and employs her as a governess. She rebuffs an amorous household servant, who then murders the child in her care. She flees again, and this time sailors, whose attentions she declines, leave her on a desolate island. She gains fame there as a healer. After the Almighty afflicts all the men who have wronged her with leprosy, they come to her to beg a cure—her husband and his brother among them. She reveals her identity to them and, after they confess their sins, returns to her husband. The tale, among the most famous in medieval European literature, enjoyed literary adaptations, and is first found in a Jewish version in a manuscript from the early thirteenth century, and thereafter in other versions.[92]

If we examine this tale against the model that makes marital status the criterion for determining the attitude towards women, we find that, like the misogynistic tales, this story commences after the wedding. Unlike them, the woman's behavior is exemplary: she risks her life, time after time, for the sake of marital fidelity. Furthermore, her image in the eyes of the surrounding society is perpetually at odds with her true nature. She is maligned unceasingly, her image as a frivolous female prompts the men around her to attempt her seduction, yet she is faithful to her principles—indeed until death. The contrast between her image and her true colors seems to be a direct reaction to that literature with a negative attitude toward women. This tale presents those derogatory depictions of women not only as false, but as an image invented by men—in accord with their own wishes and appetites—to superimpose upon women. The basic course of the tale, in which men unceasingly accuse the heroine of licentiousness, spotlights this false image, while her conduct suggests the alternative—acknowledgement of her true qualities.

Another famous tale, among the most widespread in medieval Jewish literature, is "The Bride and the Angel of Death." It also picks up the woman's story from the time of her wedding. A great holy man was told upon the birth of his only son, when he was already an old man, that the child would die on his wedding day. In due time, that day arrived; the Angel of Death appeared at the wedding in the form of a beggar and demanded the bridegroom's soul. His bride refused to part with him, and demanded that the Angel of Death obey the words of the Torah, "When a man has taken a new wife, he shall not go out to war, neither shall he be charged with any business: but he shall be free at home one year, and shall cheer his wife whom he has taken" (Deut. 24:5). In other versions, the Angel of Death was willing to take another life in lieu of the bridegroom. His father and mother refused, but the young wife agreed without hesitation to give her own soul over to the Angel of Death as ransom for the life of her bridegroom. In all the versions, the wife's intervention is accepted, and her husband enjoys an immediate pardon from heaven as a result of her arguments.

In this context, it is impossible not to also see this tale as a nearly direct response to the prevalent argument among men that women, once wed, shed their love and fidelity. The young man's marriage to his bride is perceived here as the best thing that could happen to him: her absolute devotion and cleverness lift the foreordained sentence; this marriage comes across as a kind of rebirth, as additional life given to him by his wife. Were it possible to corroborate via some other source, I would say that a woman must have composed this tale. It seems that only a woman, with her personal experience in the culture of the Middle Ages, could have reacted in this manner, couching her response in the language of narrative metaphor.[93]

The two tales "The Slandered and Banished Wife" and "The Bride and the Angel of Death," are not originally Jewish tales. They are found in general folklore prior to the appearance of the Jewish versions, and underwent a consummate process of Judaization that enabled them to blend seamlessly with Jewish culture. Not so the third example, which was apparently created within Jewish culture, its origins at least as old as the rabbinic period. I mean the tale of "The Weasel and the Well," mentioned earlier in connection with the transition of Hebrew narrative from the rabbinic period to the Middle Ages. A young man walking along a path hears cries for help from the bottom of a deep well. He consents to rescue the maiden who fell in only if she will lie with him. After he pulls her out, she persuades him in her wisdom not to sin, and to do as he will with her only after they are properly married. They appoint as witnesses to their marriage the well which she fell into and a passing weasel. Once home, the young man forgets his vow—and marries another. The young woman keeps hers faithfully. In order to reduce public pressure upon her to marry, she feigns insanity, thus putting off all suitors. The two children born to the young man are killed: one falls into a pit; a weasel bites the other. He divorces his wife and takes back the woman whom he had rescued from the well.

Like the tale of "One Man Among a Thousand," this tale is built on a comparison between the behavior of a man and a woman in the same given situation. But here the man is presented as the capricious one: he demands that the maiden commit a transgression while she is still in the pit, in other words, conditions the obligatory saving of a life on the satisfaction of his own lust; he then betrays her with the appearance of the first new woman. The maiden herself—unlike the surrounding society—does not view marriage as a means of social advancement, as, if she did, she would have married someone new. Her loyalty to the man to whom she had given her word cost her social standing, and condemned her to loneliness and alienation within her own family—just like the faithful but maligned woman (Genofeva) in the tale discussed above.

In sum, even if the medieval literature with an anti-woman bias is vaster and richer than that which offers her testimonial, it is by no means exclusive and unequivocal. At least in the realm of folk literature, it seems possible to hear the woman's voice—or perhaps the voice of men expressing an alternative understanding—in those tales constructed as antithetical to the misogynic literature. While the latter set forth marriage as an endpoint of woman's loyalty and the beginning of man's death knell, the former present it as the start of a genuine alliance, and as a new life given to him; where the latter built test situations in which the man passes heroically while the woman quickly turns traitor, the others describe the situation in reverse. In any case, folk literature's perspective on the attitude toward women—expressed primarily in the genre of the novella—indicates polyphony: even if, quantitatively, the tales expressing hatred or anxiety at women and femininity outnumber the others, the voice of the others counterbalances them with their power and authenticity.

[H] Tales of Magic and Demonology

Tales featuring magic, demons, and supernatural forces honeycomb the preceding sections that focused on other folktale themes and genres in the Middle Ages. Still, tales of magic and demonology merit a section of their own, as the demonic world pervaded the medieval consciousness, and as the rabbinic literature of the preceding age had left behind a weighty legacy in this sphere. Two key factors shaped the Jewish approach to the demonic world in this period: the cultural heritage of the rabbinic period, and the surrounding non-Jewish world. In the Middle Ages, intensive reading and study of the Talmud and Midrash became the focus of Jewish culture, hence it comes as no surprise that the rich demonic world found in these works (described in chapter 4, section H) so decidedly influenced the approach to the subject. The basic conviction of the rabbinic period, namely that "the world is full of demons" who surround mortals, lying in wait for a chance to attack, informed the worldview of medieval Jewry. This attitude comes to the fore in the realm of folk narrative. Tales of witches (such as Yokhani Bat Retivi), demons (Ketev Meriri, Bar Themalyon), and wise men who created human beings with the power of the Name, were much copied in the medieval collections of tales. They constitute further proof of the inter-period cultural transfer, a transfer that conforms to expected natural development.

The influence of foreign demonology on Judaism during this period is impressive and fascinating. It is especially prominent in the period's region of Germanic culture—in the circles of the Hasidei Ashkenaz (the medieval German pietists). Their literature—the writings of R. Judah the Pious and his pupil, R. Eleazar of Worms—contains dragons, vampires, werewolves, and a host of other demonic creatures. These tales do not echo ancient Jewish literature, but medieval German folklore. It is as if R. Judah the Pious and R. Eleazar heard these tales from non-Jews—and wove them straightaway into their own works. Over the course of hundreds of years, as the great Jewish communities consolidated in the region of the Rhine, for example, diverse elements of Germanic culture (folk elements, in the main) penetrated and became a part of the world of Jewish beliefs and folk-ideas of the period. The great majority of the tales and motifs never underwent a process of Judaization. They are told among Jews in the same manner as in Christian society.[94]

> A witch who kills with magic, or a kind of striga, continues to do harm even after her own death, if her body is anointed with that same thing that is familiar to them . . . [such a witch said to them:] "Even after my death you will not escape me." They said to her: "Tell us how to escape you after your death, and you will have expiation." She said: "Take a stake, drive it through my jaw, into my mouth, into the ground, and my spirit will not be able to harm you." (Dan, *Sippurim Demonologiim* ["Demonological Tales"], p. 14, #2)

> A tale wherein the demon appears as a cat: The man came and held on to it tightly until he [could] shut it up in a box. The next day [when he opened

the box, he saw that] it was a woman whom he recognized. He said: "I will not leave you [until you promise] not to harm me or my issue," and she swore and did no more harm. He said to her: "Who brought your body here?" She said, "First there was my spirit, then [the demons] brought my body, and my spirit entered the body, and here I am." (Ibid., p. 17, #12)

These tales date back to the twelfth and thirteenth centuries. R. Judah the Pious and members of his circle offer them as proof that the Almighty takes an active role in worldly affairs ("He has made his wonderful works to be remembered", Pss. 111:4). God's presence may not be felt in routine, daily phenomena, but it is unmistakable in the unusual, in the strange and supernatural. This is evidence of the depth of penetration of foreign folk beliefs into Jewish culture. It was so pervasive that moral leaders and circles used these 'imported' beliefs as theological proofs of the existence of God. If this was true of the learned, it was all the more so for other members of the community. These beliefs and tales served to express their anxieties over physical and spiritual maladies, disappearance in the darkness of the woods surrounding places of settlement in the Middle Ages, and menacing, perilous natural phenomena that they could not otherwise explain. Such tales are unequivocal proof of medieval Jewish society's integration into the cultural landscapes amid which it existed. The religious limitations that Judaism imposed on such beliefs were unable to prevent their dissemination among Jews. It should be noted that the tales underwent hardly any process of Judaization. They are told in the same manner, and with the same expressions and names, as in the period's non-Jewish culture.[95]

On the other hand, testimony of tales of witches that are Jewish tales in every respect survived from an earlier period and from a different region of Europe. In the eleventh-century *Scroll of Ahimaaz* from southern Italy, there are several typical tales of witches. The theme of the *Scroll* has nothing to do with magic. Rather, it chronicles the history of southern Italy's Ahimaaz family, prominent in the leadership of the Jewish community there for some two hundred years. Among tales extolling the family patriarchs are some that stress the dominance of supernatural forces, and *inter alia*, their grappling with witches:

> R. Shephatia was once walking about the streets of the city at night, and he heard the sound of wailing in the house of a neighbor and friend. He heard one woman speaking to another, the one above saying to her companion below, "Sister, take the child and keep him and together we will eat him." He listened closely to her words; he immediately went and took the child from her. Those women were not daughters of men, but demons who were passing in the night. He brought the child to his home, and showed him to his wife. They recognized him and concealed him in his bedroom. The child's father and mother had passed the entire night in anguish . . . R. Shephatia then

returned to his house with them; he told them all that had happened, and restored the child to them. (*The Chronicle of Ahimaaz*, translated by M. Salzman, New York 1924, pp. 81–82)[96]

For the most part, this is the same tale of witches-who-eat-children that we saw earlier in the traditions of Hasidei Ashkenaz. Here, however, the tale has become a Jewish tale of magic. It is told as part of a hagiographical cycle of the family patriarch, R. Shephatiah; it takes place in the Jewish street. The tale does not specify whether or not the witches (or the demons acting in their name) are Jewish, but all the other characters are, and the concluding words of thanksgiving are inarguably drawn from the Jewish culture. This tale, originally, it seems, was similar to those versions of tales copied in the writings of the Hasidei Ashkenaz (that is, devoid of any connection to Jewish culture), underwent important modifications. In this tale we see clear development, whose orientation it is to "naturalize" such beliefs and tales of magic, and turn them into part of the Jewish landscape.

A second typical tale of magic in the *Scroll of Ahimaaz* concerns another hero of the scroll, R. Aaron of Baghdad. He discovers a boy that a witch had turned into a donkey, and restores him to his father (p. 13). This tale also underwent a process of Judaization, similar to that of the above tale, but more importantly, it is a combination of the sources of magical tales that it uses. In Southern Italy, an ancient tradition is known to exist, of tales wherein a witch turns a young man into a donkey and uses him for her purposes. The earliest extant evidence of such traditions is the first-century work, *The Transformations of Lucius Otherwise Known as The Golden Ass*, by Lucius Apuleius. In this work, a tale of a witch who turns the protagonist into a donkey and sells him to a caravan of merchants serves as a framework for the entire composition. The second source of such tales is rabbinic literature, where we find the well-known tale of a sage who turns a witch into a she-ass, and rides her to market (*Sanhedrin* 67b). Such a blending of local, non-Jewish tales with traditions from the rabbinic period characterizes medieval Jewish magic tales.[97]

This tale includes yet another noteworthy factor, namely, the denunciation of the witch as a harlot, and the insinuation that she misused her young victim sexually. This is perhaps the best example of the merging of sundry origins in the period's tales of magic: the rabbinic period has already familiarized us with the conception of witches as prostitutes, and with the magic rites of antiquity that incorporated prostitution (the tale of Simeon ben Shetah and the Witches of Ashkelon, for example). The charge of harlotry leveled against the witch dovetails neatly with the earlier Jewish stereotype. Prostitution's link with magic was also a central element of medieval Christian culture, which saw every deviation from Christian doctrine as a variety of magic, and any magic that involved women as a preamble to prostitution. This was how medieval culture characteristically coped with "the other," the stranger, and the anomalous. This atmosphere assuredly influenced medieval Jewry as well.[98]

Magic, as a means of expressing social differentiation (or protest thereof), does not manifest itself only on the typological level—in the construction of "magical" stereotypes of "the other." It also comes to the fore in fashioning narrative situations that establish oppositions, struggles between "us"—the narrating society—and the other, the stranger whom society stereotypes as the "sorcerer." In medieval culture, such was the label affixed to women, lepers, homosexuals, and Jews. For the most part, Jewish narrative of the period affixed this tag to representatives of the other religion—the Christian clergy at its various levels. The use of the magic tale as a model for cultural polarization is not new to Jewish folk traditions. In chapter 4, section H, we saw how tales of "The Elders of Athens," or of the apostates, served in the folk culture of the rabbinic period to express attitudes toward Hellenistic culture and then-nascent Christianity. Such tales are also common in the Middle Ages. I would like to present two of the most widespread: R. Judah the Pious and the Bishop, and the legend of R. Meir Shatz (known as the "Akdamut Millin").

In the first tale, the Bishop of Salzburg undertakes to kill R. Judah the Pious, thereby delivering a blow to the entire Jewish community. He goes to Regensburg, where R. Judah lives, a knife hidden in his boot, and enters with his entourage. R. Judah the Pious, who knows of the plot, works his spells to trap the Bishop's head in the window of his house. He only consents to release his would-be murderer after the latter promises never to revert to his evil ways, and to treat the Jews well from then on. Ultimately, the Bishop even converts to Judaism, and becomes a righteous man. The tale appears in several versions in the traditions of Hasidei Ashkenaz, and in other sources of the period. In the second tale, a priest-sorcerer kills so many Jews that the community is moved to summon aid from across the Sambatyon River. The Jew from the Ten Lost Tribes who answers their call is a small man, and a hunchback. The priest, himself a giant, ridicules his new adversary, and faces him in a contest of magic before the king and all his ministers. The champion of the Jews successfully undoes all the priest's malevolent magic feats, then pounds his staff into the ground. With each blow, the priest sinks further into the earth, until he vanishes from sight altogether. This tale, also known as the tale of *Akdamut Millin*, after the opening words of the Aramaic hymn recited in the synagogue on the holiday of Shavuot, was very common in central and eastern Europe from at least the fifteenth century, in Yiddish and in Hebrew.

The two tales serve a similar purpose, i.e., to reproduce the religious-cultural confrontation between Judaism and Christianity on the folk level. Theological controversies between representatives of the two religions were an important component of social reality in this period. Even in places and times that were free of such debates, traditions depicting them became a part of the Jewish worldview of the period. However, these controversies—real or fictitious—took place on the elite cultural level between Jewish authorities and Christian theologians. The broad strata of the folk (in both cultures) were far from fully comprehending them. In their eyes, disputes over interpretation of Scripture, the personification of God, the chosen people, the holy trinity, and messianism, were nebulous. It seems to me that, as in the rabbinic period, the folk traditions replicate the religious polemics to a more understandable plane, one that was tangible, whose results were immediate. Thus, for the folk, the contest of magic takes the place of religious debate over the serpentine details of quotations, and provides a clear victor and vanquished instead of ambiguous resolution. In the contest of magic, the actions of each side are clear and concrete, and the hero—the representative of the narrating society—finishes first.[99]

It is also noteworthy that in both tales (and in their numerous versions), the adversaries—the bishop or priest—are sorcerers. The Jewish representative is a rabbi or a simple Jew, who employs magic only in self-defense. Again we encounter the phenomenon of "demonization of the other," this time from the Jewish perspective. The priest or bishop is the foreigner. Neither they, their actions, nor their doctrine, are understood or considered valid, and therefore they are dangerous "to us." This "alienness" translates straightaway in the folk traditions and beliefs into the stereotype of the sorcerer or demon. The difference between Judaism and Christianity in this matter lay in the consequences. The demonic stereotype of the Christian in Jewish eyes remained in the category of cultural definition; the demonic stereotype of the Jew in Christian eyes had practical ramifications: as a result, Jews were tortured and burned at the stake.

In all the tales we have looked at so far, the demonic contact is necessary to defend oneself or save representatives of the Jewish community from the hands of the demons into whose hands they had fallen. The other possibility is initiated contact, wherein the protagonist himself acts to attract the demonic forces. Aside from a few exceptional instances, such contact is considered perilous, and ends in calamity:

> [There was] one who wrote amulets, and along came the demon and lay with his wife before him and he did not see, but the wife saw. (Dan, *Sippurim Demonologiim*, p. 19, #18)

The writing of amulets for the purpose of warding off demons, or to initiate contact with them for various purposes, weakens and exposes the writer of the amulets himself to demonic attacks ("Evil spirits trouble only those who provoke them first, such as one who wrote, or whose forebears wrote amulets, or who dealt with invocations or spells, or who sought answers to his questions in dreams. Therefore one should not involve himself in such things, and he should not say, I will, for the sake of saving a life, traffic in oaths or amulets, for this is not wisdom, as [by doing so] he shortens his life and that of his seed"

[*Sefer Hasidim*, end of #379]). Contact with demons was likely motivated by the material goals of profit and pleasure, in which case it was certainly dangerous and deserving of punishment. In two similar tales, the protagonist responds to the demons' temptation: in one, he does not chop down a particular tree growing in his field, in accordance with the request of the demon who inhabits it. The demon repays him with a daily gift of silver. He prospers, but after a time his sons and servants start to die off. He appeals to a rabbi, who explains that he is being punished for his contact with demons. He then cuts down the tree, in spite of the demon's threats, and finds a great treasure beneath it. Thus he benefits without the assistance of the powers of darkness. In the second tale, a pious man finds a beautiful stone, which turns to him and asks him to care for it, wash it, put it in a fine place in his home, and so on. The stone makes him a rich man, but when it asks him to light a candle before it, he understands that he has committed the sin of idol worship. He shatters the stone and ultimately merits a vast treasure.[100]

The two tales are similar not only in their narrative course, but also in their orientation. They are exemplary tales that seek to cast dread and to forewarn (e.g., the death of the sons in the first tale), but also promise rewards to those who mend their ways. It is interesting to consider what, precisely, the caveat is in these tales. For in the period of the Middle Ages there was no longer reason to fear that Jews would turn to idol worship. The answer lies in that this concept, idol worship, in the Middle Ages, stood for Christian ritual. This was the real danger, idol worship performed by Jews being but a distant historical memory. Medieval Jews perceived Christian ritual as the worship of concrete symbols—like trees or stones—that could be seen and touched. It should be noted that this brand of idolatry was not coerced, but inadvertent—the Jews in these tales acted thus out of naivete and greed. This was the peril against which the tales seek to sound the alarm: when the Jew is compelled to openly become a Christian ("to worship idols"—to accept the tangible symbols of Christian ritual), he can cope by choosing martyrdom, which medieval Jewry polished and perfected specifically to this end. But when the road to Christianity was circuitous, or paved with avarice, the danger was greater by far. Day-to-day contact with the symbols of Christian ritual—for example, trade in Christian holy artifacts, construction of churches or their decoration, the teaching of Torah or liturgical hymns to Christian priests who would later use them in their own rites, the working of skins and their sale for parchment upon which the sacred writings of the Christians would be copied—was insidious. In many such cases the Jew, unaware of his peril, was liable to sink ever deeper, like the protagonists of the tales, until his soul was beyond salvation.[101]

Yet underlying both tales, beyond their didactic, exemplary nature, there exists the dread of contact with the demonic. One of the most important medieval compilers of tales, the thirteenth-century Cistercian monk Caesarius of

Heisterbach, argues: "Satan causes his servants to become wealthy and prosper in this world, but he always betrays them in the end." Then he offers a series of tales about people who maintained a close association with demons, who initially helped them succeed and prosper, but ultimately did them harm, and killed them with great cruelty. Caesarius also offers tales of men and women who wanted to see the demons (or Satan). Upon doing so, they faint, and are either ill for a long time or die straightaway. These tales, both in Judaism and, especially, in the Christian culture of the Middle Ages, indicate the natural human attraction to the dark side of reality, to those same strata not controlled by the official authority of the Church. This is one reason that the Church so sharply demonized heretic sects, such as the Manicheans, the Bogomils, the Cathars, and many others, whom it could not control, and who, by the same measure, exerted a strong pull on broad sections of society.[102]

In another important grouping of tales, Caesarius presents the leaders of these sects as demons or as servants of Satan (pp. 330–353, #18–25), and whosoever admires and is attracted by "their spells" is as one who worships demons. This warning against any contact with demonic forces exposes the profound concern of the official institutions (Judaism, the Christian Church) over prospective loss of authority, as the tendency of the folk strata was indeed to seek answers to the questions of their daily existence outside the normative framework that these institutions provided. In one of the tales belonging to this group, Caesarius tells of a priest who wanted to see demons. The sorcerer to whom he turned drew a circle around him and warned him not to put anything at all outside the circle. A demon, masquerading as a beautiful maiden, tempts him from beyond the circle; he sticks a finger out, and they carry him off. The sorcerer sends an emissary to the demons; it turns out that they have taken him to Hell. They are persuaded to return him, and he becomes a god-fearing monk (tale 4, pp. 318–320). An interesting variant of this tale is found in the Hebrew literature of the same period:

> It once happened that a man who was very wealthy had a very beautiful wife whom he loved exceedingly. In his courtyard were four very high and fortified walls. Therein was an opening [in the walls] to his courtyard. And there is a custom that none who enter within those walls ever leave or return home. And two satyrs dwell there. Some say that there lies the Gate of Hell. The man was very wicked and parsimonious, and his wife was wicked, and they had no sons. She desired always to approach that same opening and see what was inside. Her husband always prevented her and kept watch, for he knew that such was her inclination. One time the king required that same man, and sent for him. The man told his houseman to watch his wife and to constantly follow her wherever she might go. The man went to the king who had summoned him [and stayed there a while].

Meanwhile, the wife said to the houseman: "Listen to me and do my bidding and let me go to the opening, and I will give you whatever you wish, for if you do what I ask from you I will do you great favours." He said to her: "Please, my mistress, do not do this, you will be lost, and for nothing. My master gave me an order, saying to watch over you as the apple of his eye. For your love, to him, is wonderful and you have been very dear to him. Do not do this great wrong, and do not bring him to his grave for sorrow." She said to him: "On your life, I will go no closer to the opening then the distance of a bowshot." He did not want to let her. She persisted, until she went to the courtyard against his will and without his favor, and no one was with them in the house. The man yelled loudly and did not know what to do, and he was very grieved and ran after her. She approached the opening. As she came there, one who was inside extended his hand and pulled her in, and the door shut behind her. The man said: "And I, where shall I go from this distress that will find my master." The man went and hid in a room and was there until his master returned home.

And since the master came and did not see his wife and his servant, he fell to the floor, agitated, and he fainted. All his neighbors came to console him, but he would not be consoled. He said: "I would descend to my wife even to the netherworld." And he wept greatly for her. He went and searched fruitlessly throughout his house until he came to the room of his servant and there heard groaning and moaning. He said: "Who is groaning there—is it my servant?" He said to him: "I am your servant in your debt." He approached him and fell before him weeping and pleading. He said to him: "Where is my wife?" He stood and told him all that had happened. He said to him: "I swear I will not rest nor be still nor silent until I know where she is, in what place and what she is doing, and if I can be with her."

What did he do? He gave all he had to his kin and walked, single-mindedly, until he entered a vast forest. He went the distance of six days' walking and came across a very tall, and black, and exceedingly hideous man. He bid him good day and was bid a good day in return. The man was terribly frightened for he had never before seen his like. The tall man said to him: "I know what you seek, you seek to see your wife. If you want to come with me I will show you where she is and you can speak to her." He said to him, "For all the king's treasure, if he wanted to give it to me, I would not want to go with you." The tall man said to him: "Is there no man whom you trust in your home?" He said to him: "Yes." He said to him: "Lead him to me in eight days' time, and you will find me here."

The wealthy man left him and went on his way, and returned home. His loved ones gathered around and asked him if he had found or heard anything regarding his wife. He said to them: "Yes. Is there any man among you who would do my bidding? If ever I have done a favor for any man among you, now the time has come that you can pay me back for all I have done for you all my life." One of his young men came and said: "Master, you brought me up. Tell me whatever it is that you want and I will do your bidding, and I will take utmost care in fulfilling your instructions." He said to him: "I want you, for I have found you to be loyal and I like you, and I trust in you. Come with me and do all that I tell you." The two went together and came to the forest, to the place where he had earlier been, and the big man arrived. The young man feared him very much. His master said to him: "My son, you must go with this man and he will lead you to my wife, and you will speak to her. And if you can bring her [back] with you I will give you [vast] wealth and you will inherit all that I have." He said to him: "I will do as you have said."

He went with the big man, and he led him into Gehenna and he saw there many people he recognized suffering their judgement in Gehenna. And his master returned to his home. The young man said to him: "Show me my master's wife." He led him to a chamber and it seemed to him as if all the chamber, the walls and the ceiling, were covered in glittering gold, and the floor [was] of fine stones, red and sparkling. And he saw the wife of his master sitting in a chair of gold and dressed in golden clothing, and all her surroundings seemed to him to be of gold. Before her was a table of gold set with all sorts of golden foods and many servants, some of whom cut the food for her and others who poured white wine for her into a golden cup. When he saw her he dropped to the floor and said to her: "Praised be He who gave of his honor to beings of flesh and blood, for never have I seen any queen as honored as you [are, here]. And my master is saddened for you and has not eaten for days, he is fasting and he sent me after you [to tell you to] come back to him if you can."

She said to him: "Sir, listen to me. All that you see around me is a consuming fire. This room and the desk and all that I am wearing, and the chair in which I am sitting and all that I am eating is fire that consumes to Abaddon devouring my body and flesh. And the white wine that you see, that they are pouring for me into a cup of gold, the cup is fire. And the wine is molten lead that I drink hour after hour. And were all the world mine I would give it up happily to go outside for an hour to cool myself off, for my soul and body are burning. And tell my master thus, that all the sinners of Israel in the flesh are thus in Gehenna. And tell him to repent from his wicked deeds, for great is the power of repentance." He said to her: "And for what transgression do you [serve] such a harsh sentence?" She said to him: "For many wrongs and transgressions that I committed, for I committed adultery with another man and I desecrated the Sabbath, and I lay with my husband while menstruating, and I had no compassion for the poor and orphans, and many such deeds I did." He said to her: "Can any mortal redeem you from this judgement?" She said to him: "No. For I never had sons. Had I one son by my husband who could publicly recite, *Bless God, the blessed One,* and the public would reply, *Blessed is God the blessed One, for all eternity,* and all of the *Kaddish,* I would be redeemed at the end of my year." He said to her: "I will go and tell him all of this." She gave him a ring that was still on her finger, that he had given her, and she said to him: "Say that this should be a sign that you speak the truth regarding all you say to him."

He took leave of her and went with the man who had brought him there. He led him to the place from whence he had taken him and took his leave of him and went home. When his master saw him he rejoiced, and [he] told him all he had seen and gave him the sign, and he believed his words. What did that man do? He went to the synagogue and asked for mercy from the Holy One, blessed be He. With great weeping and a broken heart, he repented fully and did not move from there until his soul departed. And a heavenly voice said: "This man is summoned to the world to come." This is to fulfill that which is said, "That I may cause those who love me to inherit substance; and I will fill their treasures." (Ms. Oxford-Bodleiana, Or. Heb. 135, pp. 338b–339b)[103]

The tale exhibits the main characteristics of the demonic tale of the period. It is based on folk beliefs connected with demons: the danger inherent in any contact with their world—the rich man in the story maintains within his very own courtyard a dwelling-place for demons. This proximity perhaps benefits him (although not stated explicitly, it may be that his wealth and status were due to the demons' presence), but in the end, as in the other Jewish and Christian tales, suffering and catastrophe result. The tale also indicates the connection between demons and hell. In no tale, neither Jewish nor Christian, is a man dragged away or kidnapped by demons unless it is to hell. In other words, the presence of the demons can, ultimately, lead only to the abyss from whence there is no return.

One of the richest themes in medieval Christian and Jewish literature is the description of Paradise and Hell, a theme which reached its pinnacle in Dante's *Divine Comedy.* It is known that Dante based his poetical visions on a long line of folk traditions, mystical visions, and the like, in which the protagonist tours the divisions of Paradise and Hell, and describes in detail all he has seen. Our tale, which predates Dante (before the thirteenth century), takes up this same theme: the protagonist-narrator tours the various sections of the netherworld, and sees there familiar faces, suffering punishment for their sins. Another prominent element in the tale is the temptation which the woman cannot resist—as in the Christian tales—namely, to make contact with the demonic.

Here, at this precise juncture, lies the difference between the tale and its underlying folk belief. The tale uses folk belief to expose the human dimension behind the protagonist's action: the husband does not seek to prevent his wife from making contact with the demons on account of some religious taboo, but because he has her best interests at heart; a difficult internal battle rages within the woman herself between dread of the world of demons and curiosity, over whose pull she has no control. Thus the demonological beliefs here become narrative plot: the general, abstract belief is translated into the language of human feelings and emotions.[104]

Both the Hebrew tale and its Christian parallel (excerpted above in the version of Caesarius of Heisterbach) have an exemplary orientation: their protagonists—the young man in the Christian tale, the husband in the Hebrew—repent after returning from Hell (in the Hebrew tale it was not the protagonist himself who visited there, but his emissary). They acknowledge their sins and devote themselves to the monastery or to the Torah. In both, repentance and confession are the path to salvation from death, and from Hell itself. In other words, this demonic tale can be read on several levels: as an expression of the period's demonological beliefs, as a reflection of the human dimension behind contact with the demonic, and as a didactic means—in the spirit of the medieval exemplum.

Yet the boldest, most striking episode in the tale is probably the young emissary's encounter with the woman in her underworld abode. This encounter also has an exemplary dimension, as the woman confesses her grievous sins and enumerates the dreadful punishments awaiting such sinners. But the main issue in this episode is inherent in the nature of the punishment: to outward appearances, the woman lives like a queen—in a fabulous room, dressed in royal garments, and surrounded by servants and food aplenty. But it turns out that these are merely external effects cloaking a horrific punishment: everything is wrought of a fire that burns her, inside and out, without cease and without respite.

In the manner of tales of reward and punishment, this tale upholds the model of "the punishment fits the crime": hers is perfectly suited to match her transgressions. She had led a double life—appearing to be a woman like any other, who conducted her life according to conventional Jewish norms, yet in truth, she lived a wanton life of sin. This duality is replicated in her punishment: an outward appearance of glory, satisfaction, and contentment overlaying torment and terrible agony. This duality is also an expression of the more encompassing dimension of the life of that same couple—their human versus demonic lives: they broadcast a facade of human life while within, in the most concealed and protected spot of their courtyard, they lived in dangerous proximity to the forces of darkness. Their lives revolved around these forces; their prosperity emanated from them. In Hell, the same external image is preserved, even made to glow more brightly, but those same demons whose company the couple sought in life burn the sinner from within after her death. In this tale, the metaphorical form succeeds in elevating the dread of the demonic, especially its emotional expressions, to an impressive artistic peak.

Another sort of destructive contact with the demonic world is possession, wherein supernatural entities (demons, spirits of the dead) invade a human body. Such tales were also widespread, as will be recalled, in antiquity, particularly in the first centuries of the Christian era. But it was the Middle Ages that saw this narrative theme flourish. In Christianity, the New Testament's legacy to medieval saints was the idea of *imitatio Christi* (they wished to banish demons that took over a man's body, as Jesus did). Also feeding the growth of this narrative theme were social and cultural conditions that led to outbreaks of mass hysteria, interpreted as demonic possession of the stricken bodies. The profusion of such cases among nuns, and women in general, indicates their strong link to women's status in the Middle Ages, with the suppression of sexual and maternal nature, and with the existential anxieties that characterized the atmosphere of the Middle Ages.[105]

The tales of demonic possession generally follow a fixed pattern; a man discovers worsening signs of odd behavior: swooning, sensory loss, severe spasms, protruding eyes, and dangling tongue. In all descriptions of possessions, the voice motif is most recurrent: the victim speaks in a strange voice, not his own, a woman's voice emerges in deep, masculine tones, and utters things that have no connection to the individual speaking. This is generally a definitive sign that another creature—a demon or the spirit of one departed—is speaking through the victim's body. A rabbi or expert in exorcision of demons is summoned; he employs incantations, the reading of appropriate passages from the Old or New Testament, or makes the sign of the cross over the body. A conversation ensues between the demonic creature, who possesses the body, and the exorcist, in which the spirit identifies himself and enumerates the reasons that led him to invade the body in question. Ultimately, the demonic entity releases the victim and departs.

The most salient function of these tales, in both Christian and Jewish traditions, is exemplary: they testify to the existence of God, to his dominion over the world, and to the religious system of reward and punishment. In the tales of demonic possession concentrated in Caesarius of Heisterbach (chapters 9–15, pp. 330–336) the possessing demons answer the exorcist's questions. They describe Paradise and Hell, the punishment of sinners, God's grace, and the cruelty of the demons appointed to carry out the punishment of the sinners. Contact between the human and the demonic worlds comes to give voice to the demons, to reveal through them what happens in the world beyond. In Jewish culture, the tales are designed with a similar function: to expose the system of reward and punishment that is the basis for the existence of the world, to present via the demonic forces who come "from there" the punishment of the sinners. There is one main difference between the Christian and Jewish cultures:

most of the Jewish tales concern spirits of the departed who take over the body of a living being, namely, "dybbuks," not demons, whereas the latter prevail in the Christian culture. First, this indicates that the demonological obsession of the period's Christians did not carry over as is and with all its force to the Jewish world. Christian tales and beliefs saw demons in all places and in all things foreign and unfamiliar. This "demonization of the other" never reached the same level of force in the Jewish world. Second, the orientation of the tales in Judaism was to enable the sinner (whose spirit found refuge in a foreign body) to express himself, to prove that he personally acknowledged and comprehended his sins. This acknowledgement was the most important step toward reformation and gaining entrance to the world to come. It can be suggested that the orientation of the Christian tales of demonic possession is to edify through threat and intimidation (demons possess the victims). In the Jewish tales, this edification comes via understanding and self-awareness (by means of the words of the sinner himself, interlocutor of the exorcist). We will now look at one tale belonging to the end of the Middle Ages, from Safed of the sixteenth and seventeenth centuries, which can illuminate the composite sides of the Jewish dybbuk tales. A spirit enters a widow in Safed in the time of Rabbi Isaac Luria. He dispatches his disciple, R. Hayyim Vital, who demands that the spirit answer his questions:

"What was your sin and your transgression that your punishment is so great?" He [the dead man's spirit] replied, saying: "Because I sinned with another man's wife, and sired bastards. And now it has been twenty-five years that I walk in this sorrow, wandering the earth. I have no rest, for three angels of destruction walk with me wherever I go and punish me and beat me and proclaim before me: *Thus shall it be done to the man who made many bastards of Israel.*" . . . The Rabbi also asked him: "And what was done to you after your soul departed?" The spirit replied, saying, "Know that in [the city of Rosetta in Egypt], word spread of the sinking of a vessel. At once the Jews [of the city] went out to the river bank and retrieved [the bodies of] all the Jews who had drowned . . . and buried us in the cemetery. As soon as the Jews left the cemetery, a cruel angel came, a staff of fire in his hand, and beat upon my grave with that staff. At once the grave split open. . . . The angel immediately said to me: Wicked, wicked man, arise for judgement. He took me straightaway and placed me in the hollow of a sling, and in a single shot slung me from the city of Rosetta to the gate of Gehenna, that is in the desert. Upon my fall there before the gate of Gehenna . . . a thousand thousands of souls of wicked men sentenced [there] emerged, and all yelled at me and cursed me. They said to me: Here now, murderer, leave here you wicked troubler of Israel, you are not worthy even to enter here, you may not enter Gehenna. . . . "

The Rabbi said to him: "Who gave you permission to enter the body of this woman?" The spirit answered: "I spent a night in their home. In the still of the dawn this woman arose from her bed and went to strike a fire with flint and iron, but the rag did not want to catch the sparks. She persisted, but to no avail. Angered, she threw the iron and flint to the ground in anger and said: Go to the Devil. From [the moment she uttered] the word, devil, I had leave to enter her, for the angels of destruction gave me this leave." The Rabbi said to him: "For this transgression you were given leave to enter her body?" The spirit answered by saying: "Also because this woman is not as she appears, for she does not believe at all in the exodus from Egypt. On the night of Passover, when all of Israel rejoices and recites the *Hallel* [Psalms] and retells the story of the exodus from Egypt, she is laughing inside, thinking it all foolishness. In her heart she thinks this miracle never happened." The Rabbi at once said to the woman: "Do you believe with complete faith that the Holy One blessed be He created the heavens and the earth and can do anything He desires, and no one can tell Him what to do?" She replied, saying: "Yes I believe in [it] all." The Rabbi continued, saying: "Do you believe that the Holy One blessed be He took us out of Egypt and split the sea for us?" She replied: "Yes." The Rabbi also said to her: "Do you believe all of this with complete faith, and [do you] repent and regret [your] earlier [beliefs]?" And she said: "Yes," and began to weep. Our master and teacher Rabbi Hayyim Vital at once decreed a ban on the spirit and ordered it to depart via the little toe of [her] left foot, and by way of no other limb, for . . . that [departure damages the limb, rendering it] utterly useless. . . . Afterwards the spirit came at night to the windows of the house, and to the door to frighten the woman. Her kinfolk went back to the rabbi, and the rabbi at once sent his student, our aforementioned teacher and master Rabbi Hayyim Vital, to check the mezuzah and to ascertain whether or not it was kosher. He went and found the doorjamb had no mezuzah affixed to it at all. The rabbi immediately gave instructions that a mezuzah be hung on the doorjamb, and they did so. And from then on the spirit no longer came. (Nigal, *Sippurei Dybbuk* ["Dybbuk Tales"], pp. 67–70)

The tale condenses several prominent themes of demonic possession tales, first among them the exemplary orientation discussed above: the spirit describes in detail the torments it endured at the hands of the demons after death, its wanderings and its wretchedness. In this respect, the tale is very similar to the aforementioned Christian tales. The resemblance continues in the spirit's pretext to enter the woman—she uttered a curse, using Satan's name, thus allowing the spirit access. This motif is very widespread in Christian tales: a husband curses his wife, saying "the devil take her," whereupon she feels a spirit enter her ear—and take possession of her; a father, angry with his son, says, "the devil take him," whereupon a demon comes and takes him (Caesarius of Heisterbach, I, #11, 12, pp. 312–331); a girl is possessed and controlled by a demon from the age of five, because her father cursed her in the name of Satan, and so on (ibid., #26, 27, pp. 353–355). This motif also expresses the fear of proximity to the demonic world—the proximity being linguistic this time. The ancient folk belief that the spoken word, or language, has the power to act upon reality, hence great care must be taken to avoid slips of the tongue, undoubtedly underlies tales of this type. When they are told by educators and moralists—like Caesarius of Heisterbach or R. Hayyim Vital—they are transformed from folk beliefs into exemplary tales of ethics whose aim is to caution against attracting the demonic through language (or thought). Intuitive, daily repetition of the names of Satan and the demons is liable to accustom one to their presence, and thereafter even to appeal to them.[106]

The chief difference between the Christian and Jewish tales is, as aforesaid, that the latter features a dybbuk, in which the spirit of the departed can detail its sins: "I sinned with another man's wife, and sired bastards." In other words, his sins were sexual, i.e., physical; the punishment was "spiritual"—his spirit roams the world, beleaguered by angels of destruction, finding no rest. In juxtaposition, we have the widow: the dybbuk takes over her body for a spiritual transgression, "she does not believe at all in the exodus from Egypt . . . she is laughing inside, thinking it all foolishness. In her heart she thinks this miracle never happened." This reasoning apparently illuminates an important role intended for the tales of dybbuks and demonic possession in medieval culture. The woman's sin was her independent view of Jewish religion; she dared to stray in her outlook from the permitted norms of the society to which she belonged. From the perspective of Jewish society, she disassociated herself from her people. The spirit's penetration of her body and the loss of her senses are the symbolic expressions of this deviation from society's permitted boundaries. It should also be noted that such ideological deviation from the norm, i.e., intellectual independence in a woman, always carried the implication of promiscuity. It is hardly incidental that the spirit of a man who had sinned sexually "penetrated" her: this merging with a tainted, licentious being shows that her actions carried a similar taint, that of sexual independence (read: promiscuity).

The viewpoint of the widow is also germane to our analysis of this tale. The dybbuk's attack can be defined as a psychotic outburst molded by social conventions (in other words, an individual susceptible to such an outburst subconsciously "selects" a venue that conforms to the accepted traditions and beliefs of the culture to which he belongs). The woman feels she cannot go on suppressing her criticism of Judaism; no longer can she contain her spiritual independence. Jewish society of the Middle Ages did not allow women to vent deviant thoughts and opinions. The only means left her was to express them outside the conventional, rational framework, in the form of a hysterical outburst. In no way should such a phenomenon be construed as the woman's voluntary choice and decision. This is a symptom of emotional instability brought on by the acute internal tension between society's uncompromising restrictions and her own independent, critical personality. It appears that a significant portion of the tales of demonic possession of women in particular—in the Christian world as well (e.g. among nuns)—support such an explanation.

The contact between the human and the demonic takes place in dybbuk tales on two levels: in the penetration of the demonic entity into a living body, and in the tortures perpetrated by the demons on the spirit of the dead sinner. In this tale, we saw a detailed and very perceptible example of the contact with the spirits of destruction after death. Such theories are not unique to dybbuk tales, but are found even in incidental or deliberate encounters with the world of the dead. In them, the storytellers view the torments undergone by the dead sinners: the tale which we presented above about the entrance to Hell, wherein a woman dressed in royal garb suffers harrowing torment; a student of Rabbi Isaac Luria who sees sinners wrapped in chains, demons beating them mercilessly day in and day out (*Praises of the 'Ari*); the tale wherein R. Judah the Pious warned a prosperous member of his community not to shave off his beard, but in vain. After the man's death, R. Judah revived him before the eyes of the community. The dead man recounted to them that with the departure of his spirit "a demon like a great cow came and trampled on and butted my chin hairs with her muzzle, and brought a vessel full of pitch and sulphur and salt and took my spirit and put it inside, and it could not get out of there . . . [for the first letters of the verse] *You shall not round the corners of your heads, neither shalt thou mar the corners of thy beard* form the word *cows*." (Lev. 19:27)[107]

The moment of transition—or crisis—at which the certain encounter between every individual and the demonic world takes place, is the moment of death. We saw that, in the rabbinic period, this moment merited variegated narrative shaping, sometimes humorous, at other times soothing and consoling. In the Middle Ages, the encounter with the Angel of Death is always described as mysterious and dreadful, and perilous even to those who happen to be nearby. The Angel of Death appears with knife drawn, and his terrible visage is enough to chase a man's soul out of his body. After killing his victim, the Angel of Death washes his knife in a cup of water or other drink in the home, known thereafter as "the cup of poisoning." Anyone who drinks from it will surely die soon after. Out of the very fear and despair inspired by a full description of the horrific encounter with the Angel of Death—the ultimate fate of all who breathe—can spring an optimistic perception of life, death, and the beyond. Such an inversion, from the demonic to the mortal, from the dark and pessimistic perception of the world as linked to the demonic to hope and human fervor, does not exist in the realm of folk beliefs, only in the realm of the tale. As we have already seen above, it is the tale that can expose human motivations behind demonic manifestations.[108]

A typical example of such an orientation is the tale of "The Bride and the Angel of Death." Herein it is foretold of a child, before his birth, that he will die on his wedding day. The Angel of Death appears on that day to take his soul. When his parents ask him to take one of them instead:

> The Angel of Death forthwith draped [the father] in four cloaks of cruelty [and stood upon him]; Anger and rage, fury and wrath. And [the Angel] was armed as a warrior setting out to war. He unsheathed his sword, and rested his foot upon [the father's] neck to strike him. All two hundred and forty-eight organs of his body set to trembling, and he rose up and fled from beneath him. (Gaster, *Exempla*, p. 99)

The same happened with the mother. Only his fresh bride did not recoil. After he stood upon her "a second and third time, she [still] did not back away, but said: 'Finish the work of the King of all kings.' At once the Angel of Death was filled with pity for her. And a tear of mercy fell from the eye of the Angel of Death" (ibid.). In other versions of the tale, in which no such emotional response comes from the Angel of Death, he is also dissuaded by the bride's arguments. He returns to the Almighty and pleads for the groom's soul. That this tale is an offshoot of the famous myth of the Greek Alcestis and the Indian Savitry proves that before us is a phenomenon shared by diverse folk cultures distanced by time and place: the belief that the demonic threat can be diminished not only by known magical means, but also by human feelings. In the clash of demonic force with mortal beings, the individual—if he is honest and sincere—can push his demonic adversary back, overcome him, and can even mobilize him for good. It seems that such tales, which expose the human face behind the demonic phenomena, represent the few points of light in the darkness that characterized the demonological perception of the Middle Ages.[109]

The dual approach—fear and dread of the demons alongside attraction to the world of darkness that they represent—comes to its full expression in those stories featuring sexual contact between mortal and demon. Such relationships pepper all the ancient mythologies, including the Bible (Gen. 6:1–4—the sons of God and the daughters of men). In the Middle Ages, this theme enjoyed unique development. Two of the most famous tales in Jewish folklore treat this subject: Solomon and the Queen of Sheba, and the story of Lilith. In the former, whose principal development fell within the borders of Moslem culture but was well-absorbed in the Jewish world, Solomon's demon servants caution him against any sort of contact with the Queen of Sheba, as she is a demoness. By means of a glass floor (the king sits upon a floor of glass, beneath which water flows, making it appear as though he is sitting in water) he tricks her into lifting her skirts and revealing her hairy legs—the legs of a demon. He prepares a depilatory for her, and has relations with her only after she uses it—in other words, after he has shorn her of her demonic powers. Solomon's reputation as a woman-chaser, combined with his contacts with the demonic world, made him a suitable candidate for having sexual contact with a demoness.

Another famous tradition, found in the same source (*The Alphabet of Ben Sira*), is the legend of Lilith and Adam. She is apparently quite ancient—her roots date back to the period of the Ancient Near East, and she figures in the pagan beliefs and rites widespread among Jews in the cultural expanse of Babylonia-Persia in Late Antiquity. According to the tale, Lilith was not originally a demoness—she was created as Adam's first wife—but after refusing to accept his authority, she escaped and became the mother of demons. She consented to the demand of the angels (who had been dispatched to return her) not to enter any house upon which hung an amulet with the names of her and her retinue, and not to harm any who resided therein. Archeological excavation in a Jewish neighborhood of the ancient Iraqi city of Nippur uncovered the famous magic bowls—inscribed in Aramaic—upon them appeals to Lilin, Lilith, and so on. Invocations involving Lilith were, according to this evidence, tied to Lilith's sexual menace to the family. Thus Lilith came to be blamed for the erotic dreams of men and nocturnal emissions, and to be accused of endangering men who slept alone. Such beliefs were commonplace also in the Muslim east as well as in the Christian west.[110]

These relations with demons were perceived as negative and perilous. Nocturnal emissions produced the world's demons; sex with demons was considered likely to degenerate into orgiastic revelry that could only end in death and destruction. The late twelfth-century Bishop of Oxford, Walter Mapp, told in his book of exempla of men who wandered in the forest, heard voices of laughter and dancing, joined an orgy of demonesses, and never returned. He reports many similar events. We saw above, as well, the tale of Caesarius of Heisterbach, about the demon, disguised as a beautiful woman, who seduced a student. The student was then carried off to Hell. He tells other tales in the same vein, of cats who nestle erotically against monks and are later revealed to be demons; of a demoness in the guise of a nun, who caressed a monk as he lay naked in his bed—he died a short time thereafter. Still, the attitude toward this subject is not unequivocal. Relations between man and demoness can take a romantic, even human turn.[111]

The tale without which the Jewish demonical world of the Middle Ages cannot be discussed is known as "The Tale of the Jerusalemite." Its theme is the marriage of man and demoness which takes place on two different planes of existence: in the world of the demons, and in the mortal world. The protagonist is thrust into the world of the demons because he takes a wrong turn in the forest after his ship sinks in a distant land. The king of the demons forces him to marry his daughter—although the man has a family at home. According to the primary version of the tale, after the protagonist has children by the demoness, he asks her permission to visit his home town and see how his wife and children are faring. She permits him to leave for a year, but after the year is up he never returns. All the demoness's entreaties and arguments are of no avail, and after she despairs of keeping him there she kills him with a kiss. In these versions of the tale, a covert threat is not lacking—it is not possible to sunder a tie or pact made with the demonic world. But the demoness's arguments to her husband and his rabbi are so human in tone that they do not differ from the pleas of any woman whose husband would abandon her:

> She said to him, "I am your wife and you betrothed me and wed me and I have borne your sons and daughters. And when you came here you swore to me that you would return to me soon, and I gave you much silver and gold, and you broke your oath. I ask of you food and clothing and marital duty according to the law of Israel." (Ms. Oxford-Bodleian Or. 135, p. 256a)[112]

The image and conduct of the demoness are in keeping with the demonic world from which she came and to which the Jew who took a wrong turn was thrown: a big city, in whose every corner there is a study hall where men study Torah, celebrate the Sabbath lavishly, and pray publicly in synagogue. The salient human dimension in the world of the demons exists in all the many versions of this tale. It seems that, apart from the romantic factor of love between beings from different worlds, the tale's great popularity stems from this very human description of the world of the demons. Such a description has the capacity to assuage the dread and anxiety that encompassed the subject in the Middle Ages. As I emphasized above, fear of demons was in fact fear of the unfamiliar and the mysterious. By thrusting the mortal protagonist into the demons' world, the dark side of the menacing entity is illuminated. "The demons-who-are-like-people" turn the unfamiliar, the other, into the more familiar. We can now understand the other's feelings: love, jealously, loneliness—feelings fundamentally no different from our own. The tale type of "marriage between man and demoness" turns the demonological world of the Middle Ages into something more recognizable, enables its definition in human terms, and engenders an "understanding" of its motivations and behavior. Such an "understanding" is one way to mitigate and localize the dread of the demonic that was one of the foundations of the folk culture of the Middle Ages.

6 The Later Generations

The Folktale in Confrontation with a Changing World

[A] The Hasidic Story as Folk Literature

The tales that grew out of and around the Hasidic movement form one of the largest and richest veins to be mined in all of Jewish literature. They have taken both oral and written form concurrently during the last two hundred years—mostly in Eastern Europe prior to the Second World War, and thereafter in the United States and in Israel. Most evidence of this narrative's character, dissemination, and meaning has survived in small booklets that were printed cheaply and poorly in Poland, mostly in the 1860s and thereafter. More than one hundred and fifty such booklets were published, a significant portion of them in several editions. Financial expedience lay behind this form of publication for, unlike other books, these apparently did not enjoy the support of the wealthy members of the community. Moreover, the low cost facilitated their purchase by those for whom these books were intended: members of the lower classes of Jewish society. Reckoning that each such booklet contained, on average, several dozen tales, we get a glimpse of the rich repertoire of tales to grace Hasidic circles.[1]

The richness of the Hasidic tale begs a fundamental question—whence this vast development? The answer is bound firmly to the social and ideational character of the Hasidic movement. Indeed, scholars of Hasidism in recent generations underscore the tale's centrality to Hasidic culture. Hasidic doctrine imbued the tale with religious value and a role in the modes of worship. From a social perspective, Hasidism strived to reach the broadest strata of the people—including the indigent and the uneducated. The tale has always been a most convenient and effective means in the hands of any new religious movement to disseminate its ideas.

Two cardinal Hasidic notions were particularly well-suited to the tale: first, the teaching of the zaddik (i.e., righteous man, Hasidic leader). The zaddik's primary roles were to mediate between God and the Jewish individual, and "to raise the sparks from among the rinds." Such "deeds" (in Hebrew, *ma'asim,* hence the Hasidic term for the tales: "deeds of the righteous") were made tangible and "documented" through their recounting—via the telling of tales. The zaddik thus becomes a kind of mythic figure in the Hasidic tale, his actions revealed and documented in the plots of many diverse stories.

Another fundamental notion of Hasidism expressed mainly in tales is that of *devekut*, i.e., a state of "attachment" to God. This state can be achieved, *inter alia*, through corporeal means—eating, drinking, rejoicing, dancing—and, especially, through the tale. The tales, as we shall see below, serve as one of the central means, according to Hasidic teaching, of reaching a state of attachment to God. No longer deemed something of an inescapable extravagance that had somehow to be reconciled, the tale, here, perhaps for the first time in the history of Jewish culture, acquired vital religious significance.[2]

Numerous expressions relating to the social and religious function of the tale appear in Hasidic writing. Some do not differ from the attitude toward the tale evinced by the Jewish culture that preceded Hasidism. One is known as the "sweetening parable," that is to say, a spoonful of sugar helps the medicine go down. Thus, when the aim is to preach to the people, to guide them along the "bitter," arduous path of upholding burdensome precepts and prohibitions, a tale can lighten the load, make the "medicine" easier "to swallow." This comparison came to Hasidism by way of the preachers and ethicists who predated the movement, and is one of the widespread images that crystallized the Hasidic attitude toward the tale.

The therapeutic approach to the tale took root as early as the Middle Ages. The tale, by nature, is amusing and entertaining. It thus constituted a diversion from personal hardships and pain, and contributed to restoring the "balance" between the various elements held to determine a person's health (cold, warmth, moisture, and dryness), in other words, to curing illness. The prevalent, profound medieval concept of the connection between body and soul led to the description of many illnesses as psychosomatic, such that treating the soul was essential for recovery. The tale was considered by many physicians and thinkers, particularly in the Christian world, but also in medieval Judaism, to be one important avenue of such therapy.[3] A tale attributed to R. Nahman of Bratslav may indicate this notion's entryway to Hasidism:

> A tale about the daughter of our Rabbi (R. Nahman of Bratslav) of blessed memory: Our holy teacher came to her home and she was very ill. Our Rabbi sat in great sorrow and fell asleep. The Ba'al Shem Tov, of blessed memory, came to him and asked him, 'Why are you so grieved?' He said to him, 'Is not my daughter so very sick?' The Ba'al Shem Tov, of blessed memory, said to him, 'It is written in Psalms (18), *Great deliverance he gives to his king; and shows steadfast love to his anointed, to David, and to his seed for evermore. Its meaning: Great deliverance he gives to his king,* Who are the kings?— the Rabbis. That is, when the miracles and wonders God has done with the righteous are told, then the end of the verse is fulfilled—*and shows steadfast love to his anointed.* God, blessed be He, shows steadfast love to he who *re-*

counts [a word play here between *mashiakh* (messiah) and *mesiakh* (re-counts)] and tells of [the miracles and wonders] *to David, and to his seed for evermore*... And then our Rabbi, of blessed memory, told a tale of the Maharsha [Rabbi Samuel Edels] of blessed memory, and she was restored. (R. Nahman of Bratslav, *'Avaneha Barzel* # 53)

Here lies manifest the conception that recognizes the healing power of the tale, but the reasoning behind it is different from that of the Middle Ages. The tale's restorative power lies in the realm of the religious rather than the medical. It has the power to heal because through it Divine grace "emanates" to the patient:

> For the stories told about the righteous have a great power to bring wondrous salvation, as we have seen a number of zaddikim who, when they wished to bring about some salvation, would tell related tales and thus draw salvation to the matter at hand. (Zvi Moskovitch, *Otzar ha-Sippurim* ["The Treasury of Tales"], part 1, Jerusalem 1951, p. 3a)

These words seem to have been expressly intended to interpret the tale of R. Nahman of Bratslav. The tale has theurgic powers: by means of the tale that presents the hoped-for deed (salvation), one can bring about its equivalent in contemporary reality (healing the patient, for example).

Another and essential difference between the therapeutic approach to literature of the Middle Ages and that of Hasidim has to do with categories. In the Middle Ages, there was no limitation on genre, as long as it was entertaining and amusing, thereby fulfilling its medical function. In the two Hasidic citations above, it is clear that tales praising the zaddikim are called for, not just any tale. A mere symbolic recollection of the deeds of zaddikim (via telling the tale) is likely to effect that same phenomenon in contemporary reality. This is another reason that the main part of Hasidic narrative belongs to this category.

I do not intend to deal with the Hasidic tale in general below, but only with its folk manifestations. Not all Hasidic tales are folktales. A large portion of the educational stories that the teachers of Hasidism used in their sermons and conversations were created in a certain context (to explain an idea expressed in the sermon), and they were used only once. A considerable portion of the tales appearing in the collections mentioned here are compositional tales—pieced together artificially from known motifs—but did not "pass" the societal barrier, that is to say, they were not copied into other collections or told orally at other occasions, and thus cannot be regarded as folktales.

Even the celebrated tales of R. Nahman of Bratslav—an outstanding example of the great creativity to emerge from the Hasidic movement—cannot be regarded as folk literature. They make extensive use, as discovered by scholars long since, of motifs and tale types borrowed from the non-Jewish folklore of eastern Europe. But the form given them by R. Nahman was wholly original, and exclusive to the ideational and biographical orientations that characterized his spiritual world.[4]

[1] Performance Events

It is not by chance that in the writings of the Hasidic movement, relatively extensive documentation survived on the sources of the tales and the performance events at which they were told. As Hasidism saw every action, movement, or remark of the zaddik as having religious significance, it took great care to document precisely such phenomena. Naturally, not all these testimonies should be regarded as factual truth, yet they can attest to the tale's footing in Hasidic life. Since, as we have seen in the above quotations, tales of the zaddikim are so important in the Hasidic view, the question of their credibility holds tremendous significance. Only "true" tales may be told; only such have the power to act as is expected of them. The credibility of a tale handed down through several generations orally is based primarily on the trustworthiness of its bearers:

> I saw [fit] to go on telling the praise [of the Maggid (Preacher) of Kuznitz] from what I heard from the elders of our city who knew him, and what our fathers told us, as he was born in our city, the holy community of Apta (*Sefer Siftei Kodesh.* ["The Book of The Sacred Lips"], p. 3a)

> I heard more from the very old Hasid our teacher Rabbi Moses ha-Cohen, son-in-law of the zaddik Rabbi, our venerable teacher, Rabbi Issachar of blessed memory, grandson of the Rabbi the Maggid of blessed memory of Kuznitz. (Ibid., p. 4b)

> I heard from a Hasidic Torah scholar, a trustworthy individual, and old, in the city of Kuznitz, who heard [it] from his father who was a religious judge and teacher in Kuznitz that once. . . . (Ibid., p. 6a)

> I heard from an old man of about eighty years who was learned and God-fearing and trustworthy, by the name of R. Hanina from the city of Kuznitz. And he told me that he had a brother. . . . (Ibid.)

> These tales are new; only a very few have been in print. They were just collected from the mouths of men of truth, men of good deeds, who served

with the zaddikim of the generation may they rest in Paradise. (Preface to *Kehal Hasidim* ["Hasidic Assembly"]

That tale, full of feelings of woe, I heard from my father and teacher, who heard it from a man of Tarnopol, who heard it one man to another, all believers, sons of believers, God-fearing Hasidim whose thoughts are of the Almighty. (*Pe'er Mi-Kedoshim* ["The Glory of the Saints"], p. 158)

The tales written in this book are all true and evident, most of them told by wise men, zaddikim and saints and Hasidim, in order to rouse men's hearts to the ethical teaching that emerges from every tale. Before each tale I have noted who told it and from whom I heard it. (Preface to *Adat Zaddikim* ["Community of Zaddikim"], p. 17)[5]

These things speak for themselves: the repeated emphasis on the chain of transmission, on the character and credibility of the individual links in the chain, is critical to the tale's meaning and role. The tale is fit to be heard only if it is reliable, in other words, if it took place precisely as recounted. This reliability rests solely on the trustworthiness of the message-bearers. The closer they were to the event (whether from the same city, or the same time period) and, importantly, the more pious—as such most unlikely to lie, especially in regard to as sacred a topic as the deeds of the zaddikim—the more one could rely upon what they said. The preface of Menahem Mendel Bodek, one of the most important Hasidic authors, to the book, *Ma'aseh Tsaddikim* (1864) condenses these issues:

I think, too, that there is an essential difference between clarified and explained ethical remarks in the books of the pious, and the ethical teaching that comes of hearing a marvelous tale about a holy man of God. These things fly straight and unerring to the listener's heart . . . I maintain that such words are of tremendous benefit, as each and every tale has messages of great moral value, and all are true tales that I heard from Hasidim, men of good deeds. And I hope to God that this humble composition of mine will serve to augment reverence of the Almighty, which is the most sublime purpose in the world . . . And now, dear reader, put your heart into understanding some of what I have written, and may you find some merit in this unworthy work of mine. For these tales are worthwhile for all, for the small as for the great, for the wise as for the dull. Behold, the masses of simple folk, when they read an awe-inspiring tale about a great zaddik, a pillar of the world, will strain their ears to hear more of the works of God on earth as fulfilled through His servant the zaddik, and they will take note of the sheer might of the holiness of this righteous zaddik, and of the magnitude of his humility combined with the magnitude of his faith, and so on, on account of the tales. Then his spirit will break within him, and his heart will yearn to cleave unto the Almighty and to Torah scholars. (*Ma'aseh Zaddikim*, pp. 24–25)[6]

This preface, penned by someone with intimate knowledge of Hasidic story-telling, makes clear several themes of fundamental importance. First, the equivalence in the realm of religious hierarchy accorded to the literature of ethics and that of narrative. Bodek sees both as fulfilling the same religious function. And second—the credibility of the tales. Like other anthologists quoted above, Bodek emphasizes the piety of his sources, and therefrom the credibility of the tales. Nor do his remarks gloss over the social aspect of the tales: they are aimed, he points out, at the broadest strata of Hasidic society: young and old, simple folk and learned, with understandable emphasis on the simple folk. The tale is, according to this conception, the single most effective tool for spreading Hasidic doctrine (i.e., faith in zaddikim), and Judaism in general (that is, faith in God) to broad and diverse audiences.

[2] Oral and Written

The testimony brought thus far attests to the process of setting down in writing narrative traditions that circulated orally among the Hasidic communities, and of course continued to do so after the tales appeared in published collections. Descriptions of the performance events at which the tales were told aloud are further proof of the folk character of Hasidic tales. A well-known tale concerning the servant of R. Israel, the Ba'al Shem Tov, details his concern for his livelihood. The Ba'al Shem Tov instructs him that after his death he will wander among the Jewish communities, recounting the deeds he had seen with him, and in that way to make a living. But if it is clear that the platform for this tale is fictitious, there is no doubt that it elucidates one of the ways in which oral Hasidic tales spread, i.e., via professional raconteurs who made their living that way. There being, as we have seen, a great demand for such tales, clearly more than a few talented storytellers went that route. R. Nahman of Bratslav, who had a prodigious interest in tales, also attests, in a number of places, that he used to listen to tales of zaddikim at the home of the Ba'al Shem Tov, his great-grandfather in Medzibezh, and that it was they that stirred his soul to Hasidic faith. Furthermore, important testimonies survived as to how R. Nahman himself told his tales when his students visited him and discussed current events, such as the Napoleonic wars. In other words, the performance event had no established position, rather it fit in as part of everyday conversation.[7]

R. Israel ben R. Isaac Jaffe, wrote an introduction for his printing of the first edition of *Shivhei ha-Besht* ("Legends [literally, 'Praises'] of the Ba'al Shem Tov," Kopys, 1814), the first printed collection of such stories. It provides important testimony from the dawn of Hasidism on the determination of a more fixed framework for zaddik tales:

> I heard this from men of the holy land, that the first time there was a plague, Heaven be merciful, in the holy land, the holy Rabbi Menahem Mendel [of Vitebsk] of blessed and saintly memory [who went to Palestine in 1777] closed himself in with a quorum of ten men in his home, and for the duration of the confinement all of their prayers [protected them from disease]. On the holy Sabbath he did not speak words of Torah at the third meal, as was his usual custom, but instead would sit with his companions who would listen to his voice. With him was an old man, a disciple of the Ba'al Shem Tov, who would tell the praises of the Ba'al Shem Tov. One time on Sabbath, the Preacher Rabbi of blessed and saintly memory [Dov Baer, "the Great Maggid" of Miedzyrzec] came in a vision to the above-mentioned rabbi and said to him, "Are you not my student? Why do you not tell my praises as well?" And he decided to tell the praises of our great rabbi at the third meal. When the rabbi began to tell of his [teacher's] wondrous deeds, the above-mentioned old man began to tell about the Ba'al Shem Tov as was his custom and rejected his words. At once the rabbi understood that he would certainly be punished for this. Indeed it happened that immediately after the meal he became weak with intestinal disease, and it was not many days before he passed on. (*Shivhei ha-Besht*, A. Rubinstein edition, pp. 23–24)

Shivhei ha-Besht gave Hasidic narrative its basic format. All the Hasidic storytellers and writers saw and imitated it, in both form and content. Such a tale, opening the first edition of the book, must have had an important influence on Hasidic leaders as well. R. Menahem Mendel of Vitebsk introduced the practice here, in the wake of a one-time incident of plague in Tiberias, of telling tales of zaddikim at the third Sabbath meal. But if such a practice existed earlier still among the first Hasidic circles, clearly this pattern, forged at the beginning of *Shivhei ha-Besht*, created a kind of established performance framework according to which many of the Hasidic tales were told orally. By virtue of the creation of such a framework, Hasidic culture differs from the culture of every other period in the history of the Jewish folk narrative.

But the folktale is not limited, as we have already reiterated, to the oral traditions; it exists in writing as well, and in print. This holds especially true for the Hasidic folktale. The great richness of Hasidic story groupings is proof positive that the Hasidic tale's main channel of distribution, from the 1860s on, was printed material. The sanctity of the tale in Hasidism led to a situation wherein dozens, if not hundreds, of Hasidim were intensively engaged in collecting, editing, bringing to the printing house, printing, and distributing collections of Hasidic tales. Alongside the storytellers wandering among the Hasidic communities, telling tales of zaddikim, were the printers of these collections, peddling their books.[8]

The printing of a tale did not halt its narrative development. Copied repeatedly into new collections, a tale would undergo further revision and reworking, and depart the printed page to recirculate in the oral tradition. This dynamic, with which we are so familiar from the general folk narrative, also exists in Hasidic narrative. Evidence of such a process survived in the collection of tales about R. Leib Sarah's (R. Leib son of Sarah):

> I, the insignificant, saw in one book a tale about the aforementioned holy rabbi [R. Leib Sarah's]. The book is not before me to copy from precisely; I wrote what is recorded in my memory. (*Sefer Siftei Kodesh*, p. 10b)

In other words, this is evidence that sometimes a tale was not copied directly from a written collection, but through the intermediary of the oral tradition. The cheaply-printed collections lasted but a few years, thus storytellers told and copied their contents from memory long after the books themselves were dust.

The tale "*Hakhnasat Kallah*" ("Dowry for the Bride") constitutes a good example of the phenomenon we have just described. The two principal versions of the tale appear in two Hasidic collections of tales from the 1860s, the period that saw the flourishing of Hasidic narrative: *Pe'er mi-Kedoshim* (The Glory of the Saints) by Menahem Mendel Bodek (1864), and a collection in Yiddish entitled *Nissim ve-Niflaot*, attributed to roughly the same period. The protagonist of the Hebrew version is Isaiah Slotzker; of the Yiddish, Yudel Natanzhon. Both feature the same plot: the hero, a poor, meek Hasid, father of three marriageable daughters, sets out to raise money for their dowries. He borrows clothing and an elegant carriage, stays in an expensive hotel where he learns Torah, and squanders all the money he has thus far collected. The matchmaker, who's been asking about him, mistakes him for a certain man of means by the same name who lives in the same city. The protagonist consents to a match with a wealthy bridegroom, and offers a huge sum for his daughter's dowry—equivalent to that offered by the prospective in-law. When he returns home, after fixing the date of the wedding, he shuts himself up once more, in his humble room, and learns Torah. The letters of the prospective father-in-law are delivered to the man of means with the same name as the poor Hasid. Childless himself, he finds amusement in responding to the letters and sending gifts. The father-in-law, arriving in town for the wedding, finds the bride-to-be chasing after a rooster. The frightened main-course-to-be dashes into a ruined house, or a cave, where an enormous chest of coins is hidden. The poor Hasid can thus fulfill his promises, and becomes a wealthy man himself.

Although they share a common narrative plot, these versions differ in numerous ways, including the style of the tales and their scope, the personalities of their protagonists and where they live, and their realia. It is especially worthwhile to linger over the differences connected with the two secondary characters: the Hasid's wife, and the Zaddik of Apta. In the Yiddish version, the wife is the dynamic force driving the plot: she does not let her husband rest until he makes a match for his daughters; she is the one who appeals repeatedly to the Zaddik of Apta to prevail upon her husband to set out; she gets him the travelling clothes and the carriage; she goes to the Zaddik for help when her husband returns and tells her what huge sums he promised for his daughter's dowry; and again returns to him when the wealthy father-in-law arrives in their city. Conversely, in the version of the tale in *Pe'er mi-Kedoshim*, the Hasid's wife hardly appears at all, and has no role in the plot. His students look after him, advise him to set out on the journey, obtain the fine clothes and carriage for him, and more. Likewise for the Zaddik of Apta; he is pivotal to the Yiddish tale: he sends the poor man on his way and tells him to promise the same dowry sum as the father-in-law. He is involved in all stages of the plot, planting certainty in the heart of the poor Hasid family, and "pulling the strings" from many angles. The main strokes of the plot not only depend upon him, he foresees them. In the version of *Pe'er mi-Kedoshim*, the Zaddik of Apta appears only in the conclusion, where he interprets what has happened and articulates the moral of the events; in the course of the tale itself he has no role. The *Pe'er mi-Kedoshim* version does emphasize the notion of Hasidic fraternity: the Hasidim, friends and students of the protagonist, show concern for his daughters, and they see to the needs of the poor family. *Pe'er mi-Kedoshim* gives expression to this theme most clearly towards the end of the tale: The Hasid whose daughter unearthed the treasure is about to pay the father-in-law the promised sum, when the latter runs to the wealthy man of the same name, to ask him how it is that this wretched pauper has suddenly become rich. The wealthy man, a *misnaged* (that is, an opponent of Hasidism), responds, "Don't you yet know that the Hasidim can accomplish anything? I knew he was poor and destitute . . . but the Hasidim must have borrowed all this temporarily in order to glorify themselves before onlookers." Though the *misnaged* ridicules the practice of mutual assistance among the Hasidim, the storyteller clearly means to praise it.

In yet a third version of the tale, the plot develops differently. A Hasid from Palestine sets out for the diaspora to collect money for the wedding of his three grown daughters. Averse to trading on the holiness of Palestine, he wanders among the communities without revealing his origins. Upon arriving at the home of the Zaddik R. Meir of Przemyslany, the Zaddik senses "an aura of Eretz-Yisrael" about him, and gives him a chest containing six hundred gold coins which Heaven had commanded be collected on the birthdays of the Hasid's daughters. The fourth version, most famous of all, is the framework tale for S. Y. Agnon's novel *Hakhnasat Kallah* (Bridal Canopy), whose initial version is nearly a translation of the Yiddish version from *Nissim ve-Niflaot*. Not so his later versions of the novel, in which Agnon transformed the Hasidic tale into a literary classic.[9]

The transformations of this tale can lead us to an understanding of the complexity of the Hasidic tale as folk literature. Discrepancies among the versions show that they were not copied directly and precisely from one Hasidic anthology to another, but drawn from the numerous versions that circulated orally. The transition between the two languages is also typical: although the spoken language of the Hasidim was Yiddish, they tended to set their stories down in Hebrew. We cannot know today whether the Yiddish version in fact is similar to the manner in which it was told orally, but the difference between it and the Hebrew versions indicates an interesting phenomenon. The Yiddish version, which emphasizes the woman's role (alongside that of the Zaddik), may have been directed toward a female audience. Her vigorous efforts and persistence on her family's behalf emphasize to this audience the social function of the woman and her ability to influence the fate of her family. The tale in the version from *Pe'er mi-Kedoshim* has a propagandistic nature: it makes salient the brotherhood of the Hasidic community, and its advantages over the community led by the wealthy *misnaged*. Such mutual assistance is a feature of the third version as well, in which R. Meir of Przemyslany collected money all his life for the dowries of the daughters of the Hasid from Palestine. Agnon's use of the tale, his establishing it as a complex framework with multiple meanings for one of the greatest novels produced in modern Hebrew literature, is yet another instance of this tale's transformations and the vitality of the Hasidic tale in the culture of our time.

This tale has thus served to model the aspects discussed herein: the question of the performance event in the Hasidic tale; its social function; its appearance in multiple versions—in other words, its status as a folktale; its transitions between spoken Yiddish and Hebrew writing; and the link between the popular booklets, in which most of the Hasidic tales were preserved, and the elite culture—in this case S. Y. Agnon's great novel.

[3] Traditional Narrative Patterns

In the year 1896, a typical collection of tales was printed in Cracow under the title *Ma'asiyyot Peliot* ("Tales of Wonder"). It was only thirty-two pages long, printed in Rashi script on cheap paper and poorly bound, and brought to the printing house by Eleazar Shenkel from Tarnow, in Galicia. The composition of this collection is of much interest: of the twenty-four tales it comprises, the lion's share have nothing at all to do with the Hasidic world: tales of R. Abraham Ibn Ezra, R. Judah the Pious, Rabbi Moshe Isserlish, R.

Moses de Leon, R. Yehiel of Paris, Rashi. Scattered among these are tales of the Ba'al Shem Tov, R. Zusya of Hanipoli, Elimelech of Lyzhansk, R. Naphtali Ropshitser. One can clearly see that the compiler of this collection meant to intersperse tales of the most celebrated Hasidim among those of medieval Jewish luminaries. Now that the Hasidic movement was established, a major player in the Jewish world of the late nineteenth century, perhaps Eleazar Shenkel and his audience already regarded their movement as the legitimate continuation of Jewish tradition. Thus it was only natural for them to view their champions as part of the pantheon of Jewish scholars.

The connection with paragons past stands out with regard to one personality in particular—the 'Ari ("The Lion"), Rabbi Isaac Luria. The printer, in his preface to the work that led the way for all Hasidic narrative—*Shivhei ha-Besht*—lauds *Shivhei ha-Ari* (The Praises of the 'Ari) as the shining example that guided the book's compilers (Rubinstein edition, p. 25). Even without this explicit remark, the structure, orientation, and composition of tales in *Shivhei ha-Besht* exhibit a great deal of similarity to those of *Shivhei ha-Ari*, which indicates a link between the earlier work, available in numerous editions throughout Poland, and the founding myth of Hasidic storytelling. And this orientation persists as the Hasidic movement develops. *Sefer Sippurei Kedoshim* (The Book of Tales of the Saints), from the year 1865, composed mostly of Ba'al Shem Tov tales not included in the already canonized *Shivhei ha-Besht*, opens with a tale about R. Isaac Luria. From there it progresses directly to tales of the Ba'al Shem Tov and other Hasidic zaddikim. Volume 27 of a recently-published, series of Hasidic books, broad in scope, entitled *Sefarim Kedoshim mi-Talmidei ha-Besht ha-Kadosh* (Sacred Books of the Students of the Holy Ba'al Shem Tov) (Brooklyn, 1985), containing facsimiles of the important Hasidic works, opens with *Shivhei ha-Ari*, as if this work had become an organic part of the Hasidic movement![10]

The connection between Hasidism and R. Isaac Luria and other figures from Jewish history has historical, ideological, and social ramifications, but our interest is in the literary-folkloric realm. The Hasidic movement saw (or wished to present) the tales of its leaders as a link in the chain of legends about the illustrious Jews who preceded them. For this reason, Hasidic collections of tales in praise of Hasidic zaddikim always include a few stories about the heroes who preceded the movement. This ideational orientation knowingly and intentionally tied the new literary period together with the literary legacy of the one gone by.

Two basic directions come to the fore in the linkage of Hasidic tales to hagiographical tales of earlier heroes: the first is to bring the tales about earlier figures into conformity with Hasidic conception. The second adorns Hasidic zaddikim in the mantle of the traditional narrative patterns that draped the earlier figures. The tale about R. Isaac Luria that opens *Sefer Sippurei Kedoshim* can serve as an example of the first direction. It concerns R. Luria's sister, who, having no son, pleads with R. Luria until he promises her a son who will excel in study of the Torah. He warns her that if she is prideful and boasts to others about her son's erudition, the child will be punished. After the parents twice fail to restrain themselves and sing their son's praises, he loses his sight. R. Isaac Luria sends him into the dark woods, where he learns Torah from the Patriarchs. They instruct him to apprentice himself to the owner of a flour mill, and to accept the first proposal of marriage that comes his way. He is not to reveal his identity, nor to change his filthy clothes, until the Patriarchs tell him. A great rabbi, having been instructed to marry off his daughter to our protagonist, takes him home. After considerable dismay and despair over this apparently ignorant and disgusting bridegroom, R. Luria appears in the company of the Patriarchs, the bridegroom reveals his identity, and the marriage takes place in great glory and happiness.

The realia details in this tale, such as the operation of the flour mill and the wedding customs—the celebration on the Sabbath before the wedding, the jesters, the special gifts given on the occasion of the ceremonial preaching of the Torah—are of course in keeping with Eastern Europe of the nineteenth century and have absolutely no basis in the reality of Safed in the time of R. Isaac Luria. Luria is depicted as one who receives appeals in medical matters, who foresees the future and issues warnings accordingly. He evinces a high-handed attitude towards those who turn to him; court manners are the rule. These features of the tale, along with ideational themes characteristic of the Hasidic tale (like the hidden zaddik who may not reveal his identity until the time is right, inter-class marriage between a wealthy and important family and a poor Torah scholar, and the appearance of the people's most venerated historical figures [especially Elijah] at family affairs), tell us what kind of tale we have here. It is in every respect a Hasidic tale, whose protagonist happens not to be a Hasidic zaddik but R. Isaac Luria. Here, the Hasidic narrative saw fit to construct the figure of the 'Ari as a Hasidic zaddik, and in this manner to tie together two phenomena of Jewish history and present the customs and stories of the new zaddikim as another link in a chain stretching far back to the luminaries of the past.

The second direction is the use of traditional narrative patterns to fashion the Hasidic tales. The choice of the saint's legend is in keeping with Hasidic doctrine and the centrality of the Hasidic zaddik therein, but it is also a deliberate choice of a time-honored genre that figured prominently throughout the traditional narrative of the past. It does not matter whence we date the beginnings of this category, whether to the tales of the talmudic and midrashic sages or those of Rashi, Maimonides, R. Abraham Ibn Ezra, and Rabbi Judah the Pious from the Middle Ages. Clearly, Hasidic narrative established itself here on a very ancient and rich internal tradition that suited its needs and orientations. And, yet again, we can discern these trends that influenced Hasidic narrative in *Shivehei ha-Besht*.[11]

A prime example of this is the tale that opens *Shivhei ha-Besht*, concerning the Ba'al Shem Tov's father, R. Eliezer. Abducted from his home by rioters, he is sold into slavery and ends up a servant in the home of the King's second in command. When the King commands this most trusted advisor to propose a way to end the war his kingdom is fighting, R. Eliezer, who has become the minister's confidant, outlines a strategy that will lead to victory, after interpreting a dream. The minister is forced to admit that his servant is the true advisor; the king raises Eliezer to greatness and gives him his advisor's daughter's hand in marriage. R. Eliezer never consummates the union, even after years of marriage. When she asks him why, he tells her of his Jewish origins. She sends him home with a fortune, but he is robbed by highwaymen on the way. Upon his return home, Heaven informs him he is to father a son "that will give the Jewish people the light of understanding." In another version of the tale (included parenthetically in the same tale in *Shivhei ha-Besht*), it is told that the Ba'al Shem Tov's father had been sold to a mariner serving aboard a warship. When the fleet lay lengthy siege on a well-fortified harbor, he was the one to propose a way to capture the city without losses, and thus rose to greatness.[12]

The tale fits the basic narrative functions of "the biographical pattern of the cultural hero." Many heroes are made to travel far from their homes, rise from the bottommost rung of society to the summit, become military commanders or rulers, and marry the king's daughter. Ultimately, they prefer to return to their former home, and there to lead their people, provide law or a new teaching, and so on. But in this case we have no need to turn to the theoretical paradigm, as the tale about the Ba'al Shem Tov's father is surprisingly parallel to a Hebrew tale known from the medieval period, that of "Moses in Ethiopia." The tale is part of the later midrash *The Chronicles of Moses*, which appeared in many editions in manuscript and in print. According to this tale, after Moses flees from Egypt to the desert, he comes across the Ethiopian army engaged in a decade-long siege of a single city. Having hired himself to the army, Moses suggests the means to conquer the city, and thus rises to its command. After the king's death, his ministers marry him to the queen, but he does not touch her. When she complains to the ministers, they grant Moses' request and release him.[13]

In addition to the general narrative analogy, there is clear proof of the connection between the two tales in the tactics suggested by the two protagonists to conquer the city: the fortified city in the tale of Moses has gone uncaptured because there is no access to it from any side, but Moses finds a way around the obstacles and brings it down. R. Eliezer warns the king not to dispatch warships to the city, as mines lie hidden beneath the surface. He proposes an alternative method, by which the city is conquered. In spite of the many differences between the medieval tale and the Hasidic one (such as the shift from the hero [Moses] to the father of the hero [Eliezer, father of the Ba'al Shem Tov]), the correlation is clear.

It is not difficult to understand the motive behind borrowing this narrative pattern for the opening of the most important Hasidic collection of tales. The pattern, in all its forms, presents the biography of the culture hero as part of a divinely orchestrated and predetermined plan. The hero's "rise" at the king's court is meant to prepare him for the role to which his life is later dedicated: to lead the Jewish people. So it was for Moses, and so too for the Ba'al Shem Tov. This narrative paradigm was always chosen to shape the biography of founders of religions or sects, as there is nothing like it to bolster the claim of a new doctrine's divine provenance: if the life of the founder proceeded according to God's plan, it must follow that his teachings were nourished by the same spring. In other words, a distinctly propagandistic role was intended for this narrative pattern in the dissemination of Hasidic doctrine in Jewish society, and the Hasidic storytellers utilized it precisely to this end.

The following tale comes from the Hasidic collection of tales mentioned above, *Ma'asiyyot Peliot*:

> A tale about Rabbi Eliezer, father of the Ba'al Shem Tov, may his memory
> protect us, who dwelled in a village and excelled at hospitality. He would
> place [a watchman] at the outskirts of the village and instruct [him] to di-
> rect any newly arrived visitor to [his home], where he would be treated well.
> This was to spare the visitor from worrying about where to turn in a place
> where no one knew him. After the guest arrived, [Rabbi Eliezer] would give
> him a fair donation right away, before he ate, so that he could eat joyfully, for
> he knew that the needy's chief concern is to collect alms so as bring suste-
> nance back to his home. One time, in Heaven above, his fine conduct was
> praised, and it was agreed among the heavenly host to put him to a test in
> some matter. And they said, "Who will go to test him?" Samael [the Adver-
> sary] said, "I will go." Elijah of blessed memory said, "It is not good that you
> go, I will go." And Elijah of blessed memory went to him on the Sabbath af-
> ter midday in the guise of a poor man with a walking stick and a pack, and
> said Good Sabbath as was customary. It would have been fitting to cast him
> out as a desecrator of the Sabbath, but the aforementioned Rabbi Eliezer was
> a tolerant man, and did not wish to shame him. At once he gave him to eat
> the third Sabbath meal as well as the fourth Sabbath meal [eaten after the
> conclusion of the Sabbath]. Then on Sunday, at dawn, he gave him a dona-
> tion and made no mention of his desecration of the Sabbath, in order not
> to shame him. When Elijah the Prophet of blessed memory saw this fine
> conduct he revealed himself to him and said, "Know that I am Elijah the
> Prophet and I came to test you. As a reward for standing up to such a great

test, in accordance with your holiness and God-fearingness and immeasurably profound love of the Jewish people, and in reward for [observing] the precept of hospitality, you will be graced with a son that will give the Jewish people the light of understanding." His son was the Ba'al Shem Tov, may his memory protect us and all the Jewish people. (pp. 12b–13a)

This tale is akin to those describing the non-biological, spiritual "birth" of Jewish luminaries, tales that find the starting point in the deeds that the heroes themselves accomplished (Rabbi Akiva, for example) or that their fathers performed, leading the way to the birth of the great and righteous individual in question. Thus in Hasidic narrative we also find such tales about the deeds performed by the fathers of the Seer of Lublin, the Maggid (Preacher) of Kuznitz, the mother of R. Leib Sarah's, and many others. Nor is there any special innovation in the deed itself as compared to traditional Jewish narrative: the birth of a child of surpassing brilliance in Torah study as reward for acts of charity is a Jewish folk motif common since the rabbinic period. The main importance of the tale is in its attitude to R. Eliezer, father of the Ba'al Shem Tov. From the moment the story of R. Eliezer's rise in the royal court was given a fixed place in the foundation book of Hasidic literature—*Shivhei ha-Besht*—it might have been expected that the road would be closed to all other stories dealing with the same subject. But here the Hasidic tale's folk dynamic is borne out: the fact that a canonic tradition, once oral, has been set down in writing, does not block the process of continuing oral folk creation, even in subjects already "hallowed" in Hasidic tradition. It seems there is no better proof of the vitality of folk creation within any society than such a phenomenon.

[4] The Absorption of Medieval Narrative Traditions

The Hasidic tale's integration into the chronicle of the Jewish folktale manifests itself above all in its borrowing from the stock of traditional tales, and the latter's absorption into the new cultural tradition. In this respect, Hasidic narrative follows the pattern laid down by preceding periods. An important characteristic of story-craft in each period is how it absorbs and revises the tales of the past. I will therefore try to characterize the folktale that developed in the Hasidic movement by means of the ways in which it incorporated the folktales of the preceding period—the Middle Ages. Each of the three tales that follow reflects a different manner of this absorption.

First we have "The Pipe" or "The Simpleton's Prayer." The general lines of its plot are familiar, and it is told in multiple versions in a number of Hasidic story collections. A man brings his "very slow-witted" shepherd boy to the synagogue on the Day of Atonement, so that, in his ignorance, the son will not commit the sin of eating on the holy day. During the prayer, he asks his father's permission to take out the pipe that he plays in the pasture, and make music. The father forbids it, but he asks again. The father "cursed him vigorously and gave him a stern warning lest he make so bold as to, Heaven forbid, do such a thing." During the concluding service, "the lad, with great strength, wrested the pipe from his pocket, and from his father's hand, and played it very loudly." At this, the Ba'al Shem Tov shortened his prayer. He said: "This lad, with the voice of his pipe, has raised up all the prayers and made [my task] easier." He explained that, of all the prayers offered there, the fire burning in the lad's heart was what the Almighty accepted.[14]

Many variants have been proposed for this tale, in Jewish, Muslim, and Christian literature. Although some are closer in form to the Hasidic versions, the most relevant, as it can be presumed to have been familiar to the Hasidim, is the tale of the shepherd in the thirteenth-century *Sefer Hasidim*:

> Like the tale of a man who shepherded animals and did not know how to pray. Everyday he would say, "Master of the world, it is obvious and known before you, that if you had animals and gave them to me to watch over, even though I take payment from others to watch their animals, I would watch for you for free because I love you." This man was a Jew. One time a Torah scholar was passing by and found the shepherd praying in this manner. He said to him: "Fool, don't pray like that." The shepherd said to him: "How should I pray?" At once the Torah scholar taught him the order of the benedictions and the recitation of the *Shema* and prayer, so that he would no longer say what he had been accustomed to saying. After that Torah scholar left, [the shepherd] forgot what he had taught him, and did not pray. And he was afraid to say what he was accustomed to saying because that righteous man had made him stop. At night, that Torah scholar was told in a dream: "If you do not tell him that he should say what he was accustomed to saying before you came to him, and if you will not go, know that evil will befall you, because you have stolen from me one from the world to come." At once he went and said to him: "What prayer are you saying?" He said to him: "Nothing, because I forgot what you taught me and you instructed me not to say, if He had animals." The scholar said: "So and so came to me in a dream. Say what you were accustomed to saying. For in this case, [it was] not Torah and not deeds, but [his wish] to do a good deed [that] He considered it a great deed, for the Almighty sees into the heart." Therefore one should think kind thoughts to the Almighty. (*Sefer Hasidim*, Wistinetzki and Freimann edition, #5–6)

As early as the Middle Ages, the perception was common that the prayer of the unsophisticated, if offered wholeheartedly, has more intrinsic value than the normative prayer of scholars and the learned. The Almighty does not evaluate man according to the depth of his learning, but according to the depth of his faith. Ideas generally identified with Hasidic doctrine were common in Judaism many years earlier. Indeed, the saying quoted in the version from *Sefer Hasidim*, "the Almighty sees into the heart," originated in rabbinic literature, showing this perception to be more ancient still. This being the case, we should not view what the musical shepherd did as the essence, as the "revolutionary" act, as is the regular interpretation of this story. Even though the shepherd's actions in the Hasidic tale are more extreme than in the medieval version, the root of the difference lies elsewhere. If we examine these tales as two versions of a single narrative tradition, and attempt to analyze them with the help of the epic law of contrast, the result will be clearer. The model of the polarization in folk literature with respect to these two versions can be drawn as follows:

	Middle Ages:	Hasidic story:
[*binary opposition*]	shepherd < — > scholar	shepherd < — > father
	∧	∧
[*mediator*]	God	Ba'al Shem Tov

The primary polarization (or the binary opposition) in the *Sefer Hasidim* version of the tale is between the shepherd and the Torah scholar, who does not see into the shepherd's heart, and does not understand the meaning of true faith. For this reason, he is threatened with punishment unless he overhauls his entire approach. The clash is thus between the true believer and the Torah scholars, whose faith is mechanical. The force that resolves the narrative conflict here is Divine, that which reveals itself in the dream of the Torah scholar. The criticism in the medieval version is directed towards the establishment of Torah scholars who give their doctrinal skills priority over their faith. In the Hasidic tale, the polarization is between the shepherd and his father. The father himself is not of the learned camp, and it can be assumed that neither are the other worshippers in that village synagogue; all are but simple village Jews. The worshippers, who were astonished and angered upon hearing the strains of the pipe profaning their prayer, represent the community in all its preconceptions and fixed attitudes. But the more telling departure in the Hasidic version is in the figure of the neutral apex of the tale: here the Ba'al Shem Tov takes the place of the Divine force. He evinces a profound understanding of matters and interprets their meaning. The Ba'al Shem Tov, as leader of the Jews praying in that synagogue, does not stand opposed to the innocent shepherd, as does the scholar of the medieval tale. On the contrary, he alone of all those present understands the deeper significance of the action. Herein lies the fundamental difference between the medieval tale and the Hasidic one: the Hasidic zaddik is the successor to the Divine force of medieval tradition. Instead of opposing the simple, innocent Jew, he elevates his deeds to a supreme level of holiness. In other words, there is no longer any antagonism between the religious leader and "the folk," as was reflected in medieval tradition. The function of the Hasidic zaddik is to stand at his side, and raise up the sparks of holiness hidden within him.

A second example of the manner in which Hasidic literature absorbed the folktales of the past and modified them to conform to its needs and world-view is the tale of "Moses by the Well":

> It was said that Moses our Teacher struggled with this . . . he asked God, blessed be He, why it is that it goes ill for the righteous and [well for the wicked]. It is said in the midrash that when he was on the mountain he saw one man who, [when he went] to drink from the stream, forgot his purse and left. Along came another man to drink, and he found the purse, [took it,] and left. The owner of the purse returned to the stream and found [a third] man there drinking. He said to him, "You took the purse that I [left here]." Said [the third man] in response, "I saw no purse." [The owner] drew his sword and killed him. When Moses saw all this he wondered how it could be. He said to the Almighty, blessed be He, "Show me your ways, wherefore was this one killed for no wrongdoing of his own, while the thief went free?" He said to him, "The owner of the purse stole that money from he who found it, without his knowledge, and the one who was killed had killed his father and no one knew who had struck him. And *I* caused all this to happen and all my ways are true, for your ways are not mine."[15]

Several versions of the tale thread their way through Hasidic narrative. One typical version follows:

> [It happened once that] a rabbi of the Jewish people, whose teaching illumined the world, and who raised disciples who were supremely righteous, [namely,] our great teacher [Dov Baer, "the Great Maggid" of Mezhirech] came to take shelter in the holiness of the splendor and glory of Israel, his teacher the Ba'al Shem Tov may his memory protect us. The Ba'al Shem Tov told him to go outside the city, near the river, and stand there until he saw new things. He went with utmost diligence and love and affection to fulfill the words of his holy teacher, and stood there by the river until he was tired of standing. Then he saw a man come by on a horse, weary and fatigued. [The man] dismounted and washed in the river, and after that he sat down to eat a meal. After eating and drinking he took his pack and put it under his head, and lay down there to rest a while and to sleep. When he awoke from this sleep and looked at his timepiece, and he saw that he had slept for hours and had to be on his way, he hastened to mount his horse and continue on to his destination. In his haste he forgot his pack and the money inside it. On his way to the inn, he wanted to take the money to buy something to eat, and he saw that it was not with him and that it was lost. He hurried back to the river in hope of finding that his pack was still there. Meanwhile,

another man came to the river, tired and weary from the heat of the day, and he went into the water. He looked around and found the pack with the coins, took it, and hastened to ride away and flee with his find. After this one ran off with his find, a poor, old, and lame man came and sat by the river to rest from the rigors of the road. He took out his bread and ate it there. Meanwhile the owner of the lost pack came and found the old man eating. The owner told him the matter, that he had forgotten a pack with money in it there some hours before, and surely he must have found it, and asked him to return the forgotten pack. And the old man truthfully said that he did not know, and that he had found nothing, but his response was in vain, for the man did not believe him and struck him many blows, with all his might. But when he saw that striking him was in vain, he turned from there and went on his way. And so with the close of the day the Maggid of Mezhirech (may his memory protect us) returned to the house of his teacher, the holy Ba'al Shem Tov of blessed and saintly memory, [who] asked him what he had seen. He told him all [that had happened]. And the Ba'al Shem Tov replied: "The first one, who suffered the loss, in the first incarnation, unjustly and deceitfully sued the second one, who found [the pack] and ran off, for a sum that he had lost, and now God, the Primal Cause, blessed be He, has [caused] the one to lose and the second to find. And the old man was the judge that illegally ordered the payment, and now the Primal Cause, blessed be He [has caused] the one to lose and the second to find, and the old man, who had unjustly ruled [for the plaintiff], suffered many blows, and so their sin and iniquity have been redressed. Look and see that which he saw in the spirit of his holiness." (*Ma'asiyyot mi-Zaddikim Yesodei 'Olam* ["Stories of the Righteous Men, the Foundations of the World"], Podgorze, 1903, #5)

In the versions that predate Hasidism, in the Muslim branch (which, to all appearances, is the oldest) as well as the Christian, the tale is a consummately theodicean tale. A number of similar tales grew around Moses, the great rebel and skeptic of Islamic tradition. In them, Moses witnesses some act of terrible injustice, and casts doubt on Divine justice. God proves to him that the injustice was but superficial, that true justice lay hidden from the eyes of the believer. Therefore, he should not doubt even when justice is not apparent. The theological importance of the idea is fashioned clearly in this narrative plot, and is unquestionably the reason the tale was absorbed and so widely spread in both Judaism and Christianity of the Middle Ages and the early modern period. Hence it comes as no surprise that the new religious movement, one with so large a theological awareness as Hasidism, also made use of such tales. A closer examination of the Hasidic versions shows us that the theodicean conception that was at the conceptual and narrative core is here reduced to the point where it is hardly felt anymore. The *Maggid*, who takes the place of Moses in the earlier versions, does not doubt Divine justice and does not raise his voice to protest the injustice he witnessed. It should be noted that the injustice itself has also been reduced: the man who lost his money does not kill the old man, he only strikes him, and moves on. Since the apparent injustice is no longer so extreme, the preacher need not, as did Moses before him, raise his voice against it in bitter protest. Instead, he questions what he saw.

Another difference between the versions is in the connection between the hidden meaning of the event and what happens in the present: in the earlier tale, the principals are linked personally or by blood—the family connection—to the past; what took place then justifies the present event witnessed by Moses. In contrast to this, the connection between the hidden meaning of the tale and the present in the Hasidic versions is magical or mystical—that is, the linkage is a result of the transmigration of souls. The notion of reincarnation is not new to Jewish culture; it was highly developed in the Lurianic kabbalah, and many tales in *Shivhei ha-Ari*, and of R. Luria's disciple, R. Hayyim Vital, were devoted to it. The Hasidic likening of the Ba'al Shem Tov to R. Luria was what gave rise to the former's portrayal as one who could decipher the strange events of daily reality by identifying the souls who had transmigrated into beings currently living.

The principal modification made to the ancient tradition in the course of its absorption into Hasidism, and one that is connected with the previous point, is in the character of the Ba'al Shem Tov. He sends his disciple to the river, he predicts what will happen, he interprets the hidden meaning of the event. It should be noted that the narrator stresses that this was the beginning of the *Maggid*'s service with the Ba'al Shem Tov, and the very act that led him to become a devoted follower. In other words, at the heart of the Hasidic versions stands the notion of the Hasidic zaddik's omnipotence, no longer theodicy. The zaddik is the one who knows what the future holds, and he takes the place of God in interpreting the events (as in the story of "the simpleton's prayer," above). The Hasidism of the protagonist (the *Maggid*) grows out of his full, unshakable certainty in the power of the zaddik. The tale comes to prove that such certainty, even as regards unusual, or extremely strange events, has grounds. In other words, the tale's absorption by Hasidism was accompanied by changes to bring it into agreement with, above all, the Hasidic notion of the zaddik.

The last example of this process is the tale, "the three wise counsels." The prevalent version of the tale in both Hebrew and Yiddish is as follows: Three brothers come to Jerusalem to learn wisdom from King Solomon. After thirteen years in his service, he offers them their choice of wages for their labor or words of wisdom. The two older brothers chose to be paid in coin, the youngest, in wisdom. King Solomon gives him three pieces of advice: In his travels, he should always find a place to stay the night before dark; if he must cross a raging river, he should wait until the current eases; and he must never reveal a secret to his wife. The brothers begin their journey home. Although the youngest counsels making camp in a sheltered place, the two eldest brothers refuse. They continue past nightfall and freeze to death. When the youngest finds their bodies later on, he buries them and takes their money. Coming to a raging river, he resolves to bide his time. Servants of King Solomon, attempting the crossing with beasts laden with gold, drown. The youngest takes their treasure as well. But when his wife insists on knowing whence came his wealth, he cannot withstand her, and tells her it's secret. In the midst of a quarrel some time after, she screams that he murdered his brothers. The wives of the brothers, who hear her accusation, bring him before Solomon's court, where the King sentences him to death. The condemned man recounts the entire story to Solomon, who pardons him. This tale was widespread in the Hebrew narrative of the late Middle Ages (*Meshalim shel Shlomo ha-Melekh* [Parables of King Solomon]), as well as the Yiddish, and has been printed in the *Mayseh Bukh*, which was widely available in eastern Europe. It seems that the Hasidic storytellers were familiar with it from there.[16]

According to the Hasidic version of the tale, a Jewish taverner sets out to raise money for the rent on his tavern and to cover the expenses of marrying off his marriageable daughter. He wanders for twelve years, collects nine hundred rubles, and begins the journey home. On the way, he stops at the study hall of R. Levi Isaac of Berdichev, whose leadership and righteousness he admires. The Rabbi offers to teach the taverner three proverbs, each in exchange for three hundred rubles. The taverner hesitates before spending all he has toiled so long and hard to amass for a few words. After soul-searching, and out of his confidence in the zaddik, he purchases one piece of wisdom, then a second, and finally, a third, until he is bereft of all the dowry money he collected. The pieces of wisdom are: to turn only to the right, to beware of an old man with a young wife, and not to put any credence in gossip but only to believe that which he sees with his own eyes. He leaves the Zaddik's house and returns home. On the way, he directs merchants whose property was stolen to turn to the right; they get their property back, and reward him generously. He stays the night in an inn whose keeper is an old man wed to a young woman, and discovers that the wife has plotted with her lover to murder her husband. Our taverner warns the innkeeper who, thus rescued, also rewards him handsomely. When he reaches his home town, people tell him his wife has been spending every night with a young Polish squire, whom she lets into her home through a window. Our hero resolves, as per the advice he bought, to see for himself. In this way he learns that it is in fact his son, whom the Polish landowner took in return for the father's debts on the tavern. The son was raised as a Gentile but for the efforts of his mother, who persuaded him to come to her secretly each night so that she could teach him Judaism. The father redeems his son from the landowner, and the family lives from then on in comfort and prosperity.[17]

The two branches of the tale differ in many respects. I would like to dwell only on those germane to our topic of discussion. They manifest themselves primarily in the different kinds of counsel bestowed and the events stemming from them. Some differences are a consequence of the different *realia* of the two periods: the protagonist of the Hasidic tale does not wander, as was conventional in the Middle Ages, for the purpose of studying Torah or wisdom; he sets out on his travels among the communities to raise money for his daughter's wedding. Also, he earns his wealth after guiding merchants whose merchandise was stolen, not from a royal caravan carrying treasures as in the medieval versions. The motif of misogyny typical to medieval narrative is replaced in the Hasidic tale with the woman's dedication; she does her utmost to educate her son in the ways of the Torah. The Hasidic storyteller weaves into the third act of wisdom one of the most prevalent themes of Hasidic literature—"the captive child." The fact that the taverner heeded the zaddik's advice is what saved his son from the clutches of the Polish landowner, who sought to uproot him from his people.

But the chief difference lies in the figure of the one who imparts the counsels, and in his connection to the protagonist. Solomon, as in other Hebrew tales from the Middle Ages, takes the form of the wise feudal king, who judges his subjects and administers the affairs of his kingdom from on high. The wisdom motif is strongly emphasized in these tales on account of the allusion to the figure of Solomon in the Bible and post-biblical folk traditions. Levi Isaac of Berdichev, however, functions here as a typical zaddik of the Hasidic tales: he leads his followers in worship and at mealtimes he turns to them with enigmatic utterances that put them to the test of faith in his power and supernatural knowledge.

King Solomon teaches the youngest brother three general pieces of wisdom that have no connection to his life in particular, and are true at all times and situations. The zaddik Levi Isaac does not teach pieces of wisdom per se, but maxims, whose significance in the tale is as prophesy. The zaddik, unlike the wise king, is graced with supernatural knowledge and the ability to direct reality according to his will. In other words, in this tale too, as in the earlier example of the Ba'al Shem Tov, the tale fashions concretely the doctrine of the Hasidic zaddik.

Still more interesting and crucial is the link between the zaddik and his followers. The zaddik forces the protagonist to make a difficult and painful decision: to give up that for which he has labored twelve years, far from home, to accumulate, and therein his family's future, out of trust in the zaddik. The storyteller here stresses the taverner's inner struggle, which begins anew with each purchase of another "proverb" from the zaddik. Such soul-searching hardly exists in the earlier traditions (it is somewhat manifested in the split between the two older brothers, who chose material gain, and the youngest, who opts for spiritual profit). It seems that here is reflected one of the central conflicts in the life of a Hasid: reality and its demands compete with the desire for shelter with the zaddik. The issue here is not theoretical but practical, the inner struggle and decision on a day-to-day basis between these two extremes of Hasidic life. Every Hasid felt it each time he had to cut himself off from the demands of reality, family, and eking out a living, to journey to the zaddik where he would stay for long or short periods. This inner struggle also exists regarding the zaddik's advice, which often flies in the face of what logic and reality would dictate. All these are concretely manifested in this newer version of the medieval tale, wherein the core conflict of Hasidic life supplants the dualism between material and spiritual in the medieval tale.

[5] The Hidden Zaddik and Social Conflict

Among the ancient traditions most widespread in the Hasidic tales, two in particular stand out: that of the Thirty-Six Hidden Saints (*Lamed Vav Tzadikim Nistarim*), and that of the manifestations of Elijah. The ancient traditions of the thirty-six anonymous righteous men corroborate in narrative fashion the notion that in each generation thirty-six righteous men, to all appearances humble cobblers, water-bearers, tailors, coachmen, etc., are in truth the pillars upon which the world rests. Hasidic narrative developed this ancient tradition well beyond its former dimensions. Dozens of tales about simple, crude folk figures who are ultimately revealed to be hidden saints pepper the Hasidic repertoire.[18]

An interesting development took place with respect to the tales of Elijah. Stories recounting how he rescued individuals or communities in peril, and his astonishing appearances in unexpected times and places in order to punish the wicked and reward doers of good deeds, were among the most frequent in Jewish folk narrative before the advent of Hasidism. But the Hasidic tale culled from this vast treasury of folktales one tale type—the appearance of Elijah in disguise. Many Hasidic tales tell of the request of students of the Ba'al Shem Tov, or of some other zaddik, to see Elijah the Prophet. A man who steals books from the study hall, or a Gentile, a pauper, or a beggar that a group of Hasidim encounters on the road, behaves crudely. Hasidim want to castigate this individual—who is Elijah the Prophet in disguise, as their master reveals after the man disappears.[19]

The two ancient traditions that were absorbed by Hasidism reveal the same orientation: to stress the disproportion between internal and external, between the true, internal worth of a man and his external trappings. Tales of the

Thirty-Six Saints and Elijah in disguise accordingly put everyone on their guard: they had always to consider that the man before them—be he a filthy pauper or an ill-mannered or ignorant boor, might be one of the Thirty-Six, or even Elijah the Prophet. Injury to his honor, or withholding assistance, might therefore be dangerous. The argument that one may not judge the worth of an individual according to his external appearance or social status appears in the Hasidic narrative not only in the tales borrowed from the earlier Jewish traditions such as these two mentioned now, but in particular in tales created within the Hasidic world itself. The most widely scattered and famous of these concern the concealing and revealing of the Hasidic zaddikim. Here too, *Shivhei ha-Besht* apparently led the way for this development. In one of the volume's opening tales, the episode concerning the correspondence between the Ba'al Shem Tov and R. Gershon of Kutow, it is told that the Ba'al Shem Tov, not yet revealing his identity, greatly impressed the father of R. Gershon, who presided over the court in Brody. They committed to writing the terms by which R. Gershon's father would give him his daughter in marriage. After the father's demise, while R. Gershon was putting his papers in order:

> [He] found the terms relating to his betrothal of his daughter, who was the sister of our teacher and master, Rabbi R. Gershon, to some man whose name was Israel. And it was surprising in his eyes, for his father had been a man of renown, and how could he make a match with a lowly individual, with someone of little consequence and of unknown origin and family . . . [the Ba'al Shem Tov] disguised himself in the dress of the penniless in a short [fur jacket] and an old broad belt, and he changed his accent and his speech and went to the holy community of Brody to the home of our teacher and master Rabbi Gershon . . . our teacher and master Rabbi Gershon thought he was a poor man, and he took a coin and wished to give it to him, [but the Ba'al Shem Tov] said: "A word with you in private." He went with him to a room and showed him the terms, and said to him: "Bring my wife." When the above-mentioned Rabbi saw the man and his garments and his speech he was very alarmed and horrified at the appearance, what had his father of blessed memory done. (*Shivhei ha-Besht*, Rubinstein edition, p. 50)

Later Hasidic tales cast many other zaddikim in the Ba'al Shem Tov's role of holy man hiding behind a vulgar, common facade. This opening tale of *Shivhei ha-Besht* served as a narrative paradigm for dozens more Hasidic tales. From the little known of the historical Ba'al Shem Tov, it probably was not a disguise at all; he emerged from the lower, uneducated classes; his clothing and behavior were simple and crude. Apparently the later tales of his disguise and disclosure came for no other reason than to justify, in retrospect, the coarseness that characterized the founder of the movement.

Still, historical-apologetic arguments were not the impetus for disseminating tales of the Ba'al Shem Tov's concealment, or that of other zaddikim, among the Hasidic communities. Such tales spread primarily because of that same disproportion between internal and external mentioned above. In this tale, the Ba'al Shem Tov deliberately takes his graceless manners and appearance to an extreme, thereby stretching the gap between his internal worth and his external appearance. The larger this gap, the greater the test of R. Gershon of Kutow and other onlookers: could they see past the exterior to the true virtue of the zaddik? In most of the tales of concealment, as in the tale excerpted above concerning the Ba'al Shem Tov, the one tested does not pass, his suspicion of and revulsion from the poor and the base remains *in status quo*.[20]

Tales of disguise and disclosure of zaddikim are not the only ones to make manifest the chasm between what is visible to the eye and hidden spiritual nobility. R. Leib Sarah's brother is instructed to marry his son, a Torah prodigy, to the daughter of an ignorant villager known for his vulgarity. When the groom's father proposes the marriage, he rudely demands an exorbitant bride-price. He strolls through the villages on the day of the wedding and takes no part in the preparations. During the ceremony, all the honored guests look on "as he stands beside the canopy wearing a short blanket, and on it a rope belt like that carried by a porter. They scorned him in their hearts and shook their heads at him." In the end, it is revealed that the villager is one of the thirty-six saints, and he takes the groom along on his travels. In another tale, a harsh plague has struck one of the communities. Its representatives appeal to R. Baruch of Medzibezh, who sends them to a particular village, to the house of a drunkard whose blessing they must obtain to halt the plague. They find the man to be disgustingly filthy and perpetually intoxicated. Since he is never found sober, they cannot make their request of him. Tailing him, they succeed in catching him between one drunken stupor and the next, at which point he blesses them, and the plague ends. After they return to the zaddik, he tells them that that drunkard once withstood a great test: a high-placed noblewoman proposed marriage to him, but he redeemed, at risk of his own neck, the Jewish captives in her keep and fled from her after fierce inner struggle. He thus merited such status that Heaven granted any request he made. To avoid having to nullify all judgements ever made against the Jewish people, it was decreed of him that he always be drunk.[21]

In the last two examples, it is either a Hasidic community or other rank-and-file Jews who do not see the hidden saints for what they are. The zaddikim, R. Elimelech of Lyzhansk and R. Baruch of Medzibezh, are not taken in by the external behavior of these disguised saints, and perceive their spiritual nobility. But that is not always the case. In one of the tales about the Ba'al Shem Tov, he and his students are thrown together one Sabbath eve in an isolated house in the woods. Over the course of the Sabbath, his hosts, a Jew and his wife, behave in a particularly ill-mannered fashion. They light the Sabbath candles with an air of disregard, their prayers are those of ignorant boors, they repeatedly treat the Ba'al Shem Tov and his students with contempt, and the Ba'al Shem Tov suffers throughout. It ultimately becomes clear to him that the man is a hidden saint, charged to punish the Ba'al Shem Tov because his wife once scorned an orphan in his presence, and he did not stop her. He was therefore sentenced to lose one sabbath, which is regarded as a kind of world to come, instead of losing his place in the world to come. Since the event is described here as punishment of a zaddik, even the Ba'al Shem Tov is unable to make the connection between the concealed one's external facade and behavior and his true essence.[22]

The conceptual theme reflected in these tales suits the social aspect of Hasidic teaching. While tales about Rashi, R. Judah the Pious and, especially, R. Abraham Ibn Ezra, going around as paupers ignored by all were commonplace as early as the Middle Ages, the Hasidic tale intensively and deliberately directs, perhaps for the first time in the history of Jewish narrative, the point of view to the simple strata of the Jewish community. The innovation is not in attention to the poor and simple folk, but in the detailed descriptions of their behavior, emphatically different from the accepted norms of Jewish society. If this behavior can mask great spiritual virtue—as for the thirty-six saints, Elijah the Prophet, or a great Hasidic zaddik—it forces society to regard each and every such individual as if a great and noble soul resided within: "The messenger looked upon him with his mortal eyes and he seemed contemptible and good-for-nothing, and they thought him insane" (*Temimei Derekh*, Warsaw 1886, p. 9b). Such a point of view puts every man on guard, demanding his acknowledgement that things are not as they seem on the outside; Jewish society's conventional norms may severely contradict Judaism's true norms. In one tale, the Ba'al Shem Tov, reforming a zaddik who has sinned, instructs him to go into exile as a hidden figure. Abuse is heaped upon him, scorn and humiliation are hurled at him from every corner. Meanwhile a famous, wealthy preacher, esteemed and honored by all, is in fact an abject sinner. He tries to seduce the wife of the community leader who hosted him with such great honor (for which transgression they accuse the hidden zaddik). Ultimately, his true nature is disclosed (*Adat Tsaddikim*, Lemberg 1864, #9).

The shock wave that the Hasidic movement sent through the Jewish world was none other than a forced confrontation with its own insincerity. Those social norms that had taken root over the course of hundreds of years no longer suited the true hierarchy of Jewish society—the spiritual one. The marks that identified social status: class, wealth, external behavior, clothing, were no longer appropriate criteria for the evaluation of a Jew's true merit. This concept stood at the foundation of the revolution wrought by Hasidism upon Judaism of the early modern period, and it was expressed powerfully in the folktales that acquired currency within it. At the same time, it is clear that the tales do not merely reflect Hasidic teaching; they were intended to change the mentality and social psychology of the Jewish communities. If Hasidism managed to alter Judaism's social perception, even in a limited measure, there can be no doubt that the tales had a significant role.

Despite the ideological burden borne by these tales, they circulated as folk literature, and so could not be shorn of the folk mentality. This is manifested primarily in the realization of the wishful thinking at tale's end. For example, the tale of R. Isaac Luria's nephew, who wandered as a hidden zaddik until entering into a marriage agreement with a great and famous community leader. He accepted him as his prospective son-in-law despite the local community's contempt for him (*Sefer Sippurei Kedoshim* [The Book of Tales of the Saints], Warsaw[?] 1866, #1). In another tale, R. Lieb Sarah's instructs a virtuous pauper to enter into a marriage agreement with a wealthy and beautiful woman. After the wedding, the pauper rises to greatness and becomes a renowned community leader. The tale "*Hakhnasat Kallah*" (Bridal Canopy), treated above, also concludes with the poor Hasid marrying into a prosperous family, finding a vast treasure, and, once again, becoming a pillar of the community and very prosperous. In other words: although the Hasidic folktales praise the simple folk, insist that external appearance be ignored, and that the vulgar and ignoble be accepted according to their internal virtue, the personal ideal imprinted too deeply to be erased—wealth and social advantage—stands unbowed. As much as Hasidic doctrine praises simplicity and poverty, the true hidden wishes of Jewish society do not change even here. The Hasidic stories demonstrate that Hasidic teaching perhaps helped elevate the regard for the poor and lowly in Jewish society, but could not eradicate this social ideal. The desire for status and wealth remained a part of Hasidic society, just as in Jewish society from time immemorial.

[6] The Child Taken Captive to the New World

One of the most prevalent themes in the tales of Hasidism is that which tells of a Jewish child thrust into the Gentile world who succeeds, after a struggle, in returning to the bosom of his people. Almost all Hasidic story collections include at least one tale based on this theme. Like other themes of Hasidic tales, it is not new to Jewish narrative, and is known from the Middle Ages as "the captive child" (*tinok sh'e nishbah*) But the intensity of this theme in Hasidic narrative is evidence of its special significance here.

Like other tales treated above, this theme is also connected in the Hasidic tale with images that predate Hasidism, especially that of Rabbi Judah Loew of Prague. Two tales included in important story collections, *Sefer Sippurei Kedoshim* (#5) and *Pe'er mi-Kedoshim* (#5) revolve around the figure of Rabbi

Judah of Prague. The first tale—"The Chronicles of Ephraim," tells of a Jewish tenant who was, together with his family, thrown into a deep dungeon because he could not pay the landowner's rent. When his wife gives birth in captivity, the squire offers to release them, on condition that they allow him to adopt the newborn. The child grows to glory in the squire's home and excels in all studies, particularly the playing of the violin. But when the time of his Bar Mitzvah draws close, his father appears to him in a dream and instructs him to return to Judaism's embrace. On the day of his Bar Mitzvah, his father takes him to the Prague synagogue of R. Judah Loew, who knows the child has a great soul and teaches him Torah. But the squire, who is also a great sorcerer, abducts him, and a battle wages until R. Judah emerges victorious, and instructs the young man to take a wife and live as a hidden zaddik. Before his death, R. Judah instructs the Jews of Prague to put that same young man "upon his chair." In the second tale, a young prodigy is kidnapped from his father's home by two priests disguised as wealthy Jews. They imprison him in the monastery, in a room where an enchanted skull turns to him, saying that it too was once a Jewish prodigy whom the priests abducted seven years earlier. Now, continues the skull, it is the young man's turn. They intend to kill him and keep his skull there for the next seven years. Rabbi Judah, to whom the young man's father appeals, declares a public fast and special prayers, and causes a storm gale to carry the young man to the synagogue. The young man brings along the skull, which the priests used in their sorcery. Rabbi Judah gives it a Jewish burial and says *kaddish* for the victim.

Similar tales are told of Hasidic zaddikim: Jehiel Michael of Zloczow appears in a tale similar to "The Chronicles of Ephraim" (*Temimei Derekh*, pp. 9a–12a), and the Maggid of Mezehrich rescues a child who was carried off by priests. His marvelous homilies bring on a furious storm that carries the child directly to his study hall (*Seder ha-Dorot mi-Talmidei ha-Besht*, Lemberg 1865, second list, p. 11a). Even in stories revolving around Rabbi Judah of Prague, the protagonist acts as a Hasidic zaddik in every respect, as we have already seen. From this perspective, these tales are truly part of Hasidic narrative. They reflect an intensive effort to create a bond with the Jewish culture that preceded Hasidism, yet their themes reflect the world of Hasidism and its storytelling.

Another tale type, which also has roots deep in the Middle Ages, is that of "The Jewish Pope." Hasidism absorbed this tale with few modifications. Levi Isaac of Berdichev is the narrator of one version. At the core of this tale, in all its different versions, stands the motif of "the captive child." A child born of prostitution willingly converts to Christianity as Jewish society will have nothing to do with him, or else he is kidnapped by Christians. He rises through the ranks of the Church, eventually to be declared Pope. When the Jews of a community are slandered by a blood libel, he proves the lie, decries Christianity, and dies a martyr. The Hasidic storytellers' interest in this tale, shows, apparently, that in their eyes the central theme is that of a Jewish child living among Gentiles and returning to the bosom of Judaism, and not the Jewish Pope, in which they had no interest.[23]

Another tale type, also with roots in medieval Hebrew narrative, is the contest of magic. In "The Chronicles of Ephraim," Rabbi Judah of Prague vies with the squire-sorcerer over the Jewish child caught in his net. But the most widespread model in the Hasidic tales is the struggle between the Ba'al Shem Tov and the squire-sorcerer who kidnapped and murdered the child of a Jewish innkeeper on the night of his circumcision ceremony. The Ba'al Shem Tov apprehends the squire, rains blows upon him, and in the ensuing contest of magic, punishes or kills him. In these tales, as in all those preceding, the zaddik stands like a wall to protect the Jewish community from those who would kidnap their children, namely, the powers of darkness or the Gentiles with their magic. In joining battle against such forces, the zaddik employs supernatural powers, but these come under the rubric of "white magic," that is, the use of Judaism's traditional means: psalms, the ineffable name, ethical homilies and admonitions, and the like.[24]

Since the rabbinic period, as we have repeatedly shown in this work, the religious controversies between Jews and other religions have been represented on the folk level by means of tales of magic contests. Such was the case for the Jewish-Hellenistic controversy in the rabbinic period, and for the Jewish-Christian debate in the Middle Ages. Most tales of the child taken captive by Gentiles are magic tales; their significance is the same as that of the tales of magic contests between denizens of ages past. The rabbi and the Hasidic zaddik are, first and foremost, spiritual leaders; this role takes priority over their mastery of magic forces. Their principal duty is to safeguard the spiritual world of their believers. Kidnappers are of two categories: squires or priests. The former represents the socio-economic lure before the young Jew of the generation; the latter, the lurking spiritual temptation. The Hasidic zaddikim use the powers afforded them by the Jewish tradition—fasts, ritual immersions, the recitation of psalms, kabbalistic formulas—to regain the human plunder. In the tale they represent the spiritual superiority of Judaism: when the Jewish forces of holiness are exposed in all their might before the young man, he is convinced, and returns to the rock whence he was hewn.

The material and spiritual temptations of the world beyond Judaism were not the only ones confronting the young Jew. In one episode of the tale, "The Chronicles of Ephraim," the protagonist fails to withstand the temptations of Samael ("the Adversary") and, when in his hands,

> Samael said to him: "Look here, you are in my hands [I can] do with you as I please. But behold, I will allow you to return to your home if you swear to me by the name of the Almighty, the everlasting God, that you will study the

book I give you, one page each day. And when you swear to me such that no release from this vow will ever be valid, then you will return to your home, and if not—you are in my hands." R. Solomon Ephraim saw that he had no choice and he was forced to swear. He took the book from his hand and went and returned to his home, grieved and sorrowful. The very next day he studied one page, as he had been sworn to, and at once the desire to learn that had until then burned within him left his heart. And the next day he again studied one page—by now he loathed the sight of a book. On the third day he studied another page—he began to disparage the precepts and no longer came to the Rabbi's school. The rich man, with whom he stayed, saw his actions as out of character, for he had always known him to be in the habit of studying assiduously, and now he had become another person. When a few days later he began to commit some transgressions, to eat without ritually washing his hands, the householder went to the rabbi and told him about his actions. The rabbi sent for him, and he did not want to come. He sent and they took him by force. When he arrived the rabbi was astonished, and asked him: "What has happened to you?" Then he began to weep. The Rabbi warned with strict excommunication not to conceal anything from him, and he told him all that had happened. The Rabbi became greatly apprehensive, and upon seeing the unclean book in his hand his flesh crept in fear. He wrung his hands and was very grieved over the fine vessel that had fallen into the hands of the damned. (*Sefer Sippurei Kedoshim*, Nigal edition, p. 34)

This narrative episode can help us understand the full significance of this issue in the Hasidic world. The greatest peril facing "the child who was taken captive" is the book. The book causes him to loathe the study of Torah and, gradually, to stop observing the precepts. A book that leads to such results in its young reader in the mid-nineteenth century (*Sefer Sippurei Kedoshim*, printed in 1866), could only have been a book of the *Haskalah* (i.e., the Jewish enlightenment movement, and the most bitter adversary of the Hasidic way):

In the present generation the scurf from the enlightened of our people has much increased . . . for they are wise only to do evil, and have given their heart to the folly that they named enlightenment, to destroy all foundations of the religion and make a mockery of the angels of God and his zaddikim. And they have written in books their sayings and vanities to ridicule our holy Torah. And on account of our many transgressions, such sorcerers as the author of the *Moreh Nevukhei ha-Zeman* ["Guide of the Perplexed of the Time," R. Nachman Krochmal] and many more such, have now multiplied . . . May their name and memory be blotted out for generations, the purpose of all their words is to ridicule the words of the holy Talmud and the *Posekim* (that is, rabbinic authorities on halachic questions). A viper's nest lies hidden in their breast to scorn the words of our sages of blessed memory and, Heaven forfend, make of them a laughing stock. [In this way they seek] to attract the hearts of the poor folk, to get them to educate their children to follow them . . . the names of their readers are an eternal disgrace. And if not for the wise men who now dwell everywhere to stop the people, so that they will follow God and not their hearts and their eyes . . . we would all be lost, Heaven forbid. (Preface to *Kehal Hasidim*)

This passage, from one of the most important Hasidic story collections, truly sounds like a conceptual abstraction of the tales we have thus far seen: the world teems with dangers, the worst of them the peril of the Enlightenment. It wages battle with books that entice the young. The authors of these books, the leaders of the Enlightenment, are described as sorcerers, the very image of the powers of darkness in the Hasidic tales. "The poor folk"—the masses, those who were not Torah scholars—are the ones who allow their children to follow them. In other words, these are the children who were taken captive, who fell into the thrall of the forces of sorcery in the stories. Standing in the breach are those same wise men, those Hasidic zaddikim, like a bulwark throughout the Jewish communities, barring the path of the youngsters, or bringing them back after they have strayed onto this path. This is also the narrative function of the zaddikim in the tales we have seen.

The Hasidic storytellers thus use traditional patterns—the contest of magic, the captive child, the blood libel, the Jewish pope—to express one of the most deeply-seated fears disturbing the rest of nineteenth-century pious Jews: that the younger generation would flock to the Enlightenment, for in that case, in the words of the author of *Kehal Hasidim*: "we are all lost, Heaven forfend." This anxiety was not the sole province of the Hasidic community. It was manifested, for example, in the most important story collection of Sephardic Jewry of the same period, *Oseh Peleh*. The core tales of this book deal with the same theme—young men leaving their homes and facing the temptations of the non-Jewish world. After many exploits and perils, they return to the cities and the homes of their fathers, and accept the yoke of Judaism. This book also makes manifest, in distinctly folk narrative, the profound concern for Judaism's destiny in the face of the peril posed by the Enlightenment. The generation of fathers cannot sleep at night for fear that the generations of sons, evincing a clear outward predilection for the new world and its temptations, will abandon the tradition of the fathers. This anxiety was formulated plainly in hundreds of sermons, condemnatory letters, and books of ethics, and most tangibly manifested in the folktales of the period. From this perspective the Hasidic tale, with the special language it developed, joins the great campaign of religious Judaism against new directions in the evolution of Jewish culture.[25]

The Hasidic tale should not be regarded as though it only borrows tales from earlier traditions and tailors them to its world. It is also a cultural organism that builds itself through new creativity. Still, "new creativity" within the traditional culture is of a far different hue than new creation within secular culture. Most Hasidic narrative was created in the same period that saw the development of the Haskalah literature. The latter was a new creation in the full sense of the word; there had never before been its like in Jewish culture, and it relied on the creative imagination of the Enlightenment authors. Hasidic storytellers, like those of every other traditional society, base their creativity on the themes, motifs, and narrative models of the traditional narrative that preceded them. Not for want of talent, but out of a clearcut worldview. While the Haskalah authors present their narrative as fictional literature, the product of their imagination, feelings, and artistic perception, their Hasidic counterparts present their tales as unadulterated truth, of which they are not the creators (even when they were distinguished authors like Michael Levi Rodkinsohn, Menahem Mendel Bodek, or Judah Yudel Rosenberg); they merely brought it to print from reliable oral or written sources. The Hasidic storytellers' social outlook and worldview, which held that the tales be accepted by their audience as factual, also influenced their pattern. These disparate conceptions of the Hasidic storytellers, as compared to the Enlightenment authors, also influenced their choice of genre and form: while the Haskalah authors turned outward, to European literature, creating novels, short stories, satires, and romances, the Hasidic storytellers turned inward, to Jewish folk narrative, borrowing legends of the saints, the magic tale, and the wisdom novella.

Hasidic storytellers borrowed from one another, as well as from earlier Jewish and foreign traditions. Indeed, a reading of Hasidic tales demonstrates the interchange of themes, motifs, entire narrative episodes, and characters. A picture emerges of mosaics, composed of stones of predetermined colors, wherein each storyteller arranges the same materials in different ways. Since they do not correspond precisely with the motifs of folk literature, I will term as "themes" all these narrative materials that make up the stock drawn upon by Hasidic storytellers to construct their tales.

By way of example, let us consider one tale from the later legends ("praises") of the Ba'al Shem Tov: A barren woman persistently begs the Ba'al Shem Tov to pray for her. After a time, he promises her she will bear a son, and indeed, she delivers a child of unusual beauty. She brings him to the Ba'al Shem Tov to receive his blessing; he takes the child's hands, kisses him, and returns him to his mother. Upon her return home, the child dies. She goes back to the Ba'al Shem Tov, and accuses him of responsibility for the death of her son. The Ba'al

Shem Tov tells her that in a certain country there lived a king who had no sons. He turned to his Jewish advisor, who counselled him to decree that unless he had a son, the Jews would be banished from his kingdom. After following this advice, the king fathered a son who was a great prodigy. The king summoned the pope himself to tutor him. The pope stipulated that no one, including the son, might enter his room for a specified two hours each day, as during that time he rose up to study with the saints in heaven. After a time, the son, having learned all that the pope had to teach him, resolved to enter the room during the pope's self-imposed confinement. He found him wrapped in a prayer shawl, studying Torah. The prince insisted on studying *gemara* with him each day. The pope agreed and, ultimately, the prince demanded that he convert him to Judaism. The teacher went so far as to help him escape his home and join a distant Jewish community. After his death, the heavenly prosecutors determined that since he had suckled from a Gentile woman for two years, the world to come could not receive him as a holy spirit. The Ba'al Shem Tov decreed that the soul descend into the body of that same barren woman, suckle from this suitable Jewish mother for a period of two years and thus be purified, after which it would go to its rightful place.[26]

The tale is a typical example of the compositional nature of the Hasidic tale. The storyteller drew here from that same stock of narrative themes, and joined them into a single narrative plot: infertility and appeal to the zaddik, the zaddik who knows and tells hidden things, the king's edict against the Jewish community, the community saved from calamity by a miracle, a child with wondrous learning ability, a Jewish pope, a child taken captive by Gentiles, the weighing of a man's actions upon his arrival in the world to come, transmigration into a living being for the purpose of reparation, a zaddik who ordains— and God makes it so. These are all the key components of the tale, and *all* are themes that appear often in other Hasidic tales. They clearly show more than the compositional nature of the Hasidic tale; they also indicate the manner of its creation: the storyteller-author of the tale uses his society's traditional materials for his composition of a new tale. The effect, the influence of such a tale on its listeners or readers, is the end to which the Hasidic tale strives generally: it forges a sense of continuity with tales already heard, as all of the themes that compose the tale are familiar to them from other stories. Since the earlier tales were accepted by them as credible, as they heard them from people they knew to be God-fearing, or read them in holy books like *Shivhei ha-Besht*, this tale joins the hundreds of others, shoring up faith in the zaddik, in the superiority of Judaism over Christianity, and in the forthcoming reward and punishment in the world to come. In this manner a new tale is constructed from the earlier stock of Hasidic tales, simultaneously replenishing that stock by joining it as a new and dynamic link.

The use of ready-made themes does not end in the realm of narrative motifs and subjects. It extends into the plane of the active characters as well. The Hasidic tales feature four groups or types of people:

(a) the very wealthy men, community leaders, and big merchants (the *ba'aley batim*);
(b) the poor, simple folk, craftsmen, and beggars—men and women (some of them hidden saints as well);
(c) the zaddikim (and their attendants—the students and Hasidim);
(d) the gentiles—the nobility, the landed gentry, kings.

The Hasidic tales expose conflicts between (a) and (b): prosperous Jews demean the simple folk, throw them out of their homes, are loath to join their families through marriage, begrudge them honors in the synagogue (when they are hidden zaddikim) such as a sermon or prayer, and so on. The disproportion between internal and external, which we discussed in a previous section, is based on the conflict between these two types of protagonist in the Hasidic tale. Another conflict pits (a) against (d), as the Gentile kings and nobles have almost no contact with the simple folk of Jewish society. This clash involves either the Jewish tenant, the big community leaders, the Jewish court advisor, or the community rabbis. This type of conflict characterizes Jewish folktales since the medieval period, thus the Hasidic tales participate in one of the great subjects of Jewish folk narrative, namely, the clash between the Jewish people and the other nations. Busy as the Hasidic community was establishing its position within Jewish society, grappling with other streams in Judaism (as expressed in the conflict between (a) and (b)), existential anxiety about the non-Jewish world maintained a central place in the Hasidic folk consciousness. In these conflicts, type (c)—the zaddik—is a key figure. His familiar role as mediator between heaven and earth, between God and believers, broadens therefore to include mediation in the strictly mortal realm as well. He mediates between the rich and simple folk in the Hasidic tale: he reveals to the community magnates the true identity of a hidden zaddik; he is the one to whom the poor turn in their distress—and he directs them to the wealthy. He punishes the wealthy for their sins, and they become poor. In other words, movement between (a) and (b) takes place through the agency of the zaddik. In this manner, the Hasidic tale presents the zaddik as controlling the social order, as well. Such is also the case in the movement between (a) and (d). Squires send an entire tenant family to the dungeon, issue edicts against the Jewish community, abduct Jewish children, or exact heavy taxes from the community. The mediator is, once again, the zaddik: he vanquishes the squire in a contest of magic, releases the child who was taken captive, exorcises the dybbuk from his daughter and so saves the Jewish community from annihilation. In this mediation, basically defense, the zaddik is like a rampart surrounding the Jewish community and the individual, protecting them from dangers beyond.

This division of the active characters in the Hasidic tales into stereotypes shows that the Hasidic storytellers availed themselves not only of ready-made themes, but of ready-made protagonists, as well. The character of the mediating zaddik on center stage is self-explanatory and suits Hasidic doctrine. The other stereotypes are no mere technical means for the storytellers' convenience, but primarily ideational and emotional frames of reference. It is similar to the genre of the animal fable, where the active characters have fixed frames of reference: the fox is wily and the sheep naive, the lion rules and the wolf is wicked, and so on. Earlier fables, and the common concepts of that society, formed constant metaphors, frames of reference understood similarly by each society member. Thus the fable needs only to name the character in order to evoke its particular characteristics. Such is also the case in the Hasidic tale: the wealthy man, the squire, the poor craftsmen, the barren woman, and the zaddik establish fixed reference groups with which listeners or readers can identify, or from whom they can set themselves apart. Each such reference group has a clear significance in the Hasidic world.

Apart from the movement between these four types of active characters in the Hasidic tale, there is, in almost all the tales, spatial movement. The zaddik is commanded by heaven to set out on the road, the horses lead him deep into the forest or to a remote tavern; the child taken captive by the squire is kidnapped by his father, and set down in the doorway of R. Judah of Prague's study hall; R. Judah of Prague keeps him there, but the squire snatches him away a second time; he wanders in the dark forest, and again finds refuge in a study hall; a Torah scholar is commanded by the zaddik to depart into exile and wander among the various communities; a Hasid who has no resources to marry off his daughters sets out to wander and collect money for their dowries; the wealthy man who sets out on business, and innumerable examples in all the other tales. This flow between the sanctified or family structure (the synagogue, the study hall, the home) and the outside (the forest, the road, foreign locales), is so central to the Hasidic tale that its signficance must be sought out.

It seems to me that there is a connection to the social and theological perception of Hasidism which developed as a movement of opposition and protest against the social establishment and that of the Torah scholars in communities of the end of the Middle Ages. The symbol of the institution has always been a "house": the prosperous man's spacious home, the community public house in which he wields control, the house of worship, and house of study wherein the Torah scholars rule with a high hand. The protest against these institutions was also a protest against the "house" that symbolized them. Therefore the Hasidic tale breaks the boundaries of the "house": it proposes to its listeners that real, consequential life, whether social or religious, takes place "outside," beyond the four walls of the "house." That is where the hidden saints reside, there the wood choppers and water carriers, whose virtues and devotion to God surpasses that of the rulers of the "house." Therefore, almost every Hasidic tale brings its listeners outside, seeking to show them that that is where true life takes place. This is the insurgent message of the Hasidic tale: neither the wealthy and prosperous of the community, ensconced in their spacious homes, nor the Torah scholars, holing up in their ivory towers, lives a Jewish life in its truest sense. The zaddik is the mediator here, too, between the house and the outside, between the frozen institution of the past, and the life of true and dynamic faith set forth by the simple folk found beyond it.

[8] "We Saw with Our Own Eyes, in Our Own Generation"

There are still people lacking complete understanding [who are] far from believing in tales of the wonders of the zaddikim. They say, our fathers told us but we did not see it with our own eyes and we did not hear of some marvel that took place in our generation, so that it will show that there is a Law and that there is a Judge. I have already mentioned above that this is truly somewhat hidden, it is not so common as to be visible to the senses as it was once. . . . Even so, whoever wishes truly to determine that there is a Law and that there is a Judge can see that, just as numerous deeds took place before our time, [those] about which our fathers told us, so too the present holds wonders that we have seen with our own eyes. And I have said I would bring here some tales relating to this matter, for with the increase of days all is forgotten. . . . (Sefer Siftei Kodesh, 17a)

And so it is: as the Hasidic movement today is dynamic, with perhaps more political and social strength than ever before, the same is true of the Hasidic tale. In the great Hasidic centers of Israel, the United States, and Western Europe, Hasidic tales are told orally, and dozens of collections of tales are published—along with reissues of old ones with new material—as in the past. The tales are widely available throughout the present-day Hasidic courts, though they flourish especially among Chabad (Lubavitcher) Hasidism. The tens of thousands of Chabad Hasidim in the United States tell numerous so-called "Rebbe Stories" that describe appeals to the Lubavitcher Rebbe, and his responses. All matters of the modern world are addressed: medicine, livelihood, security, and education, and the Rebbe reportedly solves the problems of his believers in marvelous ways. The Chabad movement press, such as the 770 News (770 being the Rebbe's Brooklyn street address), Beit Hayyenu (The House of Our Lives), Iton Kfar Habad (The Kfar Chabad Newspaper), Are'enu

Nifla'ot (I Will Show Him Wonders), distributed by the Organization of Chabad Women, *Irgun Tzeirei Habad* (The Organization of Habad Youth) columns entitled, "I Experienced It Myself," and the like, publish hundreds of tales, each including the Rebbe's address and encouraging people to turn to him. All of these affirm the quotation heading this section: the wonders of the zaddikim have not decreased, only belief in them. Every publication of such miracles, performed day-in, day-out by the zaddikim, seeks to bring those of weak faith closer to seeing and acknowledging the daily performance of miracles. These tales, presented as "facts," naturally enrich the stock of Jewish folktales of our time in an impressive manner. Moreover, the orientation of these tales differs from the classic Hasidic narrative; they are aimed at the struggle between the different Hasidic courts, the conflict with secular Judaism, the conflict with science and modern technology and many other subjects. These are certainly worthy of encompassing collection, and of full and in-depth study.[27]

[B] Legends of the Saints and Israeli Society

[1] Saints' Legends and Contemporary Folk Literature

Folk literature is a social product. Although this determination is today perceived more narrowly than in the past, the basic notion that multiple representatives of society shape any folk creation, and that the latter must pass a "barrier,"—gain society's acceptance, or overcome its censorship—has never been contested. As a societal creation, folk literature gives expression to the processes that Jewish society has undergone in recent generations. Where Hebrew folk literature is concerned, these pertain primarily to the new life in the State of Israel. This body of literature perpetuates the long-lived tradition of writing and publishing folktales in Hebrew, though their oral recitation may have been in another language. Most of the Jewish folk literature that was originally told in Arabic, Yiddish, Judeo-Spanish, and other Jewish dialects has been committed to writing and published in Hebrew. This process is not new, having gone on continuously in Jewish culture since the Middle Ages. The new wrinkle in this field in recent generations is the revival of the oral folktale *told in Hebrew*. Since the rebirth of Hebrew as a spoken language in late nineteenth-century Palestine, narrative traditions in this language have made a comeback in the new agricultural settlements, in the old (Jerusalem, Tiberias, Safed) and new urban centers, as the official language of the political institutions, and the everyday discourse of the proto-military organizations. This shift to Hebrew did not, of course, take place all at once and, even now, some hundred years after it began, performance events still take place in other languages, as anyone engaged in field work can attest. Nevertheless, the relative quantity and intensity of live performance in Hebrew have gathered momentum, and have taken the uncontested lead in the creative folk life of modern Israel.[28]

Tales from the traditional Jewish sources, those that have been described in the previous chapters of this book, are told extensively in contemporary Israeli folk narrative. This is well attested to by the Israel Folktale Archive (IFA), founded in the 1950s by Dov Noy. The old narrative genres and themes constitute a central part of the materials collected in IFA. However, this is not an altogether new phenomenon of Jewish folklore, and does not reflect recent developments in Jewish culture and society. Much more important, for that purpose, are the traditional narrative forms that express new social and historical content. Here, as well, the traditional factors are obvious: fables and animal tales as didactic tools, exempla stories used to promote religious interests; moral tales to preach fundamentalist ideas; jokes and humorous narratives as weapons of confrontation. All these are old literary forms in Jewish folk literature, the main discourse genres of the previous periods. They were absorbed in the new Israeli reality, and are used to express it and its needs and demands.

This process is more salient in the legends of the saints than in any other genre. The revival of these tales in the new Israeli reality comes on the heels of a (relatively) short period of suppression of their creation and dissemination, when the Maghreb Jewish immigrants arrived in the State of Israel in the late 1950s and 1960s. The continuous nature of the genre is manifested distinctly in one theme: the miraculous transition of a number of saints' graves from Morocco to various locations in modern Israel. Such stories are reported in Beit-She'an, Ashkelon, Ofakim, Yeruham, and other development towns. A case in point is the room of the saint Rabbi David u-Moshe in Safed.

[2] The Reappearance of the Saints

In 1973, Rabbi David u-Moshe, a saint widely accepted among Jews of Morocco's Atlas Mountain region, appeared in a dream to Avraham Ben-Haim, a Moroccan immigrant living in a poor section of Safed. The saint instructed him to dedicate one room of his small apartment to the honor of the zaddik (saint), as a pilgrimage site. Avraham Ben-Haim followed these instructions. Since then, the room in his little apartment has become one of the most frequented pilgrimage sites in Israel. On the festival day in honor of this zaddik (the *hillulah*), more than twenty thousand faithful visitors come to pay their respects. The same process of "immigration" to the Land of Israel of long-dead saints, as it were, took place preceding the establishment of another center of adoration for Rabbi David u-Moshe. The following tale is typical, and well illustrates this theme:

Two Jews lived in Kurdani (near Haifa). On Purim night they sat and played cards. Both of them. The *Hacham* (the sage—Rabbi David u-Moshe) came to them at night and told them: Why did you forget me? They said to him: Cidi (our lord), we did not forget you. Did we forget you? How is it possible? Only the sea separates us. He said to them: No, I am not beyond the sea, I am in the old section of Ashkelon, house number so and so, at Waqnin's, at Shimon Waqnin's. They did not know him. On Purim I . . . sat with Rabbi Portal, and we ate *barkukes* (a kind of Morrocan doughnuts). I didn't sense their presence until they stood here with the car. They and their sons. They said Psalms, we ate together, and they left.[29]

A sociological analysis of the phenomenon of the transition of the saint's centers of worship to Israel indicates a clear link between "the immigration" of the saints from Morocco to Israel and the establishment of the development towns. These settlements were founded artificially in locations set aside for new immigrants, in the absence of any comprehensible ecological or financial justification. Their nearly homogeneous populations, i.e., new immigrants from a single given ethnic community had no link whatsoever to the geographical location. For many years, population exchange in the development towns was a pronounced demographic phenomenon. Many of the original immigrants, lacking any firm connection to the towns—which tended to be ugly and bereft of ways to make a decent living—moved on, and others were brought in to replace them. At the same time, during the twenty-some years since the immigration and the founding of the settlements, a firm nucleus of residents formed. These people developed a connection to the place by virtue of habit and the social ties created there over time—family, neighbors, friends. The most interesting manifestation of the sense of belonging to the place, and of nascent patriotic sensitivities, is the creation of "centers of the sacred." Perhaps these illustrate above all that the link to their new home, initially imposed upon the residents, had become a natural and desired bond. In the case of Rabbi David u-Moshe, there is direct testimony in support of this explanation: In 1973, the Ben-Haim family planned to move out of the small apartment in Safed to which they had been brought upon immigrating to Israel in 1954. The appearance of Rabbi David u-Moshe in Avraham Ben-Haim's dream prevented, at the last minute, their move to a more spacious apartment in another neighborhood. Indeed, the consecration of the room for the saint completely changed the face and image of the old neighborhood: thousands of pilgrims began to flock annually from all parts of Israel (and beyond). The consequent financial opportunities for the local populace sparked and augmented the bond between the town and its residents.[30]

The symbolic passage of the saints from Morocco to the development towns is the ultimate manifestation of the use of traditional ritual texts to express new content. Adoration of the saints, and the tales that bore and disseminated the rituals, were basic components of Jewish culture in Morocco. Arriving in Israel, Moroccan Jews encountered a new reality. The indoctrination of new immigrants via the educational system contributed to the wane of the adoration and its corresponding legends of the saints; there was nothing to link the new Israeli reality to the main components of the culture they had brought with them. Only after putting down roots, over the span of a generation, could the community restore the worship of the saints, and robustly so, to Israelis of North-African origin. One explanation of the phenomenon is that it gave religious legitimacy to the new semi-urban centers. Another derives from the community's self-image as peripheral to Israeli society. The desire to move from margin to the center is an obvious motive behind this revival of the veneration of saints in Israel. The convergence of most of the community around these "centers of the sacred," and the ways they influence the fundamental institutions of the State of Israel (the educational system, the Chief Rabbinate and the Ministry of Religion, the Security Forces, the transportation companies, the municipalities) in order to reckon with and participate in them, are typical of the phenomenon of the "ethnic revival" elsewhere in the world, as well.[31]

Another typical example of the passage of narrative forms from North Africa to Israel is the saints' tales of R. Jacob Wazanah. This saint was born near the turn of the century in the Atlas Mountains of western Morocco, and died in 1952 in the same region. Moroccan immigrants tell almost enough tales about him to put together a sort of "legendary biography" about the life of the saint. Complex and ambivalent, these tales describe his close ties to the world of the demons, including marriage to a demoness, his participation in the rituals and ceremonies of Moroccan Arabs, his association with ne'er-do-wells, living beyond the normative limits—in seclusion, not raising a family, wandering from place to place, and avoiding any kind of community position. Taken together, the tales of Wazanah indicate a striving for balance between the opposing worlds that made up Jewish life in Morocco—the sacred and the profane, earthly daily life and deep belief in the demonic world, a society with clear and rigid societal norms, and a life spent skirting them. As it happens, tales about R. Jacob Wazanah are also told today, in Israel, in settlements populated by immigrants from the areas where he was active in the western Atlas Mountains. These immigrants were settled far from the country's population centers. The sense of marginality with respect to Israeli society increased among these homogeneous populations, and with it the resurgence of tales about such sacred figures. The tales of Jacob Wazanah here lost their socio-psychological role as "balancers between worlds," as the reality had changed fundamentally. On the other hand, the problem of the marginality of the immigrants from Morocco in their new environment in Israel became a basic characteristic of their existence and self image. It seems that the tales of Jacob Wazanah, the figure who most clearly expresses marginality, here constitutes a perfect object of social identification. The many stories of his social and religious marginality clearly reflect the sensitivities of the narrating society: their economic weakness and failure to fill a respected place in the establishment of the State of Israel; customs and rituals perceived as smacking of idolatry against a background of the State's spiritual and cultural life; their being likened to despised Arabs in their customs, dress, food, and language (reminiscent of the tales of Wazanah's frequent visits among the Arabs). All these run surprisingly parallel to tales of the saint's marginality and constitute, once again, the important cultural phenomenon of resurgence of previously vanished community traditions. In their new avatar, they provide members of the community with figures of identification relevant to their needs and anxieties amid new surroundings.[32]

[3] Local Saints, Local Reality

Of utmost importance to our investigation are those tales of saints who were active primarily in Israel, as opposed to Morocco. Examples propagate before our very eyes, but here the phenomenon will be modelled with three personalities: R. Israel Abuhatzeira, the "Baba Sali" of Netivot; Rabbi Mordechai Sharabi of Jerusalem; and R. David u-Moshe who, unlike the first two, died without having set foot in Israel. The latter's faithful "brought him" to the country with the establishment of centers of homage in Ashkelon and Safed.

The Baba Sali's fame is not solely a function of his personality, being partly hereditary. He is a scion of a dynasty famed for its righteous miracle-workers and saints. Indeed, as regards one of the family's patriarchs, R. Jacob Abuhatzeira, the same process of symbolic "passage" to the State of Israel has taken place. In one typical tale included in a collection of "praises" (hagiography) of the saint, the following is told:

> I heard a wondrous story, that in the city of Ashdod in our Holy Land, there lives a family by the name of Ben Gigi. The wife is a descendent of our Rabbi Jacob [Abuhatzeira] on her father's side, and the husband is a truly pious and God-fearing man. This couple had a daughter, born under a lucky star. They live on the top floor of a three-story apartment building. Now, when the girl was about three years old, she was playing on the balcony when she fell from the third floor, God spare us. The mother called to her daughter, Rachel! but she [did] not answer. She went outside and [saw] that the child had fallen. She ran down to see her daughter, and saw that she was safe and sound. She asked her, "Who saved you?" The girl answered: "Rabbi Jacob Abuhatzeira came, and also Grandfather's father (that is, the father of Rabbi

Isaac Shitrit, the mother's father), and they caught me before I reached the ground." And all who saw [that], rejoiced, and so did all the family. May the Merciful One perform miracles and wonders for us and may we be worthy to worship wholeheartedly by virtue of the zaddikim [saints], may their virtue protect us, Amen.[33]

The *realia* herein is that of modern Israel: urban life, apartment houses, and a set of unfamiliar perils with which the immigrants must learn to reckon. The traditional apparatus of coping with the harsh circumstances of the diaspora is activated in the new Israeli surroundings: the saint skips across the voids of time and place to watch over and rescue the faithful. The geographical and spiritual distance does not stop him from departing the diaspora for modern Israel. Significantly, the manifestation in this tale takes place before a representative of the new generation, educated in the modern Israeli system. The young daughter, born in the new State, is the one to correctly interpret the significance of the miracle done for her. Therein lies an explicit assertion that faith in the righteous can pass to the next generation, notwithstanding its new circumstances that are almost diametrically opposed from those of its forbears. Life in Israel, for all its modern advances and vast sophistication, is no less needful of the power of the righteous than the diaspora.

There is no integral part of life in the State of Israel around which legends of saints have not been created. Military service and Israel's wars are among the most salient characteristics of the new reality that have no precursor in diaspora life. A typical tale in the hagiography of the Baba Sali begins as follows:

> One day a family arrived at the home of our Rabbi. All the men had long hair and beards of the mourning. You could see they were deep in grief. In reply to the question of our Rabbi's servant, they explained that their brother had gone to reserve duty, and many days had passed without their hearing word from him. The military authorities had thrown up their hands and gave notice through the town major that they had no news. . . . (*The Baba Sali*, p. 146)

The saint demanded they leave off mourning, and cited the verse: "by no means clearing the guilty," for the missing soldier will return whole and sound. Though they did not see the relevance of the verse cited (which can also mean, "the one who cleans will not be destroyed"), the family accepted his instruction. The son did indeed return home, no harm having come to him, and in the presence of the saint explained that a miracle was done him for "every Sabbath eve I clean our synagogue in Petah Tikva. The *gabbai* (i.e., a synagogue official) is the only one who knows about it." The tale includes such details of modern reality as army reserve duty, soldiers missing in action, appealing to the town major, and the involvement of the military authorities. Alongside these is an impressive array of traditional motifs from Jewish sacred legends of the past: the narrative pattern of appealing to the zaddik; his enigmatic response—whose prophetic power is revealed in the denouement; reward and rescue by virtue of a single good deed done by the hero—which is a widespread narrative motif in medieval Jewish exempla. The following tale, featuring R. Mordechai Sharabi, evinces similar characteristics:

> A story of a reservist from Bnei Brak who served his neighborhood as prayer leader for the High Holy days and as a shofar blower. On the eve of Rosh ha-Shanah, 1983, he received a call-up notice to reserve duty in Lebanon. The soldier didn't know what to do, as he was the father of five young children and his wife was almost nine months pregnant. The soldier considered asking to be released from reserve duty. However, in light of the difficult security situation on account of Operation "Peace in the Galilee" [the 1982 war in Lebanon], and the mass recruit of many citizens, he did not dare ask for release. The soldier consulted with his friends, who advised him to come to our Rabbi in Jerusalem and tell him the situation, as he would certainly be able to help him with advice and insight. The soldier saw that he had nothing to lose from visiting the kabbalist in Jerusalem, and so made his way there. He waited in line to see our Rabbi, and when he came before the Zaddik, the Rabbi said to him: "the situation in the country is difficult—this I know, and even so, you are released!" The soldier left the Zaddik encouraged, and submitted his request. Many other soldiers submitted requests for deferment or release, but all were rejected on account of the difficult situation. Only the request of the soldier from Bnei Brak was accepted, and his duty deferred to another time. The soldier attributed his release to Rabbi Sharabi, who had said to him, "You are released!" (*Rabbi Sharabi*, pp. 295–296)

This tale manifests a narrative model that was prevalent in Jewish tales of the past, wherein the regime issues an edict against a member of the community. The protagonist turns to the representative of the holy Power—the zaddik—who thwarts the decree. The proclamation of the saint, "You are released!" is twice repeated in the tale, and serves as a kind of a magic formula or invocation that successfully alters the situation. The form of the announcement is drawn from the army's official lexicon, and is not a kabbalistic formulation of any kind (it is emphasized here and in other tales that the saint is a kabbalist). It may be that this is the case in order to facilitate ready understanding among the audience of listeners, or perhaps it is meant to influence directly and literally, as by sympathetic magic, the military's written response to the request for release of the soldier from Bnei Brak.

In this example, unlike the previous one, there is an impediment to incorporating new contents into the traditional pattern, in that the military authorities against whom the saint is called in to act belong to the same people (if not the same society). The difficulty is resolved by avoiding any expression inimical to the regime (such that would figure in tales of this type that are told in the diaspora). The narrator emphasizes, in the words of the protagonist as well as those of the saint, that the release is regrettable at such a time, in order to underscore that the tale does not relate to the military as to a foreign and hostile authority. Still, the resolution of the tale is the same as that of the traditional stories. Its new content does not stem from a description of the new reality—the Lebanon War (1982) and the period following—but from the hitherto uncharted polarity between the forces active in the tale. Traditionally, the contrast in such tales was between Jews and non-Jews; contraposing Jews against the Israeli government is novel. This subrogation of a Jewish military for a non-Jewish regime gives rise to the discomfort felt by both protagonist and saint in activating the traditional methods of struggle (here—practical Kabbalah).

In another tale, a father recounts that his son deserted from the army because he wanted to serve as a military driver rather than in a combat unit. The father turns to Rabbi David ben Baruch for help after the son is caught and jailed. The rest of his unit is killed in action on the Golan Heights, after which the deserter is pardoned. The narrator adds: "I have three sons in Sinai. Each Monday and Friday, I light a candle. First I ask for the children of Israel, and after that for my sons. In the narrator's hierarchy of values, the saint's intervention is what has saved the son from a prison term. Yet he is discomfited by his understanding that this action defies the Jewish institutions of which he feels himself part. This is made clear in his apologetic conclusion to the tale, where it is claimed that the saint's action in contravention of the military authorities is at odds with the narrator's own attitude. Other events connected to security are, for example, the saint R. Mordechai Sharabi's prescience regarding the outbreak of the Six-Day War, and consequent instructions to seal up the house with sandbags, or the foreknowledge of the rescue of a pilot who had been captured by the Syrians in the Yom Kippur War, whose parents had appealed to the saint for help. Paradigmatic of the blending of ancient narrative tradition with new Israeli content is the tale of the Baba Sali and the Sabena aircraft:

> We will mention here an episode that shows the magnitude of his compassion for others. It was when, some years ago, a Sabena aircraft was seized by terrorists and landed in Lod. When he learned of the matter, he closed himself in his room and offered prayers and supplications to save the passengers' lives. Visitors to his home that day said that they were unable to see him, and he did not open the door even to members of his household. Suddenly, in the afternoon, the sound of heart-wrenching crying and wailing was heard.

Those near his room checked the time, and it turned out that this was precisely the moment that soldiers broke into the aircraft and liberated the passengers. A short time later . . . we asked him what happened to him in connection with the plane, and his response was as follows: "I heard what happened and I was greatly upset." At this point he pointed upwards and continued: "He knows that I was more sorrowful than the people in the plane, and praise God we were able to do something to help them."[34]

In this narrative pattern, the Zaddik, by means of empathy towards the suffering and through his magic powers, succeeds in influencing political or cosmic events. It has long been part of Jewish folk literature, from tales of Honi the Circle-Drawer, in which the hero's sorrow over the plight of the Jewish people brings rain, to the hasidic tales wherein zaddikim attempt, by means of staying in their rooms and dealing in mysteries, to influence the Napoleonic Wars at the start of the nineteenth century.

[4] Saints as War Heroes

Personal tales of salvation, in which the sacred power of the narrating society—the zaddik—takes action to save an individual in distress, are among the most widespread themes of past generations. War tales of the State of Israel do not differ from them in principle: the zaddik, R. David u-Moshe, informs his believers that the siren will soon begin and he must descend to the shelter; during the War of Attrition a shell falls on a military position, and a soldier who flies "seventy meters into the air" calls out the name of the saint R. David u-Moshe—and is saved; a Golani (infantry unit) soldier, lying in ambush, is surprised by enemy soldiers, but the saint R. David u-Moshe, who appears suddenly, helps him dispatch the enemy and get leave in reward; R. David u-Moshe saves a schoolgirl during the terrorist attack in Ma'alot after she appeals to him in prayer. The saint pushes her into a corner of the room, and when the shooting starts, protects her with his body. When the children jump from the windows of the building, the saint holds her and brings her to the ground without injury. The nature of the tales, and their core emotional charge, do not differ fundamentally from any tales of personal salvation in the folk literature of the past. The main difference is in the details of reality, in the occupation of the active characters (soldiers instead of merchants or craftsmen), and the nature of the given danger—real battles. Among the salient characteristics of Israeli legends of saints is the merging of traditional Jewish narrative's active forces with elements of the new Israeli reality—going off to reserve duty and the burden it places on the families, the disappearance of soldiers, the helplessness of the official security forces, and terrorist incidents.[35]

Saints' legends whose theme is war offer a glimpse of the psychological and social background of their emergence. In one tale of R. David u-Moshe, the faithful Abraham Ben-Haim of Safed relates the following:

> . . . it all happened this year, before the festival of R. Meir, three days before the festival [in Miron]. Some eight months now. [R. David u-Moshe] came and said to me: "Not many people will come [to my festival] this year." I asked him: "Why?" "Because there will be cries like war. But my feast will be all right." After I told [the men of the synagogue] . . . what did I do, I bought a calf. From Rosh ha-Shanah I bought it, and I said, this will be for the festival. In a moshav [i.e., cooperative settlement] not far from here. We bought everything. All that he said, plates, forks, and the same week that the war was supposed to begin, Yom Kippur Eve [the war began the next day], [R. David u-Moshe] came to me and said: "Listen, today they will take half the synagogue and now I am going, because the war will begin at this time. But at the festival everything will be all right." I got up in the morning and I said: "What's going to happen? If I go to the police and tell them, they will not believe me, because the people are not believers. Now we will leave it at that."
> —[the interviewer:] Did you tell anyone else?
> I told my wife, and some people in the synagogue. If there were enough faith, they could have believed such a thing. Since the war started, since that night [the zaddik] has not appeared. I lit candles and everything. (Ben-Ami, *le-Heker Folklor ha-Milhamah*, pp. 89–90)

Abraham Ben-Haim tells his tale about eight months after the 1973 Yom Kippur War. During the war, and even more so during the interval between its outbreak until the telling of the tale, the country was consumed with the question of how it could have begun without warning, without advance knowledge. Answers to this burning question were offered in military, intelligence, political, social, and psychological terms. Ben-Haim translates the question into concepts borrowed from his frame of reference—veneration of saints. He held that where the modern state's central normative institutions of the military and the political establishment failed, the traditional world, considered marginal in the State, succeeded. The saint gave ample warning, but lack of faith precluded use of the information. Most impressive is this undertaking to turn the set of beliefs of a marginal society into a legitimate component in the set of active forces in the state. Many weaknesses of the modern state could be cured, according to this conception, if only its citizens would wisely adopt the veneration of the saints as a social norm.

It is noteworthy that in the manifestation of the saint, and in the storyteller's questions, the prime concern is not connected with the war and its aftermath, but with the festival in honor of the saint—the war is liable to ruin the festival ceremony. The saint does not promise his believers that the war will end well, only that his festival will take place as usual. This is an excellent example of the manner in which military-political concepts circulating in the state undergo "translation" into concepts of belief. The results of the war and its significance for various areas of life in the country are not clear to the society of the faithful. The most important aspect, from their perspective, is the question of whether the basic structure of their lives, whose principal expression is the veneration of saints, is to be disrupted. The fears and hopes that were manifested in the central society via normative symbols and concepts found expression in the peripheral society via concepts from the realm of faith in the saints.

This process is discernible in many saints' legends: a worker in the cave of Elijah the Prophet in Haifa hears from him in a dream about the coming cease-fire during the Yom Kippur War (Ben-Ami, *Le-Heker Folklor ha-Milhamah*, p. 92); during the Six-Day War, cancellation threatened the festival in honor of R. David u-Moshe because of the blackout, which was cancelled just in time (Ben-Ami, *R. David u-Moshe*, #33); during the Six-Day War, a great light was seen emanating from the Holy Ark in the synagogue of R. David u-Moshe in Ashkelon, and immediately afterwards came the news that the war had ended.

> Here [in Safed] there was a Jewish woman who came to visit the Zaddik [R. David u-Moshe]. She said she had seen people during the war and she always lights [a candle in honor of the saint] . . . when she came, she said to me: "What shall I tell you? I had a dream." What dream? "I dreamt of two sages. One stands by Hazor and the other by Rosh Pina, and they bear rifles and stand." She asked them: "What are you old men doing here?" They said to her: "Silence! Do you know what we are or not?" They said: "This is Hanina [Honi] the Circle-Drawer. He stands by Hazor, and this is R. David u-Moshe, he stands on this side, so that the enemy will not pass." She was afraid, and lit the candles. (Ben-Ami, *le-Heker Folklor ha-Milhamah*, p. 90)

This takes place during the Yom Kippur War, a time of profound concern that the defense of the north would collapse and the Syrian army would invade the Galilee. As in the earlier examples, this tale translates the anxiety that swept the entire country into the language of faith in the saints. The apprehension was collective, but after undergoing a process of personalizaton—the narrative expression that it gets in these texts—it took on the language of religious symbols and concepts of the narrator's society. The symbolic character of the story's details is plain: She is surprised to see two elderly men bearing arms and standing guard. What are old men doing with rifles in this modern state? Who needs them where there is such a modern army? The storyteller uses her amazement to express this convention. The old men who manifested themselves before her, however, are bearers of the ancient tradition, and they successfully defend the state. Honi the Circle-Drawer, a legendary figure from the

Second Temple period, is (allegedly) buried nearby. R. David u-Moshe is the symbolic representative of the ethnic Moroccan culture. Their appearance together is the combination of the univeral Jewish forces and the ethnic, local ones. This is the symbolic way of expressing that only the traditional forces, obsolete by the conventional norms of the modern state, can contribute to that most important foundation of Israeli society—military security.

[5] Saints and Medicine

Israeli saints' legends deal with other themes besides the military and security. These include the financial well-being of the faithful, as in the purchase and sale of businesses and tax matters (Rabbi Sharabi); stock market investments and the buying of foreign currency on the black market (Rabbi Sharabi); repair and sale of cars (the Baba Sali, Rabbi Sharabi); the campaign waged against the establishment of public swimming pools allowing mixed bathing of men and women (Rabbi Sharabi); and the wave of immigration from Russia (the Baba Sali). The effort to spotlight the saint's involvement in all areas of life in the modern state has a clear objective: to prove that the zaddik's power and influence have not waned in modern technological society. Despite society's distance from the diaspora's traditional modes, the institution of the saints is strong and vital enough to keep pace with modernization.

A simple statistical evaluation of saints' legends in Israel shows that most belong to the category of healing stories. These tales also rely on ancient Jewish traditions, starting with the biblical narratives of the brass serpent in the desert (Num. 29:9), Elijah and the resurrection of the Shunammite woman's son (2 Kings 4), and Elisha curing Naaman's leprosy (2 Kings 5). However, the similarities and differences between the early traditions and those created in modern Israel can be best modelled by a famous hasidic tale in which a reputable doctor from the city of Ostraha hears that the Ba'al Shem Tov dabbles in medicine. Outraged, he gives notice that should he catch him in the act, he will kill him. An ailing rabbi calls the Ba'al Shem Tov to treat him, but his sons, lacking faith in the saint's power, send for the physician from Ostraha. The Ba'al Shem Tov gives the patient medicines, cautions him that his sons have sent for the doctor, and makes ready to depart before the doctor arrives. Upon leaving, he encounters the physician, and asks him where he learned medicine. The Ba'al Shem Tov replies, "The Almighty, blessed be He, taught me!" The physician gives the patient the very same medications as the Ba'al Shem Tov; but the patient complains that when the doctor entered his room he felt as though it was a priest who had come in.[36]

This tale is one of the first to accentuate the confrontation between scientific medicine and traditional Jewish healing in recent generations. The contrast between them is indeed manifested in the tale, but it is not absolute. The Ba'al

Shem Tov and the physician prescribe the same medication for the patient, hence neither is superior outside of the dimension of holiness that accrues to traditional medicine. This last point is brought home in both the remarks of the Ba'al Shem Tov and of the patient (the odor of apostasy, maybe even of death, fills the home when the secular doctor makes his entrance as a priest at the bedside of the dying). Hasidic narrative contains a number of tales dealing with the clash between doctors and hasidic zaddikim, but they are not numerous and do not occupy a central place in the worldview of the eighteenth and nineteenth centuries. Among the legends of saints' activity in Morocco there are also some scattered tales about children falling ill, for whom neither hospitals nor physicians can do anything, the saint alone being able to help.[37]

In contrast to the previous periods, tales of healing make up the lion's share of the hagiographical repertoire in Israeli folk narrative:

An agitated man entered our Rabbi's [the Baba Sali] waiting room and got everyone's attention. He asked to clear the way for him to bring in his ailing relative, to make room to bring in the stretcher upon which lay the suffering and disoriented patient. Shortly thereafter, the patient was brought into our Rabbi's room where he began to sob bitterly: all the doctors have already tried and failed to help him, now, in his time of need, he pleaded before our Rabbi to petition for his salvation. Our Rabbi listened to all his stories, and in a broken voice gave him a blessing for a complete and rapid recovery. From where he sat, he handed him a bottle of water and asked him to drink from the bottle every night before going to sleep. Some weeks later, the same patient arrived, walking on his own two feet, and with shining eyes told the household the following tale of wonder:

"Some days after that same evening that I was in our Rabbi's room lying on a stretcher, I had a dream. In the dream I saw our Rabbi, and in his hand was the picture of a man. Our Rabbi turned to me in the dream, showed me the picture, and said: 'This man is a physician. His name is Dr. Raphael Carasso and he lives on such and such street in Tel Aviv. Go to him and ask him to try and cure your disease.' I got up in the morning," the patient continues, "and remembered the strange dream. At once I telephoned my daughter who lives in Tel Aviv and asked her to find out if there is a doctor by that name on such and such street, the street that our Rabbi told me. My daughter did not need to think at all. On the spot she said she recognized the doctor. 'Where did you know him from?' she asked me in surprise. I described to my daughter his appearance, according to the picture that the Rabbi showed me. My daughter was surprised sevenfold and could not understand how it was that I was describing to her a man that I had never seen. I told her what had happened and that our Rabbi had come to me in a dream and showed me his picture. After apprehending the marvel of it, she hurried to the doctor's home to make me an appointment at his clinic. We made the appointment," continues the patient, "and I went to him for treatment. The doctor examined me and at once discarded every prognosis given me by the previous doctors. According to him, I was not that ill and in a few days would recover completely. He prescribed some pills for me to buy at the pharmacy, and praise God here I am, hale and hearty" . . . the recovered patient finished telling his story to the household and asked to enter our Rabbi's room to tell him his story and to thank him. When it was his turn he entered the room with our Rabbi's servant. Upon seeing him, our Rabbi's holy face shone and, with a smile on his lips, concluded, before having heard a single word: "I speak to him in a dream." (*ha-Baba Sali*, pp. 121–123)

This tale upholds the literary model of most tales in this category: a man enters the waiting room of the saint and attracts attention by his disease or unusual behavior. Next comes the appeal to the servant, who functions as mediator between "inner" and "outer," between the saint and the external world. It is especially true of tales in which the appellants are women, as the Baba Sali was in no way prepared to allow women into his sanctum. The servant transmits the request to the saint, after which the appellant provides the details. Then the Baba Sali offers him food or drink that must be taken in his presence. Alongside the corporeal activity of eating or drinking, the saint adds a blessing or biblical verse, and therein an intimation of a solution. In this tale, as well as in other tales of healing, there is no conflict between the saint and the physician. On the contrary, the saint refers the patient to the doctor, and in so doing confers authority upon him. Yet the tale that appears immediately afterward, the direct continuation of the one above, is most interesting:

Our Rabbi's servant continues, and adds to the preceding story: "Two years after the [event], a man from Tel Aviv telephoned our Rabbi's home to ask for the Rabbi's blessing for a complete recovery. I asked his name and that of his mother and he said, 'Raphael, son of so and so.' And what is your occupation?" the servant of our Rabbi asked the caller, who replied: "A physician, and my name is Dr. Raphael Carasso." R. Eliyahu heard this and recalled the story of the patient. "Tell me," he asked the doctor on the telephone, "do you live on such and such street in Tel Aviv?"—"Yes," replied the astonished doctor. Our Rabbi's servant went on to astound the doctor by describing his appearance precisely. "How do you know me?" asked the physician, who had never visited our Rabbi's house, nor had any of the household been to him for treatment. "With the Almighty's help, when you come at the next opportunity to our Rabbi's house, I will tell you," answered the Rabbi's servant, expecting him to come quickly. R. Eliyahu was curious, and wanted to be present at the encounter between our Rabbi and the physician whom he had never met yet whose picture he held in his hand. Within a few hours the doctor arrived at our Rabbi's home in Netivot with several members of his family. The excited doctor could not wait to come to the home of our Rabbi once he heard that the household knew him, though he did not know them. When he entered our Rabbi's room, our Rabbi's servant said a few words of introduction. Our Rabbi listened to his servant, and when R. Eliyahu said: "This is the doctor whose picture our Rabbi showed to that patient who recovered," our Rabbi's face glowed and he said again and again, "I speak to him in a dream" . . . and at once asked that food be brought to the table to honor the ailing physician, while assuring him a rapid and complete recovery, and also that he would be able to help the sick for many more years to come. (*ha-Baba Sali*, pp. 124–125)

Lest listeners entertain the notion that the Baba Sali sent the patient to the physician because he himself was unable to help, the second tale makes plain that the saint employs medicine when he sees fit to do so, but his supremacy in such matters is beyond question. The simple or uneducated people are not alone in recognizing his medical prowess, physicians themselves readily admit it, and on occasion require his services. In another tale, after the saint successfully cures a paralyzed young woman, a group of people come to the Baba Sali's home in Netivot and tell his servant:

Know this, that the group of people standing here are all physicians who work at Beit Levinstein Hospital in Ra'annah. We treated this young woman for four years and knew there was no chance of recovery. Her legs were paralyzed and, according to tests, within a short time the left side of her body would be paralyzed as well. When we saw what the Rabbi, whose blessing she requested, did for her . . . we could not restrain ourselves. All the doctors in the department have come to see this saint that worked such wonders. We too want to ask his blessing. (Ibid., p. 126)

In one tale, during the Baba Sali's stay in Beersheba Sorokah Hospital, a doctor from the cardiac institute brings him an infant suffering from a serious heart ailment. The baby recovers shortly after receiving the saint's blessing, and the narrator concludes: "this is not the first time that our rabbi has done what the best physicians in the hospital could not" (ibid., p. 226). Still, the tales cannot ignore the frequent clashing of scientific and traditional medicine. A sick girl from Ofakim had long been hospitalized in Beersheba when her father appealed to the saint, who instructed him to take her out of the hospital at once, against doctors' orders. On the way to Ofakim, the girl recovered. Another tale that expresses this kind of discord is transmitted as a memorat (a tale of a personal experience):

On Friday, holy Sabbath eve, [Torah] portion "*Ki Tisah*" in the year 5742 (1982), I was summoned to the neighborhood clinic in Beersheba where my wife was in severe condition on account of hemorrhaging. From there we were rushed to Sorokah Hospital. The doctors, three in number, who examined her determined unequivocally that an abortion was necessary. My wife was then three months pregnant. I hesitated, for one does not carry out an abortion so fast and a rabbi must be consulted. I asked the doctors to delay the abortion another hour and, after refusals and pleading, they consented. I set out in my car for the house of our Master and Teacher R. Israel Abuhatzeira [the Baba Sali] of blessed and saintly memory. On Friday our Rabbi was not in the habit of receiving people, and at that hour in our Rabbi's room they were reading two [portions] Scripture and one [portion] Targum [Aramaic translation of the Torah]. After explanations to his servant, R. Eliyahu Alfasi, may he be set apart for a long life, I entered, and took advantage of a short recess of the rabbis who sat with our holy Rabbi. I asked him if the abortion should be carried out. Our Rabbi blessed the bottle of water and ruled that it should not.

I left our Rabbi's house encouraged and rushed back to the hospital. I gave my wife the water to drink, and when the doctors came to continue preparations for the abortion, I suggested they reexamine her to see if it was still necessary. One of the three doctors said no further examination was required, but gave in to my wife's pleas. After the examination, all three were astounded, and one of the doctors murmured in wonder: "How is it possible? The fetus is back where it should be and the hemorrhaging stopped . . . ?" I was so happy tears streamed out of my eyes, and I read Psalms in thanksgiving to God, may He be praised. Three days later, my wife was released from the hospital in excellent health, praise God. During the Passover holiday I was one of those who went up to our Rabbi's home, and I recall that he asked his visitors to bless him that he merit seeing the face of the Messiah. I did as he asked, and the others answered, "Amen." I reminded our Rabbi of the incident and said that my wife was again not feeling well. He reassured me and said: "You have nothing to worry about," on my responsibility . . . and we had a healthy baby girl with God's help. (Ibid., pp. 132–133, told by Isaac Alush of Netivot)

The genre of legend, saints' tales included, draws its power mainly from the measure of faith that the tale inspires among the listeners. To augment the force of the tale, the storyteller employs diverse rhetorical means. Among them, a defined place and time familiar and close to the listeners, true-to-life details, and characters drawn from local reality. The tale above makes clear and bold use of all of these. The specific date on which the event takes place, the locale, and active characters all operate to build up faith in what is being told. Tales of personal experience contain another dimension, that of firsthand knowledge. This places the story above argument, as the storyteller himself attests that what happens in the tale is not something he heard from others or read in a book, but that he lived through personally. Hence this is the most lifelike narrative model in the repertoire of saints' legends. Its narrative tension lies not only in the confrontation between saint and doctors, it stems also from the urgency of the moment. The husband hasn't time to dither, as his wife's life depends on his decision. Indeed, the storyteller does a fine job of employing extremes to create narrative tension: the saint versus the physicians, the necessity of immediate decision juxtaposed with the distance to the saint's home and the obstacles he must overcome before seeing him (the distance from Sorokah Hospital in Beersheba to the city of Netivot is about half an hour; the saint is busy learning, his servant delays the husband). These multiple tensions are meant to project to the audience the full weight of decision before the protagonist, in order to highlight its critical outcome (life or death). Each member of the audience is likely to face similar decisions, perhaps of less import. The tale is meant to serve as a model of appropriate conduct in the future.

[6] The Struggle over Life and Death: Tradition vs. Modernity

Saints' legends on the theme of healing offer a glimpse of a significant current running below the surface of Israeli reality; they attest to a deep-rooted belief in supernatural forces, particularly where a sacred basis exists to support them—the supernatural power of charismatic, venerated personalities. This poses an interesting question—how can people living in a westernized country, at least as regards the modern scientific and technological achievements that are so much a part of everyday life, and who were educated primarily in the State of Israel, believe in the same traditional supernatural forces as did their forebears, whose structure of beliefs and ideas had more in common with the Middle Ages than with the modern world? It can be answered on various levels. First, belief in supernatural forces in the modern world is hardly unique to Israeli society; it appears in various manifestations throughout the eastern and western cultures. The main difference is that, in Israel, these beliefs are restored to their prominence of old; among the Atlas Jews of the eighteenth and nineteenth centuries, they were a mainstay of religious faith. This is perhaps the reason that in significant sectors of Israeli society (especially among those of North African descent) belief in the supernatural power of saints is accepted as part of normative faith, and is supported by the religious establishment.

Another possible level from which to approach an understanding of the phenomenon has to do with the very same modern education system mentioned above. It was intended primarily to strip immigrants from North African lands (and others as well) of their centuries-old diasporic culture, and to incorporate them, as fast as possible, into the new Israeli culture. The resulting changes, however, were mostly superficial. More profound cultural and psychological changes could not occur, whether because of a mistaken pedagogical concept, or because the time span was too short to allow the anticipated changes to penetrate the deepest socio-psychological layers. It is thus no wonder that approximately one generation after the great waves of immigration, a pronounced reaction has emerged against the alien values that the absorbing society sought to implant. The socio-religious baggage of the two societies is markedly different. This reaction, for the most part, takes the form of a resolute return to values and beliefs of the past (expressions such as "restore the crown to its pristine splendor" are typical of this religio-ethnic process). A prominent feature of this value system is belief in the supernatural power of charismatic leaders to influence and alter reality (veneration of the saints).

To these factors should be added a sense of disappointment in the scientific-technological world's ability to solve the problems of the individual. Paradoxically, this becomes evident via the media, itself a modern technological achievement. The media reports the strides and innovations of the science of medicine, while simultaneously lamenting the high incidence of death due to heart attacks, cancer, AIDS, various infectious diseases, and so on. These ills seem to cancel out the achievements of modern medicine, rendering it impotent in the face of innumerable health problems. Owing to the great media blitz, there seem to be many more deaths and serious diseases than ever before but, of course, in the past, people simply died without fanfare. If modern medicine has no answers to so many diseases, the folk naturally turn to those who "helped" them in the past—the sacred forces. From time immemorial, these dark and gloomy gaps where science can shed no light have given entrée to the supernatural. When the physician throws up his hands in defeat, admitting that he can offer no cure or solution, it is hardly unexpected that the patient or his family turn to the saint to ask for help. In our telecommunicative world especially, where the mass media mercilessly beats the drum of incurable diseases and science's confusion, it is only natural that the adoration of the saints enjoy a resurgence, and with it tales of healing as its primary vehicle.

Upon examination, the struggle between faith and science becomes evident as the central conflict in all saints' legends that deal with healing. In the hasidic tale told above concerning the physician and the Ba'al Shem Tov, both healers prescribe the same medicine. The naive perception that faith and modern science are not necessarily at odds is still in evidence at this juncture. More contemporary tales of healing belie this perception, highlighting the efforts of science in recent decades to supplant faith in Israel. This encroachment has taken place in all strata of life, but perhaps wreaked the most havoc in the domain of life and death that is the keystone of every religious faith. The tales of healing seek to restore control over this existential province to the world of folk belief. Life and death are in the hands of the saint, representative of the Divine on earth, as in days gone by. Medicine and science have little effect; where the physician falls short, the saint fathoms the mysteries of existence. In this instance, the growth and renewal of saints' legends had a definite purpose: to restore control to the world of faith. No mere reflection of the reality of modern Israel, these tales were designed to influence and alter it.

The militancy of these tales comes across not only in their structure, that is to say in the binary opposition of physician versus saint, but also in their direct responses. One representative tale of this sort describes an infant who suffered from severe vomiting. Doctors and medicines did not help; the parents were beside themselves:

> Then one day [the baby's mother] met a student of our Rabbi [Mordechai Sharabi] and began to mourn her misfortune in that she had to bring her son to the clinic every day for injections and treatments. The student asked her: "Have you appealed to one of the zaddikim of the generation to bless the child?" The mother answered in the negative. He said to her: "In that case, come and we will go to the zaddik, the man of God, Rabbi Mordechai Sharabi, and he will bless the child." At once the two directed their steps toward Shiloh Street [in Jerusalem], where our Rabbi lives. While walking, the student told the mother facts ['uvdot] that took place with different people who came to our Rabbi and were saved on his account. . . . (ha-Rav Sharabi, p. 222)

This describes explicitly a performance event of this typical narrative. The saint's students and followers seek to disseminate faith in the saint. In their efforts to reclaim souls, they grasp at opportunities provided by extreme personal distress and despair at the limitations of modern medicine. Tales of similar cases (termed "facts" here, to avoid the fictional connotations of the word "stories"), showcasing the saint's success where medicine failed, constitute "proof" of the saint's superiority over physicians in matters of health. The tales are thus one important weapon in the massive campaign waged by folk belief against modern science. In another tale, while a pregnant woman suffers heavy bleeding,

> the husband walked around grieving, his head bowed in concern for his wife and the fetus. When his friend learned of the matter he said to him: "Why haven't you gone to our Rabbi?" The other answered him, innocently: "For this purpose too one goes to the Rabbi?"—Then his friend explained to him that in *all matters* one should ask the advice of the great and wise ones of the Jewish people. . . . (ha-Rav Sharabi, p. 297)

The friend's reply to the husband implies that not only in matters of religion and faith should one turn to the saints, but with any difficulty or obstacle one might encounter in the course of everyday life. Indeed, the examples above illustrate how saints' legends strive to apply the saint's authority to all spheres of life, including those identified with technology and modernity, like the army and security, cars, and the stock exchange. This effort to penetrate all reaches of life and prove the validity and power of the faith there too, should thus be seen as part of a larger framework, i.e., the overall campaign to encourage a mass return to the faith, in which the struggle against modern science (as in the tales of healing) is only one component.

[7] Life as Miracle: The Religious Meaning of Society

Two large cycles of legends about R. David u-Moshe were told by Shimon Waqnin of Ashkelon and Abraham Ben-Haim of Safed. These men also established the two new centers for veneration of this saint in Israel. Many of the legends revolve around the storytellers themselves and their proximity to the saint: Shimon Waqnin tells that once while working on a road-construction crew, he fell from the water tank. As a result, his tongue was stuck outside his mouth so that he could not pull it back. No help was to be had at the hospital. Just before the start of a painful medical treatment, the saint appeared to him, and miraculously, his tongue curled back up into his mouth:

> The physician, Dr. Cohen, came and said to me, "What's your name, buddy?"
> I told him: "Waqnin, Shimon." He said to me: "Thank you . . . Are you a
> 'sage'? Are you a rabbi? Or what?" I said to him: "Not a rabbi, nor anything."
> He said: "Not a rabbi nor anything?" I said to him: "Not a rabbi nor any-
> thing." He said to me: "On your life, do you have a rabbi in the family?" I
> said to him: "I have my own synagogue, and I have a great rabbi in the fam-
> ily." He said to me: "No one is like his name. Today you were rescued." . . .
> (Ben-Ami, R. David u-Moshe, pp. 313–314)

Similarly, the tale of Abraham Ben-Haim of Safed:

> [Then there was] the one who was missing in the army. They didn't know.
> They thought him dead in the [Suez] Canal. They came on the night of the
> festival [of R. David u-Moshe] and prayed and beseeched. [His mother]
> came and brought his picture. She said to me: "You are the emissary of the
> Zaddik, ask him to find the boy. And if he is found, we will come and make
> a fine feast." I took the picture and truly began to tremble. I beseeched and I
> said: "You, R. David u-Moshe! You said you want this place [as a site of ado-
> ration and pilgrimage] and you came. I ask you that this boy return in peace
> to his parents, he and all the children of Israel and the army. That is what I
> ask." That same night [the Zaddik] came to me and said to me: "The boy re-

turns and all will be well" . . . that is how it was. The child returned. (Ben-Ami, *le-Heker Folklor ha-Milhamah*, pp. 97–98)

The two texts underscore the link and personal identification between the storyteller and the center of veneration. In the first, Waqnin identifies himself as "proprietor" of the synagogue. This is "my" synagogue. Therefore the miracle that took place thanks to the saint boosts the importance of the center of adoration and the advantages of belonging to it even in the eyes of representatives of the modern world, namely, the doctors. In the second text, this matter stands out yet more starkly when the mother of the captive soldier, in turning to Abraham Ben-Haim, calls him as the saint's emissary. The trembling that overtakes him is not only a consummate ecstatic feature, it is also an expression of the awe of the responsibility that this designation places on his shoulders. In his appeal to the saint he emphasizes that it was the saint himself who asked that he turn his home into a center of his veneration. Therein is a significant measure of veiled threat: the saint's performance of the anticipated miracle is a precondition of turning the place into a sanctuary.

The two founders of the centers of veneration do not regard the miracles performed by the saint as private events, but as a lever with which to spread belief in the saint's power among society, and to attract many more faithful to the centers of homage. Each of these hundreds of tales, spread by people near the centers of adoration—their founders, their family, or other functionaries connected to the festival in honor of the saints—serves as a means to attract more believers. In each such tale at least one more person (the protagonist for whom the miracle is performed) joins the ranks of those who believe in the saint. Among them are the young man who, along with his girlfriend, is saved from an accident while riding his motorbike (*R. David u-Moshe*, # 40); the soldier whose truck topples over the edge of the road in the Golan Heights (ibid., # 44); Waqnin's grandson, rescued from a collision with a car of Arabs (ibid., #45); the woman who is spared a Caesarian section and delivers naturally thanks to the saint (ibid., # 58).

Recruitment of the faithful is not motivated solely by spiritual altruism. Police, army officers, municipal employees, and the rest of the government authorities who become absolute believers in the saint give the center of adoration political clout as well. Indeed, in a characteristic tale of the establishment of the synagogue honoring R. David u-Moshe in Ashkelon, told by its founder, Shimon Waqnin, the authorities issue an injunction against its construction. The synagogue is built without a permit, in violation of the building code. A member of the committee sent to inspect the structure, and who opposed its completion, was hospitalized for three years in a psychiatric hospital in Be'er-Ya'akov, until he acknowledged the saint's power and was cured (*R.*

David u-Moshe, p. 308). When permission was requested to add on to the same synagogue, the Ashkelon municipality dispatched a crew to tear it down because it had been built without a permit. Synagogue functionaries turned directly to the mayor, who dropped everything, accompanied them to the synagogue, and gave them the necessary authorization (ibid., p. 316, #36).

In other words, the legend of the saints has an outright political function apart from its spiritual and social functions: that is to augment the power of the saint's court in the corridors of government, in order to achieve social and economic goals. Indeed, the financial aspect is not absent from the tales either. During the festival, candles to honor the saint, for example, are sold at the highest prices. Their purchase is considered praiseworthy indeed and confers a reward—a cure, salvation, economic prosperity—(the exaggerated prices of the candles are detailed there, pp. 307–308). There is also considerable testimony regarding economic interests linked to the center for the adoration of the Baba Sali, and their aggressive advancement via the apparatus built by his son Baruch Abuhatzeira—the Baba Baruch. The commercial venues for sacred and profane objects in the vicinity of the burial site, the various permits, the generous donations, and so on, turn the saints' tales into a very powerful means of advancing economic interests.

An examination of saints' legends in all their scope and diversity indicates their penetration into all areas of life—personal, family, and social. Hardly any important sphere of daily life in the State of Israel remains untouched. The legends address the issue of security and the military, trade and agriculture, construction, the stock market, marriage and divorce, disease and medicine, road accidents, immigration, and so on. This broad range of subjects and issues indicates that faith in the saints aspires to be the answer to all the ills that flesh is heir to. When the grandson of Waqnin of Ashkelon tells of having almost crashed into an Arab car, he adds: "I called to the saint. As a matter of course, I and everyone else, when something happens, we call to the zaddik at once, and then the zaddik takes action" (ibid., p. 322). Likewise, the woman whose daughter miscarried in spite of the physicians' efforts turned to the saint, and explained that "the zaddikim are our doctors."

In sum, legends of the saints, beyond their social or political function, came to fulfill a much more extensive and fundamental role: to give meaning to day-to-day events in Israel. In this reality, events, causes, and effects have no meaning without the guiding hand of the saints. The tales describing the driver managing to stop at the last minute before crashing into the Arab car, the young woman successfully carrying a child to term after a series of miscarriages, the soldier giving up hope of a lift when a mysterious vehicle appeared suddenly out of nowhere and took him home, along with thousands of other miniature narratives, confront the individual with an enigmatic, uncomprehended reality. The demand of normative culture in modern Israel for rational explanations conflicts with the myriad events for which no such explanation exists. All that remains is to see them as the hand of coincidence. This conflict becomes even more severe in the face of the gap between living conditions in the lands of origin and the new reality in Israel. When Shimon Waqnin of Ashkelon wanted to build a synagogue in honor of the zaddik R. David u-Moshe, he went ahead without municipal permits and blueprints prepared by structural engineers. When the injunction came to halt the construction, Waqnin did not understand what they wanted from him: "Where we lived in Morocco we also built without permits or engineers . . . ," he claims in defense against the city's representatives. The appeal to the saint in this instance is not done with intent to break the law, but in order to go back and regain that same certainty and "order" of real-life events that was his lot in the diaspora. There, any purpose for the sake of heaven, such as building a synagogue to honor the zaddik, could be carried out without the intervention and approval of the authorities. The success or failure of any action was perceived as a function of the zaddik's will and action and, as such, has an explanation and meaning.

Seeing all of life's events as a chain of miracles performed by the saint is a means to strengthen the individual's confidence and hopes, but is above all an attempt to incorporate all of life's events as part of a set of beliefs and ideas of society, and thereby to imbue them with meaning. Far from mitigating the need for the construction of such a meaning-giving-apparatus, new life in the State of Israel increased it. A comparison of the saints' legends told in Morocco to those created in Israel shows that those legends originating in the diaspora deal primarily with miracles that took place in the vicinity of the graves of the saints and pilgrimage sites, or the web of relations between Jewish and Arab society—manifested primarily in tales of the type, "the desecrator of the holy is punished" (Arabs injure the honor of the saint and are severely punished). The saints' legends created in Israel are certainly more diverse. They encompass all areas of life and society in the State, and their orientation is obvious: to prove that there is no area, not even in the modern industrialized state, where faith in saints cannot contribute. At the basis of this conscious and directed orientation there lies, to all appearances, the aspiration that the new home of the community (the Maghreb community in this case) will maintain the set of explanations and meanings that was so essential a part of its life in the past.

[C] "Return to the Faith" Stories: Religious Rhetoric in a Secular World

[1] Medium and Ideology

Legends of the saints studied in the previous passage, without exception, share a common goal beyond their functions in Israeli society as outlined in the previous section. This is to draw as many Jews as possible into the welcoming arms of the faith. One typical example suffices to illustrate this role:

A dear yeshiva student tells a story about our Rabbi that took place during [the student's] period of military service, when he had just embarked upon the path of becoming newly religious. It happened in the year 5738 [1978]: As a newly devout individual, the soldier was conscientious in matters of prayer and about upholding the other precepts. In this he crossed his commander, who did not view him with understanding: "Get up earlier in the morning to pray so you won't be late!" He was so harsh as to say that he hoped [the soldier] would be sent to jail, and that it would be easy for him to arrange. The soldier, knowing his commander "had it in for him," tried not to give him a pretext to act. "On the occasion of a new month, on account of the additional prayers, I was about half an hour late," the yeshiva student recounts today. The commander was waiting for him at the entrance: "Now you'll pay for being late" . . . and the charge went through, in the usual manner. "At the trial, I argued before the presiding officer: 'I am newly religious, and wanted to participate in public prayer on the occasion of the new month. That's why I was late' . . . I was sentenced to seven days' incarceration instead of fourteen, out of consideration . . . at the end of the trial the commander turned to me, delighted at my misfortune, and crowed about having fulfilled 'his promise' to put me in jail!

"I had not reconciled myself to the severity of the punishment in relation to the deed and the circumstances, and took advantage of an opportunity at the prison entrance to escape. I still hadn't fully digested what I had done. I ran between the hills toward the bus to Beersheba. As one might expect, the military police began to search for me, but to no avail. I took advantage of the time to visit the yeshiva and learn, to strengthen my Torah knowledge and God-fearingness. The police looked for me at our home but to no avail. From time to time I even went home, but the hand of the police did not reach me. I understood that I could not hide out for long. Friends advised me to turn to our Master and Teacher the Baba Sali . . . Our Rabbi told me to go home without fear, that everything would work out fine! I received a bottle of water that the Rabbi blessed, as was customary. The Rabbi added that one need not fear for having fulfilled the precept of praying in public, they would not have power over me. When I reached the station, the first car I stopped was going in the direction of the base where I served. I saw this as Heaven's assistance. I went right away to my commander's office. My sudden appearance startled him: 'Where did you disappear to? This time you'll be put away for a year and a half!' and he began to fill out another charge against me. Suddenly he noticed the bottle of water in my hand and asked, 'What's that?' I answered simply: 'It's water from Rabbi Abuhatzeira [the saint, Baba Sali]. And aren't you ashamed to put me in jail for arriving a few minutes late because I prayed in a public quorum? Rabbi Abuhatzeira asked that you pardon me, as the lateness was only because of the public prayers on the occasion of the new month.' My commander, obligingly, threw up his hands: 'If Rabbi Abuhatzeira is involved, I can't do a thing and, before I straighten all this out, would you give me some of the water?'

"His attitude was completely reversed—and the matter was straightened out at all the necessary echelons. My commander summed up: 'The Rabbi's blessing of you was completely fulfilled.'" (ha-Baba Sali, pp. 252–253)

The newly devout encounter myriad difficulties in daily life, including the disapproval and scorn of the secular society to which they no longer belong. Scrupulous religious observance brings the hero of this tale to the brink of criminal behavior (he is A.W.O.L.) and imprisonment. But the embrace of ultra-orthodoxy saves him from this fall from social grace, and ultimately raises the military commander's regard for him—accepting the water implies acknowledgement of sacred authority. As in tales of proselytism and martyrdom in the literature of earlier generations, the narrative poles are manned by the penitent as protagonist and the military commander as antagonist. In their confrontation it is the saint (the Baba Sali) who decides and, moreover, brings the negative persona around to submit to the saint's authority, becoming one of the faithful and thereby joining that same "holy community" of believers.

The police officers who came to reprimand the functionaries of the R. David u-Moshe synagogue for violating the blackout during the Six-Day War, and saw the light emanating from the Holy Ark heralding the war's end, also become believers in the saint (previous section). Abraham Ben-Haim's employer in Safed, of Tunisian extraction, ridiculed his belief in the saint. The road accident he suffered after expressing this scorn made him a believer too.

> I hear a lot of stories. I heard that on the Syrian border, a soldier fell asleep and his company advanced without him. Someone came to wake him, it was an old man. The soldier said to him: "What are you doing? You could get hit!" The old man replied: "Don't be afraid. Just take it upon yourself to become religious. See how I advance, and see that I help you. The staff, the support in my hand, it is a shield." The soldier did not believe. The old man advanced, and nothing happened [to them].[38]

In these texts, the connection between saints' legends and the phenomenon of returning to the faith is clear and unequivocal. Told in the company of the newly devout, these tales are meant to reinforce their faith and resolve in a hostile secular world. Told in secular society, their purpose is to encourage listeners to join the ranks of the newly religious, so that they too may benefit from the wonders of the saint.

The phenomenon of embracing ultra-orthodoxy is among the most important socio-cultural developments to take place in the State of Israel in the 1970s and 80s. Its influence is felt in all walks of life—education, the arts, the military and, especially, in the political system. Consensus holds that the great surprise of the 1988 elections and subsequent elections was the vast gains of the religious parties, especially those that focused their efforts on recruiting as many as possible to return to the faith. The pervasive appeal of adopting a religious lifestyle and the interest therein evinced (to varying degrees) by tens (if not hundreds) of thousands of Jews was not the product of a spontaneous process. It is likely that those who committed themselves to such a change were predisposed to do so, and that their erstwhile severance from the founts of the religious tradition was only temporary. It seems that modernism and the secularization of the State of Israel had an impact on only the external characteristics of their behavior and not on the core of their consciousness and beliefs. The phenomenon should perhaps be seen as part of a universal trend towards religious fundamentalism, as evidenced by the millions of new adherents in the Middle East and all over the world.

In addition to these factors, the breadth of the phenomenon in Israel can be attributed to the intensive activity of proselytizers who have employed an array of means to disseminate their ideas and attract as many as possible to their particular conception of religious tradition. As a historical phenomenon, the return to the faith deserves sociological, psychological, and theological discussion that is advanced in the great project of the study of fundamentalism. What follows herein is a description of folktales as a vehicle for promoting this revival, a perspective which was neglected in that project.[39]

"Promoters of the faith" (Hebrew: *makhazirim bi-teshuvah*) operate on the level of personal contact between believers and representatives of society, specifically those in need of medical treatment or assistance with other difficulties. An appeal to the Rabbi, saint, or hasidic zaddik is in itself an act of admission of the shortcomings of a secular life and can thus constitute a first step towards a complete return to the faith. Nonetheless, the "return to the faith" movement of this day and age gained popularity not necessarily by virtue of these personal contacts, which were the legacy of all preceding generations, but through the intensive use of the mass media. The latter can be divided into two types—direct and electronic. The direct media are essentially mass "return to the faith" evenings that take place in sports stadiums or enormous halls, featuring famous proselytizers. The shows are composed of moralizing sermons that go on for many hours, interspersed with various entertainments, such as traditional musicians, singers, and jugglers. Thousands of men and women take part in these evenings, sitting separately. Proselytizers consider the evenings an effective means of locating people with a firm predisposition to adopt a religious lifestyle. Therefore they tirelessly refer the crowd to seminars that promote religious revival and operate under their personal guidance. Notices of same are distributed and registration tables abound. The seminars are another means of direct action. Individuals and families gather for a period ranging from a day to a week in hotels in various places in the country, pay a small fee for accommodations, and participate in classes and lectures on Judaism—with special emphasis laid on the value of returning to the faith. The cardinal messages are that secular life is based on false premises and is perilous besides, and that a religious lifestyle can cure the ills of modern life.

The speeches delivered at these mass evenings, and lectures given in the format of seminars, are recorded on audio cassettes, and lately video as well. Merchants in music shops in Jerusalem and Tel Aviv told this writer, upon inquiry, that they sell hundreds of such cassettes every month. The penchant for putting such modern means of communication to sacred use has given promoters a new and powerful tool—one that reaches directly into the private domain of home and family. It also demonstrates the strategy taken up by the proselytizers: to use the most prominent symbols of the secular world—radio and television—to bring about their destruction. They seek to prove that the innovations of science and technology are not alien to the devout world, but can be employed for Godlier purposes than those embraced by the secular world.

The return to the faith movement is one of few today in which conscious, determined, and intensive use is made of folk narrative. Dozens of proselytizers wield tales to amaze and intimidate huge audiences, and to persuade them of the imperative of an uncompromising return to the faith. In this instance, the tale is not perfomed for entertainment. Revivalists devise and use the tales aggressively for direct and defined purposes. Thousands have been swept up in the return to the faith movement, a gain due in part to their virtuosity in applying this means of communication. This is a rare opportunity to examine both folk literature in action and the means used by the promoters—storytellers from the folkloristic perspective—to augment its influence and power.

[2] The Text

Inquiries for cassettes at music shops, especially the main outlet of Jerusalem's Me'ah She'arim neighborhood ("Ner le-Meah," on Hagai Street—the shop distributes a large catalog of these cassettes; its reference numbers are the basis for the cassette citations below), and conversations with the newly devout indicate that one of the most popular promoters is Rabbi Nissim Yagen of Jerusalem. More than a hundred of his cassettes (audio and video) are on sale in the shops, and thousands of copies have been sold and distributed among the public. A survey of the appearances of famous promoters shows that

Nissim Yagen makes the most use, and indeed the most interesting use, of folktales. Thus his narrative performance art deserves examination as a representative and salient sample.

The following tale was told by Nissim Yagen in the format of a long homily (lasting over an hour) delivered in Tel Aviv's Yad Eliyahu Stadium (1987) on a "return to the faith" evening. It will serve as a point of departure for a discussion of the use and function of tales in this contemporary movement:

> My dear people. Some time ago, the only son of a family in Natanya (sic!) took his parents' car and went out on the town with his friend. It was Sabbath eve, not long ago. Out he went on the coastal road. Soon after he left, a truck ran into them. Both were killed on the spot. When they told the grandmother, she, too, died on the spot. There were three funerals that bitter Friday on the same street in Natanya. A student of ours from the [religious] seminar telephoned me, he said, "Rabbi Yagen, such a terrible tragedy, you must come to comfort them. Secularists . . . to console them." I came. I want to tell you that if they had called me to comfort th'soul before the boy had died, the boy would not have died. His evil inclination would have died! In short, I came to comfort them. Dozens were there, the blow was heavy. In their fine house in Natanya, I was there. Many dozens of people. One man from Kibbutz Ashdot Ya'akov gets up, a secularist, and says: "Honored rabbi, I don't believe it, I just don't believe it," and began to argue . . . in a house of mourning. In short, listen, people, to what happened. A secular woman from Natanya gets up, I have th'phone number, th'address, and answered the man who attacked me. She says: "Listen. I don't know Rabbi Yagen, and I'll tell you. I believe there is life after death, that there is Paradise and Hell. I'll tell you what I saw with my own eyes, a shocking thing." I myself, all of us— that's how [surprised] we were. A secular woman, in pants, God save us [from women wearing pants]. She's saying that she believes in Paradise and Hell. She saw! We were all quiet in his house. "What did you see?!" She says: "My dear people, I live on a street in Natanya near the central bus station, a street of fine homes." I was there on a number of occasions. She is secular, it shouldn't happen to you. Her grandmother was a righteous woman. Many tell me: "Do you know what a religious home I come from? I'm from a religious home!" Not like us, it shouldn't happen to you, [the guy] looks like an Arab. From a religious home. He's a secularist—the home is religious. I said: "So the home they'll let into Paradise and you'll go to Hell. Why, the home is religious, you're not religious." One says to me, "You know who my Grandfather is?! Who my grandmother is?!" I said, "In heaven they won't ask who your grandfather is, they'll ask who you are!"
>
> This woman tells her story, her grandmother was a righteous woman. She died a long time ago, and the woman doesn't think of her much. Her grand-

mother came to her in a dream in a strange form, night after night. She tells her: "Saraleh, my child, get up and go quickly to the neighbor across the way. They have an eight-and-a-half-year-old daughter with a tumor in her brain. Cancer of the brain. And the girl, God preserve us, is going to die any day. Go right away to the neighbors and tell them that the reason the child has been afflicted in the core of her brain is that the parents have afflicted the core of the Jewish soul—the Sabbath. Because they desecrate the Sabbath, use electricity on the Sabbath. And tell them," in a dream this is, we all heard, "and tell the parents that if they keep the Sabbath for sixty days—the child will recover without surgery and without treatments." This woman got up in the morning and didn't know what to do. She says, "Master of the Universe, I myself am not religious, how can I go and tell her to keep the Sabbath? She'll tell me, "You go and keep it yourself first!" And besides, she'll tell me I'm nuts, I should go to a psychiatrist. She'll make me look like a fool in front of the whole neighborhood." So she didn't go. Her grandmother, may she rest in peace, came again to her granddaughter Sarah. She said, "Sarah, don't be cruel, I'm sent by God to give you this message. Go tell the parents that their daughter is dying, within two weeks she will die." A girl of eight and a half . . . Because the parents use electricity on the Sabbath. She got up, crying, and says: "Chuck [slang: husband], should I go?"—I can't believe it myself! She didn't go.

"On the third day," this woman said, in front of everyone, her grandmother told her: "You're a cruel one! A treacherous one! How can you have this on your conscience? Go tell the parents that because of their desecration of the Sabbath the girl is dying of brain cancer." She couldn't stand it anymore. She didn't know that the neighbor's daughter even had cancer. At six in the morning she got up, crying. She says [to her husband], "C'mon let's go." In pajamas, a robe, that's how they went to the neighbors. They went to the neighbors, woke them up, "Pardon us, do you have a sick daughter?" The mother burst out crying. She says: "She's not just sick anymore, she's dying. The doctors said that she'll die soon. We've already bought her a plot, the burial society, everything's in order. The cancer in her brain put pressure on the eyes. She can no longer see, she doesn't want to eat anymore, she's finished." To see a little girl finished, because of her parents' desecration of the Sabbath . . . Listen well! In short, yes, there she was, finished. "Why do you ask?"—"My grandmother. I never thought of her. She died a long time ago. She's been coming to me every night in a dream and it's weighing on my conscience, on my heart. She comes to me every night in a dream, and says to me: 'Sarah, go to the neighbor, the daughter is dying, tell her it's because of the parents' desecration of the Sabbath. And I promise,'" the grandmother promises, "'that if you keep the Sabbath for sixty days, the child will recover, without treatments, without surgery, without anything.'" The mother burst into tears, the father burst into tears. He said: "Listen, thank you very much for coming. We've tried all the doctors, we've tried all the medications, we'll try the Sabbath too! What could happen? We take it upon ourselves to keep the Sabbath." So, she was embarrassed and left.

"From the time they took it upon themselves to keep the Sabbath," the woman went on, she told us. I heard it. She said . . . "the parents took it upon themselves, the child began to get better slowly. All of a sudden her eyes opened, all of a sudden she was asking to eat, walking, little by little, without treatments, without radiation, without injections." They were ready to bury her, God preserve us. This little girl, ay-ay, this little girl (*chanting as in prayer*) . . . on the fifty-ninth day . . . they took x-rays at Tel-ha-Shomer [Hospital] . . . the professor went wild, he got a cancer in his fancy education. He says: "I don't believe it, what have you done? Where have you been?" They said: "Nothing . . . we've just been keeping the Sabbath." This child, on the fifty-ninth day they x-rayed her, saw that there was nothing, the brain was clean. On the sixtieth day, as the grandmother had said in Sarah's dream, the girl went to school as usual. She went to the neighbor, knocked on the door, said: "Thank you so much for the dream. Today, the sixtieth day, my daughter went to school." I can introduce you to the girl. My dear people! If you don't bury the evil inclination, the evil inclination buries the children. People, we must be careful. I heard it from the woman who had the dream. I heard it [directly] from her.

[3] Interpretation

My dear people. The tale was told to a vast audience (Yad Eliyahu Stadium holds some ten thousand spectators), in the format of a ranging sermon, recorded in full on two cassettes (nos. 86 and 87, "Ner le-Meah" series, under the label, *ha-Parpar ha-Kakhol* ["The Blue Butterfly"]). The general framework is homiletical, on the theme of the Pharaoh and the plagues on Egypt. Nissim Yagen dwells on each plague in turn. He demonstrates that Pharoah's blindness brought them on, that he was to blame because he shut his eyes to the plain truth that he was not a god, not on the same footing with the Almighty, Lord of Israel. The penultimate plague was that of darkness, itself a symbol of sinfulness, of a metaphorical darkness that surrounds those who refuse to see the light of truth. At this point Yagen pulls out newspaper clippings and begins reading aloud a series of items meant to prove the benighted state of the country: a child in Jerusalem from a wealthy home who murdered his parents in cold blood; horrific traffic accidents; the Left's control of the Broadcasting Authority; soldiers who refused to swear loyalty on the Bible near the Western Wall and threw the book to the ground, and so on. These incidents are Yagen's cases in point, demonstrating the consequences of what he considers a worthless secular education. The tale excerpted above comes on the heels of these items.

His intention is clear: to present the tale as part of the sequence of authentic news items, as one more actual event, that should be seen as part of the same ideational sequence—that moral decay is consuming the secular world. The media items and the tale differ on every possible level: in style, scope, source, and significance, yet the storyteller seeks to transmit them to the audience as a single semiotic sequence, whose components are merely different examples of a single reality. Similarly, in another performance (cassette 41, "*ha-dor le-an? u-Neshamot,*" [the generation, where-to? And souls] lecture given to a smaller audience at a return to the faith seminar), in Tiberias, he describes the ills of the State, "The situation in the country is grave . . . I hold newspaper clippings": terrorists kill women and children, the State establishes committees of inquiry against the soldiers who killed the terrorists; the frightful inflation; an accident at ha-Bonim Intersection in which twenty-two Petah Tikva schoolchildren on a field trip were killed when their bus was hit by a train; the IDF's Chief Education Officer whose daughter marries an Arab; a youth from the Zionist Youth Farm who roasted his girlfriend over a fire; secondary school students from north Tel Aviv who strangled an old woman to death for her money; the Minister of Education and Culture who refused to don a skullcap at the Independence Day Bible Competition. Yagen cries out that all this is the end result of education without values, without Torah, and without God-fearingness. Without pause, he continues: "One of the most troubling stories, ladies and gentlemen, that ever I heard, is the story I heard from a soldier one Friday in my office . . . I was shocked. . . . " And here he tells a tale of a seance conducted by five soldiers from Schinler army base in Jerusalem, who summoned the spirit of David Ben-Gurion. The presentation of all these tales together, in one sequence, in the same narrative tone and in the same context—that of the decline of values in the State—is designed to present the events as parts of a whole. They should not be seen as isolated events; each is an integral part of a complex system that ordinary people cannot see in its entirety. The role of the preacher-rabbi is to put the pieces together in their proper context, and show how they are interrelated as effects of a single cause. At the same time, an artistic-rhetorical perspective shows how the storyteller has built a sequence of secondary texts—the news items—that lead gradually to a peak, namely, the narrative text that is the main component of the sequence, whose source is the storyteller himself and not news items that are open to all.[40]

Friday evening . . . a truck hits them; both die on the spot. At this point in his talk, Yagen has not yet presented explicitly the connection he sees between driving on the Sabbath and the accident. That will become clear later on. The death of young people in a road accident is one of the most frequent punishments in Yagen's tales. Among the victims are Simah Akriv (cassette 41), whose children were seriously injured in the same car crash in the United States that claimed her husband's life; the train accident at ha-Bonim Junction; the son whose father took him to Holland for a tour of the red light district, who died the next day in a car accident (cassette 14); a child of two who also died in a car accident, because his mother did not immerse herself in the ritual bath; a relative of Yagen who was traditional, but continued to drive on the Sabbath, and was killed before the very eyes of his wife and children: "a car ran over his head and his brain spilled out. His wife went mad . . . " (ibid); a newly devout man who was miraculously saved from a terrible car crash, and understood that the miracle happened for him because of his return to the faith (cassette 17); an Israeli attorney who settled in the United States, married a non-Jew and ignored his father when he came from Israel to visit him, was brain-damaged in a terrible car accident, just before his dejected father was to return to Israel (cassette 86). Alongside death in car accidents, Yagen tells of death by heart attacks (the Jew who in spite of his neighbors' warnings continued his Sabbath barbecues), cancer, miscarriages, soldiers dying in the hands of terrorists. All these are a sample of the disasters that characterize modern life, the anxieties that trouble Israeli society in our time. These disasters are Yagen's confirmation that the situation must be rectified at once; in between their descriptions he asks, "Why wait until disaster strikes?!" It is clear to him, as to every good preacher and sermonizer since the world began, that in order to influence, he must use the given psychological situation to undermine existing norms and certainties—and replace them with new ones. Society's anxieties concerning death, disease, and other misfortunes were always an effective means of achieving this goal.[41]

   . . . had they called me to comfort th'soul before the child died, the child would not have died. In one evening with the newly faithful, where the participants recounted the why and wherefore of so radical a change in their lives, one woman said that after three years of suffering and treatments, her eight-year-old son died of cancer. She went on to state her conviction that, had Rabbi Yagen come to her then, her son would still be among the living. Yagen himself adds, after she is through, that it is indeed a pity the mother did not turn to him after her first dream about the child's illness for, had she done so, he would have been saved (cassette 18). Later, Yagen tells a story about a woman from Rosh ha-Nikra. It seems that a bird used to fly into her house and chirp incessantly. She ignored the omen, not taking the matter seriously. Subsequently, her husband died of a heart attack. Had she gone then to Rabbi Yagen, as she did later, her husband would have been saved. Other proselytizers do not use personal intimations of this sort to establish their position as master of powers beyond the ordinary. Via such comments Yagen creates for himself a certain

aura as one who can prevent disasters and understand messages of supernatural origin. Indeed, while little is known of saints' legends told by the saint himself, Yagen's remarks suggest that future legends (and perhaps present ones as well) told about him will have something to rely on.[42]

It goes without saying that such digressive remarks scattered in the tale are also intended to encourage potential petitioners for aid, insofar as they proclaim his ability to ease their suffering. This style of comment—had they only turned to the rabbi-storyteller, things would have unfolded differently—also creates an important narrative-psychological effect: they suggest an alternative line of development in the tale: in the story, the plot unfolded tragically, the son died. But it might have ended on a different note had the protagonist taken the one correct step—that leading to the rabbi. The storyteller's comments on what might have taken place had they but turned to him in time gives rise to a narrative undercurrent: during the recitation of the tale's tragic details, a parallel, but inverse, plot unfolds in the minds of the listeners. According to this plot, the protagonist appeals to the rabbi and is saved; the tragedy is averted. Each listener can, in his own imagination, become the hero of such a tale. The practical conclusion is obvious: he must turn to the rabbi, to the path back to the faith now, before his own life story takes a tragic turn.

A man from kibbutz . . . a secular man, says 'honored Rabbi, I don't believe it, I just don't believe it,' and began to argue. What moves this kibbutznik to confront Yagen? To what was he referring when he professed his disbelief? And, later, when the "secular woman" rises to defend the Rabbi before the gathering, what precisely is she trying to defend? Apparently, Yagen came not only to offer solace, but also to preach. It seems he articulated at this gathering in some fashion or other his conviction that " . . . had they called me to comfort th'soul before the child died, the child would not have died." The kibbutznik argued, vociferously it seems, that there was no causal relationship between the death of the child and desecration of the Sabbath. Yagen defines this as an "attack." He views the kibbutznik's statements against him as shameful, as they were made in a house of mourning. Yagen's own remarks there were permissible in his view, as they reinforce the religious norm, while the kibbutznik's remarks, repudiating it, are heretical and disrespectful.

The attribution of skepticism to the kibbutznik is also characteristic of a basic tenet of the return to the faith movement. The kibbutz is perceived as the most concrete danger to the world of the Jewish faith. It is the stronghold of the secularism that proposes an alternative to the world of tradition, and has proven for over three generations the possibility of the existence of a Jewish culture other than that developed in the diaspora. It is clear that as long as the kibbutz exists, it constitutes an example that refutes the claims of the promoters against the secular world. Therefore, these proselytizers do not refrain from noting in almost every sermon that among the newly devout are numerous kibbutzniks, or from ridiculing the kibbutz and all it stands for. The kibbutz thus constitutes a concrete address for all complaints against the secular world. These attacks on the kibbutz also have an ethnic aspect—most kibbutzniks are of Ashkenazi descent, most of the newly devout (and most of the promoters) are of Sephardi descent.[43]

A secular woman from Natanya stood up, I have th'phone number, th'address. Among the main difficulties in the reception process for tales of return to the faith is the extent of credibility. If the promoter wants his tale to shake up his listeners, and thereby encourage them to return to the faith, it must be believable. As these stories deal with outright supernatural events like the summoning of spirits, visitations, and Divinely-meted punishments, the storyteller must find the means to shore up narrative believability. Indeed, all of Yagen's stories make much and intensive use of such means: "One of the most troubling stories, ladies and gentlemen, that I ever heard is the story I heard from a woman-soldier one Friday in my office. If it was not the truth, dear brothers, I would not dare to tell you here in public. This soldier's name is Bat-el. She lives at 26 Alkavetz Street in Jerusalem. I have her phone number in my pocket, I took down word for word her story . . . I was shocked, I have her address and her phone number" (cassette 24, 41); "Did you hear about the Youth Village? In Jerusalem there is a school with thousands of pupils. A vocational high school. A vocational yeshiva . . . the head of the yeshiva told me a shocking tale a few weeks ago. He told me that he had a graduate of the yeshiva high school by the name of Eli Oistreicher. This young man Eli Oistreicher from Ofakim . . . and the Rabbi, Rabbi David Auerbach, lives at 6 ha-Pisgah Street in Jerusalem . . . Rabbi David Auerbach told me . . . (ibid); " . . . I will never forget the story that I heard. And it was recorded on cassettes. I told this on the radio as well . . . this girl, this woman, her name is Simah Akriv, and I heard the story from her. She told it at a seminar, crying like a little girl. I met her a few days earlier, this woman, I spoke with her children, a few days ago. They study together with mine" (ibid). And at the end of the story of the grandmother's visitation: "I can introduce you to the girl. . . . I heard it from the woman who had the dream. I heard it from her." In the story about the young man to whom Elijah appeared to tell him the Heavenly Tribunal had increased his years despite his having been sentenced to die that very day, and even revealed to him secrets of the redemption (cassette 87), Yagen takes the young man who told it to the Western Wall and demands that he tell the story while standing just "a meter from the Wall," in other words, Yagen adopts the most tried and trustworthy means to verify the truth of the report.

In his tales, Yagen employs a number of techniques drawn from the genre of legend to create credibility. First, the characteristics of time and place; the storyteller heard the matter just a few days previous, and the event took place in the recent past—last week or a couple of days ago. The closer in time the event to the time of its recounting, the more reliable it is, the easier it is to substantiate, and therefore the storyteller believes it will also be received as more authentic. Rare are stories of events from the distant past, like one tale about the Holocaust period and another about the snatching of Jewish children in Czarist Russia. All the rest take place at a time very close to that of the tale's telling. The characteristics of place are even more prominent: Yagen regularly offers precise addresses of the protagonists or reporters of events, their names and the places to which they have a connection. He also always emphasizes that their telephone numbers are right in his pocket, such that the matter of credibility is "closed" from all perspectives. A known phenomenon in the study of legend is that the greater the precision in the tale's local definition, the greater its credibility. Nissim Yagen makes the most of this cognitive means.

Emphasizing the unimpeachability of sources is another effective means of boosting credibility. Yagen underscores, habitually and repeatedly, the authenticity of his sources: he heard the story from one of its protagonists, other people were present when it was told, and they can testify to it, or in extreme cases, the storyteller himself was present at the time of the event. In one instance, when he tells about a boy who committed suicide because of the emptiness of the secular world, he claims that letters from that same boy happen to be on his very person, in his pocket, during the sermon. In the visitation story, Yagen uses a more complex literary technique, that of the narrative framework. The main story is told by a woman, Yagen reporting "faithfully" what she recounted at that event. The marvelous tale of the manifestation in a dream of the old righteous woman, and the cure from terminal disease out of the mouth of the secular woman augments, to Yagen's way of thinking, the believability of the tale. When a tale of this sort is told by a devout Jew, one might doubt it, as such motifs are part of the believer's world. But when a secular woman "wearing pants, God save us," tells the story in the first person, having seen it with her own eyes, as it were, even skeptical secularists, like that kibbutznik in the tale, are likely to accept it as unvarnished truth. In other words: the choice of rhetorical and stylistic forms of tales is also carefully made, so that they will contribute to the persuasive power.

This powerful effort to shore up authenticity explains a fair portion of the literal repetitions in the tale, as well as the occasionally tedious detail. The rhetorical and psychological apparatus of the return to the faith hinges upon its success.

Not like us, it shouldn't happen to you, he looks like an Arab. The nationalist extremism bordering on racism, via the construction of a stereotype of the Arab, here meets the religious aspect of return to the faith. In Yagen's interpretation of the case of the bus to Ashkelon seized by terrorists, he rails mightily against the commission of inquiry established against "our" soldiers who killed the terrorists, and in so doing defended the Jewish bus passengers. In relating to stories of mixed marriages between Jewish women and Arab men, he portrays the latter as cradle robbers who scheme perniciously to ruin young Jewish women:

> My dear people, [I'll tell you] one of the most troubling and shocking things I ever experienced, so you should know what state sons and daughters reach, our brothers and sisters, our relatives, descendants of Abraham, Isaac, and Jacob. How low one can fall! This most troubling story happened to me on a Friday morning, before I left for the yeshiva. The postman brought me an express letter. Some young woman from Kfar Saba, Miriam, has written to me. I opened the letter quickly. When I read it, I didn't know whether to laugh or cry. I called my wife to come and see what's happening in our country. This Miriam writes me in bitter tears, a Sephardi girl of eighteen. She writes, "Honored Rabbi Yagen, I heard your lecture on the radio, your broadcast, I heard that you help Jews return to Judaism. I ask you to give me some kind of crash course in Judaism." What's this? "I went out for two years with an Arab from Kfar Kassem, and this Arab decided to leave me as soon as he heard that I don't keep the Jewish Torah, the Jewish tradition." The Arab is leaving her, why? Because she's not religious! So this Miriam says to me, "Maybe Honored Rabbi, you'll teach me some Judaism so Muhammad abu Yasmin will come back to me" (*much laughter in the audience*). You hear it, it is not funny. It is not funny, people. In short, she put her phone number there. A good thing she left her number. I called my wife, I said to her, "Look, a Jewish woman wants me to teach her Judaism so Muhammad will come back to her. Why, we don't have enough little Fatah [terrorists]? She'll bring a few more Fatah [recruits] into the world." In short, I telephoned this Miriam right away, that same morning. I said: "Miriam, maybe you want to come to me?" (*In a crying voice*) "Yes, boo hoo, hoo, yes Rabbi Yagen, yes . . . Can you help me?" I said, "I can help you, with God's help, just come, come to me for the Sabbath." She said: "I'm coming." She's crying on the phone over Muhammad (*much laughter*). For him she mourned seventy days, not seven (*more laughter*). In short, she came to me for the Sabbath. I, on the Sabbath, see a lovely Sephardi girl, she needs to go marry some Muhammad to bring more Muhammads into the world? (*much laughter*). I couldn't get it through my head. I didn't say anything to her. In short, I went to pray, I came back from prayer, I began to sing *Shalom Aleichem*, Sabbath songs with all the children, the table, the lighting of candles. I said to my wife, have her light a candle. Maybe her soul will light up as well. Together with the candle. After all my little children began to tell the portion of the week, about the

wicked Esau, and Ishmael and Abu Muhammad, and more stories, all kinds of stories, the atmosphere of the Sabbath, I didn't say a single word to her (*sighs deeply*). Ay, ay, ay, Ishmael, by the way, Rashi says he became religious at the end of his days. May it soon come to pass among his grandchildren. What shall I tell you, Sabbath morning again, eating, singing songs of Sabbath, I wanted her to see the Jewish experience for herself . . . In short, the end was at the third meal, I could no longer restrain myself, I started to cry. I said to her, "Miriam, you want to go back to Muhammad?"—"Yes."—"Why, aren't there enough Muhammads? There are a hundred million, two hundred million! You are a Jew?"—"Yes." "What makes you a Jew?" She showed me a little Shield of David, but inside, inside [her shirt]. Why, [did she hide it? because] she's afraid, she goes around in Arab villages, [it's] small, unda [sic] wraps, "look" . . . I said to her: "Aren't you ashamed!" I said to her: "His grandfather killed your grandfather. That's what you need, Muhammads?" . . . In short, on Sunday morning, I didn't let her go back to . . . Petah Tikva. I brought her myself to Neveh Yerushalayim Yeshiva for girls in Bayit va-Gan. And, God be praised, she married a God-fearing yeshiva student and became a student herself at a *kollel* (i.e., an institution for adult religious education, which provides its students with all their every-day needs) in Jerusalem. (Cassette 17)

Here Yagen uses a variety of means to realize the tale's objectives. The racial humor—ludicrous names for Arabs, the children of such a couple would be "little Fatah [terrorists]," the young woman in tears over her break-up with an Arab. Threat and intimidation—there are a hundred million, two hundred million Arabs. The Arabs' forebears murdered yours, all Arabs are dangerous Fatah terrorists. The storyteller knows here precisely what kind of expressions will draw the audience's laughter, and he plies them repeatedly. Yagen also avails himself of a narrative motif that figured often in Jewish folktales in the diaspora, that of "the child taken captive": this girl, this lovely Sephardi girl, is in the Arabs' clutches and only Yagen's intervention will save her from them. His intervention, moreover, led her to her rightful destination—life in the kollel. The model of "them" and "us," the Arab murderer versus the man of integrity, the impurity of the Gentiles contrasted with the purity and beauty of the Jewish home, are brought to an extreme in this tale, but they characterize the atmosphere of all of Yagen's stories.

Her [late] grandmother came to her in a dream in a strange form, night after night. The manifestation of supernatural entities in Yagen's stories are one of the most widespread means of revealing various truths. Indeed, the use of supernatural motifs in folktales is hardly surprising, but the special manner in which Yagen employs this technique in contexts of return to the faith is of tremendous importance. Visitation in a dream is the most common form in his stories. A yeshiva student who "went heretical" and enlisted in the army was murdered by terrorists in Gaza. He was seen again and again by the principal of the yeshiva in a dream, saying that he was imprisoned in an instrument of torture (*kaf ha-kelah*); he had no respite because he had abandoned the path of the Torah (cassette 41). Simah Akriv's husband, killed in a car accident in the United States on the Sabbath, appeared to his children in a dream and thanked them and their mother for bringing him rest by virtue of having embraced religion. He tells them he is studying Gemara, there in Heaven (cassette 41). In one of the seminars, a man refused to participate in a lecture on "souls." His wife ran in tears to Yagen and told him that her father-in-law, a great zaddik, had appeared to him in a dream during the lecture, while he slept in his room in the hotel, and told him he would take him to him to the world of the dead unless he returned to the faith (cassettes 17, 24). One woman, at an evening for the newly devout, said that her sister, who had died years ago, appeared to her again and again in a dream, and told her she was coming to take her son. It turned out that the son had cancer. Each time, before the child's condition deteriorated, the departed sister would appear in the mother's dream (cassette 18).

Another type of manifestation of the departed is via seances. On a number of occasions (cassettes 17, 24, 41), Yagen talks about secularists summoning the spirits of famous people: soldiers at Camp Schneller in Jerusalem call upon the spirit of Ben-Gurion, who tells them his soul is in an instrument of torture, surrounded by "boiling excrement," for having led so many into sin. Kibbutzniks from Ginnosar recount that they called upon the spirit of Yigal Allon, who told them of a similar fate. Students Yagen knew from She'erit Yosef Yeshiva called upon the spirit of Chaim Nachman Bialik, and he too was suffering the torments of purgatory. When non-believers at one of the seminars for return to the faith went up to their room and summoned Bialik's spirit, it told them (and asked that they kindly notify Rabbi Yagen!) that he was finally released from the instrument of torture, and merited entry into Hell. At Kibbutz Beit Alpha, a seance was held. The visiting spirit identified itself as "the blue butterfly" and pronounced numbers. The participants recognized it as a telephone number, and dialed it. The rather startled woman who answered told them that she was a widow who, some years ago, had made a pact with her husband, both of them "secularists from Rehavia [a wealthy neighborhood in Jerusalem]," that the spirit of the first of them to pass away would appear in the world, transmit the code-words, "blue butterfly," and in that way prove to the survivor that there was life after death. Another story beloved by Yagen (cassettes 18, 24, 41) concerns a woman from Rosh ha-Nikra who was plagued by a bird that flew through her home, chirping incessantly and peculiarly, refusing to leave. Yagen understood that this was the spirit of the fetus that same woman had aborted, who came to tell her of the impending death of her husband from a heart attack, and of the mortal peril surrounding her son.

Direct manifestations also figure in his stories: in one seminar, a child of a participating family came and told Yagen that the Messiah had appeared to him to say that he will come and redeem his people within a few years' time (cassette 87). Another tale told at the same appearance concerns a young "Canaanite" Jew, who thought to ridicule a particular rabbi. The rabbi cursed him, and he was subsequently wounded in the Lebanon War. Crippled, he returned to the faith. Then one day an old man sat beside him on a bus. His face was that of a child, like an angel. He told him that the Heavenly Court had lengthened his years, although he had originally been sentenced to die on that very day. The messenger was none other than Elijah the Prophet, and he even described how and when the redemption would take place, but forbade him to tell others.[44]

The supernatural manifestations that take place in these stories belong to the framework of the narrating society's beliefs and views. Visitations in dreams and messages or encounters with dead souls at seances indeed deviate from ordinary, familiar reality, but not from the "expanded" borders that many in modern society accept. The enlarged borders encompass, for example, astrology, extra-sensory perception, UFOs, fortune telling, and the various magic arts. Yagen brings these occult beliefs into play precisely because they are the domain of broad circles in the secular world. The other forms of direct manifestation, such as those of the Messiah or of Elijah, are motifs rampant in the Jewish folk traditions of all generations. They are intended primarily for the audience that has already taken upon itself the full commitment of returning to the faith. If such supernatural entities appeared to our forebears, and they didn't cast doubt on the veracity of the ancient traditions that told of it, why then can it not happen likewise today?

The supernatural manifestations almost always happen (there are isolated exceptions) to secularists. They are the ones to summon spirits at a seance, they see the departed in dreams, and it is to them that the supernatural entities turn, such as the bird, the Messiah, and Elijah the Prophet. The reason for this is clear: the faithful do not require this sort of vision. The visitations occur at critical junctures in the transition from the secular world of sin to the world of the faith. The supernatural manifestation is the lever, the most powerful and convincing means of transferring the secularists to the world of the faith. This is what Yagen terms, "shock treatment." Only such a shock, that proves to the secularists that beyond their narrow and dark world there exists another, eternal world of souls and life everlasting, can redeem them.

Supernatural motifs are a characteristic element of folk narrative. As such, the proselytizers' abundant use of them is unremarkable. The supernatural motif is generally the artistic and psychological peak of the legend, and bearer of its central message. The legend takes place in the real world of home, street, workplace, car, and so on. The storyteller capitalizes on as many faith-inspiring means as possible: the names of people and places, dates, telephone numbers and additional witnesses to the event. The psychological effect created by the supernatural element amidst the realistic and believable environment carefully woven by the storytellers is that of a psychological shock: all at once, the tale thrusts its listeners into a different and disconcerting reality, that contrasts with that on display until this point in the tale—the listeners' world of daily affairs. From an artistic and psychological perspective, it is now easier to accept the supernatural occurrence as factual, as the narrative fabric has been so familiar and credible. On the other hand, the appearance of a supernatural event in the midst of everyday reality of the audience of listeners is more disconcerting and threatening, because it takes place here, among us, not somewhere in the Land of Oz. The supernatural event confronts listeners with another reality, one whose rules are different, dark, and threatening, that lies beyond the visible and the familiar. Thus, the supernatural motif fulfills its role as principal message-bearer of the tale: to prove the existence of forces beyond the commonplace. They function according to a clear and unequivocal set of rules, as revealed and interpreted by the promoters. The supernatural elements exposed in these stories are the ultimate and most reliable proof that there is one force leading and directing our world, even in the complex and chaotic reality that we live every day. Founding a belief in a guiding force in the world on supernatural manifestations (miracles, demonological appearances) is a particularly long-lived principle in the history of religions, and is well-known in medieval Judaism under the rubric of "He has made his wonderful works to be remembered." From this perspective, Yagen is breathing new life into an ancient theological technique via an interesting utilization of modern realia and well-aimed rhetorical techniques.[45]

They have an eight-and-a-half-year-old daughter with a growth in her brain. . . . To see a little girl finished, because of her parents' desecration of the Sabbath. Yagen makes much use of punishments visited upon children. These include the twenty-two children killed at ha-Bonim Junction in a collision with a train because of the Sabbath desecration in the city of Petah Tikva; the newly devout woman who recounts the death of her child because she did not repent of her secularism in time, despite the warnings of her dead sister, who appeared to her in a dream; a boy of two who died in a car crash because his mother did not ritually bathe in the *mikveh*; the woman from Rosh ha-Nikra who almost lost her son for lack of heeding the warnings of the chirping bird (only after Yagen replaced the mezuzahs in her home did the child recover); and the children of Simah Akriv who were seriously injured in a car crash in the United States because their father drove on the Sabbath. According to Yagen (cassette 41), one can learn from the biblical tale of Enoch on what account children are killed. The Almighty took Enoch to Himself so that he would not sin. It then follows that, knowing that the parents do not keep His precepts, He prefers to take them to Himself. Yagen further states that he spoke with "Hugo Bergman, the greatest philosopher in the world," and asked him why children perished in the Holocaust. Bergman replied that he did not know which was better, that they die and reach Paradise, or grow into desecrators of the Sabbath (!).

In the manner of religious preachers since the Middle Ages, Yagen taps the deepest anxieties of the society he addresses—illness and death, the death of children in particular. Yagen knows that no audience, not even the most secular, can remain unmoved by the death of children. For such secularists are the first to wonder "why did this happen to me," when their children suffer injury, with no connection to their level of education or social status. The certainty that shock treatment is the only way to reform secularists also presses Yagen to so broadly use motifs of injury to children. His repeated insistence on the necessity of returning to the faith now, before the disaster happens, before the onset of calamities such as are described in the stories, is a clear intimation that the children of the listeners, healthy and coddled though they may be, are in the same danger, unless their parents see the light and take immediate action. Influence via threat and fear is familiar to us from Jewish narrative of the Middle Ages, but in Yagen's stories it looms even larger.

Children do not appear in return to the faith stories only to suffer. One that Yagen tells at many of his appearances concerns the child who brought her parents back to the faith:

> I am reminded of a story, one that I'll never forget to tell, about how a child of four . . . I was with a group in Tel Aviv, in Neveh Sharett, where I was told that a four-year-old girl got her parents to become religious. A girl of four! There are many cases of boys and girls leading their parents back to the faith. There are children with the souls of parents and parents with the souls of children. What can be done?
>
> This girl, the parents told me, one Friday on the way home from kindergarten, she saw posters that said: "Every woman and daughter lights Sabbath candles." She comes home to her mother, a 'telligent [sic] one, she says to her mother, "Let's light Sabbath candles." The mother reacted as if she had said, "Drop dead." "Close yer mouth, shut yer mouth!" The girl was afraid, as if she had said who knows what. All she had asked was to light Sabbath candles. What did she say? The child cried, went to her room and cried. The girl was stubborn, may His name be praised, she saved her parents from a sentence to Hell. The next Friday, this little girl was stubborn, she came home:

"Oh Mommy, please, let's light Sabbath candles."—"Shut yer mouth," and gave her a slap. A pity I wasn't there. In short, the girl began to cry, and left.

On the third Sabbath she got the better of her parents. What did she do? A little girl of four! She went, she went to her mother's purse and took a hundred shekels without permission, and went to Mr. Grocer. She went to the store and said: "Mr. Grocer, Mr. Grocer (*singing*) give me two candles." He misunderstood, because Sabbath candles aren't sold singly. They come in boxes: twenty, sixteen, not singly. He heard two candles, thought two memorial candles, in tin containers that burn twenty-four hours in memory of departed souls. So he took two memorial candles and gave them to her. The girl takes the two memorial candles, comes home, goes into her room, arranges the teddy bear, the monkey, and doll, because her Mommy and Daddy don't want to, she takes the monkeys, and makes Challahs out of modelling clay, for the Sabbath, a kerchief, and lights the two memorial candles. Candles for departed souls, this is what she does. The mother sees that a half hour has gone by, an hour, and the girl hasn't been heard from, not a peep. She says to her husband: Chuck, go see what's with . . . Miri. They open the door, they're in another world. They see their daughter with two memorial candles burning and she's doing this. Then he said: "Miri, what are you doing? "Mommy, nothing." She was afraid they'd kill her.—"What are you doing?" She says: "I lit one candle for Daddy, and one for Mommy." The father told me how moved he was, so moved, that he returned to the faith that same Friday and to this day in Neveh Sharett, he buys Sabbath candles and gives them out to residents of the neighborhood for free. But why wait for the children to bring us back to the faith? (*in a crying tone*) Why wait for a father to die, why wait for a mother to die?! For a child to die?![46]

Here Yagen makes exemplary use of the notion expressed in the verse, "Out of the mouth of babes and sucklings hast thou founded strength" (Pss. 8:3). Children, being more sensitive and understanding, are also more vulnerable. They've not yet lived long enough to be tainted by the impurity of the secular world, and they are not yet impervious, like the adults, to the truth of the world of the faith. The children come home from the traditional kindergartens and schools with values unfamiliar to them. Yagen, like other revivalists, knows that this can be an efficient pipeline for the penetration of the world of the faith into the family fabric. The child is innocent and more easily influenced and can therefore be used for the first stage, the external trappings of return to the faith—the lighting of Sabbath candles, a visit to the synagogue, and so forth. Thus the gate is open for more meaningful steps, such as fastidious attention to the laws of kashrut, family purity, setting aside predetermined times for prayer and study, and from there a regular place on the yeshiva bench and residence in an ultra-orthodox neighborhood is no longer so far away.

The calculated construction of the tale and the manner in which it is told reinforce this orientation. The tale presents, side-by-side like two opposing poles, the little girl and her parents. In her innocence, persistence, and sensitivity to tradition, she represents the new generation, the hope of the Jewish people. The expressions that Yagen uses to characterize her in the story are soft, full of empathy and understanding. The many digressions he makes here ("What did she say?," "A pity I wasn't there") are also intended to establish himself, the spiritual leader, as being on the side of the little girl, along with his listeners. The characterization of the parents, the mother in particular, is deliberately crude and caustic: the mother is "an 'telligent one," short-tempered with her child, she yells, threatens, and strikes her for nothing. The deliberate contrast between the girl and her parents is manifested mostly in the concluding episode of the tale, when the parents discover what she has done in her room: Opening her door, they enter another world, the world of the Sabbath: the burning candles, the woman's hands to her face as she recites the blessing, the members of the household together in the gentle embrace of the Sabbath. But no family members graced this Sabbath tableau, only the child's toys—the teddy bear, the monkey, and doll. Having no choice, she stays with them rather than with her parents, who are not ready to take part in the sanctity of the Sabbath. It is as if the storyteller is saying here that the company of such inanimate objects as these is preferable to that of the secularists, who crudely (the mother's behavior in the story) reject any connection to the sacred tradition. Entrance into the girl's room signifies, in the most concrete form, the passage from the secular world to the world of faith, from profane to sacred.

get up and go quickly to the neighbor across the way . . . she didn't go . . . Her grandmother . . . came again to her granddaughter Sarah. . . . She didn't go. On the third day. . . . Go tell the parents. Nissim Yagen is a master of live performance. He can fascinate thousands of listeners; many thousands of his cassettes are sold to the public at large. Yagen's storycraft is composed of several techniques that serve him to build a unique atmosphere in his stories. Above all—style: Yagen speaks in the standard spoken Hebrew of modern Israel, with two main exceptions: one leaning toward high Hebrew, when he quotes biblical verses, especially sayings of the sages, and the other toward sub-standard Hebrew—when he deliberately uses colloquialisms or imperfect language: "close yer mouth, shut yer mouth," "I'm nuts," "c'mon, let's get someone," and many more of the like. Deliberate errors of gender and number agreement are frequent. From Yagen's style in his more "learned" sermons, like that on the plagues in Egypt (cassette 86) and elsewhere, it is clear that Yagen speaks a fine Hebrew. It thus follows that his use of sub-standard language is contrived. He knows that this low style of speech, in imitation of the less educated strata of the population, will appeal to them and be correspondingly more convincing.

Style is one of his tried and true ways of turning a story into a kind of (to use his own style) "slice of real life," which he reports "as it actually happened." This is the folk storyteller's primary mimetic technique to draw the listeners into the reality he is spinning.

Yagen also makes much use of dramatic techniques. He employs many dialogues and other direct responses: The grandmother's remarks to her granddaughter in her dream are offered as direct speech; the dialogue between the woman reporting the dream and her husband; the argument between the girl and her parents over the Sabbath candle-lighting issue; the dialogue between Ben-Gurion and soldiers who summoned his spirit and so on. These enable the storyteller to change his voice, to switch styles of speech, to fragment the tale and create gaps between the various units of conversation—to all appearances on account of the speakers' hesitations—and thereby turn the entire tale into a kind of little drama, as has been always the convention of folk storytellers. Yagen also "does voices": he often raises his voice and emphasizes the parts that are most important to him. When he wants to impress his listeners, he usually sighs a lot, moans "Ay-ay-ay," in order to show how near and dear the subject is to him, or how it "breaks his heart."

Another technique Yagen employs is more rare: he utters certain sentences or passages in melody. For example in our tale: "They were ready to bury her, God preserve us. This little girl, ay-ay, this little girl (*singing*) . . . on the fifty-ninth day . . . they took x-rays at Tel-ha-Shomer [Hospital] . . . they x-rayed her, saw that there was nothing, the brain was clean." And in the story quoted above about the little girl who led her parents back to the religion: "She went to the store and said: 'Mr. Grocer, Mr. Grocer (*singing*) give me two candles.' The melody is generally reminiscent of prayer melodies, in itself imbuing these bits with a tint of holiness, a hue of spiritual exaltation. Yagen always uses this technique at peak moments of the story, where the correctness of the path back to the faith is proven, or the manifestation of the Almighty is revealed in daily reality. By singing prose sentences, he seeks to bring the audience into the world of holiness shaped in the course of the tale.

Another narrative technique, also popular with folk storytellers, is the calculated construction of narrative tension. Indeed, in one passage quoted above, the grandmother reveals herself repeatedly to her granddaughter in a dream. The woman brushes aside the manifestation, each time with a new argument, and does not go to warn the parents of their daughter's mortal peril. The manifestation makes it clear that the danger is great, indeed that it grows from moment to moment. The storyteller is in no hurry; he conveys the grandmother's remarks in full detail, over and over, describes the woman's soul-searching and her exchange with her husband. These are typical means of building narrative tension; Yagen makes powerful use of them.

One of the most troubling stories, ladies and gentlemen, that I ever heard, is the story I heard from a woman soldier one Friday in my office. If this was not the truth, dear brethren, I would not dare tell you here in public. This soldier is named . . . I copied it down word for word . . . I was in shock, I have her address and telephone number . . . she and five other soldiers, one named Ronen, another by the name of. . . . She told me herself. . . .

Yagen begins the story with a declaration of how shocking and unique it is, so much so that one so well acquainted with such things as he was filled with dread. In this way, the storyteller builds up his listeners' expectations. Yet from this point, he deliberately delays the actual telling of the tale. He goes on and on about the credible sources from whom he heard it, his reactions, the details of the participants in the event, in order to draw out as much as possible the event itself, and thereby to increase the tension and the expectation of the listeners for the great truth that he is about to reveal.

They took x-rays at Tel-ha-Shomer [Hospital] . . . the professor went wild, he got a cancer in his fancy education. Humor is one of Yagen's favorite narrative techniques. He uses it at all levels: the style, the episode, and the complex anecdote. Most of his colloquialisms and grammatical errors are intended to make the audience laugh. The same is true for his derision of Arabs, secularists, and leftists. The above excerpted story, of the young woman who wanted Yagen to teach her religion so that her Arab boyfriend would return to her, displayed Yagen's masterful use of racial stereotype in cynical asides ("she cried over her Arab") to the resounding laughter of his audience. This humor, in its various manifestations, serves as comic relief in the midst of the "theological" sermons, offering a break between menacing supernatural tales. It also differentiates, via sarcastic humor, between "us" and "them," between believers and secularists. Those secularists in the audience who laughed at the folly of the secular girlfriend will no longer wish to belong to the same camp, thus humor joins the other means in the service of proselytizing. An example that shows off Yagen's comic flair is part of a long sermon about the plagues in Egypt. Coming to the plague of darkness, sent, according to Yagen, in order to give Pharaoh a chance to sit in the dark, ponder his sins, and correct his ways before the killing of the first-born, Yagen says:

There are times, man, work, wife, kids, troubles, VAT, income tax, ho, ho, ho, ho, Sick Fund, Health Fund, the other Fund . . . pension, parallel tax, direct tax, crooked tax, round tax, ho-ho! You can get really crazy. Anyone wants to be crazy, doesn't have to go to a funny farm, all he has to do is turn on the radio, open a newspaper, the radio, he'll go crazy. It's enough just to hear the news a few times. God preserve us! Why did the Almighty bring the plague of darkness down upon the Egyptians? The Egyptians might argue in the next world: "God! The plagues kept coming. The wife had an abortion, I had an abortion. The kid fell down, the car was wrecked, this happened, that happened, I got confused. I had no time to think!! And always the overdraft, always! The wife works like a dog. The husband works. . . . Couples come to me, secularists (*in a crying voice*), God preserve us, he says, "I work like a dog! Earn a thousand shekels a month. My wife works like a dog—a thousand shekels a month. And always in overdraft. Why, Rabbi?!" I said: "Why— you live like dogs! (*much laughter, applause*). He works like a dog, she works like a dog, and always in overdraft. By us [the orthodox], he doesn't work, she doesn't work, and all the time in over-plenty. Always plenty. But them, always in overdraft. He's limited, she's limited, both are limited. Ay . . . they can't get through the month, it's because the month can get along just fine without them. (Cassette 86)

In the visitation story, the object of ridicule is the professor. This one term encapsulates for Yagen all that is wrong with others: this one is secular, that one is a leftist, the other puts his faith in science instead of in the Torah. In the long sermon Yagen gave at Yad-Eliyahu Stadium, he told a typical anecdote about a professor, providing a good example of his diverse comic techniques and his attitude to all things symbolized by the "professor":

Many say (*mockingly*): "To each his own truth . . . to each his own faith . . . " they believe they're descended from apes. The luminary [ha-Gaon] R. Jacob Kaminetzki from America, may he rest in peace, was a great zaddik. He came here once with R. Moishe Feinstein for a gathering of the Council of Torah Elders, and his son was with him. When he left on the plane for America, R. Jacob Kaminetzki, luminary to the generation [ge'on ha-dor], sat with his son on the plane, back to America. Next to R. Jacob Kaminetzki sat a professor from the University [*sic*] in Israel, he too with his son. And R. Jacob Kaminetzki, his son, every minute got up, says to his father, a man of seventy-eighty, a zaddik, old, says to him, "Father, do you need anything? Father, Father can I bring you tea, something to drink? Shall I take off your shoes? Would you like a blanket?" All the way: "Father! Father! My dear father, can I bring you anything? Anything you want, I'll get for you." The professor sees all this, he's eating his heart out. Eating his heart out! His heart! The professor was also travelling with his son. Just the opposite. The professor says to his son: "My dear son, can I bring you anything?" Exactly the reverse! "Would you like a blanket? Shall I bring your shoes? How about some juice? Shall I bring some for you?" He says to his son, and the son makes a face (*much laughter*), a face he makes at his father. The silent treatment. "Why didn't he buy me a Volvo '87 instead of an '86?" Doesn't speak to him the whole flight. And the poor father, old, says to his young son: "Oh, my precious, my dear son, I'll bring you, I'll buy you a whiskey, I'll buy you whatever you want." Just . . . the silent treatment, that's it.

The professor sees how the other son, the son of R. Jacob Kaminetzki, ah, brings him, gets up all the time, all the time. Ay . . . he started to eat his heart out. The professor, before getting off the plane, said to R. Jacob Kaminetzki, head of the Yeshiva (*in a crying voice*): "Tell me honored rabbi, learned sir, I do not understand. I'm old, you're old, we are both old men. Why does your son serve you all the way, all the way! All the way! 'What would you like,' every minute, 'Father, what would you like,' everything, everything. I give him my life, my soul, he's been the death of me! The death of me! He's made me crazy. And he won't talk to me! He gives me the silent treatment!—What do you want now? He says to me: 'Shut yer mouth!' Why the difference? Why is it like this?" (*singing*) The rabbi said to him: "I'll tell you professor, professor sir, I'll tell you the truth. Your son is right, he's right. I'll tell you why your son is right. We believe, we Jews who keep the Torah and the precepts, we believe we are descended from the first man, the creation of the Almighty. We come from the first man. Thus each preceding generation is closer to the stone from which he was quarried. Closer to the Almighty. The father is closer to the Almighty, to the first man. The grandfather, closer still. The amoraim, the earlier and later authorities, the heads of the Babylonian academies, closer to God. The prophets. You believe you are descended from the ape, so the father is closer to the ape. The son is farther from the ape, you should respect him! (*much laughter and applause*). My esteemed professor," he told him, "my esteemed professor, you have to honor your son, you're a hundred years closer to the apes! He's further apart. Get up and make him tea, bathe him." What nonsense they teach the kids! Ay. . . . (Cassette 86)

Here Yagen mobilizes most of the humorous means at his disposal to create the effects he's interested in, namely, to make the audience laugh by ridiculing those they loathe, creating the contrast between the fool (the professor) and the wise man (the rabbi), and building up the audience's identification with "us", with the wise rabbi, and encouraging their mockery of "them," in this case the professor, who masquerade as wise men. The stylistic blending of high language ("the stone from which he was quarried," "luminary to the generation") with colloquialism and poor grammar (shut yer mouth, I'd give my soul, killed me, driven me crazy, the silent treatment), is above all a game in linguistic virtuosity, proof of the storyteller's control over both the world of the audience and that of the Torah scholars. The stylistic gaps created within a single sentence, the extreme transitions between the stylistic references to the different social groups (The world of Torah scholars, the simple folk and un-educated) create one of Yagen's chief humorous means.

Another is the use of a multitude of details to set up polarized situations to comic effect: The Rabbi's son, serving his father, brings him drinks, shoes, a blanket, while, in contrast, the professor kowtows to his son, offering to bring him the same things and more. This plus the frequent use of raised voice, mel-ody, rhythmic speech, imitation of the protagonist's manner of speech, and the faces (the professor's son "makes a face") lead as expected to great outbursts of laughter in the audience. Yet especially noteworthy at this juncture, as in other places in Yagen's stories, is the manner of building the narrative tension. As if working in stone, he chisels out the details of two parallel situations: that of the rabbi's family alongside that of the professor's family. The slow and detailed construction of the two situations creates a continual anticipation of a clash between the two parallel experiences found here in such cramped quarters as adjoining seats on an airplane. The confrontation, the peak of the narrative tension, takes place in the professor's meek and obsequious appeal to the rabbi. The latter's answer releases the tension so painstakingly built up through the tale, and is thus met with tremendous laughter in the audience.[47]

The construction of parallel situations in this anecdote indicates the manner of perceiving the world in other stories as well. In most of the tales, the negative protagonists, the narrative antagonists, are secularists, highly educated, kib-butzniks perhaps, who accept neither Yagen nor any of the beliefs he preaches. The story itself is generally that of a journey made by those same skeptics to the world of the faith, or proof of their folly. The secularist seeks proof, the tale is that in detail. At its conclusion, the skeptic joins the seminar for the newly devout, or becomes a student at a *yeshiva* or *kollel.* The situations constructed in most of the stories, even if they are not made explicit, pit "us" against "them." In the visitation tale, as well, the kibbutznik who "attacked" Rabbi Yagen in a bereaved home was not only a non-believer, he was utterly insensi-tive to the grief-stricken family, as opposed to Yagen and company, who came from afar to offer comfort. Likewise the woman who recounted her grand-mother's appearance in her dream—she was deaf to the incontrovertible signs, rejected the dream, and thereby jeopardized the cancer-stricken child and dis-played callousness toward the parents' anguish. The attorney who moved to the United States, where he married a "Catholic" woman and ignored his old father, who remained in Israel, was so cruel as to tell his wife and children that his old father had passed away. When the old father came to visit, his son chased him away.

News items capture a central place in the polarized view of the secular world versus the world of faith. Here Yagen regularly collects, according to his own testimony, the news items detailing the decline of the secular world, which in turn is bringing down the entire country. News of suicides, brutal murders, abuse of the elderly, scorn for the values of religion and heritage, youth addicted to drugs and prostitution, mixed marriages with Arabs, road accidents, and so on, are proof that a world without faith leads the individual and the state straight to certain destruction. His stories, and the news items from "the secular press, God preserve us," that he reads aloud at his appearances, serve the same purpose: to describe the secular world and the world of the faith as two diametrically opposed poles. One attracts all that is negative—ignorance, apostasy, crime, lust, the destruction of the family. A life of tranquility, truth, and purity of the world of the faithful gravitate to the other pole. Interestingly enough, the familiar images of light and darkness are here reversed: in contrast to the polarized world of images built by the Jewish Enlightenment of the nineteenth century, in which the world of religion and faith were defined as darkness whereas the enlightenment, daughter of the heaven, was the long-awaited light, Yagen reverses the images: he likens the secular world to darkness—spiritual, human, and ethical. The world of faith is candles on the Sabbath, the light eternally burning in the yeshivas, the purity of family life. This contrast between light and darkness has always served both religious and secular preachers and sermonizers. It also attests to the polarized way of viewing the world built by preachers of Yagen's ilk. Not only a rhetorical means, this reflects the mental structure of his reference group.[48]

[4] "Return to the Faith" Narratives and Ancient Jewish Traditions

The tales of return to the faith are one of the few examples of intentional and dynamic use of the folkloric corpus in the modern world. No mere casual performance—an encounter that leads to the telling of a few jokes, the offhand insertion of an adage in conversation—these are full-fledged performance events uncharacteristic of the modern world. The return to the faith events are organized and planned; thousands of people may participate. The deliberate spread of folkloric material—especially folk beliefs and tales—takes place all at once, to a large number of listeners. These events employ modern means of mass communication—audio- and videocassettes, powerful loudspeakers, large screens, and so on, yet they are surprisingly archaic and traditional in character. The rhetorical means Yagen uses, that were outlined above, are quite familiar from the homilies of other preacher-sermonizers of our time, especially the famous television evangelists in the United States. Yet it is difficult to imagine that proselytizers like Yagen were ever exposed to such material. Much more relevant are the early Jewish narrative traditions—especially those of the Middle Ages.

Tales of reward and punishment are the main ingredients in all religious narrative. They establish a dual and balanced narrative structure: the story of the sin balanced against the appropriate punishment, and the story of the good deed or withstanding of a trial, rewarded by the appropriate recompense. This pattern stands at the core of most of the revivalist tales: the parents who did not keep the Sabbath and were punished with the fatal illness of their daughter; the husband of Simah Akriv, who took his family for a drive on the Sabbath and died in a car crash; the attorney in the United States who ignored his father and lost his faculties after a terrible road accident; the woman whose two-year-old son died in a crash because she did not immerse herself in the ritual bath. But the most convincing expression of the reward and punishment tales is the pattern of "measure for measure." There is a correspondence between the sins and the punishments visited upon their perpetrators. The correspondence, according to the storytellers' perception, is worth a thousand eyewitnesses as evidence of the existence of a causal relationship between them. In one tale, Yagen tells of a man who customarily roasted meat "over a fire" in the yard of the apartment house where he lived, despite his neighbors' protest of his desecration of the Sabbath. He had a heart attack, and even though they explained to him that it was punishment for his desecration of the Sabbath, he continued to do so upon returning home, after convalescing. He suffered a second heart attack and died. His wife told Yagen that her late husband appeared to her every night, crying of his harsh torments in the netherworld: horrible angels cut his flesh daily and roasted it over a fire—as punishment for his actions.[49]

Another motif that was widespread in medieval narrative as well as in tales recorded from contemporary storytellers is "the desecrator of the holy is punished." Here a man (Gentile or Jew) offends a saint, who punishes him severely by way of a curse, an invocation, or the like. In one story, Yagen tells about a secular young man who wanted to mock and mistreat an elderly rabbi from Rosh ha-Ayyin. The rabbi cursed him and, subsequently, he was seriously wounded in the Lebanon War. Had he not turned back to religion in time, he would even have been killed in an accident.[50]

One of the most prevalent narrative means in folk narrative is the visitation of supernatural creatures in the world of reality for the purpose of heralding information, taking vengeance, or rendering aid. Visitations in dreams, or seances, figure prominently in Yagen's tales. The departed in these stories fill the role of mediators between the world to come and our own. They report on what is happening to them in the world to come—in consequence of their actions in this world (reward and punishment)—they warn against various perils, show the way of return to the faith, and so on. Aside from the dead, the Messiah himself appears in Yagen's stories. In one, he manifests himself to a child at a seminar on return to the faith, and informs him of his imminent arrival. So too Elijah the prophet, who appeared to the same newly devout person who had earlier done injury to the honor of the elderly rabbi, letting him know that the

Heavenly Court had ruled to pardon him, and even told him some of the secrets of the redemption.[51]

One of Yagen's most important stories goes beyond selected narrative motifs from the past, using a full narrative pattern that originated in medieval Jewish narrative. This is the tale of the yeshiva boy who decided to run off and enlist in the army, despite the opposition of the principal: "He enlisted in the IDF and was spoiled in the IDF." He was murdered by terrorists in Gaza, and began to appear regularly in the dreams of the yeshiva principal, to tell him of the awful suffering he had to endure there in the world to come for having left the yeshiva. Thus he disturbed the principal's rest for some time until the rabbi asked him how he could make amends for his soul. The dead one asked him to gather all the yeshiva students on the Sabbath, recite Psalms, Mishnah, and the *kaddish* prayer for the elevation of his soul until the end of the Sabbath, and so they did. "The next day he came to him laughing. He said to him: Rabbi, thank you so much. As you have made my soul to rest, so too will your soul rest."

The tale is a modern version of the famous "tale of the *tanna* (an authority quoted in the Mishnah) and the dead man": Rabbi Akiva (or some other sage) encounters a dead man in the forest whose custom it was to collect trees upon which he was burned the same day in the world of the dead. He told Rabbi Akiva of his sins, after which the sage lost no time searching for his widow and son, and teaching the boy to recite prayers and the *kaddish*. After the son said the prayer for the dead for his departed father, the latter appeared to Rabbi Akiva in a dream and told him that he was now saved from the torments of hell.

The differences between the two versions of the tale lie on two main planes: in the fabric of the details of the narrative reality and in the nature of the sins, but not in the deep structure of the plot. Yagen tells a modern tale: the yeshiva in Jerusalem is a "trade high school," military service and soldiers dying in the Gaza Strip are familiar features of the landscape. The sin of the wandering dead in the story of the *tanna* was that he "had relations with a betrothed maiden on the Day of Atonement," or that he impugned the honor of sages, discriminated in favor of the wealthy and burdened the poor of the Jewish people, and the like, in other words, religious-normative sin. The sin of the yeshiva boy in Yagen's tale was that he left the yeshiva to enlist in the army, and thereby was tempted to commit further transgressions. The sin of the protagonist of the medieval tale was not a "real" sin at all, but a presentation of sin taken to its extreme, such that the perpetrator has no hope of redemption. The purpose of the extremization here is to prove that a son's recitation of the *kaddish* prayer can atone for even the most foul sin. The story itself, in the manner of the medieval exemplum, serves to guide and warn against breaking a socio-religious norm. In the modern story, the sin is rather mundane: yeshiva students who opt to enlist in the IDF are a daily matter. This sin is neither alluded to nor anchored in any way in the *halachah* or in religious precepts. The fear that such a practice might empty the yeshivas of their students is the only possible explanation of the use of this ancient tradition today. The pattern of the antecedent remains in the modern version, without any modifications whatsoever, as the social purpose of the tale is the same in both periods: to caution strict adherence to the values or norms of importance to the narrating society.[52]

Yagen is in the habit of presenting his stories as an antithesis to unbelievers, to those who cast doubt on the existence of souls, of the world to come, of reward and punishment, and the like. Tales are the most convincing "answers" and "proofs" that the promoters offer in response to the multitude of questions and doubts. Here, too, Yagen uses a theological concept, dating back to the ancient world, that gained currency among both Jews and Christians in the medieval period. The supernatural phenomena that take place in the world are proofs of the existence of God and his intervention in human affairs. The manifestations of demons and dead souls, of supernatural creatures, of people possessing magical powers, and so on, are the variegated means through which God makes known his existence in the world, they are "the wonderful works" that "He has made . . . to be remembered," in the conventional terminology of medieval Jewry. The plethora of supernatural manifestations in Yagen's tales should be seen as part of this ancient notion. Over and over he declares his enthusiasm for "stories about souls," and how eager he is to investigate each such rumor, to meet with whoever had a part in it, to understand its significance. The more testimony accrues about such events, the more cogent the proof of the existence of God and His works, and the tools in the hands of the promoters to persuade and act in the secular world will be that much more effective.[53]

Did Yagen know of the "tale of the tanna and the dead soul," and the other motifs mentioned here from traditional Jewish narrative? The answer, presumably, is yes. Nevertheless, it is important to emphasize that he does not customarily use tales from the Talmud and Midrash, from the medieval literature or the later ethical literature, even though it more than likely suits his purposes. It seems the reason for this has to do with the credibility he seeks to give his stories, which he presents as "proofs" of the truth of his theological arguments. Traditional tales from the sacred Jewish literature would presumably not have the same desired effect on the secular public to whom Yagen makes his appeal as on the ultra-orthodox community of believers. Therefore Yagen's stories are drawn always from the modern reality close to the world of his listeners, and not tales of miracles from the past, that might meet with skepticism on the part of secular listeners. This is certainly also the reason for using news items, which are accepted as verified truth by a secular audience (in Yagen's opinion).

Examination of the basic narrative elements of the tale of the sick girl in search of its semiotic meaning leads to interesting results. The parents in the tale of the cancer-stricken little girl (as well as the narrator herself, the granddaughter who refused to listen to her grandmother) represent modern Israeli society, that which received a secular education and forgot its roots in Jewish tradition. The little girl, as we saw in other tales as well, represents the young generation, that which bears the future of Judaism on its shoulders. The parents' desecration of the Sabbath is the direct cause of their daughter's grave condition. In modern Hebrew, as in many other languages, the term "cancer" expresses a broad range of disasters: the verge of death, betrayal, destruction of a living organism from within. Thus the extreme right castigates leftist movements in Israel as "a cancer in the body of the nation." It seems that the cancer of the little girl signifies more than a physiological ailment. It is the destruction that the first generation of secularists in Israel has wreaked on the Jewish people. This cancer, not incidentally, targets members of the young generation, and thus quashes all hope of its rehabilitation. The girl's parents do what modern secular society expects of them: they turn to the hospital which, again, is not by chance a top-notch university institution, home of the "professors," (the significance of which term has already been established above). In order to save the nation-state from its weaknesses and failures, secular society (the parents in the story) turns to the font of secular knowledge, namely science (the hospital). But this solution is proven inadequate, it is powerless to solve anything. Science cannot help when it comes to the most important and cherished of human affairs: life and death, the spiritual existence of the nation. Since Israeli society cannot find a solution for its difficult situation, the traditional forces— "grandfather Israel"—is recruited to point out the right path. Indeed, the manifestation of the grandmother in a dream represents precisely these forces, and their typical path of solution—return to the values of the tradition (in the story, the keeping of the Sabbath). Indeed, the movement for a return to the faith sees itself as the legitimate representative of these traditional forces. Although they are pushed aside and scorned repeatedly, like the grandmother in the dream, their role is to reappear tirelessly, because it is in the soul of the people. This is the moral basis that justifies the actions of the movement for a return to the faith.

Yagen's story is essentially a new tale. Earlier folk narrative has no variants to it, as it deals with a reality and conditions unique to the State of Israel. At the same time, it is saturated with traditional motifs: religious polemic (between the rabbi and kibbutznik); the appearance of the dead in the lands of the living; manifestation in a dream; sin and its due linked according to religious norms; the sin of the fathers visited upon their children; miraculous cures—

verging on the resurrection of the dead—that reward religious activity. All these figure among the most prevalent traditional motifs in Jewish folklore, and have been touched upon numerous times in the course of this book.

The intensive use of traditional motifs in a story that is essentially new influences the listeners in two conflicting ways: on one hand, it arouses the sense that the event being recounted is entirely new, that it is part of the day-to-day world of here and now. On the other hand, ancient traditional motifs pigeonhole the new tale squarely within a system of concepts already familiar to the audience from other tales they have heard, from books they have read, and a system of beliefs and norms in which they were bred. The emotional reaction awakened in the listener is a kind of déjà vu: the story is new, but it seems familiar. This is precisely the conceptual effect the promoters seek: the events they describe are current, having taken place just now in the reality familiar to us all, and therefore they have significance for our lives. At the same time, they reverberate at a profound level and are decidedly familiar from the cultural past, a part of our collective memory.

Yagen's storytelling craft, and that of other promoters, is based on the working of simple, concrete situations, familiar to the listeners from their daily lives, into traditional narrative patterns. The result is the creation of a folk literature that is both old and new and spreads rapidly in Israeli culture among newly devout circles. The tension and contrast between Israeli cultural reality and these circles is shaped in the tales as tension and contrast between traditional motifs and modern realia. In this manner, the narrative pattern reflects fully the confrontation between ancient Jewish tradition and life in the modern world, the clash that is the spiritual basis of the movement for the return to the faith. This tension is one reason that the proselytizers' stories are among the most interesting folktales that Jewish folklore has ever known.

Notes

1. Introduction

1. The two bibliographies that span Jewish folklore research from its inception are: Noy, *The Study*; and Yassif, *Bibliography*. The history of the discipline is described in the following works: Yassif, "The Study"; Noy, "Eighty Years of Jewish Folkloristics: Achievements and Goals" in Talmage, *Studies*, pp. 1–12; B. Kirshenblatt-Gimblett, "Problems in the Early History of Jewish Folkloristics," *Proceedings of the Tenth Congress of Jewish Studies*, Division D, II (Jerusalem, 1990), pp. 21–32; G. Hasan-Rokem & E. Yassif, "Jewish Folkloristics in Israel: Directions and Goals," op. cit., pp. 33–62; H. Jason, "Study of Israelite and Jewish Oral and Folk Literature: Problems and Issues," *Asian Folklore Studies* 49 (1990): 69–108; and D. Ben-Amos, "Jewish Folklore Studies," *Modern Judaism* 11 (1991): 17–66.

2. These tensions between the elitist concept of culture and folk culture in the annals of folkloristics are described in detail by G. Cocchiara, *The History of Folklore in Europe*, trans. from Italian J. N. McDaniel (Philadelphia, 1971 [1952]); R. M. Dorson, ed., *Peasant Customs and Savage Myths. Selections from the British Folklorists* (Chicago, 1968); H. J. Gans, *Popular Culture and High Culture* (New York, 1974). The clearest expression of the social approach to literature was penned, ironically enough, by a scholar of literature: "The smallest unit, the semiotic exchange, is still inherently social, never the product of an autonomous individual, and at no level do we find the unity of a single homogeneous society speaking through a single representative individual," R. Hodge, *Literature as Discourse. Textual Strategies in English and History* (Baltimore, 1990), p. 73.

3. On the treatment of folk literature in the historical sources cf. Ben-Amos, "Distinctions," pp. 45–47, and the literature cited there. On the relationship between narrative traditions past and present, with reference to the cultures of the ancient Near East, see: H. Jason, "The Poor Man of Nippur: An Ethnopoetic Analysis," *Journal of Cuneiform Studies* 31 (1979): 189–215; H. Jason and A. Kempinski, "How Old Are Folktales?" *Fabula* 22 (1981): 1–27; in regard to Greco-Roman culture, see: A. Scobie, "Storytellers, Storytelling, and the Novel in Graeco-Roman Antiquity," *Rheinische Museum für Philologie* 122 (1979): 229–259; W. F. Hansen, "Folklore," in *Civilizations of the Ancient Mediterranean: Greece and Rome*, ed., M. Grant and R. Kitzinger, vol. 2 (New York, 1988), pp. 1121–1130; and, on a more general and conceptual level, C. Geertz, *The Interpretation of Cultures* (New York, 1973), pp. 55–86.

Hodge (1990) encapsulated brilliantly the long-standing perception at the core of studies of folk texts of the past (supra, note 2):

> "Texts from the past become problematic and unreliable, requiring a knowledge of historical rules of genre and domain which seems difficult to acquire and impossible to demonstrate. Texts survive but are meaningless: assumptions of genre and domain are the key to meaning but do not survive. A genuinely historical inquiry thus is made to seem both essential and impossible. The solution to this problem is to restate its terms, to reconnect them to a set of practices which are so functional and so widespread that they must be relatively easy to understand and grasp. The starting point for the study of genre and domain must be with

texts from the knowable present, so the relations between the interpretation of texts on the one hand and structures of genre and domain on the other can be articulated in all their complexity," p. 27.

4. On Hebrew as a spoken language, and its relationship with the other Jewish languages, cf., for example: Dan, *The Hebrew Story*, pp. 6–11; Sh. Morag, "Hebrew as an Elite Language of Culture: Processes of Consolidation and Transmission in the Middle Ages in the Mediterranean Lands," *Pe'amim* 23 (1985): 9–12 [H]; R. Drori, *Initial Contacts between Jewish and Arabic Literature in the Tenth Century* (Tel Aviv, 1988), pp. 41–54 [H]; and H. H. Paper, ed., *Jewish Languages* (Cambridge, Mass., 1978). The history of the Latin language deals with Latin as the language of culture and its relationship with the spoken languages of the Middle Ages, but compare especially: E. R. Curtius, *European Literature and the Latin Middle Ages*, trans. from German by W. R. Trask (Princeton, 1973); and E. Auerbach, *Literary Language and its Public in Late Antiquity and in the Middle Ages*, (London, 1965).

2. The Biblical Period

1. On the extensive scholarship published on the subject, compare the surveys of: J. W. Rogerson, *Myth in Old Testament Interpretation* (Berlin, 1974); idem, *Anthropology and the Old Testament* (Oxford, 1978); P. G. Kirkpatrick, *The Old Testament and Folklore Study* (Sheffield, 1988); "Altes Testament," *Enzyklopädie des Märchens*, vol. 1, pp. 419–441; S. Talmon, "The Comparative Method in Biblical Interpretation: Principles and Problems," *Vetus Testamentum Supplements* 29 (1977): 320–356; and Yassif, "The Study", pp. 4–16. Very interesting, and almost unknown, is H. J. D. Astley, *Biblical Anthropology: Compared with and Illustrated by the Folklore of Europe and the Customs of Primitive Peoples* (Oxford, 1929), which deals with questions of animism and the supernatural, folk dancing, and clothing, in the spirit of British folkloristics of his time.

On the contribution of Gunkel, considered the father of this school, cf. Kirkpatrick, and also: P. Gibert, *Une théorie de la légende: Herman Gunkel (1862–1932) et les légendes de la Bible* (Paris, 1979) and W. Klatt, *Herman Gunkel: Zu seiner Theologie der Religionsgeschichte und zur Entstehung der formesgeschichtlichen Methode* (Göttingen, 1969). Gunkel himself points to earlier scholars who dealt with the folkloric aspects of Scripture: H. Gunkel, *The Folktale in the Old Testament*, trans. M. D. Rutter (Sheffield, 1987), p. 34.

Among the general introductions to the biblical literature, the contribution of two in particular to the definition of biblical tales as folk narrative deserve emphasis: O. Eissfeld, *The Old Testament: An Introduction. The History of the Formation of the Old Testament* (New York & London, 1965 [German Original, 1934]) and R. H. Pfeiffer, *Introduction to the Old Testament* (New York, 1948).

A limited survey, but one of vast interest, as it was written in the very period of the emergence of Gunkel's method, yet apparently with no connection to it, is: I. F. Wood, "Folktales in Old Testament Narratives," *Journal of Biblical Literature* 28 (1909): 34–41.

An important survey of the status of biblical folktales among tales of the ancient Near East is found in H. Jason and A. Kempinski, "How Old Are Folktales?" *Fabula* 22 (1981): 1–27; D. Damrosch, *The Narrative Covenant: Transformations of Genre in the Growth of Biblical Literature* (San Francisco, 1987); E. Greenstein, "On the Genesis of Biblical Prose Narrative," *Prooftexts* 8 (1988): 347–354, and most recently, and with understanding of the folkloristic method: S. Niditch, *Folklore and the Hebrew Bible* (Minneapolis, 1993).

2. Gunkel was the first biblical scholar to make direct use of the folkloristic method to prove the folk origin of biblical tales. These were the epic laws of Olrik, and cf. Olrik, *Laws;*

Holbeck, "Laws." However, Olrik himself, as we now know, used his "epic laws" to analyze some of the legends in Genesis: A. Olrik, *Principles for Oral Narrative Research*, (Bloomington and Indianapolis, 1992), pp. 116–133.

On the study of motifs and tale types, see Thompson, *Motif Index*; Arne and Thompson. Biblical scholars generally preferred the structural approaches of Vladimir Propp and Claude Lévi-Strauss to indicate the similarity between universal narrative patterns and the biblical tale. A. Dundes, "Structuralism and Folklore," *Studia Fennica* 20 (1976): 75–93; B. Holbeck, "Formal and Structural Studies of Oral Narratives," *Unifol* (Copenhagen, 1978), pp. 149–194, and also the general discussion of the methods of Greimas, Barthes, et. al. in connection with Scripture in D. C. Greenwood, *Structuralism and the Biblical Text* (Berlin, New York, and Amsterdam, 1985) and J. Blenkinsopp, "Biographical Patterns in Biblical Narrative," *Journal for the Study of the Old Testament* 20 (1981): 27–46. P. J. Milne, "Folktales and Fairy Tales: An Evaluation of Two Proppian Analyses of Biblical Narratives," *Journal for the Study of the Old Testament* 34 (1986): 35–60 criticizes Blenkinsopp and his predecessor J. Sasson for using the Proppian structural approach further than Propp himself intended— analysis of the fairytale genre. Such criticism cannot be justified, as such a seminal approach as the Proppian (and the Levi-Straussian, as well), should be applied, with care and caution, to other genres, and both Sasson and Blenkinssop were correct in doing so. See also P. J. Milne, *Vladimir Propp and the Study of Structure in Hebrew Biblical Narrative* (Sheffield, 1988).

Another research approach prevalent among biblical scholars is that of "oral poetry" established by Parry and Lord. Cf. also Y. Zakovich, "From the Oral to the Written Tale in the Bible," *Mekhkrey Yerushalayim be-Folklor Yehudi* [Jerusalem Studies in Jewish Folklore] 1 (1981): 9–43 [H] and R. C. Culley, "Oral Tradition and Biblical Studies," *Oral Tradition* 1 (1986): 30–65. On these schools and their methods in biblical scholarship, see Yassif, "The Study."

3. On the genre approach in the study of folk narrative, compare the general discussions of Ben-Amos, *Genres*, and Dégh, "Narrative." The application of the doctrine of folkloristic genres in biblical research also began with the works of Gunkel on legends of the Book of Genesis and on the fairy tale in the Hebrew Bible (supra, note 1). A broad generic classification of the biblical tales is found in Eissfeld (supra, note 1), G. W. Coats, *Saga, Legend, Tale, Novella, Fable: Narrative Forms in Old Testament Literature* (Sheffield, 1985). The last, however is flawed in its lack of understanding of the generic classification in modern folkloristics. More successful attempts to distinguish biblical tales generically were made by Rofé, *Tales of the Prophets*, and Kirkpatrick (supra, note 1), which tries to resolve the general confusion over this problem among biblical scholars.

4. The literature published on the myth, its origins, and meaning is quite extensive, and need not be cited here. There is a direct connection to the present discussion in the classic book of G. S. Kirk, *Myth. Its Meaning and Function in Ancient and Other Cultures* (Cambridge, 1970). For aspects of the myth as a folk genre, see P. Maranda, ed., *Mythology. Selected Readings* (Harmondsworth, 1972); A. Dundes, ed., *Sacred Narrative. Readings in the Theory of Myth* (Berkeley and Los Angeles, 1984), and the extensive literature mentioned in the latter. The link between the study of myths and biblical literature began as early as the Solar school in nineteenth-century folklore studies (on this see Yassif, supra, note 1), and grew stronger with the discovery and study of mythological texts from the ancient Near East. Compare the classic books of H. Gunkel, *Schöpfung und Chaos in Urzeit and Endzeit* (Göttingen, 1895); A. T. Clay, *The Origin of Biblical Traditions. Hebrew Legends in Babylonia and Israel* (New Haven, 1923); Y. Kaufmann, *The Religion of Israel: From Its Beginnings to the Babylonian Exile*, trans. and abridged by M. Greenberg (Chicago, 1960), pp. 60–147; F. M.

Cross, *Canaanite Myth and Hebrew Epic: Essays in the History of the Religion of Israel* (Cambridge, Mass., 1973); T. H. Gaster, *Myth, Legend and Custom in the Old Testament* (New York, 1969); F. Blanqart, ed., *La Création dans l'Orient Ancient* (Paris, 1987); and U. Cassuto, *Biblical and Canaanite Literature* (Jerusalem, 1983) [H]. The texts from the ancient Near East were collected in J. B. Pritchard, ed., *Ancient Near Eastern Texts Relating to the Old Testament* (Princeton, 1969).

Yehezkel Kaufmann's well-known argument, that mythological elements in the Hebrew Bible are borrowed from other nations of the ancient Near East, while the ancient Hebrews, the framers of monotheism, never created myths, is apologetic and does not bear close scrutiny. On the contrary, if not for the rigid censorship of mythological materials in biblical literature, we would undoubtedly have much more numerous and developed Hebrew myths. On Kaufmann's hypothesis and its critical treatment, see: M. Halbertal and A. Margalit, *Idolatry*, (Cambridge, Mass. and London, 1992), pp. 67–107.

On the concept of demythologization, cf. Z. Levi, "Demythologization or Remythologization," *Bar-Ilan University Yearbook* 22–23 (1988): 205–228 [H]; "Entmythisierung," *Enzyklopädie des Märchens*, Vol. 4 (Berlin, 1982), pp. 21–42; M. Lüthi, *The European Folktale: Form and Nature* (Philadelphia, 1982), pp. 66–80; and L. Honko, "The Problem of Defining Myth," in Dundes (op. cit. n. 4), pp. 42–44. On the demythologization that began in myths of the ancient Near East with the transition to biblical literature, cf. Kaufmann, *History*, ibid.; Eissfeld, *An Introduction* (supra, note 1), pp. 36–37; M. Weinfeld, *Deuteronomy and the Deuteronomic School* (Oxford, 1972), pp. 190–209; and T. Frymer-Kensky, *In the Wake of the Goddesses: Women, Culture, and the Biblical Transformation of Pagan Myth* (New York, 1992), pp. 83–186.

Scholarship has approached the myth of God's battle with the primeval monsters from various points of view: K. Wakemann, *God's Battle with the Monster. A Study in Biblical Imagery* (Leiden, 1973); J. Day, *God's Conflict with the Dragon and the Sea. Echoes of a Canaanite Myth in the Old Testament* (Cambridge, 1985); J. H. Gronbaek, "Baal's Battle with Yam—A Canaanite Creation Fight," *Journal for the Study of the Old Testament* 33 (1985): 27–44; C. Westermann, *Genesis 1–11. A Commentary*, trans. J. J. Scullion (London, 1984), pp. 363–383, and the vast literature cited in the latter.

Many dealt with the story of the Garden of Eden as a myth, indicating variants in the ancient Near East, analyzing its mythic structure, and ascertaining its significance. Compare the extensive literature cited in Westermann, ibid.; S. Niditch, *Chaos to Cosmos. Studies in Biblical Patterns of Creation* (Chico, Cal., 1985); D. Jobling, *The Sense of Biblical Narrative: Structural Analysis in the Hebrew Bible* (Sheffield, 1986) (morphological analysis in the Proppian approach); S. G. F. Brandon, *Creation Legends of the Ancient Near East* (London, 1963); E. R. Leach, *Genesis as Myth and Other Essays* (London, 1969) (Lévi-Straussian approach); and H. N. Wallace, *The Eden Narrative* (Atlanta, 1985) (according to the Parry-Lordian approach to oral poetry).

On the tale of the Tower of Babel, cf. Westermann, pp. 537–540, and the literature there cited. An important Sumerian variant of this tale was published by S. Kramer, "The 'Babel of Tongues': A Sumerian Version," *Journal of the American Oriental Society* 88 (1968): 108–111.

The myth of the sons of God and the daughters of man is discussed at length in Westermann, ibid., pp. 363–383; Niditch, ibid., pp. 38–40; U. Cassuto, "The Story of the Sons of God and the Daughters of Man," in *Biblical and Canaanite Literature* (op. cit.) pp. 98–107 [H]; P. D. Hanson, "Rebellion in Heaven," *Journal of Biblical Literature* 96 (1979): 195–233; O. Davidson, "The Mythical Foundation of History: a Religious-Semiotic Analysis of the Story of the Fall," *Linguistica Biblica* 51 (1982): 23–36; and R. S. Hendel, "Of Demigods and Deluge: Toward an Interpretation of Genesis 6:1–4," *Journal of Biblical Literature* 106 (1987): 13–26.

On the development of this myth after the Bible and later versions, see M. Delcor, "Le myth de la chute des anges et de l'origine de géants comme explication du mal dans le monde dans l'apocalyptique juive: Histoire des traditions," *Revue d'Histoire des Religions* 190 (1976): 3–53.

The story of the Flood is discussed at length in all the books that dealt with a comparison of Scripture and the ancient Near East. The comparison focused primarily on the Babylonian Epic of Gilgamesh. See also the texts in Clay and Pritchard (supra). Also: W. G. Lambert & A. R. Millard, *Atra-hasis: The Babylonian Story of the Flood* (Oxford, 1969); Westermann, ibid., pp. 384–458, and the exhaustive literature cited therein; and S. Loewenstamm, "The Flood," *The N. H. Tur-Sinai* Book (Jerusalem, 1959/1960), pp. 3–26 [H]. Y. M. Grintz, in *Yihudo ve-Kadmuto shel Sefer Bereshit* [*The Singularity and Antiquity of the Book of Genesis*] (Jerusalem, 1983), pp. 42–46 [H], compares in detail the biblical tale to the Babylonian one. A broad comparative look at flood stories in different cultures can be found in R. Andrée, *Die Flutsagen* (Braunschweig, 1891) and E. Böklen, "Die Sintflutsage. Versuch einer neuen Erklärung," *Archiv für Religionswissenschaft* 6 (1903): 1–6, 97–150.

For an analysis of the flood story according to the Lévi-Straussian approach, see M. Casalis, "The Dry and the Wet: A Semiological Analysis of Creation and Flood Myths," *Semiotica* 17 (1976): 35–67.

For a folkloristic approach to another typical etiological myth in Genesis, see D. Noy, "The Transformations of Lot's Wife," in *A Volume in Honor of Zalman Shazar* (Jerusalem, 1972–1973), pp. 20–37 [H], and A.D. Aycock, "The Fate of Lot's Wife," in *Structuralist Interpretations of Biblical Myth*, E. Leach and A.D. Aycock eds. (Cambridge, 1983), pp. 113–119.

5. On the myth of the creation of the first woman cf. Westermann (supra, note 4), pp. 225–236; A. Krappe, "The Birth of Eve," *Occident and Orient, Moses Gaster Anniversary Volume* (London, 1936), pp. 312–322; P. Schwartz, *Die Neue Eva: Der Sündenfall in Volksglauben und Volkserzülung* (Göttingen, 1973); and R. Graves, *Adam's Rib and Other Anomalous Elements in the Hebrew Creation Myth* (London, 1955).

A student of Freud devoted a monograph to a psychoanalytical approach to the myth of the creation of woman: T. Reik, *The Creation of Woman* (New York, 1960). On the medieval tale of Lilith as "the first Eve" and its links to the biblical tale, see Yassif, *Ben Sira*, pp. 63–71. On other myths connected with the women in Genesis, see N. Wander, "Structure, Contradiction and Resolution in Mythology: Father's Brother's Daughter Marriage and the Treatment of Women in Genesis 11–50," *Journal of the Ancient Near Eastern Society* 13 (1981): 75–99.

On the tale of Jacob's struggle with the angel, see Gunkel, *The Folktale* (supra, note 1), pp. 83–87; and on the structuralist analysis according to the structural approach of V. Propp, R. Barthes, "The Struggle with the Angel," in his *Image-Music-Text. Essays Selected and Translated by Stephen Heath* (Glasgow, 1977), pp. 125–141; S. A. Geller, "The Struggle at the Jabbok: The Uses of Enigma in Biblical Narrative," *Journal of the Ancient Near Eastern Society* 14 (1982): 37–50; and C. Westermann, *Genesis 12–36: A Commentary*, trans. J. J. Scullion (Minneapolis, 1985), pp. 512–521. Westermann points out the similarities of style and pattern to the tale of the bloody bridegroom (Exod. 4:24–26), yet another typical combat-myth. Compare also the additional literature on this tale and the interesting use of rabbinic Midrash for its interpretation in Y. Avishur, "On the Fictional Character of the Bloody Bridegroom Tale," *Eshel Beer-Sheva* 2 (1980): 1–10 [H]. The author makes interesting use here of formulas of Babylonian incantations for desert travellers (such as Moses and his family), and of tales of demons who swallowed their victims as far as the missing foreskin (if they were circumcised), to interpret Zipporah's remark "Surely a bloody bridegroom art thou to me/A bloody bridegroom thou art, because of the circumcision," which recalls the style of these invocations of defense. A broad analysis of the studies of this demonic tale is found in B. P.

Robinson, "Zipporah to the Rescue: A Contextual Study of Exodus IV 24-6," *Vetus Testamentum* 36 (1986): 447-461.

6. Since the Grimm Brothers' classic definition of the legend (*sage*) as a "historical" genre, study of it has developed along several lines. For general definitions, see Dégh, "Narrative," pp. 72-80; W. Seidespinner, "Sage und Geschichte: Zur Problematik Grimmscher Konzeptionen und was wir daraus lernen können," *Fabula* 33 (1992): 14-38; L. Röhrich, *Folktales and Reality*, trans. P. Tokofsky (Bloomington and Indianapolis, 1991), pp. 9-26. On the legend as sacred history, cf. W. R. Bascom, "The Forms of Folklore: Prose Narratives," *Journal of American Folklore* 78 (1965): 3-20 and the general surveys and extensive bibliography in Ben-Amos, *Genres*; also note 69 in Chapter 4, below (the rabbinic period); W. D. Hand, ed., *American Folk Legend: A Symposium* (Berkeley, 1971); L. Petzoldt, ed., *Vergleichende Sagenforschung* (Darmstadt, 1969); L. Röhrich, ed., *Probleme der Sagenforschung* (Freiburg and Breisgau, 1973), and the book which covers most aspects of the genre: H. P. Ecker, *Die Legende—Kulturanthropologische Annäherung und eine literarische Gattung* (Stuttgart and Weimar, 1993).

7. Gunkel discerned the tales' independence within the patriarchal story cycle (cf. supra, note 1). Many studies have been published on the tale of Avram and Sarai in Egypt, and compare the discussion of these in Westermann (supra, note 5), pp. 159-168. Of unique importance from the perspective of folkloristic discussion is the study of J. Van Seters, *Abraham in History and Tradition* (New Haven, 1975); S. Niditch, *Underdogs and Tricksters: Prelude to Biblical Folklore* (San Francisco, 1987), pp. 23-69; and Coats (supra, note 3), pp. 71-81. Van Seters regards the version in Genesis 12 as the ur-text from which descended the other versions. Niditch, conversely, sees a separate orientation in each of the versions: the version in Genesis 12 is "popular," that in Genesis 20 is "courtly," and that in Genesis 26 is "homiletical." On the later developments of the tale in the Midrash and the use made of them to understand the scriptural text, see Y. Zakovich and A. Shinan, *Avram and Sarai in Egypt. Genesis XII 10-20 in the Bible, in the Ancient Targums and in the Early Jewish Literature* (Jerusalem, 1983) [H].

8. The important discussion of the legendary and literary aspects of the tales of Elijah and Elisha is Rofé's book, *Tales of the Prophets* (supra.), which distinguishes between various sorts of prophetic legend—the historical legend, the vita, and the literary legend—that underwent revision by the scribes. L. Bronner, *The Stories of Elijah and Elisha* (Leiden, 1968), points out the connection between these tales and motifs from the Ugaritic and Canaanite mythology. Her conclusion from these parallels is that the author of the tales wrote them as a polemic directed against the Canaanite mythology. In her opinion, these are not folktales but a theological polemic against the folk beliefs in Baal (pp. 139-140). Even if it is so (and her conclusions do not seem convincing to me), the theological polemic was created only in the transmission stage of the folk traditions to the biblical literature. The motifs that Bronner indicates prove their dispersion in the folk traditions of the ancient Near East, and the fact that Canaanite mythological motifs became legendary motifs in the Hebrew folk literature of the biblical period (in other words, they were demythologized).

9. Gunkel ascertained the legendary nature of the patriarchal tales in the introduction to his interpretation of the Book of Genesis: "Die Sagen der Genesis," in *Genesis. Übersetzt und erklärt von Herman Gunkel* (Göttingen, 1910). Compare the detailed discussion in Kirkpatrick (supra, note 1), pp. 81 ff., who argues that the patriarchal stories were created in a period in which the family was the basic sociological unit. Only in the monarchical period were these traditions set down in writing. For an overview of the entire subject, including an analysis of the tales and the studies made of them, see Westermann (supra, note 4), pp. 30-58. Westermann emphasizes here that approaching the stories of the Book of Genesis as

folktales is the most convincing explanation of their literary form. Westermann also discusses the socio-historical role of the patriarchal tales—to give generations to come a connection to their past. Folk legend scholars defined its social role in exactly the same manner.

10. On the folkloric motifs in the Book of Jonah and their variants in the medieval folklore, see H. Schmidt, *Jona—Eine Untersuchung zur vergleichenden Religionsgeschichte* (Göttingen, 1907) and U. Steffen, *Das Mysterium von Tod und Auferstehung: Formen und Wandlungen des Jona-Motives* (Göttingen, 1963). For a generic discussion of the Book of Jonah, defining it as "a tale with a lesson" instead of as a legend (as the prophet performs no miracle—rather miracles are done for him), see Rofé, *Tales of the Prophets*, pp. 128–143. For another definition of the composition, as a satire that evolved from the myths of a monster swallowing the hero, a satire whose barbs were directed toward the Jewish people's tendency to isolate itself from the other nations, see A. Lacoque and P. E. Lacoque, *Jonah. A Psycho-Religious Approach to the Prophet* (Columbia, South Carolina, 1990).

On the framework of the Book of Job as a folktale, see Pfeiffer (supra, note 1), pp. 668–670, and the literature cited there. On the epic laws of Olrik employed in analyzing the framework of the Book of Job, see note 2, above. A different approach to this story, one that sees in it an artistic creation of literature, is formulated in M. Weiss, *The Story of Job's Beginning: Job 1–2, a Literary Analysis* (Jerusalem, 1983). On Job as a legendary figure in the ancient Near East, compare N. H. Tur-Sinai, "Job," *Biblical Encyclopedia*, vol. 1, pp. 245–246 [H]. Here he turns to Accadian variants on a king of one of the Babylonian cities, his fall from greatness and the sickness he suffered through no fault of his own, his subsequent cure, and return to his high position. Likewise, an ancient Indian legend about a contest-wager among the gods, who put a righteous king to the test. In spite of the injuries done him, he withstands all trials.

11. Gunkel, *The Folktale* (pp. 135–138), locates the tale of David and Goliath between similar stories in the Bible itself and international folklore. Likewise, the clash between the youth and the older man (David and Saul), the success of the youngest son in fraternal rivalries, the youngest son saving his tribe. An important work analyzing the tale according to the Russian Formalist method is that of H. Jason, "The Tale of David and Goliath: Folk Epic?" *Hasifrut* 23 (1976): 23–41 [H]. Compare this to "Deborah and Barak—What Do They Have in Common with an Epic?" *Shnaton le-Mikra u-Mizrah Kadum* 5–6 (1980/1981/1981/1982): 79–87 [H]. A. Rofé sees the origin of the tale in the genre of fairytale, when the theological dimension added to it only at a later stage. An analysis of the tale according to the Russian Formalist method proves that the structure of the tale of David and Goliath parallels that of the fairytale. Nonetheless, the version before us, as well as the variant on Elhanan, the son of Yaare-oregim, is a legend par excellence, anchored in time and in place. Compare also S. Hon, "Who Killed the Philistine?" *Beit Mikra* 29 (1979/1980): 88–92 [H] and A. Rofé, "David's War against Goliath—Legend, Theology and Eschatology," *Eshel Beer Sheva* 3 (1986): 55–90 [H]. On additional folkloric motifs in the tales of David see D. M. Gunn, *The Story of King David: Genre and Interpretation* (Sheffield, 1978).

12. The terms "memorat" and "chronikat" were first defined as folkloric genres by C. W. von Sydow, *Selected Papers on Folklore* (Copenhagen, 1948), esp. pp. 60–85, 127–145; L. Dégh, "The Memorat and the Proto-Memorat," *Journal of American Folklore* 78 (1974): 225–239; and J. Pentikäinen, "Grenzprobleme zwischen Memorat und Sage," *Temenos* 3 (1968): 137–167.

The first to describe "le loi de crystallisation" was A. Van Gennep, *La Formation des Legends* (Paris, 1917). Also see L. Dégh, "Process of Legend Formation," *Fourth International Congress for Folk-Narrative Research in Athens* (Athens, 1965), pp. 77–87 and S. K. D. Stahl, "The Oral Personal Narrative in its Generic Context," *Fabula* 18 (1978): 21–34.

13. The classic theoretical discussions of the fable are considered to be Ben E. Perry,

"Fable," *Studium Generale* 12 (1959): 17–37; E. Leifried, *Fabel* (Stuttgart, 1976); R. Dithmar, *Die Fabel* (Paderborn, 1974); Thompson, *The Folktale*, pp. 217–224; Noy, *Animals*, pp. 138–169, and the extensive literature there cited.

On "The Tale of Etana," compare the texts in Pritchard, pp. 114–118; I. Levin, "Etana," *Fabula* 8 (1966): 1–63; J. V. Kinnier Wilson, "Some Contributions to the Legend of Etana," *Iraq* 31 (1969): 8–17; H. Freydank, "Die Tierfabel im Etana-Mythus," *Mitteilungen des Institutes für Orientforschung* 17 (1971–2): 1–13; and J. V. Kinnier Wilson, *The Legend of Etana. A New Edition* (Wiltshire, Eng., 1985).

On the fable and the animal tale in the Bible, see Gunkel, *The Folktale*, pp. 37–72; A. M. Vater Solomon, "Fable," in Coats (ibid., note 3), pp. 114–125; R. J. Williams, "The Fable in the Ancient Near East," in *A Stubborn Faith*, ed., E. C. Hobbs (Dallas, 1956), pp. 3–26; and Y. Zakovich, "Aesop's Fables and Biblical Literature," *Yeda Am* 20 (1981): 3–9 [H]. Our discussion of the fable deals only with the narrative fable (fabula) as opposed to the exemplary fable (parable) that, for the most part, does not come under the rubric of folktale. On the distinction between these types of fables, compare Meir, "Fable," and below in chapter 4, section I, the discussion of the fable and the animal tale in rabbinic literature.

14. Gunkel, *The Folktale*, pp. 38–40, regards the Jotham fable as a satire of the monarchy, in that the least suitable candidate ascended to the throne. A full literary analysis of the fable in its historical context is that of U. Simon, "The Fable of Jotham—the Fable and Its Interpretation and their Narrative Framework," *Tarbitz* 34 (1965): 1–34 [H], and earlier literature therein as well. On the ancient Near Eastern variants to the Jotham fable, see Pritchard, pp. 410–411, 592–593. Gaster (supra, note 4), pp. 423–428, offers a variant from the Alexandrian poet Calymachus, on the altercation between the olive and the laurel. When the prickly bush tries to reconcile the pair, they scorn him as inferior (pp. 424–425). On other key fables in the Hebrew Bible, see U. Simon, "The Poor Man's Ewe-Lamb," *Biblica* 48 (1967): 207–242 and Y. Gitay, "The Place and Function of the Song of the Vineyard in Isaiah's Prophecy," in *The Bible*, ed., H. Bloom (New York, 1987), pp. 195–204.

15. German literary theory dealt at length with definitions and development of the novelistic genre. For general definitions and study of the novella, as well as extensive literature, see B. von Weise, *Novelle* (Stuttgart, 1963) and K. K. Polheim, *Novellentheorie und Novellenforschung* (Stuttgart, 1965); and R. J. Clements & J. Gibaldi, *Anatomy of the Novella* (New York, 1977).

On the novella in antiquity (within the sphere of Greek culture), see S. Trenkner, *The Greek Novella in the Classical Period* (Cambridge, 1958); and, on the novella in the study of folk literature, E. Yassif, "The Novella as an Ethnopoetic Genre," *Papers of the Eighth Congress of the International Society for Folk-Narrative Research* (Bergen, 1984), pp. 283–289.

16. On this text and its background, see: M. Lichtheim, *Ancient Egyptian Literature* (Berkeley and Los Angeles, 1976), vol. 2, pp. 203–211. On the link between the biblical tale of Joseph and the realia and culture of ancient Egypt as proof of Egyptian origin of the tale, see Grintz, *The Singularity and Antiquity* (supra, note 4), pp. 100 ff. See especially S. T. Hollis, *The Ancient Egyptian 'Tale of Two Brothers.' The Oldest Fairy Tale in the World* (Oklahoma, 1990). The definition of the Joseph tale as a novella began, not surprisingly, with the biblical studies of Gunkel and Gressman: H. Gressmann, "Ursprung und Entwicklung der Josefsage," *Eucharisterion, Herman Gunkel Festschrift* (Göttingen, 1923), pp. 1–55 and D. B. Redford, *A Study of the Biblical Story of Joseph* (Leiden, 1970) (VTS Vol. 20). He sees the tale as a hybrid genre, a cross between fairy tale and novella, and thus defines it as "novellenmärchen." Gunkel defined it similarly: "Zwischen Sagenkranz und Novelle." Cf. H. Donner, *Die literarische Gestalt der alttestamentlichen Josephsgeschichte* (Heidelberg, 1976) and G. W.

Coats, *From Canaan to Egypt. Structural and Theological Context for the Joseph Story* (Washington D.C., 1976).

For a general discussion of the novella in the Hebrew Bible that puts the genre at the center of the discussion of the Joseph story cycle, see W. Lee Humphreys, "Novella," in Coats (ibid., note 3); idem, *Joseph and His Family. A Literary Study* (Columbia, S.C., 1988).

17. Niditch (supra, note 4), pp. 126–145, contains an analysis of the folkloric elements of the Scroll of Esther. She emphasizes the great density of folk motifs of wicked men, beautiful maidens, foolish kings, betrayals, and deceptions, relative to the other books of the Bible. She also makes salient the "fairytale" construction of the tale, with Esther as a "Jewish Cinderella" who rises to greatness. On this matter, Niditch points out the similarity to the tale of Joseph, brought out earlier, and cf. M. Gan, "The Scroll of Esther as Viewed Through Joseph's Experiences in Egypt," *Tarbiz* 31 (1962): 144-149 [H]. The similarity of themes and literary construction in the tales of Joseph and Esther bolsters my argument that both belong to the same genre—that of the novella.

On the tale of Esther as "the rise of the wise courtier," see S. Niditch and R. Doran, "The Success Story of the Wise Courtier," *Journal of Biblical Literature* 96 (1977): 179-193; W. Lee Humphreys, "The Story of Esther and Mordechai: An Early Jewish Novella," in Coats (supra, note 3), pp. 97-113, and the detailed and careful comparison of the Hebrew and Greek versions of the book: L. M. Wills, *The Jew in the Court of the Foreign King: Ancient Jewish Court Legends* (Minneapolis, 1990), pp. 153-192—"Esther: From Court Legend to Novella"; and in a more text-based argument, Wills, *The Novel*, pp. 93-131.

For a detailed comparison of the Scroll of Esther and the tale of Scheherazade (the framework tale of *The Arabian Nights*), see E. Cosquin, "Le Prologue-Cadre des Mille et Une Nuits, Les légends Perses et Les Livre D'Esther," *Revue Biblique* N.S. 6 (1909): 7-49, 161-197.

18. The first to point out the folk character of the tale and gather more than twenty variants, mostly from India, was H. Gressman, "Das Salomonische Urteil," *Deutsche Rundschau* 130 (1907): 212-228. Compare the interesting article of E. Lipinski, "Ancient Types of Wisdom Literature in Biblical Narrative," *I. L. Seeligmann Volume*, 3 (Jerusalem, 1983), pp. 39-50, that places the tale in the category of "King's Bench Tales." He offers variants from Babylonia and Sumer for tales of the King's wisdom revealed in court, and especially trials of simple folk presided over by the king, whose wisdom is thereby revealed publicly.

19. On folk story cycles see, for example, J. L. Fischer, "The Sociopsychological Analysis of Folktales," *Current Anthropology* 4 (1963): 235-295.

Important contextual research has proven that folk storytellers in Tunisia favor story cycles over isolated tales. They customarily string together tales of the cycle on a particular theme, or associatively (a saying popular among them is, "one tale leads to another"). The tales of the cycle explain each other, and their intention is to substantiate a moral idea, historical event, or the like. Compare S. J. Webber, *Romancing the Real: Folklore and Ethnographic Representation in North Africa* (Philadelphia, 1991), pp. 112-115, 128 ff. Rofé, in *Tales of the Prophets*, pp. 48-49, also claims that the tales of Elisha existed as a cycle of tales told orally prior to their being set down in writing in the Bible. On the concept of the story cycle in the Hebrew Bible, see Z. Weissman, *The Story Cycle of Jacob and its Introduction into the History of the Nation's Patriarchs* (Jerusalem, 1986), pp. 37-38 [H]. Cf. also Wills (op. cit. note 17), pp. 150-151.

20. Extensive literature has been published on the saga, both as the beginning of Scandinavian literature, and because of the form's importance in the history of folk literature. Compare, for example, S. Einarsson, *A History of Icelandic Literature* (Baltimore, 1967), pp. 122-151; K. Liestol, *The Origin of the Icelandic Family Sagas* (Oslo, 1930); T. M. Andersson,

"The Icelandic Sagas," in *Heroic Epic and Saga*, ed., F. J. Oinas (Bloomington and London, 1978), pp. 144–171; J. L. Byock, *Medieval Iceland: Society, Sagas and Power* (Berkeley, 1988), and the vast literature cited in the latter two. Some works have been published on the saga in the Hebrew Bible, most of which confused the generic term "sage" (the German equivalent of legend) with the "saga," that is, the Nordic story cycle. The first to define the patriarchal story cycle as a saga was Jolles, and compare, regarding the issue as a whole, Kirkpatrick (supra, note 1), p. 81. A. Jolles, *Einfache Formen: Legende, Sage, Mythe etc.* [Halle, 1956] claimed that the patriarchal tales, as opposed to other story cycles in the Bible, are not interested in events and matters of state, but rather in family ties. In his opinion, the patriarchal story cycles were created in a period in which the family was the basic sociological unit. Compare Westermann (supra, note 5), pp. 30–58, who views the patriarchal tales as "Sagen" and the inclusive unit as "Saga," a distinction that is very reasonable. In the chapter devoted to the saga in Coats (supra, note 3), pp. 26 ff., he stumbles over all the obstacles trumpeted before the publication of his work.

21. On the components of truth and fiction in historical writing in antiquity, see J. Van Seters, *In Search of History* (New Haven and London 1983); R. E. Friedman, ed., *The Poet and the Historian. Essays in Literary and Historical Biblical Criticism* (Chico, 1983); and the methodological discussion on the problem of "history as literature" in E. Weinryb, *Historical Thinking, Chapters in the Philosophy of History* (Tel Aviv, 1986), pp. 389–454 [H].

On the saga's claim of historical truth, compare the important discussion in Liestol (supra, note 20), pp. 233–254 ("The family Sages claim to be history").

On the general problems connected with the historicity of oral traditions, see R. M. Dorson, "The Debate over the Trustworthiness of Oral Tradition History," *Volksüberlieferung. Festschrift für Kurt Ranke* (Göttingen, 1968), pp. 19–35; J. Vansina, *Oral Tradition. A Study in Historical Methodology* (Harmondsworth, 1973); and P. Thompson, *The Voice of the Past: Oral History* (Oxford, 1978). On this question from the point of view of biblical scholarship, see J. Van Seters, *Abraham in History and Tradition* (New Haven and London, 1975); idem, *In Search of History* (supra); and K. R. Andriolo, "Myth and History: A General Model and its Application to the Bible," *American Anthropologist* 83 (1981): 261–284.

22. Abundant literature has been published on folk saints' legends, addressing itself primarily to material from the medieval period on. The classic work in this field is still considered to be H. Delehaye, *The Legends of the Saints* (New York, 1962 [first published 1905]); R. Aigrain, *L'Hagiographie. Ses Sources, ses méthodes, son histoire* (Paris, 1953). Compare also the encompassing and annotated bibliography on the subject (containing more than 1,300 entries) in Wilson, *Saints*. Also see Loomis, *White Magic* and Ben-Ami, *Saints*, pp. 56–69.

"The biographical pattern" of the cultural hero has been an object of folkloric inquiry since the nineteenth century, when various such patterns were suggested to describe the similarity of the biographies of cultural heroes of different peoples. Compare also the history of scholarship on this subject and the extensive literature in A. Dundes, "The Hero Pattern and the Life of Jesus," in his *Interpreting Folklore* (Bloomington and London, 1980), pp. 223–262, 282–287; D. Noy, "The Figure of the Messiah as Folk Hero," *Mahanayyim* 124 (1970): 114–125 [H]. In his classic study of "the biographical pattern," Lord Raglan treated three biblical figures: Joseph, Moses, and Elijah: L. Raglan, "The Hero of Tradition," in *The Study of Folklore*, ed., A. Dundes (Englewood Cliffs, 1965), pp. 142–157. On the role of this pattern in the patriarchal cycle of legends, consult A. Brenner, "Female Social Behavior: Two Descriptive Patterns Within the 'Birth of the Hero' Paradigm," *Vetus Testamentum* 36 (1986): 257–273.

On matching the "pattern" to the tale of Samson, see Zakovich (supra, note 4), p. 230. Much has been published on Samson as a mythic figure and a comparison of his biography with that of Heracles-Hercules. Works representative of the various approaches include: H. Stainthal, "Die Sage von Simson," *Zeitschrift für Völkerpsychologie und Sprachwissenschaft* 2 (1862): 129–178; A. S. Palmer, *The Samson Saga and Its Place in Comparative Religion* (New York, 1913); H. Gunkel, "Simson," *Reden und Aufsätze* (Göttingen, 1913), pp. 38–64; O. Margalith, "Samson's Foxes," *Vetus Testamentum* 35 (1985): 224–229; idem, "Samson's Riddle and Samson's Magic Locks," ibid. 36 (1986): 225–234; and idem, "More Samson Legends," ibid., 397–405.

Plentiful literature has also been published on the hero in folk literature. Compare, for example: E. E. Klapp, "The Folk Hero," *Journal of American Folklore* 62 (1949): 17–25; D. Norman, *The Hero: Myth, Image, Symbol* (New York, 1969); on the figure of the hero in the Hebrew Bible, see H. Gunkel, *Israelitisches Heldentum und Kriegsfrömigkeit im Alten Testament* (Göttingen, 1916).

On the figure of the hero in the Scroll of Esther, and the literary model of "the rise of the wise Jewish courtier," cf. note 17, above.

23. On the comparison of biblical tales to myths of antiquity and the process of demythologization in biblical literature, cf. note 4, supra. On the mythological and anti-mythological processes taking place in the story of the binding of Isaac, see the classic work of S. Spiegel, *The Last Trial* (New York, 1967); H. C. White, "The Initiations Legend of Isaac," *Zeitschrift für alttestamentliche Wissenschaft* 91 (1979): 1–30, and the additional literature on this subject cited in E. Yassif., ed., *The Binding of Isaac. Studies in the Development of Literary Tradition* (Jerusalem, 1978) [H].

The monologue of Sargon, King of Agade, is quoted in Pritchard (supra, note 4), p. 119; cf. also Ch. Cohen, "Hebrew tbh: Proposed Etymologies," *Journal of Near East Studies* 4 (1972): 46–51; S. E. Loewenstamm, "Die Geburstgeschichte Moses," *Studies in Jewish Religious and Intellectual History Presented to Alexander Altman* (Alabama, 1979), pp. 195–213. On the mythological figure of Samson, see note 22, above.

24. On the intentionally didactic nature of Jewish folktales, see B. Heller, "Tendences et idées juives dans les contes Hebreux," *Revue Des Etudes Juifs* 77 (1923): 97–126 and D. Noy, "Folklore," *Encyclopedia Judaica* (Jerusalem, 1974), 6, cols. 1374–1410.

3. The Second Temple Period

1. On literature of the Second Temple period, see the general introductions and extensive literature contained in N. de Lange, *Apocrypha: Jewish Literature Between the Bible and the Mishnah* (London, 1981); J. H. Charlesworth, *The Pseudepigrapha and Modern Research* (Ann Arbor, 1981); M. E. Stone, ed., *Jewish Writings of the Second-Temple Period* (Philadelphia, 1984); Schürer, *History*, 3, Part 1, pp. 170–469; and M. De Jonge, ed., *Outside the Old Testament* (Cambridge, 1985). On the folk genres in this period among Christian circles, cf. R. Bultman, *History of the Synoptic Tradition* (New York, 1963), pp. 209–244 and J. Quasten, "The Beginnings of Christian Romance, Folk Stories and Legends," in his *Patrology* (Westminster, Md., 1990²). The standard editions of the books in English are: R. H. Charles, ed., *The Apocrypha and Pseudepigrapha of the Old Testament* (Oxford, 1913) and J. H. Charlesworth, ed., *The Old Testament Pseudepigrapha* (London, 1983–1985).

2. On these Hebrew texts that survived from the medieval period, see Dan, *The Middle Ages*, pp. 22–23; Flusser, *Josippon*, pp. 148–153; I. Lévi, "L'histoire 'De Suzanne et les Deux Vieillards' dans la littérature juive," *Revue des Etudes Juives* 95 (1933): 157–158; A. M. Dubarle, *Judith. Formes et sens des diverses Traditions* (Rome, 1966); and idem, "L'authenticité des textes Hébreux de Judith," *Biblica* 50 (1969): 187–211.

3. On the *Book of Ahikar* and the *Book of Joseph and Asenath*, compare the general intro-

ductions cited in note 1, above. The Aramaic version from Elephantine is translated in Charlesworth, *Pseudepigraph*, 2:479–508. Cf. also F. C. Conybeare, J. Rendel-Harris, and A. Smith Lewis, *The Story of Ahikar* (Cambridge, 1913). The tale of Ahikar is classified as tale type AT 922. Compare also the literature cited in Aarne and Thompson, ibid., as well as: A. H. Krappe, "Is the Story of Ahiqar the Wise of Indian Origin?" *Journal of the American Oriental Society* 61 (1941): 280–284 and R. Degen, "Achikar," *Enzyclopädie des Märchens* (Berlin, 1977), 1: cols. 53–59.

V. Aptowitzer, "Asenath, the Wife of Joseph—a Haggadic, Literary-Historical Study, *HUCA* 1 (1924): 239–306, studies its Jewish sources and parallels. Wills, *The Novel*, pp. 158–183, treats it as part of the Joseph traditions of the Second Temple period.

4. On the historical background of the period, cf. Schürer (supra, note 1) and I. Gafni, "The Historical Background," in Stone (op. cit. n. 1), pp. 1–32. H. Kreissig, *Die sozialen Zusammenhänge des Judäischen Krieges* (Berlin, 1970), boldly raises interesting social questions regarding the class tensions in Jerusalem during the period of the Great Revolt, the folk strata of craftsmen, wanderers, beggars, prostitutes, and the like. On the relationship between Jews and pagans in the ancient world, see the important survey of L. H. Feldman, *Jew and Gentile in the Ancient World* (Princeton, 1993).

On the historical legends in the literature of the Second Temple period, Bickerman argues, "Jewish literature of the Hellenistic age belongs in great part to the genre of historical fiction," E. Bickerman, *The Jews in the Greek Age* (Cambridge, Mass., 1988), p. 203; cf. G. W. E. Nickelsburg, "Stories of Biblical and Early Post-Biblical Times," Stone (op. cit. n. 1), pp. 33–88.

On the historical legend as genre, and its position between history and folklore, see Yassif, *The Study* (1988), pp. 3–11, and the literature cited there, and note 6 to chapter 2, above, and to chapter 4, below, note 69.

5. The "defiler of the sacred is punished" is the Jewish tale type AT 771*, see A. Marcus, "The Defiler of the Sacred is Punished (AT 771*)," *Studies in Agaddah and Jewish Folklore in Honor of Dov Noy's 60th Birthday*, ed. J. Dan and I. Ben-Ami (Jerusalem, 1982, *Mekhkarey ha-Merkaz le-Heker ha-Folklor* [Studies of the Center for Folklore Research], 7), pp. 337–366 [H]; on tales of the confrontation between the Jewish people and the other nations, see Noy, "Yemen" and Marcus, "Confrontation."

6. Nickelsburg (in Stone, supra, note 1), pp. 82 ff., presents the folk background of the tale, as does Charlesworth, *Modern Research* (supra, note 1), pp. 149–151; and see H. Jason, "A Tale of Anti-Semitism in the Ancient Period," *Mahanayyim* 76 (1963): 130–135 [H] and Bickerman (supra, note 4), pp. 234–236. Wills, *The Novel*, pp. 193–206, defines these stories as "historical novels," and their main function as "temple propaganda." However, they have nothing in common with the novel genre.

7. On the motif of miraculous rescue of the Jewish community and the communal "Second Purim" celebrations, see Marcus, "Confrontation," pp. 346–349; T. Alexander, "A Second Purim—A Family's Reflection: Literary Tradition, Self Image, and Ethnic Identity," *Mehkarei Yerushalayyim be-Folklor Yehudi* [Jerusalem Studies in Jewish Folklore] 13–14 (1991–1992): 349–370 [H]; chapter 2, above, note 17; and M. Ginzburger, "Deux Pourims locaux," *Hebrew Union College Annual* 10 (1935): 445–450.

8. On the Book of Judith and its historical background, cf. Y. M. Grintz, *The Book of Judith* (Jerusalem, 1957) [H]; L. Alonso-Schökel, "Narrative Structures in the Book of Judith," *The Center for Hermeneutical Studies in Hellenistic and Modern Culture*, Colloqui II (Berkeley, 1975), pp. 1–20; Wills, *The Novel*, pp. 132–157, and the additional literature cited in note 2, above. On the Book of the Maccabees III cf. note 6, above; Schürer (supra, note 1).

9. C. C. Torey, "The Story of the Three Youths," *American Journal of Semitic Languages*

and Literatures 23 (1907): 177–202; S. A. Cook, in the Charles edition (supra, note 1), pp. 29–34, emphasizes the folk-novelistic origin of the tale, and cf. also Nickelsburg, in Stone (supra, note 1), pp. 131–135.

The *Letter of Aristeas* was published in the aforementioned collections of pseudepigrapha (note 1), and cf. Schürer (ibid.), p. 474 and the extensive literature cited therein; see also H. St. J. Thackery, *The Letter of Aristeas*, trans. with an "Appendix of Ancient Evidence of the Origin of the Septuagint" (London, 1918); N. Meissner, *Untersuchungen zum Aristeasbrief*, 2 vols. (Berlin, 1971). On the tale in rabbinic sources, see E. Tov, "The Rabbinic Tradition Concerning the 'Alterations' Inserted into the Greek Pentateuch and their Relation to the Original Text of the LXX," *Isak Leo Seeligmann Volume*, ed. A. Rofé and Y. Zakovitch (Jerusalem, 1983), pp. 371–394 [H]; and the discussion below, chapter 4, section C. For a brilliant and daring discussion of a learned Jew of the sixteenth century on the talmudic and apocryphal versions of the tale, see Azariah Di-Rossi, *Selected Chapters from Sefer Me'or einayin and Matsref la-Kessef*, ed. R. Bonfil (Jerusalem, 1991), pp. 271–283 (*Imrei Binah*, ch. 7) [H].

10. The transition from the folk novellae and folk legend to historiography and novelistic writing starts as early as Herodotos. See W. Aly, *Volksmärchen, Sage and Novelle bei Herodot und seinen Zeitgenossen* (Göttingen, 1921); J. N. Kazazis, *Herdotos' Stories and History: A Proppian Analysis of His Narrative Period* (Cambridge, 1958); A. E. Wardman, "Myth in Greek Historiography," *Historia* 9 (1960): 403–413; and Wills, *The Novel*, pp. 28–38.

On Josephus Flavius: S. Rappaport, *Agada und Exegese bei Flavius Josephus* (Frankfurt, 1930); S. Niditch, "Father-Son Folktale Patterns and Tyrant Typologies in Josephus," *Journal of Jewish Studies* 32 (1981): 47–55; and D. Golan, "Josephus and Alexander's visit to Palestine: Legend and History," in *Josephus Flavius—Historian of Palestine*, ed. U. Rappaport (Jerusalem, 1983), pp. 29–55 [H]. Wills, *The Novel*, pp. 187–193, deals briefly with the story of the Tobiads.

On the superlative and the contest riddles in general, cf. A. Taylor, *A Bibliography of Riddles* (Helsinki, 1939); idem, *The Literary Riddle Before 1600* (Cambridge, 1949); R. Abrahams, *Between the Living and the Dead* (Helsinki, 1980, FFC No. 225); D. Noy, "Riddles at a Wedding Feast," *Mahanayyim* 83 (1963): 64–71 [H]; and D. Pagis, *A Secret Sealed. The History of the Hebrew Riddle in Italy and Holland* (Jerusalem, 1986), pp. 34–110 [H].

11. On the expanded biblical tale in the Bible itself, see: Y. Zakovitch and A. Shinan, *The Book of Genesis in the Ancient Targumim and in the Ancient Jewish Literature* (Jerusalem, 1983) [H], and further publications in the same series; and the seminal work by M. Fishbane, *Biblical Interpretation in Ancient Israel* (Oxford, 1985).

On the expanded biblical tale as a literary genre, cf. Heineman, *Paths*; Halevy, *Gateways*; W. Wright, *The Literary Genre Midrash* (New York, 1967); G. Vermes, *Scripture and Tradition in Judaism. Haggadic Studies* (Leiden, 1961); and D. Boyarin, *Intertextuality and the Reading of Midrash* (Bloomington and Indianapolis, 1990).

On the expanded biblical tale in the literature of the Second Temple period, see Nickelsburg in Stone (supra, note 1), pp. 89–156. ("The Bible Rewritten and Expanded"); de Lange (supra, note 1), pp. 53–102; Schürer, *History*, 1, pp. 308–341; 2, pp. 706–749, 757–786 ("Biblical Midrash"); P. S. Alexander, "Retelling the Old Testament," in *It is written: Scripture Citing Scripture—Essays in Honour of Barnabas Lindras* (Cambridge, 1988), pp. 99–121; D. J. Harrington, "Abraham Traditions in the Testament of Abraham and in the 'Rewritten Bible' of the Intertestamental Period," in *Studies on the Testament of Abraham*, ed. G. W. E. Nickelsburg (Missoula, 1976), pp. 165–172. An innovative approach is suggested now by: E. S. Gruen, *Heritage and Hellenism: The Reinvention of Jewish Tradition* (Berkeley, Los Angeles, London, 1998).

12. For a condensed list of studies on the story of the Akedah, see E. Yassif, ed., *The Bind-*

ing of Isaac. Studies on the Development of a Literary Tradition (Jerusalem, 1978) [H]; R. Hayward, "The Present State of Research into the Targumic Account of the Sacrifice of Isaac," Journal of Jewish Studies 32 (1981): 127–150, and the insightful: J. D. Levenson, The Death and Resurrection of the Beloved Son (New Haven and London, 1993). On the development of the figure of Satan from the Second Temple literature to early Christianity, see: E. Pagels, The Origin of Satan (New York, 1995), pp. 35–62.

13. On the trial of Job in post-biblical literature see Y. S. Licht, Testing in the Hebrew Scriptures and Post Biblical Judaism (Tel Aviv, 1973) [H]; H. E. Kaufmann, Die Anwendung des Buchs Hiob in der Rabbinschen Agada (Frankfurt, 1893).

On the tale of Placidas and its background, cf. H. Delehaye, "La Legende de Saint Eustache," in Delehaye, Mélange D'hagiographie Greque et Latine (Bruxelles, 1966), pp. 213–239 and E. Yassif, "The Man Who Never Swore an Oath: From Jewish to Israeli Oikotype," Fabula 27 (1987): 216–236.

On the testaments genre and The Testament of Job in particular, see Nickelsburg, Tales; Charlesworth, Modern Research (ibid.), pp. 134–137; H. Kee, "Satan, Magic and Salvation in the Testament of Job," Society of Biblical Literature 1 (1974): 53–76; S. Spiegel, "Noah, Daniel and Job," Louis Ginzberg Jubilee Volume (New York, 1945), pp. 305–351; Y. S. Licht, "The Meaning of the Testament of Job," Proceedings of the Sixth World Congress of Jewish Studies, 1 (Jerusalem, 1977), pp. 147–156 [H].

14. On the pseudepigraphic Book of Joseph and Asenath, see in extenso the introductions cited above in note 1, and Aptowitzer and Wills (supra, note 3). On the Greco-Latin romance genre see, for example, B. Edwin-Perry, The Ancient Romances. A Literary-Historical Account of Their Origins (Berkeley and Los Angeles, 1967); T. Hägg, The Novel in Antiquity (Oxford, 1983), and Wills, The Novel.

On the theme of conversion, the central interest of this work, see: R. D. Chestnutt, From Death to Life: Conversion in Joseph and Asenath (Sheffield, 1995).

15. The comparison of The Testament of Joseph to the tragedy of Hippolytus was first offered and analyzed by M. Braun, History and Romance in Graeco-Oriental Literature (Oxford, 1938); R. I. Perro, "The Testament of Joseph and Greek Romance," in Studies in the Testament of Joseph, ed. G. W. E. Nickelsburg (Missoula, 1975), pp. 15–28; M. Hengel, Judaism and Hellenism. Studies in Their Encounter in Palestine during the Early Hellenistic Period (London, 1974), pp. 110–111; M. Niehoff, "The Figure of Joseph in the Targums," Journal of Jewish Studies 39 (1988): 234–250; H. W. Hollander and M. De Jonge, The Testament of the Twelve Patriarchs. A Commentary (Leiden, 1985), pp. 362–410; and H. W. Hollander, Joseph as an Ethical Model in the Testament of the Twelve Patriarchs (Leiden, 1981). It is to be regretted that J. L. Kugel does not take into account this analogy, in his In Potiphar's House. The Interpretive Life of Biblical Texts (San Francisco, 1990).

16. J. G. Gager, Moses in Greco-Roman Paganism (Nashville and New York, 1972); A. Shinan, "Moses and the Ethiopian Woman: Sources of a Story in the Chronicles of Moses," Scripta Hierosolymitana 27 (1978): 66–78; and T. Rajak, "Moses in Ethiopia: Legend and Literature," Journal of Jewish Studies 29 (1978): 111–122.

17. On the martyrological literature in Christianity, see, for example, Delehaye, Martyrology; H. Delehaye, Les Origines de Culte des Martyrs (Bruxelles, 1933); W. H. C. Frend, Martyrdom and Persecution in the Early Church. A Study of a Conflict from the Maccabees to Donatus (Oxford, 1965); and the considerable literature on martyrology at the dawn of Christianity in Wilson, Saints, pp. 329–336, and in Judaism of the Second Temple period: H. W. Surkau, Martyrium in jüdischer und frühchristlicher Zeit (Göttingen, 1938); E. Tcherikover, "Jewish Martyrology and Jewish Historiography," YIVO Annual of Jewish So-

cial Science 1 (1946): 9–23; H. A. Fischel, "Martyr and Prophet," *Jewish Quarterly Review* 37 (1947): 265–280, 363–386; M. Simon, "Les Saints d'Israél dans la dévotion de l'église Ancienne," *Revue d'Histoire et de Philosophie Religieuses* 34 (1954): 98–127; D. F. Winslow, "The Maccabean Martyrs: Early Christian Attitude," *Judaism* 23 (1974): 78–86; G. W. E. Nickelsburg, *Resurrection, Immortality, and Eternal Life in Intertestamental Judaism* (Cambridge, Mass., 1972). According to the latter, literary-martyrological forms begin in the Hebrew Bible as early as the story of the Servant of God in the Book of Jeremiah and the Book of Daniel, but there is no clear evidence of the genre's penetration to folk literature at so early a stage. Compare also in: *Holy War and Martyrology in the History of the Jewish People and the Nations—Collected Lectures* (Jerusalem, 1965), pp. 7–92 [H], especially the articles of Y. Efron, D. Flusser, and M. D. Hertz. Compare also the collection of articles devoted to the Second Temple period: J. W. Van Henten, ed., *Die Entstehung der Jüdischen Märtyrologie* (Leiden, 1989).

18. The two classic studies of the tale are Y. Gutmann, "The Mother and Her Seven Sons in Aggadah and in the Books of the Hasmoneans II and IV," *Sefer Yohanan Levi* [Book of Yohanan Levi] (Jerusalem, 1949), pp. 25–32 [H]; G. D. Cohen, "The Story of Hannah and Her Seven Sons in Hebrew Literature," *Jubilee Volume for M. M. Kaplan* (New York, 1953), pp. 109–122 [H]; and see also Nickelsburg (supra, note 17), pp. 93–111; E. Bickerman, "Les Maccabées de Malalas," *Byzantion* 21 (1951): 63–83; M. Hadas, "The Third and Fourth Books of Maccabees," in *Jewish Apocryphal Literature*, ed. S. Zeitlin (New York, 1953), pp. 127–135; I. Lévi, "Le Martyre des Sept Macchabées dans la Pesikta Rabbati," *Revue des Etudes Juives* 54 (1907): 138–141; and J. Obermann, "The Sepulcher of the Maccabean Martyrs," *Journal of Biblical Literature* 50 (1931): 250–265.

19. The versions of the work were published in Charles, *Apocrypha*, 2:155–162, and Charlesworth, *Pseudepigrapha*, 2:143–176. For versions of the tale in the Christian literature of the period, see Schürer (supra, note 1), pp. 335–341, and in rabbinic literature—below in chapter 4, notes 25–27; Nickelsburg, in Stone (supra, note 1). The variants in Near Eastern literature can be found in the Persian compositions *Bundahish*, and *King Djemshad and the Diwas* (Charles, *Apocrypha*, p. 158), and a comparative analysis in Gaster and Heller (7: "Der Prophet Jesajah und der Baum," pp. 32–52). On the suppositions that the work originates in the Judean Desert sects, see D. Flusser, "The Apocryphal Book of Ascensio Isaiah and the Dead Sea Sect," *Israel Exploration Journal* 3 (1953): 30–47; M. Philonenko, "Le Martyre d'Esaie et l'historie de la Sect de Qoumran," *Cahiers de la Revue et de Philosophie religieuses* 41 (1967): 1–10.

20. C. C. Torrey, *The Lives of the Prophets* (Philadelphia, 1946); M. Simon, "Les saints d'Israel dans la dévotion de l'Eglise ancienne," *Revue d'histoire et de Philosophie Religieuses* 34 (1954): 98–127; Charlesworth (op. cit. n. 1), pp. 379–400; D. Safran, "The Lives of the Prophets," in Stone (op. cit. n. 1), pp. 56–60; and Schürer, *History*, 3: 783–786. S. Klein was among the first to discern the folkloristic importance of the book in relation to the local traditions in Palestine in the Second Temple period: "On *Vitae Prophetarum*," *Sefer Klausner* [Joseph Klausner Jubilee volume] (Tel Aviv, 1937), pp. 189–209 [H]. Klein's approach was expanded and developed in the excellent study of ancient Jewish folk religion by J. Jeremias, *Heiligengräber in Jesu Umwelt: Eine Untersuchungen zur Volksreligion der Zeit Jesu* (Göttingen, 1958). On the saints' graves at the dawn of Christianity and their ritual importance, see H. Delehaye, "Loca Sanctorum," *Analecta Bollandiana* 48 (1930): 5–64.

21. On the story cycle as a literary form, see chapter 2 above (The Biblical Period), section E, and the literature cited there; and below, chapter 4, section K. Nickelsburg suggested that the Daniel tales form a story cycle (supra, note 1), pp. 19–30. Nickelsburg quotes the tenth

(questionable) tale from *The Prayer of Nabonidus* in Stone (ibid.), pp. 35–37. On the variants to the Daniel tales in rabbinic literature, see Yassif, "Traces." Wills, *The Novel*, pp. 40–67 defines this cycle of stories as a novel. I find no justification for that in his argument.

On the Book of Susannah, see W. Baumgartner, "Susanna. Die Geschichte einer Legende," *Archiv für Religionswissenschaft* 24 (1926): 259–280; H. Engel, *Die Susanna-Erzählung* (Freiburg, Schweiz, 1984); Wills, *The Novel*, pp. 53–60; and J. J. Collins, "The Sage in the Apocalyptic and Pseudepigraphic Literature," in *Seers, Sybils and Sages in Hellenistic-Roman Judaism* (Leiden, 1997), pp. 339–350. S. Sered and S. Cooper, "Sexuality and Social Control: Anthropological Reflections on the Book of Susanna," in E. Spolsky ed., *The Judgment of Susanna: Authority and Witness* (Atlanta, 1996), pp. 43–56, make the distinction between "structural strength" of the elders and "moral strength" of Susanna, an observation I fully support. However it can be applied only to the Theodotion version of the story, and so cannot cover the whole range of possible interpretations. S. Lasine, "Solomon, Daniel, and the Detective Story: The Social Function of a Literary Genre," *Hebrew Annual Review* 11 (1987): 247–266, presents an interesting approach to the Susannah story—as a detective story. Yet it seems unnecessary to back-date the appearance of the genre of the detective story. The tale of Solomon and the two women in the Bible, as well as the Book of Susannah, belong to the novelistic genre, whose definition includes the solution of narrative conflict via cleverness and wile.

On Christian saints' legends as variants of the Daniel tales, see Loomis, *White Magic*, index, "Daniel." On the Daniel tales as a route in the rise of the wise courtier, see Hengel (supra, note 15), pp. 29–32; W. Lee Humphreys, "A Life-Style for Diaspora: A Study of the Tales of Esther and Daniel," *Journal of Biblical Literature* 92 (1973): 211–223; and L. M. Wills, *The Jew in the Court of the Foreign King: Ancient Jewish Court Legends* (Minneapolis, 1990). On the Daniel tales in Rabbinic literature and their variants, see Ginzberg, *Legends*, 4: 326–334, 337–340, 345–350, and the notes therein and Y. M. Grintz, *Chapters in the History of the Second Temple* (Jerusalem, 1969), pp. 66–78 [H].

On tales of King Solomon and their variants in Near Eastern literature, see E. Yassif, "Parables of King Solomon," *Mehkarei Yerushalayyim be-Sifrut Ivrit* [Jerusalem Studies in Hebrew Literature] 9 (1986): 357–373 [H]. For the testimony of Origen, who heard the story of Susannah told among Jews in Palestine in the third century C.E., see B. Heller, "The Additions to the Book of Daniel," in A. Kahana ed. *Ha-Sefarim ha-Hitzonim*, 2 vols (Jerusalem 1970²), 1:556 [H].

22. Versions of the Septuagint and Theodotion are laid out side by side in most versions of the Book of Susannah published in editions of the Apocrypha (supra, note 1). Heller's work is particularly important (supra, note 21). Compare also I. Lévi, "L'historie de Suzanne et les deux vieillards dans la littérature juive," *Revue des Etudes Juives* 95 (1933): 157–171; B. Heller, "Die Susannaerzählung: ein Märchen," *Zeitschrift für die alttestamentliche Wissenschaft* 54 (1936): 281–287, and the additional literature cited in Wills, *The Novel*, pp. 53–60.

23. On the *Book of Ahikar* and the story of "The King's Three Bodyguards," see notes 3 and 4, above. On the folk novella, structure, and orientations, see supra, chapter 2, note 15, and E. Yassif, "The Novella as an Ethnopoetic Genre," *Papers of the Eighth Congress of the International Society for Folk-Narrative Research* (Bergen, 1984), pp. 283–289.

On the narrative pattern of the courtier's rise to greatness, see the works of Hengel, Humphreys, and Wills (supra, note 21).

24. The literature published on the folk fairytale is especially vast—see, for examples, the bibliography in Ben-Amos, *Genres*, pp. 250–276; Lüthi, *Once*; and Lüthi, *The Fairytale*.

On the epic structure of the biblical David story, see chapter 2, above, note 11. Scholars have also noted the paucity of the magic fairytale in the period's Greek and Roman literature. See W. F. Hansen, "Folklore," in *Civilizations of the Ancient Mediterranean: Greece and Rome*, ed. M. Grans and R. Kitzinger (New York, 1988), 2:1125.

Versions of the Book of Tobit can be found in all editions of the apocryphal literature (supra, note 1), and see especially B. Heller's important introduction in Kahana (supra, note 21), pp. 295–347. Grintz takes issue with the folkloristic approach (supra, note 21), pp. 47–65. I disagree with Wills, *The Novel*, pp. 68–92, who attempts to approach the Tobit fairytale as a "comic book", or a "romantic comedy." There is also no justification to the attempt to claim that the tale type "the grateful dead" is not central to the structure of the story—it is exactly here that its meaning and socio-religious function lies, and see also the next note.

25. On the structure of the magic fairytale, see Propp, *Morphology*; Jason, "School." The tale type "the grateful dead" is AT 506, and see G. H. Gerould, *The Grateful Dead* (London, 1908); L. Liljeblad, *Die Tobiasgeschichte und andere Märchen mit toten Helfern* (Lund, 1927); F. L. Ruppert, "Das Buch Tobias—ein Modell märchgestaltender Erzählung," in *Festschrift J. Ziegler*, ed. J. Schreiner (Würzburg, 1972), 1:109–119; W. Soll, "Tobit and Folklore Studies, with Emphasis on Propp's Methodology," in *Society of Biblical Literature, 1988 Seminar Papers*, ed. D. J. Lull (Atlanta, 1988), pp. 39–53, idem, "Misfortune and Exile in Tobit," *Catholic Biblical Quarterly* 51 (1989): 209–231, and the works of Milne (supra, notes to chapter 2, note 2); C. A. Moore, *Tobit: A New Translation with Introduction and Commentary* [The Anchor Bible], (New York, 1995), pp. 11–14, deals with the two central folkloric themes of the book: The Grateful Dead and The Dangerous Bride.

26. A great deal has been published on the demonic possession of mortals. See, for example, Nigal, *Dybbuk*; Bilu, "Dybbuk"; T. K. Oestereich, *Possession Demoniacal and Other among Primitive Races in Antiquity, the Middle Ages and Modern Times* (New York, 1930); S. V. McCasland, *By the Finger of God: Demon Possession and Exorcism in Early Christianity in Light of Modern Views of Mental Illness* (New York, 1951); G. Scholem, "Dibbuk," *Encyclopedia Judaica* (Jerusalem, 1972), 6:19–20; H. A. Kelly, *The Devil, Demonology and Witchcraft* (Garden City, N.Y., 1968), pp. 67–96; I. M. Lewis, "A Structural Approach to Witchcraft and Spirit-Possession," in *Witchcraft: Confessions and Accusations*, ed. M. Douglas (London, 1970), pp. 293–309; V. Crapanzano and V. Garrison, eds., *Case Studies in Spirit Possession* (New York, 1977); and G. Erickson, "The Enigmatic Metamorphosis: From Divine Possession to Demonic Possession," *Journal of Popular Culture* 11 (1977): 656–681.

27. The tale type of "the predestined bride" has been the object of several studies in general and in Jewish literature. See Schwarzbaum, *Folklore*, pp. 143–172; A. Taylor, "The Predestined Wife," *Fabula* 2 (1957): 45–77; and Shenhar, *The Folktale*, pp. 134–154. On the wife who is responsible for the death of her husbands in Jewish traditions, see: M. A. Friedman, "Tamar, A Symbol of Life: The 'Killer Wife' Superstition in the Bible and Jewish Tradition," *Association of Jewish Studies Review* 15 (1990): 23–61.

28. The transition from myth to fairytale was discerned and defined by the brothers Jakob and Wilhelm Grimm. See *The German Legends of the Brothers Grimm*, ed. and trans. D. Ward (Philadelphia, 1981), 2: 362–371; Lüthi, *European*, pp. 66 ff., 114 ff.; M. Eliade, "Myths and Fairy Tales", in his *Myth and Reality*, trans. W. R. Trask (New York, 1975^2), pp. 195–202; A. Birgitta Rooth, "Motive aus griechischen Mythen in einigen europäischen Märchen", W. Siegmund ed., *Antiker Mythos in unseren Märchen*, (Kassel 1984), pp. 35–41; and J. Zipes, *Breaking the Magic Spell, Radical Theories of Folk and Fairy Tale* (Austin, 1979), pp. 4 ff.

On the process of demythologization, compare chapter 2, above, note 4. The figure of Satan in the Second Temple period and at the dawn of Christianity, and his role as antagonist, was described by L. Röhrich, "Teufelsmärchen und Teufelsagen," in *Sagen und ihre Deutung*, ed. Lüthi-Röhrich-Fohrer (Göttingen, 1965), pp. 28–58; H. A. Kelly, *Towards the Death of Satan: The Growth and Decline of Christian Demonology* (London, 1968); J. B. Russell, *Satan in Early Christian Tradition* (Ithaca and London, 1981); idem, *The Devil: Perceptions of Evil From Antiquity to Primitive Christianity* (Ithaca, 1977); and Pagels, *Satan* (supra, note 12).

4. The Rabbinic Period

*The translations from the main Rabbinic sources are from the following editions: Babylonian Talmud [by name of the tractate]: *The Babylonian Talmud*, trans. I. Epstein (London, 1938–1952).

Midrash (by name of each midrash): *Midrash Rabbah*, trans. H. Freedman and M. Simon (London and New York, 1983).

Palestinian Talmud (PT and name of tractate): *The Talmud of the Land of Israel*, ed. and trans. J. Neusner (Chicago and London 1982).

The editions and translations from the other rabbinic sources are given in the following notes.

1. L. Zunz formulated the chronological principles upon which the study of rabbinical literature is based: L. Zunz, *Hadrashot be-Yisrael ve-Hishtalshelutan ha-Historit [The Homilies of the Jewish People and Their Evolution]*, ed. and supplemented by H. Albeck (Jerusalem, 1954) [H]; Steinschneider, *Literature*, pp. 2–54; H. L. Strack and G. Stemberger, *Einleitung in Talmud und Midrasch* (München, 1982); J. N. Epstein, *Introductions to the Amoraic Literature*, ed. E. Tz. Melamed (Jerusalem and Tel Aviv, 1963) [H]; *Encyclopedia Judaica*: "Aggadah," "Midrash," 2: 354–366, 11:1507–1514, and the literature cited therein.

2. The known discussion of the aggadic story as an "artistic creation" is found in J. Fraenkel, *Studies in the Spiritual World of the Aggadic Story* (Tel Aviv, 1981) [H]; and idem, *The Ways of the Aggadah and the Midrash* (Givataim, 1991) [H]. Unfortunately, these works, aside from commentaries on some stories, have little value as a literary theory of the Rabbinic story. The much older, Heinemann, *Pathways*, is still the most insightful and instructive "theory of midrash," and should be considered, still, the best statement of its kind. Also G. Hasan-Rokem, *Web of Life: Folklore in Rabbinic Literature* (Tel Aviv, 1996) [H], adds many important contributions to this trend of the literary study of Rabbinic stories. On this, see also: I. Jacobs, *The Midrashic Process: Tradition and Interpretation in Rabbinic Judaism* (Cambridge, 1995).

3. On the synagogue and the academy in the rabbinic period, see D. Urman, "The Synagogue and the Academy—Are They One and the Same?" in *Ancient Synagogues—Collected Studies*, ed. A. Oppenheimer, E. Kasher and U. Rapaport (Jerusalem, 1988), pp. 53–75 [H], and the literature cited therein; Z. Safrai, "The Communal Roles in Synagogues in Palestine in the Time of the Mishnah and the Talmud," in *Memorial Volume for Mordechai Weizer*, ed. S. Schmidt (Jerusalem, 1981, pp. 230–248 [H]; Sh. Safrai, *Palestine and Its Sages in the Period of the Mishnah and the Talmud* (Jerusalem, 1984) [H]; Idem, "The Uniqueness and Importance of the Phenomenon of Synagogues in the Period of the Mishnah and the Talmud," in *Synagogues in the Period of the Mishnah and the Talmud*, ed. Z. Safrai (Jerusalem, 1986), pp. 15–42 [H], and the important discussion and vast bibliography in Schürer, *History*, 2: 415–454 ("School and Synagogue").

On the status of the public sermon, cf. J. Haineman, *Public Sermons in the Talmudic Period* (Jerusalem, 1971) [H]; idem, *Legends*, pp. 17–48; and O. Meir, *Darshanic Story in Genesis*

Rabbah (Tel Aviv, 1987), pp. 11–42 [H]. On translations and the translators' role in the transfer and creation of folk traditions, see A. Shinan, *The Targumic Aggadah* (Jerusalem, 1979) [H]; idem, *The Embroidered Targum: The Aggadah in Targum Pseudo-Jonathan of the Pentateuch* (Jerusalem, 1992), pp. 120–167 [H].

4. On the concept of "the folk" in folklore, see A. Dundes, "Who Are the Folk?" in his *Essays in Folkloristics* (Meerut, 1978), pp. 1–21; and on the concept in the rabbinic period, see A. Oppenheimer, *The Am ha-Aretz: The Social History of the Jewish People in the Hellenistic-Roman Period* (Leiden, 1977); M. Goodman, *State and Society in Roman Galilee A.D. 132–212* (Totowa, N.J., 1983), pp. 64–89; R. A. Horsley with J. S. Henson, *Bandits, Prophets and Messiahs—Popular Movements at the Time of Jesus* (San Francisco, 1985); Schürer, *History*, pp. 322–337; and A. Kobelman, "The Folk in Rabbinic Literature", *Jewish Studies* 36 (1996): 111–132. E. E. Urbach, "The Laws of 'Avodah Zarah and the Archeological and Historical Reality in the Second and Third Centuries," in Urbach, *World*, pp. 125 ff., claims that the sages were as familiar with folk and magic beliefs as were the other social strata of the folk, and therefore no separation should be made between the world of the sages and daily reality in the matter of pagan beliefs.

5. On the theoretical principles of the definition of folklore genres, see Ben-Amos, *Genres*, pp. 249–274, and the considerable literature cited there. In his article, "Generic Distinctions in the Aggadah," in Talmage, *Studies*, pp. 45–72, Ben-Amos seeks to apply his well-established distinction between ethnic genres and analytical categories to material from rabbinic aggadah, and asks how the sages themselves distinguished between the various genres. His method lies at the heart of the "synthetic" perception proposed here. Compare also section K, below.

6. The contextual school in folkloristics dealt at length with the importance of the performance event. Compare the programmatic collection of articles, D. Ben-Amos and K. Goldstein, eds., *Folklore: Performance and Communication* (The Hague, 1974); D. Ben-Amos, "New Trends in the Study of Folklore," *ha-Sifrut* 20 (1975): 1–7 [H]. On the concept of "Sitz im Leben" with respect to narrative, see B. O. Long, "Recent Studies in Oral Literature and the Question of 'Sitz im Leben,'" *Semeia* 5 (1976): 35–50.

7. On the aggadic traditions on "Zechariah's blood," see B. Marmelstein, "The Aggadah of the Blood of Zechariah the Prophet—Its Roots and Branches," *Sefer ha-Yovel le-Shmuel Krauss* [Jubilee Volume in Honor of Samuel Krauss] (Jerusalem, 1933), pp. 161–168 [H]; Heineman, *Legends*, pp. 31–38; Sh. Blank, "The Death of Zechariah in Rabbinic Literature," *Hebrew Union College Annual* 12–13 (1937–1938): 237–346; Gaster and Heller (1936), pp. 44–48; B. Halpern Amaru, "The Killing of the Prophets: Unravelling a Midrash," *Hebrew Union College Annual* 54 (1983): 166–170.

On the history of Jews' travels to Palestine, see the introduction to A. Yaari's anthology, *Mas'ot Eretz Yisrael* [Journeys in Palestine] (Tel Aviv, 1946) [H]; J. Prawer, "Hebrew Travelogues in Palestine in the Crusader Period," *Katedra* 40 (1986): 31–62, (1987): 65–90 [H]; E. Reiner, "Pilgrims and Pilgrimage to Palestine 1099–1517," (Ph.D. diss., The Hebrew University, Jerusalem, 1988) [H]; R. A. Bascom, *Prolegomena to the Study of the Itinerary Genre in the Old Testament and Beyond* (Ph.D. Thesis, Claremont Graduate School, 1986) and note 49, below.

8. On the figure of Bar Kappara and his rivalry with Rabbi Judah the Patriarch, see Bacher, *Legends*, vol. 2, part 2, pp. 163–176 [H]; E. E. Halevy, *The Historical-Biographical Aggadah in Light of Greek and Latin Sources* (Tel Aviv, 1975), pp. 567–570 [H]. On group meals in the rabbinic traditions of the period, cf. A. Oppenheimer, "Havurot that Were in Jerusalem," in *Chapters in the History of Jerusalem in the Days of the Second Temple* (Volume in

Memory of Abraham Schalit), ed. A. Oppenheimer, E. Rapaport, and M. Stern (Jerusalem, 1981), pp. 178–190 [H] and P. H. Peli, "Havurot that Were in Jerusalem," *Hebrew Union College Annual* 55 (1984): 55–74.

9. On these two important fables, see the variants and the extensive scholarly literature cited in Schwarzbaum, *Berechia*, pp. 25–47, 51–56. On the use of the fable at historical and communal events, see B. E. Perry, "Fable," *Studium Generale* 12 (1959): 17–37; D. Daube, *Ancient Hebrew Fables* (Oxford, 1973); Schwarzbaum, *Berechiah*, pp. vii–xiii, and also the discussion and literature cited below in section I of this chapter. On the notion of "true performance," compare the discussion in D. Hymes, "Breakthrough Into Performance," in *Folklore: Communication and Performance*, ed. D. Ben-Amos and K. Goldstein (The Hague, 1975), pp. 11–74 and E. C. Fine, *The Folklore Text. From Performance to Print* (Bloomington, 1984), p. 13.

10. On tales of the Sodomites, see below, section [K].

11. See Heinneman, *Public Sermons* (supra, note 3), pp. 7–11; Shinan, *The Targumic Aggadah* (supra, note 3), pp. 1–38. On antisemitic street theater during the Roman period, cf. M. B. Lerner, "Anti-Semitic Theater in the Roman Empire," *Mahanayyim* 76 (1963): 128–129 [H]; M. D. Herr, "Hatred of Jews in the Roman Empire in Light of Rabbinic Literature," *Volume in Memory of Benjamin de-Vries* (Jerusalem, 1969), pp. 149–159 [H]; D. Gilula, "Jokes about Jews in Roman Literature," *Jerusalem Studies in Jewish Folklore* 9 (1986): 7–37 [H] and I. Heinemann, "Antisemitismus," *Realenziklopädie der Klassischen Altertumswissenschaft*, supp. 5 (Stuttgart, 1931), pp. 3–43.

12. On the expanded biblical tale in the Second Temple period, see chapter 3, above, and the literature cited there in note 11—which bears on the rabbinic period as well. In addition, Heinemann, *Pathways;* Halevy, *Gates;* G. Vermes, *Scripture and Tradition in Judaism. Haggadic Studies* (Leiden, 1961); D. Boyarin, *Intertextuality and the Reading of Midrash* (Bloomington and Indianapolis, 1990) and O. Meir, *The Homiletical Tale* (supra, note 3).

13. On the versions of the story of Cain and Abel in Aggadah and other literatures, see V. Aptowitzer, *Kain Und Abel in der Agada* (Vienna, 1922); Ginzberg, *Legends*, 1: 107–113, and accompanying notes; A. Oppenheimer, "Cain and Abel: The Evolution of the Motif from the Ancient Near East, by Way of the Bible and on to the Aggadic Literature and the Books of the Church Fathers," *Gedalyahu Alon Memorial Volume* (Tel Aviv, 1970), pp. 27–68 [H]; N. Stillman, "The Story of Cain and Abel in Midrashic Thought," *Mekhkarei ha-Mercaz le-Heker ha-Folklor* [Studies of the Center for Folklore Research] 3 (1972): 159–165 [H]; S. H. Hooke, "Cain and Abel," *Folklore* (1939), pp. 58–65; D. Jassine, "Caïn et Abel Selon le Midrash," *Nouveaux Cahiers* 25 (1971): 33–40; N. A. Stillman, "The Story of Cain and Abel in the Qur'an and the Muslim Commentators," *Journal of Semitic Studies* 19 (1974): 231–240 and J. Illies (Hrsg.), *Brudermord—Zum Mythos von Kain und Abel* (München, 1975).

On the epic laws as evidence of the folk origin of narrative texts, see Olrik, "Laws" and Holbeck, "Laws." On the use of binary opposition as a structural device, see C. Lévi-Strauss, "The Structural Study of Myth," *Structural Anthropology* (New York, 1963), pp. 206–231. On the oral foundations of written texts, see W. J. Ong, *Orality and Literacy—The Technologizing of the Word* (London and New York, 1982); W. A. Graham, *Beyond the Written Word: Oral Aspects of Scripture in the History of Religion* (Cambridge, 1987) and J. Goody, *The Interface Between The Written and the Oral* (Cambridge, 1987).

14. On Flood stories as folktales, see the literature cited in chapter 2, above, note 4. Noah and the Flood in rabbinic literature appear in Ginzberg, *Legends*, 1: 143–182 and notes. On Noah's drunkenness, see Ginzberg, ibid. (on different versions of the tale); B. Heller, "Ginzberg's Legends of the Jews," *Jewish Quarterly Review* 24 (1933–1934): 410, note 35, defines the story as a folktale; J. Perles, *Zur Rabbinischen Sprach und Sagenkunde* (Berlin, 1901),

pp. 46 ff.; A. I. Baumgarten, "Myth and Midrash. Genesis 9:20–29," in *Christianity, Judaism and Other Graeco-Roman Cults. Studies for Morton Smith at Sixty*, ed. J. Neusner (London, 1975), part 3, pp. 55–71; H. H. Cohen, *The Drunkenness of Noah* (Alabama, 1974); O. Dähnhart, *Natursagen* (Leipzig und Berlin, 1907–1910), 1: 298–314; M. Grünbaum, *Gesammelte Aufsätze zur Sprach-und Sagenkunde* (Berlin, 1901), pp. 435–41; J. P. Lewis, *A Study of the Interpretation of Noah and the Flood in Jewish and Christian Literature* (Leiden, 1966); L. Feldman, "The Portrait of Noah in Josephus, Philo, Pseudo-Philo's Biblical Antiquities and Rabbinic Midrashim," *Proceedings of the American Academy of Jewish Research* 55 (1988): 31–58, and the recent: N. Cohn, *Noah's Flood. The Genesis Story in Western Thought* (New Haven and London, 1996).

15. For variants of the tale in rabbinic literature, see Ginzberg, *Legends*, 1: 193–203; B. Beer, *Leben Abraham nach Auffassung jüdischen Sagen* (Leipzig, 1859); Halevy, *Gates*, pp. 72–78. On the story of Abraham and Nimrod in the Middle Ages, see: Eisenstein, *Midrashim*, 1:1–9; H. Speyer, *Die Biblischen Erzählungen im Koran* (Hildesheim, 1961²), pp. 120–186; H. Schützinger, *Ursprung und Entwicklung der arabischen Abraham-Nimrod Legende* (Bonn, 1961²).

The youngest brother rising to greatness is tale type AT 550–551 (or the parallel motif H1242). On this typical tale type, see H. Jason, "The Tale of David and Goliath: Folk Epic Creation?" *ha-Sifrut* 23 (1976): 23–41 [H].

The "reductio ad absurdum" is narrative motif J1191.1, which appears, for example, in tale types AT 875 ("the wise farmer's daughter") and AT A920 ("the princess and the farmer's daughter"). See K. Ranke, "Ad Absurdum führen," *Enzyklopädie des Märchens*, 1:79–85.

On the martyrological typology that appears in the tale, see Delehaye, *Martyrology*; Loomis, *White Magic*, pp. 30–37, and for an example of the tales on Saint Eustacius (Placidas) and Saint Alexis, see Jacobus de Voragine, *The Golden Legends* (New York, 1969), pp. 351–374, 555–561; Tubach, *Index*, #2041, 2035, 2038, 5146, and motif H1573.4.1.

On the typology of "the good and the bad sister" or "the unsuccessful repetition," see W. E. Roberts, *The Tale of the Kind and the Unkind Girls* (Berlin, 1958); A. Dundes, "The Binary Structure of the 'Unsuccessful Repetition' in Lithuanian Folktales," *Western Folklore* 21 (1962): 165–174 and H. Jason, "The Tale of the Mountain of the Sun—the Model of the Unsuccessful Repetition," *Mehkarim be-Toldot Yehudei Irak u-be-Tarbutam* [Studies in the History and Culture of the Jews of Iraq] 1 (1981): 169–185 [H]. On the "chain" type narrative or the contest of superlatives cf. motifs H631–H633 (superlative riddles); Schwarzbaum, *Berechia*, pp. 167–178, and the extensive literature cited there.

16. On the wars of the sons of Jacob in the apocryphal literature, see *The Testaments of the Twelve Tribes*, "The Testament of Judah" (Charlesworth, *Pseudepigrapha*, 2: 795–802), the general introductions cited in chapter 3 above, note 1, and especially Nickelsburg, in Stone (ibid.), pp. 121–125, and additionally, H. W. Hollander and M. De Jonge, *The Testaments of the Twelve Patriarchs—A Commentary* (Leiden, 1985), pp. 25–27.

On the argument between Joseph and Judah in Egypt, see Ginzberg, *Legends*, 2: 103–110, and the accompanying notes and Halevy, *Portions*, pp. 161–162. On the folk beliefs connected with giants, see Bächtold-Stäubli, "Zwerge und Riesen," 9:1008–1138, and the literature there mentioned and Thompson, *Motifs*, motifs G100–G199.

17. On the tale and its variants, see Ginzberg, *Legends*, 4: 107–109. On the folk motifs see in Ginzberg, ibid., note 100; Noy, *Index*, and the supplemental texts in M. Higger, *Halakhot ve-Aggadot* [Halacha and Aggadah] (New York, 1933), pp. 77–80 [H]; and Grünbaum, *Studies*, pp. 189 ff. On the Devil masquerading as various animals in order to lead mortals astray, see M. Rudwin, *The Devil in Legend and Literature* (La Salle, Il., 1973). On the "life token," see B. Heller, "Notes de folk-lore juif," *Revue des Etudes Juives* 82 (1926): 301–316 ('le life

token'). On the journey abridged via use of the Ineffable Name, see A. Marmorstein, "Legendenmotive in der rabbinischen Literatur," *Archiv für Religionswissenschaft* 16 (1913): 160–175; Grünbaum, ibid., pp. 238 ff.; Trachtenberg, *Magic*, pp. 78–103; Urbach, *Sages*, pp. 102–114; Thompson, *Motifs*, D2122.5. The recent M. Verman and S. H. Adler, "Path Jumping in the Jewish Magical Tradition," *Jewish Studies Quarterly* 1 (1993/94): 131–148, is rather informative, and does not know of previous studies of the theme.

The motif of suspending a person or object in air magically is found as early as *The Book of Ahikar* and its variants among the sages. See Yassif, "Traces," pp. 228–229; "Ahikar," in Charles, *Apocrypha*, pp. 756–757, 762–763 and Babylonian Talmud, *Berachot* 8b.

18. On the legend of Androgenous among the sages, see Urbach, *Sages*, pp. 228–229, and the literature cited therein; Halevy, *Portions*, pp. 31–41; supra, chapter 2, note 5; F. Lenovmand, *The Beginnings of History According to the Bible and the Traditions of Oriental Peoples* (New York, 1882); A. Krappe, "The Birth of Eve," *Occident and Orient, Gaster Anniversary Volume* (London, 1936), pp. 312–322; T. Reik, *The Creation of Woman* (New York, 1960), pp. 24 ff.; M. Eliade, *Mephistopheles and Androgyny* (New York, 1965): "The Divine Androgyny," pp. 158 ff. and W. E. Meeks, "The Image of Androgyny," *History of Religion* 13 (1974): 165–208.

On the Pandora myth, see R. Graves, *The Greek Myths* (Harmondsworth, 1960), I:144–145; H. Türck, *Pandora und Eva—Menschwerdung und Schöpfertum im griechischem und judischem Mythos* (Weimar, 1931); S. S. Lachs, "The Pandora-Eva Motif in Rabbinic Literature," *The Harvard Theological Review* 67 (1974): 341–345; Z. Kagan, "Pandora's Box in Greek Mythology and in Jewish Aggadah," *Mahanayyim* 112 (1967): 130–135 [H]; Halevy, *Portions*, pp. 51–59.

19. On the folkloric traditions on King Solomon in Jewish culture and their dispersal in the Arab traditions of the Middle Ages, see Ginzberg, *Legends*, 4: 123–176; Y. Rosenberg, *Sefer Divrei ha-Yamim asher le-Shlomo* [The Book of Chronicles of Solomon] (Piotrkow, 1904) [H]; G. Weil, *Biblical Legends of the Mussulmans* (New York, 1846); R. Faerber, *Salomon in der Tradition* (Wien, 1902); St. J. Seymour, *Tales of King Solomon* (London, 1924); G. Salzberger, *Die Salomo-Sage in der semitischen Sagenkunde* (Berlin, 1907); idem, *Salomos Tempelbau und Thron in semitischen Sagenkunde* (Berlin, 1912) and J. B. Prichard, ed., *Solomon and Sheba* (London, 1974).

20. On the legend of Solomon and Ashmedai, see Ginzberg, *Legends*, 4; 165–169, and the accompanying notes; Goebel, *Motifs*, pp. 55 ff.; I. Lévi, "L'Orgueil de Salomon," *Revue des Etudes juives* 17 (1888): 58–65 and A. Kohut, *Über die Jüdische Angelologie und Däemonologie in Parsismus* (Leipzig, 1866): 80 ff. Krappe compares the tale of Solomon and Ashmedai to a story of Herodotus (3:68–69), about the Persian sorcerer Semardis, who seized power by assuming the guise of the king. He was exposed after the women in the harem were questioned: A. H. Krappe, "Solomon and Ashmodai," *The American Journal of Philology* 54 (1933): 260–268. For an interesting monograph that posits an Indian origin for the tale in the spirit of the Indo-European school, see H. Varnhagen, *Ein indisches Märchen auf seiner Wanderung durch die asiatischen und europäischen Literaturen* (Berlin, 1882). Most of the works mentioned in the preceding note also deal with this legend, as do P. Falk, "Di Talmudishe Aggadah fun Shlomo ha-Meilekh mitten Ashmedai un der Shamir in Tzvei Altyiddishe Nusha'ois" [The Talmudic Aggadah of King Solomon and Ashmedai with the Shamir in Two Old Yiddish Versions] 13 (1938): 246–274; Ben-Yehezkiel, "The Book," pp. 365–367; Halevy, *Gates*, pp. 236–239; R. Kushelevski, "Solomon and Ashmedai," in *The Thematology Index to the Literature of the Jewish People*, ed. Y. Elstein (Bar-Ilan University, Ramat-Gan, 1986) [H]. The task of bringing a wondrous item or cure to the ailing king belongs to tale types AT 550–551. The narrative type of the miraculous deeds of a supernatural creature accompanied

by a questioning mortal is known in international folklore as "the angel and the monk" (AT 759). On this legend in Jewish literature, see I. Lévi, "La légende de l'ange et l'ermite dans les écrits Juives," *Revue des Etudes Juives* 8 (1884): 64–73; S. Krauss, "A Moses Legend," *Jewish Quarterly Review* 2 (1912): 339–364; and the vast literature in Schwarzbaum, *Folklore*, pp. 75–126. The narrative type of the fallen pride of the wealthy man after a pauper or demon dons his garb and appears in his place is AT 757, and motif L411—a supernatural creature takes the place of a proud king, and K1934.1—an imposter (a demon or sorcerer) replaces the king. See Bolte and Polivka, 2:418 ff.; Varnhagen, ibid.

21. The link between rabbinic and apocryphal literature has been much discussed, see, for example, L. Ginzberg, "Some Observations on the Attitude of the Synagogue to Apocalyptic-Eschatological Writings," *Journal of Biblical Literature* 41 (1922): 115–136; M. Hengel, *Judaism and Hellenism* (London, 1979), 1:110 ff. and G. Alon, "Did the Jewish People and its Sages Cause the Hasmoneans to be Forgotten?," in his *Jews, Judaism and the Classical World* (Jerusalem, 1977), pp. 1–17. Among the first to propose a folkloristic process as explanation for the transfer of narrative traditions from one period to the next was I. Lévi, "L'histoire de 'Suzanna et les Deux Vieillards' dans la Littérature Juive," *Revue des Etudes Juives* 95 (1933): 157–158; M. Stone, "Introduction," in *Jewish Writings of the Second Temple Period*, ed. M. Stone (Philadelphia, 1984), pp. xx–xxiii.

22. The tale in the apocryphal literature was discussed above in chapter 3, especially note 15. For variants to the tale in rabbinic literature, see Ginzberg, *Legends*, 2: 44–58, and the accompanying notes. Grünbaum, *Studies*, pp. 515–593; J. Yohanan, *Joseph and Potiphar's Wife in World Literature* (New York, 1968); J. L. Kugel, *In Potiphar's House—The Interpretive Life of Biblical Texts* (San Francisco, 1990).

23. On the role and status of Satan as protagonist in the literature of the Second Temple period, see the literature cited above, chapter 3, note 28. On scholarship on the theme of the binding among the sages cf. *The Binding of Isaac—Studies in the Development of a Literary Tradition*, ed. E. Yassif (Jerusalem, 1978 [H] and R. Hayward, "The Present State of Research into the Targumic Account of the Sacrifice of Isaac," *Journal of Jewish Studies* 32 (1981): 127–150. Different versions of the tale and the confrontation with Satan appear in Ginzberg, *Legends* 1: 276–279, and the accompanying notes.

24. On the tale of Moses in Ethiopia and its successive forms, see chapter 3, note 16. See also M. Abraham, *Légendes juives apocryphes sur la vie de moïse* (Paris, 1925) and S. Brock, "Some Syriac Legends Concerning Moses," *Journal of Jewish Studies* 29 (1979): 237–256. An interesting explanation defining the ancient tales that deify cultural heroes as a means of religious propaganda deserves note: E. Schüssler-Fiorenza, "Miracles, Mission and Apologetics," in *Aspects of Religious Propaganda in Judaism and Early Christianity*, ed. Schüssler-Fiorenza (Notre-Dame, 1976), p. 11, and J. J. Collins, *Between Athens and Jerusalem: Jewish Identity in the Hellenistic Diaspora* (New York, 1983).

25. On *The Martyrdom of Isaiah* and the apocryphal *Vitae Prophetarum* see supra chapter 3, and especially the literature cited there in note 19. On the transformations of the tale in early Christian literature, see Schürer, *History*, 3: 335–341. On the targumic versions of the story, see G. Grelot, "Deux Tosephtas targumique sur Isaïe 66," *Revue Biblique* 89 (1972): 511–543; Ginzberg, *Legends*, 4: 278–279 and B. Halpern-Amaru, "The Killing of the Prophets—Unravelling a Midrash," *Hebrew Union College Annual* 54 (1983): 170–174. Variants to the tale in international folklore were uncovered in the work of two of the great Jewish folklorists: Gaster and Heller, pp. 32–52.

26. For hypotheses on the origin of the composition among the Judean Desert sects, see D. Flusser, "The Apocryphal Book of Ascencio Isaiah and the Dead Sea Sect," *Israel Exploration Journal* 3 (1953): 30–47 and M. Philonenko, "Le Martyre d'Isaïe et l'histoire de la sect

de Qoumran," *Cahiers de la Revue d'histoire et de Philosophie religieuses* 41 (1967): 1–10. For a literary analysis similar to that proposed here, see Nickelsburg, in Stone (supra, note 21), pp. 52–56.

27. In addition to Thompson's standard index, *Motifs*, Noy's *Index* lays out the motifs below in their talmudic-midrashic context: the Ineffable Name—A138, and see note 17 above, and also H. L. Held, "Der Schem ha-mephorasch," *Das Gespenst des Golem* (München, 1927), pp. 163–214; and Urbach, *Sages*, pp. 124–134. The tree that opens to swallow the fugitive—D1393.1; trees that hide escapees in a miraculous manner—R311.1; runaways exposed within a tree—R351. All of chapter Q582 is devoted to the motif of *lex talionis*—which proves its vast dissemination in folk thought. Ginzberg, too, in *Legends*, ibid., claims that Isaiah was punished measure for measure. The fact that his ritual fringes gave him away proves the possibility that other versions of the tale involved a transgression against the precept of ritual fringes. The motif of murder of the hero by sawing him in two was widespread in the literature of the Near East, and is found in the Persian work known as *The History of King Djemchid and the Devas*. See also Gaster and Heller (supra, note 25) and Charles, *Apocrypha*, 2:158.

28. On the tale and its variants in the apocryphal literature, compare the discussion in chapter 3, above, and note 20 therein. Compare also R. Doran, "A Synoptic View of the Mother and her Seven Sons," in *Ideal Figures in Ancient Judaism*, ed. G. W. E. Nickelsburg and J. J. Collins (Ann Arbor, 1980), pp. 189–222.

29. The paradigmatic comparison of Hellenistic and Hebrew narrative styles is E. Auerbach, *Mimesis. The Representation of Reality in Western Literature* (Princeton, 1953), ch. 1. Auerbach, however, draws a comparison between the Bible and the Odyssey. In the story of the mother and her seven sons, the two cultures' respective versions of the tale can be likened and therefore the comparative study here is stronger and even more convincing. On the role of biblical verses in the fashioning of aggadic tales, see J. Fraenkel, "Bible Verses Quoted in Tales of the Sages," *Scripta Hierosolymitana* 22 (1971): 80–99.

30. On *The Letter of Aristeas* see chapter 3, above, and the literature cited there in note 9, and E. Tov, "The Rabbinic Traditions," and the important literature cited therein. On the controversy among the sages on the matter of forbidding Greek wisdom, see Lieberman, *Greek*; Hengel (supra, note 21).

31. On the narrative cycle of Daniel in the biblical and apocryphal literature, compare the discussion above in chapter 3 and the literature cited there in note 21. See also B. Heller, "The Additions to the Book of Daniel," in *The Apocrypha and Pseudepigrapha translated into Hebrew*, ed. A. Kahana (Tel Aviv, 1956), 1:554–560 [H]; F. Zimmerman, "Bel and the Dragon," *Vetus Testamentum* 8 (1958): 438–440, suggests that this story is a later development of the Marduk and Tiamat myth. On the different versions of the tale in Midrash Genesis Rabbah, compare the Theodor-Albeck edition, p. 790, with the printed Venetian version and the later printings. Even the most reliable manuscript of the Midrash (*Midrash Genesis Rabbah, Ms. Vatican Ebr. 30*, ed. M. Sokoloff [Jerusalem, 1971], p. 1176 [H]), contains only the short version and not the tale itself.

32. On the differences between how tales were told in the two Talmuds, see E. Karlin, "Narrative Characteristics in the Two Talmuds," *Divrei Sefer* (Tel Aviv, 1952), pp. 5–42 [H]; S. Safrai, "Tales of the Sages in the Palestinian Tradition and the Babylonian Talmud," *Scripta Hierosolymitana* 22 (1971): 209–232. The folk motifs that sustain these tales are: F911.4.1.2—a serpent swallows ships with all hands; F911.6—a monster swallows everything put in front of it; F912—a victim tears apart the monster from within. On tales of marvelous journeys of the period, see M. C. P. Schmidt, *Zur Geschichte der geographischen Literatur bei Griechen und Römern* (Berlin, 1887) and J. Richard, *Les Récits de Voyages et de Pèlerinages* (Turnhout,

1981). On the important story cycle of Alexander the Great in Talmudic narrative, see S. J. Rapoport, *Erekh Millin* (Prague, 1852), 1:120–170 [H] and Halevy, *Gates*, pp. 115–137.

33. On the structure of the story cycle in *Lamentations Rabbah*, see Hasan-Rokem, "Riddles," and the literature cited there in note 3; see also the discussion in section K, below. On allegorical interpretations of the riddles, and on the view of it as a polemic against Christianity, see Bacher, *Legends*, vol. 1, part 1, p. 125. On the character of the stories as "fools' tales," see K. Dietrich, "Jüdischgriechische Schnurren," *Mitteilungen zür judischen Volkskunde* 23 (1907): 69–75. Twisting a rope out of sand is tale type AT 1174.

34. On *The Book of Ahikar* and its folkloristic importance, see the discussion above, chapter 3, and the literature cited there in note 3, and Nickelsburg (supra, note 26), p. 284; L. M. Lindenbergen, "Ahikar," in Charlesworth, *Pseudepigrapha*, I:479–492.

35. On the phenomenon of renewal of tales from the Second Temple literature in Hebrew literature of the Middle Ages, cf. Flusser, *Josippon* 2:148–153 [H]; A. M. Dubarle, "L'authenticité des textes Hébreux de Judith," *Biblica* 50 (1969): 187–211; and Yassif, "Leisure," pp. 894–895.

36. On the apocryphal *Book of Tobit* and its folkloristic nature, see the discussion above in chapter 3, and the literature cited there in notes 25 and 26. The international motifs of "the grateful dead" are: E341.1—the dead man grateful that his uninterred corpse was given an honorable burial; T66.1—the grateful dead man helps the hero win the princess. See the story of "R. Reuven's Bride" texts and variants, in Gaster, *Exempla*, tale 139, and pp. 85, 215. Cf. also Schwarzbaum, *Folklore*, pp. 143–172; Shenhar, *The Folktale*, pp. 134–154.

37. One interesting example can be clearly indicated: Origen, the third-century Church Father, testifies that he closely questioned the Jews in Palestine about their familiarity with the story of Susannah and the elders. Those questioned recognized the tale, and identified by name the two elders who testified falsely against her—Ahab and Zedekiah. Cf. D. Heller, "Additions to the Book of Daniel," note 31 above, 2: 556–557 [H], and Kay in Charles, *Apocrypha*, 1: 644. The folk imagination apparently equated the elders of the Susannah story with the two false prophets, Ahab ben Kuliyah and Zedekiah ben Ma'asiyah. Jeremiah tells how Nebuchadnezzar burned them alive for committing adultery with their neighbors' wives (Jeremiah 29:21–29), and the expansions of the tale: *Sanhedrin* 93a; *Tanhuma*, Leviticus, 6; *Tanhuma Buber*, Leviticus 10; and additional sources listed in Ginzberg, *Legends*, 4: 336–337, and note 108. Ginzberg also alludes to the possible connection between Ben Zakkai's painstaking interrogation of witnesses (*Sanhedrin*, 5b) and Daniel's similar questioning in the Book of Susannah (ibid., 6: 426–427, note 79). In any case, these are proof that, although the rabbinic literature contains no mention of the story of Susannah, the tale was well-known to Jews in third-century Palestine.

38. A conception sharply formulated by A. Wesselski, *Märchen des Mittelalters* (Berlin, 1925), pp. xi–xxiii; E. Keifer, *Albert Wesselski and Recent Folk-Tale Theories* (Bloomington, 1941); and Gaster, *Studies*, pp. 1005–1039.

39. On the general hagiography, see the extensive literature of primary sources and the research literature cited in Wilson, *Saints*, pp. 370–396, and also the editor's thorough summary, ibid., pp. 1–55. The biographical legend in folkloristics is discussed at length in Ben-Amos, *Genres*, pp. 249–274 (bibliography); A. van Gennep, *La Formation des Légendes* (Paris, 1912), pp. 121–131, 183–200; O. Klapp, "The Folk-Hero," *Journal of American Folklore* (1949): 17–26; K. Horn, *Der aktive und der passive Märchenheld* (Basel, 1983), and the literature cited in the following notes.

The studies of heroes' and saints' legends in Hellenistic culture and at the dawn of Christianity have special importance and bearing on the discussion below. One important conclusion of these studies is that the ancient biographies had a central role in the extensive propaganda for dissemination of the various religions in the pagan world. On this, see A. Momigliano, *The Development of Greek Biography* (Cambridge, Mass., 1971); C. W. Votav, *The Gospels and Contemporary Biographies in the Greco-Roman World* (Philadelphia, 1970); D. Georgi, "The Records of Jesus in Light of Ancient Accounts of Revered Men," *Society of Biblical Literature. Proceedings of 108th Annual Meeting* (Philadelphia, 1972), 2: 527–542; D. L. Tiede, *The Charismatic Figure as Miracle Worker* (Missoula, 1972); W. S. Green, "What's in a Name?—The Problem of Rabbinic 'Biography,'" in *Approaches to Ancient Judaism: Theory and Practice*, ed. W. S. Green (Missoula, 1978), no. 1, pp. 77–96; and P. Cox, *Biography in Late Antiquity. A Quest for the Holy Man* (Berkeley and Los Angeles, 1983). On the question of differences between the adoration of the saints in Christianity and in Jewish culture, and why such a ritual did not develop in Judaism, see P. Brown, *The Cult of the Saints. Its Rise and Function in Latin Christianity* (Chicago, 1981), pp. 1–22; P. S. Alexander, "Rabbinic Biography and the Biography of Jesus: A Survey of Evidence," in *Synoptic Studies: The Ampleforth Conference of 1982–1983*, C. M. Tuckett ed. (Sheffield, 1984), pp. 19–50; R. L. Cohn, "Sainthood on the Periphery: The Case of Judaism," in *Sainthood: Its Manifestations in World Religions*, ed. R Kieckhofer and G. D. Bond (Berkeley and Los Angeles, 1988), pp. 43–68.

For a concentration of biographical legends in rabbinic literature, see Bacher, *Legends*; H. N. Bialik and Y. H. Ravnitzky, eds., *The Book of Legends. Sefer Ha-Aggadah*, trans. W. G. Braude (New York, 1992), pp. 201–332 ("The Deeds of the Sages"); Halevy, *The Historical-Biographical Aggadah* (supra, note 8), as well as collections on individual sages. On these, see J. Bergmann, *Die Legenden der Juden* (Berlin, 1919), pp. 31–42, 109–121.

40. Scholars of medieval Christian hagiography differentiate between saints' legends that were created and spread by *simplices* and those created and employed by the *literati*. Cf. Gurevich, *Culture*, p. 52; E. Yassif, "Rashi Legends and Medieval Popular Culture," in *Rashi 1040–1990*, ed. G. Sed-Rajna (Paris, 1993), pp. 484–492. On tales of rain-making, see the large collection of tales in the Babylonian Talmud, *Ta'anit* 23a-25b and the discussion that follows. On the story of Hillel and the Sons of Bathyra, see S. Lieberman, *Tosephta Kifshutah*, Pesahim, ch. 4 (New York, 1962), pp. 566–567 [H]; Palestinian Talmud *Pesahim*, ch. 33, 1, BT *Pesahim*, 66a; Bacher, *Legends*, vol. 1, part 1, pp. 2–3; Urbach, *Sages*, pp. 576–593 ; Halevy, *The Historical-Biographical Aggadah* (supra, note 8), pp. 111–113. On the legends created around Hillel, see: N. Glatzer, *Hillel the Elder* (New York, 1957); C. Safrai, "Sayings and Legends in the Hillel Tradition" in J. H. Charlesworth and L. L. Johns eds., *Hillel and Jesus: Comparative Studies of Two Major Religious Leaders* (Minneapolis, 1997), pp. 306–320.

41. For the history of scholarship on this issue since the studies of von Hahn in the third quarter of the nineteenth century, see A. Taylor, "The Biographical Pattern in Traditional Narrative," *Journal of the Folklore Institute* 1 (1964): 114–129; Raglan's famous work was published in 1934, and was later included in his book, Lord Raglan, *The Hero—A Study in Tradition, Myth and Drama* (New York, 1956). Another interpretation of the hero's life that acquired currency over the years is that of J. Campbell, *The Hero with a Thousand Faces* (New York, 1949). The important summation of the subject with an exhaustive bibliography is that of A. Dundes, "The Hero Pattern and the Life of Jesus," in his *Interpreting Folklore* (Bloomington, 1980), pp. 223–262, 282–287. The biographical pattern of the Jewish folk hero was formulated in D. Noy, "R. Shalem Shabazi be-Aggadat ha-Am shel Yehudei Teyman," in *Bo'i Teyman*, ed. Y. Ratzaby (Tel Aviv, 1967), pp. 106–133 [H]; Idem, "The Death of Rabbi Shalem Shabazzi in Yemenite Folk Legend," in *Studies in The Heritage of Yemenite Jewry*, ed. Y. Tobbi (Jerusalem, 1976), pp. 132–149 [H], and the more detailed pattern suggested by T. Alexander, "Saint and Sage: The 'Ari and Maimonides in Folktales," *Jerusalem Studies in Jewish Folklore* 13 (1992): 29–64 [H].

42. For the sources of biographies of these sages, with notes and detailed variants, see

Bacher, *Legends*. On Raban Johanan ben Zakkai cf. J. Neusner, *The Development of a Legend—Studies on the Traditions Concerning Yohanan Ben Zakkai* (Leiden, 1970). On Rabbi Eliezer ben Hyrcanus, see Z. Kagan, "Divergent Tendencies and their Moulding in the Aggadah," *Scripta Hierosolymitana* 22 (1971): 151–170 and R. D. Aus, "Luke 15:11–32 and R. Eliezer ben Hyrcanus's Rise to Fame," *Journal of Biblical Literature* 104 (1985): 443–469. For the traditions on Rabbi Akiva, see L. Finkelstein, *Akiba—Scholar and Martyr* (New York, 1936); Y. Kanovich, *The Complete Collection of Rabbi Akiva's Sayings in the Talmudic and Midrashic Literature* (Jerusalem, 1965), pp. 27–40 (the biography) [H]; and S. Safrai, ed., *R. Akiva ben Yosef—His Life and Thought* (Jerusalem, 1971) [H].

43. These tales may be found in *Avot de-Rabbi Nathan*, Schechter edition, version A, 6; version B, 12 [The Fathers According to Rabbi Nathan], translated by Judah Goldin, New Haven, 1955, p. 41. For the sources and variants to the biographical legends of Rabbi Akiva, see the previous note and J. Goldin, "Toward a Profile of the Tanna Akiba ben-Joseph," *Journal of the American Oriental Society* 96 (1976): 38–56; C. Kolitz, *Rabbi Akiva: Sage of All Sages* (Woodmore, N.Y., 1989).

44. On the Torah–water of life analogy see "Water signifies Torah, as stated: everyone that thirsteth, come ye to waters" (*Bava Kamma* 17a), and other related comments (including *Ta'anit* 7a, *Song of Songs Rabbah* portion 1, *Sifrei*, portion "Ekev," 48, *Seder Eliyahu Rabbah*, portion 18 [Ish-Shalom edition, pp. 91, 105]). This analogy is particularly interesting in connection to Rabbi Akiva himself in the famous tale of his death, when he told the fable of the fox and the fishes that was based on the Torah–water of life equation (*Berachot* 61b). For an attempt to construct a biography for Rabbi Akiva according to remnants of legends about him, see Safrai (supra, note 42), pp. 13 ff. On the structure of this tale, see A. Goldberg, "Das Martyrium des Rabbi Akiva—Zur Komposition einer Märtyrererzählung (b. Ber. 61b)," *Frankfurter Judaistische Beiträge* 12 (1984): 1–82; J. Fraenkel, *Studies* (supra, note 2), pp. 48–52.

45. For versions of the tale, cf. Safrai, ibid., pp. 68–70 and Halevy, *The Historical-Biographical Aggadah* (supra, note 39), pp. 373–376. On the novella, its literary nature, and social roles, see chapter 2, above, note 15; J. Elbaum, "Models of Storytelling and Speech in the Stories about the Sages (The Attestations about Rabbi Akiva in Avot de-Rabbi Nathan)," *Proceedings of the Seventh World Congress of Jewish Studies* (Jerusalem, 1977), vol. 3: 71–77 [H]; Kagan (supra, note 42), p. 158, note 6, and p. 168, note 12; and S. Safrai, "Tales of the Sages in the Palestinian Tradition and the Babylonian Talmud," *Scripta Hierosolymitana* 22 (1971): 223–229. The recent T. Ilan, *Mine and Yours are Hers: Retrieving Women's History from Rabbinic Literature* (Leiden-New York-Köln, 1997), attempts to "hunt" for the facts in Rabbinic stories about women, and mainly in the story about Rabbi Akiva's wife. Although the discussion is at many times erudite and insightful, the attempt to look at these tales as if they are built on "factual details," and that it is possible to point at these details, is not only an attempt to revive the most simplistic positivistic historical research, but also methodologically unacceptable.

46. On the tale of Rabbi Akiva and the deserted corpse (*met mitzvah*), see S. Lieberman, *Tosephta Kifshutah—Mo'ed* (New York, 1962): 3:325, note 31 [H]; Safrai, *R. Akiva* (supra, note 42), p. 71. The relationship between Torah study and performance of good deeds is discussed by Urbach, *Sages*, pp. 603–620 and Halevy, *The Historical-Biographical Aggadah* (supra, note 8), pp. 413–415.

For the sages' attitude toward *Am ha-Aretz* (the simple folk), see Urbach, *Sages*, pp. 630–648 and A. Oppenheimer (supra, note 4), pp. 170–198. Scholars of ancient Roman folk culture found there the same kind of rivalry and mutual scorn between the educated and the broad strata of the folk. Quintilian, for example, snubs the "boors" and "crude of spirit" who enjoyed hearing Aesop's fables! Strabo claims that "every boorish and uneducated man is, in a certain sense, a child, and like the child loves stories, and so too is the half-educated man—his ability to think is not fully developed, and as regards his spiritual level, he is still but a child," A. Scobie, "Story-Tellers, Storytelling and the Novel in Graeco-Roman Antiquity," *Rheinische Museum für Philologie* 122 (1979): 232.

47. For the tale of R. Akiva's corpse, see *The Midrash on Proverbs*, translated by B. L. Visotzky, New Haven and London, 1992, ch. 9, p. 50. On tales of the death of cultural heroes, see the final paragraphs in Raglan's pattern (supra, note 41); Noy, "The Death of Rabbi Shalem Shabazi" (supra, note 41), as well as the classic study of Ph. Aries, *The Hour of Our Death*, trans. H. Weaver (New York, 1981); and S. Cohen, "The Origin of Death," *Journal of Jewish Lore and Philosophy* 1 (1919): 371–396. On tales of the death of Rabbi Akiva, see Safrai, *R. Akiva* (supra, note 42), pp. 109–124. S. Lieberman brought to light Christian variants of the day to the tale of Rabbi Akiva's death in "The Martyrs of Caesarea," *Annuaire de l'Institut de Philologie et d'Histoire orientales et slave* 7 (1939–1944): 395–446.

48. On the death of Rabbi, see H. A. Kulitz, *Our Holy Rabbi—His Lineage, His Time, and the Force of His Thought* (Jerusalem, 1989), pp. 301–312 [H].

A great deal has been published on the connection between nature and man in ancient mythology. See, for example, G. S. Kirk, *Myth. Its Meaning and Functions in Ancient and other Cultures* (Cambridge, 1970); idem, *The Nature of Greek Myths* (Harmondsworth, 1974), pp. 42 ff., 69–91; Lüthi, *Europe*, pp. 66–80; and M. Eliade, *Myth and Reality*, trans. W. R. Trask (New York, 1963), pp. 54–74.

On the appearance of the mythological tales in aggadah and the curbing of their mythological character, see the monumental and enduring study, M. Grünbaum, "Beiträge zur vergleichenden Mythologie aus der Hagada," *Zeitschrift der Deutschen Morgenländischen Gesseltschaft* 31 (1877), pp. 183–359. Extensive literature has been published on the poetic use of mythological concepts. See, for example, the works included in J. B. Vickery, ed., *Myth and Literature: Contemporary Theory and Practice* (Nebraska, 1966) and the literature cited there, and the entry "Myth" in S. S. Jones, *Folklore and Literature in the United States—An Annotated Bibliography of Studies of Folklore in American Literature* (New York and London, 1984); F. E. Baer, *Folklore and Literature of the British Isles. An Annotated Bibliography* (New York and London, 1986) ("myth patterns").

49. The apocryphal *Vitae Prophetarum* is yet more ancient evidence of the practice of visiting the graves of saints in Palestine—as early as the first century B.C.E.—and of tales of the frequent miracles surrounding them. See also on this chapter 3, above, note 20. On legends of the graves of saints at the dawn of Christianity and late antiquity cf. the considerable literature cited in Wilson, *Saints*, pp. 338–342; H. Delehaye, 'Sanctus'—*Essai sur le culte de Saints dans l'Antiquité* (Brussels, 1954); E. D. Hunt, *Holy Land Pilgrimage in the Later Roman Empire AD 312–460* (Oxford, 1984), and the important material cited in the last work.

50. For discussions on the perception of death by the sages, see A. P. Bender, "Beliefs, Rites and Customs of the Jews Connected with Death, Burial and Mourning," *Jewish Quarterly Review* (o.s.) 6 (1894-5): 317–347, 664–671, 7 (1895-6): 101–118, 259–269; S. Klein, *Tod und Begräbnis in Palästina zur Zeit der Tannaiten* (Berlin, 1908); J. Preuss, *Biblisch-Talmudische Medizin* (Berlin, 1911); W. Hirsch, *Rabbinic Psychology: Beliefs about the Soul in the Rabbinic Literature of the Talmudic Period* (London, 1947); A. J. Saladrini, "Last Words and Deathbed Scenes in Rabbinic Literature," *Jewish Quarterly Review* 68 (1977): 28–45; Fraenkel, *Studies* (supra, note 2), pp. 41–61; and O. Meir, "A Study of Eulogy Tales in Rabbinic Literature," *Sinai* 47 (1983): 123–137 [H]. For sources and variants to the legend of the death of David, see Ginzberg, *Legends*, 4; 113–114 and notes.

51. Compare also A. Büchler, *Types of Jewish-Palestinian Piety* (London, 1922); Y. Baer,

"The First Hasidim in the Writings of Philo and the Hebrew Tradition," *Zion* 18 (1953): 91–108 [H]; G. B. Tzarfati, "Pious Men and Men of Deeds and the First Prophets," *Tarbitz* 26 (1957): 126–153 [H]; Urbach, *Sages*, pp. 506–511; Oppenheimer, *The Am ha-Aretz* (supra, note 4); Halevy, *The Historical-Biographical Aggadah* (supra, note 8), pp. 88–96; L. Jacobs, "The Concept of Hasid in the Biblical and Rabbinic Literature," *Journal of Jewish Studies* 8 (1957): 143–154; D. Daube, "L'enfant terrible (Honni, Hanina ben Dosa)," *Harvard Theological Review* 68 (1975): 371–376; G. Vermes, *Jesus the Jew* (New York, 1973), pp. 58–82; E. Werner, "Traces of Jewish Hagiolatry," *Hebrew Union College Annual* 51 (1980): 39–60; Y. Baer, *Israel Among the Nations* (Jerusalem, 1955) [H], developed a view that saw the first hasidim as a kind of "exemplary community" (pp. 116 ff.), similar to that of the first Christians, that had rules and social organization. See E. E. Urbach's reservations on this view in "Status and Leadership in the World of the Palestinian Sages," in Urbach, *World*, pp. 306–329. On the term "the chapter of piety," see Tzarfati, "Pious Men and Men of Deeds."

52. On tales of the pious men and men of deeds, see the literature cited in the preceding note and O. Meir, "The Donkey of R. Phinehas ben Jair," *Mehkarei ha-Merkaz le-Heker ha-Folklor* (Dov Noy volume), 7 (1983): 117–137 [H]; Halevy, *The Historical-Biographical Aggadah* (supra, note 8), pp. 278–283 (Hanina ben Dosa), pp. 540–543 (Phinehas ben Jair); G. Vermes, "Hanina Ben Dosa," *Journal of Jewish Studies* 23 (1972): 28–50, 24 (1973): 51–64; D. L. Tiede, *The Charismatic Figure as Miracle Worker* (Missoula, 1972); B. M. Bokser, "Wonder Working and the Rabbinic Tradition: The Case of Hanina ben Dosa," *Journal for the Study of Judaism* 16 (1985): 42–92; and J. Neusner, *The Wonder-Working Lawyers of Talmudic Babylonia* (Lanham, N.Y., 1987).

53. The sources of the tales of Honi and his descendants are found in the Babylonian Talmud, *Ta'anit* 23a–b; Tzarfati, "Pious Men" (supra, note 51), pp. 126–130; Z. Kagan, "Honi's Circle—The Path of Mythic Structure from the Aggadic Literature to Modern Hebrew Literature," *Jubilee Volume for Shimon Halkin* (Jerusalem, 1975), pp. 489–502 [H]; R. Patai, "The Control of Rain in Ancient Palestine," *Hebrew Union College Annual* 14 (1939): 251–286; W. S. Green, "Palestinian Holy Men—Charismatic Leadership and Rabbinic Tradition," *Aufstieg und Niedergang der römischen Welt* 19.2 (1979): 619–647. The latter regards the Honi legend's development from the anonymous tale of the *Tosephtah* to the amoraic literature as "manipulation of the charisma" on the part of the rabbinical establishment in order to take control of beliefs connected to the power of folk saints. Other tales of the rivalry between representatives of the simple folk and the sages are found in the Palestinian Talmud *Demai* 1, 3 (Pinhas ben Yair), *Pe'ah* 1, 1 (honoring one's father and mother), *Ta'anit* 21b (righteous men and simple folk); tales of rain-making in *Ta'anit* 23a ff., *Berakhot* 33a ff. (Hanina ben Dosa), and elsewhere. On the rivalry between the sages and the "simple folk," see the discussion and literature cited above in note 46.

54. Palestinian Talmud *Demai* 70, 3; Palestinian *Hullin* 1, 3; on the rivalry between Rabbi Judah the Patriarch and the other sages, see above, note 48. Urbach discussed at length the question of the sages' ties to folk culture, and concluded that claims of alienation were not justified, see E. E. Urbach, "The Laws of Idol Worship and the Archeological and Historical Reality in the Second and Third Centuries," in Urbach, *World*, pp. 125–178. On the heavenly fire sent to bring the devout to God or to punish sinners, see E. Nourry (P. Saintyves), *Essais de folklore Biblique* (Paris, 1922); and T. H. Gaster, *Myth, Legend, and Custom in the Old Testament* (Gloucester, Mass., 1981), pp. 511–512.

55. On the magic circle in folklore, see, for example, Tubach, *Index*, nos. 1068–1071; "Magical Circle," *Encyclopedia of Religion and Ethics* (Edinburgh, 1927), pp. 321–324; J. Campbell, *The Hero* (op. cit. n. 41), pp. 261–269; Trachtenberg, *Magic*, p. 169; and Thompson, motif D1272.

It is worth comparing the Palestinian version of the tale of the river to that which appears in *Hullin* 7a:

> Once R. Pinhas ben Yair was on his way to redeem captives, and came to the river Ginnai. "O Ginnai," said he, "divide thy waters to me, that I may pass through thee." It replied, "Thou art about to do the will of thy Maker; I, too, am doing the will of my Maker [to flow to the sea]. Thou mayest or mayest not accomplish thy purpose; I am sure of accomplishing mine." He said: "If thou wilt not divide thyself, I will decree that no waters ever pass through thee." It, thereupon, divided itself for him. There was also present a certain man who was carrying wheat for the Passover, and so R. Pinhas once again addressed the river: "Divide thyself for this man, too, for he is engaged in religious duty." It thereupon, divided itself for him too. There was also an Arab who had joined them [on the journey], and so R. Pinhas once again addressed the river, "Divide thyself for this one, too, that he may not say, 'Is this the treatment of a fellow traveller?'" It, thereupon, divided itself for him too. R. Joseph exclaimed: How great is this man! Greater than Moses and the sixty myriads of Israel! For the latter [the sea divided itself] but once, whilst for the former thrice!

With the disappearance of the magic formula of twice calling out the river's name (although the threat to do so remains here, too), the magic character of the tale is blurred almost completely. More important is the fact that, in the Babylonian version, the miracle is performed even for individuals not learned in miracles, such as R. Pinhas ben Yair. It would seem that this concluding episode in the Babylonian version comes to confirm the tales's conclusion in the Palestinian version, where R. Pinhas ben Yair explains to his students that it was not magic qualities that caused the river to part before him, but the precept which he was about to perform: the part about the two other people in the Babylonian version confirms this. The tale in the Babylonian version is a kind of reaction to or completion of (via the addition of a narrative episode) the Palestinian version (on the differences between the versions of the tales in the two Talmuds, see the studies enumerated above). In other words, we are witnesses here to an evident process of the tale's movement from the magical to the ethical realm. Cf. Fraenkel, *Studies* (supra, note 2), pp. 24–25 and L. Jacobs, "The Story of R. Pinhas ben Yair and his Donkey" in B. Hullin 7a–b," in *A Tribute to Geza Vermes*, ed. P. R. Davies and R. T. White (Sheffield, 1990), pp. 193–205. On the sages' efforts to obscure the magical character of these tales, see the broad-scoped discussion in Urbach, *Sages*, pp. 97–123, and section H below (Tales of Magic).

56. On the legends of Elisha ben Avuyah, see Bacher, *Legends*, vol. 1, part 2, pp. 139–142; Urbach, *Sages*, pp. 465–467; Halevy, *The Historical-Biographical Aggadah* (supra, note 8), pp. 420–432; S. Back, *Elisha ben Abuya—Acher* (1891); and A. Büchler, "Die Erlösung Elisa b. Abujahs aus dem Höllenfeuer," *Monatschrift für Geschichte und Wissenschaft des Judentums* 76 (1932): 412–456. The concept of "anti-legend" is discussed in the scholarly literature in M. Lüthi, *The European Folktale: Form and Nature* (Philadelphia, 1982), pp. 87–88 and D. Miron, "Folklore and Antifolklore in the Yiddish Fiction of the Haskalah," in Talmage, *Studies*, pp. 219–250.

57. Much has been published on the genre of exemplum and its history. See the principal works, which also contain extensive bibliographies: J. L. Welter, *l'Exemplum dans la littérature religieus et didactique du moyen age* (Paris, 1927); H. Bausinger, "'Exemplum' und 'Beispiel,'" *Hessische Blätter für Volkskunde* 59 (1968): 31–43; R. Schenda, "Stand und Aufgaben der Exemplaforschungen," *Fabula* 10 (1969): 69–85; D. O. Via, "Parable and Example Story—A Literary-Structural Approach," *Semeia* 1 (1968): 105–133; C. Bremond-Le Goff-

Schmitt; C. Daxelmüller, "Exemplum," *Enzyklopädie des Märchens* (Berlin, 1982), vol. 4, cols. 627–649; J. D. Lyons, *Exemplum—The Rhetoric of Example in Early Modern France and Italy* (Princeton, 1989), and the bibliography given below, chapter 5 ("The Middle Ages"), notes 41, 43.

58. The first serious discussion of rabbinic aggadah as exemplary genre is found in Ben-Amos, "Distinctions," in Talmage, *Studies*, pp. 62–66. Ben-Amos views the biographical legends as belonging to the genre of exemplum, and so claims that the message and social function of the exemplary tales are hidden in the tale itself and not transmitted overtly. Such a conception of the genre is perhaps appropriate for the medieval exemplum, but is liable to miss the phenomena unique to rabbinic literature. Such a definition of the genre will in truth include all types of tales in aggadah—the magic tale and the novella, the anecdote and the historical legend. I will attempt to make salient in the remarks below the unique nature of the rabbinic exemplum that stems from its independent qualities, even if there is some discrepancy between its nature and standing in this period and the conception of the genre in later theory.

59. *Leviticus Rabbah*, Margolies edition, p. 856; *Tanhuma*, "Kedoshim," 8; Gaster, *Exempla*, # 368. Urbach, *Sages*, pp. 440–441, regards the story as a folktale, and defines its function precisely as that of the exemplum, despite the fact that he does not use this terminology. The tale is a combination of two tale types: AT 653*C—the two wooers, and AT 1689*A—two presents for the king. Cf. also A. Shinan, "'The Tale of the Citrons'—A Story from the Midrash [*Leviticus Rabbah*, 37, 2] and Some of the Forms it Took," *Jerusalem Studies in Jewish Folklore* 13–14 (1992): 61–79 [H].

Another example of the delicate line between the novelistic tale and the exemplum is the story of the adulteress in Midrash *Numbers Rabbah* 9, 9. The midrash relates to Numbers 5:12–24: "Speak to the children of Yisra'el, and say to them, If any man's wife go aside, and commit a trespass against him, and a man lie with her carnally, . . . and she be undetected. . . . And the priest shall bring her near, and set her before the Lord. . . . and he shall cause the woman to drink the bitter water that causes the curse. . . . ":

> A story is told of two sisters who looked like each other, and one of whom was married in another town. The husband of one them grew jealous against her and sought to make her drink the bitter water in Jerusalem. So she went to the city where her married sister lived. Said her sister to her: "What is your reason for coming here?" "My husband," she told her "wishes to make me drink the bitter water and I am defiled." Her sister said: "I will go in your place and drink." "Go," replied the other, "and do so." What did she do? Donning her sister's garments, she went and drank the bitter water and was found to be clean. When she returned home, her sister, who had played the harlot, came out to meet her and they embraced and kissed each other. As they kissed each other the harlot smelled the bitter water and instantly died. This is to confirm what it says, "There is no man that has power over the spirit" (Eccles. 8, 8) . . . For this reason it says, "And act unfaithfully against him."

The tale can be seen as a caution to women not to commit the sin of adultery. But the structure of the midrashic text that opens and closes with the same verse, the blending of additional verses from various sources, and the linkage to the biblical text indicate that it should be seen as a homiletical illustration of the given verse, and not necessarily as an exemplary text intended to teach a rule of ethical conduct.

60. On the tale, see M. Gaster and B. Heller, "Der Schüler und das Mädchen," *Monatsschrift für Geschichte und Wissenschaft des Judentums* 78 (1934): 334–343; W. Z. Harvey, "The

Pupil, the Harlot and the Fringe Benefits," *Prooftexts* 6 (1986): 259–264; A. Goshen-Gottstein, "The Zizit Commandment, the Whore and the Homiletical Story," in Z. Grunner and M. Hirschman, eds. *Rabbinic Thought: Proceedings of the First Congress* (Haifa, 1990), pp. 45–58 [H]; Gaster, *Legends*, # 35 (and the variants cited in the note to the tale). On the sages' conception of repentance see Urbach, *Sages*, pp. 461–471. For the distinction between tales whose context is the learned culture (literati) and those of folk origin (simplices), see note 40, above. On Moses's appeal to the forces of nature before his death, see Ginzberg, *Legends*, 3: 448–453.

61. For the distinction between the model of "exemplary behavior" and the narrative model cf. Bremond–Le-Goff–Schmitt. On the changing of protagonists from exemplary figures to anonymous ones see ibid., p. 45. The anonymous nature of the heroes in some of the rabbinic exempla was stressed by Ben-Amos, "Distinctions." For variants to the tale of Yosef the Shabbat Lover, cf. Gaster, *Exempla*, #380; Schwarzbaum, *Studies*, pp. 269–270, 272, and the literature cited there. For a concentration of other rabbinic tales on the theme of Sabbath observance, see Bialik and Ravnitzky, *Sefer ha-Aggadah* (supra note 39), pp. 486–493.

62. On animals who keep religious precepts, see Noy, *Index*, ch. B, and Noy, *Animals*.

63. On the modus operandi of the "exemplary apparatus" and its use of psychological tools to enforce its values, see Bremond–Le-Goff–Schmitt; E. Yassif, "The Exemplary Tale in *Sefer Hasidim*," *Tarbitz* 57 (1988): 225–232 [H], and the literature cited there.

64. On the question of the place and importance of the talmudic *ma'aseh* (casus) in the emergence of the halacha and the aggadah, see A. Kaminka, "The *Ma'aseh* as a Source of Halacha," in his *Studies in Scripture, Talmud and the Rabbinic Literature* (Tel Aviv, 1951), 2:1–41 [H]. On the *casus*, its definition and history, see A. Jolles, *Einfache Formen* (Tübingen, 1982²), pp. 171–199; K. Stierle, "L'Histoire comme example, l'example comme histoire," *Poétique* 10 (1972): 188–189. On the tale of Rava's Reed cf. Y. A. Klausner, *Ha-Novela ba-Sifrut ha-Ivrit* [The Novella in Hebrew Literature] (Tel Aviv, 1947), pp. 26–28 [H] and Goebel, *Motifs*, pp. 196–197.

65. For variants to the tale, see Gaster, *Exempla*, # 33 and *Piska* 22, translated by William G. Braude, New Haven and London, 1968, p. 465. On court and law tales in international folklore, see E. Nourry (P. Saintyves), *Les Cinquante jugment de Salomon ou Les Arrêts des Bons juges d'apres la tradition populaire* (Paris, 1933); A. Dundes Renteln and A. Dundes, eds., *Folk Law: Essays in the Theory and Practice of Lex Non Scripta* (Wisconsin, 1994), 2 vols.

66. There aren't many fundamental discussions of rabbinic attitude to historiography. Compare Steinschneider, *Literature*, pp. 42–43; I. Sonne, "The Use of Rabbinic Literature as Historical Sources," *Jewish Quarterly Review* 36 (1945): 147–169; M. D. Herr, ed., *The History of Palestine—The Roman-Byzantine Period* (Jerusalem, 1985), pp. 377–379 [H] and idem, "The Concept of History among the Sages," *Proceedings of the Sixth World Congress of Jewish Studies* (Jerusalem, 1977), 3: 129–142[H]. The most comprehensive study of the cultural and literary aspects of the sages' historiographical outlook is still the pioneering work of I. Heinemann, *Pathways of Legend* (Jerusalem, 1954) [H], wherein he develops the notion of "the creative historiography." A collection of articles by E. E. Urbach on "Midrash and History" appears in his book, *World*, pp. 349–436. More specific questions are treated in H. A. Fischel, "Story and History: Observations of Greco-Roman Rhetoric and Pharisanism," *American Oriental Society*, Middle West Branch, Oriental Series 3 (Bloomington, 1969), pp. 59–88; S. Y. Friedman, "Historical Legend in the Babylonian Talmud," offprint from *Memorial Volume for Rabbi S. Lieberman* (Jerusalem, 1989), pp. 1–46 [H]; Yassif, "The Study" (1988), pp. 3–8.

67. For the extensive literature on this subject see above, chapter 3 [B], and below, chapter 5 [E], and the accompanying notes.

68. Owing to the centrality of the event depicted in this legend—the destruction of the Temple and the transition from Temple rites to Torah study in the sages' academies—studies focusing on it are numerous. I will mention only some of the more recent: the comparison of the first four versions in G. Alon's seminal article, "Raban Johanan ben Zakkai's Emergence to Yavneh," *Zion* 3 (1938): 183-214 [H]. Y. Baer analyzes the tale from another, somewhat apologetic point of view, in "Jerusalem in the Great Revolt," *Zion* 36 (1971): 178-190 [H]; A. Schalit, "The Prophecies of Josephus and Raban Johanan ben Zakkai on the Ascent of Vespasian to the Throne," in *Salo Baron Jubilee Volume*, ed. S. Lieberman (Jerusalem, 1975), pp. 397-432 [H]; J. Neusner, *The Development of a Legend. Studies on the Traditions Concerning Yohanan Ben Zakkai* (Leiden, 1970) [on this see Ilan (supra note 45), pp. 9-16]; P. Schäfer, "Die Flucht Johanan b. Zakkais aus Jerusalem und die Gründung des 'Lehrhauses' in Jabne," *Aufstieg und Niedergang der römischen Welt* 19.2 (1979): 619-647; A. J. Saladrini, "Johanan Ben Zakkai's Escape from Jerusalem—Origin and Development of a Rabbinic Story," *Journal for the Study of Judaism* 18 (1987): 69-80; and see also S. Safrai, "Ancient Historiographical Palestinian Sources in the Tradition of the Babylonian Talmud," in *Studies in Historiography*, ed. M. Zimmerman, M. Stern, and J. Salmon (Jerusalem, 1988), pp. 82-83 [H].

69. On the formation of legend according to folkloristic theories, see W. D. Hand, ed., *American Folk Legend: A Symposium* (Berkeley and Los Angeles, 1971); L. Dégh, "Process of Legend Formation," in *Fourth International Congress for Folk-Narrative Research in Athens*, ed. G. Megas (Athens, 1965), pp. 77-87; S. Bernfeldt, "The Legend and the History of the Jewish People," *Sefer ha-Yovel le-Nahum Sokolov* [Jubilee Volume for Nahum Sokolov] (Warsaw, 1904), pp. 211-221 [H] ("We must be extremely conscious in taking evidence from legend, as it would be all too easy to err, and twice so: We do a disservice to the legend itself, as in our desire to make of it history we must, perforce, strip it of its poetic garb. Yet on the other hand, we build a grand edifice on a ramshackle foundation, as in essence the legend is not history, but a natural, poetic, activity of the folk"); J. Wolfsberg, "Aggadah and History," in *Minha li-Yehudah, Presented to Rabbi Yehudah Leib Zlotnick on His Sixtieth Jubilee*, ed. S. Assaf, J. Even-Shmuel and R. Benjamin (Jerusalem, 1950), pp. 31-39 [H]; Bergmann, *Legends*, pp. 5-16; and J. Bergmann, "Geschichte und Legende," *Festschrift Adolf Schwartz zum siebzigsten Geburstage* (Wien und Berlin, 1917), pp. 89-108. Important methodological developments took place in the definition and meaning of oral history as well. See J. Vansina, *Oral Traditions as History* (Madison, Wisc., 1985) and P. Thompson, *The Voice of the Past—Oral History* (Oxford, 1978).

70. On various aspects of the figure of Bar-Kokhba and the rebellion he led, see two collections of articles: A. Oppenheimer, ed., *The Bar-Kokhba Revolt—Collected Articles* (Jerusalem, 1980) [H]; idem and E. Rappaport, eds., *The Bar-Kokhba Revolt, New Studies* (Jerusalem, 1984) [H], and the exhaustive bibliography in the latter, pp. 243-251. On the Bar-Kokhba legend among the sages, see S. Krauss, "The Regiments of Bar-Kokhba," *Jubilee Volume for Alexander Marks* (New York, 1950), pp. 391-399 [H]; R. G. Marks, *The Image of Bar Kokhba in Jewish Literature Up to the Seventeenth Century: False Messiah and National Hero* (Ph.D. Thesis, University of California, Los Angeles, 1980), and idem., *The Image of Bar-Kokhba in Traditional Jewish Literature* (University Park, Pa., 1994), compares versions of the legend in the Palestinian Talmud and Midrash Lamentations Rabbah, and proposes similar distinctions. See also the notes below.

71. The historiosophic concept of "history as narrative" developed along parallel lines in Europe, in the mentalité school, see A. Gurevich, "Medieval Culture and Mentalité According to the New French Historiography," *Archives europénnes de sociologie* 24 (1983): 167-195; R. Chartier, "Intellectual History and History of Mentalities—A Dual Re-Evaluation," in his *Cultural History Between Practice and Representation* (Ithaca, N.Y., 1988); P. Carrard, *Po-*

etics of the New History: French Historical Discourse from Braudel to Chartier (Baltimore, 1992); and in the United States following Hayden White and others and cf. the latter's fundamental works, H. White, "The Historical Text as a Literary Artifact," Clio 3 (1974): 277–303; idem, Tropics of Discourse (Baltimore, 1978); idem, Metahistory (Baltimore, 1973); and L. O. Mink, "Narrative Form as a Cognitive Instrument," in The Writing of History, ed. R. H. Canary and H. Kozicki (Madison, Wisc., 1978), pp. 129–149. For the implementation of these principles to the folkloric text, see R. M. Hurst, "History and Folklore," New York Folklore Quarterly 25 (1969): 243–260; G. Lutz, "Volkskunde und Geschichte—Zur Frage einer als 'historische Wissenschaft' verstandenen Volkskunde," Volkskultur und Geschichte—Festgabe für Josef Dönninger zum 65 Geburstag (Berlin, 1970), pp. 14–26; H. G. Ellis Davidson, "Folklore and History," Folklore 85 (1974): 73–92; N. Belmont, Arnold Van Gennep—The Creator of French Ethnography (Chicago and London, 1979), pp. 113–121; R. Bauman, Story, Performance and Event. Contextual Studies of Oral Narrative (Cambridge, 1986); E. C. Fine, The Folklore Text. From Performance to Print (Bloomington, 1984); S. D. Stahl, Literary Folkloristics and the Personal Narrative (Bloomington and Indianapolis, 1989); and C. Rearick, Beyond the Enlightenment: Historians and Folklore in Nineteenth Century France (Bloomington, 1974). On mythological motifs that parallel the Bar-Kokhba legend, and especially in Greco-Roman culture, see E. E. Halevy, The World of the Aggadah: The Aggadah in Light of Greek Sources (Tel Aviv, 1972), pp. 112–114 [H]; idem, The Historical-Biographical Aggadah (supra, note 8), pp. 440–445. The tale type of the revolt against heaven and "pride punished" is AT 836 and its various offshoots.

72. On the narrative theme of "the rise of the wise courtier," see above, chapter 3, section [E].

S. Lieberman determines, according to testimony in the apocryphal books, that the name of the Arab officer who besieged Jerusalem was Avgar, not Pangar, and cf. his book Midrashey Teiman (Jerusalem, 1970), p. 15 [H]. A. Yisraeli-Taran, The Legends of the Destruction (Tel-Aviv, 1997), p. 29 observes that the official rank of dux is Byzantine, and so the versions using it cannot be earlier than the third century, and compare also ibid. p. 109, note 2.

73. On the first narrative model, fleshed out in the tale of Nathan de-Zuzita and its variants, see Sanhedrin 31b (Mar-Ukbah) although the tale was not itself preserved, Rashi cites it there; R. Nissim of Kairouan, Hibbur Yafeh Mih-ha-Yeshu'ah, Hirschberg edition (Jerusalem, 1970), pp 73–76 [H] and on Arab variants to the tale cf. ibid., p. 63; Gaster, Exempla, #35; Jellinek, Beit ha-Midrash, part 5, pp. 142–144. On the second narrative model, in which the husband is forced to cooperate with his wife and her lover, cf. Yassif, Golem, pp. 217–222. Cf. also M. Gaster, "Seder Ma'aseh Ukbah," Ha-Tzofeh le-Hokhmat Yisrael 9 (1924/1925): 158–161 [H]; Gaster and Heller, pp. 334–343.

74. On Jewish historical consciousness after the destruction of the Temple, see M. D. Herr, "The Nation of Israel after the Destruction of the Second Temple," in The History of the Land of Israel—The Roman Byzantine Period, ed. M. Stern (Jerusalem, 1984), pp. 286–301; R. Goldberg, "Early Rabbinic Explanations of the Destruction of Jerusalem," Journal of Jewish Studies 33 (1982): 517–525; A. L. Mintz, Hurban: Responses to Catastrophe in Hebrew Literature (New York, 1984), pp. 49–83; D. G. Roskies, Against the Apocalypse: Responses to Catastrophe in Modern Jewish Culture (Cambridge, Mass., 1984); and idem. (ed.), The Literature of Destructions: Jewish Responses to Catastrophe (Philadelphia, 1988), pp. 49–70. The legend of "Kamza and Bar Kamza" and the causes of the Temple's destruction are discussed in Halevy, Gates, pp. 203–228 and Baer, "Jerusalem in the Days of the Great Revolt" (supra, note 68), pp. 169 ff.

75. See A. Schalit, Herod the King, the Man and his Achievements (Jerusalem, 1978) [H]; J. Levin, "The History of the Herodian Period," in Stern (supra, note 74), pp. 25–78; G. Allon,

"The Attitude of the Pharisees to the Roman Government and the House of Herod," *Scripta Hierosolymitana* 7 (1961): 53–78; H. W. Hoehner, *Herod Antipas* (Cambridge and London, 1972); Schürer, *History*, 1: 282–329. On the legend of Herod and Mariamme, reference to the Greek and Roman sources, see Halevy, *The Historical-Biographical Aggadah* (supra, note 8), pp. 102–109; Schürer, *History*, I: 283–284, 302–303. On the comparison between this legend and its parallel in Herodot, see Ilan (supra note 45), pp. 152–154. On sexual intercourse with corpses as a folkloric motif, see Thompson, motif T466.

76. On the tale of the mother and her seven sons in the literature of the Second Temple period, cf. that cited above in chapter 3, note 18.

On The Ten Martyrs, and *Midrash Eleh Ezkerah*, see Urbach, *Sages*, pp. 520–523; S. Krauss, "The Ten Martyrs," *ha-Shiloah* 44 (1925), pp. 10–22, 106–117, 221–233 [H]; S. Tudor, "The Ten Martyrs—The Tale and Its Background," *ha-Umah* 9 (1972): 199–206 [H]; H. Graez, "Die hadrianische Verfolgung und die zehn Märtyrer," *Monatschrift für Geschichte und Wissenschaft des Judentum* 1 (1852): 307–322; L. Finkelstein, "The Ten Martyrs," in *Essays and Studies in Memory of Linda Miller*, ed. I. Davidson (New York, 1938), pp. 29–56; W. H. C. Frend, *Martyrdom and Persecution in the Early Church—A Study of a Conflict from the Maccabees to Donatus* (Oxford, 1965). A synoptic edition was prepared by G. Reeg, *Die Geschichte von den zehn Märtyren* (Tübingen, 1985).

77. On the demonic world in the rabbinic period and its connection to neighboring cultures, see M. Margaliot, *Sefer ha-Razim: A Book of Magic from the Talmudic Period* (Jerusalem, 1967), pp. 1–62 [H]; Urbach, *Sages*, pp. 97–123; J. Bazak, *Beyond the Senses: On Supernatural Phenomena in Jewish Traditions and in Contemporary Studies* (Tel Aviv, 1986) [H]; Bergmann, *Legends*, pp. 43–54, 60–72; G. Brecher, *Das Transcendentale Magie und magische Heilarten im Talmud* (Wien, 1850); A. Kohut, *Über die judische Angelologie und Däemonologie in Parismus* (Leipzig, 1866); L. Blau, *Das altjüdische Zauberwesen* (Berlin, 1914); P. Fiebig, *Rabbinische Wundergeschichten des neutestamentlichen Zeitalters* (Bonn, 1933); E. Langton, *Essentials of Demonology: A Study of Jewish and Christian Doctrine, its Origin and Development* (London, 1949); G. Theissen, *Urchristliche Wundergeschichte* (Gütersloh, 1974); L. Sabourin, "Hellenistic and Rabbinic Miracles," *Biblical Theology Bulletin* 2 (1972): 281–307; J. Goldin, "The Magic of Magic and Superstition," in *Aspects of Religious Propaganda in Judaism and Early Christianity*, ed. E. Schüssler Fiorenza (Notre Dame, 1976), pp. 115–147; J. Naveh and S. Shaked, *Amulets and Magic Bowls: Aramaic Incantations of Late Antiquity* (Jerusalem, 1985, bibliography on pp. 242–264); P. S. Alexander, "Incantations and Books of Magic," in Schürer, *History*, 2, part 1, pp. 342–379; and P. Schäfer, "Jewish Magic Literature in Late Antiquity and Early Middle Ages, *Journal of Jewish Studies* 41 (1990): 75–91. The most complete, detailed, and reliable survey is still H. L. Strack & P. Billerbeck, "Zur altjüdischen Dämonologie," in *Kommentar zum Neuen Testament aus Talmud und Midrasch* (München, 1922), 4: 1, pp. 501–535. A good and updated survey of most themes connected with magic in the Talmud is G. Veltri, *Magie und Halakha*, (Tübingen, 1997).

78. On magic in ancient Greece and Rome, see J. C. Baroja, *The World of the Witches* (Chicago and London, 1965), pp. 17–40, and the literature cited there. Baroja points to the writings of Plato, Ovid, Petronius, Lucian, Apuleius, and others, in which testimony survived as to the demonic beliefs of their time, and on the complex attitude towards these manifestations. See ibid., pp. 19, 31, 38–39. On the social status of the magician in ancient Rome, see F. Graf, *Magic in the Ancient World*, trans. by F. Philip (Cambridge, Mass. and London, 1997).

A cluster of magic traditions from the tannaic period appears in chapters 6–7 of *Tosefta Sabbath*, and cf. the important interpretation of S. Lieberman, *Tosefta Kifshutah* (New York 1962), 3:79–105 [H], and the literature cited there. On the texts from tractate *'Avodah Zarah* see E. E. Urbach, "The Laws of 'Avodah Zarah in Light of the Archeological and Historical Reality of the Third and Fourth Centuries," *Eretz Yisrael* 5 (Benjamin Mazar Volume, 1959): 189–209 [H]; idem, *Sages*, pp. 97–123; and S. Lieberman, *Greek*, pp. 245–252. Folk medicine has always been the main arena for dabbling in magic. See the classic study of J. Preuss, *Biblisch-Talmudische Medizin* (Berlin, 1911) [*Biblical and Talmudic Medicine*, trans. by F. Rosner (New York, 1978)]. On the use of symbols and magic objects in this period, see the monumental compendium of E. R. Goodenouph, *Jewish Symbols of the Greco-Roman Period*, 13 vols. (New York, 1953–1968).

    79. On locations haunted by demons, see Strack and Billerbeck (supra, note 77), pp. 518–519; Noy, *Index*: G302.9: Deeds of the Demons; G302.15: Places Haunted by the Devil. The serpent who sees or touches the shadow of a flying bird—and the bird's wings drop off, *Mekhiltah be-Shalah*, Va-Yisah ch. 1 (Weiss edition, p. 53) [H]; *Tanhuma be-Shelah* 18 (Buber edition, p. 64). See also the monograph on the shadow in Jewish folklore: A. Löwinger, "Der Schatten in Literatur und Folklore der Juden," *Mitteilungenn zur jüdischen Volkskunde* 13 (1910): 1–5, 41–57. The chief cause of the various diseases (especially those linked to emotional disturbance) is demonic injury, and cf. Preuss (supra, note 78); Y. Bilu, "The Place of the Demon in Explanations of Illnesses and Ills among Israelis of Moroccan Descent," *Jerusalem Studies in Jewish Folklore* 2 (1982): 108–123; and idem, "The Taming of the Deviants and Beyond: An Analysis of Dybbuk Possession and Exorcism in Judaism," *The Psychoanalytical Study of Society* 11 (1985): 1–32.

    80. On a similar encounter between Elijah (or another supernatural entity) and Lilith as she haunts the homes of mortals with injurious intent to children, see Strack and Billerbeck (supra, note 77), pp. 514 ff., 764 ff.; Yassif, *Ben Sira* pp. 63–71; G. Vermes, "Hanina ben Dosa," *Journal of Jewish Studies* 23 (1972): 28–50. On the unicorn cf. O. Shepard, *The Lore of the Unicorn* (London, 1929) and J. Einhorn, *Spiritualis Unicornis. Das Einhorn als Bedeutungsträger in Literatur und Kunst des Mittelalters* (München, 1971). The body of the demon (or dragon) is covered with a protective, impenetrable layer. See Noy, *Index*, motifs G302.4 and ff. On the demon Ketev Meriri and his place in the development of Jewish folklore, cf. A. Löwinger, "Der Windgeist Keteb," *Jahrbuch für Jüdisch Volkskunde* 2 (1924–25): 157–170; Noy, *Index*, motif G302.2; and Thompson, *Motifs*, G369.7 Demon with one eye; D1402.2 Magic eye kills all who see it. Folk beliefs similar to these that are found among the sages, and tales reporting on them and on dangerous encounters in city streets with demons or witches and so on, were quite widespread in the Roman folklore of the period, see Scobie (supra, note 46), pp. 248–249. On folk beliefs about "the evil eye" and ways of combating its peril in Greece and Rome of the first century B.C.E. and on, see Baroja (supra, note 78), p. 38, and the full survey in E. S. McCartney, "Praise and Dispraise in Folklore," in *The Evil Eye—A Casebook*, ed. A. Dundes (Madison, Wisc., 1981), pp. 9–38.

    81. In recent years, folkloristic scholarship has focused on the urban legend, and cf. G. Bennet et al., ed., *Perspectives on Contemporary Legend* (Sheffield, 1987); and especially: G. Bennet and P. Smith, *Contemporary Legend: A Folklore Bibliography* (New York and London, 1993). On linkage between modern legend and ancient legends, see B. af Klintberg, "Do the Legends of Today and Yesterday Belong to the Same Genre?" in *Storytelling in Contemporary Societies*, ed. L. Röhrich & S. Wienkler-Piepho (Tübingen, 1990), pp. 113–126. On the traditional approaches to the study of folklore in remote border regions and "primitive" societies, see R. M. Dorson, ed., *Peasant Customs and Savage Myths*, 2 vols. (Chicago, 1968); on the demonic element's infiltration into daily life in the tales and beliefs of the rabbinic period, see H. Lewy, "Zum Dämonenglauben," *Archiv für Religionswissenschaft* 28 (1930): 241–252; D. Ben-Amos, "A Formal and Structural Study of Legends in the Talmud and the Midrash,"

Proceedings of the Fourth World Congress of Jewish Studies (Jerusalem, 1969), pp. 357–359 [H]; idem, "Distinctions," in Talmage, *Studies*, pp. 45–72. The esthetic and psychological effects of the *märchen* and the *sage* were discussed at length by M. Lüthi, "Aspects of the Märchen and the Legend," *Genre* 2 (1969): 162–178; idem, *Volksmärchen und Volkssage—Zwei Grundformen volkstümlicher Erzählung* (Bern, 1966).

82. Thompson, *Motifs*, B11.23.1: Seven-headed dragon; Noy, *Index*, motif G302.16 and the tale type AT 300: The Dragon Slayer. On Christian saints who do battle with dragons (especially the legend of Saint George and the Dragon), see J. B. Aufhauser, *Das Drachenwunder des Heiligen George in der grieschischen und lateinischen überlieferung* (Leipzig, 1911); J. Fonterose, "Saint George and the Dragon," in his *Python: A Study of Delphic Myth and Its Origin* (New York, 1974), appendix 4; Loomis, *White Magic*, pp. 65, 118–119, and the literature cited in Wilson, *Saints*, p. 320.

83. Important evidence of the existence of tales about demons who attack in synagogues survived in the New Testament:

> And [Jesus] came down to Capernaum, a city of Galilee, and taught them on the sabbath days. And they were astonished at his doctrine; for his word was with power. And in the synagogue there was a man, which had a spirit of an unclean devil, and cried out with a loud voice, saying, Let us alone; what have we to do with thee, thou Jesus of Nazareth? Art thou come to destroy us? I know thee who thou art; the Holy One of God. And Jesus rebuked him, saying Hold thy peace, and come out of him. And when the devil had thrown him in the midst, he came out of him, and hurt him not. And they were all amazed, and spake among themselves, saying, What a word is this! for with authority and power he commandeth the unclean spirits and they come out. (Luke 4:31–36; Mark 1:21–34; Matt. 8:14–17)

It should be noted that in stories in the New Testament, the magical perfomance takes place before all the worshippers in the synagogue, since the outright objective of the tale is missionary. See, for example, H. C. Kee, *Miracle in the Early Christian World* (New Haven and London, 1983). On the negative attitude toward heroes and tales of heroism in rabbinic aggadah, and their replacement with tales of belief and ethics, see R. G. Marks, "Dangerous Hero: Rabbinic Attitudes Toward Legendary Warriors," *Hebrew Union College Annual* 54 (1983): 181–194.

84. On the tale of Solomon and Ashmedai, see above in note 20; Ben-Yehezkiel, "The Book," pp. 365–367; Halevy, *Portions*, pp. 236–239, and the discussion above in this chapter, section C (The Expanded Biblical Story); I. Lévi, "L'Orgueil de Salomon," *Revue des Etudes Juives* 13 (1888): 58–65; Grünbaum, *Studies*; Goebel, *Motifs*. On "Joseph Shiddah," see *Eruvin* 43a.

85. On the tale of Bar Themalyon, see I. Lévi, "Légendes Judeo-Chrétiennes," *Revue des Etudes Juives* 8 (1884): 197–205, who considers this legend to be borrowed from the Christian legend of Saint Bartholomew. J. Halévy expressed reservations to this conclusion in "Ben-Thymélion et Bartholomée," *Revue des Etudes Juives* 10 (1885): 60–65. On this tale cf. the discussion in M. Geller, *Joshua B. Perahia and Jesus of Nazareth: Two Rabbinic Magicians* (Ph.D. Thesis, Brandeis University, 1973), pp. 176–178. The tale type, "miraculous rescue of a Jewish community," is one of the most common in Jewish folktales. Cf. also Marcus, "Confrontation," pp. 9–204. Tales of rescue of the Jewish community after exorcising the demon from the emperor's daughter are found in the eleventh-century *Scroll of Ahima'atz* (*The Chronicle of Ahimaaz*, trans. M. Salzman [New York, 1924], pp. 71–73), and cf. E. Yassif, "Folk-

tales in the Scroll of Ahima'atz." *Yad le-Heiman. Collected Articles in Memory of A. M. Habermann* (Lod, 1984), pp. 46–48 [H]. Edifying evidence of the popularity of the beliefs in possession and exorcising of demons among Jews in Palestine of the first century C.E. is extant in Josephus Flavius:

> God also enabled him [Solomon] to learn that skill which expels demons. . . . And he left behind him the manner of using exorcisms, by which they drive away demons, so that they never return, and this method of cure is of great force unto this day; for I have seen a certain man of my own country whose name was Eleazar, releasing people that were demoniacal in the presence of Vespasian, and his sons, and his captains, and the whole multitude of his soldiers. The manner of the cure was this:—He put a ring that had a root of one of those sorts mentioned by Solomon to the nostrils of the demoniac, after which he drew out the demon through his nostrils; and when the man fell down immediately, he abjured him to return into him no more, making still mention of Solomon, and reciting the incantations which he composed. And when Eleazar would persuade and demonstrate to the spectators that he had such a power, he set a little way off a cup or basin full of water, and commanded the demon as he went out of the man to overturn it, and thereby to let the spectators know that he had left the man; and when this was done the skill and wisdom of Solomon was shewn very manifestly. (Flavius Josephus, *The Antiquities of the Jews*, Book VII, ch. II, part 5, in *Josephus Complete Works*, trans. William Whiston [Michigan, 1978], p. 173).

So too in tales of the New Testament (and see note 83, above). According to other testimony from Josephus, it becomes clear that the demons who took possession of mortal bodies were themselves spirits of the wicked. In describing a root called "Baaras," he writes, "one virtue it hath, that if it only be brought to sick persons, it quickly drives away those called Demons, which are no other than the spirits of the wicked, which enter into men that are alive, and kill them, unless they can obtain some help against them" (*The Wars of the Jews*, Book 7, ch. 6, part 3, in *Josephus Complete Works*, ibid., pp. 595–596). On the history and antiquity of this phenomenon, see T. K. Oesterreich, *Possession, Daemonical and other Among Primitive Races in Antiquity, The Middle Ages and Modern Times* (New York, 1930); S. V. McCasland, *By the Finger of God: Demon Possession and Exorcism in Early Christianity in Light of Modern Views of Mental Illness* (New York, 1951); Geller, ibid., pp. 172 ff.; chapter 3, above, note 26.

86. On folktales containing the motif of a mortal wed to a demoness, see Y. L. Zlotnick, *Ma'aseh Yerushalmi* [The Story of the Jerusalemite] (Jerusalem, 1947), esp. pp. 30–33 [H], with its important supplemental material from rabbinic literature. See also the history of this prominent tale: S. Zfatman, *The Marriage of a Mortal Man and a She-Demon: The Transformation of the Motif in the Folk Narrative of Ashkenazi Jewry in the Sixteenth–Seventeenth Centuries* (Jerusalem, 1987) [H], and the literature cited there.

87. M. Hengel, *Rabbinische Legende und früphrisäische Geschichte: Schimeon b. Schatach und die achtzig Hexen von Askalon* (Heidelberg, 1984); J. Efron, "The Deed of Simeon ben Shatah in Ascalon," in A. Kasher, ed. *Jews and Hellenistic Cities in Eretz Israel* (Tübingen, 1990), pp. 318–341, reconstructs the orgiastic rites in the caves surrounding the city of Ashkelon, and interprets the tale as recounting the war against the shrine of Aphrodite-Ishtar (Astrate), and the reservations on both in Ilan (supra, note 45), pp. 32–35; Halevy, *The Historical-Biographical Aggadah* (supra, note 8), pp. 72–85. On women in witchcraft and the link to prostitution, see Blau (supra, note 77), pp. 18 ff.; Baroja (supra, note 78), pp. 31 ff.; Geller (supra, note 85), pp. 18–19; and S. Fishbane, "'Most Women Engage in Sorcery': An Analysis of Sorceresses in the Babylonian Talmud", *Jewish History* 7 (1993): 27–42. The de-

monization of the members of other religions and beliefs started already in early Christianity: E. Pagels, *The Origin of Satan* (New York, 1995), pp. 63–88, 149–178.

88. This is the first part of the "biographical pattern" of the cultural hero. On this subject in general, see supra, note 41. On the birth of R. Judah ben Beteirah as the beginning of a "legendary biography," see Bin-Gorion, *Mimekor*, #248–249, and the corresponding notes. On deliberate sexual incapacitation as a magic phenomenon, cf. A. Marmorstein, "Beiträge zur Religionsgeschichte und Volkskunde," *Jahrbuch für jüdische Volkskunde* 1 (1923): 280–319, 2 (1924/5): 344–383; and Bazak (supra, note 77), pp. 52–56, and, in the corresponding Arabic culture, Y. Tzoran, "Magic, Theurgic, and the Science of the Letters in Islam," *Jerusalem Studies in Jewish Folklore* 18 (1998): 33–36. For an analysis of the tale according to the hypothesis of the "relationship between the natural and supernatural," see Ben-Amos, "Distinctions," pp. 55–56. Geller (note 85, above), p. 157, suggests that the woman whom R. Joshua ben Hananiah pulled by the hair was the demoness Lilith. However Lilith, unlike witches, who were part of Jewish society, was not afraid of being exposed. Lilith was the "mother of the Demons," with a host of spirits at her beck and call, and it is hard to believe that folk beliefs would have her "drawn up" in such a manner from the table of some ordinary Jew in Rome. For the historical background to visits of the sages in Rome, see S. Safrai, "The Sages of Yavneh in Rome," *Memorial Volume for Shlomo Umberto Nahon* (Jerusalem, 1978), pp. 151–167 [H]. On witches in the Hellenistic world who, driven by jealousy, rendered their lovers impotent, and on the connection between witchcraft, women, and jealousy, see Baroja (supra, note 78), pp. 31–36.

89. On R. Joshua ben Hananiah's involvement in magical events, see W. S. Green, *The Traditions of Joshua Ben Hananiah* (Leiden, 1981), pp. 11–13, and also Geller (supra, note 85), pp. 152 ff. On the story cycle of R. Joshua and the Elders of Athens, see Yassif, "Traces," pp. 227–229.

90. R. T. Herford, *Christianity in Talmud and Midrash* (London, 1903), pp. 112–115, 211 ff. and A. Segal, *Two Powers in Heaven: Early Rabbinic Reports About Christianity and Gnosticism* (Leiden, 1977). On the image of Jesus as magician in the Hebrew sources of the period, see: " . . . in the scant reports about Jesus and his disciples in Rabbinic literature they are primarily described as enchanters and sorcerers," Urbach, *Sages*, pp. 115–116; M. Smith, *Jesus the Magician* (New York, 1977); M. Geller, "Jesus's Theurgic Powers: Parallels in the Talmudic and Incantation Bowls," *Journal of Jewish Studies* 28 (1977): 141–155; and P. J. Achtenmeir, "Jesus and the Disciples as Miracle Workers in the Apocryphal New Testament," in *Aspects of Religious Propaganda*, ed. Schüssler-Fiorenza (op. cit. n. 24), pp. 149–186.

91. Some view the tale of the creation of a man by Rabbah as the starting point for the rich and important tradition of the *golem*. Cf. G. Scholem, "The Idea of the Golem," *On the Kabbalah and Its Symbolism*, trans. R. Manheim (New York, 1969), pp. 158–204; M. Idel, *The Golem. Jewish Magical and Mystical Traditions of the Artificial Anthropoid* (Albany, 1990), pp. 27 ff.; and the literature cited in Yassif, *Golem*, notes 58–60.

92. J. Bazak, "The Laws of Witchcraft and the Laws of Planting Squash," *Bar-Ilan* 6 (1968): 156–166 [H]; Veltri, *Halakha* (supra, note 77). On the positive, sanctified magic cf. Loomis, *White Magic*, supra note 82. The learned of Greece and Rome also drew a distinction between professional sorcerers who deserved to be executed for their deeds and those who performed tricks for the purpose of entertainment, who should be pardoned, cf. Baroja (supra, note 78), p. 19, 31. On Maimonides's approach to magic, on the one hand, and the place of the heroes of magic tales, on the other, see Bazak, *Beyond the Senses* (supra, note 77), pp. 91–98; T. Alexander and E. Romero, eds., *Erase una Vez . . . Maimonides* (Cordoba, 1988), and below, chapter 5, note 78.

93. Compare the variants and extensive scholarship cited in Schwarzbaum, *Studies*, pp.

278–290, and the literature mentioned there, and Schwarzbaum, *Folklore*, pp. 143–171. On the role and importance of charity, see F. Rosenthal, "Sedaka, Charity," *Hebrew Union College Annual* 23 (1950–51): 411–430.

94. *Toseftah, Shabbat*, chapters 6–7; *Shabbat* 66b–67a; ibid., 109b and ff.; *Gittin* 68b–69a; *Pesahim* 110a–111a; *Avodah Zarah* 28a. On these texts, see those studies cited in note 78, above.

95. On folk medicine in the talmudic period, its dissemination, and foundations, see Preuss's classic study (supra, note 78); H. C. Kee, *Medicine, Miracles and Magic in New Testament Times* (Cambridge, 1986); D. Noy, "The Talmudic-Midrashic 'Healing Stories' as a Narrative Genre," *Koroth* 9 (1988): 124–146. Folk cures and various magic means that employ the name of Jesus are known from yet an earlier period (the first and second centuries C.E.), and see the literature cited above, note 90, and especially Geller (supra, note 85), pp. 144–152, which presents and compares five versions of this tale.

96. This is not the venue for bibliographical notation of the vast literature on the study of humor and jokes, such as can be found in every subject index of humanities and the social sciences. The outline of the chapters on humor and anecdote in Thompson, *Motifs* (Chapter 10) and in Aarne and Thompson (the types included in the third chapter of the classification—1200–1999), represent the different categories of folk humor. I will only address the study of Jewish humor and jokes: E. Druyanow, "The Jewish Folk Joke," *Reshumot* 2 (1927): 303–357 [H]; D. Noy, "Is There a Jewish Folk Joke?" *Mahanayim* 67 (1962): 49–56 [H]; A. Stahl, "Lines of Development in [Jewish] Humor," *Mehkarei ha-Merkaz le-Heker ha-Folklor* 3 (1973): 189–204 [H]; E. Yassif, "The *Chizbat*: Israeli Folklore or Jewish Folk Tradition?" *Kiryat Sefer* 57 (1982): 141–147 [H]; A. Ziv, *The Psychology of Humor* (Tel Aviv, 1981) [H]; idem, *Humor and Personality* (Tel Aviv, 1984); E. Simon, *Zum Problem des Jüdischen Witzes* (Berlin, 1929); H. Loewe, *Alter Jüdischer Volkshumor aus Talmud und Midrasch* (Frankfurt, 1931); T. Reik, *Jewish Wit* (New York, 1962); H. Jason, "The Jewish Joke: The Problem of Definition," *Southern Folklore Quarterly* 31 (1967): 48–54; D. Ben-Amos, "The Myth of Jewish Humor," *Western Folklore* 21 (1973): 112–131; E. Oring, *Israeli Humor—The Content and Structure of the Chizbat of the Palmah* (Albany, 1981); idem, *The Jokes of Sigmund Freud—A Study in Humor and Jewish Identity* (Philadelphia, 1984); I. Ch. Bermant, *What's the Joke?—A Study of Jewish Humor Through the Ages* (London, 1986); and S. B. Cohen, ed., *Jewish Wry—Essays in Jewish Humor* (Bloomington and Indianapolis, 1987).

97. R. Piddington, *The Psychology of Laughter—A Study in Social Adaptation* (London, 1933); D. H. Monro, *Argument of Laughter* (Carlton, Australia, 1951); also the main studies included in the collection of A. J. Chapman and H. C. Foot, eds., *Humor and Laughter—Theory, Research and Applications* (London, 1976); Oring, *Chizbat* (supra, note 96), pp. 39–56; Ziv, *Psychology* (supra, note 96). See the detailed discussion of "the mechanism of the joke" and the technical means that stimulate humor in S. Freud, *Jokes and Their Relation to the Unconscious* (London, 1960), pp. 16–89.

98. For the tale of Korah, see *The Midrash on Psalms*, 1, 15, translated by William G. Braude, New Haven, 1959, pp. 20–21. For additional sources and variants to the unique parodies of Korah and his wife, see Ginzburg, *Legends*, 4:332–333, notes 566–567; Halevy, *Portions*, pp. 243–250; B. Barnea, *Legends of Korah through the Rabbinic Looking Glass* (Tel Aviv, 1984), pp. 123–127 [H]; M. Bar, "The Riches of Moses in Rabbinic Aggadah," *Tarbitz* 43 (1974): 70–87 [H]; idem, "Korah's Quarrel in Rabbinic Aggadah," *Mehkarim le-Zekher Yosef Heinemann* (Jerusalem, 1981), pp. 9–33 (esp. pp. 25 ff.) [H].

We have a great deal of evidence on the sages' use of humor to serve didactic needs. Note for example, *Pesahim* 117a: "Even as Rabbah used to say something humorous to his scholars before he commenced [his discourse], in order to amuse them; after that he sat in awe and commenced the lecture."

99. On the motif of *reductio ad absurdum*, see above, note 15. The wretched, good-for-nothing hero who outwits society's tyrants and exposes its injustices is known as the trickster, a folk hero who occupies an important place in the folklore of many societies. See below as well.

100. On misogynist narrative motifs, see Aarne and Thompson, tale types 1440–1524. On the vast literature on misogyny in world literature, see K. M. Rogers, *The Troublesome Helpmate: A History of Misogyny in Literature* (Seattle, 1966); H. R. Hayes, *The Dangerous Sex: The Myth of Feminine Evil* (New York, 1964); and K. M. Wilson and E. M. Makowski, *Wykked Wyves and the Woes of Marriage—Misogynous Literature from Juvenal to Chaucer* (New York, 1990). And in Jewish literature, see below, chapter 5, note 89. The story of R. Judah the Patriarch and the woman who was raped is analyzed in depth by M. L. Satlow, "'Texts of Terror': Rabbinic Texts, Speech Acts, and the Control of Mores," *AJS Review* 21 (1996): 276–280, who adds also another variant to this story in Nidah 45a. On the humor of double entendre, see D. Navon, "On the Characterization of the Joke—The Unseemly that Appears Seemly," *Jerusalem Studies in Jewish Folklore* 4 (1983): 125–146 [H].

101. For humorous motifs on the theme of drunkenness, see Thompson, *Motifs*, X800–X899; on the demonic origin of drunkenness, motif A1386. On the sources of Noah's drunkenness see Ginzburg, *Legends*, 1:167–170, and especially note 58. On the analogy between stages or situations in a man's life and various animals, see the broad comparative discussion in Schwarzbaum, *Folklore*, pp. 215–238: "The Zoologically Tinged Stages of Man's Existence"; M. Grünbaum, *Gesammelte Aufsätze zur Sprach- und Sagenkunde* (Berlin, 1901), pp. 435–441; D. Almagor, "The Seven Ages of Man," *Yediot Aharonot*, 30 September 1977, weekly supplement, pp. 16–17 [H]; and Ch. Shmeruk, *Yiddish Literature—Chapters in its History* (Tel Aviv, 1978), pp. 75–76 [H].

102. On the story of the drunk in the graveyard, see Gaster, *Exempla*, #305 (and the literature cited there); the pious man with a drunken father, Ben-Yehezkiel, *Ma'asiot*, 2:701 ("And He Shall Turn the Heart of the Fathers to the Children"); Noy, *Iraq*, #96; J. Elbaum, "Tales of the Drunk and the Ugly in Our Literature and in Greek Legend," *Mahanayyim* 102 (1967): 122–129 [H]. The tale is classified in the motif index as J1321.1, and as tale type AT 835, and is found as early as ancient Greece: B. E. Perry, ed., *Babrius and Phaedrus* (Cambridge, Mass., 1965), pp. 470–471, note 246. On the sociological phenomenon of the dominant society viewing subcultures as 'other,' and the latter's demonization, see, for example, J. Richards, *Sex, Dissidence and Damnation. Minority Groups in the Middle Ages* (London and New York, 1990) and the considerable literature cited there.

103. These comic motifs are known to have existed in ancient Near Eastern culture, as evidenced by *The Book of Ahikar*. See the comparison to this work above in section [B], and notes 33–34. On the structure of the story cycle of "The Wisdom of the Jerusalemites," cf. the discussion below in section K (The Story Cycle), and the literature cited there in the notes.

104. On the nature and meaning of coarse humor, see G. Legman, *The Rationale of the Dirty Joke: An Analysis of Sexual Humor* (New York, 1968); A. Dundes, *Cracking Jokes: Studies of Sick Humor Cycles and Stereotypes* (Berkeley, 1987); and Ziv, *Psychology* (supra, note 96), pp. 27–36, 69–73. Following his visit to Rome, the Church Father Augustine (354–430 C.E.) tells of (female) innkeepers in Italy, known for their spells, who were in the habit of serving their guests cheese—and turning them into beasts of burden (*De Civitate Dei* 18, 1), and cf. Baroja (supra, note 78), pp. 43–44.

105. On antisemitic humor in Roman culture (chiefly among the spiritual elite) see D. Flusser, "The Blood Libel against the Jews in Light of the Views of the Hellenistic Period," *Sefer Yohanan Levi* (Jerusalem, 1949), pp. 104–124 [H]; and D. Gilulah, "Jokes about Jews in

Roman Literature," *Jerusalem Studies in Jewish Folklore* 9 (1986): 7–37 [H]. The historical background of the antisemitic theater in Caesaria is described by M. D. Herr, "Hatred of the Jewish People in the Roman Empire in Light of Rabbinic Literature," *In Memory Book for Benjamin de-Frieze* (Jerusalem, 1969), pp. 149–159 [H]. On the cultural-historical background of these tales, see I. Heinemann, "Antisemitismus," *Realenzyclopädie der classischen Altertumswissenschaft* (Stuttgart, 1931), supplement 5, pp. 3–43. On pagan rites in Rome attested to in rabbinic literature, see M. Hadas-Lebel, "Le Paganism a travers les sources rabbiniques des IIe et IIIe siécles—Contribution a l'étude du syncrétism dans l'empire romain," *Aufstieg und Niedergang der römischen Welt* 19.2 (1979): 619–647 (esp. p. 636); J. N. Sevenster, *The Roots of Pagan Antisemitism in the Ancient World* (Leiden, 1975). On the ridicule at the Sabbath, the circumcision, and the poverty of Jews, see also: L. H. Feldman, *Jew and Gentile in the Ancient World* (Princeton, 1993), pp. 153–172.

106. Aarne and Thompson classify tall tales as narrative types 1875-1999; Thompson, *The Folktale*, pp. 214–217; R. M. Dorson, *Davy Crockett—American Comic Legend* (New York, 1939); and Bauman (op. cit. n. 71), pp. 20–32.

107. The main discussion of rabbinic tall tales is D. Ben-Amos, "Talmudic Tall-Tales," *Folklore Today. A Festschrift for R. M. Dorson* (Bloomington, 1976), pp. 25–43. On the tall tales of Rabbah bar Bar Hana, cf. Loewe (supra, note 96), pp. 60–69; S. Klein, "The 'nehutei' and Rabbah bar Bar Hannah," *Zion* (Annals of History and Ethnography) 5 (1933): 1–13 [H]; A. Karlin, "Tales of Wonders of Rabbah bar Bar Hannah," *Sinai* 20 (1947): 56–61 [H]; N. Shalem, "Rabbah bar Bar Hannah and Tales of Wanderers," ibid., 24 (1949): 108–111 [H]. A contemporary of Rabbah bar Bar Hana, Lucian (second century c.e.) provides important evidence as to the nature and dissemination of the genre of lies in the ancient world. In his *Verae Historiae*, he formulates the principles of the genre (I quote him from the Loeb edition):

> Well, on reading all these authors, I did not find much fault with them for their lying, as I saw that this was already a common practice even among men who profess philosophy. I did wonder though, that they thought that they could write untruths and not get caught at it . . . and I had nothing true to tell, not having had any adventures of significance, I took to lying. But my lying is far more honest than theirs, for though I tell the truth in nothing else, I shall be at least truthful in saying that I am a liar . . . I am writing about things . . . which in fact do not exist at all . . . Therefore my readers should on no account believe in them (Lucian, *Verae Historiae*, The Loeb Classical Library, Cambridge, Mass., 1961, vol. 1, pp. 250–253, 1:3–4).

Lucian's remarks are edifying in several respects: 1) the genre of "tales of lies," was accepted and well-known among writers and the learned in his day. While in the passage excerpted above, he takes a mostly cynical tone against "serious" writers whose writings are entirely contrived, it is clear from his words here and elsewhere in the work that he had already encountered such tales; 2) the power of the genre is in the overt lie, in the fact that the author (or storyteller) and his audience are all aware that lies and exaggerations are the stuff of the tale. On these see: C. P. Jones, *Culture and Society in Lucian* (Cambridge, Mass. and London, 1986), pp. 46–58. It is worthwhile to compare Lucian's comments to those of a famous teller of tall tales from the Palmach period (1946-1948), Dan Ben-Amotz, in his introduction to *Yalkut ha-Kezavim* (Bag [or collection] of Lies): "There is a worthy difference between a tall tale, a lie, and a stretching of the truth. A lie is when no one knows the truth except for the one telling it. Stretching the truth is when everyone knows the truth, except for the victim of the practical joke. And a tall tale is when everyone knows the story is nothing but fabrication yet they happily come back to hear it again and again." D. Ben Amotz and H. Hefer, *Yalkut ha-Kezavim*, Tel Aviv, 1956, p. 6 [H]); 3. The topics of rabbinic tall tales have much in common with those Lucian tells concerning the marvelous journeys of seafarers, ascension to heaven in craft harnessed to eagles, descent to the depths of the ocean inside the belly of a whale, and a journey through Paradise where he encounters great figures of the past—Homer, Socrates, and Helen of Troy. On the use of mythic themes in Jewish tall tales, see below.

108. The distinction between fabula—the narrative fable—and parable as exemplary tale originated with Aristotle's theory of rhetoric. See Aristotle, *The 'Art' of Rhetoric*, ed. and trans. J. H. Freese (Loeb Classical Library, Cambridge, Mass., 1926), 2.20, 1393a-b, and the studies dealing with the distinction between this pair of terms: E. Leibfried, *Fabel* (Stuttgart, 1967); D. Stern, "Rhetoric and Midrash: The Case of the Mashal," *Prooftexts* 1 (1981): 263–265, and especially his *Parables in Midrash: Narrative and Exegesis in Rabbinic Literature* (Cambridge, Mass. and London, 1991); J. D. Lyons, *Exemplum: The Rhetoric of Example in Early Modern France and Italy* (Princeton, 1989), pp. 6–11; and especially Meir, "The Fable", where she defines these terms similarly. Below is just such a typical rabbinic parable:

> [In the beginning God created.] R. Oshaya commenced [his exposition thus]:
> Then I was by Him, as a nursling (amon); and I was daily all delight (Prov. 8, 30)
> . . . Another interpretation: "amon" is a workman (uman). The Torah declares: "I
> was the working tool of the Holy One, blessed be He." In human practice, when
> a mortal king builds a palace, he builds it not with his own skill but with the
> skill of an architect. The architect moreover does not build it out of his head, but
> employs plans aand diagrams to know how to arrange the chambers and the
> wicket doors. Thus God consulted the Torah and created the world (*Genesis
> Rabbah*, 1,1).

The sermon seeks here to flesh out, by means of the parable, the notion that the Torah was the plan that preceded the creation of the world, that the Almighty built the world according to this plan, just as a builder works from his blueprints. In this parable, the story has a literary existence by virtue of the analogy between the acts of the builder and the creation of the world. Imagine a folk storyteller telling his audience that when a builder is busy at his craft, he looks at his blueprints, and does his work! Is there even a kernel of a tale in that? Such is the nature of the parable whose raison d'être stems from its link to the ideic theme it is meant to substantiate, and which lacks any status independent of this context. Such are most parables in rabbinic literature. Narrative fables, by contrast, are likely to exist free of their context or the attached epimythium, and they can be told independently at a performance event. Only the latter can be defined as folk fable.

The classic study of king parables (which constitute the majority of exemplary mashal in rabbinic literature) is I. Ziegler, *Die Königsgleichnisse des Midrasch, beleuchtet durch die römische Kaiserzeit* (Breslau, 1903). Also see A. A. Feldman, *The Parables and Similes of the Rabbis: Agricultural and Pastoral* (Cambridge, 1924); R. Pautrel, "Les canons du mashal rabbinique," *Recherches de science religieuse* 26 (1936): 1–45; R. M. Johnston, "The Study of Rabbinic Parables—Some Preliminary Observations," *Society of Biblical Literature* 10 (1976): 337–357; and the insightful Stern, *Parables in Midrash* (supra, this note).

Modern scholarship on the parable is sustained chiefly by the intensive treatment of the parables of Jesus in the New Testament. This scholarship is discussed in W. S. Kisinger, *The Parables of Jesus—A History of Interpretation and Bibliography* (Metuchen, N.J., 1979). For a comparison of these with those of the sages, see D. Flusser, "Jesus's Parables and the Mashal of Rabbinic Literature," in *Judaism and the Origins of Christianity* (Tel Aviv, 1982), pp. 150–209 [H]; P. Fiebig, *Der Erzählungsstil der Evangelien im Lichte des rabbinischen Erzählungstils* (Leipzig, 1925); D. Flusser, *Die rabbinischen Gleichnisse und der Gleichniserzähler Jesus* (Bern, 1981).

109. Publications on the narrative fable are numerous and diverse. Compare the exhaustive bibliographies in R. Dithmar, *Die Fable: Geschichte, Struktur, Didaktik* (Paderborn, 1974); P. Hasubek, ed., *Die Fabel—Theorie, Geschichte und Rezeption einer Gattung* (Berlin, 1982); P. Carnes, *Fable Scholarship: An Annotated Bibliography* (New York and London, 1985); Schwarzbaum, *Berechia*; and H. J. Blackman, *The Fable as Literature* (London and Dover, 1985). The influential theory on the emergence and evolution of the fable from the ancient Near East was formulated by B. E. Perry, "Fable," *Studium Generale* 12 (1959): 17–37; idem, "Introduction," *Babrius and Phaedrus* (op. cit. n. 102), pp. xix–xxxiv. On the narrative mashal among the sages, compare Steinschneider, *Literature*, pp. 35–42; S. Back, "Die Fabel im Talmud und Midrasch," *Monatschrift für Geschichte und Wissenschaft des Judentums* 24 (1876): 540–555; 25 (1877): 27–38, 126–138, 195–204, 276–285, 493–504; 29 (1880): 24–34, 68–78, 102–114, 225–230, 267–274, 374–378, 417–421; 30 (1881): 124–130, 260–267, 406–412, 453–458; 32 (1883): 317–330, 521–527, 563–567; 33 (1884): 23–33. Also see D. Daube, *Ancient Hebrew Fables* (Oxford, 1973). Variants to the tale types of mashal are to be found in Noy, *Animals*.

110. On the myth of Etana see chapter 2, above, and note 13. On the connection between Aesopian literature and the parables and animal tales of the ancient Near East, see Perry, *Babrius* (supra, note 109) and W. Wienert, *Die Typen der griechischrömischen Fabel* (Helsinki, 1925) (FFC no. 56). The quotations from Aesop's fables here and below are from *Aesop without Morals*, trans. L. W. Daly (New York and London, 1961).

111. The relationship between the tale and the proverb was discussed in Hasan-Rokem, *Proverbs*, and the literature cited there. The main theoretical discussion is still G. L. Permiakov, *From Proverb to Folk-Tale*, trans. from the Russian by Y. N. Fillipov (Moscow, 1979). On the proverbial fable in ancient Near Eastern literature and its connection to Aesopian literature, see Perry's remarks (note 109, above, from where the citations are also taken), and O. Crusius, *Paroemiographica—Textgeschichtlisches zur alten Dichtung und Religion* (München, 1910); E. I. Gordon, *Sumerian Proverbs. Glimpses of Everyday Life in Ancient Mesopotamia* (Philadelphia, 1959); H. von Thiel, "Sprichwörter in Fabeln," *Antike und Abendland* 17 (1971): 105–118. An affinity also exists in the Bible between the fable and the proverb, there termed "mashal." On this see M. Haran, "Mashal," *Encyclopedia Biblica* (Jerusalem, 1968), 5:548–553 [H]. On Rava's Reed, compare the variants and the vast literature cited in Schwarzbaum, *Berechia*, pp. 163–166.

112. Other tales in common to Aesop and the sages include: the man whose young wife plucks out his white hairs while his not-so-young wife plucks the black ones, leaving him entirely bald—Aesop, #231, and in the Talmud, *Bava Kamma* 60a; the fable on the creation of iron—Aesop, #247, *Genesis Rabbah* 5, 10; and the fable of the lion and the Egyptian, see the discussion below. On the link between these two treasuries of fables in the ancient world cf. H. Schwarzbaum, "Aesop's Fables and Rabbinic Mashal," *Mahanayim* 112 (1967): 112–117 [H]; A. Shenhar, *From Folktale to Children's Literature* (Haifa, 1982), pp. 101–120 [H]; J. Jacobs, *History of the Aesopic Fable* (London, 1889); and Schwarzbaum, *Folklore*, pp. 197–214: "Talmudic-Midrashic Affinities of Some Aesopic Fables." On the link between other fables of Greco-Roman literature and rabbinic mashal, see Lieberman, *Greek*, pp. 110–123; E. E. Halevy, *The World of the Aggadah* (supra, note 71), pp. 232–246. On the fable of the fox and the vineyard, see Schwarzbaum, *Folklore*, p. 205; Noy, *Animals*, p. 249, tale type AT 41*.

113. On the fable of the young donkey, her mother, and the sow, compare the literature suggested by Schwarzbaum, *Folklore*, pp. 208–209; idem, *Berechia*, pp. 314–321; and Halevy, ibid., pp. 241–243. On the bird who sought to relocate the sea, see Halevy, ibid., pp. 243–245. For the fable of the lion who invited the other animals to a feast and hung pelts on the walls of his home, see Schwarzbaum, ibid., pp. 207–208.

114. On the polemic and political functions of the fable, see Schwarzbaum, *Berechia*, pp. i–xviii; Noy, *Animals*, pp. 194–197.

115. On this fable, see Urbach, *Sages*, pp. 223–225; J. Scheftlowitz, "Ein Beitrag zur Methode der vergleichenden Religionsforschung," *Monatschrift für Geschichte und Wissenschaft des Judentum* 65 (1921): 123–127. For variants in international folklore see Thompson, *Motifs*, N886. The cycle of tales about Antoninus and Rabbi is discussed at length in S. Krauss, *Antoninus und Rabbi* (Frankfurt, 1910); L. Wallach, "The Colloquy of Marcus Aurelius and the Patriarch Judah I," *Jewish Quarterly Review* 31 (1940–1941): 259–286.

116. This fable is tale type AT 76. See also Schwarzbaum, *Berechia*, pp. 51–56, and the abundant literature offered there and D. Noy, *Introduction to Aggadah* ed. M. Ganan (Jerusalem, 1970), pp. 73–75 [H].

117. On the fable of the fox and the fishes, see Schwarzbaum, *Berechia*, pp. 25–47, who includes all the relevant literature. His attempts to prove that this fable has variants that predate the talmudic version are not convincing. See also A. Singer, "An Analysis of Fox Fables in Rabbinic Literature," *Jerusalem Studies in Jewish Folklore* 4 (1983): 80–83 [H]; T. Gutmann, *Ha-Mashal be-Tekufat ha-Tannaim* [The Mashal in the Time of the Tannaim] (Jerusalem, 1949), pp. 53–54 [H].

118. This view on the development of the fable from animal tales was crisply formulated by Perry (supra, note 109). See also Thompson, *The Folktale*, pp. 217–220; C. Johnston, "Assyrian and Babylonian Beast Fables," *American Journal of Semitic Languages and Literature* 28 (1911–12): 81–100; B. E. Perry, "The Origin of the Epimythium," *TAPA* 71 (1940): 391–419; E. Gordon, "Sumerian Animal Proverbs and Fables," *Journal of Cuneiform Studies* 12 (1958): 43–75; F. Harkort, "Tiervolkserzählungen," *Fabula* 9 (1967): 87–99; and G. Hasan-Rokem, "Fable," *Encyclopedia Judaica* (Jerusalem, 1971), 6:1125–1133.

119. Mythological animal tales from rabbinic literature are collected in Ginzburg, *Legends*, 1: 30–42, and the corresponding notes; E. Levine. "In the Ram's Footsteps," in *Research and Analysis in Jewish Studies*, ed. Y. Bahat (Haifa, 1976), pp. 135–148 [H]; and the ground-breaking work of M. Grünbaum, "Beiträge zur vergleichenden Mythologie aus der Hagada," *Zeitschrift der Deutschen Morgenländischen Gesselschaft* 31 (1877): 183–359. Also see O. Dähnhardt, *Natursagen—Eine Sammlung naturdeutender Sagen, Märchen, Fabeln und Legenden* (Leipzig und Berlin, 1907–1912), 3 and A. Marmorstein, "Legendenmotive in der rabbinschen Literatur," *Archiv für Religionswissenschaft* 16 (1913): 160–175.

120. The story cycle in aggadah has not yet been treated thoroughly. See, for example, M. Güdemann, "Agada und Midrasch-agada—ein Beitrag zur Sagengeschichte," *Jubelschrift zum neunzigsten Geburstag des Dr. L. Zunz* (Berlin, 1884), pp. 111–121. Güdemann offers evidence of groupings of aggadah that, in his opinion, predated the Talmud and Midrash; H. Fischel, "Studies in Cynicism and the Ancient Near East—The Transformation of a *Chria*," *Religions in Antiquity. Essays in Memory of E.R. Goodenough* (Leiden, 1968), pp. 372–411, and especially the observations made by Hasan-Rokem, "Riddles," and Sh. Valler, *Women and Womanhood in the Stories of the Babylonian Talmud* (Tel-Aviv, 1993), pp. 156ff. [H].

121. See Bin-Gorion, *Paths*, pp. 169–170; Gaster, *Exempla*, and the summation of the controversy over this subject in Braude's introduction to this edition, pp. xxv–xxx. S. J. Friedman mentions additional literature on the subject in "On the Historical Aggadah in

the Babylonian Talmud," offprint from *In Memory of Rabbi Shaul Lieberman* (Jerusalem, 1989), p. 2, n. 5 [H]. On the development of story groupings in the Middle Ages, see Yassif, "Narrative."

122. On the story cycle in *Midrash Lamentations Rabbah*, see Hasan-Rokem, "Riddles," pp. 540–544. The second tale does not appear in the printed editions of the Babylonian Talmud, but in several manuscripts, and on this see ibid. Mordecai Margolies, in his discussion of the two story cycles in *Genesis Rabbah* and *Leviticus Rabbah*, leans to "aggadic tales more ancient from which both of them drew." His reasoning, however, is not convincing, at least as regards this example. Also see, in his edition of *Leviticus Rabbah*, "Introduction, Appendices and Indices to Midrash Leviticus Rabbah" (Jerusalem, 1960), p. xiii [H].

123. On this figure in international folklore, see P. Radin, *The Trickster* (New York, 1956), and especially the appended essays of Kerenyi and Jung. On similar figures in the aggadah, see K. Dietrich, "Jüdische-griechische Schnurren," *Mitteilungen zur jüdischen Volkskunde* 23 (1907): 69–75.

124. On the pair of terms, "analytical categories" and "ethnic genres," see Ben-Amos, "Categories." On the tale of Joseph, see D. B. Redford, *A Study of The Biblical Story of Joseph* (Leiden, 1970 [Vetus Testamentum Supplements, vol. 20]), pp. 66–105. On the stories of Elijah and Elisha, see Rofé, *Tales of the Prophets*, pp. 48–50, 155–165. Z. Weissman, *The Story Cycle of Jacob and its Place in the History of the Nation's Patriarchs* (Jerusalem, 1986), esp. pp. 37–38 ("the kyklos") [H]. On the framework tale in *The Book of Ahikar* and in the Middle Ages, see Yassif, "Traces," pp. 227–229; idem, "Pseudo Ben-Sira and Medieval Tradition of the 'Wisdom Questions,'" *Fabula* 23 (1983): 48–63; S. J. Fajardo, "The Frame as Formal Contrast," *Comparative Literature* 36 (1984): 1–19; and K. S. Gittes, "The Canterbury Tales and the Arabic Frame Tradition," *Proceedings of the Modern Language Association* 98 (1983): 237–251. A translation of the Aramaic version of *The Book of Ahikar* from the fifth century B.C.E., found in Elephantine, was published in *The Old Testament Pseudepigrapha*, ed. J. H. Charlesworth (London, 1985), II: 479–508.

125. On the contest of riddles and tasks, consult for example, Thompson, *The Folktale*, pp. 105–108; Campbell, *The Hero* (op. cit. n. 41), pp. 49–244; J. F. Ringel, *Patterns of the Hero and the Quest—Epic, Romance, Fantasy* (Ph.D. Thesis, Brown University, Providence, R.I., 1979).

126. These tales and an analysis of their humorous character were treated above in section I (The Comic Tale). On tales of lies or exaggeration, see tale types, AT 1875–1999; Thompson, *The Folktale*, pp. 214–217; and the discussion of the genre among the sages in Ben-Amos, "Talmudic Tall-Tales" (supra, note 107). Hasan-Rokem, "Riddles," classifies the tales in the cycle of "The Wisdom of the Jerusalemites" as belonging to the genre of riddle.

127. Other tales on Rabbi Eleazar ben Simeon are found in the Palestinian Talmud tractate *Ma'aserot* 3, 4; *Pesikta de-Rav Kahane*, portion *Vayehi be-Shelah*, Mandelbaum edition, pp. 193 and ff. Also see Friedman (supra, note 121), pp. 4–21, and the literature cited there; O. Meir, "Unworthy Scion of a Righteous Father—From Tradition to Renewal," *Dappim le-Mehkar be-Sifrut* 4 (1988): 9–18 [H]; and D. Boyarin, "Literary Fat Rabbis: On the Historical Origins of the Grotesque Body," *Journal of the History of Sexuality* 1 (1991): 551–584.

128. For a preliminary discussion of the subject, see Steinschneider, *Literature*, pp. 37–38; Noy, "Versions." For treatment of the subject from another perspective, see J. Fraenkel, "Bible Verses Quoted in Tales of the Sages," *Scripta Hierosolymitana* 22 (1971): 80–99. Some key aspects of the subject were discussed by G. Hasan-Rokem, "The Biblical Verse as Proverb and as Quotation," *Jerusalem Studies in Hebrew Literature* 1 (1981): 155–166 [H].

129. For example: the story of the four Jerusalemites who stay with an innkeeper in Athens is tale type AT 655—the clever brothers prove to the king that he is illegitimate; the

story of the blind slave who knows there is a caravan of camels before him, belongs to tale type AT 655A, which is also widespread in various cultural regions; the twisting of sand into rope is comic tale type AT 1174; and the first tale in the cycle, about the clever division of the chicken, is tale type AT 1533. Dietrich (supra, note 123) proposed a similar view of this story cycle.

130. On folkloric motifs relating to fabulous fish who drag or overturn ships, see Thompson, *Motifs*, B541.5, B551.1. For an analysis of the link between the tale and the verse in Ecclesiastes see Noy, "Versions."

131. Compare Coleridge's well-known definition: "Ideas by having been together acquire a power of recalling each other; or every partial representation awakes the total representation of which it had been a part," S. T. Coleridge, "On the Law of Association—Its History Traced from Aristotle to Hartly," *Biographia Literaria* (Princeton, 1983), 1:102–103. On the role of association in Scripture, see Rofé, *Tales of the Prophets*, p. 49; Y. Zakovich, "The Associative Principle in the Structure of the Book of Judges and Its Use as a Tool in Discerning Stages in the Crystallization of the Book," *The Isaac Arieh Zeeligman Volume* (Jerusalem, 1983), Hebrew section, pp. 161–183.

132. My friend Professor David Rosenthal offered additional possibilities for the description of the ties between tales in some of the story cycles treated here, among them "technical" links such as the inclusion of tales only after the repetition of "leading" words, combining subjects "on account of their ending" and so forth. See his article, "Ancient Redactions Within the Babylonian Talmud," *Proceedings of the Ninth World Congress of Jewish Studies*, Division C (Jerusalem, 1986), pp. 7–14 [H].

133. A general discussion of this subject appears in Fraenkel, ibid., pp. 99–115. Sh. Valler, "The Grouping of Tales in Ketubbot 62b–63a," *Tura. Collected Writings on Jewish Thought and Scholarship Presented to Professor Shlomo Greenberg* (Oranim, 1989), pp. 95–102 [H], discerns three story pairs that display opposing positions on the subject under discussion, arranged in ascending order of severity. The whole book of Ilan, *Mine and Yours* (supra, note 45), deals, on and of, with various aspects of the tale of Rabbi Akiva's wife.

134. S. Lieberman, *Greek*; Fischel (supra, note 120), and, on the entire matter, Yassif, "The Study" (1987), pp. 19–20.

135. Cf. Urbach, *Sages*, pp. 102–108.

136. *Leviticus Rabbah*, 24, 4, *Avot de-Rabbi Nathan*, version B, chapter 7. For a discussion of further versions of the tale of Titus and its variants, see I. Lévi, "La Mort de Titus," *Revue des Etudes Juives* 15 (1887): 62–69; G. Hasan-Rokem, "Within Limits and Beyond: History and Body in Midrashic Texts," *International Folklore Review* 9 (1993): 5–12. The tale type AT 836—Pride is Punished; also Thompson, *The Folktale*, pp. 130–134, and motifs C50—taboo: offense to the sanctity of the gods; C51.1—taboo: desecration of a holy place.

137. On tales of "charity delivers from death" see the Jewish oicotype AT 934*F, A. Shenhar, *The Folktale*, pp. 48–55; Schwarzbaum, *Folklore*, pp. 143–172.

138. The section known as "Perek Helek" in the Babylonian Talmud is built according to a similar structural conception (*Sanhedrin* 90a). The gemara goes on, by means of sages' remarks, fables, expanded biblical tales, and various folktales, to detail the reasons why each such group enumerated at this point in the Mishnah has no portion in the world to come. This section, however, as aforesaid, is not a story cycle according to our definition.

139. For the point at which belles lettres meets folkloric creation, see the key arguments proposed by R. Jakobson and P. Bogatyrew, "Folklore as a Special Form of Creation," trans. J. M. O'Hara, *Folklore Forum* 13 (1980): 1–22.

Claims as to the fragmented nature of the aggadah were made by Ch. N. Bialik and Y. Ch. Ravnitzky, *Sefer ha-Aggadah* (Tel Aviv, 1960), Introduction [H, not included in the English translation of the book]. Compare to this and to earlier literature on this subject: J. Elbaum, "The Book of Aggadah—Introductory Chapters," *Jerusalem Studies in Hebrew Literature* 10–11 (1987–1988): 377, 384 [H].

5. The Middle Ages

1. For a basic discussion of the chronological boundaries of the "Jewish Middle Ages," see H. H. Ben-Sasson, "The Jewish Middle Ages—What Are They?" and "Objectives of and Obstacles to Jewish Chronography of the Middle Ages," in H. H. Ben Sasson, *Continuity and Change* (Tel Aviv, 1984), pp. 359–401 [H]; idem, *The History of the Jewish People* (Tel Aviv, 1969) 2:13–22 [H]; M. D. Herr, "On the Significance of the Term, 'Middle Ages' in Jewish History," *Culture and Society in Medieval Jewish History—Collected Articles in Memory of Haim Hillel Ben-Sasson* (Jerusalem, 1989), pp. 83–98 [H]. The paramount historiographic venture of our day also recognizes this overall demarcation: Baron, *History*, vols 3–8. On the approach that rejects any demarcation of boundaries between antiquity and the Middle Ages (with reference to Jewish culture), see the approaches mentioned in Herr, ibid., pp. 87–88, note 25.

2. The separation of the disciplines, as far as is known, originated in early Islamic culture in the tenth century. See L. Gardet, "The Organization of Knowledge into its Constituent Disciplines" in *The Cambridge History of Islam*, eds. P. M. Holt, A. K. S. Lambton and B. Lewis (Cambridge, 1970), 2: 587–603. Muhammad ibn al-Nadim, for example, catalogued the various disciplines in which books were written in the three hundred years since the establishment of Islam. He lists languages, religious law, theology, history, poetry, philosophy, the natural sciences, medicine, geometry, fiction bedtime stories, invocation of spirits, magic, and sleight of hand. See also A. Giladi, *Baghdad—Gateway to Medieval Islamic Culture* (Tel Aviv, 1981), pp. 53–54 [H]. On the phenomenon in Jewish culture, see E. Fleischer, "A New Look on the Early Hebrew Fable Literature," *Bikoret u-Parshanut* 11–12 (1978): 19–24 [H]; Steinschneider, *Literature*, pp. 60 ff. On the emergence of Hebrew narrative in the Near East at the start of the Middle Ages, see Yassif, "Narrative." For evidence of the antiquity of *The Midrash of the Ten Commandments* and *The Alphabet of Ben Sira*, see Zunz, *Homilies*, p. 66; Gaster, *Exempla*, pp. 7–9; E. Yassif, "The Tale of the Man Who Never Swore an Oath," *Fabula* 27 (1987): 216–236; idem, *Ben Sira*, pp. 19–29; and M. B. Lerner, "On the Midrash to the Ten Commandments," in *Studies in Talmud. Collected Studies in Talmud and Related Fields*, ed. Y. Zussman and D. Rosenthal (Jerusalem, 1990), pp. 217–236 [H]. On the phenomenon of story groupings, found mostly in rabbinic literature, see above chapter 4, section K. On Jewish-Persian-Arabic groupings of the framework tales of the day, see C. Brockelman, "Kalila we-Dimna," *The Encyclopedia of Islam*, New Edition (Leiden, 1974), 4: 503–506; K. S. Gittes, "The Canterbury Tales and the Arabic Frame Tradition," *Publications of the Modern Language Association* 98 (1983): 237–251; S. J. Fajardo, "The Frame as Formal Contrast," *Comparative Literature* 36 (1984): 1–19; H. R. Runte and J. K. Wikeley, *The Seven Sages of Rome and the Book of Sindbad—An Analytical Bibliography* (New York and London, 1984); F. Geissler, "Das Panchatantra und seine mitteleuropäischen Fassungen," *Fourth International Congress for Folk-Narrative Research in Athens* (Athens, 1965), pp. 117–125; M. I. Gerhardt, *The Art of Story-Telling: A Literary Study of the Thousand and One Nights* (Leiden, 1963). Proof of *Kalila we-Dimna*'s influence on medieval Hebrew literature is found in J. Derenbourg, *Deux Versions Hebraiques du Livre de Kalilah et Dimnah* (Paris, 1881); Steinschneider, *Translations*, pp. 872–883. Stored in the Cairo Genizah were many texts, including Arabic romances such as 'Antar, tales of morals and of thieves from *The Arabian Nights*, animal tales and fairy tales from medieval Arabic folklore, that were written in Arabic in Hebrew

letters, and constitute invaluable proof of medieval Jewish society's absorption of Arabic folk literature. Compare V. Lebedev, "Cats, Mice, Thieves and Heroes in 'Arabian Nights' Genizah Tales," *Genizah, Fragments* 24 (October, 1992): 2. R. Drori, *The First Contacts of Jewish Literature with Arabic Literature in the Tenth Century* (Tel Aviv, 1988) [H] treats the same period and theme from a different angle.

3. A preliminary, insufficient description of the narrative works of the period is Dan, *Middle Ages*. Cf. also Yassif, "Narrative"; idem, *Ben Sira*; idem, "Studies in the Narrative Art of the Scroll of Ahimaaz," *Jerusalem Studies of Hebrew Literature* 4 (1984): 18–42 [H]; idem, "The Transformation of Folktales into Literary Works in the Hebrew Literature of the Middle-Ages," *ARV—Scandinavian Yearbook of Folklore* 46 (1990): 175–187. On the same process—the transition from folk traditions to the consciousness of the artist-creator—that takes place around the twelfth century, see R. Kellogg, "Varieties of Tradition in Medieval Narrative," in *Medieval Narrative: A Symposium,* ed. H. Bekker-Nielsen et al. (Odense, 1979), pp. 120–129; J. Bumke, *Courtly Culture: Literature and Society in High Middle Ages,* trans. T. Dunlop (Berkeley and Los Angeles, 1991), pp. 488–517.

4. Drori (supra, note 2), pp. 143–145, offers examples of eleventh-century sages wandering Tiberias's markets and streets in order to hear Hebrew as it was commonly spoken, and thereby learn the correct pronunciation of biblical words. Jerahme'el ben Shlomo, the eleventh-twelfth-century Italian author and poet, also explains to his readers that he translated the Aramaic portions of the Book of Daniel into Hebrew as more people know that language (Oxford-Bodleian manuscript Heb. d. 11, p. 68a). A number of important proofs of the matter survive in *Sefer Hasidim* (Wistinezki-Freimann edition): "An old man was asked how it was that he had lived so long. He said, 'because there were guests in my home who did not speak my language. They spoke to me in the Hebrew language in the bath house, but I never spoke the Hebrew tongue in the bath house, or in the outhouse, nor even regarding everyday matters even though it is permitted, for I made a fence and [so I was given] more years" (#799); "Jews came to that place with an officer and [he] heard them speaking in the holy tongue. He asked them to rescue him from there. They told him, 'do not speak to us in the holy tongue lest you be recognized as a Jew" (#902); M. Brauer, "The Wanderings of Students and Sages—Preface to a Chapter on The History of the Academies," *Culture and Society in Medieval Jewish History: Collected Articles in Memory of Haim Hillel Ben-Sasson* (Jerusalem, 1989), p. 467 [H] offers testimony on the gathering of students from various places in one academy, which indicates that the language of study was Hebrew. Compare Baron, *History,* 7: 3–61; I. Zinberg, *A History of Jewish Literature,* trans. and ed. B. Martin (Cleveland, 1972–1978), 7: 3–28; Sh. Morag, "Hebrew as the Elite Language of Culture: Processes of Crystallization and Transmission in the Middle Ages in the Mediterranean Lands," *Pe'amim* 23 (1985): 9–21 [H]; H. Z. Hirschberg, "Jewish Society in the Diaspora on the Eve of the Geonic Period," *Religion and Society: Lectures Delivered at the Ninth Convention of Historians* (Jerusalem, 1964), pp. 68–80 [H]; M. Simonsohn, "The Hebrew Revival among Early Medieval European Jews," *S. W. Baron Jubilee Volume* (Jerusalem, 1974), pp. 831–858; A. Grossman, "Communication among Jewish Centers During the Tenth to the Twelfth Century," in *Communication in the Jewish Diaspora: The Pre-Modern World,* ed. S. Menache (Leiden, 1996), pp. 107–126. On similar problems in the relationship between Latin and the languages spoken in the Middle Ages, and the modes of communication between the learned Church elite and the masses, see, for example, M. Richter, "Kommunikationsprobleme im lateinischem Mittelalter," *Historische Zeitschrift* 222 (1976): 43–80.

5. On the Arabic origins of *The Midrash of the Ten Commandments* and *The Alphabet of Ben Sira,* see D. Noy, "International and Jewish Tale-Types in *The Midrash of the Ten Commandments*," *Proceedings of the Fourth Congress of Jewish Studies* (Jerusalem, 1969), 2: 353–355

[H]; *The Alphabet of Ben-Sira:* E. Yassif, "On Interpretation and the Ideational Traces in a Literary Work," *Eshel Be'er Sheva* 2 (1980): 97–118 [H]. On the link between Yiddish and Hebrew as regards literary creation, see Ch. Shmeruk, *Yiddish Literature: Aspects of Its History* (Tel Aviv, 1978), pp. 9–24 [H]; Zfatman, *Narrative*, pp. 79–86, 105–116.

6. The citations from the *Scroll of Ahimaaz* are taken from *The Chronicle of Ahimaaz*, trans. M. Salzman (New York, 1924). On the composition of Menahem ben Peretz ha-Hevroni, see J. Prawer, "Hebrew Travelogues in Palestine in the Crusader Period," *Katedrah* 41 (1987): 69–73 [H]; Yassif, "Leisure," pp. 890–892, and the literature cited there.

7. On the large and important collection of fables of Berechia ha-Nakdan, see Schwarzbaum's broad work, *Berechia*. On *Pirkei de-Rabbi Eliezer* and its connection to Arabic literature, cf. Zunz, *Homilies*, pp. 134–140 and Haineman, *Legends*, pp. 181–200; on *Genesis Rabbati*, compare H. Albeck's introduction to his edition (Jerusalem, 1940), pp. 1–37 [H]; M. Himmelfarb, "R. Moses the Preacher and Testament of the Twelve Patriarchs," *AJS Review* 9 (1984): 55–78. For critical editions and basic discussions of *The Chronicles of Moses, Midrash va-Yissa'u,* and *Sefer ha-Yashar,* see A. Shinan, "The Chronicles of Moses," *ha-Sifrut* 24 (1977): 100–116 [H]; J. B. Lauterbach, "*Midrash va-Yissa'u* or the *Book of the Wars of the Sons of Jacob.* Published for the First Time according to Various Manuscripts with an Introduction and Notes," *Ma'amarim le-Zekher R. Zvi Peretz Hayyot* [Articles in Memory of R. Zvi Peretz Hayyot of Blessed Memory] (Vienna, 1933), pp. 205–222 [H]; T. Alexander and J. Dan, "The Complete *Midrash va-Yissa'u,*" *Mehkarei ha-Merkaz le-Heker ha-Folklor* 3 (1972): 67–76 [H]; *Sefer ha-Yashar,* ed. and introduced by J. Dan (Jerusalem, 1985/1986) [H]. On *Ma'aseh Avraham Avinu,* see B. Chapira, "Legends Biblique attribuées a Ka'b el Ahbar," *Revue des Etudes Juives* 69 (1919): 86–107; J. Finkel, "An Arabic Story of Abraham," *Hebrew Union College Annual* 12–13 (1937–1938): 387–410. The most important collection of small Midrashim from the Middle Ages is that of A. Jellinek, *Beit ha-Midrash* (Jerusalem, 1967²). Compare J. Elbaum, "Between Revision and Rewriting: On the Nature of the Late Midrashic Literature," *Proceedings of the Ninth World Congress of Jewish Studies* (Jerusalem, 1986), 3:57–62 [H].

8. On the high percentage of rabbinic legends in story groupings from the Middle Ages, such as Gaster's edition of *Sefer ha-Ma'asiyyot,* see Gaster, *Exempla,* pp. 185–270; P. S. Alexander, "Gaster's Exempla of the Rabbis: A Reappraisal", *Rashi 1040–1990,* ed. G. Sed-Rajna (Paris, 1993), pp. 793–805; and in *Hibbur Yafeh min-ha-Yeshu'ah:* Rabeinu Nissim ben R. Ya'akov of Kairouan, *Hibbur Yafeh min-ha-Yeshu'ah,* H. Z. Hirschberg edition (Jerusalem, 1970), pp. 56–61 [H]; and on *Sefer ha-Ma'asim,* Oxford manuscript: E. Yassif, "*Sefer ha-Ma'asim:* The Character, Origins and Influence of a Collection of Stories from the Time of the Tosaphists," *Tarbitz* 53 (1984): 412–417 [H]. On the influence of rabbinic sources on the Yiddish *Mayseh-Bukh,* see S. Zfatman, "*Mayseh-Bukh*—A Genre in Old Yiddish Literature," *ha-Sifrut* 28 (1979): 128–132 [H]. On "internal," as opposed to "external," influences on the Hebrew tale of the Middle Ages, see L. Landau, "R. Akiva and the Matron—Between a Close Reading and an Genetic Approach," *Dappim le-Mehkar be-Sifrut* 7 (1991): 293–304 [H].

9. The following pointed out the variants to these tales, and dozens more: M. J. Bin-Gorion, *Mimekor,* pp. 507–511; Gaster, *Exempla.* In the abridged edition of the English translation of *Mimekor Yisrael,* the editor, Dan Ben-Amos, points out additional medieval variants to these tales, cf. Ben-Amos, *Mimekor Yisrael,* pp. 125–162.

10. On versions of the tale in rabbinic literature, and its research, see the discussion above in chapter 4, section F, and note 60. On versions from the medieval period, see Ben-Amos, *Mimekor Yisrael,* pp. 181–183. On the halachic controversy over conversion for the sake of marriage, see the entry, "Conversion," *Encyclopedia Talmudica: A Digest of Halachic Lit-*

erature and Jewish Law, ed. Sh. Zevin (Tel Aviv, 1954), 6:426–427 [H]: "If a person comes to convert, man or woman, it is appropriate to investigate them . . . lest [the request for conversion comes because] the woman has set her sights on a Jewish man. And if after investigation it becomes clear that this is indeed the reason for conversion, they are not accepted."

11. For the midrashic version, see *Midrash Proverbs*, ed. B. Visotski (New York, 1990), pp. 190–192 [H]. Shenhar compares the tale's versions, *The Folktale*, pp. 48–55.

12. For the medieval versions of the tale, see Gaster, *Exempla*, note to story 332; Ben-Amos, *Mimekor Yisrael*, p. 185. The version of *Hibbur Yafeh Min-ha-Yeshu'ah*, Hirschberg edition, pp. 4–5. Bin-Gorion indicates several differences between the versions, *Paths*, pp. 59–61. Schwarzbaum, *Folklore*, pp. 81–82, points to the version of this tale in *Vitae Patrum* concerning a God-fearing monk who is torn to pieces by wild animals, and of a wicked wealthy man who died the same day. The latter's sumptuous funeral was well attended, in stark comparison to the monk's procession. The monk's student, who questioned the justice of the situation, saw an angel in a dream who explained that the rich man had now received his reward for the one good deed he did in his life, and the monk his punishment—in this world, in order to arrive in the next in a pure state. This version of the *Vitae* had much influence on the dissemination of the tale in the Chrisitan folklore of the Middle Ages.

On the tale of Rabbi Joshua ben Levi and Elijah, cf. Schwarzbaum, ibid., pp. 87 ff., which mentions variants in the international folklore and compares the tale in detail to the Islamic version from the Koran. Ben-Amos, *Mimekor Yisrael*, p. 188. On theodicean tales in Judaism and Islam, see B. Heller, "Chadhir und der Prophet Elijahu als wundertätiger Baumeister," *Monatschrift für Geschichte und Wissenschaft des Judentums* 81 (1937): 76–80; E. L. Ormsby, *Theodicy in Islamic Thought* (Princeton, 1984); D. Noy, "The Jewish Theodicy Legend," in *Fields of Offerings. Studies in Honor of Raphael Patai*, ed. V. D. Sanua (Cranbury, N.J., 1983), pp. 65–84.

13. On the tale, "Joshua ben Levi and the Angel of Death," cf. I. Lévi, "La conte du Diable dupé dans le folklore juif," *Revue des Etudes Juives* 85 (1928): 137–163; H. Schwarzbaum, "Elijah the Prophet and R. Joshua ben Levi," *Yeda Am* 7 (1960): 22–31 [H]; and Ben-Amos, *Mimekor Yisrael*, pp. 211–212. On variants to this tale in Arabic culture, see H. Schwarzbaum, *Biblical and Extra-Biblical Legends in Islamic Folk-Literature* (Walldorf-Hessen, 1982), pp. 146–147, note 122.

14. On the *totentanz* in medieval European culture, see J. M. Clark, *The Dance of Death by Hans Holbein*, with an Introduction and Notes (London, 1947); G. Knox, "The Totentanz in Ellison's *Invisible Man*," *Fabula* 12 (1971): 168–178, and the important analysis of: J.-C. Schmitt, *Ghosts in the Middle Ages: The Living and the Dead in Medieval Society*, trans. T. L. Fagan (Chicago and London, 1998), pp. 214–215. On the travels to Eden and to Hell, theories on their origins in Jewish culture, and peak in Dante's poetry, see Gurevich, *Culture*, pp. 104–152; J. Le Goff, *The Medieval Imagination*, trans. A. Goldhamer (Chicago, 1988), pp. 67–77; M. Himmelfarb, *Tours of Hell: An Apocalyptic Form In Jewish and Christian Literature* (Philadelphia, 1983); E. Gardiner, *Medieval Visions of Heaven and Hell: A Sourcebook* (New York and London, 1993), and with special emphasis on the folkloristic aspect: G. Gatto, "Le Voyage au Paradise: La christianisation des traditions folkloriques au Moyen Age," *Annales E.S.C.* 34 (1979): 929–942.

15. For rabbinic sources on Rabbi Akiva's beginnings, see S. Safrai, *R. Akiva ben Joseph— His Life and Teaching* (Jerusalem, 1971), pp. 65–97 [H] and chapter 4, above, section E. On versions of the tale from the Middle Ages, see Gaster, *Exempla*, note to no. 147 and Ben-Amos, *Mimekor Yisrael*, pp. 131–132.

16. See the previous chapter, section K, for a discussion of the cycle of tales of drunks;

Jacob ben Isaac Luzzato, *Sefer Kaftor va-Ferah* (Amsterdam, 1709), p 99a [H]. On the sources of this version, see *Tanhuma, shmini*, 11. For the international versions, see Schwarzbaum, *Berechia*, pp. 538–541; Ben-Amos, *Mimekor Yisrael*, p. 179.

17. On the stories of R. Hanina ben Dosa in rabbinic literature, cf. the discussion above in chapter 4, section E, and the literature cited there in note 52. On tales of R. Hanina ben Dosa in the Middle Ages, see *Mimekor Yisrael*, no. 347; Ben-Amos, *Mimekor Yisrael*, p. 136. The version of *Hibbur Yafeh min-ha-Yeshu'ah*, Hirschberg edition, pp. 24–26.

18. For the most basic and comprehensive discussion of this tale, including its modern versions in the folktales of ethnic communities in Israel, see Noy, "Versions." For other versions from the Middle Ages see Yassif, *Ben Sira*, pp. 159–162.

19. To these tales we should add the tales of Yokahni bat-Retivi (BT Sotah 22a), and Beruria wife of Rabbi Meir (BT 'Avodah Zara 18b), where the story itself appears only in Rashi, in situ. On the tale of "the weasel and the well," cf. D. Sadan, "On the Aggadah of the Weasel and the Well," *Molad* 15 (1957): 367–381, 467–476 [H]; Z. Kagan, "From Aggadah to Novella," *ha-Sifrut* 3 (1971/1972): 242–248 [H]; and R. Meyer, "Geschichte eines orientalischen Märchenmotivs in der rabbinischen Literatur," *Festschrift Alfred Bertholet zum 80 Geburstag* (Tübingen, 1950), pp. 365–378.

On the literary character of Rashi's stories, see L. Landau, "Rashi's Tales in the Babylonian Talmud," *Eshel Be'er Sheva* 3 (1986): 101–117 [H]. Rashi's version is found in his commentary to *Ta'anit*, 8a. The long version in B. M. Levin, *Otzar ha-Geonim le-Masekhet Ta'anit* [Treasury of the Ge'onim to Tractate Ta'anit] (1933), 5, *in situ* [H]; *Sefer Arukh ha-Shalem*, A. Kohut edition (Vienna, 1926), 3:395–396 [H].

20. Rashi's version is found in his commentary corresponding to the location in the Babylonian Talmud, and the version of Rav Hai Gaon in *The Geonic Responsa to Tractate Sanhedrin*, B. M. Levin edition, p. 343 [H]. On studies that treated these versions cf. Landau, "Rashi" (supra, note 19); Schwarzbaum, *Berechia*, pp. 550–558, which compares at length the various versions of the fable among the European fabulists of the period; Z. Shukry, "The Wolf and the Fox in the Well," *Laographia* 22 (1965): 491–497, analyzes in detail the realia of the fable.

21. The main medieval text of this tale is found in *The Alphabet of Ben Sira*, and cf. Yassif, *Ben Sira*, pp. 71–76, and also the detailing of the other versions from the medieval period, ibid. Another important version appears in *Midrash Psalms*, Buber edition, Psalm 34, p. 123a, and in *Yalkut Shimoni* to Samuel # 131 [H] also, it seems, from the Middle Ages. For details of the folkloric motifs of which the tale makes much use, see *Ben Sira*, ibid.

22. On the tale of Samuel's father, see the responsa of Rav Hai Gaon in *Teshuvot ha-* [Responsa of the] Ge'onim, J. Musafia edition (Lyck, 1864), no. 92, pp. 29b–30a [H]; Ben-Amos, *Mimekor Yisrael*, p. 125; A. Marmorstein, "Beiträge zur Religionsgeschichte und Volkskunde," *Jahrbuch für jüdische Volkskunde* 1 (1923): 315–319. On the tale of the birth of Rabbi, see the commentary of the Tosaphot on *Avodah Zarah* 10b; Jellinek, *Beit ha-Midrash*, 6:130–131; and additional versions listed in *Mimekor Yisrael*, no. 245. The general motifs dealing with this theme are F 317—Fairy predicts future greatness of (newborn) child; M 311—Prophecy: future greatness of unborn child. J 2342.2.1—Woman gives birth to child fourteen months after husband's departure. K 1920-1930—Substituted children; K 1921—Parents exchange children.

23. Almost all the works of Jewish history deal with the cultural contacts between Jews, Christians, and Muslims in the medieval period. See especially Güdemann, *Learning*; Baron, *History*, vol. 4 ("Meeting of East and West"); idem, "The Jewish Factor in Medieval Civilization," *Proceedings of the American Academy of Jewish Research* 12 (1942), pp. 1–48; J. Parkes, *The Jew in the Medieval Community* (London, 1938); B. Blumenkranz, *Juif et chrétiens dans*

le monde occidentale, 430–1096 (Paris, 1960); R. Chazan, *Medieval Jewry in Northern France: A Political and Social History* (Baltimore and London, 1973); M. Kriegel, *Les Juifs a la fin du Moyen Age dans l'Europe méditerranénne* (Paris, 1979); J. R. Marcus, *The Jew in the Medieval World. A Source Book: 315–1791* (New York, 1979).

24. The classic work on Jewish translations in the Middle Ages is Steinschneider, *Translations*. Compare the interesting thesis of J. Jacobs, *Jewish Contributions to Civilization* (Philadelphia, 1920), pp. 138–163 ("Medieval Jews as Intellectual Intermediaries"), and the important discussion of C. C. Lehrmann, *Jewish Influence on European Thought* (London, 1976), pp. 50–80 ("Medieval Judeo-Romance Literary Relations"). On translations of *Kalilah we-Dimna* into Hebrew, see Derenbourg (supra, note 2). On *The Tales of Sendebar*, see M. Gaster, "The Tales of Sendebar," in *vezot le-Yehuda. Sefer ha-Yovel le-Y. L. Landau* [For Yehuda. Jubilee Volume for Y. L. Landau] (Tel Aviv, 1937), pp. 7–39 [H]; E. Epstein, "Mishle Sendebar: New Light on the Transmission of Folklore from East to West," *Proceedings of the American Academy of Jewish Research* 27 (1958): 1–17; idem, *Tales of Sendebar* (Philadelphia, 1967). On *The Romance of Alexander the Great*, see G. Cary, *The Medieval Alexander* (Cambridge, 1967); I. J. Kazis, ed. and trans., *The Book of the Gests of Alexander of Macedon: A Medieval Hebrew Version of the Alexander Romance* (Cambridge, Mass., 1962); R. Reich, ed. and trans., *Tales of Alexander the Macedonian. A Medieval Hebrew Manuscript* (New York, 1972). On the composition-translation of Kalonymus ben Kalonymus, *Iggeret Ba'alei Hayyim*, cf. the Toporovski-Habermann edition (Jerusalem, 1949) [H]. On the romance of the knights of the round table in Hebrew, see J. Dan, "Hebrew Versions of Medieval Prose Romances," *Hebrew University Studies in Literature* 6 (1978): 1–9; C. Leviant, ed. and trans., *King Artus. A Hebrew Arthurian Romance of 1279* (New York, 1969); Z. Malachi, ed., *The Adventures of Sir Amadis de Gaula* (Tel Aviv, 1981) [H]. On the texts in Judeo-Arabic that survived in the Cairo Genizah, see note 2, above. For the translations and revisions into Yiddish of the romances, see I. Zinberg, *A History of Jewish Literature*, trans. and ed. B. Martin (Cleveland, 1972–1978), vols. 1: 185–206; 7: 49–86; Shmeruk (supra, note 5), pp. 89–104 (on the contribution of Elijah Bakhur in translating the texts); Zfatman, *Narrative*, 1:69–76, and the important literature cited there; L. Landau, *Arthurian Legends: Or the Hebrew-German Rhymed Version of the Legend of King Arthur* (Leipzig, 1912).

25. On the tale of R. Joshua ben Levi and Elijah, its variants, its comparison to the version of the Koran, and theories as to its origins, see above, note 12. On the legend of "Solomon and Ashmedai," see the discussion above, chapter 4, section C, and the detailed literature offered there in note 20.

26. On the tale, see Yassif, *Ben Sira*, pp. 166–168. On the Arabic version cf. Y. Ratzhabi, *Sikhot 'Arav* [Arabian Traditions] (Tel Aviv, 1967), pp. 40–41 [H]; A. Stahl, "On Development of Humor," *Mehkarei ha-Merkaz le-Heker ha-Folklor* 3 (1973): 198 [H]. The story merited cataloguing as international tale type AT 830c, and as motif N385.1 ("If God Wills"). For variants in Muslim and Jewish folklore, see Schwarzbaum, *Studies*, p. 271–272; and cf. J. Nacht, "If God Wills," *Sinai* 24 (1948/1949): 72–79 [H].

27. G. Scholem proposed a mystical interpretation for this story, and cf. "Garments for Souls and the Rabbinic Robes," *Tarbitz* 24 (1955): 290–306 [H]. D. Z. Bannet revealed the origins of the tale in Islamic culture in "The Rabbis' Robe: Hibbur Yafeh me-ha-Yeshu'ah and Islamic Tradition," *Tarbiz* 25 (1956): 331–336 [H].

28. The tale was published from an Oxford manuscript in Gaster, *Exempla*, pp. 197–206. On variants in world literature, see Gaster, ibid., in the note; Ginzburg, *Legends*, 5: 148, note 49 (which posits an Indian origin for the tale), and Heller (*Jewish Quarterly Review* 24 [1933–34]), who rejects this theory. M. Piekarwz, in his remarks to the Hebrew edition of Zinberg (supra, note 24 [Tel Aviv, 1958]), pp. 254–255, points to the tension between mythic and Jew-

ish elements in the story, and compares the manuscript version to the Yiddish version that appears in the *Mayse-Bukh*. Compare E. Yassif, "Intertextuality in Folk literature: Pagan Motifs in Early Modern Jewish Folktales," *Jerusalem Studies in Jewish Folklore* 19-20 (1998): 287-309(H). The motif of the golden hair that causes a man to fall in love with its owner was widespread in the Middle Ages as part of the romance of Tristan and Isolde, but dates back much farther, appearing as early as the tales from ancient Egyptian literature. See Y. M. Grintz, ed. and trans., *Tales, Songs, and Fables from Ancient Egyptian Literature* (Jerusalem, 1975), pp. 60-61 [H].

29. The tale of Joshua ben Nun appears in Abraham ben Eliyahu of Vilna, *Rav Pe'alim* (Warsaw, 1894), p. 12a [H]. Ben-Amos offers an important bibliographical note to the tale, *Mimekor Yisrael*, pp. 25-26. The vast literature published on the Oedipus myth and its variants is summed up in L. Edmunds and A. Dundes, eds., *Oedipus. A Folklore Casebook* (New York and London, 1984), L. Edmunds, *Oedipus: The Ancient Legend and Its Later Analogues* (Baltimore, 1985), which also treats the Jewish versions of the tale (pp. 68-69, 199-206). In medieval traditions, Judas Iscariot, the Jewish traitor of Christian culture, takes Oedipus's place, and see P. F. Baum, "The Medieval Legend of Judas Iscariot," *Publications of the Modern Language Association* 24 (1916): 481-632; P. Lehmann, "Judas Iscariot in der lateinischen Legendenüberlieferung des Mittelalters," *Studi Medievali* 4 (1930): 289-346; G. Zuntz, "Ödipus und Gregorius," *Antike und Abendland* 4 (1954): 191-203; H. Maccoby, *Judas Iscariot and the Myth of Jewish Evil* (London, 1992). On the medieval versions and the hasidic narrative, see Ben-Yehezkiel, *Ma'asiot*, p. 427, and an important note on p. 700; B. Heller, "Über Judas Iscariot in der jüdischen Legende," *Monatschrift für Geschichte und Wissenschaft des Judentums* 76 (1932): 33-42; Y. Elstein, "The Gregorius Legend: Its Christian Versions and Its Metamorphosis in the Hasidic Tale," *Fabula* 27 (1986): 195-215. On the anthropological connection between the prohibition of cooking a calf in its mother's milk and incest, see H. Eilberg-Schwartz, *The Savage in Judaism* (Bloomington and Indianapolis, 1990), pp. 128-134; E. Cosquin, "Le Lait de la Mere et le Coffre Flotant," *Revue des Questions Historiques* 83 (1908): 353-425; I. Lévi, "Le Lait de la Mere et le Coffre Flotant," *Revue des Etudes Juives* 59 (1910): 11-13.

One important distinction between AT 931 (Oedipus) and AT 933 (Gregorius)—the two main branches of the tale—is that in the Gregorius legend, mother and father are siblings, and Gregorius sleeps with his mother but does not murder his father. In the Jewish version, the opposite takes place: Joshua bin Nun kills his father—but does not sleep with his mother. This illustrates the different sensitivities of the Jewish and Christian societies. In the latter, incestuous relations between brother and sister can be forgiven, so that the protagonist can go on to become the greatest of popes (Gregorius). In Jewish society, sexual relations with one's mother are unforgivable, if not on account of the sin itself, then because of their consequences: children born of such a union have no future within Jewish society. Therefore, apparently, the Jewish storytellers chose to change this particular detail in the prevalent narrative traditions of the tale. Conversely, in most of the *Israel Folktale Archives* versions (the Hebrew, contemporary variants) appearing in translation in Edmunds, ibid. (pp. 199-206), the protagonist does indeed lie with his mother, but the child born thereof dies as a result of an accident (he falls into a soup pot and is hence eaten by his unwitting father).

30. The classic discussion of ways of Judaizing the international tale types is found in Noy's work, "Versions." On additional means of Judaization with reference to medieval narrative, see Yassif (supra, note 8).

31. The tale is known as the legend of Crescentia or Genofeva and is classified in the international index as tale types AT 712 and AT 883*. On versions of the tale in international folklore, see A. Wallensköld, *Le conte de la femme chaste convictée par son beau frére*

(Helsinki, 1907); H. L. Uther, "Crecentia," *Enzyklopädie des Märchens* (Berlin, 1981), 3:167–171; and I. Dan, "The Innocent Persecuted Heroine: A Female Fairy Tale," in *Patterns in Oral Literature*, ed. H. Jason and D. Segal (The Hague, 1977), pp. 13–30. A poetic version of the tale that weaves together poems and long rhetorical passages, yet is astonishingly similar in plot to the Hebrew version, is found in Zia u'd-Din Nakhshabi, *Tales of the Parrot (Tuti-Namah)*, trans. and ed. M. A. Simsar (Ohio and Gratz, 1978), pp. 201–208 ("Utarid and Khorshid"). On the Hebrew version of the tale found in the grouping of tales entitled *Sefer ha-Ma'asim* in an Oxford manuscript, see Yassif (supra, note 8), pp. 418–419; Ben-Amos, *Mimekor Yisrael*, pp. 386–387. On the tensions between didactic tendencies and artistic enjoyment in the European novellae of the Middle Ages, see E. Hermes, "The Answer of the Physician and Theory of the Novella," *The Disciplina Clericalis of Petrus Alfonsi*, trans. E. Hermes (Berkeley and Los Angeles, 1977), pp. 14–20; R. Dickinson, "Didacticism in the Fifteenth Century Novella and Folktale," *Southern Folklore Quarterly* 30 (1966), 264–270.

32. On the talmudic fable of "the fox and the fishes," cf. above, chapter 4, section J, and note 117. For the text of *The Alphabet of Ben Sira* and how it was revised, see Yassif, *Ben Sira*, pp. 100–104; also M. Steinschneider, "Zu Kalila We-Dimna," *Zeitschrift der Deutschen Morgenländischen Gesellschaft* 27 (1873): 553–565; M. Gaster, "Das Herz auf dem Lande," *Monatschrift für Geschichte und Wissenschaft des Judentums* 29 (1880): 475–480; and B.C. Kirtley, "Remarks on the Origin and History of an 'Alphabet of Ben Sira' Fable," in *Studies in Biblical and Jewish Folklore*, ed. F. L. Utley, D. Noy, and R. Patai (Bloomington, 1960), pp. 29–37.

33. The Vatican manuscript version is reproduced in M. Hirschler, "Anthology of Tales and Legends," *Genuzot* 2 (1985): 179–180 [H]. For a more widespread version of the tale subsequent to *Meshalim shel Shlomo ha-Melekh* [Parables of King Solomon], see E. Yassif, "Parables of King Solomon," *Jerusalem Studies in Hebrew Literature* 9 (1986): 357–373 [H] and Ben-Amos's note on this version, *Mimekor Yisrael*, p. 28.

34. On the origins of and variants to the tale in medieval narrative, see Schwarzbaum, *Studies*, pp. 65–71; idem, *Folklore*, pp. 369–375; Y. Dishon, *Joseph ben Meir ibn Zabara's Sefer ha-Sha'shu'im* (Jerusalem, 1985), pp. 63–70 [H]; Yassif, "Parables of King Solomon," ibid., pp. 364–365; Ben-Amos, *Mimekor Yisrael*, pp. 57–58. On international versions cf. G. Paris, "Die undankbare Gattin," *Zeitschrift des Vereins für Volkskunde* 13 (1903): 1–24, 129–150; J. Bolte und G. Polivka, *Anmerkungen zu den Kinder- und Hausmärchen der Brüder Grimm* (Leipzig, 1913–1932), 1:126–131, and see the literature cited in Aarne and Thompson for tale types AT 612–612A.

35. The first version of the tale of "Solomon and the Thief" in Hebrew literature appears in *Midrash of the Ten Commandments*, eighth commandment (G. Hasan-Rokem edition, pp. 26–28); Gaster, *Exempla*, tales 111–112, and the variants listed there in the note to the story; M. Gaster and B. Heller, "Salomon und der Dieb," *Monatschrift für Geschichte und Wissenschaft des Judentums* 78 (1934): 273–278. For Boccaccio's version of the tale in his book, *Filocolo*, see its translation in R. P. Miller, ed., *Chaucer: Sources and Backgrounds* (New York, 1977), pp. 122–135; A. C. Lee, *The Decameron. Its Sources and Analogues* (London, 1909), pp. 322–328. Chaucer's marvelous version is the famous "Franklin's Tale," and see W. H. Schofield, "Chaucer's Franklin's Tale," *Modern Language Association of America* 16 (1901): 405–449. As to the question of Near Eastern versions of the story, see J. Schick, "Die ältesten Versionen von Chaucers Frankeleynes Tale," in *Studia Indo-Iranica. Ehrengabe für Wilhelm Geiger*, ed. W. Wüst (Leipzig, 1931), pp. 89–107; W. F. Bryan and G. Dempster, eds., *Sources and Analogues of Chaucer's Canterbury Tales* (New York, 1958), pp. 377–397. On the tale of "the weasel and the well," see the discussion above in this chapter, section B, and note 19.

36. On versions of the tale in Jewish narrative, see Yassif, "The Tale" (supra, note 2); Ben-

Amos, *Mimekor Yisrael*, p. 361. For international versions of the tale, see G. H. Gerould, "Forerunners, Congeners and Derivatives of the Eustace Legend," *Publications of the Modern Languages Association* 19 (1904): 335–448; A. Monteverdi, *I testi della Leggenda di S. Eustachio*, 2 vols. (Bergamo, 1909–1910); A. Hilka und W. Meyer, "Ueber die neu-aramäische Placidus Wandergeschichte," *Nachschriften* (1917): 80–95; H. Delehaye, "La Legende de Saint Eustache," in his *Mélange D'Hagiographie Greque et Latine* (Bruxelles, 1966), pp. 213–239.

37. On the novella of Solomon and the Queen of Sheba, see the literature cited in Yassif, *Ben Sira*, pp. 50–59; A. Chastel, "La Legende de la Reine de Saba," *Revue de l'Histoire de Religions* 119 (1939): 204–225, 120 (1940): 27–44, 160–174; J. B. Pritchard, ed., *Solomon and Sheba* (London, 1974); A. H. Johns, "Solomon and the Queen of Sheba: Fakhr al-Din al-Razi's Treatment of the Quranic Telling of the Story: Sura 27 (al Nami): 15–44," *Abr-Nahrain* 24 (1986): 58–82; and the socio-historical interpretation of J. Lasner, *Demonizing the Queen of Sheba: Boundaries of Gender and Culture in Postbiblical Judaism and Medieval Islam* (Chicago, 1993). The *Second Targum to Esther* appeared recently in a critical edition: *The Targum Sheni to the Book of Esther: A critical edition based on MS. Sasson 282 with critical apparatus*, by B. Grossfeld (New York, 1994), pp. 30–33.

38. On the history of the exemplum in European literature, see Bremond—Le-Goff—Schmitt; J. L. Welter, *L'Exemplum dans la littérature religieuse et didactique du moyen age* (Paris, 1927); J. A. Mosher, *The Exemplum in the Early Religious and Didactic Literature of England* (New York, 1911); M. D. Howie, *Studies in the Use of Exempla with Special Reference to Middle High German Literature* (London, 1923); C. Daxelmüller, "Exemplum," *Enzyklopädie des Märchens* (Berlin, 1982), vol. 4, col. 627–649; R. Schenda, "Stand und Aufgaben der Exemplaforschungen," *Fabula* 10 (1969): 69–85, and the recent bibliography cited in: J. Berlioz and M. A. Polo de Beaulieu, eds., *Les Exempla médiévaux. Introduction a la recherche* (Carcassonne, 1992); B. Engler and K. Müller, eds. *Exempla: Studien Zur Bedeutung und Funktion exemplarischen Erzählens* (Berlin, 1995). A collection of texts dealing with themes discussed here is: J. Young Gregg, *Devils, Women and Jews: Reflection of the Other in Medieval Stories* (Albany, 1997). On *Sefer Hasidim*, see the important collection of articles and literature cited therein (pp. 279 ff.): I. G. Marcus, ed., *Religion and Social Ideas of the Jewish Pietists in Medieval Germany* (Jerusalem, 1986) [H].

39. On the *adab* and the *farag* in Islamic literature, cf. A. Wiener, "Die Parag ba'd as Sidda-Literatur," *Der Islam* 4 (1913): 270–298, 387–420; F. Gabrieli, "Adab," *The Encyclopedia of Islam*, New Edition (Leiden and London, 1960), 1:175–176. On the connection between these genres in Arabic literature and *Hibbur Yafeh min-ha-Yeshuah*, see *An Elegant Composition Concerning Relief after Adversity*. Trans. from the Arabic with an introduction and notes by W. M. Brinner (New Haven and London, 1977), pp. xxiv–xxix. On the important work of Petrus Alfonsi and his links to Islamic culture, cf. Schwarzbaum, *Folklore*, pp. 239–358; E. Hermes, *The Disciplina* (op. cit. n. 31), pp. 3–99; G. Constable and J. Kritzeck, eds., *Petrus Venerabilis (1156–1956): Studies and Texts* (Rome, 1956); J. Tolan, *Petrus Alphonsi and his Medieval Readers* (Gainesville, 1993).

40. Güdemann mentioned the exemplary nature of *Sefer Hasidim* in *Learning*, pp. 99 ff. See also I. F. Baer, "The Religious-Social Orientation of 'Sefer Hasidim,'" *Zion* 3 (1938): 6–7, 19 [H]. T. Alexander-Frizer, *The Pious Sinner. Ethics and Aesthetics in the Medieval Hasidic Narrative* (Tübingen, 1991); E. Yassif, "The Exemplary Tale in 'Sefer Hasidim,'" *Tarbitz* 57 (1987/1988): 217–255 [H]. Passages from *Sefer Hasidim* were translated from *Sefer Hasidim al-pi Nosah Ktav-Yad asher be-Parma* [Sefer Hasidim according to the Parma Manuscript], (Y. Wistinetski and J. Freimann edition, Frankfurt, 1924) [H].

41. On the concept of the exemplum in antiquity and the ways of using it in Hellenistic rhetoric, see J. D. Lyons, *Exemplum. The Rhetoric of Example in Early Modern France and*

Italy (Princeton, 1989). The definition most widely accepted by medieval writers was that of thirteenth-century Jean de-Garland: "Exemplum est dictum vel factum alicuius autentice persone dignum imitatione" ("The exemplum is a true story about an exemplary figure whose deeds should be emulated"). Thus these guiding terms are accepted in the perception of the genre: the exemplum is a tale that illustrates (*ilustrare*) an abstract idea, which comes to persuade us (*persuasio*) that the entertaining (*delectare*) story is an example worthy of note (*demonstrare*) and imitation (*imitatio*). Compare to this Daxelmüller (supra, note 38), p. 627, and especially the basic critical discussion of the genre: Bremond—Le-Goff—Schmitt.

42. This outlook was also developed in the preceding chapter, in the discussion of the exemplum in rabbinic literature, and cf. the discussion and corresponding literature, ibid., section F, and notes 58, 59.

43. On the "analogous" and "paradigmatic" nature of the exemplum, see Bremond–Le-Goff–Schmitt, p. 54; H. Bausinger, "'Exemplum' und Beispiel," *Hessische Blätter für Volkskunde* 59 (1968): 31–43; D. O. Via, "Parable and Example Story: A Literary-Structural Approach," *Semeia* 1 (1968): 105–133; T. Whitesell, "Fables in Medieval Exempla," *Journal of English and Germanic Philology* 46 (1947): 348–366.

44. Another tale that belongs to the type concerning a dead person who returns to our world and reports his fate in the next in order to caution the living or guide them concerning the fulfillment of a precept or ethical norm, is that offered by the son of R. Judah the Pious, R. Zaltman, in *Sefer ha-Gan* (the tale is reproduced and discussed below in this chapter, section [F]). Another interesting tale is offered in Jerusalem manuscript Heb. 8°3182, and reproduced in N. Brüll, "Beiträge zur jüdischen Sagen- und Sprachkunde im Mittelalter," *Jahrbücher für jüdische Geschichte und Literatur* 9 (1889): 1–85: "A story heard from the mouth of Rabbi Judah the Pious, who told of Mrs. Yuta. This Mrs. Yuta passed on a few days before, and those sitting did not see [anything; they only heard] a voice. And when they went out Mrs. Yuta said [in the language of Ashkenaz], 'Achh' [i.e., that she was suffering in the next world]. Then Rabbi Judah the Pious [asked her how she had sinned to be so punished]. She said to him: 'Once we were playing with a ball and the boys with us, and I fell on the ball, and one boy jokingly touched my thigh, I did not shame him, rather I laughed. And each and every day now [the rest is missing]" (p. 21). It seems that Rabbi Judah the Pious had a particular affection for this type of tales, as he believed it had the power to influence his listeners. On the spread of the narrative theme of the dead who returns to the lands of the living, see Thompson, *Motifs*: E200–E399: Return from the dead, and Tubach, *Index*: "Dead, return from"; L. Petzold, *Der Tote als Gast: Volkssage und Exempel* (Helsinki, 1968), and the socio-historical analysis of J. -C. Schmitt, *Ghosts in the Middle Ages: The Living and Dead in Medieval Society*, trans. T. Lavender Fagan (Chicago and London, 1998). On oral poetry's use of the ready-made epic pattern, consult the classic work of A. B. Lord, *The Singer of Tales* (New York, 1978) and J. M. Foley, *The Theory of Oral Composition. History and Methodology* (Bloomington and Indianapolis, 1988).

45. On the tale type, "the neighbor in Paradise" see, for example, Z. Kagan, "A Craftsman as a Neighbor in Paradise," *Mahanayyim* 91 (1964): 42–47 [H]; T. Alexander, "'A Neighbor in Paradise' in *Sefer Hasidim*: A Folktale in Its Ideational Context," *Jerusalem Studies in Jewish Folklore* 1 (1981): 61–82 [H]; B. Heller, "'Gott wünscht das Herz': Legenden über einfältige Andacht und über den Gefährten im Paradise," *Hebrew Union College Annual* 4 (1927): 365–404.

46. On the dialectic nature of the European exemplum that confronts its protagonists with a choice between good and evil, life and death, see Bremond–Le-Goff–Schmitt, pp. 80–81; F. C. Tubach, "Strukturanalytische Probleme des mittelalterlichen Exemplum," *Hessische*

Blätter für Volkskunde 59 (1969): 31–43. Sh. Werses, "On Clarification of the Structural and Generic Traits of the Tales of 'Sefer hasidim,'" *Studies in Kabbalah, Jewish Philosophy and Ethical Literature, Presented to Isaiah Tishbi on his Seventy-Fifth Birthday* (Jerusalem, 1986), pp. 357–360 [H] On the versions of the tale, "R. Akiva and the Wandering Dead," and its avatars in Hebrew literature, see M. B. Lerner, "The Story of the Tanna and the Dead: Its Literary and Halachic Transformations," *Asufot* 2 (1988): 29–70 [H].

47. On the tale of the innocent shepherd and its versions, cf. M. Ben-Yehezkiel, "Prayer of the Simpleton," *La-Mo'ed* 2 (1946): 112–139 [H] and D. Noy, "The Simpleton's Prayer Brings Rain," *Mahanayyim* 51 (1960): 34–45 [H]. Alexander (supra, note 40), pp. 58–86, places the tale in the context of the teaching of the Medieval Jewish Pietists and their attitude to prayer and devotion, and this is surely one way of understanding the meaning of the tale in this particular context. Other tales that deal with similar subjects of prayer customs and the recitation of liturgical hymns attest to the use of the exempla in the controversy within the religious and social leadership of the community. Compare, for example, this typical tale:

> A story of Rabbana Eliezer bar Nathan, may his memory be for a blessing, who was the leader of Mainz [Jewish community]. Once there was a community leader from Cologne, and his father was a rabbi and his grandfather was a rabbi and his grandfather's father was a rabbi—and his grandfather's father was from a family of converts and not of distinguished lineage. And he abolished all the liturgical hymns [from being recited in the synagogue, as was the custom of that community], and no man was authorized to do anything without his permission. Now this same community leader had a special room into which a mouse could not gain entry. One time, after he shut the door and lay upon his bed, a rooster got in and stripped all the flesh from his face. The next day, the Sabbath, the community leader went to Master of the Name (a miracle worker) who lived there, and asked him what it was about, and requested that he seek out the answer in a dream. [The Master of the Name] said: "That was Rabana Eliezer bar Nathan, may his righteous memory be for a blessing, the Rabbi of Mainz." So he went to Mainz and asked, "What have I done to you? And if I've done something to you forgive me." He answered him: "All that I did to you I had to do against my will because thus instructed me my holy fathers who produced the liturgical hymns. [They] do not want you to continue abolishing the liturgies they created. And if, heaven forfend, you do continue, you and all your seed will perish for all eternity." And he made a solemn vow that he would not leave off from saying [these hymns] and that wheresoever he found them, he would store and protect them, and so he did (Brüll, supra note 44, p. 23).

48. On the tale of "the half friend," see E. M. Habermann, "The Faithful Friends—Three Tales of Friendship," *Mahberot le-Sifrut* 5 (1951): 80–93 [H]; E. Yassif, "The Contribution of *Sefer Oseh Pele* to Jewish Folk Narrative," *Jerusalem Studies in Jewish Folklore* 3 (1982): 54–56 [H]; and H. Schwarzbaum, "Petrus Alfonsi's 'Disciplina Clericalis,'" *Sefarad* 21 (1961): 283–294 (reprinted in Schwarzbaum, *Folklore*, pp. 255–266). The tale first appears in the writings of the eleventh-century convert, Petrus Alfonsi, and cf. *Die Disciplina Clericalis des Petrus Alfonsi—nach allen bekanten Handschriften*, Hrsg. A. Hilka and W. Söderhelm (Heidelberg, 1911), pp. 3–6.

49. The version of *Midrash of the Ten Commandments* is found in all the editions in the seventh commandment (Hasan-Rokem edition, pp. 23–25), and in *Hibbur Yafeh me-ha-Yeshuah*, Hirschberg edition, pp. 68–70. For additional variants cf. Gaster, *Exempla*, no. 384;

Ben-Amos, *Mimekor Yisrael*, pp. 145–146. In the version cited by S. A. Wertheimer, *Batei Midrashot* (Jerusalem, 1968), pp. 184–186 [H], the woman "kept giving him wine until he did not know his right hand from his left and that night was Purim night," and so R. Meir is exonerated from the transgression of drinking too much, as well! Compare also Shenhar, *The Folktale*, pp. 95–102. On the figure of the sinner who repents in medieval legends, see E. Dorn, *Die Sündigen in der Legende des Mittelalters* (München, 1967).

50. On the sources of and variants to this tale in Hebrew literature and Islamic culture, see Hirschberg, *Hibbur Yafeh*, p. 65–67; Ben-Amos, *Mimekor Yisrael*, p. 141. On the designation, "Tzutzita," see D. Boyarin, "To the Talmudic Lexicon," *Tarbitz* 3 (1981): 164–175 [H].

51. On the attitude of medieval Christian preachers and thinkers toward the exemplum, see Mosher, *The Exemplum* (supra, note 38), pp. 6, 10–13; Bremond–Le-Goff–Schmitt, pp. 30–31; and T. F. Crane, "Medieval Sermon Books and Stories," *Proceedings of the American Philosophical Society* 21 (1883), pp. 56 ff. Caesarius of Heisterbach (thirteenth century), author of one of the largest and most influential collections of exempla in Christian Europe, describes the power of the exemplum in the introduction to one of his stories as follows (the dialogue is between the monk and the novice): "Monk: . . . Would you like to hear of the peril of some who desired to him (The Devil) in his own person?—Novice: Indeed I greatly desire it, *because the more horror and malice that I hear about him, so much the more shall I fear of sin!*" (Caesarius Heisterbacensis Monachi, *Dialogus Miraculorum*, translated from the Latin by H. von E. Scott and C. C. S. Bland [New York, 1929], book 5, chapter 28, vol. 1, p. 357).

52. For a list of the folktales in *Sefer Hasidim* and a discussion of how they differ from the original stories of R. Judah the Pious, see Yassif, "The Exemplary Tale" (supra, note 40). On the ideological tension at the heart of the *Sefer Hasidim* tales, see Alexander (supra, note 40). On the nature and history of the collections of exempla mentioned here, see note 38, above, and J. Matuszak, *Das Speculum Exemplorum als Quelle volkstümlicher Glaubensvorstellung des Spättmitelalters* (Siegeburg, 1967); A. Kaufmann, *Caesarius von Heisterbach. Ein Beitrag zur Kulturgeschichte des zwölften und dreizehnten Jarhundert* (Leipzig, 1974). Christian exempla also contain more than a few examples of the ideational tension that influenced the nature of the tales, and see P. Assion, "Das Exemplum als agitatorische Gattung," *Fabula* 19 (1978): 225–240.

53. The problem of "factual truth" as opposed to "historical truth," and the function of the historical legend in historiography, is one of the most discussed in historical theory in recent years. I refer here only to some of the latest discussions in which extensive literature is cited: H. White, "Historicism, History and the Figurative Imagination," "The Fictions of Factual Representation," in *Tropics of Discourse* (Baltimore, 1978), pp. 101–120; P. Ricoeur, "L'histoire comme récit," in *La Narrativité*, ed. D. Tiffeneau (Paris, 1980), pp. 3–24; J. M. Beer, *Narrative Conventions of Truth in the Middle Ages* (Geneva, 1981); S. Fleischman, "On the Representation of History and Fiction in the Middle Ages," *History and Theory* 22 (1983): 278–310, as well as chapter 4, above, note 71. On the development of this perception in the field of French historiography, see the important survey-criticism of A. J. Gurevich, "Medieval Culture and Mentality According to the New French Historiography," *Archives européennes des sociologie* 24 (1983): 167–195. Regarding Jewish culture, we must cite principally Baron, *History*, 6: 188–198, 232–234 ("Josippon and Historical Folklore," "History and Folklore"); R. Bonfil, "Myth, Rhetoric, History? A Look at the Scroll of Ahimaaz," *Culture and Society* (supra, note 1), pp. 99–136; I. G. Marcus, "History, Story and Collective Memory: Narrativity in Early Ashkenazic Culture," *Prooftexts* 10 (1990): 365–388. I will articulate elsewhere the main differences between the approach of the latter two articles and my own.

The main work to develop the notion of "collective memory" in the sphere of Jewish culture is that of Y. H. Yerushalmi, *Zakhor: Jewish History and Jewish Memory* (Seattle, 1982). On the folkloristic perception of the historical legends of the Middle Ages, see B. A. Rosenberg, "Folklore Methodology and Medieval Literature," *Journal of the Folklore Institute* 13 (1976), pp. 311–329; J.-C. Schmitt, "Les Traditions Folkloriques Dans la Culture Médiévale," *Archives des Sciences Sociales der Religion* 52 (1981): 5–20, and the considerable literature cited there; Yassif, "The Study" (1988), pp. 3–10, and the additional literature on "History and Folklore" cited above in chapter 2, note 6, and chapter 4, note 69. The perception at the core of my approach to the historical legends was formulated by one of the leading French historians of the medieval period: "Thus structuralism (and comparative history) not only helps us to do away with the fallacious historicism of an 'event-ridden' history of tales and legends (which sought the explanation and, worse still, the origin of a tale or legend in a historical event or character). It also makes it possible, if we pay attention not only to form but also to changing content, to comprehend the historical function of both, in relation not to an event but rather to social and ideological structures themselves," J. Le Goff, *Time, Work, and Culture in the Middle Ages*, trans. A. Goldhamer (Chicago, 1980), p. 219.

54. On the historiographic works and the studies on them, see M. A. Shulvass, "The Knowledge of History and Historical Literature in the Cultural Sphere of Medieval Ashkenazic Jewry," *Jubilee Volume for Hanokh Albeck* (Jerusalem, 1963), pp. 465–495 [H]; Yerushalmi, *Zakhoer* (supra, note 53); Yassif, "The Study"; R. Bonfil, "Jewish Attitudes Toward History and Historical Writing in Pre-Modern Times," *Jewish History* 11 (1997): 7–40. References to *Shevet Yehudah* are from E. Shochat edition (Jerusalem, 1947) [H]. On the reactions of the exiles from Spain to their exile, see the classic essay of H. H. Ben-Sasson, "A Generation of Exiles from Spain Speaks," in *Continuity and Change* (Tel Aviv, 1984), pp. 198–238 [H], and: D. G. Roskies, ed., *The Literature of Destruction: Jewish Responses to Catastrophe* (Philadelphia, 1988), pp. 89–106.

55. On verisimilitude in medieval historiography, see the works cited above in note 53, and especially that of Beer, *Narrative Conventions of Truth*. All the scholars who treated it ascertained the a-rhetorical nature of the legend, beginning with the classic definition of the Brothers Grimm at the start of the nineteenth century (and cf. the vast literature cited in *The German Legends of the Brothers Grimm*, ed. and trans. D. Ward [Philadelphia, 1981], II), and the theoretical literature cited above in chapter 4, section G ("The Historical Legend"), and note 69, ibid.

On the literary interest in the book *Shevet Yehudah*, see the works of I. Loeb, "Le Folk-Lore Juif dans la chronique du Schébet Iehuda d'Ibn Verga," *Revue des Etudes Juives* 24 (1892): 1–29; Zinberg, *History*, 4: 65–72; Y. H. Yerushalmi, *The Lisbon Massacre of 1506 and the Royal Image in the Shebet Yehuda* (Cincinnati, 1976); and J. D. Abramsky, "On the Essence and Content of *Shevet Yehudah*" in his *On the Paths of the Eternal Jew* (Tel Aviv, 1985), pp. 46–65 [H]. On the story-craft of *The Book of Josippon* see Flusser, *Josippon*, 2:185–216 ("The Book of Josippon as a Work of Art").

56. The basic texts on the Massacres of 1096 were taken from A. M. Habermann, ed., *The Massacres of Ashkenaz and France. Chronicles and Liturgical Hymns* (Jerusalem, 1971) [H]. A great deal has been published on the literary shaping of the 1096 massacres (and other massacres), the utilization of biblical and rabbinic tales of martyrdom, and the molding of these tales into a "collective memory" for generations to come. See I. F. Baer, "The 1096 Massacres," *Assaf Volume* (Jerusalem, 1953), pp. 126–140 [H]; S. Spiegel, "From Proverbs of the 'Akedah: *The Murdered of Blois* and the Revival of the Blood Libels," *Jubilee Volume for M. M. Kaplan* (New York, 1953), pp. 267–285 [H]; J. Katz, "Between 1096 and 1648–49," *Jubilee Volume for Yitzhak Baer on His Seventieth Birthday* (Jerusalem, 1961), pp. 318–337 [H]; J. Hacker, "On the 1096 Massacres," *Zion* 31 (1966): 225–231 [H] and the exhaustive litera-

ture cited there in note 1; S. Schwartzfuchs, "The Place of the Crusades in the History of the Jewish People," *Culture and Society* (supra, note 1), pp. 251–268; R. Chazan, "The First-Crusade Chronicles," *Revue des Etudes Juives* 133 (1974): 237–254; and I. Marcus, "From Politics to Martyrdom: Shifting Paradigms in Hebrew Narratives of the 1096 Crusade Riots," *Prooftexts* 2 (1982): 40–52 (which also treats the likening of the suicide to the sacrifice in the Temple). Especially important for the study of the recurrent topic in these chronicles is: R. Chazan, "Representation of Events in the Middle Ages," *Essays in Jewish Historiography*, ed. A. Rapoport-Albert (Atlanta, 1991), pp. 40–55.

57. On medieval tales of blood libels, see D. Noy, "Tales of Blood Libels in Jewish Communities," *Mahanayyim* 110 (1967): 32–51 [H]; Marcus, "Confrontation"; S. Spiegel, "From Proverbs of the 'Akedah," ibid., and the literature cited in the following works: R. Po-chia Hsia, *The Myth of Ritual Murder, Jews and Magic in Reformation Germany* (New Haven and London, 1988); W. P. Eckert, "Vehängnisvolle Legenden als Ausdruck und als Grund christilich-jüdischen Gegensatzes," in *Monumenta Judaica*, ed. K. Schilling (Köln, 1964), pp. 154–160; A. Dundes, ed., *The Blood Libel Legend* (Madison, Wisc., 1991). The legends collected by Yuzpa Shamash, the synagogue caretaker in the community of Worms in the seventeenth century, includes two realistic tales of blood libels. In both, the apologetic-conciliatory aspect towards the Christian overlords stands out, characterizing the status of the community leaders. Compare S. Eidelberg, ed., *R. Yuzpa, Shammash of Worms* (Jerusalem, 1991), pp. 82–84 [H].

58. On the tale type, "miraculous rescue of a community," and the "second Purim" tales, see in detail above, chapter 3, section B, and note 7, ibid. The tale here was excerpted from *Divrey Yoseph* by R. Joseph ben Isaac Sambari, in E. Neubauer, *Medieval Jewish Chroniclers* (Oxford, 1895).

59. On *Toledot Yeshu* ("The Life of Jesus") see the main texts and philological discussion in S. Krauss, *Das Leben Jesu nach jüdischen Quellen* (Berlin, 1902); and additional texts found thereafter in the *Genizah* and other sources: L. Ginzberg, *Ginzey Schechter* (New York, 1928), pp. 324–338 [H]; Z. Falk, "A New Fragment from 'Toledot Yeshu,'" *Tarbitz* 46 (1976/1977): 319–322 [H]; D. Boyarin, "A Corrected Reading of the New Fragment of 'Toledot Yeshu,'" *Tarbitz* 47 (1978): 249–252 [H]; S. Weissenberg & A. Marmorstein, "Über eine Toledot Jeschu Handschrift," *Mitteilungen zur jüdischen Volkskunde* 15 (1912): 95–97; B. Heller, "Über das Alter der jüdischen Judas Sage und des Toldot Jeschu," *Monatsschrift für Geschichte und Wissenschaft des Judentums* 77 (1933): 198–201; W. Fischel, "Eine jüdische-persische 'Toldoth Jeschu' Handschrift," *Monatschrift für Geschichte und Wissenschaft des Judentums* 78 (1934): 343–350; W. Horbury, "The Trial of Jesus in Jewish Tradition," in *The Trial of Jesus*, ed. E. Bammel (Naperville, 1970), 3: 103–121; S. Légasse, "La légende juive des Apotres et les rapports judéo-chrétiens dans le haut Moyen Age," *Bulletin de Littérature Ecclésiastique* 75 (1974): 99–132; B. Blumenkranz, *Juifs et chrétiens* (Paris, 1977), pp. 169 ff.; G. Schlichting, *Ein jüdisches Leben Jesu* (Tübingen, 1982) (Wissenschaftliche Untersuchungen zum Neuen Testament, no. 24) [includes Hebrew texts].

The versions of the legend of "Simon Cephas" are cited in Jellinek, *Beit ha-Midrash*, 5:60–62, 6:9–14, 155–156. Zunz cites testimonies to the effect that the tale was known as early as the time of Rashi and the Tosaphists in L. Zunz, *Literaturgeschichte der Synagogalen Poesie* (Berlin, 1865), pp. 5–6, and see also, M. Güdemann, *Geschichte des Erziehungswesens und Kulture der abendländischen Juden* (Vienna, 1884), II:44–52; K. Kohler, "Simon Cephas," *Jewish Encyclopedia* (New York, 1906), 11:366–368; J. H. Greenstone, "Jewish Legends About Simon-Peter," *Historia Judaica* 12 (1950): 89–104, which claims, following Jellinek (*Beit ha-Midrash*, 6:x–xi), that the tale was intended to bring together Jews and Christians and lead to more Christian tolerance toward Jews. However, the claim can have no basis in reality, as the tale was meant for Jewish society and for Jews, where it was indeed told. It is noteworthy to mention in this context that among the Islamic legends of Ka'b Al-Ahbar, a Jew who converted and was considered to be among the founders of Islam, are some that present him as also having been sent on a similar mission by the Jewish elders, and cf. M. Perlmann, "A Legendary Story of Ka'b Al-Ahbar's Conversion to Islam," *The Joshua Starr Memorial Volume* (New York, 1953), pp. 85–99. In connection with this tale, S. D. Luzzatto writes in his introduction to the Italian prayer-book about the development of his "folkloristic" consciousness—a consciousness quite advanced in relation to the Jewish culture of the early nineteenth century:

> Thus, in his words, 'Since the names of the first *paytannim* [composers of liturgical poems] have been lost to memory, it has happened that liturgical poems have been attributed to people who never thought to write [them]. Now this was not done by mistake, but with the good intention of strengthening the faith. And here I have been shocked and amazed for some twenty-four years since seeing in the *Mahzor Vitry* (manuscript belonging to my wise and dear friend Joseph Almanzi may the Lord watch and keep him) the responsa of Rabbenu Tam. It states that Simon Cephas wrote the *seder* for the Day of Atonement entitled *Eten Tehilah*. And after twenty years my astonishment evaporated, for I saw, in a manuscript of a commentary to the *Mahzor* that I have (p. 155), [regarding] *Eten Tehilah*, [that] Simon Cephas, also called St. Peter of Rome . . . made this praise after instituting the faith . . . [missing in the original—E.Y.]. Then he put himself in the Roman tower for the rest of his days with meager bread and scant water, and sent them this praise to notify them that he did not believe at all in . . . [as above] but to quiet the wicked that rioted against the Jews deliberately.' This ends the quotation. Then I comprehended that the remarks of Rabbenu Tam are based on a false rumor that spread among the Jews in days of old, in the time of the troubles and devastations, with good intention to strengthen the faith of the masses, for they would hear that the first Apostle wrote liturgical hymns in praise of the Jewish faith, and that his intention when he found the new faith was only for the sake of Heaven and for the welfare of the Jews. (S. D. Luzzatto, *Mavo le-Makhzor Bnei Roma* [Introduction to the Italian Rite Prayer Book], Livorno, 1856, p.16 [H])

On the legend of "The Jewish Pope," see the texts in Jellinek, *Beit ha-Midrash*, 5:148–152; and other versions from manuscripts noted in A. David, "On the Legend of the Jewish Pope," *Yad le-Heiman. Collected Articles in Memory of A. M. Habermann* (Lod, 1984), pp. 17–26 [H]. On the historical background to this legend and the polemic of the popes in Rome in the twelfth century, see Güdemann, *Learning*, part 2, pp. 58–64; I. A. Klauzner, *Ha-Novella ba-Sifrut ha Ivrit* [The Novella in Hebrew Literature] (Tel Aviv, 1947), pp. 41 ff. [H]; E. Grossman, *The Early Sages of Ashkenaz* (Jerusalem, 1989), pp. 89–90 [H]; E. Grabois, "From 'Theological' Anti-Semitism to 'Racial' Anti-Semitism: The Polemic of the Jewish Pope in the Twelfth Century," *Zion* 47 (1982): 1–16 [H]; M. Steinschneider, "Zum Judenpapst," *Israelitische Letterbode* 7 (1881–2): 170–174; S. Krauss, "Die jüdischen Apostel," *Jewish Quarterly Review* 17 (1905): 370–383; M. Stroll, *The Jewish Pope: Ideology and Politics in the Papal Schism of 1130* (Leiden, 1987).

60. The main historical studies of these texts are A. Grabois, "The Legendary Figure of Charlemagne in the Hebrew Sources of the Middle Ages," *Tarbitz* 36 (1967): 22–58 [H]; A. Grossman, "The Emigration of the Kalonymus Family from Italy to Germany," *Zion* 40 (1975): 154–185 [H], and in his book, *The Early Sages of Ashkenaz* (Jerusalem, 1989), pp. 29

ff. [H]. Additional texts were published from manuscripts by A. David, "Tales of the Persecutions in Germany of the Middle Ages," *Shai le-Heiman. Studies in Medieval Hebrew Literature* (Jerusalem, 1977), pp. 69–83 [H]. Marcus (supra, note 53), pp. 371 ff., looks at these
texts in a manner similar to that which I propose below.

61. The classic study of the legend of "the four captives" is G. D. Cohen, "The Story of
the Four Captives," *Proceedings of the American Academy of Jewish Research* 29 (1960–1961):
55–131, and the discussion of it and its contribution to the study of Jewish historiography in
Marcus (supra, note 53), pp. 368–371. On the legend of "Aharon of Baghdad and the Lion"
see the works of R. Bonfil, "Between the Land of Israel and Babylonia: Guidelines for the
Study of the History of Jewish Culture in Southern Italy and Christian Europe in the Early
Middle Ages," *Shalem* 5 (1987): 1–30 [H]; idem, "Myth" (supra, note 53). Another tale that
reflects the tensions between the Torah centers of medieval Jewry, this time between the
academies of Babylonia and the center in the German lands, was preserved in manuscript
and published by Brüll (supra, note 44), pp. 36–37. According to this account, R. Meshullam
the Great, son of R. Kalonymus, was kidnapped and sold into slavery in Babylonia. There
he served in the home of the head of the academy, concealing his wisdom while covertly
solving the sage's difficulties in halachah. After his secret is exposed, the head of the academy admits that R. Meshullam is his superior in Torah knowledge, and thus recognizes indirectly the supremacy of the new center in the German lands over the ancient Torah centers
of Babylonia.

62. The text is cited by A. David (supra, note 60), pp. 80–81, from a sixteenth-century
Warsaw manuscript. He equates it with Joseph ha-Cohen's description in *Emek ha-Bakha*,
in order to prove that in fact it refers to a period much later than that of Charlemagne.

63. Much has been published on the messianic awakening in medieval Jewry, mostly historic and ideational discussions that have no place here. The main texts were collected in
A. Z. Aescoly, *Ha-Tenu'ot ha-Meshikhiot be-Yisrael* [Jewish Messianic Movements] (Jerusalem, 1956), pp. 93–417 [H]. The articles gathered in the collection, *Messianism and Eschatology—Collected Articles*, ed. T. Baras (Jerusalem, 1984), pp. 169–324 [H], represent, in general,
the philosophical, mystical, and historical approaches to the messianic movements; and the
sociological approach is presented by: S. Sharot, "Jewish Millenial-Messianic Movements: A
Comparison of Medieval Communities," T. M. Endelman ed., *Comparative Jewish Societies*
(Ann Arbor, 1997), pp. 61–88, and the vast literature listed there. The text here is cited from
Sefer Me'oraot Zvi (Warsaw, 1903), pp. 35a–37b [H], among eleven tales of false messiahs told
according to the same pattern that I proposed, and in a similar style.

64. On these traditions, see Sh. Eidelberg, "The Antiquity of the Jewish Settlement in
Germany," *World Union of Jewish Studies Newsletter* 17–18 (1981): 9–25 [H]; Sh. Eidelberg,
"The Origins of Germanic Jewry: Reality and Legend," in *Ashkenaz. The German Jewish
Heritage*, ed. G. Hirschler (Yeshiva University, 1988), pp. 5–7; J. Shatzmiller, "Politics and
the Myth of Origins: The Case of the Medieval Jews," in *Les Juifs au Regard de L'Histoire.
Mélanges en l'honneur de B. Blumenkranz*, ed. G. Dahan (Paris, 1985), pp. 49–61; J. Kaffiah,
The Jews of Yemen (Jerusalem, 1976), p. 30 [H] and the commentaries of Isaac Abrabanel to
the Book of Obadiah verse 20, and to Zechariah 12:7. The Legend of the Worms Community
is found in the book of Yuzpa Shamash (caretaker of the synagogue) *Ma'aseh Nissim* (S.
Eidelberg edition, supra, note 57, p. 59) [H].

On the medieval journeys to the Land of Israel, see A. Ya'ari, *Mas'ot Eretz Yisrael* [Jour-
neys to the Land of Israel] (Jerusalem, 1946), pp. 31–322 [H], and Ya'ari's exhaustive introduction there; J. Prawer, "Hebrew Travelogues of the Land of Israel in the Crusader Period,"
Katedrah 40 (1986): 31–62 [H], 41 (1987): 65–90 [H]; the important work of E. Reiner, *Immigration and Pilgrimage to the Land of Israel 1099–1517* (Ph.D. diss., The Hebrew University,

Jerusalem, 1988) [H]; and the collection including comparative studies of Jewish and Christian travel: R. Outerhout ed., *The Blessings of Pilgrimage* (Urbana and Chicago, 1990). For an anthropological point of view, consult the approach of G. Bowman, "Pilgrimage Narratives of Jerusalem and the Holy Land: A Study of Ideological Distortion," A. Morinis ed., *Sacred Journeys: The Anthropology of Pilgrimage* (Westport, Conn., 1992), pp. 149–168. The most famous instance of moving to the Land of Israel during this period as a result of the messianic impulse is the immigration of R. Judah ha-Levi. Compare B. Z. Dinur, "The Immigration of Rabbi Judah Ha-Levi to the Land of Israel and the Messianic Fervor of his Day," in his *Be-Ma'avak ha-Dorot* (In Struggle of Generations) (Jerusalem, 1975), pp. 202–248 [H].

65. For sources of and variants to "The Legend of Bustenai," see Ben-Amos, *Mimekor Yisrael*, p. 223, and the studies cited there on the historical backdrop to the tale. Likewise M. Gil, "The Babylonian Encounter," *Tarbitz* 48 (1979): 35–73 [H] M. Steinschneider, *Die Geschichtsliteratur der Juden* (Frankfurt, 1905), pp. 9–10.

66. The tale of exorcising the demon from the daughter of Byzantine emperor Basil I is found in *Megilat Ahima'az*, B. Klar edition, pp. 17–20. On the tale and its versions, and on the folkloric quality of *The Scroll of Ahimaaz*, see my article, "Folktales in the Scroll of Ahimaaz," *Yad le-Heiman. Collected Articles in Memory of E. M. Habermann* (Lod, 1984), pp. 41–56 [H]; also M. Ben-Sasson, "Community Leaders in North Africa. The Figure and the Image: Literary Creation as Historical Source," *Pe'amim* 26 (1986): 152–162 [H].

67. The texts of the legends about the persecutions in Halle and Mainz were reproduced from the Warsaw manuscript in A. David's article (supra, note 60). He offers other traditions, as well, that identify the place with the city of Fulda (ibid., no. 8). A tradition about active vengeance against the rioters survived among the Jews of Worms: when, during the time of the black plague, the Jews of Worms were accused of poisoning the wells, the Christians set a date to wipe out the community. The Jewish community leaders, summoned to the city council, hid butcher knives in their clothing. When the judges accused them of the blood libel, they locked the courtroom door, fell upon the dishonorable magistrates, and killed the lot. Other Jews, armed with swords and spears, attacked and killed Christians outside the courthouse, then they set fire to the municipal granaries (Yuzpa Shamash, *Ma'aseh Nissim*, S. Eidelberg edition [supra, note 57], p. 75). H. H. Ben-Sasson, in "The Singularity of the Jewish People according to Denizens of the Twelfth Century," *Perakim* 2 (1968–1974): 165–167, 172–177 [H], points to the existence of two approaches to Jewish resistence in the twelfth century: one passive, espoused by R. Judah ha-Levi, for example, and the other, active, whose outstanding proponent was R. Abraham ibn Ezra: "two giants of Jewish religious philosophy—Rabbi Abraham ben David and Maimonides, the great chronographers of that century—Rabbi Abraham ben David in Spain, tellers of the stories about 1096 in Ashkenaz, the commentator, the philosopher, and poet R. Abraham ibn Ezra . . . and lastly R. Eleazar Ba'al ha-Rokeah, of the masters of the Hasidei Ashkenaz, all agree on one thing—they all equally reject outright the willing acceptance of degradation as something of intrinsic value and wish, each in his own way, for an active, fighting response" (P. 167).

68. For biographical information on Rashi, see Leopold Zunz, *Toldot Rashi* (The Life of Rashi), translated into Hebrew by Shimshon Bloch (Warsaw, 1862). There has been a great deal of research on Christian hagiography, whose scope and diversity are enormous. For a full description and exhaustive list, including some 1,300 entries arranged according to subject and period, see Wilson, *Saints*, and the important work not yet included therein: R. Aigrain, *L'Hagiographie. Ses sources, ses méthodes, son histoire* (Poitiers, 1983). H. Rosenfeld makes special reference to the medieval period in Germany in his *Legende* (Stuttgart, 1961).

The question of historical authenticity of the saints' legends was recently discussed by F. Lotter, "Methodisches zur Gewinnung historischer Erkenntnisse aus hagiographischen Quellen," *Historische Zeitschrift* 229 (1979): 298–356; D. Weinstein and R. M. Bell, *Saints and Society: The Two Worlds of Western Christendom, 1000–1700* (Chicago and London, 1982), pp. 1–15; T. J. Heffernan, *Sacred Biography. Saints and Their Biographies in the Middle Ages* (New York and Oxford, 1988), pp. 38–71. The last three criticize the "positivist" approach of nineteenth-century scholars of hagiography, who look for the factual "kernel" in saints' legends, and their criticism of these tales when they cannot find one, much the same as Zunz. Gurevich formulates keenly the difference between this approach and that of the modern historians in *Culture*, p. 51: ". . . from the point of factual reliability, very few hagiographical texts bear critical examination. But if we see in them monuments of culture reflecting the spiritual life of the environment which generated them for which they were created, our assessment will be completely different." Of special importance for the beginning of the phenomenon, and especially regarding the miracles in the domain of healing, see: R. Van Dam, *Saints and their Miracles in Late Antique Gaul* (Princeton, 1993), and the importance of the period's art as evidence in: B. Abou-El-Haj, *The Medieval Cult of Saints: Formations and Transformations* (Cambridge, 1994). There is a tendency in medieval studies to forget that in medieval Islam, as well, the veneration of saints had a central place, and in the case of Jewish culture, it is of primary importace, and compare: I. Goldziher, "On the Veneration of the Dead in Paganism and Islam," in *Muslim Studies*, ed. S. M. Stern (London, 1967), 1: 209–239; H. Bar-Itzhak, "Modes of Characterization in Religious Narrative: Jewish Folk Legends about Miracle Worker Rabbis," *Journal of Folklore Research* 27 (1990): 205–230.

69. On *Shalshelet ha-Kabbalah* [The Chain of Tradition], see A. David, *The Historiographic Enterprise of Gedaliah ibn Yahya, Author of Shalshelet ha-Kabbalah* (Ph.D. diss., The Hebrew University, Jerusalem, 1976) [H]; Zinberg, *History* (supra, note 24), 4: 82–86. The citations are from Gedaliah ibn Yahya, *Shalshelet ha-Kabbalah* (Warsaw, 1881) [H].

70. On the reciprocity between oral sources and written texts in saints' legends of the Middle Ages see, for example, B. Stock, *The Implications of Literacy: Written Language and Models of Interpretation in the Eleventh and Twelfth Centuries* (Princeton, 1983), pp. 12–87; J. M. H. Smith, "Oral and Written: Saints, Miracles, and Relics in Brittany, c. 850–1250," *Speculum* 25 (1990): 309–343; and A. M. Kleinberg, *Prophets in Their Own Country: Living Saints and the Making of Sainthood in Later Middle Ages* (Chicago, 1992), and the vast literature cited in them.

71. On saints' rites in medieval Christian Europe, see above, note 68, and especially Wilson, *Saints*. On the *reliquia* and pilgrimages in Christianity, see the extensive literature cited in Wilson, ibid., pp. 338–344, and also R. and C. Brooke, *Popular Religion in the Middle Ages* (London, 1984), pp. 14–30; and especially: N. Hermann-Mascard, *Les Reliques des Saints: Formation coutumeive d'un droit* (Paris, 1975); P. J. Geary, "Sacred Commodities: The Circulation of Medieval Relics," A. Appaduri, ed., *The Social Life of Things: Commodities in Cultural Perspective* (Cambridge, 1986). Testimony regarding an unintentional visit to the (fictive) grave of Rashi in Prague is offered in *Shalshelet ha-Kabbalah*: "Before me testified Jewish merchants from Mantua who were on their way to the court of the emperor in the Germanic kingdom. In the city of Prague they saw the burial place of Rashi, with a grave stone. They could not understand what was written on it because [the letters were] worn" (22b). On pilgrimages to saints' graves in Palestine as early as the Second Temple period, see above, note 64.

72. The structural scheme of Jewish hagiographical tales was formulated by D. Noy, "R. Shalem Shabazzi in the Folk legend of Yemenite Jewry," *Bo'i Teiman* (Tel Aviv, 1967), pp. 106–133; and was followed by T. Alexander, "Saint and Scholar: The 'Ari and Maimonides in

Folk Tales," *Jerusalem Studies in Hebrew Literature* 13 (1992): 29–64. On the application of the formula to Rabbinic Agadah, see above, chapter 4, section E, and the literature cited there in the notes. On the birth legends surrounding Maimonides, see I. Berger, "Maimonides in Folk Legend," *Massad* 2 (1936): 216–238 [H] (the quote is taken from p. 220); T. Alexander and E. Romero, *Erase una vez . . . Maimonides—Cuentos tradiciones hebreos* (Cordoba, 1988). On the birth legend of R. Samuel the Pious, see *Ma'aseh Book*, trans. M. Gaster (Philadelphia, 1981 [1934]), no. 161, and also J. Meitlis, *The Praises of Rabbi Samuel and Rabbi Judah the Pious* (London, 1961), pp. 161–163 [Yiddish]. Another birth legend of R. Judah the Pious makes use of the widespread folk motif of "fulfilling the wish": "A story of our Rabbi Samuel the Pious of blessed and saintly memory. Walking along the road with two others, our Rabbi Samuel of blessed and saintly memory lifted his eyes to heaven and it seemed to him that he saw the skies open. Our Rabbi Samuel said to his companions: Ask of the Creator at this time whatever you desire and it will come true, as I see the skies are open and a man can have but one wish and the blessed Almighty will grant it. One asked for sons and one for wealth, and our Rabbi Samuel asked for issue like himself. And upon his return home his wife immersed herself and conceived our Rabbi Abraham and after that our Rabbi Judah the Pious" (Brüll [supra, note 44], p. 24). On Rashi: *Shalshelet ha-Kabbalah*, ibid., p. 22b, and also I. Berger, "Rashi in Folk Legend," in *Rashi—His Teaching and Personality*, ed. S. Federbush (New York, 1958), pp. 147–179 [H]. On the use of biblical models in Christian saints' legends, see M. van Uytfanghe, "Modeles bibliques dans l'hagiographie," in *Le Moyen Age et la Bible*, ed. P. Riché and G. Labrichon (Paris, 1984), pp. 449–487.

73. The death of R. Judah the Pious, *Ma'aseh Book*, no. 183, Brüll (supra, note 44), p. 43, Meitlis (supra, note 72), pp. 140–141. On Maimonides, *Shalshelet ha-Kabbalah*, pp. 26b, Berger, "Maimonides" (supra, note 72), p. 224. On the death of Nahmanides, ascertained from the splitting of his mother's gravestone, see *Shalshelet ha-Kabbalah*, p. 26a.

74. On the travels of Rashi, see Berger, "Rashi" (supra, note 72), pp. 156–166; J. Ben-Hillel, "Rashi in the Legend-Lore, *Rashi-Bukh* [Book of Rashi] (Buenos Aires, 1940), pp. 336–346 [Yiddish]. On Maimonides, *Shalshelet ha-Kabbalah*, pp. 20a–20b; Alexander and Romero (supra, note 72), pp. 61–74. On R. Samuel and R. Judah the Pious, Meitlis (supra, note 72), pp. 24 ff.; on R. Abraham ibn Ezra, N. Ben-Menahem, *Abraham ibn Ezra: Sihot ve-Aggadot Am* [Abraham ibn Ezra: Traditions and Folk Legends (Jerusalem, 1943), pp. 11–62 [H]. On the atmosphere of wandering in medieval Jewish communities and its causes see, for example, I. I. Yuval, "Ashkenazic Autobiography of the Fourteenth Century," *Tarbitz* 55 (1986): 541–566 [H]; I. A. Agus, *The Heroic Age of Franco-German Jewry* (New York, 1969), pp. 23–51.

75. On these tales, see Berger, "Maimonides" (supra, note 72), p. 221; on ibn Ezra, N. Ben-Menahem, "Folk Legends on R. Abraham ibn Ezra," *Minkhah li-Yehudah. Presented to Rabbi Y. L. Zlotnik on His Sixtieth Jubilee* (Jerusalem, 1950), pp. 141–161, no. 6 [H]. On R. Judah the Pious, see *Ma'aseh Book* (supra, note 72); Brüll (supra, note 44); J. Dan, "The History of 'The Story of the *Akdamut*' in Hebrew Literature," *Bikoret u-Parshanut* 9–10 (1976): 197–213, and especially appendices B, D, and E [H]. On the use of the Ineffable Name in medieval legend see, for instance, Trachtenberg, *Magic*, pp. 78–103; M. Grünbaum, "Über Schem Hammephorasch," *Zeitschrift der Deutschen Morgenladischen Gesselschaft* 39 (1885): 543–616, 40 (1886): 234–304; H. L. Held, "Der Schem ha-mephorasch," in his *Das Gespenst des Golem* (München, 1927), pp. 163–214.

76. The legend of "Maimonides and the Physicians" appears in *Shalshelet ha-Kabbalah*, p. 20a, and cf. Berger, "Maimonides" (supra, note 72), pp. 226 ff.; Alexander and Romero (supra, note 72), pp. 99–114. The legend of Nahmanides and Abner (of Burgos) in *Shalshelet ha-Kabbalah*, p. 26a. On the correspondence between the saint's spiritual legacy and the leg-

ends surrounding him, see L. Sheppard, *The Saints Who Never Were* (Dayton, Ohio, 1969), and in Jewish domain: Berger's note, "Rashi" (supra, note 72), pp. 147–149; E. Yassif, "The Interrelationship Between Biography and Hagiography: The Case of Judah the Pious," C. Daxelmüller ed., *R. Judah He-Hasid of Regensburg* (Regensburg, 1999).

77. The legend appears for the first time in *Shalshelet ha-Kabbalah* (p. 23a), and thereafter in many versions, and see Berger (supra, note 72), pp. 169–171.

78. On the controversy between rationalists and mystics during this period, and that over Maimonides's books, see Güdemann, *Learning*, 1:45–71; Zinberg, *A History* (supra note 24), 2: 103–134; H. H. Ben-Sasson, *History of the Jewish People in the Middle Ages* (Tel Aviv, 1969), pp. 151–158 [H]; C. Sirat, *Jewish Philosophy in the Middle Ages* (Jerusalem, 1975), pp. 292–299 [H]; J. J. Dinstag, "The Conceptual Relationship between the Kabbalistic Sages and Maimonides—An Annotated Bibliography," *Da'at* 25 (1990): 53–84 [H]. On Rabad's view of *Mishneh Torah*, see I. Twersky, *Rabad of Posquieres. A Twelfth Century Talmudist* (Cambridge, Mass., 1962), pp. 128–196; G. Scholem, "From Scholar to Kabbalist (The Kabbalists' Legend of Maimonides)," *Tarbiz* 6 (1935): 334–342 [H]; M. Idel, "Maimonides and Kabbala," in *Studies in Maimonides*, ed. I. Twersky (Cambridge, Mass., 1990), pp. 31–82; M. E. Shmidman, "On Maimonides's Conversion to Kabbalah," in *Studies in Medieval Jewish History and Literature*, ed. I. Twersky (Cambridge, Mass., 1984), pp. 375–386. The legend according to which Maimonides converted to Islam appears in D. S. Margoliouth, "The Legend of the Apostasy of Maimonides," *Jewish Quarterly Review* 13 (1901): 539–541.

79. On legends about the medieval wanderers, see above, note 74. For the tale of R. Samuel the Pious collecting alms, see *Ma'aseh Book*, Gaster edition (supra, note 72), no. 162; Meitlis (supra, note 72), p. 48. On R. Samuel nullifying the edict against the community, Meitlis, ibid., p. 52. For the tale of Rabbi Abraham ibn Ezra concealing his identity from Rashi and R. Judah ha-Levi see Ben-Menahem, *Abraham ibn Ezra* (supra, note 74), pp. 22–27, 38–41; Ben-Menahem, "Legends" (supra, note 75), no.1; idem, "R. Judah ha-Levi and Rabbi Abraham ibn Ezra," *Areshet* (1944): 366–369 [H]. On the social tension in Spain in this period, see J. T. Assis, "Poor and Rich in Jewish Society in Mediterranean Spain," *Pe'amim* 46–47 (1991): 115–138 [H], and the literature cited there.

80. On the figure of R. Judah the Pious as it arises from his writings and from testimony of his day, see Yassif, "The Exemplary Tale" (supra, note 40), pp. 236–246; J. Dan, "On the Historical Figure of R. Judah the Pious," *Culture and Society in Medieval Jewish History. Collected Articles in Memory of H. H. Ben-Sasson* (Jerusalem, 1989), pp. 389–398 [H].

On the shaving of one's beard in the Middle Ages, the related controversies, and the relevant rulings, see "Destroying the Beard. The Ban on Shaving Facial Hair," *Encyclopedia Talmudica* (Jerusalem, 1965), vol. 11, cols. 118–128 [H]; I. Abraham, *Jewish Life in the Middle Ages* (New York, 1973), pp. 283–284; T. and M. Metzger, *Jewish Life in the Middle Ages* (Freibourg, Switz., 1982), pp. 147–148; and "Beard and Shaving," *Encyclopedia Judaica* (Jerusalem, 1971), vol. 4, cols. 356–358.

On the tension between the religious leaders and the community's wealthy members, see H. H. Ben-Sasson, "The Medieval German Pietists on the Distribution of Material and Spiritual Possessions," in *Religion and Social Ideas of the Jewish Pietists in Medieval Germany*, I. G. Marcus, ed. (Jerusalem, 1986), pp. 217–236 [H]; I. G. Marcus, *Piety and Society: The Jewish Pietists of Medieval Germany* (Leiden, 1981), pp. 55–108. Similar tension in the Jewish communities of Spain in the thirteenth century is described by I. F. Baer, *History of the Jews in Christian Spain* (Tel Aviv, 1965), pp. 126 ff. [H].

81. On the thriving of Torah study in France and the German lands in the wake of Rashi and his students, see Güdemann, *Learning*, 1:3–44; E. E. Urbach, *The Tosaphists, Their History, Works, and Method* (Jerusalem, 1955) [H]. On opposition to the study method of the

Tosaphists, see H. Soloveichik, "Three Themes in the Sefer Hasidim," *AJS Review* 1 (1976): 311–358.

82. On such studies in medieval Christian culture, see Gurevich, *Culture*, p. 52; Heffernan (supra, note 68), pp. 21 ff.; H. Grundmann, "Litteratus-Illitteratus. Der Wandel einer Bildungsnorm vom Altertum zum Mittelalter," *Archiv für Kulturgeschichte* 40 (1958): 1–65.

83. The legend was published by Y. Ratzhabi, "The Birth of Rashi in Yemenite Legend," *Ba-Mishor* 1 (1940): fol. 27–28 [H] and cf. Berger, "Rashi" (supra, note 72), pp. 153–155. Also see the literature cited in B. Toelken, "The Folklore of the Academe," in *The Study of American Folklore*, ed. J. H. Brunwand (New York and London, 1986), pp. 502–528.

84. On the social and ideational background of the notion that "virtue is its own reward," current as far back as the time of the sages, see the important discussion in Urbach, *Sages*, pp. 269–270: "'There is no reward for (the fulfillment of) precepts in this world' (BT Hullin 142a) . . . precepts are not rewarded in this world . . . Such a doctrine concerning the reward given for the fulfillment of the precepts could be held by few individuals only."

Yuzpa Shamash, in the seventeenth century, offered an important variant to the legend of Nahmanides, learning the wisdom of Kabbalah from an elder who was none other than R. Eleazar of Worms, and cf. *Ma'aseh Nissim*, Eidelberg edition (supra, note 57), pp. 67–70; J. Dan, "On the Study of Legends Surrounding R. Eleazar of Worms," *Sinai* 74 (1974): 171–177 [H].

85. A small representation of the vast scholarship published on the genre follows: J. A. Klausner, *Ha-Novellah ba-Sifrut ha-Ivrit* [The Novella in Hebrew Literature] (Tel Aviv, 1947) [H]; B. von Weise, *Novelle* (Stuttgart, 1963); K. K. Polheim, *Novellentheorie und Novellenforschung* (Stuttgart, 1965); A. Semponx, *La Nouvelle* (Tournhout, 1973); J. Clements and J. Gibaldi, *Anatomy of the Novella* (New York, 1977); M. Ellis, *Narration in the German Novella—Theory and Interpretation* (Cambridge, 1979). In the domain of folk literature: P. N. Boratav, "The Tale and the Epico-Novelistic Narrative," *Studies in East European Folk Narrative*, L. Dégh ed. (Bloomington, 1978), pp. 3–48; and E. Yassif, "The Novella as an Ethnopoetic Genre," *Papers of the Eighth Congress for the International Society for Folk Narrative Research* (Bergen, 1984), pp. 283–289.

86. A borderline genre—the *Novellenmärchen*—was proposed as early as the eighteenth-century German Romanticists, as it suited their ideational and aesthetic orientations. See, for example, von Weise, *Novelle* (op. cit. n. 85), p. 6; Thompson, *The Folktale*, p. 8; Dégh, "Narrative," pp. 67–68. On the grouping of stories that includes this tale and its context, see Yassif, *Sefer ha-Ma'asim* (supra, note 8), pp. 409–430.

87. A. Marx, ed., "The Correspondence between the Rabbis of Southern France and Maimonides about Astrology," *Hebrew Union College Annual* 3 (1926): 311–358; *The Letters of Maimonides*, J. Shilat edition (Jerusalem, 1988), 2:478–490 [H].

The notion of "a match made in heaven" existed as early as the rabbinic period (*Mo'ed Katan* 18b; *Sotah* 2a; PT *Kiddushin* 3, 3).

On converse trends in the novella, see the remarks of E. Hermes, "The Answer of the Physician and the Theory of the Novella," in *The Disciplina Clericalis of Petrus Alphonsi* (op. cit. n. 31), pp. 14–20. For versions of the tale of "Solomon's Daughter in the Tower" see Ben-Amos's headnote, *Mimekor Yisrael*, pp. 70–71.

88. On the portrayal of women in the folktale and in folklore see, for example, C. Farrar, ed., *Women and Folklore* (Austin, 1975); R. Jordan and S. Kalcik, eds., *Women's Folklore, Women's Culture* (Philadelphia, 1985); K. E. Rowe, "To Spin a Yarn: The Female Voice in Folklore and Fairy Tale," in *Fairy Tale and Society*, ed. R. B. Bottigheimer (Philadelphia, 1986), pp. 53–74; K. F. Stone, "Feminist Approaches to the Interpretation of Fairy Tales," ibid., pp.

229–236; M. Mills, "Feminist Theory and the Study of Folklore: A Twenty Year Trajectory," *Western Folklore* 52 (1993): 173–192.

89. On the misogynistic literature, especially in the Middle Ages, see the literature cited above in chapter 4, note 100. On this literature in Jewish cultural spheres of the Middle Ages, see Schwarzbaum, *Folklore*, pp. 173–196; D. Pagis, "The Poetic Polemic on the Nature of Women," *Jerusalem Studies in Hebrew Literature* 9 (1986): 259–300 [H]; J. Dishon, *Sefer ha-Sha'ashu'im* (supra, note 34), pp. 53–91; A. Neubauer, "Zur Frauenliteratur," *Israelitische Letterbode* 10 (1884): 97–105, 113–133; 11 (1985): 62–69, 88–92; 12 (1886): 49–83; N. Roth, "The 'Wiles of Women' Motif in the Medieval Hebrew Literature of Spain," *Hebrew Annual Review* 2 (1978): 145–165; T. Rosen, "On Tongues Being Bound and Let Loose: Women in Medieval Hebrew Literature," *Prooftexts* 8 (1988): 67–88; T. Fishman, "A Medieval Parody of Misogyny: Judah ibn Shabbetai's 'Minhat Yehudah sone hanashim,'" ibid., pp. 89–112; J. R. Baskin, "Jewish Women in the Middle Ages," *Jewish Women in Historical Perspective*, J. R. Baskin, ed. (Detroit, 1991), pp. 94–114.; ibid., "From Separation to Displacement: The Problem of Women in Sefer Hasidim," *AJS Review* 19 (1994): 1–18, and the general picture arising from L. Davidman and S. Tenenbaum, eds., *Feminist Perspectives on Jewish Studies* (New Haven and London, 1994).

90. On the *Parables of King Solomon* and the sources of its tales, see Yassif, "Parables" (supra, note 33); Ginzberg, *Legends*, 4: 130–142; Ben-Amos, *Mimekor Yisrael*, pp. 35–36, 59–63.

91. Sh. Shahar, *The Fourth Estate: A History of Women in the Middle Ages*, Trans. Ch. Galai (London and New York, 1983); S. M. Stuart, *Women in Medieval Society* (Philadelphia, 1976); D. Baker, ed., *Medieval Women* (Oxford, 1989); E. Ennen, *The Medieval Woman* (Oxford, 1989); J. Bumke, *Courtly Culture. Literature and Society in the High Middle Ages*, trans. T. Dunlap (Berkeley and Los Angeles, 1991), pp. 325–414; A. Blamiris, ed., *Woman Defamed and Woman Defended: An Anthology of Medieval Texts* (Oxford, 1992); C. W. Bynum, *Fragmentation and Redemption: Essays on Gender and the Human Body in Medieval Religion* (New York, 1991); and the issue of *Speculum* 68/2 (1993).

92. Tale 20 in the grouping, *Sefer ha-Ma'asim*, mentioned above in note 8. On the tale, see A. Wallensköld, *Le conte de la femme chaste convictée par son beau-frére* (Helsinki, 1907); R. M. Walker, *"La chanson de Florence de Rome* and the International Folktale," *Fabula* 23 (1982): 1–18; and Ben-Amos, *Mimekor Yisrael*, pp. 386–387.

93. For a ranging discussion of this tale, its sources, and variants, see Ben-Amos, *Mimekor Yisrael*, pp. 207–209; Schwarzbaum, *Folklore*, pp. 143–172; G. Megas, "Die Sage von Alkestis," *Archiv für Religionswissenschaft* 30 (1933): 1–33.

94. On Jewish magic of the rabbinic period, see chapter 4, above, section H. Güdemann describes medieval Jewish magic's link to the magic beliefs of the European cultures, *Learning*, especially 1:140–156, 2:196–202; Baron, *History*, 8: 3–54; S. Shaked, "On Jewish Magic Literature in the Lands of Islam," *Pe'amim* 15 (1983), p. 15–28; Trachtenberg, *Magic*; J. von Ins, ed., *Abraham von Worms. Das Buch der wahren Praktik in der göttlichen Magie* (München, 1988). The ancient Germanic beliefs in vampires, strigae, werewolves, and so forth are described at length in Bächtold-Stäubli and C. Kappler, *Monstres, demons et merveilles a la fin du moyen age* (Paris, 1982). On some demonological tales in the Rhinelands in the twelfth and thirteenth centuries, see J. Dan, "Demonological Tales in the Writings of R. Judah the Pious," in his *Studies in the Literature of the Medieval German Pietists* (Ramat Gan, 1975), pp. 9–25 [H].

95. On the theological basis of "He has made his wonderful works to be remembered," see J. Dan, *Torat ha-Sod shel Hasidei Ashkenaz* [The Mysticism of the Medieval German Pietists] (Jerusalem, 1968), pp. 194 ff. [H]. Urbach, *Sages*, pp. 102–106 emphasizes, "The mir-

acle corroborates the truth and existence of the divinity—this was an accepted principle in antiquity." Pope Gregory the Great (late sixth century), in his stories of various wondrous acts, also declares that these tales are "the realization of God's words everyday" (*Saint Gregory the Great: Dialogues*, trans. O. Zimmerman [New York, 1959], p. 31). Walter Mapp, Bishop of Oxford at the close of the twelfth century, after offering a series of typical demonological tales, also concludes that "the deeds of God (which are exposed through such tales) cannot be comprehended by man's mind, and His creation is above all our studies" (Walter Mapp, *De nugis Curialium*, ed. M. R. James [Oxford, 1983], p. 160). An important treatise of R. Judah the Pious, where he discussed in depth his understanding of this theological principle, has been published recently by I. Ta-Shema, "The Tractate *He has made his wonderful works to be remembered* by R. Judah the Pious," *Kovetz Al-Yad* 12 (1994): 122–146 [H].

96. The Hebrew original of the *Scroll of Ahimaaz* was published in *Megillat Ahima'atz ve-Hi Megilat Yuhasin le-Rabbi Ahima'atz be-Rabbi Paltiel* [The Scroll of Ahimaaz: the Scroll of the Lineage of Rabbi Ahimaaz son of Rabbi Paltiel], B. Klar edition (Jerusalem 1974^2) [H], and was translated to English by M. Salzman, *The Chronicle of Ahimaaz* (New York, 1924). On this work, see the literature cited in Yassif, "Studies in the Narrative Art" (supra, note 3) and Bonfil, "Myth" (supra, note 53).

97. Apuleius's work, *The Golden Ass*, from the first century C.E., is one of the earliest known groupings of folktales. The text is offered in English translation in *The Transformations of Lucius otherwise known as The Golden Ass by Lucius Apuleius*, trans. R. Graves (Harmondsworth, 1950); See also E. Simon, "The Riddle of Apuleius's *Golden Ass*," *Eshkolot* 1 (1954): 11–24 [H]; B. E. Perry, *The Ancient Romances. A Literary-Historical Account of Their Origins* (Berkeley and Los Angeles, 1967), pp. 236–284; and especially: A. Scobie, *Apuleius and Folklore* (London, 1983).

98. The social perception of magic in the Middle Ages is formulated in J. B. Russel, *Witchcraft in the Middle Ages* (Ithaca and London, 1972); H. Webster, *Magic. A Sociological Study* (New York, 1973); V. I. J. Flint, *The Rise of Magic in Early Medieval Europe* (Princeton, 1991), and especially: R. Briggs, *Witches and Neighbors: The Social and Cultural Context of European Witchcraft* (New York, 1997), and the extensive literature cited in these works. The demonization of the Jew in the medieval ages as the embodiment of "the other" was described in great detail by J. Trachtenberg, *The Devil and the Jews. The Medieval Conception of the Jew and Its Relation to Modern Anti-Semitism* (New Haven, 1943); Baron, *History*, 11: 122–191, as well as by: N. Cohn, *Europe's Inner Demons* (Bungay and Suffolk, 1975); J. Richards, *Sex, Dissidence and Damnation. Minority Groups in the Middle Ages* (London and New York, 1990); D. Nirenberg, *Communities of Violence: Persecution of Minorities in the Middle Ages* (Princeton, 1996). The tale of Rabban Simeon ben Shetah and the Witches of Ashkelon is discussed above in chapter 4, section H.

99. The tale of R. Judah the Pious and the Bishop of Salzburg is reproduced from manuscript in Jellinek, *Beit ha-Midrash*, 6:139–141, and variants to this tale are found in abundance in the traditions of the medieval German Pietists, as indicated by Dan, "Demonological Tales" (supra, note 94), p. 24; idem, "The History of 'the Story of the *Akdamut*'" (supra, note 75). On the tale of "The *Akdamut*," featuring R. Meir Shatz, see the preceding article, and also J. Rivkind, "Di Historische Alegoriye fun R. Meir Shatz" [The Historical Allegory of R. Meir Shatz], *Filologishe Schriften* 3 (1929): 1–42 [Yiddish]; Ch. Shmeruk, "The Beginning of Yiddish Narrative Prose and Its Center in Italy," *Memorial Volume for A. L. Karpi* (Jerusalem, 1967), pp. 123–126 [H]; E. Yassif, "An Early Translation and Hebrew Version of 'The Story of the Akdamut,'" *Bikoret u-Farshanut* 9–10 (1976): 214–228 [H].

100. "The Pious Man and the Carob Tree" was copied in Oxford-Bodleian manuscript Or. 135, p. 303a–b (no. 8), and published in *Hibbur ha-Ma'asiyyot ve-ha-Midrashot ve-ha-Haggadot* [Composition of Tales and Midrash and Legends] (Venice, 1599), tale 15 [H]; in the Yiddish *Mayseh Bukh* (Gaster Edition), no. 190, and in Eleazar Araki's *Sefer ha-Ma'asiyyot* [Book of Tales] (Baghdad, 1892), no. 15 [H], and cf. Gaster, *Exempla*, nos. 307, 395, and the corresponding notes. The tale of the stone used for idol worship was also published in *Hibbur ha-Ma'asiyyot*, no. 16, and in the Araki's edition of *Sefer ha-Ma'asiyyot*, no. 16, and cf. Gaster, *Exempla*, no. 396. Walter Mapp (supra, note 95), pp. 141–142, also tells of a monk who fed crumbs from his table to a small snake that came to beg food. The snake grew from day to day, becoming so large that he filled up the monk's little dwelling. At this point the monk realized that the snake was, in fact, Satan. He prayed to God for forgiveness. God dispatched a messenger who counseled him to wait forty days, at which time Satan disappeared, never to return. More stories from the domain of exemplary literature appears in: J. Young Gregg, *Devils, Women, and Jews: Reflections of the Other in Medieval Sermon Stories* (Albany, 1997), pp. 61–68.

101. On the Jewish image of Christianity in the Middle Ages see, for example, J. Katz, *Between Jews and Gentiles. The Jewish Attitude toward their Neighbors in the Middle Ages and the Dawn of the Modern Age* (Jerusalem, 1960) [H]; B. Blumenkranz, *Juifs et Chrétiens dans le monde occidental 430–1096* (Paris, 1960); H. Liebeschütz, "Relations between Jews and Christians in the Middle Ages," *Journal of Jewish Studies* 16 (1965): 35–46. The ban on trading in Christian holy artifacts and in contributing, as merchants, to their rites, is discussed in detail in Katz, pp. 35–45.

102. Caesarius of Heisterbach, *The Dialogue on Miracles* (op. cit. n. 51), book 5, chapter 34, pp. 313–320, 355–363, 365–366. On the demonization of the heretical Christian Cults, see the literature in note 98, above, and also C. Ginzburg, *The Night Battles. Witchcraft & Agrarian Cults in the Sixteenth and Seventeenth Centuries* (Baltimore, 1983) and J. L. Nelson, "Religion in 'histoire totale': Some Recent Work on Medieval Heresy and Popular Religion," *Religion* 10 (1980): 60–85.

103. The tale was first published and translated into French by I. Lévi (*Revue des Etudes Juives* 35 [1897]: 76–81); Eisenstein, *Midrashim*, pp. 350–351; Gaster, *Exempla*, note to no. 338 (the references to variants are of little importance). On the folk beliefs in the matter of the gate to the other world being located in the Valley of Hinnom (with roots as early as the rabbinic period: *Eruvin* 19a) see S. Klein, "The 'Nehutei' and Rabbah bar Hana on Issues of Eretz Yisrael," *Zion* (*Annals of History and Ethnography*) 5 (1933): 5–13 [H]; Lerner, "The Story of the Tanna and the Dead" (supra, note 46), pp. 43 ff. On this motif in world literature, see G. D. Schmidt, *The Mouth of Hell in Medieval Art and Thought* (Ph.D. diss., University of Illinois, 1985).

104. On journeys to Paradise and Hell before Dante's account, see Gurevich, *Culture*, pp. 104–152; J. Le Goff, *The Birth of Purgatory*, trans. A. Goldhamer (Chicago, 1984); E. Gardiner, *Visions of Heaven and Hell Before Dante* (New York, 1989), and note 14, above. One sentenced to Hell who preaches religious observance is motif E 367.1. On the diversity of punishments in Hell, see Thompson, motifs Q560ff. In the Jewish domain, M. Gaster, in 1893, was the first to collect and interpret these texts: M. Gaster, "Hebrew Versions of Hell and Paradise," in his *Studies and Texts* (London, 1928), I: 124–161.

105. Of the extensive literature published on the subject, see above, chapter 3, note 26, Tubach, *Index*, nos. 1440, 1624, 3384; D. P. Walker, *Unclean Spirits. Possession and Exorcism in France and England in the late Sixteenth and Early Seventeenth Century* (London, 1981) and in the Jewish world: G. Nigal, *Dybbuk*; Y. Bilu, "Dybbuk"; S. Zfatman, "'A Tale of a Spirit in

the Holy Community of Koretz—A New Stage in the Development of a Folk Genre," *Jerusalem Studies in Jewish Folklore* 2 (1981): 17–65 [H]; idem, "The Exorcism of Spirits in Prague in the Seventeenth Century," ibid., 3 (1982): 7–35 [H].

106. Motif C12, and tale types AT 813, 813A–B; A Rash Remark, or A Curse Leads to Kidnapping of the Cursed (a child, or the one who uttered the curse himself) by the Demon or Satan, and Tubach offers the variants, *Index*, no. 1440.

107. The tale of the students of Rabbi Isaac Luria can be found in M. Benayahu, *Sefer Toldot ha-'Ari* (Jerusalem, 1967), pp. 232–234 [H]. The tale of the wealthy man who shaved off his beard despite R. Judah the Pious' warning is quoted in the tradition attributed to the latter's son in *Sefer ha-Gan* of R. Isaac ben R. Eleazar of Worms (Venice, 1606), pp. 9b–10a [H].

108. On tales of death, see Dan, "Demonological Tales" (supra, note 94), nos. 15, 16. On the perception of death in medieval culture, cf. Gurevich, *Culture*, pp. 146 ff., especially p. 241, note 1; Ph. Aries, *Western Attitudes to Death From the Middle Ages to the Present* (Baltimore, 1976); P. J. Geary, *Living with the Dead in the Middle Ages* (Ithaca and London, 1994). J.-C. Schmitt, *Ghosts* (supra, note 14) deals extensively with the perception of death in the Middle Ages.

109. For the different versions of this tale type in Jewish culture and international folklore, see H. Schwarzbaum, "The Hero Predestined to Die on His Wedding Day," in Schwarzbaum, *Folklore*, pp. 143–172.

110. On these two tales, see Yassif, *Ben Sira*, pp. 50–59, 63–70, and the literature there cited.

111. These stories of Walter Mapp are grouped in his book of exempla (supra, note 95), part two, chapters 12, 13, 14, part four, chapter 9. The tales of Caesarius of Heisterbach (supra, note 51), no. 33, p. 362.

112. A great deal has been published on this tale. See, for example, Y. L. Zlotnik, N. Aloni and R. Patai, *Ma'aseh Yerushalmi* [The Story of the Jerusalemite] (Jerusalem, 1947); J. Dan, "Five Versions of the Story of the Jerusalemite, *Proceedings of the American Academy of Jewish Research* 35 (1967): 99–111; S. Zfatman, *Marriage*, and the vast literature cited in the latter. The most impressive version of "The Story of the Jerusalemite" appears in Dan, "Demonological Tales" (supra, note 94), no. 19 (p. 19): Here the demoness passes over to the mortal world—she is faithful to and loving of the hero until the moment of her death. Yuzpa, caretaker of the community of Worms in the seventeenth century, in his collection of tales, *Ma'aseh Nissim*, assembled a number of fascinating demonic stories. One of them ("A Tale of the Queen of Sheba"), tells how the Queen of Sheba appeared before a wretched pauper, slept with him daily, and made him wealthy. Ultimately, she takes away all his possessions and kills his children (Eidelberg, *R. Yuzpa Shamash* [supra, note 57], pp. 85–86). The tale combines two of the motifs mentioned several times in this chapter: daily submission to demons, in return for which the demons endow him with great wealth, yet ultimately do him severe harm, and the marriage—i.e., sexual relations with the demoness. One of the most important Tosaphists, R. Isaac ben R. Moses, in his book, *Or Zaru'a* (Zhitomir, 1862), part 1, no. 124, p. 22b) [H], also offers an interesting tale that shows, *inter alia*, that even the most learned men of the day accepted this as within the realm of the possible, so much so that they formulated Halacha in connection with this folk belief:

> . . . however, with regard to the spirits, "You shall not commit adultery" does not apply . . . Hence they said: Whosoever lays with the spirits bears no [taint] even if he ejaculated in a nocturnal pollution. [It is written that] you should not commit adultery with mortals or with an animal or with hand and foot [i.e., mastur-

bation]. But [if it is with] the spirits, then it is not fornication. And furthermore, there is that which happened to that pious man who encountered a demoness. She seduced him and coupled with him, and it was the Day of Atonement. Afterward this pious man regretted this action very much, until he met Elijah of blessed memory who asked him, "Why are you sorrowful?" He told him of all that had happened to him. He said to him: "You are exempt; she was a demoness." And his mind was eased. And had he been culpable, then Elijah of blessed memory would not have appeared to him and spoken with him, and exonerated him. From this you learn that it was not fornication, and was exempt.

6. The Later Generations

1. On Hasidic story collections in Yiddish, see C. Shmeruk, *A History of Yiddish Literature* (Tel Aviv, 1978), pp. 198–234 [H]; and in Hebrew, G. Nigal, *Hasidic Narrative: Its History and Themes* (Jerusalem, 1981) [H]. Nigal also compiled an important bibliographic list arranged according to the order of publication of the collections, ibid., pp. 304–308, but it is incomplete. On another approach to book-craft in the Hasidic culture, and its treatment of Hasidism as emerging oral culture, see Z. Gries, *On Books, Authors and Tales at the Dawn of Hasidism. From the Ba'al Shem Tov to Menahem Mendel of Kotzk* (Tel Aviv, 1992) [H]. An important group of stories collected by a modern scholar is Ben-Yehezkiel, *Ma'asiot*. The book includes comparative notes to the tales, but the texts have been lightly revised.

2. These remarks were formulated mainly by M. Pierkarz, *On the Founder and Writings of Bratslaver Hasidism* (Jerusalem, 1972), pp. 83–131 [H]. This is how Gries (supra, note 1) views the network of relations between the folktale and the story collection in Hasidism, an approach that basically corresponds to the way I seek to present matters below: "I believe that the tales passed on and transmitted orally throughout the history of the movement contributed decisively to the Hasidic masses' feeling of belonging and identification with their community, and with the Zaddik at its forefront. Furthermore, the publication of different versions of these tales, especially since the 1860s, in no way hampered the continuous, torrential, and influential flow of the oral tales" (p. 37).

3. On the "sweetening parable," see Piekarz (supra, note 2), pp. 87 ff. On literature's perceived therapeutic role in the Middle Ages, see G. Olson, *Literature as Recreation in the Later Middle Ages* (Ithaca and London, 1982); Yassif, "Leisure."

4. Vast scholarship has been published on the tales of R. Nahman. Cf., for example, Piekarz (supra, note 2), ibid.; Y. Elstein, *Pa'amei Bat-Melekh* [Footsteps of a Princess] (Ramat Gan, 1983) [H]; idem, *Ma'aseh Khoshev—Studies in the Hasidic Story*, pp. 143–191 [H]; A. Green, *Tormented Master: A Life of Rabbi Nahman of Braslav* (University, Alabama, 1979), pp. 337–372, and the extensive literature cited there.

5. *Sefer Siftei Kodesh* ["The Book of the Sacred Lips"], reproduced and republished in a series by New York Hasidim under the title, *Holy Books from Disciples of the Holy Ba'al Shem Tov* (Brooklyn, 1985), vol. 24 [H]. The preface to *Kehal Hasidim* ["Hasidic Assembly"] is reproduced in Dan, *Hasidic*, pp. 200–202. A new edition of the collection of tales of Michael Levi Rodkinson (Frumkin), *Adat Zaddikim* ["Community of Zaddikim"] was published by G. Nigal, *The Stories of Michael Levi Rodkinson* (Jerusalem, 1989) [H]; *Pe'er Mi-Kdoshim* ["The Glory of the Saints"] also in an edition by G. Nigal: *Menahem Mendel Bodek, Hasidic Stories* (Tel Aviv, 1991) [H].

6. *Hasidic Stories*, Nigal edition (supra, note 5). On Bodek's undertaking in Hasidic narrative, see Nigal's introduction, ibid.

7. See the tale of the Ba'al Shem Tov's servant in J. Dan, *The Hasidic Novella* (Jerusalem,

1966), pp. 30–35 and corresponding note [H]. On R. Nahman's custom of telling stories to his students, see Dan, *Hasidic*, p. 49; Green (supra, note 4), pp. 346–347.

8. According to testimony on Michael Levi Rodkinson (Frumkin), one of the most prolific Hasidic authors, quoted in Nigal, *Stories of Michael Levi Rodkinson* (supra, note 5), p. 9.

9. The Yiddish version was discovered and published by A. Holtz, *The Story of R. Yudel Hasid, from its Beginning in Nissim ve-Nifla'ot until S. Y. Agnon's* Bridal Canopy (New York, 1986) [H]. The author also compares the versions in detail. The version from *Pe'er Mi-Kdoshim* was published by Dan, *The Hasidic Novella* (supra, note 7), pp. 65–72; and the Nigal edition, *Hasidic Stories* (supra, note 5), pp. 182–186. The third version is reproduced in Ben-Yehezkiel, *Ma'asiot*, pp. 346–347.

10. On editions of *Shivhei ha-Ari* see M. Benayahu, "*Shivhei ha-Ari*," *Areshet* 3 (1961): 114–165 [H] idem, "*Shivhei ha-Ari* in Yiddish," ibid., 4 (1962): 481–489 [H].

11. On ancient Hebrew hagiography, see the studies enumerated above in chapter 5 ("The Middle Ages"), section F.

12. *Shivhei ha-Besht*, A. Rubinstein edition (Jerusalem, 1992), pp. 36–39 [H]. For a discussion of the tale from another angle, see Elstein, *Ma'aseh Khoshev* (supra, note 4), pp. 63–128.

13. On "the biographical pattern of the culture hero," see the extensive literature above in chapter 4, section E. The edition of *The Chronicles of Moses* was published by A. Shinan, "The Chronicles of Moses," *ha-Sifrut* 24 (1977): 100–116 [H]. It was M. J. Berdyczewski who noticed the similarity between the tale of the Ba'al Shem Tov's father and *The Chronicles of Moses*, in his *Ma'amarim* (Tel Aviv, 1966), p. 284 [H].

14. *Kvutzat Ya'akov* (Przemysl, 1897), 53a. Additional versions of the tale in the general literature are offered in Elstein, *Ma'aseh Khoshev* (supra, note 4), pp. 7–40; T. Alexander, *Narrative and Thought in "Sefer Hasidim"* (Ph.D. diss., Los Angeles, 1977), pp. 62–101, 299–306 [H].

15. The citation is from the story's first Hebrew version, Joshua Ibn Shuaib, *Drashot al ha-Torah* [Sermons on the Torah] (Cracow, 1573), photostat (Jerusalem, 1969), beginning of parasht Devarim, p. 76a. For additional versions of the tale see; Bin-Gorion, *Mimekor*, no. 38 and Ben-Amos, *Mimekor Yisrael*, p. 23, no. 13. On early Arabic versions, see Schwarzbaum, *Folklore*, pp. 101–102, note 141. Ginzberg, ibid., and Krauss (S. Krauss, "A Moses Legend," *Jewish Quarterly Review* 2 [1911–12]: 339–364) point to the Yiddish translations of Ibn Shuaib's version of the tale, and claim that the tale made its way to the hasidim by way of these translations.

16. For the versions and sources of the tale, see E. Yassif, "Parables of King Solomon," *Jerusalem Studies in Hebrew Literature* 9 (1986): 365–366 [H].

17. *Eser Orot* [Ten Lights] (Piotrkow, 1907) [H]; Ben-Yehezkiel, *Ma'asiot*, pp. 284–286, and additional variants, ibid., p. 697.

18. Compare also J. Jacob (Klapholtz), *Lamed-vav Zadikim [The Thirty-Six Hidden Saints]. A Collection of Tales of the Hidden Saints Compiled from Reliable Sources and Arranged According to Topic*, 2 vols. (Bnei Brak, 1977) [H]; Ben-Yehezkiel, *Ma'asiot*, pp. 109–131, and corresponding notes; Nigal, *Hasidic Narrative* (supra, note 1), pp. 259–263; G. Scholem, "The Thirty-Six Hidden Saints in Jewish Tradition," in his *'Od Davar* (Tel Aviv, 1989), pp. 199–204 [H]; H. Schwarzbaum, "The Thirty-Six Saints in Jewish Folklore," *Yeda Am* 18 (1977): 20–28 [H].

19. Nigal, *Rodkinson* (supra, note 5), p. 45, and note 192, p. 89; Yehuda Yudel Rosenberg, *Sefer Eliyahu ha-Navi* [The Book of Elijah the Prophet], (Piotrkow, 1911) [H]; Nigal, *Hasidic Narrative*, ibid., pp. 264–279; *Sefer Sippurei Kedoshim* [The Book of Tales of the Saints], G. Nigal edition (Jerusalem, 1977), pp. 42–43 [H].

20. On the "revelation" tales see *Sefer Hitgalut ha-Zaddikim* [Book of the Revelation of the Zaddikim] (Warsaw, 1905) [H]; A. Rubinstein, "The Story of the Revelation in *Shivhei ha-Besht*," *Alei Sefer* 6–7 (1979): 157–186 [H]; Nigal, *Hasidic Narrative* (supra, note 1), pp. 84–103.

21. The first tale is quoted from Ben-Yehezkiel, *Ma'asiot*, p. 122. The second, about the drunken saint, is from Bodek, *Hasidic Stories*, Nigal edition (supra, note 5), p. 32.

22. From Ben-Yehezkiel, *Ma'asiot*, p. 116.

23. On the tale type, "the Jewish Pope" in medieval narrative cf. chapter 5, above, section [E].

24. Ben Yehezkiel, *Ma'asiot*, p. 327; *Adat Zaddikim*, Nigal edition (supra, note 5), no. 4; and cf. the discussion of the tale type in Dan, *Hasidic*, pp. 191–195, and his, "The History of 'The Story of the *Akdamut*' in Hebrew Literature," *Bikoret u-Farshanut* 9–10 (1977): 197–213 [H].

25. See E. Yassif, "The Contribution of *Sefer Oseh Pele* to Jewish Folk Literature," *Jerusalem Studies in Jewish Folklore* 3 (1982): 47–66 [H].

26. As cited by Dan, *Hasidic*, pp. 261–263.

27. B. Z. Dinur produced a brilliant socio-historical analysis of the enduring tension between rich and poor, Torah scholars and simple folk, and between them and the Gentile landowners at the time Hasidism flourished: "The Dawn of Hasidism and Its Social and Messianic Foundations," in his *Be-Mifneh ha-Dorot* (Jerusalem, 1972), pp. 139 ff. [H]. Gries (supra, note 1), pp. 61–62, rejects the claim that Hasidism recoiled in any way from Torah study, and views the traditional study hall as a spiritual center in Hasidic culture as well. I do not care to enter into the historical debate between these two, however I will make the claim that the literary-folkloristic analysis of the Hasidic tales supports Dinur's approach. The current tendency to emphasize the religious aspects of Hasidism and undermine its social origins seems to me unproper and unfounded. On this issue, see also M. Piekarz, "Hasidism—A Socio-Religious Movement as Seen through *Devekut*," *Da'at* 25 (1990): 127–144 [H].

M. Roseman, "The History of a Historical Document: Shivhei ha-Besht and Its Compilation," *Zion* 58 (1993): 213–214 [H] discusses the Hasidic healing stories and their relation to modern medicine. In her work on tales of healing in Chabad Hasidism, my student, Miriam Aharoni (Beersheba, 1991), collected more than a hundred and forty tales from these written sources. On tales of modern Hasidim, see also J. R. Mintz, *Legends of the Hasidim: An Introduction to Hasidic Culture and Oral Tradition in the New World* (Chicago and London, 1968); Y. Eliach, *Hasidic Tales of the Holocaust* (Oxford, 1982).

28. Folk literature scholarship has recently become interested in the characters of individual storytellers, their world view, and the influence of their biography on the nature of their stories, in order to temper the trend of folklore research toward the collective conception. See, for example, J. Pentikäinen, *Oral Repertoire and World View. An Anthropological Study of Maria Takalo's Life History* (Helsinki, 1978 [FFC no. 219]); S. Erdész, "The World Conception of Lajos Ami, Storyteller," *Acta Ethnographica* 10 (1961): 327–344; D. Noy, "The Universe Concept of Yefet Shvili, A Jewish Yemenite Storyteller," *Acta Ethnographica* 14 (1964–5): 259–275; Y. Bilu and G. Hasan-Rokem, "Cinderella and the Saint: The Life Story of a Jewish Moroccan Female Healer in Israel," *Journal for the Psychoanalytical Study of Society* 14 (1989): 227–260.

29. On moving away from the rites of saints in the first years of Jewish immigration from Morocco to Israel, see Ben-Ami, *Saints*, pp. 702 ff.; Y. Bilu, "Veneration of Saints among Moroccan Jews in Israel—Content and Meaning," in *New Directions in the Study of the Problem of Ethnicity* (Jerusalem Institute for Jewish Studies no. 8, Jerusalem, 1984) [H]. S. N.

Eisenstadt also alludes to such a hiatus in his introductory article to this collection. The text quoted was told by Shimon Vaknin, founder of the center of the rite in Ashkelon, and cf. I. Ben-Ami, "The Folk Veneration of Saints Among Moroccan Jews. Tradition, Continuity and Change," in *Studies in Judaism and Islam*, ed. S. Morag and I. Ben-Ami (Jerusalem, 1981), p. 311, no. 15. The daily press of late 1989 reports on actions taken to bring saints' remains to Israel: "In a secret operation the bones of four saints were brought from a country in the Middle East . . . and interred in a cemetery of a municipality in the south . . . The Chief Rabbi of the municipality in the south, who yesterday confirmed the story, added that in question were the four rabbis held to be the most holy by descendants of the Sephardic communities in Israel, [rabbis] who died 250 years ago. According to the Rabbi, were the names of the rabbis made known, thousands of believers in Israel and the diaspora would come to prostrate themselves on the graves. He noted that among those in question were miracle-workers, of whom legends were told even during their lifetimes" (*Yediot Aharonot*, Nov. 15, 1989). For further studies of the theme in Israeli folk culture, see: H. Bar-Itzhak, "Modes of Characterization in Religious Narrative: Jewish Folk Legends about Miracle Worker Rabbis," *Journal of Folklore Research* 27 (1990): 205–230; S. Sered Starr, "Rachel's tomb: Societal liminality and the revitalization of a shrine" *Religion* 19 (1989): 27–40; idem, "Rachel's Tomb: The Development of a Cult," *Jewish Studies Quarterly* 2 (1995): 103–149; Y. Bilu and E. Ben-Ari, "The Making of Modern Saints: Manufactured Charisma and the Abu-Hatseiras of Israel," *American Ethnologist* 19 (1992): 672–687.

30. Ben-Ami, "Folk-Veneration" (supra, note 29), offers the relevant material from Safed and Ashkelon, including Ben-Haim's detailed testimony; E. Ben-Ari and Y. Bilu, "Saints' Sanctuaries in Israeli Development Towns: On a Mechanism of Urban Transformation," *Urban Anthropology* 16 (1987): 243–272, develop the basis of the theses presented herein.

31. The programmatic formulation of the phenomenon appears in the collection of E. Hobsbawm and T. Ranger, eds., *The Invention of Tradition* (Cambridge, 1983); A.D. Smith, *The Ethnic Revival in the Modern World* (Cambridge, 1981). On the phenomenon in Israel, see the fundamental works of S. N. Eisenstadt, *Israeli Society* (London, 1967), pp. 154–230; idem., *Integration and Development in Israel* (New York, 1970), and the more recent: H. Herzog, "Is Ethnic Segregation Political?" *Megamot* 28 (1984): 332–352 [H]; H. Goldberg, "Historical and Cultural Dimensions of The Communal Phenomena," *Megamot* 28 (1984): 233–249 [H]; and the recent collection, H. E. Goldberg ed., *Sephardy and Middle Eastern Jewries* (Bloomington and Indianapolis, 1996).

32. H. Jason, "Rabbi Wazana and the Demons: Analysis of a Legend," in *Folklore Today, Feschtshrift for R. M. Dorson*, ed. L. Dégh et. al. (Bloomington, 1976), pp. 273–290. The analysis here is based on the findings of Y. Bilu, "Life History as Text," *Magamot* 29 (1986): 349–371 [H].

33. *Sefer Ma'aseh Nisim: The Chronicles and Wonders of our Teacher and Rabbi . . . Jacob Abuhatzeira . . . the Almighty favored me and I collected and copied and wrote and edited what I have heard from preachers of truth, a summary of his life history, his deeds and wonders, by my insignificant and ignorant self, Abraham Mugrabi, may the Lord watch and keep me* (Jerusalem, 1968). Other hagiographical collections treated below are *Our Holy Rabbi the Baba Sali. His Holiness, Teaching, Leadership and Marvels . . . Rabbi Israel Abuhatzeira . . .* by Rabbi Eliyahu Alfasi, former attendant to the holy man (Jerusalem, no date); *Rabbi Sharabi. Chronicles of his Life, Teaching, and Miracles . . .* The Illustrious Rabbi Mordechai Sharabi, of blessed and saintly memory, comp. and ed. Yona Refaeli (Jerusalem, 1984).

34. On these army and war tales, see I. Ben-Ami, "On the Folklore of War, the Motif of the Saints," *Dov Sadan Festschrift* (Jerusalem, 1977), pp. 95–96 [H]. The story about the Sabena aircraft is from *Baba Sali* (note 33), pp. 236–237.

35. The tales mentioned appear in Ben-Ami, "Folklore of War" (supra, note 34), p. 92; tales of R. David u-Moshe in Ben-Ami, "The Folk Veneration of Saints" (supra, note 29), tales 41, 43. On stories of mysterious rescue, see Marcus, "Confrontation"; Noy, "Yemen."

36. The tale is quoted in *Shivhei ha-Besht*, S. E. Horodetzki edition (Tel Aviv, 1968), p. 109 [H]; *Kehal Hasidim* ["Hasidic Assembly"], p. 11. On tales of healing in biblical and talmudic literature, see J. Preuss, *Biblische-Talmudische Medizin* (Berlin, 1911). On hasidic tales of healing, consult Nigal, *Hasidic Narrative*, pp. 165-171. While working on her research paper, my student, Miriam Aharoni, collected some hundred and forty tales of healing of Chabad Hasidim. Some had been published in the Chabad movement's press; she collected others from the oral traditions. The book, H. W. Polsky and Y. Wozner, *Everyday Miracles: The Healing Wisdom of Hasidic Stories* (London, 1989), is a curious blend of hasidic texts concerning appeals to zaddikim on medical matters (generally psychological in nature), along with interpretation and psychological guidance. On the conceptualization of medicine as a cross between miracle and science in the nineteenth century, see W. Theopold, *Mirakel Heilung zwischen Wissenschaft und Glauben* (München, 1983).

37. Ben-Ami, "The Folk Veneration of Saints" (supra, note 29), p. 294, nos. 2, 3. The remarks of the great French historian, Marc Bloch, are especially edifying with regard to medical miracles connected with saints: "what created faith in the miracle was the idea that there should be a miracle. It was this idea too which allowed it to survive, plus, as the centuries passed, the accumulated testimony of generations who had believed and whose evidence, founded it seemed upon experience, one could not doubt (from *Les Rois Thaumaturges* [Paris, 1925], p. 429, as cited in Thomas, *Religion* [below], p. 205). In the Middle Ages and the dawn of the modern age, tales of healing were among the most important subjects treated by tales of the Christian saints. See also Wilson, *Saints*, pp. 17-21, 150-152; K. Thomas, *Religion and the Decline of Magic. Studies in Popular Beliefs in Sixteenth and Seventeenth-Century England* (London, 1971), pp. 209-251. Confirmed testimony attests to some three-quarters of the miracles in the hagiographical narrative being connected with the healing of illnesses! See J. M. H. Smith, "Oral and Written: Saints, Miracles and Relics in Brittany c. 850-1250," *Speculum* 65 (1990): 329. On similar tales of healing in the fundamentalist movements in the United States, W. Clements, "Ritual Expectation in Pentecostal Healing Experience," *Western Folklore* 40 (1981): 139-148; idem, "Faith Healing Narratives from North-East Arkansas," *Indiana Folklore* 9 (1976): 15-39; V. Romano and I. Octavio, "Charismatic Medicine, Folk Healing, and Folk Sainthood," *American Anthropologist* 67 (1965), 1151-1173; B. G. Alver, "The Bearing of Folk Belief on Cure and Healing," *Journal of Folklore Research* 32 (1995): 21-33; T. Selberg, "Faith Healing and Miracles: Narrative about Folk Medicine," ibid. 35-48.

38. See such typical tales in Ben-Ami, "The Folk Veneration of Saints" (supra, note 29), nos. 43 and 75. The text cited here is from Ben-Ami, "Folklore of War" (supra, note 35), p. 39.

39. The weekly *Politika* devoted its issue no. 42 (January, 1989) to the political, social, and cultural aspects of the fundamentalist revival in Israel. Typical recollections on the path taken by penitents from the secular world to the sheltering wings of religion are quoted in S. Meislesh, *Return to Religion: Phenomenon and Individuals* (Givatayyim, 1984) [H] and M. J. Levin, *Journey to Tradition: The Odyssey of a Born-Again Jew* (Hoboken, N.J., 1986). For a primary analysis of the phenomenon, undertaken before the dramatic developments of the second half of the 1980s and the '90s, see J. Aviad, *Return to Judaism: Religious Renewal in Israel* (Chicago, 1983). On the development of fundamentalism from a comparative point of view, see M. E. Marty and R. S. Appelby, eds., *The Fundamentalism Project* (Chicago and London, 1991-1995). While this impressive project includes many aspects of the fundamentalism phenomenon, it neglects the folkloristic aspects, especially the most important one—

fundamentalism as folk-religion. Some papers in this project deal with fundamentalism in Israel: An important survey of the political developments is C. S. Liebman, "Jewish Fundamentalism and the Israeli Polity," Vol. 3 (Chicago and London, 1993), pp. 68–87. A comparison of Jewish, Moslem, and Christian fundamentalisms is presented by E. Sivan, "The Enclave Culture," *Fundamentalisms Comprehended* (Chicago and London, 1995), pp. 11–70. Compare also: I. S. Lustick, *For the Land and the Lord. Jewish Fundamentalism in Israel* (Washington D.C., 1988) (focusing mostly on the *Gush Emunim* movement); and B. Lawrence, *Defenders of the Book: The Fundamentalist Revolt in Islam, Judaism and Christianity* (San Francisco, 1990) examine from a comparative perspective the phenomena that characterize Jewish, as opposed to Christian and Islamic, fundamentalism. The works of W. C. Booth, "The Rhetoric of Fundamentalist Conversion Narrative," in ibid, pp. 367–392, and J. L. Peacock and T. Pettyjohn, "Fundamentalisms Narrated: Muslim, Christian, and Mystical," in ibid, pp. 115–134, use rhetorical and literary methods to deal with the fundamentalist phenomena, as I do here. On the process of distributing religious-fundamentalist texts and sermons on cassettes, and their being played at private gatherings, see the important testimony of L. Dégh, "Are Sectarian Miracle Stories Contemporary American Folk Legends?" in *Storytelling in Contemporary Societies*, ed. L. Röhrich and S. Wienker-Piepho (Tübingen, 1990), pp. 71–90 (esp. p. 82); idem, "Tape-Recording Miracles for Everyday Living: The Ethnography of a Pentecostal Community," in L. Dégh, *American Folklore and the Mass Media* (Bloomington and Indianapolis, 1994), pp. 110–152.

40. Another revivalist, Emanuel Tehilah (*Mo'ah ve-Lev* cassette no. 4), in a lecture delivered to a vast audience in Netanyah, opens his sermon with a similar inventory of disasters in the State of Israel: drug abuse, young suicides, divorce, theft, and murder. "What's happened to the nation of Israel?!" he thunders. At sermon's end, he describes the matriarch Rachel arising from her grave, looking around, and seeing the State of Israel befouled by those horrendous crimes and lowered morality. Aviad (supra, note 39) shows that these examples of the flaws of the secular world are among the most prevalent means employed by the Jewish revivalists as well as American Christian preachers, pp. 28–30, 39, 49, 128; Sivan (supra, note 39). Yagen and Amnon Yitzhak (cassette no. 3, lecture at a Holon synagogue before an audience of some six hundred listeners) make much of the same play on words— in Hebrew, the words for secular (*hiloni*) and sickly (*holani*) have similar pronunciations— to convey the notion that the secular world is diseased.

41. Thus Aviad (supra, note 39), pp. 40 ff., describes performances by Reuven Elbaz, one of the first and foremost proselytizers, in Jerusalem neighborhoods. A similar phenomenon among the medieval religious leaders is described in E. Yassif, "The Exemplary Tale in *Sefer Hasidim*," *Tarbitz* 57 (1987/1988): 217–255 [H], and see also the literature cited there.

42. Likewise in the hagiography of the medieval Jewish pietists, which apparently began in the tales they themselves told (particularly R. Judah the Pious), and see J. Dan, "On the History of *Shevahim* Literature," *Jerusalem Studies in Jewish Folklore* 1 (1981): 82–101 [H]. The more recent tales of R. Nahman of Bratslav revolve around R. Nahman himself. See A. Green, *Tormented Master* (supra, note 4), pp. 338–342; Dan, *Hasidic*, pp. 132–188.

43. On rifts of this sort with secular Israeli society, see Aviad (supra, note 39), pp. 128–132, 137–143, and on similar phenomena in the United States, Dégh (supra, note 39). The famous speech given by the head of the Council of Torah Sages deserves mention at this juncture: Rabbi Eliezer Schach, who is in fact the main leader of ultra-orthodox Jewry, delivered this speech in 1991. In a live broadcast on Israeli television, Rabbi Schach claimed that the kibbutzes, by virtue of their conduct, were alienating themselves from the Jewish people. Similarly, the former Minister of Absorption, Rabbi Yitzhak Peretz, in the same year, stated that

the kibbutzes were corrupting Israel's youth, for which reason he refused to direct new immigrants there.

44. Aviad (supra, note 39) names other revivalists who make ample use of dreams. On the dream in Jewish folk culture, see Yassif, *Bibliography*, index, "dreams"; Y. Bilu, "Dreams and the Wishes of the Saints," in *Judaism Viewed From Within and From Without*, ed. H. Goldberg (New York, 1986), pp. 285–313; idem and H. Abramovich, "In Search of the Sadiq: Visitational Dreams Among Moroccan Jews in Israel," *Psychiatry* 48 (1985): 83–92; V. Lanternari, "Dreams as Charismatic Significance: Their Bearing on the Rise of New Religious Movements," in *Psychological Anthropology*, ed. T. R. Williams (The Hague, 1975), pp. 221–235.

An entire issue of the journal *Representations* was devoted to the seance in modern culture: *Representations* 22 (1988): *Seance and Suicide: The Media of Somatic History*.

A categorization of revival tales in the Christian world according to the supernatural elements found therein was proposed by R. Kvideland, "Christian Memorates in Norwegian Revival Movements," in *Storytelling in Contemporary Societies* (op. cit. note 39), pp. 61–70. The author proposes the following categories: tales of miraculous rescue, supernatural notification of disasters to come (road accidents, ship-sinking, etc.)—particularly via dreams, prayers answered at once, near-death experiences featuring religious visions, and the like.

45. In one appearance (cassette no. 42), Yagen says, "An entire *sefer Torah* [Scroll of the Law] could be written on the miracles and wonders that I see each and every day. They could fill [all three divisions of the Scriptures:] the Pentateuch, Prophets, and Writings." And again, in the same speech, "The Almighty uses overt miracles, maybe they [the unbelievers] will come back to Judaism." In a videocassette made for the *el ha-Ma'ayyan* ["To the Wellspring"] foundation of the *Shas* ["Torah Guardians"] Party in 1991, Uri Zohar, the former comedian and film director who was 'born again,' recounts events of the past year: on the holiday of Shavuoth, terrorist boats tried to reach Israeli shores and murder people on the beach. The security forces were not prepared for defense but, thanks to a miracle, the terrorists failed. The great rescue followed upon the Jews' having studied the *Book of the Zohar* all the previous night. Radio and television pundits tried to explain how it happened that no one was hurt, concealing the fact that it was a miracle. Then there was the incident that marked the holiday of Simhat Torah. Hundreds of Arabs threw thousands of stones upon the crowds of people who were praying at the Wall, and yet no Jew suffered injury. "The cruel Arabs" had overlooked one crucial detail: the Priestly Blessing had been conferred at the Wall only minutes before: "The Lord bless thee, and keep thee." Newspapers and the radio ignored this miracle as well. The third incident was the Gulf War. How was it possible for SCUD missiles to fall without killing anyone? Yet again, the press deliberately hid the truth, that it was a miracle. In other words, the sin of the secular world is that it seeks rational interpretation of reality and ignores the simple, obvious explanation for which Judaism has stood from time immemorial. Kvideland (supra, note 44) reports similar remarks from his informants. One of them states, "As I told you, I had innumerable experiences like this during my lifetime. I also think many people have them, but not everyone is conscious of it" (p. 66). A popular book that attempts the same argument, and includes many personal narratives of informants who had these everyday experiences is: D. Wakefield, *Expect a Miracle: The Miraculous Things that Happen to Ordinary People* (New York, 1955). Dégh, "Tape-Recording Miracles for Everyday Living" (supra, note 39), suggests that this search for everyday miracles is a type of socio-psychological cure for the altered state of consciousness emerging from modern life. On the psychological function of the legend, and the role of the supernatural element, see L. Dégh and A. Vazsonyi, "Legend and Belief," *Genre* 4 (1971): 281–

304 and A. Dundes, "On the Psychology of the Legend," in *American Folk Legend: A Symposium*, ed. W. D. Hand (Berkeley and Los Angeles, 1971), pp. 21–36.

On the principle of "he has made his wonderful works to be remembered" in the Rabbinic and Medieval periods, see chapter 5, above, note 95.

46. Cassette no. 41. Yagen retells the tale several times in different versions, as documented in cassettes nos. 18 and 24. Other revivalists, such as Reuven Elbaz, Amnon Yitzhak, and Emanuel Tehilah, tell it too.

47. Other revivalists also boast considerable comic talent. In his sermon in Holon, Amnon Yitzhak tells the talmudic anecdote concerning two men walking alongside a donkey. Passersby ridiculed them for not riding the beast. Each subsequent action they took provoked more mocking comments until they hoisted the donkey onto their own backs. Yitzhak changes the tale to tell of a bride and groom so concerned with what others think of them that they ultimately carry the donkey on their backs. His intimation is to those who do not return to the faith for fear of ridicule. Yagen, in the previous tale, also employs the image of a couple living like dogs. Amnon Yitzhak tells with great flair a long anecdote about a man who did not fear sin, for he planned that when he appeared before the Heavenly court, he would claim that, not knowing how to read, he had never learned Torah. The Court pardoned him, and he was taken to Paradise. After a full tour, he wanted to descend to Hell, where his friends were. There Yitzhak comically describes the torment of the sinners, and the manner in which the protagonist, too, is punished. The audience's reaction is raucous laughter and scorn and thus these comic tales achieve their purpose. Yitzhak employs the same witticisms and comic wordplay as Yagen: secular-sickly, the secularists believe they are descended from apes, they ought to call their fathers "Monkey-face," and visit their relatives in the zoo, "the secularists go with the flow, they shouldn't get electrocuted in the end." Needless to say, a revivalist like Uri Zohar, who was a professional entertainer in an earlier, secular stage of his life, makes full use of his professional skill, now redirected to a sanctified goal. On these humorous aspects of the revivalist movements, and especially their manipulation of humor to 'demonize the other,' see: G. Aran, "What's so Funny about Fundamentalism?" in *Fundamentalisms Comprehended* (supra, note 39), pp. 321–352.

48. All the tales of the newly religious in cassettes nos. 17 and 18, and the testimony in Aviad (supra, note 39), p. 44, and Meislesh, pp. 41–90, belong to this model of the transition between the secular and religious worlds. Other preachers make use of the same symbols of light and darkness. See Aviad, ibid., pp. 40, 43. On similar testimony of newly religious in the Christian world, and the tale of the traumatic event that brought them to that turning point, see S. D. Rose, "Conversations of Conversions: Interviewing American Evangelical Women," *International Journal of Oral History* 8 (1987): 28–40; W. Clements, "I Once Was Lost: Oral Narratives of Born-Again Christians," *International Folklore Review* 2 (1982): 105–111; and E. Lawless, "The Night I Got the Holy Ghost . . . Holy Ghost Narratives and the Pentecostal Conversion Process," *Western Folklore* 47 (1988): 1–19. Dégh, "Tape-Recording Miracles" (supra, note 39) found that in the community she studied in southern Indiana, "most conversion stories include a supernatural experience" (pp. 119–120).

49. This tale has a parallel among the hagiographical tales of R. Judah the Pious, told by his son, R. Zaltman. It tells of an affluent man of Regensburg whom R. Judah the Pious warned against continuing to shave off his beard. This man of means ignored the warning, and some time later passed away. In the presence of members of the community, R. Judah the Hasid employed the Ineffable Name and revived the corpse that lay before them. It told them of the terrible agonies he suffered in that world as demons in the shape of cows tortured him. The first letters of the biblical verse: "You shall not round the corners of your

heads, neither shalt thou mar" ("the corners of thy beard") form an acrostic for the Hebrew word for 'cows' (R. Isaac ben R. Eleazar of Worms, *Sefer ha-Gan* [Venice, 1606], pp. 9b–10a).

50. On these tales in Jewish folklore, see E. Marcus, "The Desecrator of the Holy is Punished (AT 771)," *Mehkarei ha-Mercaz le-Heker ha-Folklor* 7 (1983): 337–367 [H]; Noy, "Yemen."

51. On similar manifestations of the dead before living beings for the purpose of foretelling their punishment or reward in the world to come—and, in so doing, shaping conduct in our world, see Tubach, *Index*, "Dead, Return of"; L. Petzoldt, *Der Tote als Gast: Volkssage und Exempel* (Helsinki, 1968), and the comprehensive survey of the theme in the middle ages: J. -C. Schmitt, *Ghosts in the Middle Ages: The Living and the Dead in Medieval Society*, trans. T. Lavender Fagan (Chicago and London, 1998). On the tale of "the Tanna and the Dead Man" see the next note.

52. For compiled versions of the tale and their evolution, see M. B. Lerner, "The Tale of the Tanna and the Dead Man: Its Literary and Halachic Variants," *Asufot* 2 (1988): 29–70 [H].

53. See note 45, above, for a fuller discussion.

Abbreviations Used in the Notes

Bibliographical entries appearing in two or more chapters have been cited in shortened form:

Aarne and Thompson	A. Aarne and S. Thompson, *The Types of the Folktale, A Classification and Bibliography* (Helsinki, 1961, FFC no. 184).
Bacher, *Legends*	B. Z. Bacher, *Aggadot ha-Tannaim* [Legends of the Tannaim] (Berlin, 1922) [H].
Bächtold-Stäubli	H. Bächtold-Stäubli, ed., *Handwörterbuch des deutschen Aberglaubens*, 13 vols. (Berlin und Leipzig, 1927).
Baron, *History*	S. W. Baron, *A Social and Religious History of the Jews*, 18 vols. (New York, 1952–1985).
Ben-Ami, *Saints*	I. Ben-Ami, *Saint Veneration among the Jews in Morocco* (Jerusalem, 1984) [H].
Ben-Amos, "Categories"	D. Ben-Amos, "Analytical Categories and Ethnic Genres." *Genre* 2 (1969): 275–301.
Ben-Amos, "Distinctions"	Idem, "Generic Distinctions in the Aggadah," in *Studies in Jewish Folklore*, ed. F. Talmage (Cambridge, Mass., 1980), pp. 45–72.
Ben-Amos, *Genres*	Idem., ed., *Folklore Genres* (Austin, 1976).
Ben-Amos, *Mimekor Yisrael*	Idem, *Mimekor Yisrael. Classical Jewish Folktales*, trans. I. M. Lask, prepared with an introduction and headnotes by D. Ben-Amos (Bloomington and Indianapolis, 1990).
Ben-Yehezkiel, "The Book"	M. Ben-Yehezkiel, "The Book *And It Came to Pass*", in *Bialik: Critical Essays on his Work*, ed. G. Shaked (Jerusalem, 1974), pp. 337–370 [H].
Ben-Yehezkiel, *Ma'asiot*	Idem. ed., *Sefer ha-Ma'asiyyot* [The Book of Legends], 2 vols. (Tel Aviv, 1965³) [H].
Bergmann, *Legends*	J. Bergmann, *Die Legenden der Juden* (Berlin, 1919).
Bilu, "Dybbuk"	Y. Bilu, "The Taming of the Deviants and Beyond: An Analysis of Dybbuk Possession and Exorcism in Judaism," *The Psychoanalytical Study of Society* 11 (1985): 1–32.
Bin-Gorion, *Mimekor*	M. J. Bin-Gorion [Berdyczewski], *Mimekor Yisrael. Ma'asiyyot ve-Sippurei Am* [From the Spring of Israel, Legends and Folktales] (Tel Aviv, 1965/1966) [H].
Bin-Gorion, *Paths*	E. Bin-Gorion, *The Paths of Legend. An Introduction to International Folktales and of the Jewish People* (Jerusalem, 1950) [H].

Bolte and Polivka	J. Bolte and G. Polivka, *Anmerkungen zu den Kinder-und Hausmärchen der Brüder Grimm*, 5 vols. (Leipzig, 1913–1932).
Bremond–Le-Goff–Schmitt	C. Bremond, J. Le-Goff and J. C. Schmitt, *L'Exemplum* (Typologie des sources du Moyen Age Occidental, no. 40) (Turnhout, 1982).
Charlesworth, *Pseudepigrapha*	J. H. Charlesworth ed., *The Old Testament Pseudepigrapha*, 2 vols (Garden City, 1983–1985)
Dan, *Hassidic*	J. Dan, *The Hasidic Story—Its History and Development* (Jerusalem, 1975) [H].
Dan, *Middle Ages*	Idem, *The Hebrew Story in the Middle Ages* (Jerusalem, 1974) [H].
Dégh, "Narrative"	L. Dégh, "Folk Narrative," in *Folklore and Folklife—An Introduction*, ed. R. M. Dorson (Chicago and London, 1972), pp. 53–84.
Delehaye, *Martyrology*	H. Delehaye, *Les Passions des martyrs et les genres littéraires* (Brussels, 1921).
Eisenstein, *Midrashim*	Y. D. Eisenstein, ed., *Otzar Midrashim: A Library of Two Hundred Minor Midrashim*, 2 vols (New York, 1915) [H].
Flusser, *Josippon*	D. Flusser ed., *The Book of Josippon*, 2 vols. (Jerusalem, 1978–1980) [H].
Gaster and Heller	M. Gaster and B. Heller, "Beiträge zur vergleichenden Sagen- und Märchenkunde," *Monatschrift für Geschichte und Wissenschaft des Judentums* 77 (1933): 431–435; 78 (1934): 273–278, 343–532; 80 (1936): 35–52, 127–128.
Gaster, *Exempla*	M. Gaster, *The Exempla of the Rabbis* (New York, 1968²).
Gaster, *Studies*	Idem, *Studies and Texts in Folklore, Magic Medieval Romance, Hebrew Apocrypha and Samaritan Archaeology*, 3 vols. (London, 1928).
Güdemann, *Learning*	M. Güdemann, *Sefer ha-Torah ve-ha-Hayyim be-Artzot ha-Ma'arav bi-yemei ha-Beinayyim* [The Learning and Life in Western Europe in the Middle Ages], translated from the German by A. Sh. Friedberg, 3 vols. (Warsaw, 1897) [H].
Ginzberg, *Legends*	L. Ginzberg, *The Legends of the Jews*, 7 vols. (Philadelphia, 1909–1938).
Goebel, *Motifs*	F. M. Goebel, *Jüdische Motive im märchenhaften Erzählungsgut* (Gleiwitz, 1932).
Grünbaum, *Studies*	M. Grünbaum, *Neue Beiträge zur semitischen Sagenkunde* (Leiden, 1893).
Gunkel, *The Folktale*	H. Gunkel, *The Folktale in the Old Testament*, trans. M. D. Rutter (Sheffield, 1987).
Gurevich, *Culture*	A. Gurevich, *Medieval Popular Culture: Problems of Belief and Perception* (Cambridge, 1988).
Halevy, *Gates*	E. E. Halevy, *Gates of the Aggadah in Light of Greek and Latin Sources* (Tel Aviv, 1982²) [H].

Halevy, *Portions*   Idem, *Portions of Aggadah of Light of Greek Sources* (Tel Aviv, 1973) [H].

Hasan-Rokem, "Riddles"   G. Hasan-Rokem, "'Spinning Threads of Sand': Riddles as Images of Loss in the Midrash on Lamentations," *Untying the Knot—On Riddles and Other Enigmatic Modes*, eds. G. Hasan-Rokem and D. Shulman (New York, 1996), pp. 109–124.

Hasan-Rokem, *Proverbs*   Idem, *Proverbs in Israeli Folk Narratives: A Structural Semantic Analysis* (Helsinki, 1982, FFC no. 232).

Haineman, *Legends*   Y. Hineman, *Aggadah and Its Development. Studies in the Evolution of Traditions* (Jerusalem, 1974) [H].

Heinemann, *Pathways*   I. Heinemann, *Pathways of the Aggadah* (Jerusalem, 1954) [H].

Heller, "Ginzberg"   B. Heller, "Ginzberg's Legends of the Jews," *Jewish Quarterly Review* 24 (1933–34): 51–66, 165–190, 281–307, 393–418; 25 (1934–35): 29–52.

Holbeck, "Laws"   B. Holbeck, "Epische Gesetze," *Enzyklopädie des Märchens*, Bd. 4 (Berlin, 1982), cols. 58–69.

IFA   The Israel Folktale Archives, Haifa University. Tale numbers according to the Archive's classification or its publications (see Jason, "Types").

Jason, "School"   H. Jason, "The Formalist School in the Study of Folk Literature," *ha-Sifrut* 3 (1971): 53–84 [H].

Jason, "Types"   Idem, "Types of Jewish Oriental Oral Tales" (part 1), *Fabula* 7 (1965): 115–224; Part 2 (Jerusalem, 1975).

Jellinek, *Beit ha-Midrash*   A. Jellinek, *Beit ha-Midrash*, 6 parts (Jerusalem, 1967^2) [H].

Lévi-Strauss, *Anthropology*   C. Lévi-Strauss, *Structural Anthropology*, trans. M. Layton (New York, 1963).

Lieberman, *Greek*   S. Lieberman, *Greek and Hellenism in Palestine* (Jerusalem, 1963) [H].

Loomis, *White Magic*   C. Grant Loomis, *White Magic. An Introduction to the Folklore of Christian Legend* (Cambridge, Mass., 1948).

Lüthi, *European*   M. Lüthi, *The European Folktale: Form and Nature*, trans. J. D. Niles (Philadelphia, 1982).

Lüthi, *Once*   Idem, *Once Upon a Time. On the Nature of Fairy Tales*, trans. L. Chadeayne and P. Gottwald (Bloomington and London, 1976).

Lüthi, *The Fairytale*   Idem, *The Fairytale as Art Form and Portrait of Man*, trans. J. Erickson (Bloomington, 1984).

Marcus, "Confrontation"   E. Marcus, "The Confrontation Between the Jewish People and the Nations in the Folktales of Jews from the Lands of Islam," 2 vols. (Ph.D. diss., The Hebrew University, Jerusalem, 1978) [H].

Meir, "Fable"   O. Meir, "The Fable of the Wheat," in *Research and Analysis in Jewish Studies*, ed. Y. Bahat (Haifa, 1976), pp. 149–160 [H].

Nickelsburg, *Tales*	W. E. Nickelsburg, "The Bible Rewritten and Expanded," in *Jewish Writings of the Second Temple Period*, ed. M. E. Stone (Philadelphia, 1984), pp. 89–156.
Nigal, *Dybbuk*	G. Nigal, *The "Dybbuk" Tales in Jewish Literature* (Jerusalem, 1983) [H].
Noy, *Animals*	D. Noy, *The Jewish Animal Tale of Oral Tradition* (Haifa, 1976) [H].
Noy, *Index*	D. Neuman (Noy), *Motif Index to the Talmudic-Midrashic Literature* (Ph.D. Thesis, Indiana University, Bloomington, 1954).
Noy, *Iraq*	Idem, *The Beautiful Maiden and the King's Three Sons: 120 Folktales of Iraqi Jewry* (Tel Aviv, 1965) [H].
Noy, *The Study*	Idem, *The Study of Folk Literature in Judaism and Other Peoples—A Selected Bibliography* (Jerusalem, 1969) [H].
Noy, "Versions"	Idem, "The Jewish Versions of the 'Animal Languages' Folktale (AT 670)—A Typological-Structural Study," *Scripta Hierosolymitana* 22 (1971): 171–208.
Noy, "Yemen"	Idem, "Israel and the Nations in the Folk-Legends of Yemenite Jewry," in *Studies in Geniza and Sephardi Heritage*, ed. Sh. Morag and I. Ben-Ami (Jerusalem, 1981), pp. 229–295 [H].
Olrik, "Laws"	A. Olrik, *Principles for Oral Narrative Research*, trans. K. Wolf and J. Jensen (Bloomington and Indianapolis, 1992), pp. 41–61.
Propp, *Morphology*	V. Propp, *Morphology of the Folktale* (Austin and London, 1968).
Rofé, *Tales of the Prophets*	A. Rofé, *Tales of the Prophets. Prophetic Narrative in The Bible* (Jerusalem, 1983)[H].
Schürer, *History*	E. Schürer, *The History of the Jewish People in the Age of Jesus Christ (175 B.C.–A.D. 135),* A New English Version revised and ed. G. Vermes, F. Millar and M. Goodman (Edinburgh, 1986).
Schwarzbaum, *Berechia*	H. Schwarzbaum, *The Mishle Shu'alim (Fox Fables) of Rabbi Berechia Ha-Nakdan* (Kiron, 1979).
Schwarzbaum, *Folklore*	Idem, *Jewish Folklore Between East and West—Collected Papers*, ed. E. Yassif (Beersheba, 1989).
Schwarzbaum, *Studies*	Idem, *Studies in Jewish and World Folklore* (Berlin, 1968).
Shenhar, *The Folktale*	A. Shenhar, *The Folktale of Israeli Ethnic Groups* (Tel Aviv, 1982) [H].
Steinschneider, *Literature*	M. Steinschneider, *Jewish Literature, From the Eighth to the Eighteenth Century* (London, 1857).
Steinschneider, *Translations*	Idem, *Die hebräischen Uebersetzungen des Mittelalters und die Juden als Dolmetscher* (Berlin, 1893).
Talmage, *Studies*	F. Talmage, ed., *Studies in Jewish Folklore* (Cambridge, Mass., 1980).

Thompson, *Motifs*	S. Thompson, *Motif Index of Folk-Literature*, 6 vols. (Copenhagen-Bloomington, 1955–1959).
Thompson, *The Folktale*	Idem, *The Folktale* (Berkeley and Los Angeles, 1977).
Trachtenberg, *Magic*	J. Trachtenberg, *Jewish Magic and Superstition. A Study in Folk Religion* (New York, 1939).
Tubach, *Index*	F. C. Tubach, *Index Exemplorum. A Handbook of Medieval Religious Tales* (Helsinki, 1969, FFC no. 204).
Urbach, *Sages*	E. E. Urbach, *The Sages—Their Concepts and Beliefs*, trans. I. Abrahams (Jerusalem, 1979).
Urbach, *World*	Idem, *The World of the Sages—Collected Studies* (Jerusalem, 1988) [H].
Wills, *The Novel*	L. M. Wills, *The Jewish Novel in the Ancient World* (Ithaca and London, 1995).
Wilson, *Saints*	S. Wilson, ed., *Saints and Their Cults. Studies in Religious Sociology, Folklore and History* (Cambridge, 1983).
Yassif, *Ben Sira*	E. Yassif, *Tales of Ben Sira in the Middle Ages* (Jerusalem, 1984) [H].
Yassif, *Bibliography*	Idem, *Jewish Folklore: An Annotated Bibliography* (New York and London, 1986).
Yassif, "Cycle"	Idem, "The Story Cycle in Rabbinic Aggadah," *Mehkarei Yerushalayyim be-Sifrut Ivrit* 12 (1990): 103–146 [H].
Yassif, *Golem*	Idem, *Judah (Yudel) Rosenberg—the Golem of Prague and Other Tales of Wonder*, newly ed. and annotated, and with an introduction by E. Yassif (Jerusalem, 1991) [H].
Yassif, "Narrative"	Idem, "The Emergence of Hebrew Narrative in the East and Its Transition from the Middle Ages to the Modern Times," *Pe'amim* 26 (1986): 53–70 [H].
Yassif, "Leisure"	Idem, "*Leisure* and *Generosity*: Theory and Practice in the Emergence of the Hebrew Tale at the Close of the Middle Ages," *Kiryat Sefer* 62 (1988–1989): 887–905 [H].
Yassif, "The Study"	Idem, "The Study of Folklore and Jewish Studies: Directions and Goals," *The World Congress of Jewish Studies Newsletter* 27 (1987): 3–27; (1988): 3–26 [H].
Yassif, "Traces"	Idem, "Traces of Folk Traditions of the Second Temple Period in Rabbinic Literature," *Journal of Jewish Studies* 39 (1988): 212–233.
Zfatman, *Narrative*	S. Zfatman, "Yiddish Narrative Prose from Its Beginnings until 'Praises of the Besht' (1504–1814)," 2 vols. (Ph.D. diss., The Hebrew University, Jerusalem, 1983) [H].
Zfatman, *Marriage*	Idem, *The Marriage of a Moral Man and a She-Demon: The Transformation of the Motif in the Folk Narrative of Ashkenazi Jewry in the Sixteenth–Seventeenth Centuries* (Jerusalem, 1987) [H]

Zunz, *Homilies*   L. Zunz, *The Homilies of the Jewish People and Their Historical Development*, ed. and supplemented by H. Albeck, trans. from the German by M. E. Z'ak (Jerusalem, 1954) [H].

Index

Aaron, 168, 169

Abbaye, 146, 148, 149, 151, 152–54, 228

Abel, 47, 48, 80–82

Abraham, 16, 18, 31, 36, 49, 201; Nimrod and, 82–83, 84; Sarah and, 220; testing of, 48

Abram, 16

abridged journey, 86, 264

academy, 71, 72, 78, 79, 106, 187; common people and, 264; demons in, 152–53; Isaiah's death and, 95; as ivory tower, 117; tosafist, 338

Adam, 12, 47, 87, 228, 271; burial cave of, 220; Lilith and, 369

Adam and Eve, Book of, 80, 90

Adversary. *See* Satan

Aesop's fables, 23, 193–98, 200, 202, 206, 488n46

Against Apion (Josephus), 43

aggadah, 241, 243, 263, 264, 265, 272; biblical verse and, 223; birth legends and, 326; as folk narrative, 250–65

aggadic literature, 72, 78, 87, 227; comic tales and, 180; Daniel story cycle and, 100; death in, 114; eastern motifs in, 101; expanded biblical stories, 79, 90; fables, 194; Flood story in, 82

Agrat bat Mahlath (demon), 148, 150

agriculture, 11, 189–90, 191, 197, 204

Ahikar, 39, 63, 64, 102–103, 105, 214

Ahimaaz (family), 318–19, 353

Akiva, R., 90, 136, 144, 209, 325, 385; daughter of, 163–64, 224–25; death of, 3, 112–13, 276, 487n44; "emergence" of, 109–11; fox-and-fishes fable, 76, 205, 206, 207, 275–76; Kalba Savua's daughter and, 71, 234, 258; magician and, 160; medieval tales about, 258–59; sage stories and, 108, 218; story cycles about, 226; tall tales and, 185; *tanna* and the dead man, 457; as Torah scholar, 206, 327; wandering dead and, 290

Alexander the Great, 101, 219, 266

Alexandria, 45, 51, 98

Allah, 266–67, 270

Alphabet of Ben Sira, 246, 247, 248, 251, 275, 282

amoraic period, 109, 115

analogy, 286

anecdotes, 190, 269, 284

Angel of Death: bride and, 103, 285, 350, 368; encounter with, 367–68; R. Joshua ben Levi and, 256, 257–58, 267; Torah study and, 114

angels, 36, 42, 279, 280, 303, 369; Jacob and the angel, 12–13; Raphael, 65; rebel, 68; in *Susannah and the Elders,* 62

animal tales, 26, 193, 284, 408; Bible and, 33; disappearance of, 249; fables and, 23, 24, 208; Hasidic tales and, 405; Indian, 266; Middle Ages, 263; Sabbath in, 125

animals, 12, 23, 49, 192; language of, 260, 271; in service to God, 237–38

antagonist, 91, 138

anthropomorphism, 192, 208

anti-Christian legends, 306

anti-heroes, 138, 139, 143. *See also* heroes

anti-Jewish humor, 180–82

Antiquities of the Jews (Josephus), 51, 92

anti-saints, 119–20

antisemitism, 78, 330

Antoninus Pius (Roman emperor), 204–205, 221, 264

Apocrypha, 38–40, 46, 84, 96

Apuleius, Lucius, 354

Arab culture, 246, 283, 284; in modern Israel, 411, 429, 441–43

Arabian Nights, The, 246, 266, 276, 346

Arabic language, 253, 265, 275; Bible in, 38, 39; spoken by Jews, 247, 248, 407. *See also* Judeo-Arabic language

Aramaic language, 5, 55, 369; Bible in, 38, 39, 103, 214; in comic tales, 171–72; fables in, 198; Moses in Ethiopia story, 92; proverbs in, 195; spoken by Jews, 247; story cycles in, 219; Torah in, 71, 77

Ark of the Covenant, 41

Armenian language, 38, 39

Artapanus, 51, 52, 92

Arthur, King, 266

Ashmedai (King of Demons): as anti-hero, 68; Benaiah and, 267; in *Book of Tobit,* 65, 66, 67; Solomon and, 87–89, 154, 482n20

associative accumulation, 227–44, 240

Assyria, 65

astrology, 162–64, 224

Athens, Elders of, 101–102, 160, 214–15, 241, 355
Atonement, Day of, 173, 174, 233, 270, 331, 385
authenticity, 15, 16, 32; of exemplary tales, 121,
    284–85, 287; of fairy tales, 151; of foundation
    myths, 188; of historical legends, 132, 133; of
    Patriarchal tales, 22, 23
Avimelekh, 16–17, 24, 25, 201

Ba'al, prophets of, 36
Ba'al Shem Tov, Israel, 372, 376, 381, 383, 384;
    captive-child motif and, 399; hidden zaddik
    and, 393–96; "Moses by the Well" story, 388–
    89; physician and, 418–19, 424; "praises" of,
    402–403; R. Isaac Luria and, 390; in shepherd
    tale, 386–87
Baba Sali, 418–22, 428, 430, 431
Babylonia, 4, 8, 30, 246; academy in, 98; in
    Daniel story cycle, 58, 59, 101; demons in,
    150; fables in, 192; as Jewish center, 38, 172,
    310, 316; priests of, 57; rainmaking in, 230;
    victory over Egypt, 63
Babylonian Talmud, 70, 75, 90, 97, 252, 255;
    Angel of Death in, 256; expanded biblical
    stories in, 79; Isaiah in, 93–94; King Solomon
    tale in, 87; magical tales in, 215–16; R. Akiva
    story in, 109; role of synagogue in, 71; Sab-
    bath in, 124; sages in, 115; saints' deaths, 112;
    story cycles in, 218, 223, 234–35; tall tales in,
    183–84. See also Palestinian Talmud; Talmud
Baghdad, 281
Balaam's ass, 24
balance, 20, 24, 25, 42, 372
Bar Daroma, 134–35, 136
Bar Hana, Rabbah bar, 183–89, 217, 228–29
Bar Kappara, 75–76
Bar Kokhba Revolt, 85, 135–37, 142, 144, 196, 301
Bar Mitzvah, 163
battle/war tales, 85, 157
Beit ha-Midrash, 71
Bel (god), 58, 60
Belchira the Samaritan, 54, 94–95
Benaiah, 267
Berdyczewski, Micha Josef, 1, 251
Bible: biblical verse in story cycles, 223–27; crys-
    tallization of legend and, 23; folk literature
    and, 3, 4, 6, 8–10, 33; as history of Hebrew
    people, 15; multiple authors of, 8; mythologi-
    cal elements in, 464; purposeful character of,
    37; witches and magicians in, 144; woman's
    creation stories, 12. See also Scripture; specific
    books of Bible
Biblical Antiquities, The, 47, 80, 90
biblical period, 3, 4, 6, 8–10, 39; developments
    and transitions, 33–37; fable, 23–26; legend,

15–23; myth, 10–15; novella, 27–30; retreat
    into, 87; story cycle, 30–33
biblical research, 31
binary opposition, 20, 29, 63, 81, 387
biographical legends, 17–19, 30–31, 218; as exem-
    pla, 491n58; rabbinic period, 106–20; of
    saints, 322–42
biographical story cycles, 218–23
birth legends, 325–26, 526n72
Black Plague, 299, 320
blood libels, 299–300, 303–305, 319, 342, 401;
    Jewish pope legend and, 398
Boccaccio, Giovanni, 278
Buber, Solomon, 103
burials, 113–14
Byzantine Empire, 318, 319, 325

Cain, 47, 48, 80–82
Cairo Genizah, 266, 293
Canaan, 8, 12, 13, 18, 28; in Joseph story, 27;
    Moses and, 123; mythology of, 466n8;
    Patriarchs in, 31; sons of Africa and, 219; war
    against Canaanite tribes, 84, 90
Canterbury Tales, The (Chaucer), 346
captive-child motif, 307, 397–401, 443
castle-in-the-air motif, 102–103
casus, 108, 130, 131–32
cedar tree, 196
censorship, 14, 18, 55
Cephas, Simon, 306–307, 308
chain of tradition, 250–51, 323
Chaldeans, 56
charity, 122, 163, 164, 226, 238, 345, 385; halakha
    and, 270
Charlemagne, 297, 299, 309–10, 316–17, 318
Chaucer, Geoffrey, 278, 346
childbirth, 11, 14, 157–58, 159
children, 18, 71, 216; as audience for folktales,
    266, 343; captive-child motif, 307, 397–401;
    in "return to the faith" stories, 446–50
Chmielnicki massacres, 56–57
Christianity, 39, 55; Church Fathers, 52, 60, 121,
    160, 284; conflict with Judaism, 99, 160–61,
    265, 300, 303–308, 355–57, 399, 403; conver-
    sion to, 50, 307, 308, 320; demonological tales
    and, 361, 362–63, 366; exemplary tales and,
    283, 284, 295–96; hagiography and, 339; he-
    retical sects, 358; Isaiah's death in, 93; Jewish
    diaspora and, 265; Jewish pope legend, 306,
    307, 308, 398–99; Letter of Aristeas and, 45;
    martyrological narrative in, 52–53, 83–84,
    96, 143–44; Middle Ages concept and, 245,
    246; rise of, 38; saints, 49, 50, 60, 84, 153, 325–
    26, 328, 363, 476n21; seen as idolatry, 357;

Solomon and Queen of Sheba, 281; spirit possession tales and, 155; theodicean tales, 389; view of folk heroes, 280; view of magic and women, 354; view of marriage, 348

chronicle, 22, 32

Chronicle of Ahimaaz, The, 318–19, 353–54

Chronicles of Moses, The, 52

circumcision, 52, 119, 182, 264, 399, 465n5

class distinctions, 2, 268, 335–37, 472n4; exemplary tales and, 291; Hasidism and, 371, 393–97, 535n27; interclass marriage, 382; Torah scholars and, 264

collective memory, 301–303

comic tales, 166–91

commentaries, 251, 309, 311

Common Era, 60

concubines, 29, 36, 64

contests, 31, 63–64; of magic, 160, 355, 401, 404; performance events as, 73; of riddles, 84, 215; of wisdom, 214–15; of wits, 101–102

context, 4, 16; aggadic deliberation, 210; biblical, 9; historical, 24, 40; legal, 210; of rabbinic period tales, 120; removal from, 240

conversion: to Christianity, 50, 307, 308, 320; to Islam, 522n59; to Judaism, 43, 50, 111, 123, 125, 218, 253–54, 271, 403

core meaning, 26

creation stories, 11, 14, 33, 34, 35

Crusades, 56, 299, 301, 315, 331–33

crystallization, 22–23, 30, 46, 73, 88; of biographical legends, 332; of historical legends, 135, 136–37, 138; of new cultural patterns, 250; of rabbinic literature, 39; of story cycles, 234

culture heroes, 31, 36, 384, 470n22

Cyclops, 149

Cyrus (Persian king), 46

Daniel, 22, 57–61, 68, 83; crocodile and, 100; lions' den story, 57–58, 60; story cycle of, 99–100; Susannah and, 62

Daniel, Book of, 40, 57, 59, 509n4

Dani'el, 22

Dante, Alighieri, 258, 361

Darius (Persian king), 46, 57, 58, 64, 84, 100

"Darius's Three Bodyguards," 45–46, 63

David, 34, 80, 276, 317; Goliath and, 22, 36, 83, 467n11; pretense of insanity, 263; warriors of, 34; Yishbi and, 85–86

Davidic dynasty, 22, 141, 317, 318

death, 10, 17, 125, 163; car accidents, 437–38, 444, 446–47; fear of, 127, 150; origin of, 11, 34; of talmudic heroes, 112–15. *See also* Angel of Death

Deborah, 34

Decameron (Boccaccio), 346

demigods, 11, 36

demonological tales, 14, 35, 36, 144–66, 322, 351–70

demons, 13, 65–66, 105, 145, 228, 319; Queen of Sheba as, 281; travelers and, 465n5. *See also* dybbuks

demythologization, 11, 18, 35–36, 113

denouement, 16, 139, 413

deserted corpse, 109, 110

Devil. *See* Satan

diaspora, 29, 69, 247, 281; messianism in, 313; modern Israel and, 412, 418, 423; wandering legends, 328–30

didacticism, 36–37, 64, 78–79, 87; exemplary tales and, 121; fables and, 194; story cycles and, 211; Torah study and, 110. *See also* exemplum/exempla

dietary laws, 14, 239

Divine Comedy (Dante), 258, 361

divine parentage, 35, 36

divine voice, 48, 53

dragons, 149, 153, 154

dreams, interpretation of, 57, 59, 60, 177, 241, 242, 318

drunkards, 174–77, 259, 395

dualistic religion, 68

dybbuks, 66, 147, 155, 319, 364–67, 404. *See also* demons

Ecclesiastes, Book of, 197, 198

Egypt, 4, 8, 28, 42, 63, 84; Abram and Sarai in, 16; exodus from, 3, 229; fables in, 192; Hellenistic, 45; Islamic, 305; Israelites in, 35; Jeremiah buried in, 56; as Jewish center, 38; *khons* tale, 66; Moses in, 51; plagues on, 436, 451–52; wanderers in, 329, 330; war against Ethiopia, 92

Eleazar, R., 113, 114, 158, 159, 190

Eleazar ben Simeon, R., 212, 221–23, 232

Eleazar (Maccabees), 142, 144

Eliezer, 212, 220, 235

Elijah, 20, 30, 43, 274, 305; Angel of Death and, 104, 105; Elisha and, 17, 18, 19, 31, 34, 36, 61, 214, 466n8; in Hasidic tales, 393–94; as healer, 221; Israeli secularist and, 445; Maimonides and, 327, 328; modern Israel and, 417; ox buyer and, 289; R. Akiva and, 112; R. Joshua ben Levi and, 256, 266–67; Rashi and, 340

Elisha, Elijah and, 18, 31, 214; evolution of story cycle, 36; folk hero and, 34; as miracle (wonder) workers, 17, 61; mythology and, 466n8; Patriarchal tales and, 19

Enlightenment (Haskalah), 400–402, 455

entertainment, 77, 78, 167

epic laws, 25, 53, 71, 86, 101, 462–63n2

epic poems, 288

epimythium, 192, 201, 204; as ethical conclusion, 208; fabulists and, 197, 206; in Jotham's fable, 25; in poor man's ewe lamb, 24

eroticism, 27, 33, 37, 45, 51, 231, 253; in *Book of Tobit*, 66; in demonological tales, 157; in novellae, 343; Solomon and Queen of Sheba, 282; *Susannah and the Elders*, 61

Esau, 13, 193

Esdras, Apocryphal, 41, 63, 106

Esther, 28, 29, 34. *See also* Scroll of Esther

ethical tales, 37, 109, 118, 121, 208

Ethiopia, 51–52, 92, 281, 383

Ethiopian language, 38

ethnology, 214

etiological tales, 32, 40, 175; as legend, 139–40, 142; as myth, 10, 11, 12–13

etymologies, 13

Eve, 12, 87, 272

evil, good and, 20, 130

evil eye, 149

exegesis, 78, 87, 239; homiletic interpretation and, 185, 186; *mashal* and, 201–202, 203; Moses in Ethiopia story, 92

exemplum/exempla, 108, 408, 457, 491n58; definition, 517n41; Middle Ages, 283–97; rabbinic period, 120–32, 148, 150, 156. *See also* didacticism

exilarch, 64, 317

exile, 40, 67

Exodus, 3, 30, 188, 229

exorcism, 155, 363, 404, 497–98n85

expanded biblical tales, 40, 46–52, 67, 68; in Middle Ages, 250; in rabbinic period, 79–89

expulsions, 10, 329

Ezekiel, 21–22, 56

fables, 284, 408; biblical period, 23–26, 32, 34; disappearance of, 249; Middle Ages, 261–62; rabbinic period, 191–209; types of, 468n13

fabulists, 262

factual tales, 121, 131

fairy tales, 16, 72, 284, 344; authenticity and, 151; magical, 13, 33, 343; in Second Temple period, 64–67

false prophets, 54, 94

families, 31, 32, 455, 466n9, 470n20; chronicles of, 247; loss of, 127; of Torah scholars, 235

fate, 163, 164

fiction, truth and, 32, 217, 234

flames, rescue from, 57, 83, 84

Flood story, 11, 14, 35, 80, 82, 465n4

folk consciousness, 309, 311, 312

folk medicine, 165

folktales, 2, 3, 4, 28, 49; alternating storytellers, 30; Arab, 60, 266; biblical tales and, 9; developmental lines, 34–35; epic laws of, 71, 86; "Hebrew" and "Jewish," 4–5; international, 12, 136, 263, 265–82; legal, 130–32; literary works and, 70–71, 156, 243, 247; motifs in, 48; of non-Jewish origin, 55, 79, 86, 122, 271, 273–82, 292, 350, 354; originating in academy, 108–109; urban population centers and, 151; variants of, 60

folkloristics, 1, 22, 132, 297, 463n3

food taboos, 13, 14

formulaic numbers, 20, 48

fox and fishes, parable of, 3, 112, 207, 275–76, 487n44; fabulists and politics of audience, 205, 206; as performance event, 76

framework grouping, 67, 214–15

France, 248

Garden of Eden, 48, 209, 255; as myth, 10, 11, 14, 34, 464; "Pandora's Box" theme and, 87

gender stories, 351–70

generic classification, 9–10, 215–17

Genesis, Book of, 12, 15, 16; Avimelekh and Sarah, 17; biblical research and, 463n3; *Book of Jubilees* and, 48; Joseph story, 27–28; Patriarchal tales, 22–23, 31–32, 277

genres, 6, 15, 34, 67, 240; in Hasidic literature, 402; in Middle Ages, 249–50; transitional forms, 33

Gentiles, 20, 225–26, 305; captive child among, 397–99; in comic tales, 178–82; divine intervention against, 56; economic and cultural ties to, 304; in Hasidic tales, 404; Jewish conflict with, 46, 166, 236, 239, 331–33, 342; Jewish courtier and, 29, 68–69, 138, 139; Jewish leaders and, 317–18; Jewish messianic movements and, 312, 313, 314; perception of Judaism, 218

geography, 31, 32, 42, 299; legend and, 17; etymology and, 13; miracles and, 56

Germanic culture, 352

giants, 11, 22, 36, 64, 85, 263, 355

Gideon, 24, 25, 34

God of Israel, 49, 58, 578; animals and, 237–38; attachment to, 372; creation of, 34; daughters of men and, 10, 11; Gentile rulers and, 99; as hero, 15; men rebelling against, 10–11; name of, 130, 303, 304, 307, 330; Pharaoh and, 16; Solomon's wisdom and, 30; in story of

Esther, 29; struggles with monsters, 10, 14, 35; supernatural forces and, 458; will of, 209

God-fearingness, 116, 117, 430, 437

Godrey of Bouillon, Duke, 331–33

gods, 10, 12, 15, 33, 35, 89

Goliath, 22, 36, 83, 86, 467n11

good, evil and, 20, 130

grandmother tales, 74

"grateful dead" motif, 66, 67, 105, 485n36

grave robbers, 228

Great Revolt. See Bar Kokhba Revolt

greatness, rise to, 271, 280, 383, 469n17; biblical Joseph story, 27; youngest son, 28, 33, 83, 109

Greece, ancient, 146, 183; culture, 236; language, 38, 39, 45, 61, 98, 198; literature, 180, 195–96; mythology, 21, 50–51, 85

Gregory the Great, Pope, 273, 295, 530n95

Grimm, Jakob and Wilhelm, 10, 466n6

guardian angel, 13

Hadrian, 135, 136, 181, 223

hagiography, 17, 40, 250, 330; biographical cycles and, 218; Christian, 339; factual kernel and, 525n68; in modern Israel, 411–12, 419–21; Second Temple period, 57–61, 68

halakha, 4, 110–11, 246, 342; academy and, 78; actions alien to, 270; biblical verses and, 223; context and, 3, 121; as legal ruling, 107; oath taking and, 130; permission and prohibition, 141; treatises, 323

Haman, 29, 199, 200, 202

Hanina ben Dosa, R., 133, 260, 325, 345

Hasidei Ashkenaz, 352, 354, 355

Hasidic stories, 371–74, 402–406; captive-child theme, 397–401; contemporary, 406–407; hidden zaddik, 393–97; medieval narrative traditions and, 385–93; narrative patterns, 380–85; oral and written, 376–80; performance events, 374–76

Hasidim, 115, 118, 273, 419

Haskalah. See Enlightenment

Hasmonean Revolt, 38, 54, 301

heaven, ascent to, 18, 36

Hebrew Bible. See Bible

Hebrew language, 5–6, 55, 61, 103; Apocrypha and Pseudepigrapha in, 38; fables in, 198; Hasidic tales in, 380, 390; history of narrative in, 67–69; in Middle Ages, 247–48, 509n4; rebirth of, 407; spoken in modern Israel, 408, 449; story cycles in, 219; translations into, 265, 266

Heliodorus, Temple Treasures and, 41

Hellenistic culture, 38, 42, 51, 355; apocryphal

literature and, 96; battle stories, 85; eroticism in, 90; exemplary literature and, 121, 284; fables and, 208; Jewish conflict with, 160, 178–79, 236, 399; romances, 50; saints' legends, 485n39

Hercules, 13, 85

heresy, 119, 268, 358

hermeneutics, 196, 199, 200

Hermes, 51

Herod, 141–42

heroes, 13, 15, 27, 34; anonymous, 128; biographical *vs.* historical legend, 322; biography of, 31, 79; denunciation of, 119–20; destruction of Jerusalem and, 216; divine intervention and, 16; downfall/death of, 73, 143, 484n27; in fairy tales, 64; good and bad, 208; hero-king, 101; lesser known, 22; negative image of, 85; Patriarchs as, 18; triumph over Gentiles, 46; types of, 34. See also anti-heroes

Hillel the Elder, 107, 108, 218–19, 325, 327

Hippolytus (Euripedes), 50

historical kernel, 22, 23, 138, 297, 323

historical legends, 17, 40–46; Middle Ages, 297–321; from novellae to, 45–46; rabbinic period, 132–44

historiography, 132, 136–37, 251, 298–99, 309

Holocaust, 441, 447

Holofernes, 43, 46

holy men, 115–16, 117–18, 120, 232

Holy of Holies, 41, 237

homiletics, 3, 47, 51, 77, 80, 91; exemplary tales and, 121; fables and, 195; interpretation, 70, 71, 82, 185–86, 191; techniques, 75

homilies, 241, 287, 288, 399; in academy, 78; didacticism and, 275; rabbinic aggadah and, 251

homosexuals in medieval culture, 355

Honi the Circle Drawer, 115, 116, 117, 243, 415, 417–18

house, theme of, 405–406

humor, 37, 189, 206; "return to the faith" movement and, 443, 453–54, 540n47

Iceland, 31

idolatry, 18, 36, 49, 50; Abraham and, 83; Christianity as, 357; Daniel and, 58, 59, 100; magic and, 164, 165; shift to monotheism, 60

Iliad, 243

Imitatio Christi, 52, 363

immortality, 11

impotence, 157

incest, 126, 514n29

India, 30, 55, 262, 271, 274, 279

injustice, 26, 169, 200, 389–90

Iraq, 262, 312

Isaac, 16, 17, 18, 48; binding of, 35, 80, 91–92; Sarah and, 201

Isaiah, 54–55, 92–95, 105, 484n27

Islam, 255, 274, 281; exemplary literature and, 283, 284; expanded biblical tales and, 68; Jewish diaspora and, 248, 265, 305; Jews converted to, 522n59; Koran and, 266–68; martyrological narrative and, 68; Middle Ages concept and, 245–46; separation of disciplines and, 508n2; theodicean tales, 389

Israel, ancient, 4, 30, 86, 189; Israelite culture, 14, 15, 33, 34

Israel, modern state of, 1, 41, 245, 371; "return to the faith" stories in, 429–60; saints' legends in, 407–29

Israel, name of, 12, 13, 14

Israel Folktale Archives (IFA), 2, 408

Israel (nation/faith community), 13, 19, 26

Italian language, 265

Italy, 318, 319

Jacob, 16, 18, 228; angel and, 12–14, 17; Esau and, 193; name of Israel, 12, 14; sons and, 84

Jeremiah, 56

Jerusalem, 45, 55, 56, 74–75; Crusaders and, 331–33; destruction of, 213, 242–43; in modern Israel, 433, 440, 457; Roman siege of, 132–33, 137; social unrest in, 314

"Jerusalemite, Story of the," 156

Jerusalemites, Wisdom of the. See Wisdom of the Jerusalemites

jesters, 76, 169

Jesus, 49, 161, 165, 306, 307, 330, 497n83; martyrology and, 52–53

Jewish Christians, 160, 177

Jewish community: Alexandrian, 42–43; Ashkenazi and Sephardic Jews, 440; in Assyrian exile, 67; as the chosen people, 204; conflict with Arabs, 441–43, 539n45; covenant with Christian rulers, 310; destruction and rebuilding of, 311; dispersion of, 265; edicts against, 301, 319, 404; in Egypt, 98, 99; fate of, 28, 29, 34; hatred toward, 42, 59, 68, 138, 300; in Hellenistic world, 68; intellectual elite of, 248–49; internal tensions of, 311–21, 333–37; miraculous rescue of, 43, 69, 154, 304–305; Muslim culture and, 266–70; redemption of captives, 289; relations with non-Jews, 20, 125–26, 129, 131, 177–82, 202, 219, 225–26; violent resistance of, 321, 524n67. See also Judaism

"Jewish humor," 189

Job, Book of, 19–22, 48, 49, 68, 91

Johanan, R., 114, 188, 262; birth legend, 108; death of, 119; idolatry and, 164; Resh Lakish and, 221, 232, 238; on sorcerors, 156

Johanan ben Zakkai, Raban, 132–33, 137–39, 140–41

jokes, 167, 171, 174

Jonah, Book of, 19, 34, 467n10

Joseph, 27, 29, 31, 32, 34, 214; Asenath and, 39, 49–50, 90; brothers and, 80; Judah and, 85; Potiphar's wife and, 50, 90–91

Josephus Flavius, 43, 51, 52, 92, 133, 498n85

Joshua ben Hananiah, R., 160, 161, 162, 166, 179; children and, 241, 242; Elders of Athens and, 101–102, 214–15; Lilith and, 499n88; Lion and Partridge fable, 205; tall tales and, 184

Joshua ben Levi, R., 256–58, 266–67

Jotham's fable, 23, 24–26, 76, 468n14

Jubilees, Book of, 47–49, 57, 80, 90, 91

Judah, 84, 85

Judah the Patriarch, R., 75, 77–78, 173, 174, 205; Antoninus Pius and, 204–205, 264; biographical story cycle, 212; story cycles about, 221

Judah the Pious, R., 248, 284, 285, 287, 295, 296, 324, 380; attempt on life of, 355; birth legends, 326, 526n72; class confrontation and, 336–37; in demonological tales, 352, 353, 367; Hasidic tales and, 382; as pauper, 396; as Torah scholar, 328

Judaism: collective unconscious of, 188; conflict with Christianity, 160–61, 300, 303–308, 355–57, 399, 403; conversion to, 43, 50, 111, 123, 125, 218, 253–54, 271, 403; demonology and, 352; Enlightenment and, 401; fate and, 164; foreign influences on, 266; Gentiles' conception of, 218; Hasidism as revolution upon, 396–97; Hellenism and, 160, 236; Jewish guilt and, 282; monotheism and, 145; narrative elements alien to, 272; "return to the faith" stories, 429–36; secular, 407; view of marriage, 348. See also Jewish community

Judaization, 79, 271, 350; of demonological tales, 153; Germanic culture and, 352–53; of international narrative types, 273–74, 275, 279; of novellae, 122; of pagan myths, 86

Judean Desert sects, 55, 94–95

Judeo-Arabic language, 5, 267. See also Arabic language

Judeo-Spanish language, 5, 407

Judges, Book of, 24, 25, 30–31, 277

Judith, Book of, 40, 43, 45, 46, 57, 105

justice, divine, 263, 267

Kabbalah/kabbalism, 286, 299, 327; Maimonides and, 322, 334–35; in modern Israel, 413, 414;

Nahmanides and, 341–42; R. Isaac Luria and, 390
Kalba Savua, 109, 110, 111
Kalonymus, R., 297, 309–11, 316
Ketev Meriri (demon), 148–50
khons tale, 66
kibbutzim, 439–40, 444, 538–39n43, 545
king of flesh and blood (parable), 200, 205
Kings, Book of, 15, 17, 30
knowledge, tree of, 47
Koran, 266–68, 281
Kurdistan, 312

Lamentations, Book of, 101
land, ownership of, 33
language-of-animals motif, 260
languages, 5, 10, 14, 38, 39, 407. *See also specific languages*
Late Antiquity, 52
Latin language, 5, 38, 39, 247, 462n4
Law, scholars of, 110
law of contrast, 20–21, 28–29
Lebanon, cedar of, 23
Lebanon War, 414, 445, 456
legal tales, 151–52
Letter of Aristeas, 41, 45, 98, 99
Leviathan (monster), 10, 188, 189, 260, 261, 275
Lewinski, Y. T., 1
life token motif, 86
Lilith, 368, 369, 465n5, 496n80, 499n88
linguistics, 4
literature: Akkadian, 25; biblical, 3, 9, 26; Canaanite, 18; Christian, 68; Egyptian, 25, 66; Islamic, 68; of Middle Ages, 4; rabbinic, 3, 156; as a saga, 31; Ugaritic, 18, 22
liturgy, 4
local legends, 17
Loew, R. Judah, 68, 397
love potions, 51
love stories, 253, 277
loyalty, 27, 48, 208–209
Lubavitch Hasidim, 406–407
Luria, R. Isaac, 324, 364, 367, 381–82; hidden zaddik theme and, 397; kabbalism of, 390

Maccabees, Books of the, 57, 96, 105; historical legends and, 40, 41, 42–43; martyrological narratives and, 53, 142, 144
madness, 263, 351
magic, 43, 117, 118, 215–16, 490n55; contests of, 404; Divine Name and, 86; of Gentiles, 399; prostitution and, 354
magical tales, 37, 331, 343; Bible and, 33, 40, 64; captive-child motif, 399; in Middle Ages,

351–70; in rabbinic period, 144–66; structure of, 13
magicians, 144, 160, 161, 179, 214, 230
Maimonides, 5, 29, 68, 316, 322, 324; birth legend of, 325–26; controversy surrounding, 334–35; funeral of, 328; Hasidic tales and, 382; magic and, 162; Rashi and, 323; as Torah scholar, 328; as wanderer, 329
Man of God motif, 18
Manasseh, King, 54, 93, 95
marketplace, 72, 75, 78, 179, 265
marriage, 123–24, 253, 271, 348, 350, 382
Martyrdom of Isaiah, 93, 94–95
martyrological narrative: in Middle Ages, 302, 321; in rabbinic period, 83–84, 95, 142–43; in Second Temple period, 40, 52–57, 67, 68, 69
mashal, 23, 191, 194, 196–99, 206–209, 286
medicine, saints and, 418–23
memorat, 421–22
messianic movements, 311–16
metaphor, 23
metonymy, 227, 286
Middle Ages, 32, 61, 85, 164; Christian narratives in, 52; demonological tales in, 156; exemplary literature of, 121, 283–97; historical legends, 297–321; international folklore, 265–82; in Jewish history, 245–50; Latin and Hebrew languages in, 5; literary originality in, 243; magical and demonological tales, 351–70; novellae and gender stories, 343–51; rabbinic aggadah, 250–65; revival of Second Temple literature, 106; saints' legends, 321–42; seafarers' tales, 227; separation of disciplines and, 4; story cycles in, 211; view of God's greatness, 209
Middle East, ancient. *See* Near East, ancient
Midrash, 10, 57, 90, 92; biographical legends in, 106, 107; comic tales in, 175; demonological tales in, 145; folk humor and, 167; folk literature and, 3, 4; isolated verses and, 80; literature *vs.* folktales in, 70–71; in Middle Ages, 352; rabbinic aggadah in, 252; story cycle in, 209, 210; tale in context, 129; tall tales in, 183
Midrash of the Ten Commandments, 246, 248, 279; exemplum/exempla in, 283, 285, 289, 292; "language of animals" motif in, 260; novellae in, 345; rabbinic aggadah in, 251
minim (Jewish Christians), 160, 177
miracles, 45, 56, 57, 407, 446; medical, 537n37; messiahs and, 312, 313; in modern Israel, 426–29; performed by holy men, 116
miracle-workers, 17–18, 34, 61, 106
Miriam, 144, 216, 224
Mishnah, 108, 234, 235

misogyny, 171, 346–49, 351, 392

mistaken identity, 141

modernity, tradition and, 423–26, 459

monotheism, 60, 145, 464; censorship and, 14, 18; myth and, 11, 15; romances and, 50

monsters, 10, 14, 22, 35, 64, 100, 229

morality, 23, 123, 126, 291–92

Mordecai, 28, 29, 34

Morocco, 408, 409–11, 418, 419, 429

morphology, 13, 22

mortality, 11, 14

Moses, 30, 80, 107, 123; in comic tales, 168–69; Divine justice and, 388–90; in Ethiopia, 51–52, 92, 383; infant, 35; in the Koran, 266–67; parted sea and, 160; Torah and, 45

"Mother and Seven Sons" story, 53–54, 96–98, 105, 142, 144, 224

motifs, 14, 15, 18, 22, 240; abridged journey, 86; captive child, 307, 443; castle in the air, 102–103; in demonology, 149; erotic, 29; folkloric, 48; "grateful dead," 66, 67, 105; greatness, 28; in Hasidic tales, 402; of international folklore, 105–106, 263; language of animals, 260; life token, 86; mythical, 40; pagan, 271; "predestined bride," 67; rescue from flames, 57, 83; study of, 463n2; supernatural, 16, 17; tempest, 228

Muhammad, 330

mysticism, 284, 334, 335. See also Kabbalah/kabbalism

mythopoesis, 14

myths, 72, 229, 271, 284; authentication of, 188; in biblical period, 10–15, 32; Canaanite, 466n8; "decline" of, 68; disappearance of, 249; Job story as, 21; Oedipus, 273. See also demythologization

Nahmanides, 324, 341–42

narratives, 4, 6; biblical, 37; climax, 16; exemplary, 124; fixed stages of, 13; genres, 9; in Hasidic stories, 380–93; historical, 22; international, 104; patterns of, 51, 308; structure of parables and fables, 192

nationalism, 33, 178

nature, forces of, 31, 153, 161, 253, 291

Near East, ancient, 4, 30, 193; biblical literature and, 8, 9, 34; eagle-and-serpent tale in, 23; Elijah/Elisha stories and, 18; fables in, 24, 26; fairy tales in, 65; folktale genres in, 33, 67; Job as legendary figure in, 467n10; Lilith legend, 369; mythology of, 10, 35, 68, 464

Nebuchadnezzar, 43, 46, 57, 59, 248, 282

New Testament, 93, 121, 155, 284, 363, 497n83

Nissim, R., 260, 267, 289, 294, 296

Noah, 82, 174–75

nomadic tribes, 8

Norway, 31

novellae, 27–30, 34, 45, 51, 72; international type, 122; Second Temple period, 61–64; transformation to historical legend, 45–46

Noy, Dov, 1, 107, 408

Odyssey, 243

Oedipus myth, 273

oicotype, 43, 104

oral transmission, 8, 14, 15–16, 19, 31, 95

Origen, 60, 485n37

otherness, 355

paganism: fairy tales and, 68, 344; as idolatry, 59, 60; Judaization of, 86, 271; magic and, 165; residues in Jewish culture, 271, 273; Roman, 181

Palestine, 38, 53, 54, 55, 60; academy in, 98; Aesop's fables known in, 194; Arab conquest of, 70; demons in, 150; Hellenistic rule in, 198; as Jewish center, 310; Jewish community in, 172; in Middle Ages, 247–48, 249, 315; modern, 407; saints' resting places in, 56; travel tales and, 188; wanderers in, 329

Palestinian Talmud, 70, 74, 79; condensed narratives in, 100; demonological tales in, 155–56, 160; Isaiah in, 93; parental honor in, 128–29; R. Akiva story in, 109; saints' deaths in, 223, 238; tall tales in, 183. See also Babylonian Talmud; Talmud

Paltiel the Patriarch, R., 68

Pandora's box, 87

Pangar the Arab duke, 137–38, 139

parables, 64, 71, 137, 503n108; analogy and, 286; rabbinic period, 191–209; in sacred service, 70

Parables of King Solomon, 61

Paradise and Hell, 361, 363

parental honor, 128–29

paternity, 232, 347

Patriarchs, tales of the, 15, 16, 220, 470n20; as biographical legends, 18–19; folk hero and, 34; "historicity" of, 22; saga genre and, 31–32

performance events, 72–79, 187, 374–76

Persia, 246, 262, 279; folk narratives of, 55; hero-king tales in, 101; literature of, 85; messianic legends in, 312; mythology of, 271; Purim miracle in, 29, 202

Persian language, 266, 275

Phaedra and Hippolytus, 50–51, 90, 91

Pharaoh, 16, 27, 51, 92, 201; Ahikar and, 102–103; infant Moses and, 35; plagues on Egypt, 436

Pharisees, 63

Philistines, 17, 22, 36, 263
Philo, 47
Phoenicia, 8
pietists, German, 352, 354, 355
Pinhas ben Yair, 116, 117, 118, 125
plant tales, 23, 24–25, 26, 207
Plato, 45
plot, 25, 27, 42, 99, 439; progression of, 192, 288; resolution of, 64
pogroms, 301–303, 311, 314–15, 319–20
Poland, 371, 381
polemics, 203
poor man's ewe lamb, fable of, 23, 24
pope, legend of Jewish, 306, 307, 308, 398–99
posthumous legend, 107
praises. See hagiography
prayers, 386, 518n47
"predestined bride" motif, 67
prenatal legends, 107–108, 159
pride laid low, 89, 135, 136, 137, 237
priests, 41, 239, 330, 399; pagan, 58, 60; sacred history and, 18; wicked, 55
Prince of Hatred. See Satan
promiscuity, 366
prophets, 15, 17, 56
prostitutes/prostitution, 252–53, 291, 354, 455; Solomon's judgment of, 29–30; witchcraft and, 157
protagonist, 138, 212, 240; in exemplary tales, 288–89; redemption of, 280; in story cycles, 219, 221
Provence, 309, 310
proverbs, 23, 63, 71, 82, 194–96
Proverbs, Book of, 23
Pseudepigrapha, 38–40, 46, 49, 50
punishment, 20, 40, 123, 455; body/soul separation and, 205; for breaking Sabbath, 456; of Cain, 81; of children, 446–47; for defilement of the sacred, 41, 42–43, 68, 429; destruction of Temple and, 315; in exemplary tales, 125–30; reward and, 19, 280; by Satan, 49; sin and, 33, 238–39, 242, 285, 289, 290, 362; of a zaddik, 396
Purim, 29, 45

Queen of Sheba. See Sheba, Queen of
Qumran texts, 57, 59

Rabbah (sage), 146
rabbinic period, 3, 4, 7, 39, 70–72; aggadic traditions of, 54; biographical legends, 106–20; comic tales, 166–91; exemplum/exempla, 120–32; expanded biblical stories, 47, 79–89; historical legends, 132–44; magical and de-

monological tales, 144–66; magic and religious controversies, 399; misogynist tales, 346; narrative traditions from Second Temple period, 89–106; parables and fables, 191–209; performance events, 72–79; story cycles, 209–44
rabbis, 41, 71, 90, 164, 489n53
Raglan, Lord, 107
Rahab (monster), 10
rainbow, 11
rain/rainmaking, 18, 141, 190, 240; divine control of, 11; Honi the Circle Drawer and, 116, 243; in story cycles, 230, 231, 232; in Talmud, 115
Raphael (angel), 65, 67
Rashi, 252, 255, 256, 310, 339–40, 381; birth legend of, 326, 341–42; fables and, 261, 262–63; Godfrey of Bouillon and, 331–33; Hasidic tales and, 382; legends about, 322–23; pessimism of, 261; as wanderer, 329, 338
rebbe stories, 406–407
Rebecca, 16, 17
reincarnation, 390
religion, 140, 150, 283, 432
repentance, 124
repetition, 19–20, 24, 84, 101
Resh Lakish, 221, 232, 238
responsa, 247, 251, 308, 309
"return to the faith" stories, 439, 458–60; ancient Jewish traditions and, 455–58; confrontations with Arabs, 441–43
reward, 123, 285, 289, 455; body/soul separation and, 205; in exemplary tales, 127, 129; punishment and, 19, 280; by Roman emperor, 154; withstanding trials and, 20, 49
riddle contests, 31, 63–64, 84, 215, 234
Roman Empire, 95, 146, 154, 222, 223; circumcision and, 182, 264; culture of, 74, 76, 487–88n46; Jewish resistance to, 132–37; literature of, 180, 183, 195–96; relations with Jewish community, 204–205, 206
romances, 266
romantic love, 50, 259, 343, 344, 348, 370
romanticism, folkloristics and, 1, 297
"rose among the thorns" motif, 192
Russia, 418, 441
Ruth, Book of, 33, 34

Sabbath, 122, 288, 345; desecration of, 435, 438, 447, 459; return to faith and, 447–49; reward for keeping, 124–25; reward for virtue and, 254–55
sacred legends, 17–18, 21, 29, 40, 60–61
sacrifices, 97, 158

Sadducees, 63

sagas, 31–33, 34, 469–70n20

sages, 70, 71, 75, 76, 77, 80; Bar Kokhba and, 85; biographical legends about, 259; debates with Greek philosophers, 236; demons and, 145, 148, 150, 158–59; in exemplary tales, 120–21, 128–29; Herod and, 141; Isaiah's death, 96; legends about, 325, 328; miracle-workers and, 106; origins of, 108; position in society, 150; religious debates of, 99; Romans and, 132; Sabbath and, 124; Samuel's father and, 264; Second Temple literature and, 90, 92, 105; story cycles and, 215; systematic context and, 243; tall tales and, 184–86, 187–90

saints, 34, 56, 89, 220, 382; anti-, 119–20; burial grounds of, 220; Christian, 49, 50, 60, 84, 153, 325–26, 328, 363, 476n21; death of, 143; graves of, 107, 112, 119, 305, 408, 488n49; hidden, 20, 43, 393–96, 404; Jewish, 20, 43, 59, 393–96; legends of Middle Ages, 60, 321–42; in modern Israel, 407–29; prenatal legends about, 107–108

Samaritans, 60

Samson, 13, 17, 35, 85; birth of, 36; story cycle of, 30–31, 34

Samuel, Book of, 65, 277

Sanhedrin, 274, 277

Sarah, 16–17, 36, 65, 67, 201, 220

Sargon, 35

Satan, 67, 68, 358, 531n100; binding of Isaac and, 48, 91–92; in Book of Job, 20, 21; David and, 85; Isaiah's death and, 54, 55; Noah and, 82, 175

Saul, King, 276

scholars. See Torah scholars

science, 423–26, 452, 459

scribes, 14, 323

Scripture, 9, 10, 28, 39; cultural dependence on, 79; eroticism and, 50; fables and, 203; "hidden" and "external" books and, 38; interpretation of, 356; medieval folktales and, 247; monotheistic censorship of, 14; struggle against myth, 11. See also Bible

Scroll of Esther, 40, 43, 138, 202, 282, 318; Divine Plan and, 200; fairytale construction of, 469n17; as novella, 28; rescue-of-Jewish-community theme, 45, 68, 304; romantic triangle in, 29; theodicy and, 199. See also Esther

Scroll of Ruth, 33

sea, land and, 14

seafarers, 188, 189, 217, 227, 228, 229, 232

seances, 437, 444–45

"Second Purim" tales, 43, 304–305

Second Temple period, 4, 6–7, 304, 418; apocrypha and pseudepigrapha, 38–40; expanded biblical tales, 46–52; fairy tales, 64–67; hagiographical cycles, 57–61; historical legends, 40–46; history of Hebrew narrative, 67–69; influences on rabbinic period, 89–106; martyrological narratives, 52–57; novellae and wisdom tales, 61–64

sects, 95

secularism, modern Israel and, 434, 436–37, 439–41, 444, 447, 448, 451, 452–55

Sefer ha-Ma'asim, 251, 344, 345

Sefer Hasidim, 283–84, 286, 288, 290, 296, 340, 386, 387

Sefer ha-Yashar, 52

Seleucus, 41

separation of disciplines, 4, 246, 508n2

Septuagint, 38, 45, 59, 61–63, 105, 476n22; sanctity of, 98–99

sermons, 77, 210

Serpent (monster), 10

sexes, polarization of the, 171–74

sexuality/sexual relations, 43, 232, 234, 296; in folk humor, 180; between gods and mortals, 10, 11; between humans and demons, 156, 366, 368–70, 532–33n112; incest, 273; in medieval literature, 346–51

Shabbetai Zevi, 312, 313

Shahpur I (Persian king), 101

Sheba, Queen of, 281–82, 368–69, 532n112

sin, 253, 457–58, 459, 485n37, 491n59; fathers and sons, 290; incest, 273, 514n29; lust, 140; pride, 136, 137; punishment and, 33, 238–39, 242, 285, 289, 362

Six-Day War, 414, 417, 431

Slavic languages, 38

snakes (serpents), 137, 163, 179, 208; Bar Kokhba and, 136; eagle and, 193; in fables, 204, 207; food and, 232, 238; in Garden of Eden, 209; Satan as, 531n100; in tall tales, 184

social protest, 169–71

Sodom/Sodomites, 77, 170, 173, 212, 217, 235

Solomon, King, 61, 63, 80, 274, 276–78, 349; Ashmedai and, 87–89, 154, 482n20; daughter of, 344; judgments of, 29–30, 278; Queen of Sheba and, 281–82, 368–69; three wise counsels and, 390–91, 392

Song of Songs, 57, 59, 192

sorcerors/sorcery, 161, 215, 304, 330; Enlightenment (Haskalah) as, 401; goal of, 156; Greco-Roman view of, 499n92; Judaism and, 162–63; Kabbalah and, 322; meaning of, 355

Spain, 315, 316, 338
Spanish language, 265
spirits. *See* demonological tales; demons;
  dybbuks
stereotypes, 207, 208, 355, 356, 405; of Arabs,
  441, 443, 451
story chain, 73, 101
story cycles, 13, 15, 16, 30–33, 469n19; David, 22;
  hero-king, 101; rabbinic period, 209–44
"Story of the Jerusalemite," 156
storytellers, 2, 25–26, 75; altering of stories, 263;
  alternating, 30; as moralists, 275; multiple,
  70; of rabbinic period, 101; skill of, 184
street theater, 78, 182
structuralism, 463n2, 520n53
substitution, 35
Sukkot, festival of, 122
Sumer, 4, 8, 30, 192, 469n18
supernatural events/forces, 16, 17, 21, 27, 151,
  353; animism and, 462n1; divine punishment,
  41, 42–43; heroes and, 280; modern Israeli belief in, 423; in "return to the faith" stories,
  445–46
survival tales, 69
Susannah, Book of, 41, 57, 59, 105, 106, 476n21
Susannah and the Elders, 58, 60, 349, 476n21;
  different versions of, 60, 61–63; Origen and,
  485n37
sweetening parable, 372
symbols, 308
Symposium (Plato), 45
synagogues, 41, 71, 72, 78, 79; conduct in, 126–
  28; demons in, 152, 497n83
syncretism, 51

taboos, 13, 14
tall tales, 167, 182–86, 187–90, 502–503n107
Talmud, 3, 4, 40, 80, 90; biographical legends
  in, 106, 107; demonological tales in, 145, 147;
  folk humor and, 167; Isaiah's death in, 55;
  literature *vs.* folktales in, 70–71; in Middle
  Ages, 247, 264, 352; rabbinic aggadah in, 252;
  story cycles in, 209, 210; tale in context, 129.
  See also Babylonian Talmud; Palestinian
  Talmud
tannaitic period, 109
Tannin (monster), 10
tempest motif, 228
Temple, 41, 68, 76; destruction of, 85, 140, 142,
  181, 188, 189, 196, 216–17, 301, 314; rebuilding
  of, 46, 141, 206
Ten Martyrs, 56, 95, 144, 181
Ten Tribes, 43

terrorism, 437, 438, 444, 457, 539n45; Baba Sali
  and Sabena aircraft, 414, 415; Jewish-Arab
  intermarriage and, 442, 443
Testament of Job, 40
Testaments of the Twelve Patriarchs, 40, 49, 50,
  80, 84, 90, 91
theodicy, 20, 89, 200, 263, 389, 390
Theodotion, 61–62
theology, 18, 161, 250, 306, 458; antisemitism
  and, 314; ethics and, 205; hermeneutics and,
  200; Israelite, 15; Jewish-Christian debates
  and, 355
Theseus, 50
Thirty-Six Hidden Saints, 20, 43, 393–96
thistle and cedar, fable of, 23, 26
Titus, 41, 237
Tobias, 65, 66–67, 105
Tobit, Book of, 40, 65–67, 104–105, 106
Torah, 92, 239, 290, 326–27; Aramaic translations, 77; centers of, 316, 523n61; demonological tales and, 150, 153–54; encounter with
  death and, 114–15; in German lands, 297,
  309, 310; in Greek, 45; issue of originality
  and, 337–38; martyrological tales and, 144;
  mother's milk and, 273; preachers and, 80;
  public reading of, 48, 71; R. Akiva's study of,
  109, 110; science and, 452; simple piety and,
  116
Torah scholars, 255, 256, 259, 295, 344; demons
  and, 148; folk healers and, 147; folk literature
  and, 251; issue of originality and, 337–38; opposition to, 405, 406; poor folk and, 401;
  prostitutes and, 123, 252–53; Rashi stories
  and, 337–38; reward for, 253; in story cycles,
  230–31; talmudic scholarship and, 264; in
  western Europe, 248; women and, 235, 259,
  327
Tower of Babel story, 10, 14, 34
transitional folktales, 33–37
travel tales, 32, 186–87, 217
trees, 24–25, 26, 135; demons in, 357; Isaiah and,
  54–55; magic and, 146–47; Tree of Knowledge, 272
triangle, romantic, 29
tribes, 8, 19, 23, 31
trickster, 212, 217
truth, 32, 217, 234, 308
Tur Malka, destruction of, 133–34, 140, 242
turning points, 27
*Twelve Patriarchs, Testaments of the. See Testa-
  ments of the Twelve Patriarchs*
Two Brothers, tale of, 28
"two to the scene," 20, 101

Ugaritic literature, 18, 22, 466n8
unicorns, 149
United States, 371, 438, 444, 454, 455, 456
urban legends, 151

Vespasian (Roman emperor), 132, 137, 138, 139, 498
vineyard, fable of, 23, 26
Vitae Prophetarum, 54–56, 57, 59, 75, 93
Vitry, Jacques de, 295

wandering dead man, 290, 457
wandering legends, 328–30, 335
warnings, 120–21
Wazanah, R. Jacob, 410–11
weasel and the well, 261–62, 263, 278, 350–51
weddings, 135, 163
well, weasel (or wolf) and. *See* weasel and the well
wilderness, journey through, 30
wiliness, 27, 29, 43, 206
wisdom, 87, 102, 138, 243, 259, 331
Wisdom of the Jerusalemites, 101–102, 177–78, 211, 215, 225–26, 235–36, 239, 240–42
wisdom tales, 23, 30, 46, 61–64, 69, 208
wise courtier, rise of, 68
witches, 156–57, 159, 264, 499n88; Ahimaaz chronicle and, 353–54; banned in the Bible, 144; erotic aspect of, 157–58; as part of Jewish society, 166
woman/women, 14, 20; comic tales and, 171–74;

creation of, 11–12, 465n5; as demoness/dybbuk, 366–67; devil in guise of, 155–56; erotic power of, 45; folk medicine and, 74; literacy and, 266; in medieval literature, 346–51; in modern Israel, 434, 440–41, 442–43; pregnant, 107–108, 120; as rescuers of Jewish community, 43; status in Middle Ages, 363; strength of, 64; superior in righteousness, 255; synagogues and, 71; wives, 29, 36, 274–75, 349, 365
written transmission, 16

Yagen, R. Nissim, 433–60
Yamm (monster), 10
Yemen, 5, 334
Yiddish language, 5, 266, 355, 407; Hasidic tales in, 379–80, 390, 391; in Middle Ages, 247
Yohanan, R., 271–72, 280
Yom Kippur War, 414, 416–17

zaddikim, 256, 272, 288, 294–95, 371–93; captive-child theme and, 398–99; hidden, 382, 393–97; Lubavitcher movement and, 406–407; as mediators, 404–406; medieval tradition and, 387–88; in modern Israel, 413, 415, 418–19, 426–27, 428, 432
Zealots, 85, 132, 133, 196
Zechariah, 55, 56, 75
Zedekiah, 60
Zerubavel, 43, 64, 68, 84, 138
Zion, Return to, 38, 45, 46, 315–16

ELI YASSIF is Professor of Hebrew literature and Jewish Folklore at Tel Aviv University. He is the founder of Jewish folklore studies at Ben-Gurion University in Israel and has served as visiting professor at UCLA, University of Maryland, Oxford University, University College in London, University of California at Berkeley, and the University of Chicago. He is the author of many books, including *The Study of Jewish Folklore: An Annotated Bibliography*, *The Golem of Prague*, and *The Knight, the Demon and the Virgin: An Anthology of Hebrew Stories from the Middle Ages*.